France and Its Empire
Since 1870

France and Its Empire Since 1870

ALICE L. CONKLIN
Ohio State University

SARAH FISHMAN
University of Houston

ROBERT ZARETSKY
University of Houston

New York   Oxford
OXFORD UNIVERSITY PRESS
2011

Oxford University Press, Inc., publishes works that further Oxford University's
objective of excellence in research, scholarship, and education.

Oxford   New York
Auckland   Cape Town   Dar es Salaam   Hong Kong   Karachi
Kuala Lumpur   Madrid   Melbourne   Mexico City   Nairobi
New Delhi   Shanghai   Taipei   Toronto

With offices in
Argentina   Austria   Brazil   Chile   Czech Republic   France   Greece
Guatemala   Hungary   Italy   Japan   Poland   Portugal   Singapore
South Korea   Switzerland   Thailand   Turkey   Ukraine   Vietnam

Copyright © 2011 by Oxford University Press, Inc.

Published by Oxford University Press, Inc.
198 Madison Avenue, New York, New York 10016
http://www.oup.com

Oxford is a registered trademark of Oxford University Press

ISBN   978-0-19-973518-1 (pbk)
ISBN   978-0-19-973517-4 (hbk)

Printing number: 9 8 7 6 5 4 3 2 1

Printed in the United States of America
on acid-free paper

To our students—past, present, and future

CONTENTS

ILLUSTRATIONS AND MAPS

ILLUSTRATIONS

MAPS

PREFACE

Alexis de Tocqueville, known to most Americans for his classic study of the emerging democracy of the U.S., described France in the mid-nineteenth century as "of all European nations . . . the best qualified to become, in the eyes of other peoples, an object of admiration, of hatred, of compassion, or alarm, never of indifference." The anger that flashed across America in 2003 when France refused to support U.S. military action in Iraq proved Tocqueville's point. Americans were not, and are not, indifferent to France.

While no longer a leading world power, France holds a unique status in the world. Despite occupying a territory smaller than the state of Texas, it boasts the second largest economy in Europe and is home to vibrant industrial and technological sectors ranging from civilian nuclear power and high-speed trains to aeronautics and aerospace research. The nation ranked number one in the World Health Organization's most recent survey of health care systems, turning it into a medical destination for the citizens of other nations—including those of the United States—in search of answers to their health care conundrums. France was a driving force for European integration and enjoys, with Great Britain and Germany, the status of first among equals in the European Union. French governments on the Left as well as the Right still embrace the Gaullist insistence on an independent foreign policy—much to the irritation of American presidents from Franklin Delano Roosevelt to George W. Bush. France sits in one of the five permanent seats in the United Nations Security Council and has its own nuclear military force.

But these impressive industrial, technological, and geopolitical achievements are not what spring to mind for many Americans, when the name of France is invoked. In his memoirs, Charles de Gaulle observed that he had always had a "certain idea of France." So do many others, both French and foreigners. The cultural sway of France is particularly impressive. From cinema and theater to literature and philosophy, from high fashion to luxury manufacture to some of the world's truly great cuisines, France has been a global touchstone of both the arts and the art of living (and eating) well. It is, after all, the nation that coined the term "intellectual," as well as "entrepreneur," and it remains the nation where "intellectuals" still play a dramatic role in public and political life. These well-known attractions explain why France continues to be the world's leading tourist destination.

Recently, France has made headline news around the world for other less flattering reasons. In 2005, rioting youth from Paris and other cities' dilapidated suburbs called attention to a long-festering problem of racism in France. Young citizens whose parents had emigrated from France's former empire—once the largest in the world after Great Britain's—face systematic discrimination and economic if not cultural exclusion, particularly if their families are Muslim. These frustrated youths exploded in rage, mostly directed at cars and buildings, not innocent by-standers. The riots point indirectly to a lesser known aspect of France's history: Its active pursuit of imperialism for much of the last two centuries. France's global empire was mostly undone after World War II, but its complex influence lives on. On the one hand, France nurtures economic and cultural ties with its former colonies, enhancing its international prestige; on the other hand, racist habits of mind acquired through decades of authoritarian rule overseas linger on in contemporary French society and surface in times of economic difficulty. Meanwhile, millions of people today live in a francophone world created by French expansion and many of the students we teach at our respective universities have roots in places that were once French territories.

Tocqueville, however, had in mind yet another vision of France when he penned his famous lines quoted here. Since the Revolution of 1789, France has claimed no less important a role than the United States as a beacon of democracy and human rights in the world. Progenitor of the great Revolution of 1789, France insisted at the time—and the French Republic has maintained this position ever since—that its revolutionary axioms and aspirations, although the particular invention of one part of the French nation, were and are universal. As a result, the great trinity of revolutionary values that was first pronounced in French—*Liberté, Egalité, Fraternité,* or Liberty, Equality, Fraternity—has remained no less valid and vital when cast in other languages. The tremors unleashed by revolution and regicide reached across the globe at the end of the eighteenth century and continue to do so today. The countless invocations of 1789 as the walls of communism collapsed across central and east Europe in 1989 are but one sign of the abiding relevance of Tocqueville's observation. Throughout the world, France inspires hope among the oppressed and fear among the oppressors—but never indifference.

Our book takes up all these "Frances"—as well as others perhaps even less familiar to our readers—to provide an up-to-date synthesis of the history of an extraordinary nation that has been shrouded in myths, many of its own making. We seek both to understand the myths and to uncover the complicated and often contradictory realities that underpin them, based on the most recent historiography. We begin with the premise that France and the United States are sister Republics, joined at the hip since Lafayette crossed the Atlantic to serve the struggle against tyranny, and yet display profound differences that are as compelling as the apparent similarities. The great appeal of French history is that it offers the spectacle of different responses than those of America to some of the same great challenges that faced, and still face, citizens struggling to create genuinely democratic polities and cultures in the era of modern global capitalism.

This "American" viewpoint has determined our starting point and principal themes. Above all, we frame this book around the contested emergence of the French Republic, a form of government that today—finally—appears permanent in France, yet whose birth pangs were much more protracted than those of the American Republic. While both the French and American Republics were forged in the maelstrom of revolution, the first French Republic lasted scarcely a decade, and succumbed first to a military dictator and then to an entrenched Old Regime determined to extirpate any challenge to the king's monopoly on power. Only in 1870 did the advocates of "Liberty, Equality, Fraternity" finally prevail, with the founding of the French Third Republic. Yet even the Third Republic could not survive defeat at the hands of the Germans in 1940. For four "dark" years, a new military dictator collaborated with the German occupiers before the people's representatives founded a Fourth, and then the current Fifth, Republic. Still, if the consolidation of their Republic could not have been more different than the American experience, French democrats, just like their counterparts across the Atlantic, never abandoned their lofty ideals, even if they repeatedly fell short of their founding myths. Women were not enfranchised in France until 1944. Existing colonies were not shed in 1789, and a vast new empire was acquired from 1870 onward and was retained until 1962. A messianic but often intolerant French republicanism insisted that regional and cultural differences be banished from the public sphere in the name of creating a secular unitary nation. Our book explores these paradoxes, without ever losing sight of the fact that some segment of the French population has always been willing to fight, and often die for the principle of basic human rights for all.

We have written this book with two principal goals in mind. The first—as the title suggests—is to offer a truly global history of modern France in order to contextualize better many of the events that have landed France in the news internationally in the first decade of the twenty-first century. These include the integration of Europe, periodic anti-American sentiment among French and vice versa, race riots, French military interventions in Africa, Corsican nationalism, superb social services, and the rise of extremism on the far Right. Too often histories of modern France have limited themselves to what has been known since the era of decolonization as the "Hexagon"—that is to say, French national boundaries within Europe. Yet for most of the modern era, French territory spanned the globe, and France was commonly referred to as home to 100 million French men and women, only half of whom lived in the Hexagon (or "metropole," as it was known before 1962). The republican nation-state was always imperialist, and although the last "colony," Algeria, won its independence from the Fifth Republic in 1962, France still possesses overseas territories and departments in the Caribbean, the Indian Ocean, and the South Pacific.

The pages that follow consistently integrate the history of the empire into that of France. We examine the consequences of overseas expansion, emphasizing in particular the ways in which the French have absorbed and reshaped their ideas, political practices, and tastes through contact with other cultures and peoples, particularly in the exploitative context of empire and postcolonial immigration. This approach has the advantage of not only restoring to view an often ugly history that the French themselves have tended to try to forget but also of making available to a wider public the results of what has become one of the most dynamic fields of French history in the last 30 years.

Yet our interest in a "global France" is not limited to empire. Born of a military defeat at the hands of the Prussians in 1870, the French Third Republic (as well as the Fourth and Fifth) shares an intertwined history with Germany that has been by turns bloody and intimate. In addition, while military rivalry between Britain and France dated back centuries, after 1870, despite continuing and intense colonial rivalries, Britain and France have been thrown together as allies, a fraught but unavoidable forced marriage. Last but not least, from World War I on, France embarked upon a new relationship with the United States, one characterized equally by French fears of and desire for "Americanization." Our global history consistently follows these foreign entanglements as well.

Our second goal is to provide a lively and coherent narrative of the major developments in France's tumultuous and—to outsiders anyway—hopelessly confusing political life; indeed, the chapters are organized around the many political turning points and confrontations that litter the landscape of a nation that has often earned the reputation of being "exceptional" in its inability to reach consensus. Since republicanism only slowly won over the majority of the French, we pay especially close attention to other political ideologies—charting the rival claims of monarchists, anti-Semites, and fascists; socialists and communists; *gauchistes* and feminists; Greens and human rights activists. Yet if a strong political narrative guides this history, we also underpin it with detailed analysis of economics, society, and culture. For example, we consider not just political, cultural, and economic elites but men and women from every background—working class and bourgeoisie, immigrants, Catholics, Jews and Muslims, Bretons and Algerians, rebellious youth, gays and lesbians—in the firm belief that the rich diversity of France can never be overemphasized.

Among these groups, we have nevertheless made the deliberate choice to give full attention to the forgotten half of the population: French women. From 1789 on, a few enlightened men like Antoine-Nicolas de Condorcet, together with activist women like Théroigne de Méricourt and Olympe de Gouges, challenged the exclusion of women from the category of citizen, insisting that universal ideals should truly be universal. Women played key roles in each of France's revolutionary upheavals, and suffered the consequences. While the Third Republic established in 1870 denied women political and civil rights, still, nineteenth-century feminists—a word invented by a French woman—viewed the Republic as the best hope for progress. Meanwhile, French women of all backgrounds played a critical role in the French economy, in their families, and in the two world wars. Still, in one of the many ironies of French democracy, among the first to adopt universal male suffrage, women in France were among the last in Western Europe to gain the franchise in 1944, voting for the first time in 1945. Their experiences are thus emblematic of the struggles of many groups in French society to bring practice in line with the Republic's professed ideals, whose history we seek to highlight.

Finally, a word about about where we begin and where we end. Although our story of modern France and its empire begins with a brief recap of the events of 1789, since the eruption of the Revolution shaped all subsequent political struggles and social, economic, and cultural development, our real jumping off point is the Franco-Prussian War of 1870 and the surrender of Louis Napoleon Bonaparte to the Prussians at Sedan. The fall of Napoleon III marked the birth of the Third Republic, but it also heralded, in the unfolding of the Paris Commune, the great clash of several antagonistic Frances: Paris and the provinces, Left and Right, workers and bourgeoisie. While the Franco-Prussian War pitted French against Germans and the Commune pitted French against French, in 1871, an uprising in Kabylia rocked French Algeria and set the French against one of their colonized peoples, the Algerians. This revolt represented the last gasp of Algerian resistance to the wave of French land confiscation and settlement that began with the invasion of 1830. These Franco-French, Franco-German, and Franco-Algerian (or Franco-African, Franco-Asian) confrontations continued in various guises through the rest of the nineteenth century and well into the twentieth. With the dawn of the twenty-first century, some of these confrontations are again reinventing themselves, and provide the greatest challenge facing President Nicolas Sarkozy, elected in 2007.

We have incurred many individual and collective debts in writing this book, including to those who first taught us French history. Robert Zaretsky thanks Patrick Hutton, Lenard Berlanstein and the late Hans Schmidt; Alice Conklin thanks Philip Nord, Geoffrey Parker, the late J.H.M. Salmon and the late Alain Silvera; and Sarah Fishman thanks Patrice Higonnet, Stanley Hoffmann, Dominique Veillon and Robert Soucy. For specific help at critical moments, thanks also to Hannah Ewing, Lisa Hoffman, John Goins, Jacques Weber, and Bob Buzzanco. Mircea Platon's research assistance and critical reading helped shape the manuscript at key stages. At Oxford Press, we wish to thank Bruce Borland, Peter Coveney, Danniel Schoonebeek, George Chakvetadze, Barbara Mathieu, Charles Cavaliere, and, most especially, Brian Wheel.

In preparing the first edition of this book, we benefited from the comments of several readers: Amy Forbes, Millsaps College; Gillian Glaes, Carroll College; Nathanael Greene, Wesleyan University; Donald Reid, University of North Carolina, Chapel Hill; Todd Shepard, Johns Hopkins University; Leonard V. Smith, Oberlin College; Michael S. Smith, University of South Carolina; Mary Dewhurst Lewis, Harvard University.

ABOUT THE AUTHORS

Alice L. Conklin teaches Modern European History, with a particular focus upon nineteenth- and twentieth-century France and its Empire, at Ohio State University. She received a B.A. from Bryn Mawr College in 1979, an M.A. in French Studies from NYU in 1984, and a Ph.D. in History from Princeton University in 1989. Conklin is the author of *A Mission to Civilize: The Republican Idea of Empire in France and West Africa, 1895–1930* (Stanford, 1997), which won the 1998 Book Prize of the Berkshire Conference of Women's Historians. Her 1998 article "Colonialism and Human Rights, A Contradiction in Terms? The Case of French West Africa, 1895–1914" published in the *American Historical Review,* won the Koren Prize for the best article in French History from the Society for French Historical Studies. She is also the co-author of *European Imperialism, 1830–1930: Climax and Contradictions,* Problems in European Civilization Series (Houghton Mifflin, 1998), and has co-edited a special issue of *French Historical Studies,* "Writing Colonial Histories" (2005). She is currently completing a cultural, political, and intellectual history of French anthropology as a colonial science, tentatively entitled *In the Museum of Man: Ethnography, Race Science and Empire in France, 1930–1950,* which questions whether a newer "culture concept" replaced the older biological concept of "race" in the era of the two world wars. Conklin has held research fellowships from the John Simon Guggenheim Foundation, the Fulbright Commission, the German Marshall Fund, and the Mershon Center for International Studies and the History Department at the Ohio State University.

Sarah Fishman, Professor of History at the University of Houston, earned her B.A. from Oberlin College in 1979, an M.A. in International Relations from the University of Southern California in 1980, and a Ph.D. in History from Harvard University in 1987. Fishman is the author of *We Will Wait: Wives of French Prisoners of War 1940–1945* (Yale, 1992) and *The Battle for Children: World War II, Youth Crime, and Juvenile Justice in Twentieth-Century France* (Harvard, 2002). She also co-edited, along with Laura L. Downs, Ioannis Sinanaglou, Leonard V. Smith and co-author Robert Zaretsky, *France at War: Vichy and the Historians* (Berg, 2000). Her current research explores the impact of France's rapid post-war economic transformation, a period known as the "thirty glorious years," on ordinary people's lives, focusing on women, gender, and family life.

Robert Zaretsky teaches in the Honors College, University of Houston. He received a B. A. in Philosophy from McGill University in 1978, on M. A. in History from the University of Vermont in 1983, and a Ph.D. in History from the University of Virginia in 1989. He is author of *Nîmes at War: Religion, Politics and Public Opinion in the Department of the Gard 1938–1944* (Penn State 1995), *Cock and Bull Stories: Folco de Baroncelli and the Invention of the Camargue* (Nebraska 2004), *Albert Camus: Elements of a Life* (Cornell 2010) and, with John Scott, *The Philosophers' Quarrel: Hume, Rousseau and the Limits of Human Understanding* (Yale 2009). He has also translated Tzvetan Todorov's *Voices from the Gulag: Life and Death in Communist Bulgaria* (Penn State 1999) and, with John Scott, *Tzvetan Todorov's Frail Happiness: An Essay on Rousseau* (Penn State 2001). He is currently writing a book with John Scott on the clash of reason and religion in 18th century Europe, tentatively titled *Boswell's Enlightenment.*

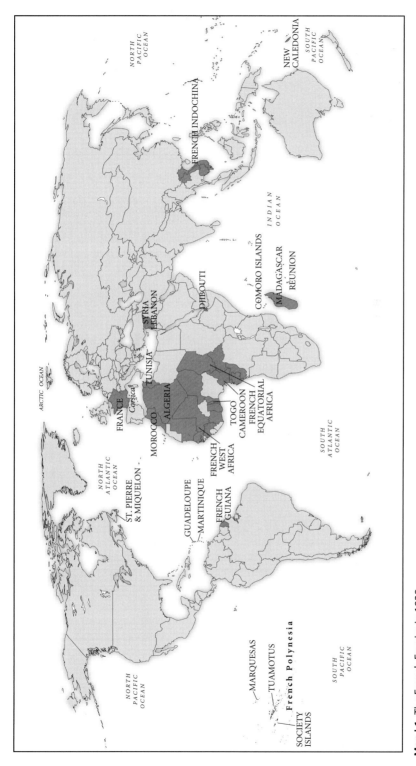

Map I.1 The French Empire in 1939.

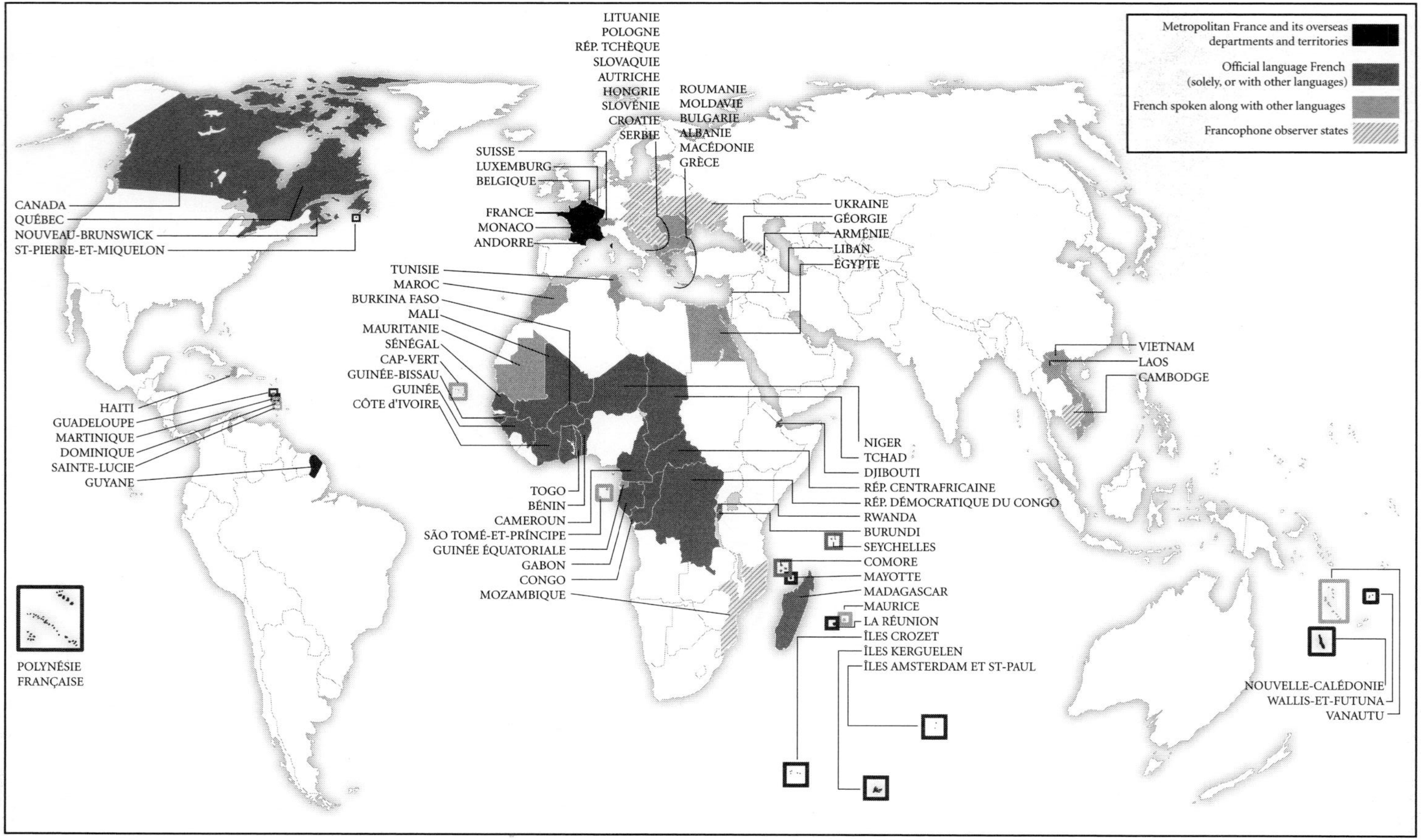

Map I.2 The Francophone world in 2006.

Metropolitan France and its overseas departments and territories
Official language French (solely, or with other languages)
French spoken along with other languages
Francophone observer states

CANADA
QUÉBEC
NOUVEAU-BRUNSWICK
ST-PIERRE-ET-MIQUELON

LITUANIE
POLOGNE
RÉP. TCHÈQUE
SLOVAQUIE
AUTRICHE
HONGRIE
SLOVÉNIE
CROATIE
SERBIE
ROUMANIE
MOLDAVIE
BULGARIE
ALBANIE
MACÉDOINE
GRÈCE

SUISSE
LUXEMBURG
BELGIQUE
FRANCE
MONACO
ANDORRE

UKRAINE
GÉORGIE
ARMÉNIE
LIBAN
ÉGYPTE

VIETNAM
LAOS
CAMBODGE

NIGER
TCHAD
DJIBOUTI
RÉP. CENTRAFRICAINE
RÉP. DÉMOCRATIQUE DU CONGO
RWANDA
BURUNDI
SEYCHELLES
COMORE
MAYOTTE
MADAGASCAR
MAURICE
LA RÉUNION
ÎLES CROZET
ÎLES KERGUELEN
ÎLES AMSTERDAM ET ST-PAUL

TUNISIE
MAROC
BURKINA FASO
MALI
MAURITANIE
SÉNÉGAL
CAP-VERT
GUINÉE-BISSAU
GUINÉE
CÔTE d'IVOIRE

TOGO
BÉNIN
CAMEROUN
SÃO TOMÉ-ET-PRINCIPE
GUINÉE ÉQUATORIALE
GABON
CONGO
MOZAMBIQUE

HAÏTI
GUADELOUPE
MARTINIQUE
DOMINIQUE
SAINTE-LUCIE
GUYANE

NOUVELLE-CALÉDONIE
WALLIS-ET-FUTUNA
VANAUTU

POLYNÉSIE FRANÇAISE

xxii

CHAPTER 1

The Embattled Republican Tradition
1792–1870

On March 28, 1871, a great crowd began to form outside Paris' City Hall, the Hôtel de Ville. The air was charged with expectation. Since the preceding autumn, the French nation had been battered by a series of events, beginning with a catastrophic war against Prussia. The rapid advance of Prussian forces into France, and their encirclement of Paris, had led to the overthrow of the French ruler, Louis Napoleon Bonaparte, and the birth of a new Republic—France's third since 1789. But history was not yet done. On that clear and cold spring day, from the balcony of the Hôtel de Ville, the creation of the Republic was announced to great roars of approval. Thousands of soldiers raised their bayonet-topped rifles into the air as the military bands and crowd, awash with French tricolored flags, launched into a thunderous rendition of "La Marseillaise."

Clearly, for the people on the streets of Paris in 1871, there was no better way to signal the birth of a new Republic in France than singing "La Marseillaise," an anthem that reflects the complex history of modern France. Written in 1792 by Joseph Rouget de Lisle, a military officer, the song began its life as a battle hymn for the citizen army just born in the crucible of the French Revolution. Quickly spreading across France, the song reached the southern city of Marseille just as volunteers were preparing to join the revolutionary army. The men of Marseille, belting out the song during their march northward, thus immortalized it as "La Marseillaise" by the time they reached Paris.

Ever since 1792, the anthem's fortunes have reflected the turbulent history of France. Throughout the nineteenth and into the twentieth century, the explosive words of "La Marseillaise" inspired either dread or devotion:

Arise children of the fatherland
The day of glory has arrived
Against us tyranny's
Bloody standard is raised
Listen to the sound in the fields
The howling of these fearsome soldiers

1

They are coming into our midst
To cut the throats of your sons and consorts

To arms citizens
Form your battalions
March, march
Let impure blood
Water our furrows[1]

The throng of Parisians singing "La Marseillaise" outside the Hôtel de Ville on March 28 welcomed more than the creation of a new democratic government. Their singing signaled their desire to re-create the 1789 Revolution—an event they believed, as did their foes both within and without France, remained very much alive, and which had inaugurated the republican tradition in France. Nearly a century later, the fires of the 1789 Revolution continued to burn.

FRANCE'S OLD REGIME

The French Revolution produced a new group of political leaders who took the Enlightenment's abstract ideas about politics and society and, through the crucible of revolution, forged a French republicanism that would be fiercely egalitarian, universal, and anticlerical. These leaders contrasted themselves, their political philosophy, and the world they hoped to create with what came before, which they named the "Old Regime" as a convenient foil to differentiate it from the ideals of 1789. The relevance of the Old Regime cannot be ignored, then, because for more than a century after the 1789 revolution, French republicanism contended with its alternative vision of France.

France under the Old Regime was a monarchy. Kings (by law, a woman could not ascend to the throne of France) were vested by God with the right to rule, the foundation of divine-right monarchy. In reality, however, even absolute kings relied on key advisors with expertise in various areas. Moreover, the king's divine writ did not always extend into the reality of social and economic facts. Every man, woman, and child under the Old Regime was born into a status that entailed both duties and privileges. Two powerful institutions in particular controlled extensive national resources that gave them considerable local authority: the Catholic Church and the nobility.

France, although it had very small Protestant, Jewish, and Muslim communities, was officially Catholic; indeed, with the baptism of Clovis back in 496, it had become the Church's "eldest daughter." A powerful institution just below the king, the Catholic Church not only ensured the salvation of souls but also controlled a significant portion of France's wealth; provided the state with educated servants; monitored society by registering births, baptizing babies, overseeing marriage, and burying the dead; and assisted the people in distress by providing alms for the poor and administering hospitals and schools. The French Catholic Church was hardly uniform in nature. Under one roof this powerful institution included bishops who lived on huge estates and collected tithes and poor parish priests who barely scraped by. The Church reinforced royal authority by preaching obedience to the kings and was exempt from land taxes because its land and wealth provided in theory for the spiritual and physical well-being of the people.

Just behind the clergy in rank was the nobility, hereditary elites responsible for much of the day-to-day operation of the country and who possessed large landed estates and controlled much of the country's wealth. Nobles represented less than 2 percent of France's population but owned more than 25 percent of the land. By the 1700s, nobles made up the entire army officer corps and filled nearly all of France's public positions, from high ministries to local judges to tax collectors. Because the nobility provided either military or civil service to the kings, they too were exempt from many taxes. Aside from royalty, clergy, and nobility, nearly everyone else, or 75 percent of the population, was a peasant, someone who lived and worked on the land. Peasants leased or sharecropped their land and paid their lord rent, either in kind, a certain amount of grain for example, or in money. Peasants also owed their landlords a motley array of obligations that dated back to the medieval period. For example, inhabitants from one small town each owed the landlord a hen on the first day of Lent. Manor rolls listed all rents, dues, and obligations.

Townspeople represented the newest element of Old Regime society. The French word for town, *bourg,* gave this group its name, the bourgeoisie. Forming the bourgeoisie, a notoriously elusive and broad term, were craftsmen, merchants, and those in the professional classes, such as lawyers, notaries, and bankers. From about 700,000 people in 1700, the bourgeoisie had increased dramatically to about 2.3 million people by 1789, or about 8 percent of the population. Some members of the bourgeoisie were wealthier than many nobles. Bourgeois families interested in the status conferred by nobility had two pathways of upward mobility: either by marrying a daughter to a noble's son, presumably a noble family needing an infusion of money, or by purchasing a venal office that carried a title of nobility. Townspeople in France included not just these wealthy, highly educated members of the upper bourgeoisie but also many small-scale shopkeepers and skilled craftsmen, who formed the ranks of the lower, or petty bourgeoisie At the bottom of the urban social hierarchy were day laborers and the unemployed.

Women's status was determined by birth but also by marriage. Marriage required a dowry in keeping with the family's wealth and status. The Church provided an outlet for women who did not or could not marry; such women could enter holy orders. Noble and wealthy bourgeois families used marriage for strategic purposes, to create or solidify alliances and safeguard property. In both peasant and bourgeois households, wives played a critical role in the household, which represented a productive and not just a reproductive unit. While by law and tradition women were subservient to their husbands or fathers, their critical contribution to the success of the household gave them a certain status. Wives often developed critical skills that could enable them to keep a family business or farm going if they were widowed.

CAUSES OF THE FRENCH REVOLUTION

This picture of Old Regime France greatly simplifies a country undergoing massive changes in the eighteenth century. While the cumbersome political system no longer corresponded to France's economic and social structures, the system still appeared to be functioning in 1789. Why France experienced an event as major, shattering, and novel as revolution in 1789 will forever be debated by historians. Rather than one, simple cause, a number of factors contributed to the system's collapse.

The quintessential embodiment of the French absolute monarchy, Louis XIV, who reigned from 1643 to 1715, had a Machiavellian intelligence and confidence lacking in his successors. When Louis XV and Louis XVI met resistance in their dealings with various influential groups and people, they first resisted, then yielded, a dangerous pattern of inconsistency. Equally destabilizing to Old Regime society and politics was the Enlightenment, a vigorous intellectual movement that challenged the status quo ever more radically over the course of the eighteenth century.

While hardly a unified movement with a single philosophy—it embraced thinkers as diverse as the materialist Denis Diderot and theist Voltaire—the Enlightenment was fundamentally a new and critical orientation to the existing world, a belief in the power of science and rational thought and the goal of progress. The Enlightenment's *philosophes,* the French word for philosopher, left their mark less by their own original theories than by popularizing other thinkers, most notably the great trio of Englishmen: Francis Bacon, Isaac Newton and John Locke. *Philosophes* rejected traditional sources of knowledge such as religious authority and revelation. They argued that logic and rational thought would make existing social and political systems more just and humane. While the *philosophes,* with the possible exception of Jean-Jacques Rousseau, were not revolutionaries, their critical attitude called existing political systems to account and questioned the way things had always been done. In adopting Locke's claims that every human being has certain natural rights, including the right to liberty, some *philosophes* undermined the very foundations of divine-right monarchy.

Mediocre kings challenged by the Enlightenment also contended with the collapse of France's fiscal machinery as a result of a massive debt crisis, further eroding the Old Regime's stability. The fiscal system faced tremendous pressures, largely owing to France's highly ambitious, expansionist foreign policy. France under Louis XIV had become Europe's greatest power in terms of population, economic clout, and military might and was also a global power with extensive colonies in North America and the Caribbean. To maintain its status France needed both a powerful army to counter its continental rivals—the Hapsburgs, Russia, and Prussia—and an expensive navy to compete with Great Britain in North America. The Seven Years War, 1756–1763, fought both in Europe and in North America—where the struggle against the British was called the French and Indian Wars—proved extremely costly and resulted in the loss of nearly all of

France's overseas possessions. The most important exception was St. Domingue, now known as Haiti, an enormously lucrative sugar colony that relied on slave labor. In 1776, the French saw a perfect opportunity to reduce Britain's power by providing financial and military support to the American revolutionaries seeking independence. However, financial support for the American rebellion bankrupted the French monarchy.

Paying for France's global ambitions meant raising taxes and provoking public anger. In Old Regime France, there was no generally accepted view about who had the power to raise taxes and who should pay them. Most taxes in France in the 1700s were based on land, and nearly all the largest landowners, nobles, and the Church were exempt from land taxes, leaving small peasant farmers struggling to meet the burden. At the same time, the French economy in the 1700s was generating enormous commercial profits, increasing the size and expectations of the bourgeoisie. For the most part, the monarchy proved ineffective at tapping this new source of potential revenue. Instead, the bourgeoisie's growing size and wealth presented another challenge to the system, as their rising economic clout grew increasingly incommensurate with their feeble political power.

To try to resolve the budget crisis, when Louis XVI came to the throne in 1774, he drew on progressive thinkers like the economist A. R. J. Turgot. At this critical juncture, the monarchy's fiscal crisis raised the explosive issue of reforming taxation. The state's half-hearted efforts to fix things only succeeded in angering various groups. When Louis tried to end the noble exemption from land taxes, some nobles, following the bourgeoisie's lead, adopted an Enlightenment argument. They would be willing to pay their share of taxes, but only if the interests of the French people were represented in any decisions about taxation. The nobility's interests differed from those of the bourgeoisie and the peasants, but their argument cast the king's attempt to change the system of taxes, which would have spread the tax burden more equitably, as despotism. Nobles began to demand that the king consult with the closest thing France had to England's Parliament, the Estates-General, an ancient assembly that had not met in over 150 years.

The French Estates-General consisted of three separate estates. The First Estate was the Clergy, the Second Estate was the Nobility, and the Third Estate was equivalent to the Commons—or, in the famous phrase of the Abbé Siéyès, everyone else. By the 1780s, the archaic Estates-General no longer reflected the growing complexity of French society. The Third Estate, once only peasants, now included a hugely diverse group, from poor peasants to middling shopkeepers to wealthy merchants, lawyers, and bankers. Still, the Estates-General was the only representative body France had and, after resisting, Louis XVI gave in and agreed to convene the Estates-General in May 1789.

Unwittingly, the Old Regime had crossed the Rubicon, as the fossilized institution of the Estates-General became the vehicle of revolution. Disputes quickly erupted over the issue of representation, with demands that the Third Estate, given the size of its constituency, should have twice as many seats as any other estate. Leading voices also demanded that all three estates, rather than voting separately, convene as a single body and that the members vote "by head" and not "by estate."

By June 1789, the situation had reached a critical impasse when, on June 10, the Third Estate invited the other two to join them and form a single assembly. With some reform-minded members of the First and Second Estates joining them, on June 17, the Third Estate, to reflect its new self-definition, changed its name to the National Assembly. On June 23, Louis angrily locked the National Assembly out of its meeting room. In defiance, members of the National Assembly found an empty royal indoor handball court, convened, and swore an oath, the Tennis Court Oath, to continue meeting until they had written a constitution for France.

Outmaneuvered, Louis ordered all the nobles and clergy of the first two estates to join the National Assembly. Yet at the same time, rumors began to circulate that the king was raising an army to put down the people of Paris and disband the National Assembly. In search of arms and ammunition, on July 14, 1789, the people of Paris stormed the Bastille, a medieval fort that had once served as both a prison and, more to the point, an armory. This date was eventually enshrined by the popular imagination, and republican commemorations, as the start of the French Revolution.

THE BIRTH OF A REPUBLIC (1789–1793)

Thus a noble rebellion against royal power launched the Revolution that overthrew the monarchy. Paradoxically, this result was unintentional. The common goal in 1789 was to create a constitutional monarchy loosely modeled on that of England, with a king who retained the right to appoint his ministers and conduct foreign policy but who would consult with a representative body such as the National Assembly to determine taxation and pass legislation. Once the National Assembly had come into existence, it thus insisted on a constitution to delineate the powers of the various branches of government.

Initially, Louis XVI surrendered to the prospect of a constitutional monarchy, less from conviction than necessity. But the Revolution soon established its own dynamic and moved away from its initial and modest proposals. Over the summer of 1789, wild rumors about the nobility's violent intentions against the peasantry sparked a peasant uprising known as the "Great Fear." Across France, peasants besieged the sites and symbols of the Old Regime, killing local representatives of the nobility and torching the manor rolls that listed their rents and honorific dues. Culminating on the night of August 4, 1789, the National Assembly ratified the peasants' actions, abolished the "feudal system," and declared defunct all privileges that set nobles apart from commoners. With the large estates broken up and all honorific and most monetary dues erased, small family farms became the norm across rural France. In one of its most enduring legacies, the 1789 Revolution left France with a large, independent peasantry.

The next step taken by the Assembly also reflected the sweeping desire to end privilege and create a system founded on equality. On August 27, 1789, these "representatives of the French People" set forth its guiding principles: "[C]onsidering ignorance, forgetfulness or contempt of the rights of man to be the only causes of public misfortunes and the corruption of Governments, [we] have resolved to set forth, in a solemn Declaration, the natural, unalienable and sacred rights of man." Informed by Enlightenment ideals, like the American colonists' Declaration of Independence, France's Declaration of the Rights of Man and Citizen insisted that "Men are born and remain free and equal in rights."[2]

Some members of the clergy supported the National Assembly, but events would drive a lasting wedge between the revolutionaries and the Catholic Church. The fiscal pressures that forced Louis XVI to convene the Estates-General remained, and the new government had financial obligations to meet. To raise money, in November 1789 the National Assembly voted to sell land owned by the Catholic Church, justifying the vote as the means of covering the costs of replacing Church-run hospitals and orphanages with public ones. Not surprisingly, this move infuriated the Catholic clergy, as well as the nobility and the king. Tensions were ratcheted up yet again in 1790 when the Assembly passed a Civil Constitution of the Clergy requiring that priests take an oath of allegiance. These early revolutionary actions laid the foundations for a bitter, longstanding division between the Catholic Church, the Revolution, and its republican heirs. Alarmed by the National Assembly's actions vis-à-vis "feudal dues" and Church property, some nobles saw the writing on the wall and left France, becoming émigrés who hoped that the Revolution would fail and they could return to the old ways.

A constitution establishing a constitutional monarchy was formally adopted in September 1791. A new representative body, the Legislative Assembly, elected under the 1791 Constitution, replaced the National Assembly. Although it restricted suffrage to adult males who paid at least three days' wages in taxes, the Legislative Assembly passed some measures that were quite radical for its time. For example, it created the Committee of Public Instruction that, in theory, would provide education for all children. Nothing much came of this committee, but other actions proved lasting. The Assembly also emancipated Protestants and Jews, giving them full political rights. Also in 1791, the Assembly enacted a Penal Code that intentionally omitted restrictions on private sexual conduct between consenting adults, making France the first to abolish sodomy laws. In March 1791, the assembly abolished all guild restrictions on exercising trades and all tolls and trade restrictions inside France. It created an entirely new administrative division of France, replacing the old, traditional provinces with new departments of roughly equal size. Wanting the state to replace the Church in family matters, the revolutionaries in 1791 made marriage a civil contract. For the family to reflect France's new foundation of liberty and equality, the Assembly ended primogeniture and mandated that family property be divided equally amongst heirs. Finally, the Legislative Assembly on September 20, 1792 legalized divorce, putting an end, in family life, to arbitrary authority.[3]

While it did desire greater equality within the family, the Legislative Assembly never considered granting women the vote. Women's exclusion from full citizenship frustrated Olympe de Gouges, a middle-class woman who had long been active in enlightened circles. In 1791, she published the Declaration of the Rights of Woman and the Female Citizen, which paralleled point by point the 1789 Declaration of the Rights of Man and Citizen. Her attempt to extend the concept of citizenship and equality to women had little effect. Also inspired by the language of liberty emanating from France, slaves in St. Domingue (Haiti) revolted in 1791 and in 1793 won their freedom and, temporarily, the island's independence. In 1794, the Revolutionary government abolished slavery throughout the French empire, but Napoleon restored slavery in Haiti in 1802. Still, from 1792 on, abolition of slavery became a key tenet of French republicanism.

De Gouges' declaration and the slave revolt in St. Domingue underscored the potential for radical change that the Revolution had unleashed. Foreign powers, watching events in France unfold, grew increasingly unsettled. Monarchs across continental Europe could not help but feel threatened by the notion that the people might rise up and limit their power, forcing them to consent to a constitution and parliamentary rule. Aware that France was distracted by internal turmoil, Prussia and Austria tried to scare their traditional nemesis into reversing some of the Legislative Assembly's new policies with a joint declaration in August 1791 that they would intervene if necessary to protect Louis XVI. After vigorous debates in France as to how to respond to the Prussian/Austrian declaration, a pro-war group took control of the Assembly. The Jacobins, so-called for the political club most of them came from, believed that war with Prussia and Austria would unify the country. On April 20, 1792, France declared war on Austria, followed shortly by a draft of newly minted citizens into the army.

In June 1792, the men from Marseilles arrived in Paris, ready to serve in the army, singing their soon to be famous song. On July 28, 1792, the German Duke of Brunswick issued a hostile declaration holding the inhabitants of Paris responsible for any attack on the king. This attempt at foreign intervention again only escalated tensions in France, in effect dooming the monarchy. In Paris, a bloody and violent popular uprising on August 10, 1792 led to the suspension of the king, Louis XVI. The constitutional monarchy instituted a year earlier could not work. The Legislative Assembly called all men over age 25 to elect representatives to a Convention that would write a new constitution and determine Louis XVI's fate. Assembling for the first time in September 1792, the Convention, in a truly radical break, immediately deposed Louis, proclaiming France a Republic. It is to this moment that a new political tradition of republicanism in France can be officially dated—one inseparable from the Revolution that spawned it.

FRANCE'S FIRST REPUBLIC (1793–1804)

Overturning the king was bound to anger the Prussians and Austrians already at war with France. The Convention's next step only further escalated tensions. In November and December 1792, the Convention issued two "Propaganda Decrees." The first promised "fraternity and help to all peoples who wish to recover their liberty";

the second stated that France would establish "free and popular" governments in any territory it occupied.[4] In other words, facing military disaster, France's new republican leaders threatened to export their revolution to other parts of Europe. The Propaganda Decrees represented the first articulation of what French republicans would call their *mission civilisatrice,* or civilizing mission. Based on the assumption that the values of the French Revolution—Liberty, Equality, and Fraternity—were not specific to France but were universal human rights, the French men who came to power in 1792 insisted that they could and should be spread by force of arms if necessary. Obviously, every other power in Europe had much to lose.

Louis XVI and the revolutionary leaders were at a critical impasse. Even among the members of the Convention, the question of what to do with Louis himself was controversial. Foreign armies were invading France and threatening to restore the king by force. The French army, missing most of its noble officer corps, faced a series of military defeats. Some members of the newly elected Constitutional Convention argued in favor of sparing Louis' life. A radical faction in the Convention disagreed; they managed to take control, and in January 1793 the Convention voted 380 to 310 to execute Louis XVI. France would remain a Republic, at least for the time being. Nine months later the former queen, Marie Antoinette, was also tried and executed for treason. Their son died in prison in 1795, leaving no direct heirs.

Depending on one's perspective, it was either the best or the worst of times to guillotine a king. Six months after Louis XVI's execution, in June 1793, the Convention completed France's new constitution. The 1793 Constitution abolished slavery and created a truly egalitarian and democratic Republic based on universal male suffrage. Yet this very radical constitution never went into effect: With the very survival of the new Republic at stake, leaders of the Convention decided to set the constitution aside and create an emergency government to deal with the extreme circumstances France faced.

On the military front, disaster was imminent. Both rapidly advancing foreign armies and an internal, pro-Catholic counter-revolutionary uprising in a western region known as the Vendée threatened the regicide Convention in Paris. With 749 deputies making effective government impossible, the Convention appointed 12 of its members to a smaller governing body called the Committee of Public Safety, which took over running the war against foreign powers, the fight against the counter-revolution in the Vendée, and ensuring adequate distribution of food to the cities. Eventually one member of the Committee of Public Safety, a provincial lawyer named Maximilien Robespierre, unofficially took charge of the Committee, becoming, in effect, a dictator.

With his fellow Jacobins, Robespierre established the "Reign of Terror" in order, as they saw it, to save the Revolution. During the Reign of Terror, which lasted from September 5, 1793 to July 28, 1794, the Convention confiscated the land of nobles who had left France, requisitioned food from peasants, and froze prices and (eventually) wages. Thus the Revolution came full circle. From contesting royal despotism, by 1793 the Revolution resulted in an extreme dictatorship of the Left, a repressive system of top-down control and violence to support an all-out war against both internal and external foes. "No liberty for the enemies of liberty," exclaimed Louis de Saint Just, a member of the Committee of Public Safety.

Blaming France's military and social crises on secret plots and conspiracies to overthrow the Revolution, the Committee passed the Law of Suspects on September 17, 1793, giving it the power to arrest and punish anyone for anti-revolutionary acts, speech, or writings. Thus the Law of Suspects targeted not just counter-revolutionaries bearing arms but also peasants who grumbled about food requisitions, relatives of the émigrés, and even people with "no visible means of support." To deal with the huge number of cases, the Committee of Public Safety created special tribunals across France to try cases quickly and to send those found guilty of anti-revolutionary activity to the Reign of Terror's ultimate expression, the guillotine, considered by revolutionaries to be the "scythe of equality." "Terror" wrote Robespierre, "is nothing other than prompt, severe, inflexible justice." Estimates of those killed during the Reign of Terror range from 20,000, counting only those executed through the legal process, to over 200,000, including those killed in the suppression of the counter-revolutionary revolt in the Vendée. In Paris alone, during the Reign of Terror about 100 people a month were executed, but in its final month the Terror sent some 1,300 Parisians to the guillotine, feeding the legend of streets running red with blood. Although it lasted less than a year, the Reign of Terror would have traumatic consequences for French politics and society; in many people's minds, republicanism and terror became irrevocably associated.

While some people initially supported the Terror to save the Revolution from its enemies, once France turned the tide against both external and internal threats, defeating the Vendée and pushing back the foreign invaders in 1794, the Terror's days were numbered. Eventually Robespierre, increasingly isolated, lost control of the Convention. After he and the members of his circle were arrested, accused of plotting against the revolution, and executed for treason on July 28, 1794, the Terror came to an end. The Convention disbanded the Revolutionary Tribunals, freed thousands of prisoners, lifted the strict wage and price controls, and closed the Jacobin club.

A new kind of Republic then emerged in 1795, the Directory, with a new constitution. To prevent the excesses of the Terror, rather than a single house controlling all functions, the Directory rested on a separation of powers. The executive, a five-man committee, had limited powers over the two-house legislature. While it overturned the Convention's most radical policies, the Directory maintained two fundamental aspects of the Revolution, a constitution and representative government, while it continued to wage war, demonstrating to those willing to be persuaded that a republic in France could rule effectively without terror. With most of its formerly noble army officers in emigration, the army promoted a new class of men who ordinarily would never have become officers. One such officer, a talented Corsican named Napoleon Bonaparte, gained wide notoriety in military campaigns against the Austrians. He had carefully promoted his image through a series of newspapers ostensibly directed at soldiers that circulated in France. Given his rising popularity and renown, a group conspiring to overthrow the Directory contacted him for support. In 1799, Napoleon helped them overthrow the Directory, replacing it with a system called the Consulate, with himself as the First Consul. In 1804, he put an end to the republican phase of the French Revolution that had begun in 1792, declared France to be an Empire, and crowned himself emperor of France.

NAPOLEON'S EMPIRE (1804-1815)

Even before he officially took the title of emperor, Napoleon governed France as a dictator. In some ways he was the first modern dictator, complete with a secret police, press censorship, and preventive detention. Yet, in recognition of the new forces in French society that had brought him to power, Napoleon was careful to maintain a republican façade. First, there continued to be elected consultative assemblies, three of them in fact, but they were largely rubber stamps, since only the Council of State, appointed by Napoleon, could initiate legislation. When he crowned himself emperor, Napoleon looked to Imperial Rome for his inspiration, introducing the plebiscite, in which the public was asked to approve Napoleon as emperor in a simple yes/no vote.

In addition to extending France's power across the continent, and indeed the globe, Napoleon worked to end France's bitter civil strife. His goal was to neutralize the passions stirred by the Revolution and convince all parties to work within his system. To do so, Napoleon had to persuade the French people that the Revolution was both alive and also over. This delicate balancing act is reflected, for example, in Napoleon's 1801 Corcordat with the Papacy. Rather than reestablishing Catholicism as France's official religion, the Concordat instead recognized Catholicism as the religion of the majority of the French people. It formalized the system of public salaries for clergy, but in exchange the Church acknowledged the toleration of other religions and accepted the loss of its former lands and of its monopoly over schools and charity. Napoleon also encouraged émigré nobles to return to France, welcoming all who took an oath of loyalty to him.

Ultimately Napoleon's political system did not outlast his rule, but three of Napoleon's creations proved profound and continue to operate to this day: the Napoleonic Code, the centralized civil service, and a national secondary school system. First, Napoleon completed the revolutionary project of imposing uniform laws and standards on France. Prior to 1789, the law varied from region to region and rested largely on customary practices, most of which had never been written down. Modeled on Roman law, the Napoleonic Civil and Penal Codes set down between 1804 and 1810 many of the Revolution's legal changes. For example, the Code eliminated all legal privileges associated with the Old Regime, such as titles of nobility, and largely left in place the equal inheritance law. While French men were said to be equal before the law, the Code created two "less than equal" groups, workers and women. Under the Code, anyone paid a wage was required to carry a small booklet that listed his or her work history. Workers needed permission from their employers to change jobs; in a court of law, an employee's word counted less than that of an employer. The Revolution's abolition of guilds in 1791 also made workers' organizations illegal. Facing even greater legal disadvantages, women became minors under the law; they were treated like children, placed under their husbands' control, unable to control property or work for wages without their husbands' consent, prohibited from testifying or serving as witnesses in court, and excluded from voting.

Second, in addition to codifying law, Napoleon created a centralized, rational bureaucracy to administer France. Based on training and merit, all civil servants across France worked for the national government. The central government in Paris appointed a prefect to oversee each department's administration. Third, Napoleon both centralized and secularized the secondary educational system, now dedicated to the formation of the Empire's civil servants and military officers through a national system of secondary schools, called *lycées*, a term that derived from the Latin Lyceum. Napoleon's move created a lasting institution, but it also transformed education into a great point of contention between Church and State throughout the nineteenth and twentieth centuries.

Napoleon is surely most famous for his conquest of much of Europe, which eventually led to his downfall. By 1810 French power extended south to Spain and east to the border of Prussia, with Russia and Austria forced allies of Napoleon. But by 1815, the revolutionary ideals he had ridden for so long finally toppled Napoleon. His conquests had conjured the genie of anti-French nationalism from the Spanish Pyrenees to the steppes of Russia, spurring peoples across the continent to emulate the French, even or especially if it meant resisting them. When Napoleon finally conceded defeat at the Battle of Waterloo in 1815, a quarter-century of warfare had left nearly 1 million French men dead, but both hopes for and fear of revolution were very much alive.

LEGACIES OF THE 1789 REVOLUTION

Since 1789 on, French law has rested on the basic legal equality of men. No future government, including monarchies and empires, tried to reestablish nobility with hereditary legal privileges. With Napoleon, noble émigrés mostly returned to France, where although they no longer had hereditary legal privileges, they and their families continued to play important roles in their regions as leading and influential citizens, permitted to use their now entirely honorific titles. Other kinds of inequalities persisted, including the less than equal status under the law of employees and women. Also, the right to vote was restricted to men of property. Some subsequent regimes placed further restrictions on groups of people, especially in Algeria, but for the most part the nineteenth century witnessed struggles to expand civil, legal, and political rights to include all French citizens.

Although nineteenth-century France held rehearsals for nearly every form of government, ranging from constitutional monarchy to republic to dictatorship to empire, from 1789 on every government has rested on a written constitution that set out the government's structure and functions as well as the limits of its power. In addition to a constitution, every government after 1789, with the brief exception of the Vichy years from 1940 to 1944, has boasted a publicly elected assembly, even though the assemblies varied greatly in actual powers.

While pre-Revolutionary France entertained a variety of political philosophies, the Revolution crystallized political alliances along a fundamental dividing line between, for lack of a better designation, the Right and the Left. Prior to 1789, very few people questioned whether or not France should have a king. The dynasty simply existed; its authority was divine. As new political philosophies emerged during the Enlightenment, some debated the idea of monarchy in theory, but few thinkers challenged the existence of the Bourbon dynasty. Criticism of Louis XVI focused on the nature of his rule, not on his right to rule. After 1789, monarchism became a political movement of the Right. Although over the nineteenth century monarchism splintered, pitting Bourbon diehards, known as Legitimists or Ultras, against moderates who eventually aligned themselves with the Orleanist branch of the royal family, all monarchists opposed a republic.

Against monarchists on the Right, the Revolution's most important legacy was the republican Left. Often referred to as Jacobins, a political club whose members made up the leading politicians during the most radical phase of the Revolution, French republicans opposed a monarchy of any kind, deeply distrusted the Catholic Church, disliked privilege, and championed representative government and liberal freedoms like freedom of speech, religion, and press. Republicans had indeed ended the legal privileges of nobility and lifted restrictions on various minority groups, including Jews, Protestants, and homosexuals, and, with prodding from colonial subjects, republicans had ended slavery. Women would have to wait, and French republicans initially also allowed for legal biases against working people. However, by the mid-twentieth century, French republicans had come to consider the government an essential tool for correcting economic and social inequalities.

In addition to those fundamental beliefs, throughout the nineteenth century, three key characteristics dominated French republicanism. First, republicans were profoundly anti-clerical. While most of them were Catholic on a personal level, they did not trust the Catholic Church as an institution and worked to limit its authority, its political power, and its dominance over primary education. Republicans, often for good reason, viewed the Catholic Church as a hostile and powerful institution that was pro-monarchy and fostered obedience to authority, not reason. The mistrust, even hatred, was mutual. The revolutionary government's confiscation of Church lands and imposition of the oath of loyalty, along with the struggle over schools, alienated the Catholic Church from republicans. This conflict would, somewhat paradoxically, begin to heal only after 1905, when the Third Republic imposed official separation between Church and State.

Second, although they desperately wanted to restore a democratic system, republicans were left after 1794 with an intense fear of another Reign of Terror, which curbed their willingness to contest nonrepublican governments in the nineteenth century. Fear of another Terror also limited how far republicans would bend to the demands of the more radical urban working class who got involved in upheavals. The fear that guillotines would reappear and the streets would again run red with blood terrified both urban republicans and the great mass of provincial small landowners and townspeople. Maintaining property qualifications for the vote was one way to limit popular pressure over elective officials. Fear of another Terror also led republicans, when opportunities arose to gain power, to refuse radical measures either to fight their enemies on the Right or to gain the support of more militant allies on the Left. They favored democracy, but with limits.

Third, France's republicans were profoundly nationalistic, as well as universalist; in fact the two tendencies reinforced each other. The 1789 Revolution came to define itself by the enemies it fought. The Revolution made ordinary French men into citizens who owned land and played an active civic role. In return, those ordinary French men were eager to fight to defend those rights and their nation. At the same time, the Declaration of the Rights of Man articulated the idea that the revolutionary

Liberty Leading the People, Eugène Delacroix (1830).

values of freedom and equality were universal and not specifically French, and encouraged citizens to believe that it was the French Republic's mission to bring those values to other peoples suffering repression. The combination of a firm belief in the right of all peoples to freedom with the expansionist goal of exporting those "universal" values by military force was a contradiction inherent to French republicanism from the start. Through much of the nineteenth century both French nationalism and expansionist notions of universalism were firmly entrenched on the Left of the political spectrum.

Fourth, on the Left, the Revolution's legacy included not just republicans but also a more radical left-wing group that derived from its revolutionary street fighters. Working people, artisans, tradesmen, and small shopkeepers—both men and women in Paris and other cities—proved critical to key events, like the storming of the Bastille, which changed the course of the Revolution. This diverse group of people came to be called the *sans culottes* (those without breeches), a reference to the fact that the men wore the long pants of the working man and not the short knickerbockers worn by aristocrats. The *sans culottes* often articulated the Revolution's most radical demands, pressing for price controls and insisting on direct, popular democracy. The *sans culottes* believed that they, the people, should be involved in the political process. They insisted on being present to witness legislative sessions and demanded the ability to recall unpopular representatives. Alongside the *sans culottes,* their wives and daughters also got involved, articulated their demands for equality, and created their own political clubs until they were outlawed in October 1793.

Repressed after the Reign of Terror, the *sans culottes* disappeared from history. In Paris, nevertheless, the popular radicalism they expressed lived on among working people, under the surface of ordinary life. Rather than exhibiting fear of revolutionary extremes, the working people of Paris romanticized the most radical era of the Revolution, passing down stories and legends. As the 1871 singing of "La Marseillaise" signaled, when subsequent revolutions broke out over the nineteenth century, popular radical traditions, techniques, symbols, language, clubs, and newspapers that referred back to the 1789 Revolution quickly resurfaced.

FROM NAPOLEON I TO NAPOLEON III (1815–1852)

Napoleon's defeat and exile to Saint-Helena in 1815 ushered in a half-century of political instability, in which the French retried every phase of the Revolutionary era. Under the watchful aegis of the European monarchs who had defeated France and whose interest was stability, the Bourbon kings were restored to the throne in 1815. While the victors over Napoleon might have preferred turning back to the Old Regime, in fact the restored Bourbon monarchy more closely resembled the constitutional monarchy that first emerged after 1789. The Restoration kings would have to abide by a written constitution, the Charter, and would have to share power with an elected assembly, although the franchise was limited by high property qualifications. Again linking family and polity, the Restoration revoked the legalization of divorce. As one monarchist explained, just as political democracy "allows the people, the weak part of political society, to rise against the established power," so divorce, "veritable domestic democracy," allows the wife, "the weak part, to rebel against marital authority." Thus, he argued, "in order to keep the state out of the hands of the people, it is necessary to keep the family out of the hands of wives and children."[5]

Another event of great future importance started at the very end of the Restoration period when the last Bourbon king, Charles X, invaded and conquered the port of Algiers, in Algeria. This act of aggression set in motion a policy of overseas expansion in Africa and Asia that would continue intermittently for the next 50 years, before climaxing in a burst of imperialism at century's end. Charles X's motivations were several, including deepening financial concerns, worries over the activities of the Barbary pirates based on the Algerian coast, and a desire to replace the loss of St. Domingue in the Caribbean. But this was not all. If the British gained their nineteenth-century empire in a fit of absent-mindedness, the French launched their second imperial career in a fit of desperation. With hold on power increasingly precarious, Charles tried to rally the nation to the throne by sending a military expedition to Algeria. The French fleet overwhelmed the defenses erected by the local Ottoman ruler, the Dey. The Bourbon flag was raised over occupied Algiers on July 5, 1830, fluttering over a city ransacked by French troops. Not only did the state-sanctioned pillaging of Algiers herald France's policy toward the rest of Algeria—which it would gradually and with extraordinary difficulty continue to "pacify"—but the transfer of physical property to Europeans also founded a constituency that would undermine future efforts at the social and political assimilation of the Arab and Berber populations.[6]

While the immediate imperial operation in Algiers was a success, the patient nevertheless died. Charles X was thrown from power less than a month later in a limited revolt led by disgruntled monarchists who quickly replaced the Restoration monarchy with a new monarchy, this one under the kingship of Louis Philippe of Orléans, cousin to the Bourbons. The July Monarchy, so called after its birth month, adopted a slightly more liberal constitution that reduced property qualifications and more than doubled the electorate, if only to 250,000 electors in a population of nearly 30 million. One significant aspect of the July Monarchy's existence is the rift it created within the right-wing monarchist camp between Legitimists or Ultras, angry at the overthrow of the Bourbon dynasty, and the more liberal Orleanist monarchists. Louis-Philippe's regime proved friendly to business, and France experienced a period of rapid economic growth, spurred in part by a state-supported program of railroad construction. It also continued the conquest of Algeria, where the French encountered a brilliant adversary in a charismatic young holy man, Abd el-Kader, who called for a jihad against the unbelievers. In 1839, Louis Philippe authorized an all-out war against Abd el-Kader and his followers, who seemed to melt into the desert in the face of French columns. Atrocities escalated, as an increasingly brutalized French army resorted to scorched-earth policies and the murdering of women and children to break

Algerians' resistance—a pattern of violence that would become a defining feature of French rule in Algeria. Only in December 1847 was Abd el-Kader defeated and captured.

Victory in Algeria was nevertheless not enough to save Louis Philippe from the same fate as his predecessor. When the king and Prime Minister François Guizot clumsily tried to stop a burgeoning protest movement in February 1848, another revolution broke out, and France's second experiment with a Republic began. While it barely lasted four years (1848–1852), the Second Republic left a deep imprint on France. Slavery was abolished for good in all territories in 1848; this decree targeted certain *vieilles colonies*, or old colonies, in the West Indies and the Indian Ocean, which had been acquired under the Old Regime and had long relied on slave labor: Martinique, Guadeloupe, and Réunion. The small French colonies on the coast of Senegal and French Guiana were also affected. The Second Republic instituted, again once and for all, universal male suffrage without any property qualifications in France, a change that ultimately, ironically, led to its own destruction. Citizenship and suffrage rights were also extended to all male inhabitants of France's *vieilles colonies* regardless of race—a group that included, in addition to those territories just listed, the tiny islands of St. Pierre et Miquelon off the coast of Newfoundland.

Beyond democratic expansion, the Second Republic adopted a series of social policies that no other government in the world had ever tried. Concerned not just with political and civic rights such as suffrage, freedom of press, and assembly, the Second Republic turned its attention to the economic welfare of its working-class citizens. It created a commission to study conditions and set policies for working people and started a program to provide jobs for unemployed workers in Paris, the National Workshops. While greatly appreciated by the working people in Paris, the National Workshops were extremely unpopular with the vast majority of voters from provincial France, who elected an assembly determined to put an end to this socialist experiment. Tragically, the closing of the National Workshops sparked a secondary popular uprising in June 1848. During the so-called June Days, Parisians not only took to the streets, but tore them up as well to build barricades. Piling up cobblestones and benches, ordinary people attempted in this way to keep government soldiers out of various parts of the city. Even though they only held out for a week, barricades, which had appeared in 1832 and 1834 in uprisings in Paris and Lyons, reappeared in in 1848, 1871, 1944, and 1968.

Karl Marx, in something of an exaggeration, described the June Days of 1848 as the "most colossal event in the history of European civil wars." More accurately, he also noted that the ruling powers of Europe "trembled at the June earthquake."[7] The French government quickly and brutally defeated the June uprising by the people of Paris. Government soldiers killed some 2,000–3,000 Parisians, arrested about 15,000 people, and eventually deported around 4,000 of them, many to Algeria. The quick repression of the uprising calmed the ruling powers, but the June Days also highlighted another critical aspect of France. While there had long been differences between the capital city, Paris, and the many and extremely diverse provinces of France, each with its own history, culture, traditions, and even language, over the nineteenth century the political gap widened between the radicalism of the people of Paris and the conservatism of the vast majority of people living in the provinces, most of them in small towns and rural areas.

The violent clash in June 1848 between Paris radicals and conservatives elected to the national assembly by universal suffrage weakened the Second Republic, making it easy prey for its popularly elected president, none other than Napoleon Bonaparte's nephew. In 1851, Louis Napoleon Bonaparte overthrew the Second Republic; in 1852, he declared France once again to be an empire, the Second Empire, and himself to be Napoleon III.

NAPOLEON III AND THE SECOND EMPIRE

According to nineteenth-century French historian and politician François Guizot, the Second Empire found its longevity, if not legitimacy, from the uneasy marriage of three qualities, as the guarantor of the French Revolution, the pledge of social order, and the symbol of national glory. The name Napoleon alone symbolized national glory; an authoritarian system would naturally maintain order, but it might seem a stretch to link the Second Empire to the French Revolution. In fact, opposition to Napoleon III came primarily from republicans on the Left. Still, like his uncle, Napoleon III posed as guarantor of the Revolution by creating a two-house legislature and leaving in place universal male suffrage. This democratic impulse might have challenged Napoleon III's rule but for his ingenious solution. In each electoral district one official candidate was named, often a local leader viewed as likely to win. Only the official candidate appeared on the ballot. The legislature, forbidden from proposing laws or even debating the emperor's proposals, had little if any real power, and for the first few years, given that they owed their legislative seats to Napoleon III's support and patronage, few elected legislators challenged his power. Still, the Second Empire was nominally democratic.

Rather than restricting suffrage, the Second Empire maintained the second quality, social order, with strict control over the press and careful police surveillance. Lacking a free press or other outlets for their views, republicans, many of whom considered themselves inheritors of the Jacobin tradition, lurked in silent opposition from the start of the Second Empire. There were other inherent conflicts in Napoleon III's ideological mix. Only the most adept political juggler could keep in the air, for instance, the revolutionary emphasis on liberty, equality, and fraternity with the elite's attachment to an inequitable and oppressive economic and social status quo. To garner the Catholic Church's support, the conservatives who dominated the Second Republic after June 1848 had passed the Falloux law in 1850, allowing the Church to set up secondary schools. The Second Empire's conservative social order also rested on nearly universal small-scale peasant farming, a key legacy of the Revolution that centered on the family as the source of labor and subsistence. Anyone, however, who challenged Napoleon III's power too overtly faced imprisonment or banishment. One of the emperor's first gestures in

1851 was to establish the infamous penal colony of Devil's Island in French Guiana. Two years later, Napoleon III took over the island of New Caledonia in order to have a penitentiary in the South Pacific.

SOCIETY AND ECONOMY UNDER THE SECOND EMPIRE

Republicans and radicals on the Left lived almost exclusively in the cities or larger towns. Peasants and city-dwellers held vastly different political priorities. Louis Napoleon's overwhelming rural support was due to more than a familiar name recalling an earlier glory. Equally important, Napoleon's birthright also guaranteed order and the sanctity of private property. The peasants, haunted by vague yet persistent memories of the Revolution, "gave the emperor their votes, and in return expected solicitude, generosity, and possibly concrete rewards."[8]

Clearly, those who left for Paris and other cities eased the situation of those who stayed behind, thus relieving the pressure on land and lessening the poverty that had been endemic to the countryside. Yet dramatic regional differences in the levels of economic prosperity persisted. Northern and central France prospered under the Second Empire, yet more distant regions like Brittany and the Pyrenees stagnated. To complicate matters even further, economic inequities appeared and grew within individual regions and departments. For example, the silkworm industry in the southern department of the Gard was crippled by disease, while its wine growers enjoyed unprecedented profits.[9]

Linguistic variations further contributed to the diversity. In revolutionary France, the singing of "La Marseillaise" was not only a glorious event, but also a peculiar one: Most of those marching, and many more of those listening, did not understand a single word.[10] French was a foreign language in much of France under the Old Regime; only with the Revolution and its new conception of politics was a single language, French, identified with the nation. Yet nearly a century later, barely half of the population spoke French as their primary language. One education official noted with some despair in 1864, "Despite all efforts, the French language spreads only with difficulty."[11] France's periphery, in particular, hardly seemed French. From the Atlantic coast to the Pyrenees and from the lowlands of the North to the southern Alpine foothills, Frenchmen and Frenchwomen spoke Breton, Basque, Flemish, German, Italian, Provençal, and Corsican. Even in the "French" parts of France, local dialects or *patois* flourished. Parisians in working-class districts and in the suburbs also spoke an *argot,* or slang, that set them apart from the middle and upper classes.

Regardless of the region and language, rural life remained primitive; farming technology and methods, as well as housing, clothing, and hygiene had changed little since the previous century. France's equal inheritance law threatened to divide farms into plots too small for subsistence. In the nineteenth century, rural families averted that disaster by limiting their family size. Nevertheless, the farm as patrimony created a strong attachment to the land and dampened ambition. Farms would stay small and in the family, conditions that discouraged each generation from taking out loans either to expand or to modernize operations. Some enterprising farmers, tenant farmers in particular, managed to enrich themselves. But life for most rural Frenchmen and women remained harsh, structured by tradition and memory. Meat was rare, literacy rarer, and hygiene rarest of all. Realist painter Gustave Courbet powerfully depicted the complex social hierarchies that dominated rural France during this period. His massive work *Burial at Ornans* rejects the temptation to impose a comforting myth or narrative upon rural France, instead documenting the many tensions among the nation's social classes. The painting's grim palette, conveying a large group of townspeople united only in their common battle against nature, is a far cry from efforts to romanticize rural life.[12]

The small farm's ascendancy in the nineteenth century slowed the growth of industry. For one thing, the stability of French rural society, with its very slowly growing population, failed to provide the huge, uprooted pool of labor that both drove demand for industrial production and gave it a labor force in England. Harsh as it was, rural life guaranteed sustenance and, clearly for many people, compared favorably with conditions in coal mines or large factories. Thus French economic development bore little resemblance to that of Great Britain, whose industrialization has often been used as the model. While Great Britain hosted a revolution in agriculture and industry, a dramatic shift of manpower from the countryside to the cities, and rapid growth of a domestic and overseas market for its burgeoning textile industry, France in the nineteenth century instead saw much slower and more erratic growth. But French commerce and industry in fact adapted well to its own particular circumstances.

Although France did not compete with the other European economies in capital goods, it remained the leader in luxury goods, such as silk, lace, fine china, and the so-called *articles de Paris* (furniture, books, jewelry, clothing, and the like). As these traditional, artisanal industries indicate, France's economic growth, which, measured per capita, kept pace with other major European economies, occurred within a stable social and technological context. France's productivity remained high because French manufacturing, which grew slowly under Napoleon III, responded to domestic demand and provided France with export goods that could compete on the global market.

The peculiarities of French manufacturing shaped the nature of France's working class. While estimations of the size of the working class in the 1860s vary, it is fair to say that roughly one-quarter to one-third of the active population, both men and women, were manual laborers. Yet the term "laborer" included master artisans, like the glassworkers of Carmaux or porcelain makers of Limoges, along with coal miners at Decazeville and construction workers in Paris. Salaries fluctuated as wildly as did levels of skill and geographical location; "aristocrats" of the working class, like the metal workers at Le Creusot, earned five to seven times more than the weavers of Mulhouse. In general, while workers' wages rose during the 1850s and 1860s, the marketplace remained volatile and job security precarious. Such fragility was compounded in the cities by the absence of a social safety net and restrictions on workers' ability to organize, much less strike. Extended kin networks and paternalistic employers still buffered the lot of rural workers. Napoleon III hoped to gain support by directing some attention to the working class, promoting the creation of popular banks that would extend credit to ordinary working people and public works projects to provide jobs. Yet Napoleon III also feared popular radicalism, and most working people viewed the Second Empire with equal suspicion.

Thus the Second Empire, despite its half-hearted efforts at economic and social justice, ultimately served the social and economic interests of the bourgeoisie, who most benefited from the modernization of banking, extension of credit, burgeoning of industry, growth of the railway network, and liberalization of trade laws. Early in the Second Empire, protectionist tariffs kept international competitors at bay, while the creation of France's first investment bank funneled capital to French business. The regime witnessed significant economic expansion, with a 300 percent increase in industrial plant and machinery. Even as beneficiaries of the Second Empire's economic expansion, most members of the bourgeoisie nevertheless felt frustrated by its authoritarian structure and advocated a return to more liberal government. The bourgeoisie, however, was hardly homogeneous, either in terms of income or political outlook.

In part, to be bourgeois entailed a certain level of income. At one end of the spectrum stood the *haute bourgeoisie,* whose ranks were heavy with bankers and industrialists, while at the other end were state employees and professionals like lawyers and doctors. This said, to be bourgeois in the nineteenth century perhaps depended less on one's income than on the way in which the income was spent. The bourgeoisie was, in a sense, a practitioner of a certain style of life—a style grounded in a general culture and attached to the domestic virtues of duty and fidelity. The bourgeois of this era "did not aim to outdo other bourgeois but to keep up with them. . . . Do as others do: that was the level he worked up to. Do not be common: that was the barrier he had to maintain."[13] With the economic prosperity of the Second Empire, the ranks of the bourgeoisie began to expand, particularly at the bottom. New upwardly mobile groups from France's provincial towns, who by dint of hard work had managed to acquire an education, moved in ever greater numbers into the professions or the civil service as well as into business and commerce. These "new social strata," as they would later be dubbed, were among the nation's most ardent supporters of republicanism, especially compared to most longstanding members of France's *haute bourgeoisie*—whose members continued to worry about the dangers of extending the franchise to all males regardless of income or education.

NAPOLEON III AND THE CITY OF PARIS

During the Second Empire, Paris was the magnet for both workers and the bourgeoisie from the provinces. During the first half of the century, the city's population soared from 500,000 to more than 1 million, doubling again by 1870. While the capital's impossibly dense streets grew ever more prone to social unrest and medical epidemics, France's successive regimes mostly dithered over urban renewal projects. It was only with the Second Empire that the political will of Napoleon met its administrative genius in Georges-Eugène Haussmann. Appointed by Napoleon as prefect of the Seine, and thus the effective ruler of Paris, Haussmann's task was to remake the city into a capital worthy of the new Second Empire's ambitions.

An engineer by training, Haussmann treated Paris as a giant machine. His goal was to improve circulation of goods, people, water, and sewage. With the chaotic and winding streets a hindrance to that, Haussmann envisioned and then created the modern street system, first linking a series of north-south streets and east-west streets to create intersecting axes bisected by connecting streets to form a series of concentric rings. These major arteries were widened and lined with trees. To create a capital fitting an empire, open spaces were created to set off the city's monumental structures, including Notre Dame and the Arc de Triomphe. The city began to stretch westward along the Seine as new neighborhoods were built for an eager and ambitious bourgeoisie.[14]

At the same time, to make all this possible, many working-class districts in central Paris were destroyed and rebuilt according to the new imperial aesthetic. This process, called *éventrement,* or disemboweling, drove the residents, most often artisans and small merchants unable to afford the rents in their rebuilt neighborhoods, to outlying districts to the north and east.[15] Prior to Haussmann, social segregation in Paris had traditionally been vertical. Before the elevator, wealthy families lived on the lower floors, working families on the upper floors, and the very poor, day laborers, and students in tiny attic garrets. Across the city, people of varied social background crossed paths. With Haussmann a new form of geographical segregation, with each social class restricted to particular areas of the city, overtook the tradition of vertical segregation. Neighborhoods in eastern and northern Paris like Belleville were largely ignored by the regime, despite the fact that the skilled workers and shopkeepers who were moving there had historically been the ferment to the city's earlier revolutions. Meanwhile, central and western Paris, girded with wide boulevards lined by the uniform and sober facades of apartment buildings, became home for an ascendant bourgeoisie and showcase for the Second Empire's pretensions. Haussmann's undeniably great achievements— which also encompassed his modernization of the roads, sewers, and water supply—came at an equally great price in rising social resentments that would soon erupt.

A FAILED LIBERALIZATION

Starting in 1860, Napoleon III introduced modest economic and political reforms, hoping to further stimulate the economy, stem rising discontent, and gain wider support. These goals, however, proved impossible to reconcile. In 1860, in keeping with the tenets of laissez-faire that previous French governments had shunned, Napoleon III signed a free trade agreement with Great Britain. Absent the traditional state protection of import tariffs and quotas, economic sectors ranging from luxury goods to metallurgy could not compete with British firms, and French industry began to stagger. Particularly in Paris and provincial cities, workers' salaries lagged behind the cost of living; the working class resented its precariousness, and even the bourgeoisie feared for its prosperity. When worker unrest escalated, Napoleon III at first responded with the proverbial carrot. He legalized strikes in 1864—a remarkable concession for any nineteenth-century regime, not to mention an authoritarian one. By 1868 he went a step further and announced that the government would tolerate workers' organizations. Yet far from stemming discontent, each of these attempts to reach out to workers fueled demands for further rights.[16] Ultimately, the Second Empire could not reconcile its need to maintain social order with its desire for social equality, and when workers pushed back, the regime once again wielded the stick. To just cite one example, when miners went on strike in 1869 and 1870 at St. Etienne and Aubin, Napoleon III responded with deadly force.

The emperor's attempts at political reform met the same fate. In the 1860s, the legislature gained the right to debate state policy and to publish those debates, and some press restrictions were lifted. Such liberalization only whet the opposition's appetite for a return to a genuinely representative government. As newspapers gained greater freedom, openly republican papers like Henri Rochefort's *La Lanterne*

French school in Algeria, circa 1860. Private Collection/Archives Charmet/The Bridgeman Art Library.

relentlessly ridiculed and criticized the regime. *La Lanterne* announced in its very first issue, "France has 36 million subjects, not counting the subjects of discontent."[17] Even in the legislature, Napoleon III's attempt to appease the growing opposition from Orleanists, Legitimists, and republicans of various stripes failed. The legislative elections of 1869 resulted in striking gains for the republican opposition. This led both to the formation of a new ministry under the young opposition leader Emile Ollivier and to the renewal of doubts about the Second Empire's future. As Napoleon III himself observed forlornly to English reformer Alfred Cobden, "[W]e make revolutions in France, not reforms."[18]

The emperor's plans for liberalization also extended to recently "pacified" Algeria, with equally contradictory results. In the 1850s, the army was administering France's newest overseas territory, which was now opened to colonization. By 1849, 35,000 settlers had arrived in the fertile coastal regions of Algeria from Europe, fleeing poverty and seeking land at the expense of the estimated 3 million native and predominantly Muslim inhabitants, made up of both Arabs and Berbers. These same settlers were determined to keep native Algerians subjugated. At first Napoleon III went along with the settlers' wishes, but in 1860 he changed his mind and declared that Algeria was an Arab kingdom under French protection and that Algerians' religion and land had to be respected. Only through such respect could the Algerian people be brought, or so the emperor maintained, to accept their new *patrie* or fatherland—France.

Such pro-Arab sentiments only turned the settlers against the emperor and made them, too, into ardent republicans. Ironically, the very Arab kingdom that was supposed to protect natives' interests and traditions guaranteed that France would henceforth treat Algerians as subjects rather than citizens. In a landmark decision in 1865 Napoleon III decreed that Algerians were French but could not acquire citizenship without first renouncing the right to be governed by Muslim law and agreeing to live under the French Civil Code. For a Muslim such renunciation would be an act tantamount to apostasy, and few applied to become citizens. Yet without citizenship, Algerians would never see their rights either acknowledged or upheld by the colonizer.[19]

THE EMPIRE AND EUROPE

The Second Empire's ideological contradictions were most marked in the realm of foreign affairs. As domestic economic and social pressures threatened the regime, Napoleon III increasingly relied on the "splendor" of French glory abroad; his throne became hostage to a "politics of grandeur" that had neither an administration nor an army capable of carrying it out. The timing of his decision to seek glory abroad could hardly have been worse, given the ambitions of Prussian chancellor Otto von Bismarck. While the French emperor increasingly looked abroad in order to maintain cohesion at home, the Prussian chancellor first had to create a nation in order to impose domestic order. Bismarck had concluded that Prussia could lead the mosaic of small states to German unification only if he succeeded in fomenting a war with France.[20]

Before 1870, France, not Germany, was the great threat to the continental balance of power. Whether monarchical, republican, or imperial, since the reign of Louis XIV in the 1600s, France had pursued an aggressive diplomacy on the continent. However, France's political, military, and economic dominance began to suffer in the nineteenth century. Great Britain's rapid industrialization, followed later in the century by Prussia then Germany, quickly outstripped French growth, whose essential raw materials like coal and iron ore were located in northern and eastern regions along the border with Germany. The vulnerability of these resources was underscored by demographic trends; compared to Germany, France's birth rate was anemic. Prussia's stunning military victory over the Austrian empire in 1866 led to the creation of the North German Confederation, whose population nearly equaled that of France, with an army one-third larger and coal production three times greater. A number of French observers, alarmed by the relative nature of national greatness, were unnerved by the appearance of this young giant on their eastern frontier. Even moderate and liberal opponents of the Second Empire began to argue in the 1860s on behalf of a preemptive war against Prussia, echoing historian and Orleanist minister Adolphe Thiers' assertion that the only way "to save France is to declare war on Prussia immediately."[21] As Louis Napoleon's blunt-spoken wife, Empress Eugénie, told the Prussian ambassador: "We are in danger of finding you in Paris one day unannounced. I will go to sleep French and wake up Prussian."[22]

Eugénie's native Spain happened to set in motion the chain of events that led to the empress' waking up, if not Prussian, at least as an exile in England. Intent on completing German unification under the aegis of Prussia, Bismarck spied his chance south of the Pyrenees. He persuaded Prussian King Wilhelm to propose a member of his royal family as candidate to the vacant Spanish throne, knowing full well that it would alarm France. Though Wilhelm soon withdrew the candidacy at the behest of the other European powers, Napoleon and his closest advisors were not mollified. On the defensive back home, Napoleon III desperately needed a foreign policy success to rally the nation. As a result, the French foreign minister, the Duc de Gramont, demanded that Wilhelm foreswear any future role in the Spanish succession. Bismarck transformed the king's refusal into a diplomatic slap in the face. National honor demanded immediate satisfaction and, on July 19, 1870, France declared war on Prussia. A new chapter in the history of French republicanism was about to begin.

CHAPTER 2

L'Année Terrible
1870–1871

War broke out on July 19, and by October 3, 1870, Prussian forces had encircled Paris. The city's residents gathered around green posters plastered across the city. They announced the formation of 10 battalions of women, called the Amazons of the Seine, who would be trained and armed to defend Paris. Moreover, they would be garbed in dashing black and orange uniforms, complete with hats. Women were invited to sign up at 36 rue Turbigo, the office of Félix Belly, the entrepreneur behind the scheme. The one requirement was that the applicant bring along a member of the National Guard to vouch for her patriotic character. Women flocked to the office, but the National Guard quickly quashed the project.[1]

Félix Belly soon disappeared—it turned out he was charging each applicant an "enrollment fee"—but the image of Amazons rallying to the defense of Paris had a much longer life. In the wake of an armistice, the victorious Prussians pulled back, only to be replaced by French troops who in turn besieged a rebellious Paris. War against Prussia became a civil war between the city of Paris, which declared itself the Commune and inheritor of France's revolutionary tradition, and the rest of France.

What had mostly been a fiction during the Prussian siege became briefly a reality during the short-lived Commune: Women achieved unprecedented social and political prominence. Their newfound freedom reached as far as military activity. Women were seen carrying arms and wearing uniforms in the streets, and newspapers followed the activities of Louise Michel, whose name became indelibly linked to the Commune: "Citizen Michel picked up the wounded under the royalist shells and, when necessary, returned fire."[2] She later explained in her memoirs that while she "loved the smell of gunpowder," it was devotion to the Revolution that inspired her to fight.

This was undoubtedly the motivation of many other women; as one prominent participant, André Léo, declared: "Great causes excite the same sentiments in all human hearts." This "great cause," for Michel, Léo, and countless other women, meant the freedom to enjoy the same rights that 1789 had promised men. At the same time, this "great cause" horrified most of the rest of France. Recalling the

26

Woman at the Hôtel de Ville, Second Day of the Paris Commune, 1871, Daniel Urrabieta
Vierge. Musée de la Ville de Paris, Musée Carnavalet, Paris/Lauros/Giraudon/The Bridgeman Art Library.

bloody events of 1871, Jules Claretie was appalled by the image of "squads of women, armed, uniformed . . . running through the streets." "We can only wonder," he lamented, "from what slime the human species is made and what animalistic instincts, hidden and ineradicable, still crouch in the dark soul of mankind."[3]

Past and present, revolution and reaction, gender and class made for a perfect storm in 1871. Fear of social disorder and hope for a new political order collided in the streets and on the barricades of Paris. For its enemies, the Commune and its train of evils were epitomized by women; their sudden prominence—in the streets, political clubs, newspapers, and various institutions—was proof of a world turned upside down. For its defenders, the Commune heralded the fulfillment of the history first unleashed in 1789; for Léo, the "struggle [was] finally beginning between what is usual and what is right, between the ways of the old order and the spirit of the new era."[4] Though the path was longer and more torturous than Léo and Michel believed it would be, ironically the disasters of the Franco-Prussian War and the Paris Commune eventually led to the completion of the work of the French Revolution, a century after its birth.

THE FRANCO-PRUSSIAN WAR

History offers few more striking examples of politically disastrous and morally egregious statements than Prime Minister Emile Ollivier's declaration in July 1870 that he accepted the decision to go to war with Prussia "with a light heart."[5] While this statement could serve as the epitaph of the Second Empire, it is unclear how widely it reflected public opinion. Either through prudence or patriotism, few politicians protested the regime's decision. One notable exception was Adolphe Thiers, former prime minister during the July Monarchy and in the opposition during the Second Empire. Thiers lambasted the childish justifications and lack of preparations that would lead to his own ascent to power.[6] Etienne Arago, a republican deputy, was equally outraged: "The civilized world will condemn you when this comes to light. Indeed if you make war on this basis it is because you want war at any price."[7] More spectacular though equally ineffective was the protest by Lucien-Anatole Prévost-Paradol, French ambassador to the United States. Prévost-Paradol's *La France nouvelle,* published in 1868, foresaw the collision between France and Prussia, lamenting the "rivers of blood and tears [that] will flow when it takes place." These rivers, regardless of the war's outcome, would overwhelm France. While defeat would leave it fatally weakened, victory would leave it prey to an undying German desire for revenge. Victim of his own lucidity, Prévost-Paradol shot himself through the heart in his Washington home on July 20.[8]

By then, a feverish bellicosity was sweeping much of Paris. The streets no less than the opera halls resounded with the singing of "La Marseillaise," which had until then been outlawed by the Second Empire.[9] Groups of young men marched along the boulevards "with arms linked together or waving their sticks over their heads and shouting 'Marchons! Marchons!' at the top of their voices." Once in uniform, the men were "invariably saluted with cheers, to which they responded with cries of 'Vive la France!' and 'To Berlin!' "[10]

Beyond Paris—and even there, the working class-districts were more subdued than central and western districts—the news of war failed to spark the same fervor. From his Norman redoubt, Gustave Flaubert wrote to George Sand that he was "nauseated" by the news, foretelling a "frightful butchery" because of the "stupidity of my countrymen."[11] And while the provincial cities and towns staged patriotic events, the countryside appeared far less enthralled. War inevitably announced hardship—a realistic attitude on the part of rural Frenchmen more preoccupied by the dim prospects for the upcoming harvest than by abstract values like the nation.[12] Anxiety over the crops was compounded by the sacrifices imposed by military conscription. If you pulled the short straw, the term of service was five years—an eternity for peasants. Rural families most often lacked the resources of the urban bourgeoisie, which could pay for the conscripted man's exemption from service by buying a replacement.

Consequently, it is not surprising that official reports noted widespread apathy, diffidence, and fear among the peasantry. Ignorance of current events, too, was common. Observers frequently underscored the surprise evoked among the peasantry by the official declaration of war. In a sense, Paris no less than Berlin was a faraway country inhabited by people of whom the peasants knew nothing.[13] This helps explain the contrast novelist Georges Sand noted in her journal between the ebullience in Paris and fear and anxiety that had overcome her rural neighbors in the Berry region.[14] In the end, although public opinion fluctuated, many Frenchmen and Frenchwomen either seemed resigned to the war or were driven by a kind of patriotic determination.[15]

As the French marched to war in the summer of 1870, the fixation on past glories blinded them to the shortcomings of their military preparation for war. By 1870, the many inadequacies of the military had been transformed into a sort of national genius embodied in *"le système D,"* for *se débrouiller*—to make do. In contrast, the Prussian military establishment had fully made use of the gains of its more advanced industrialization. For example, they brilliantly adapted the railway system, exploiting it for speed of troop concentration. This allowed the Prussian commanders to concentrate their forces at decisive points—ironically, a basic principle of Napoleonic strategy.[16] Unlike their Prussian counterparts, the French military command not only failed to assume control over the rail system but also concocted a plan of staggering complexity that sent regiments, reservists, and supplies circling across the country in search of one another. As a result, by the third week of mobilization, only half of the French reserves, most often bereft of their equipment, had joined their regiments, while the other half, hostages of rail snarls and marooned far from their destination points, "spent their days sleeping, drinking, begging, and plundering army stores."[17]

France was at an equally critical disadvantage in terms of the numbers and quality of its soldiers. With its reserve and guard contingents, the ranks of the Prussian army, overwhelmingly conscripts, exceeded 1 million. The French army, on the other hand, was half the size and depended largely on professional soldiers, the *grognards* (or grumblers, a term of affection for Napoleon's troops) who had once been the nation's glory. But those days were past. In 1867, the blunt-spoken general Jules Trochu, who would assume control of the army during the last phase of the war, lambasted French soldiers, in a book titled *The French Army,* as too old, too drunk, and too cynical to defend the nation.[18] France's embrace of a small, professional army during the Second Empire partly resulted from the fear inspired by the example of the revolutionary citizen army of 1792 that cast its shadow across the entire continent. Moreover, the Second Empire found itself in a position similar to the governments of most modern liberal societies, unwilling to alienate its bourgeois supporters by the imposition of either a draft or universal military service. The depth of differences between civilians and military planners was plumbed in an exchange during the regime's ill-fated effort to reform military conscription in 1869. When opposition politician Jules Favre protested that the army was intent on turning France into one vast complex of barracks, the chief of the French Army, Marshal Niel, replied caustically, "As for you, take care that you don't turn it into a cemetery."[19]

If armies rose and fell on the quality of armaments and materiel alone, then France was in good shape. While the French muzzle-loading brass cannons did little more in 1870 than offer target practice for the Krupps breech-loading cannons, the *chassepot* rifle outclassed its Prussian equivalent, and France had actually built and tested an early rapid fire machine gun, the *mitrailleuse*. France's fundamental problems were elsewhere. Training, tactics, and organization, not technology, were the crucial differences between Prussia and France. The *chassepot* was only as good as the men who wielded and commanded it. The machine gun's development was so swaddled in secrecy that its efficient use remained an utter mystery. The new weapons served as little more than symbols of institutional incompetence or paralysis of will when abandoned *chassepots* littered the muddy banks of rutted roads along which streamed demoralized and retreating troops.

The French commanders also showed they had neither learned nor forgotten anything from earlier wars. The military command was a throwback to an earlier century, filled with men who most often owed their commissions to family or social influence.[20] The density of intellectual mediocrity, strategic incompetence, and organizational ineptitude at the top, when added to a widespread indifference to the Second Empire and Napoleon III among the troops, suggests that France had lost the war before it was begun. In contrast, Prussia's political, military, and industrial leaders had catapulted their country from a provincial backwater to continental power, one that carefully harvested the lessons of earlier wars and no less methodically planned for the next one.

On July 28, 1870, under the intent gaze of the Empress Eugénie, Napoleon III headed east from Paris to assume command of his disorganized forces. Harried by spasms of pain from a huge bladder stone, Napoleon could barely master his horse, much less the quickly moving events on the front. A series of rapid and bloody battles at the towns of Wissembourg, Froeschwiller, and Spicheren, while of negligible strategic importance, nevertheless sapped the morale of French troops, undone by weeks of poor logistics and incompetent leadership.

As with the declaration of war, the public's response to the news of the initial Prussian victories varied dramatically. While the countryside, particularly those areas most distant from the battles, reacted with a combination of anxiety and confidence, Paris burst with disbelief, then anger. On August 7, crowds spilled into the boulevards, demanding the arming of the populace—an event, with its deliberate echoes of 1792 and the violent birth of the First Republic, that hardly reassured an increasingly embattled imperial entourage. The following day, the republican legislators, prodded by the crowds—several thousand protesters milled in front of the National Assembly calling for the overthrow of the Second Empire —demanded the resignation of Prime Minister Ollivier, the cashiering of the general staff, and the creation of a war committee. These demands reflected a dramatic shift for the Left: The "regime was now being attacked, not for being bellicose, but for being incompetent."[21]

On August 9, 1870, Eugénie, having sent a terse message to her husband that insurrections were imminent in Paris, oversaw the overhaul of the government, now under the leadership of the Comte de Palikao. The new ministry attempted to galvanize the nation's defenses by reforming the army and mobilizing a National

Guard that, until then, existed mostly on paper. The Palikao ministry also began the crucial task, given the increasing likelihood of a siege, of stockpiling essential supplies in the capital. Yet, while Paris prepared to continue the war, Napoleon III's forces, given the unhappy moniker "Army of the Rhine," lurched in retreat, prey to deepening confusion and uncertainty. On August 17, a listless emperor turned over supreme command to François Achille Bazaine, a general whose popularity was based on his humble origins, not his strategic brilliance, and whose middle name proved as hollow as the name of the army he now led.

Barely installed as commander, Bazaine saw his army cut in two by Prussia's inexorable advance. The forces led by Marshal MacMahon, under the nominal command of Napoleon III, were paralyzed by conflicting orders. MacMahon's efforts to defend the Second Empire by retreating to Paris were countermanded by Eugénie, convinced that any such move would have the opposite effect. Paris, she feared, would then fall not to the Prussians, but to irate and rebellious Parisians. As the empress asked her husband, who had initially agreed with MacMahon's strategy, "Have you considered all the consequences which would follow from your return to Paris under the shadow of two reverses?"[22] The conflicting political and military imperatives thus spurred a cascade of commands and counter-commands that fatally delayed any effective strategy. MacMahon finally led his demoralized and exhausted troops to the eastern fortress city of Sedan, while Bazaine's forces were forced back on Metz.

General Ducrot famously described the situation of MacMahon's army: "We're in a chamber pot and about to be shat on." Indeed, Moltke's forces quickly enveloped Sedan on September 1 and overwhelmed French efforts to defend their outlying positions. The battle quickly turned into a slaughter; frantic soldiers fell back upon the city, jostling against ambulances and bewildered citizens in the narrow, overcrowded streets of the medieval town. In his novel La Débâcle, Zola conveys the event's hellishness through his description of the ground outside the city's military hospital: At "the feet of the dead were the heaps of arms and legs, and in fact anything cut or hacked off on the operating tables, the sweepings of a butcher's shop when he had swept the refuse of flesh and blood into a corner."[23]

By late afternoon, Napoleon, who failed even in his attempt to die earlier in the day by riding his horse across the battlefield, ordered that the white flag be raised above the city. After brief negotiations, the French surrendered on September 2, 1870. The French "Army of the Rhine" lost more than 17,000 men at the Battle of Sedan, and Prussia captured more than 100,000 French soldiers, who were parked for a week in huge outdoor pen erected on a nearby plain without shelter or adequate food before their transfer to Prussia. The French officers, on the other hand, were able to return to France upon giving their word they would not again take up arms against Prussia. All the while Napoleon, with his imperial suite in tow, was allowed to pass through Belgium on his way to captivity, thus avoiding the humiliation of passing in front of the men he had so horribly failed. Bismarck's terse observation—"There is a dynasty on its way out"—was accurate, but blind to his victory's far-ranging consequences for France, Europe, and the world.

THE FALL OF THE EMPIRE

On September 4, 1870, when news of Sedan's fall and Napoleon's captivity reached Paris, the city's residents filled the streets and then the government buildings in protest. Critic and writer Edmond de Goncourt, whose journal offers a wealth of observations during this period, noted, "Everywhere around me I hear people greet each other feverishly with the remark: 'This is it!' . . . From all this throng there comes a deep, dull murmur."[24] The murmur soon reached a crescendo; Parisians swept across the Place de la Concorde and surged into the Palais Bourbon. There, the legislature was frantically debating the Second Empire's future—a discussion rendered moot by the implosion of protesters into the chamber. Boisterous cries for the declaration of a Republic, amplified by the thousands more outside the building, could not be ignored. The legislature abandoned its final, half-hearted efforts to salvage what remained of the past, and a disguised empress fled Paris the following day in the coach of a wealthy American dentist.

Keeping a semblance of sangfroid, the legislature's republican leaders, Léon Gambetta and Jules Favre, tried to master the surge of popular anger by changing its course. They led the crowd from the Palais Bourbon to the Hôtel de Ville, the official starting line of the revolutions of 1789, 1830, and 1848. Elbowing aside members of the radical Left, already circulating lists of possible ministers, Favre and Gambetta formed a "Government of National Defense." The government was staffed almost entirely by representatives from Paris; the ministers were all committed republicans, the moderate Favre assumed the thankless task of foreign minister, and the radical Gambetta swept into the ministry of the interior. The Parisian deputies made one concession to their right-wing colleagues in the legislature, appointing as president the Orleanist, Catholic, and Breton general, Louis Trochu. Having made its arrangements and named a president, the National Assembly left the rest of the Government of National Defense (GND) in Paris and installed itself safely in Bordeaux. Eventually, to maintain links to the outside world, the GND in Paris sent a small delegation to establish a government office in the city of Tours.

The events of September 4, 1870, while remarkable, left many issues unresolved. First, neither Bismarck, who insisted upon a dependable interlocutor with whom to strike a deal, nor the French legislators accepted the newly proclaimed government's legitimacy. Second, this revolution veered from the historical template. A hated regime's overthrow was not accomplished, as in 1830 and 1848, by the taking of arms or shedding of blood. Truth be told, there was no need for arms to be taken or blood to be shed. The events of September 4 were less a "birth than a certification of death."[25] The Second Empire simply dissolved, leaving behind an institutional vacuum. The provisional government, confronted with an enormous task of national defense, threw itself into that vacuum, firmly believing, with their Parisian supporters, that Napoleon III and not France had been defeated and that the new Republic stood as insurance for the nation's ultimate victory.[26]

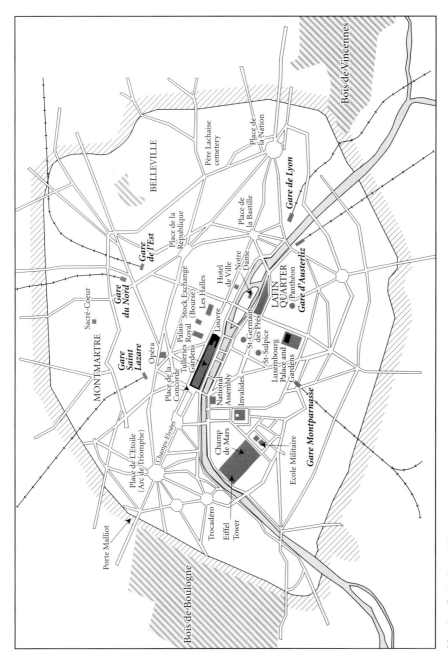

Map 2.1 Paris since 1889.

33

Third, a number of southern cities, rooted in a long revolutionary tradition, also rallied to the Republic as self-proclaimed Committees of Public Safety hoisted red flags over their city halls. Thus, in Lyons, local republicans invaded city hall, released all political prisoners, and toppled the statues of Napoleon III and Eugénie.[27] Similar events unfolded in Marseilles, Bordeaux, and Nîmes. Prefects in several rural departments reported that peasants, still loyal to the defunct regime, worried over the urban revolutionaries' intentions for their property and livelihood. Rural support of the GND was provisional and pragmatic; despite the momentary unity, there remained deep ideological fault lines running through the nation.

After September 4, Paris became the war's focal point not just because of its traditional domination over France, but also because of a series of decisions made by the GND. The cancellation of national elections, originally scheduled for October 1870, deprived the government of legitimacy in provincial eyes. More critically, having sent a small delegation to Tours, a temporary secondary seat of power, and the legislature to Bordeaux, the people actually running the GND hunkered down in Paris. This decision, though unsurprising, was not inevitable. Gambetta, for example, had argued for a stronger governmental presence in Tours so that France would not be taken hostage should Paris be captured. Gambetta's counsel was ignored, however, and the encirclement of Paris by the Prussians, completed in late September, had heavy strategic consequences. National resistance was now yoked irrevocably to Parisian resistance. Should the city fall, almost certainly would France too. As a result, the rescue of Paris became the great goal for the nation's armies. Bismarck welcomed this strategy; the knowledge that the "relief of Paris, rather than attrition and defeat of the German armies, was the objective at which the Delegation aimed" greatly simplified his planning.[28]

As Prussian forces approached Paris in mid-September, Jules Favre, without informing his fellow ministers, met with Bismarck. The inexperienced minister, who had earlier declared that France would not surrender "an inch of her soil or a stone of her fortresses," found that Bismarck expected France to do that and a good deal more. Under the illusion that Prussia considered the Second Empire, and not France, her enemy, and would show leniency in the negotiations, Favre was driven to tears by Bismarck's demands. Intoning that while regimes came and went in France, France's hostility to Germany would never abate, Bismarck informed the minister that Prussia intended to annex Alsace and part of Lorraine. Deprived of a common ground for negotiations, a deeply shaken Favre took his leave and sighed: "It is to be an endless struggle between two peoples who ought to stretch out their hands to each other."[29]

Once encircled by the Prussian forces, Paris after September 1870 was cut off from France and the world. Along with crucial tactical consequences, there were also great material and psychological ramifications. The authorities, anticipating a siege, had ingeniously improvised. The Bois de Boulogne, for example, became a vast holding pen for sheep and cattle (though the authorities overlooked the need for cows, creating a desperate situation for infants and children during the latter stages of the siege). A pond in a wealthy district of Paris, Auteuil, which had once been an artificial setting of bucolic calm for the aristocracy, was "half dried up by the sheep which kneel there, drinking, in the weeds."[30] Still, given the insatiable needs of a population far too great for the city's resources—the provisional govern-ment had based its calculations on a population of 1.5 million individuals, yet there were in fact more than 2 million inside the city walls—food, and no less critically, firewood and coal, grew increasingly scarce as the siege continued from autumn to winter.

The flocks of sheep shrank and soon disappeared from the parks, as did the trees, felled for firewood. By early fall, there occurred one of the more curious transformations in this capital of gastronomy: the appearance of horsemeat in butcher's windows and restaurant menus. At first it was scarcely accepted. In October a waiter assured Goncourt that his dish was roast beef, but Goncourt knew better—the meat "was watery, without fat, and striped with white nerves; my painter's eye discerned the blackish red color, so different from the rose red of beef." By November, waiters were proud to serve horsemeat, now itself a rare deli-cacy and replaced by even less likely candidates. Soon taking the place of a donkey whose abdomen is cut out "in festoons and lace and garlanded with leaves and roses" in a horse butcher's window were the former denizens of the Paris Zoo. One frigid evening, Goncourt admired the "trunk of young Pollux, the elephant in the Zoo" as well as camel kidneys, in a butcher's window. Cats and rats, made strange bedfellows by the siege, eventually became staples.

By early December, as Goncourt grimly noted, "You talk only about what is eaten, can be eaten, or can be found to eat. Conversation does not go beyond that."[31] Food scarcity eventually prompted the Academy of Science, which gave its imprimatur for properly cooked rat, to estimate the city's rodent population. It was placed at 25 million, translating to 12 rats per Parisian.[32] There was surely an ele-ment of self-dramatization, however, in accounts like Goncourt's. Dishes made from exotic animals were done less of necessity than a kind of patriotic exhibition-ism, while Goncourt himself reports that traditional foods were always available for the well-to-do.[33] By ordering a well-prepared plate of kangaroo meat, diners displayed the ingenuity of a cultured people besieged by German barbarians.[34] Poorer Parisians, needless to say, could hardly exhibit such bravado. Moreover, gender no less than social class determined the distribution of shortages. Men were, in general, better fed than women, if only because men could join the National Guard and thus be guaranteed three square meals a day, while women were burdened with the daily task of finding food and fuel for themselves and their families.

Like the city walls, the psychological ramparts of its male population were besieged. Women increasingly participated in various aspects of the siege, work-ing as nurses or making military uniforms in textile workshops. Though these changes mostly implicated working-class women, they were not alone. For example, Juliette Adams, the wife of the prefect of police, ran a hospital and enlisted other bourgeois women in her cause. These roles may well have politicized Parisian women, who increasingly considered themselves as participants in the defense of the city, rather than mere observers. In fact, their determination and energy contrasted sharply with an embattled and self-doubting military and political class that, failing to win a single battle, impotently watched the city slowly starve and freeze to death.[35]

No less crucially Paris, the capital of the nineteenth century, the intellectual and artistic heart not just of France, but Europe and the world, was walled in and isolated. With the withering of news, rumors, fears, and hopes flourished. Dwelling on the city's complete isolation, Goncourt wrote in late October: "Not an inhabitant who has had any news from his family for the last forty days! Never before have two million people been shut up in so absolute a prison." Better a prison, for a Parisian like Goncourt, than the provinces. For Goncourt, "To vegetate in this brutal and monotonous condition of war means for the Parisian to suffer in Paris boredom like that of a provincial city." Setting aside the element of snobbery, there remains the great emotional impact of this total isolation upon Parisians. Nothing is crueler, Goncourt lamented in December, "than to live in darkness, in night, in ignorance of the tragic fate which threatens, surrounds, and stifles you."[36]

Darkness quickly became a reality. Under Haussmann, the city had seeded its new boulevards and public places with nearly 24,000 gas lamps, transforming Paris into the "café" of Europe. During the siege, Parisian boulevards, falling back on oil lamps and candles, again dimmed to medieval times. But, as with food shortages, the eclipse of Parisian lighting was not experienced in an identical fashion. While fashionable newspapers like Le Gaulois asked if Paris, this "lugubrious city without illuminated windows, open cafés, and gaiety," was still Paris, the poor and working-class quarters hardly posed the question. Largely untouched by urban renewal, the general lack of public infrastructure in these districts entailed continuity rather than rupture during the siege.[37]

The ingenuity of Paris' response to these deprivations was not limited to gastronomy. Most famously, there were balloon flights over the city walls and Prussian forces. Prompted by the photographer Nadar, who had earlier used balloons for aerial shots of imperial Paris, the provisional government began to manufacture and launch balloons in late September as a means of maintaining not just communication, but Paris' control over the rest of the nation. By February, 65 balloons had floated above and away from Paris, carrying on these obviously one-way trips more than 10,000 kilograms of messages. Writer Théophile Gautier reflected on the precarious nature of such contact with the outside world: "On a piece of thin paper more than one man . . . has dropped a tear. Shall we ever again see those to whom we write, now that the letter-box is a balloon and the postman the wind?"[38]

Léon Gambetta was one of more than 160 passengers who reentered the world via balloon, landing near Tours in early October. Charged with the task of mobilizing southern France to relieve Paris, Gambetta took over the ministry of war and quickly pulled together a collection of veterans and conscripts dubbed the Army of the Loire. In light of the monumental logistical and institutional obstacles that

The Departure of Léon Michel Gambetta (1838–1882), in the balloon "L'Armand-Barbès," October 7, 1870, Jules Didier and Jacques Guiaud. Musée de la Ville de Paris, Musée Carnavalet, Paris /Giraudon/The Bridgeman Art Library.

Gambetta confronted, the Army of the Loire's very existence was as remarkable as the fact that it actually won one battle—chasing the Prussians from Orleans in early November. Although the Prussians retook the city a few weeks later, the significance of Gambetta's army lay not in its military fortunes but in its symbolic power. His use of mass conscription, harkening back to the glory of the people defending their nation in 1792, helped establish the new Republic's legitimacy. As one German military analyst later commented, "Above all, the spectacle was intended to impress: The German barbarians were to be defeated not by armed force but by their amazement at free France's tremendous capacity for sacrifice."[39]

The French revolutionary myth of the people in arms also consumed Paris. Fired by memories of the 1793 draft, the city's National Guard grew to nearly 200,000 men, encompassing nearly every able-bodied Parisian male. In the words of one historian, the Guard became a "popular army—or at least an armed horde."[40] Men were assigned to battalions based on their neighborhoods, resulting in a military force with strongly contrasting political values: moderate in the western and bourgeois districts, radical in the eastern and working-class areas. The latter battalions in particular, with their calls for offensive sorties— a prescription of dire futility—represented a thorn in the side of the military and political leadership. With the last offensive spasms of January 1871, Trochu most probably aimed less at breaking through the Prussian lines than at silencing this faction.

Caught between the Prussian forces from without and Parisian revolutionary forces within, the provisional Government of National Defense had no respite.

The situation worsened in late October when France's Marshal Bazaine surrendered the remaining half of the Army of the Rhine, comprising more than 100,000 men holed up in Metz since August. France's original military forces were either dead, wounded, or captured, leaving the Prussian high command free to turn its full attention to Paris. The situation inside the city was critical by the end of 1870. The city's material difficulties, compounded by the daily bombardment of the city through January and a restless populace demanding a reply of 1792, made for combustible politics.

As head of the government, Trochu's position had become untenable. Scarcely sympathetic to the moderate republicans, much less the extreme Left, he had to swallow deeply and accept their presence in order to avert civil war. As for the war against Prussia, Trochu's prudent response to the immense tactical and strategic handicaps he faced was interpreted by his republican foes as cowardice or, worse yet, treason. Hounded by a bellicose Left, which exerted pressure through newspapers, journals, and republican clubs, Trochu ordered a series of military sorties in December and January. The National Guard's lack of training and cohesion, made worse by the severe cold, turned these attacks, difficult in the best of conditions, into suicidal gestures designed to appease a militant Parisian population committed to war.

The bloody climax came in mid-January 1871 with the Battle of Buzenval. More than 4,000 Frenchmen lost their lives in a vain effort to overrun the Prussian artillery batteries. The survivors of the carnage fell back on Paris. The confusion on the battlefield was then duplicated within the city walls. In a dress rehearsal of sorts for the Commune, the same military forces that had been defeated by the Prussians just days before now repressed an uprising fomented by the more extreme republican clubs. Once they dispersed the crowds, the reality of the army's hopeless predicament was starker than before. Favre and the Government of National Defense finally concluded that Paris had to surrender.

FROM ONE SIEGE TO ANOTHER

More than three months after their earlier meeting at Fèrrieres, Bismarck and Favre again sat across from one another on January 23, 1871, meeting at the German headquarters established at the symbolic site of Versailles. But the nature of the war had also changed. On both sides of the Rhine, leaders of the professional armies that had faced one another in 1870 as tools of traditional diplomacy found themselves overwhelmed by great surges of nationalism. Bismarck and the French republican leaders had both released mass and irrational sentiments that, impossible to control, they could only hope to ride. On January 18, the new German Empire had been declared, finalizing a long movement for unification, and the German public was unwilling to accept anything less than the annexation of Alsace and part of Lorraine and a punishing war indemnity. The German military, harried by French *francs-tireurs* (partisans) shared this animosity to France. While the impact of French guerrillas on the Prussian war effort is debatable, French civilians clearly paid a terrible price. Prussian commanders held them responsible and destroyed entire towns and villages, acting on Bismarck's injunction that he wanted "no laziness in killing."[41] The same tendency to blur civilian and military realms carried over, as well, in the Prussian bombardment of Paris.

The French urban population was also under the thrall of nationalism. News of the Government of National Defense's decision to seek an armistice, while greeted with relief in the countryside, largely exempt from the war's destruction, was glumly received in Paris, a city that had sacrificed so much on behalf of France. As one guardsman wrote, "Paris suffered so greatly, yet was willing to accept death. Now, we have been turned over to the enemy without being consulted by those who failed to defend us."[42] Yet such feelings of shame and disgust, just as common among civilians, especially in the working-class districts, as among soldiers in Paris, could not trump reality. Under the Prussian threat to recommence the shelling and begin negotiations with the disgraced Bonaparte, the French government had no choice but to accept Bismarck's terms.

Signed by Favre and Bismarck on January 28, 1871, the Armistice agreement stipulated that France would, after a three-week period, hold national elections. Both sides expected that elections would create a fully representative national assembly with which Prussia could then conclude peace terms. In the ensuing electoral frenzy, the monarchists—both Legitimists and Orleanists—framed the vote in terms of war and peace. Even though a Bonaparte had led France into war, by January 1871 monarchists represented the peace party and portrayed republicans as hawks. "Those who want war to the bitter end will vote for the Jacobin list, which . . . wishes to have the last man killed and the last crown spent. Those who want an honourable peace will vote for the peace list."[43]

The identification of the republicans with the war was not entirely unjust. The Republic had, after all, insisted on pursuing the war after Napoleon III's capture, and certain republicans like Gambetta expressed in no uncertain terms their bitter opposition to the Armistice. However, the vast majority of Frenchmen, ensconced in their farms and villages, largely indifferent to Paris politics, wanted the war to end. The results of the elections on February 8, 1871 were dramatic. Republicans scarcely won 150 seats, mostly hailing from Paris and the provincial cities. Supported overwhelmingly by the rural vote, the right-wing monarchist "peace party" swept most of the remaining 645 seats. But the greatest victor of the elections was Adolphe Thiers. A small man whose physical energy and intellectual vigor belied his 70 years of age, Thiers had made his reputation during the July Monarchy, having both served Louis-Philippe as prime minister and undermined him as a political opponent. His renown, enhanced by the tragic clarity of his warnings against going to war against Prussia, thrust him to victory in 26 departments (French electoral rules allowed a single candidate's name to be placed on multiple ballots). No one was more convinced of the importance of his role than Thiers himself, declaring that his task was to "shield France from German vindictiveness, rebuild the power of the state, and give the country lasting political institutions."[44]

Though the monarchists held an overwhelming majority, they accepted Thiers as president. His official title, "Chief of the Executive Power of the Republican State," nevertheless reflected the monarchist majority's distaste for republicanism—an uneasiness perhaps felt by Thiers. While he himself had served the Orleanist king Louis-Philippe, Thiers was a realist who foresaw the irresistible rise of popular democracy. Already, during the short life of the Second Republic (1848–1852), Thiers had concluded that a Republic was the government that divided Frenchmen the least. Tellingly, Thiers appointed just one monarchist to his cabinet, while filling the rest of the ministries with moderate republicans, appointing Favre Minister of Foreign Affairs and Picard Minister of Interior. Yet even Thiers could not soften Bismarck's fundamental demands. In the end, France was forced to accept Prussia's annexation of Alsace and part of Lorraine (including the ill-starred Metz), as well as payment of a 5 billion franc war indemnity (with Prussian soldiers remaining on French soil until it was paid in full). The one concession Thiers squeezed from Bismarck was retaining the Alsatian city of Belfort, but in a humiliating quid pro quo, Prussian soldiers were allowed a victory march down the Champs-Elysées.

In retrospect, the treaty terms Bismarck insisted upon were not as draconian as many contemporaries thought. Apart from the territorial losses in the east—which amounted to more than 15,000 square kilometers of prime real estate rich in mineral resources and industry and 1,600,000 inhabitants—and sundry humiliations, France avoided any constraints on its national sovereignty, its military power, or its economic power, once having paid the indemnity, which was itself an element of traditional treaty-writing.[45] Yet Parisians, emerging from a traumatic siege, could not adopt such a dispassionate perspective. Rather than a sigh of relief, Paris would soon respond to the peace terms with the event known as the Paris Commune.

THE PARIS COMMUNE

On March 1, 1871, the newly elected National Assembly, still temporarily housed in Bordeaux, ratified the terms of the peace treaty. The February elections and resulting settlement with Germany only deepened the chasm between Paris and the rest of the nation. While the end of the war provoked a great sigh of relief in rural France, which could now go about its business, it compounded the shame and anger of Parisians, who had assumed not just the burden of the siege but also the heritage of the 1789 Revolution. For Parisian workers, the experience of the Prussian siege awakened long-repressed memories of the glory days of the *sans culottes*—as the working people of Paris had been called during the first Republic of 1792—and these memories began to shape their reactions to events.

Such memories, periodically revived in the revolution of 1830 and again during the June Days of 1848, represented the deep and tangled roots of the Paris Commune. However, by March 1871, the conflicting motivations behind the war and experiences during it provided the immediate catalysts. Experiences of the war that differed according to geography, gender, and generation were in turn sifted through different historical and ideological sieves. Emphasizing the historical continuity of events, Paris returned to its revolutionary and republican past, with political clubs and radical newspapers springing up, often named after their historical predecessors. Meanwhile, in the provinces, fearing those revolutionary tendencies in Paris as much, if not more, than Prussian demands, many ordinary people turned to conservative and traditional authorities as a counterweight. In the end, the monarchists and moderate republicans sitting in Bordeaux chose to ignore Gambetta's warnings against a humiliating peace: "Revolution will break out in Paris. . . . The unfortunates [in the assembly] fail to understand that what comes next will be worse than the war itself." Gambetta concluded that Paris "will be forced to create an independent government over which the National Assembly . . . will have no power. . . . Out of the still-glowing ashes of the war, a far more terrible civil conflict will be born."[46]

By March 1871, the dissonance between these two Frances had reached critical mass; as one monarchist observed, "Very bravely but not with impunity had the Parisians suffered . . . the privations and emotions of the siege. At first we provincials couldn't reason with them. It seemed as if we did not even speak the same language and that they were prey to a kind of sickness, what we called 'fortress fever.'"[47] The National Assembly stoked the fires with several moves between March 10 and 11, suspending pay to National Guardsmen in Paris unless they could prove poverty and closing down all clubs, all public meetings, and five newspapers. Most provocatively, the Assembly, without warning, ended a measure taken during the Prussian siege, a temporary moratorium on rents, debt payments, and pawnshop sales that helped tide people over during the siege when commerce had largely ground to a halt. Not only did the Assembly lift the moratorium, it decreed that all overdue rents be paid in full immediately, sharpening animosity between Paris and the National Assembly. In its final blow, the National Assembly, fearing the National Guard's militancy and its continued control over cannons, enflamed the "passionate patriotism" of Paris and fears of a restoration of the monarchy, by moving from Bordeaux not to Paris, but to the former royal headquarters, Versailles.[48] Thiers, determined to reassure the Assembly's concern that he would be lenient with the Parisians, wanted to "finish with" the agitators before the Assembly reconvened in Versailles on March 20.[49] Temperatures in both Paris and Versailles (shorthand for France's national government) were rising.

On March 18, 1871, the fever spiked. Early that morning, Thiers ordered troops into the working-class neighborhood of Montmartre to remove several cannons that had been under local National Guard control. For once, Thiers had miscalculated. Working-class residents resisted giving up the cannons. In a confrontation between the army and the rapidly mobilized residents, the troops refused General Lecomte's orders to fire on the civilians. As the troops fraternized with the civilians, an angry crowd lynched both the commanding general, Lecomte, and a second general who happened onto the scene. Thiers quickly ordered the removal of the regular troops from Paris, then with his cabinet he also fled Paris for the haven of Versailles. As in September 1870, in Paris, a new and makeshift government, the Central Committee of the National Guard, filled the vacuum left by a national government in flight. Faithful to historical precedent, the committee announced its birth from the windows of the Hôtel de Ville.

The National Guard committee members were republicans, not revolutionaries. From the perspective of Versailles, however, it was hardly reassuring to observe the radical posturing of a city that, in its view, had already humiliated the nation. The mutual and deadly incomprehension of both sides stunned observers like Zola: Torn between "the dissidents of City Hall and the blind bigots of the Assembly, France lies bleeding. . . . If one day history tells us how the insurrection pushed her over the edge, it will add that the regular and legitimate power did everything to make her plunge fatal."[50]

Elections for a new city council on March 26 confirmed the city's militancy, as well as the declining power of moderate republicans (reflected in the high abstention rate among voters, particularly in the western, mostly middle-class districts). Two days later, on March 28, 1871, with one eye on the revolutionary past and the other on a utopian future, the Paris municipal council, freed of its more conservative members, baptized itself the Paris Commune. The Commune's name referred not to Marx's ideas but to the municipal government of Paris, called the Commune, during the 1789 Revolution. The flush of millennial optimism exploded in other cities with similar political traditions; Marseilles, Narbonne, Toulouse, and Lyons also declared themselves communes. Yet the provincial Communards, unlike their Paris brethren, barely had the time to familiarize themselves with the levers of power before their fingers were pried off by Versailles, whose forces soon reimposed order. The "Republic of Paris" faced alone a country whose citizens by and large accepted the legitimacy of the elected government in Versailles and not that of a city whose ambitions they had long resented.

Radicals like writer Jules Vallès hailed the advent of the Commune, seeing in it the revival of the radicalism of the *sans culottes* of 1792. A participant in the events of March 18—the raising of the red flag over the Hôtel de Ville and the chanting of "La Marseillaise"—Vallès praised "a revolutionary and patriotic festival, peaceful and joyous, a day of intoxication and solemnity, of grandeur and merriment, worthy of those witnessed by the men of '92."[51] On the other hand, Goncourt, who dismissed Vallès as a "bohemian of the beer hall" (a description the young and bohemian Vallès would probably not dispute), expressed the fears of the Parisian bourgeoisie: "The unbelievable rules. . . . [T]he cohorts of Belleville [a working-class district] throng our conquered boulevards [the middle-class's public space] . . . going along in the midst of a somewhat mocking astonishment which seems to embarrass them and makes them turn their eyes toward the toes of their shoes, worn mostly without socks."[52]

These antithetical perspectives nevertheless point to important elements of the Commune. Vallès' depiction of the Commune highlights its initially festive character. Throwing off the oppressive weight of unjust political and economic regimes, the people of the Paris Commune threw themselves a party that expressed their will "to become masters of their lives and histories in the realms of politics and everyday life."[53] An undeniably, if at times overly dramatized, festive element to the Commune resulted from its spontaneous and collective assumption of a city's freedom.

Goncourt's scorn for the shabby, working-class Parisians who suddenly appeared on middle-class, Haussmann-created boulevards points to another factor. The Parisians who unexpectedly found themselves in power seemed determined to reclaim the city from the authoritarian rule of earlier regimes. This assertion of local control found voice in the new government's adoption of the term "commune," the supreme expression of self-government. The uprising of March 1871 represented a mass movement in which the Communards thought of themselves as Parisians first, workers second. It is not a coincidence, perhaps, that the "largest urban revolution in modern history occurred on the heels of the first experiment with urban planning in an industrial city"—namely, Haussmann's transformation of the city.[54] By reshaping Paris, Haussmann also reshaped the collective consciousness of working-class Parisians.

Thiers, attempting to lead a country wracked by war and unrest, could not abide the Commune's claims of local control. Invoking the recently ended civil war across the Atlantic, he declared that the capital must be brought to heel and that "any attempted secession . . . will be energetically repressed in France as it has been in America."[55] And as in the United States, this confrontation led ineluctably to civil war, not between North and South, but between France and Paris.

The Commune, a 66-man governing body for the city of Paris that combined executive and legislative functions, lasted scarcely two months, from a surprising birth on March 28 to a violent death on May 28. Paradoxically its very brevity makes it difficult to summarize. Enveloped in a thicket of actions and aspirations, undertaken by amateurs under the unrelenting pressure of the popular opinion from within and the Versailles army from without, the Commune's actions and what they meant are still debated. Yet a number of elements are clear. First, the Commune was an experiment in radical popular government, harkening back to the *sans culottes,* similarly operating in time of civil war. Though never short of frequently inspiring, occasionally maddening rhetoric, the Commune lacked resources and time. More than three-quarters of the Commune's budget, about about 42 million francs, went to war-related needs (mostly salaries for the National Guard). The rest was spread among all other services (including, critically, the bureau of military supply). While the Commune insisted on the importance of public education, its education department had a budget of just a few thousand francs.

Second, though hobbled by the imperatives of war, the Commune's great social measure, as Karl Marx announced, "was its own working existence."[56] Inevitably, many of its economic measures were dictated by the Commune's dire circumstances: the cancellation of overdue rents, suspension of sale of objects hocked at pawnshops, pensions paid to common-law wives of National Guardsmen killed in battle. In a measure that seemed quite radical at the time, the Commune created workers' cooperatives to take over businesses whose owners had left Paris.

Even more radical, some of the workers' cooperatives involved women. However, even these measures were spurred less by ideological conviction than by the imperatives of the moment and the desperate lot of most Parisians. The Commune needed uniforms, artillery shells, and other goods produced; out-of-work Parisians needed jobs. The Commune intended not to expropriate private property, but only to get production going again; in theory, property owners who returned were to be compensated. In general, the Commune's decrees, in their attempt at balancing conflicting interests with adherence to existing property rights, were far more moderate than its rhetoric.[57]

Third, the Commune was fueled less by economic than by political concerns, reflecting the fundamental belief that political injustice was the source of all other ills. This notion imbued the Commune's "Declaration of the French People," published in mid-April 1871. The document's authors, including Jules Vallès, insisted that republicanism was the only legitimate form of government—indeed, how could it be otherwise since everything just and good flowed from the mere existence of the Republic? Moreover, the declaration clarified the Commune's federalism, or desire for decentralized government with local autonomy. The Declaration affirmed that each and every commune, the name for the lowest-level administrative district in France, from Paris to the smallest village, should be equal and absolutely autonomous—a dizzying claim to make on behalf of a nation with 36,000 communes. The document also announced the complete separation of Church and State—a central concern of the French Left ever since the Revolution and a great symbolic step toward their goal of a fully secularized society.

Fourth, when not paying the bills for its defense, the Commune advanced a number of original and important social and cultural projects. Though deprived of time and money, educational reformers were encouraged in their attempts to rid the schools of religious influence and to extend basic and technical education to working-class children, both boys and girls. As this project indicates, in terms of gender politics, the Commune clearly tilted toward greater equality. The Commune decreed equal wages for male and female educators and also created a significant public space for women. Women, like writer André Léo, published in many of the Communard newspapers and spoke before political clubs, some of which were exclusively female. Working women created cooperatives to produce uniforms for National Guardsmen, provided nursing and ambulance services during the fighting. They challenged their subordinate position as both workers and women. Contemporaries were clearly aware of this sea change: "I have seen," wrote a journalist for Le Vengeur, "three revolutions, and for the first time I have seen women involve themselves with resolution. . . . It seems that this revolution is precisely theirs, and that in defending it, they defend their true future." The actions and ideas of female public actors and intellectuals like Léo; Elisabeth Dmitrieff, who organized the Women's Union for the Defense of Paris and Care for the Wounded; and Paule Mink, who wrote scathing critiques of socialist and misogynist thinkers like Pierre-Joseph Proudhon, represented an important, if temporary, leap forward for women's activism.

Finally, the attention to gender inequality was part of something fundamental to the Commune—its desire to overthrow all political and social hierarchies of power. That fellow Parisians no longer addressed one another as *monsieur* or *madame*, but as *citoyen* or *citoyenne;* that the poor and disenfranchised could, if only for a few weeks, enjoy economic rights and political power; that women were treated as the equal of men—these were great changes indeed.

THE FALL OF THE COMMUNE

The Commune achieved historical and mythical stature owing both to the millennial expectations it broadcast and to the waves of blood in which they were drowned. Its response to the looming shadow of the national government in Versailles was rhetorical, not tactical. The Commune invoked the memory of 1792–1793, of a people in arms. Imbued with the historical legend, the Commune's leaders believed that such a force would, by its very nature, overcome a counter-revolutionary force held together solely by fear or self-interest. One of the leading Communards, Charles Delescluze, declared, "When the People have rifles in their hands and paving stones under their feet, they have no fear of all the strategists of the monarchist school."

The hollowness of such appeals soon became tragically clear. On April 3, 1871, the Commune launched an attempt to stream out of Paris and sweep over Versailles; the attack quickly turned into a frantic backwash against the city's walls thanks to the ineptitude of the officers and indiscipline of the troops. This fiasco was a sickening sign of things to come. The national government's Versailles army occupied the siege positions only recently vacated by the Prussians. The Commune's military commanders and political leaders, thrown back on the defensive, descended into confusion and internal strife.

Finally, on the night of May 21 the national army entered Paris through an unguarded section of the wall, inaugurating the final phase of the Commune—known ever since by its accurate description, *la semaine sanglante,* or Bloody Week. More than 120,000 strong, the national troops systematically and brutally took over the city. As the streets grew thick with the mass of invading troops, many Communards—despite the heroic legends of every street defended to the last man or woman—simply tossed away their guns, surrendered their barricades, and melted back into their neighborhoods. Nevertheless, Communards fiercely defended a number of districts, particularly in eastern Paris, which became the defenders' last redoubt. Heavy with revolutionary associations, the Place de la Bastille offered the most effective resistance.

The remaining knots of Communards were eventually pushed back to the dense and recalcitrant working-class neighborhoods of Ménilmontant and Belleville, as well as the cemetery of Père Lachaise, where the last defenders were shot or surrendered on May 28, 1871. That same day, Marshal MacMahon, having earlier surrendered Sedan to the Prussians, could now boast of having retaken Paris from his fellow French: "Paris has been delivered. . . . [O]rder, work and security will reign once more"[58]

Children killed by a bombardment during the Siege of Paris, 1870–1871. Musée de la Ville de Paris, Musée Carnavalet, Paris /Lauros/Giraudon/The Bridgeman Art Library.

This bare narrative of Bloody Week scarcely conveys the event's ferocity and violence. While the national army suffered approximately 3,500 killed or wounded, there were, according to conflicting sources, between 10,000 and 20,000 deaths among the Communards. The majority of these deaths resulted not from battle but from the army's systematic killing of those, including the wounded, suspected of having fought with the Commune. Many men were simply shot on sight, while hundreds of others were rounded up, tried by hastily assembled military courts, then taken off to barracks or parks where they were dispatched by firing squads. Hundreds of prisoners, for example, were trundled to Père Lachaise, lined against a wall, shot, and buried in mass graves, establishing the *Mur des fédérés,* or Wall of the Federals as one of the great sites of commemoration for the French Left. More than 40,000 men and women were arrested and marched to Versailles; the dismal sight evoked pity in an otherwise unforgiving Goncourt, who thought, "They seem already half undressed for execution."[59] Reentering Paris in the wake of Bloody Week, Emile Zola described, "the corpses heaped high under the bridges . . . that frightful mound of bleeding human flesh, thrown haphazardly on the tow paths. Heads and limbs mingle in horrible dislocation. From the pile emerge convulsed faces. . . . What a lugubrious charnel house."[60]

Both Communards and soldiers of the national Versailles army were guilty of excess. On May 24, in the midst of Bloody Week, Communards executed the Archbishop of Paris, Georges Darboy, and three other hostages at the prison of La Roquette. More killings, planned or spontaneous, followed and reached a crescendo when 50 hostages—a mixture of priests and policemen—were hauled to Belleville and massacred by a crowd of men and women. Although it does not lessen the horror, the comparative rarity of such events nevertheless makes for a telling contrast with Versailles' systematic and sustained killings of Communards and civilians (a distinction necessarily blurred by the nature of the conflict.) Also, while Commune leaders often attempted to stop such summary executions, no such humanity was ever evinced by the officers fighting for Versailles, who saw their task as ridding "the country of all the scum that is spreading grief and ruin everywhere."[61]

Nevertheless, through arson the Communards unleashed their hatred of the regime on the city they sought to hold. Communards set fires, in theory, as a defensive tactic to prevent advancing soldiers from penetrating a neighborhood. Not accidentally, the Commune's fires destroyed structures closely associated with state power and gave rise to the legend of the *pétroleuses,* fearsome female incendiaries roaming the streets of Paris with cans of gasoline.[62] Nearly one-third of the city was burned down; the ashes and smoke shrouded the city, according to Goncourt, resembling an eclipse.[63] Several historic buildings, most notably the Tuileries, Hôtel de Ville, and Palais de Justice, were destroyed by fire; yet others, like Notre Dame, were saved only through the intervention of Communard officials. These buildings were closely linked to the detested rulers of the past and, it now seemed, the immediate future; the battle, lost militarily, would at least be continued symbolically.

MAY 1871

Even as the ruins of the Tuileries and Hôtel de Ville still smoldered, the tricolor flag was again flying above Paris, and bourgeois strollers were again walking along Haussmann's boulevards (whose paving stones, pried loose for barricades, had quickly been returned to their earlier function.) As he strolled along the streets, Goncourt reflected on the import of the Commune—or, more precisely, its violent suppression: "The solution has restored confidence to the army, which learned in the blood of the Communards that it was still able to fight. Finally, the bloodletting was a bleeding white; such a purge, by killing off the combative part of the population, defers the next revolution by a whole generation."[64]

Historians of the Commune have, wittingly or not, largely echoed Goncourt's interpretation. The French army's action flowed, in part, from its recent experience. An institution steeped in the glory of its revolutionary and Napoleonic successes failed to win a single battle against Prussia. More humiliation was heaped upon the army's leadership when, in the wake its defeats at Sedan and Metz, a hastily mobilized civilian army defended France with far greater resolution and daring than that shown by the French officer corps. When confronted by a radical and recalcitrant Paris, the army hid or perhaps purged its shame through the massacre of those who stood as witness to its shortcomings.

The army's shame dovetailed with Thiers' determination to rid the newborn Republic of threats from its most radical partisans. Once Paris was retaken, Thiers shed no tears over the carnage for which he bore ultimate responsibility: "The ground is strewn with their corpses; may this dreadful sight serve as a lesson."[65] The Commune's sudden rise and shattering fall marked the apotheosis of the French revolutionary tradition, and in particular the popular radicalism of its urban working people, the *sans culottes* of 1789. From the taking of the Bastille through the revolutions of 1830 and 1848 to the Paris Commune, institutional and popular forms of violence pulse through the political history of France. Once the French state lost its monopoly of legitimate violence in 1789, there ensued a series of popular challenges to established regimes over the next century, which met them with even greater ferocity. Not only were monarchies challenged by republicans, but in turn, each "Jacobin" Republic found itself challenged by more radical demands for true, direct popular sovereignty issuing from working men and women. The so-called founding massacres committed by the July Monarchy in 1832, the Second Republic in June 1848, the Second Empire in December 1851, and, finally, the nascent Third Republic in May 1871, proved the state's willingness to shed blood and the capacity and determination not just of monarchists on the Right but also of republicans on the Left to stamp out popular uprisings. As it turned out, aside from the considerably less deadly right-wing rioting in the 1930s and the internecine bloodletting during World War II, France would never again see such explosions of popular violence.[66] Ultimately, it was the brutally thorough nature of the Commune's death, rather than its short and ambiguous life, that prepared the ground for the Third Republic. Not only was popular radical republicanism sidelined by the state's resolute response, but so too were the reactionary and monarchist movements jostling one another for another shot at mastery. The majority of Frenchmen preferred their order and stability served not by kings, but by conservative republicans.

CHAPTER 3

The Return of the Republic
1871–1885

In his painting of the July 14, 1878, celebrations in Paris, Impressionist master Claude Monet depicts the rue Saint Denis awash in a sea of blue, white, and red flags. The festive scene celebrates, in a seemingly straightforward manner, the French nation's embrace of the Republic. The blur of French *tricolores,* or the tricolored flag, tied ever since the French Revolution to republican ideals, does not seem to cast either literal or metaphorical shadows across the street.

Yet shadows appear upon closer inspection. Scrawled across the flag on the right is the phrase "Vive la République"—or, rather, the beginning of such a phrase: The letters trail off into illegibility. And barely noticeable is the banner strung across the street, announcing "Vive la France." Less ambivalent in his own rendering of the same holiday was Monet's colleague Edouard Manet. Here, as one critic has observed, the contrast of the flags fluttering above both a bourgeois couple descending from a horse-drawn carriage and the crippled figure hobbling down the other side of the street—a veteran of 1848? 1870? Or 1871?—poses hard questions about the fledgling Republic.[1]

Both paintings reveal the problematic ties between France and the newly born Third Republic.[2] How could it be otherwise when the same republican devotion that inspired the Communards also drove the forces of repression? In the decade that followed the great collision of 1871, opposing attitudes toward the Republic shaped France's politics, society, art, and diplomacy, with important consequences for its citizens and subjects—women and men; workers, peasants, and the bourgeoisie; Bretons, Corsicans, and Algerians, as well as Parisians. Even republicans differed on the social ends of the state and on the line between the politics of the possible and the ideal.

THE EARLY REPUBLIC

French republican ideology, as it developed in the 1870s and 1880s, emphasized the primacy of the nation, of man's (and, eventually, feminists insisted, of woman's) capacity to reason, of the role of education and the rule of law.[3] That this political creed, embodied in the tricolor flag, would eventually be accepted by most Frenchmen and Frenchwomen was itself a remarkable turn of events. Given republicanism's association throughout the nineteenth century with the Reign of Terror, the odds seemed to be against the return of republicanism, particularly after the horrors of 1871.

Nevertheless, important historical trends during the first two-thirds of the century helped bring the Third Republic into being. Key elements of the revolutionary legacy had been absorbed by successive regimes. The 1814 Charter, which restored the Bourbon dynasty, also guaranteed legal and religious equality and reintroduced parliamentary practice, beginning a long apprenticeship in the arts of democracy. No less importantly, France developed a strong and independent public sphere, girded by "dense and intertwined networks of communication and sociability" —a sine qua non for an open and democratic state.[4] In addition, for specific historical and philosophical reasons, the small but influential Protestant and Jewish communities embraced the republican values of secular education, a clear separation between Church and State, and the use of critical reason. The Freemasons, from whose ranks nearly half of the Third Republic's ministers came, shared these same values and democratic practices, as did the academic, medical, and business communities. As a result, the raw material and laborers for a revived

The Triumph of the Republic, 1879–1899, **Aimé Jules Dalou.** Place de la Nation, Paris/The Bridgeman Art Library.

Republic remained intact throughout the Second Empire under the rubble of post-war and post-Commune France.

Still, given that monarchists controlled the legislature by a large majority in 1871, the turn to a republican form of government was unexpected. For many contemporaries, after the Commune's fall, a royal restoration seemed likely. A nation exhausted by foreign and civil war seemed at the very least indifferent to such a turn of events. The unlikely midwife to the Third Republic's birth was Adolphe Thiers, the one indispensable politician in the grim and uncertain days during and after the repression of the Commune and the German occupation. In part, it was his decisive actions during this period that made him irreplaceable—to the frustration of his foes on both the political Left and Right.

Thiers completed the critical task of "wearing out the Revolution."[5] He was not only resolute, but also prescient. A supporter of the Orleanist monarchy, Thiers nevertheless came to the reluctant realization that only a Republic could ride the late nineteenth-century's surging wave of democratic practice and sentiment. Thiers, who once famously declared that the Republic would be conservative or would not be at all, also firmly believed by 1871 that France would be republican or would not be at all.

The by-elections of July 1871 reflected Thiers' realism. In 117 contests for the lower house Chamber of Deputies, republicans won all but five seats. In Paris and large provincial cities with a radical tradition like Lyons and Marseilles, voters rallied to Gambetta's name. Even the rural areas that had voted overwhelmingly for the monarchist "peace ticket" a half-year before now also voted for the republican list, confident that Thiers could control both the royalists and radical republicans.

The confidence of rural and bourgeois France was well placed. Named president of the Republic in August 1871, Thiers quickly ended the German occupation and restored France's economy and prestige. Through the successful floating of loans, France paid the last installment of its war indemnity to Germany in mid-1873, nearly a year before the deadline. At the same time, despite calls for the introduction of a direct tax, Thiers revealed his conservatism by raising indirect taxes and imposing protectionist tariffs.

It was also under Thiers' watch that order was restored in Algeria. The new colony underwent its own bloody uprising and repression in the wake of France's defeat by Prussia, for reasons, however, that were only partially related to events in Europe. In 1867, an estimated 300,000 Algerians died in a famine induced by the expropriation of their lands by settlers. To add insult to injury, the new Third Republic on October 24, 1870, passed what became known as the Crémieux decree, granting all Algerian Jews—who numbered around 5,000—French citizenship on the grounds that they could be more easily assimilated into French culture than Algeria's Muslim majority could. This decision inflamed both the settlers and Algeria's Muslims, albeit for different reasons. The settlers were outraged that any group of native inhabitants would be granted the same status that they had, and Algerian Muslims resented that the Jews were granted political privileges that were denied to them.

In this tense political climate, France's defeat at the hands of the Prussians was taken as a sign from God that Algerian Muslims should rise up against their colonial oppressors. On March 16, 1871, coincidentally just two days before the outbreak of revolution in Paris, an important tribal leader, Muhammad al-Hajj-ak-Muqrani went on the attack against the French, and within a month several hundred thousand Algerians responded to the call for jihad. The rebellion, however, was no match for the French army in Algeria, and by early October it had collapsed. In a vicious set of reprisals, pro-rebellion tribes saw their lands confiscated and leaders deported, and European settlers had a new opportunity to extend their influence at the expense of the interests of the indigenous populations.[6]

In laying the foundations for a Republic in the wake of rebellions at home and overseas, Thiers was aided by the disarray of his monarchist opponents. The Second Empire's disastrous handling of the war against Prussia had thoroughly discredited Bonapartism. And though the monarchists had swept into the Assembly in early 1871, they were fatally divided between the Orleanists, committed to Louis-Philippe's offspring, the Count of Paris, and the Legitimists, devoted to the Count of Chambord, the heir of the Bourbon dynasty. The two men and their followers shared little apart from the desire to return the monarchy to France. Whereas the Orleanists had long accepted many of the institutional and political acquisitions of the French Revolution, such as a constitution and an elected legislature, the Legitimists denounced every aspect of the Revolution and its foul spawn. Fittingly, the Bourbon heir had spent nearly his entire life in Austrian exile, divorced not just from the realities of French history and society but even from the tasks of everyday life; it appears that Chambord was unable to tie his own shoes.

Led by this otherworldly figure, the Legitimists reminded the nation they never missed the opportunity to lose an opportunity. At first, negotiations between the two branches of the royal family seemed to lead to a happy result, Legitimists were willing to agree that upon the death of their leader, the childless Chambord, the Orleanist Count of Paris would succeed to the throne. Yet the agreement quickly unraveled when Chambord announced his political credo. In two letters published that summer and fall, he declared that as long as France flew the tricolor flag, the symbol of those forces that twice overthrew his ancestors, he would never reclaim his throne. He would rule only under the white flag associated with the Bourbon monarchy: "I can return to France only with my principle and my flag."[7]

And so, Chambord remained in exile, with his principle intact but the agreement with the Orleanists in tatters. His obstinacy forced the Orleanists to find a new way to retain power. By mid-1873, their hopes for the restoration of the monarchy were boosted, ironically, by the early withdrawal of German soldiers from French soil that same year. As a result, Thiers was no longer essential. Scarcely tolerated by monarchists on the Right who were persuaded that Thiers wished for a Republic, distrusted by many moderate republicans as secretly wanting a monarchy, and detested by the radical Left, for whom he would always be the Commune's executioner, Thiers was caught between opposing political forces joined only by the desire to be rid of him.

Their opportunity came in May 1873, when a republican legislative candidate defeated the incumbent Orleanist foreign minister, Charles de Rémusat, in a Paris by-election. The vote shocked the ranks of the Right. The leading Orleanist politician, the Duc de Broglie, observed, "We thought we were seeing the resurrection of the Commune."[8] The Right's attention was immediately concentrated and they prepared a vote of no confidence in Thiers' ministry. From the opposite side of the Chamber, Gambetta's group of radical republicans joined them and succeeded in bringing down the government. After four decades of public life, Thiers finally exited the stage of French politics.

Marshal MacMahon replaced Thiers as president but was dwarfed by him in every respect save actual height. Responsible for the surrender of Sedan, MacMahon was chosen less for his military or political genius—he had none—than for his distaste for republicanism and lack of imagination. He could usefully serve as a placeholder for an eventual restoration. In October, Prime Minister Broglie persuaded the Chamber to extend the period of presidential rule to seven years, hoping that MacMahon would outlive the last Bourbon, Chambord, and then would transfer power to the Orleanist Count of Paris. Under MacMahon's dull gaze, the government outlawed activities that smacked of republicanism, such as celebrating July 14 (not yet made a national holiday); displaying busts of Marianne (a female allegory of the Republic widely used in images during the Revolution), which had long been the embodiment of republican France in city halls; and even holding civil burials (which by definition fell outside the control of the Church).

More broadly, Broglie's ministry introduced a new "Moral Order"—MacMahon's phrase that became the shorthand for his regime. A critical factor to the launching of the "Moral Order" was *dénatalité,* the term used for the nation's faltering birthrate. Few subjects more consistently preoccupied politicians, doctors, and social scientists, especially when they compared France's birthrate to their neighbor east of the Rhine. Between 1871 and 1911, France's population rose from 36 million to 39.5 million; during the same period, Germany added more than half a million citizens *every* year.[9] While the reasons for France's comparatively sluggish birthrate remain vague, it is clear that the nation's paired preoccupations with a waning birthrate and a waxing Germany contributed to a revival of religious enthusiasm, replete with pilgrimages, prophecies, and purported miracles. At the same time, these concerns spurred the call for national regeneration among the professional and political classes. While the republican Left shared these worries about the nation's moral fiber, the extreme Right saw its opponents as the disease for which they pretended to be the cure.

The question over the place of the Catholic Church in politics and society, dating from the early days of the 1789 Revolution, thus became more pressing. The claims made by Moral Order policies confirmed the fears of radicals like Gambetta that the Church would always be an obstacle to the spread of republicanism and its closely related creed of rationalism. One advocate of republicanism, Paul Bert, remarked that the task of the Republic was to create "a secular religion of moral idealism, without dogmas, without miracles, without priests."[10]

In the end, however, it was not republican opposition but dissension among the forces of the Right that undermined Broglie's holding action. Like Thiers before him, the moderate Orleanist, challenged by radical republicans, was brought down by unreconstructed Legitimists—known as the *chevau-légers,* or light horsemen—who refused to stray from their faith in a Catholic king and nation. Unable to straddle the conflicts amongst the monarchist rank and file, the Broglie government fell in 1874, followed by an intensifying struggle between the republican Left and monarchist Right over the fate of a regime that edged ever closer to confirming its republicanism.

CONSTITUTIONAL LAWS AND CRISIS

The Third Republic was officially born with neither trumpet blasts nor sounding of tocsins, but in the flurry of tactical jockeying. Citizens of Paris proclaimed a Republic on September 4, 1870; the French elected a legislature, which chose a president and a prime minister, but hopes for a monarchist restoration precluded any attempt to produce a constitution. Dwindling hopes for a monarchy left unclear what would happen after President MacMahon's term ended, given the continued split between a monarchist Right and a republican Left.

At the center of the republican Left were three men, Jules Simon, Jules Ferry, and Jules Grévy—known as "the three Jules"—who shared much more with pragmatic Orleanists like Thiers and Henri Wallon than with unruly southerners like Léon Gambetta, a more radical republican. The three Jules feared the potential excesses of popular democracy and wrestled with the challenge of making a place in politics for the masses. There were several forms of political activity that were considered, ever since 1789, to be legitimate expressions of the republican spirit. "Public meetings, strikes, parades, memorial ceremonies, even riots"—all of these activities flowed from the revolutionary tradition. Moderates like the three Jules sought to control this potentially explosive energy through formal democratic mechanisms, most importantly voting. The great goal of the first generation of republican politicians in the Third Republic, who would come to be known as the Opportunists, "was to find a way to be both republicans, with its legacy of violence, and men of order." In due course they found some monarchists who were willing to meet them halfway.

Yet the lack of true consensus was so strong that the nascent Third Republic never adopted an actual constitution. No grand political or philosophical principles were broadcast in 1875, no single document was published then or after. There was no French equivalent of the Federalist Papers, much less an American Constitution. Rather, Orleanist Henri Wallon in 1875 offered a key amendment concerning the method of presidential election—"The president of the Republic is elected by a majority of votes by the Senate and the Chamber met together as a national assembly." The motion was approved by a vote of 353 to 352. By a single vote on a seemingly bland amendment confirming that the president was the executive, the Third Republic began to take legal shape.

A constitution was perhaps too much to expect from the collection of fractious and mutually suspicious movements, yet in the wake of the Wallon amendment, they did agree upon a critically important series of constitutional laws establishing the new Republic's structure and mode of operation. Most difficult for the Left to swallow was the very creation of the presidency—a concept that ran against the grain of republican political theory and historical experience. According to the constitutional laws, the president functioned as a monarch in everything but name and lineage, accountable neither to the senators nor deputies, able to appoint his cabinet and dissolve the Republic's lower house, the Chamber of Deputies, at will. He was "*irresponsable*": Neither beholden to nor bound by the will of the National Assembly. Many republicans, attached to the revolutionary tradition of a single house legislature, also frowned upon, though were unable to halt, the creation of an upper house, the Senate. Elected by colleges made up of local representatives, one-quarter of all Senators would become "life members." Thus, along with a strong presidency, the Senate served as a brake on the sudden and violent lurches of a people the lawmakers feared in 1875.

This uneasy consensus between moderate republicans and monarchists failed to satisfy the more radical elements in either camp. Both the radical Left and extreme Right had good reason to revolt. The series of laws enacted in the wake of the Wallon amendment created a state that was, according to one's taste, either too republican or not republican enough. Nevertheless, Gambetta and the republican Left happily grabbed the opportunity that presented itself. Indeed, so eagerly did they grab it that die-hard radical republicans, known as the "Intransigents," derisively called them "Opportunists," a term Gambetta and his partisans soon embraced.

Gambetta understood that the times no longer called for commandeering hot air balloons as he had during the Prussian siege, or cursing compromise as a betrayal of republican principles. Instead, the Republic could only survive through concessions, leading Gambetta to declare, "My policy is in accord with my philosophy, I deny the absolute everywhere, and so you can well imagine that I am not going to recognize it in politics. I belong to a school which believes only in the relative, in analysis, in observation, in the study of facts."[11] Gambetta's speech was welcomed with repeated gusts of "Vive la République! Vive Gambetta!"—an enthusiastic response that, ironically, reminded Gambetta's centrist allies of the potential dangers of republicanism. Despite his newfound opportunism, Gambetta would always be "a reminder of the possibilities of popular mobilization," a speaker whose passion inevitably raised the specter of Jacobin violence.[12]

The Republic was thus born from an assembly whose original purpose, scarcely four years before, was to resurrect the monarchy. Yet the true nature of this pact with reality should not be mistaken. The 60 or so Orleanists who voted on behalf of the laws of 1875 had hardly converted to republicanism. Instead, they too were converts to realism, seeking to stem the excesses of republicanism by erecting as many institutional limits as they could against an electorate that seemed as unpredictable as it was powerful. In a word, the Right saw maintaining manhood suffrage as regrettable but irresistible, while the Left greeted its formalization as the long-awaited culmination of 1789.

The inability of the Right and Left in post-war and post-Commune France to agree on the legitimacy of the 1789 Revolution, and thus the Republic, had tremendous consequences. The laws that established the Third Republic in 1875 merely papered over the political, ideological, and religious divisions issuing from the 1789 Revolution. Herein lies a crucial paradox. The Third Republic "would be in many ways conservative, but it would never be centrist: it would always be ideologically a regime of the Left."[13]

Upon the constitutional establishment of the Republic in 1875, President MacMahon's position became untenable. MacMahon was a military man who had climbed the ranks under Napoleon III and been placed in office by the monarchists, but whose republican opponents would now outflank him. Senate elections returned a precariously small Rightist majority, while elections to the lower house, the Chamber of Deputies, resulted in an overwhelming republican victory. Gambetta led the new republican majority and prudently imposed a moderate platform on his followers.

By October 1876, paralysis had settled on relations between the Senate and the Chamber of Deputies. In an attempt to drive a wedge between Jules Simon's conservative wing of the republicans and the Gambettist wing, MacMahon asked Simon to become prime minister and form a government. Yet when an embattled Pope Pius IX sought to rally Catholics to his side in his struggle with a revolutionary and unified Italy, republican deputies in France loudly criticized French Catholics who responded to the pope's call. As tempers flared, Gambetta threw himself into the fray. In a famous speech of May 4, 1877, he declared that the French detested clericalism as much as they did the old regime. "Clericalism" he roared, "is the enemy!" ("Le cléricalisme, voilà l'ennemi!").

Gambetta targeted here not Catholicism, but clericalism, the term coined for the Catholic Church's active participation in the political affairs of the nation. The distinction, however, was lost in the ensuing turmoil. When the Chamber passed a resolution that condemned demonstrations on behalf of the Vatican, MacMahon was caught between a stubborn and hostile government and his own equally stubborn base. On May 16, 1877, MacMahon dismissed Simon's government. The president had acted within his constitutional authority in dismissing Simon, yet most republicans on the Left interpreted his decision as a parliamentary coup, especially when, two days later, MacMahon appointed a new ministry stocked with conservatives and led by the Orleanist Duc de Broglie.

Predictably, the lower house legislators remained at odds with the Senate and president. After a month-long stalemate, President MacMahon dissolved the Chamber and called for new elections. For Broglie, the choice could not be clearer: Frenchmen were called upon "to choose between Marshal MacMahon and [Gambetta] who scarcely controls the agitated masses of radicalism and spasms of the new social classes."[14] Which Gambetta, though? This was the rub for the conservatives. Would a majority of Frenchmen conclude that Gambetta and his followers were still the fiery radicals of 1869–1870, or the moderates they had since become? Never had the French electorate, this "unprecedented and powerful force still unaware of itself," in the words of one contemporary, seemed so unpredictable.[15]

When the results of the new elections were announced in October 1877, MacMahon suffered what would be his final defeat. The voters elected 326 republicans, a bit short of Gambetta's prediction of 400 seats but far more than the 200 or so monarchists on the Right. After a moment's hesitation, MacMahon was persuaded by the Orleanists to accept the results and asked the conservative republican, Jules Dufaure, to form a new ministry. Less than two years later, in January 1879, with a republican majority also now in control of the Senate, MacMahon acknowledged his institutional irrelevance. He resigned from the presidency before the end of his term and quickly was replaced by the moderate republican and reassuringly bland Jules Grévy. The "Moral Order" thus ended not in war or on the streets, but in the ballot box.

THE REPUBLIC TRIUMPHANT

The series of events triggered by MacMahon's dismissal of Simon came to be known as the "crisis of May 16." Ironically, that crisis marked the birth of what has been called the "Absolute Republic."[16] The monarchist, anti-republican Right, by the number of votes cast in the election, still represented nearly half of the electorate. Yet MacMahon's defeat heralded not just the Left's ascendancy, but also the effective exile of the monarchist Right from political leadership for the Third Republic's duration.

In fact, though the constitutional laws of 1875 were neither rewritten nor revisited, the practice of the various institutions changed dramatically. MacMahon's act was the first and last time a president would exercise his constitutional prerogative to dissolve the National Assembly and call for new elections. Though in theory presidents retained this power, in practice they could not employ it. The Left, which had always worried about the potential excesses inherent in presidential power, given the experience of two Napoleons, now succeeded in imposing their ideal of a weak executive and powerful legislature.

Moreover, the Left's victory introduced the tradition of "republican discipline." Gambetta persuaded the Left to present a unified front by agreeing that all republican candidates, regardless of their particular affiliation, would run unopposed in their districts. This discipline, embraced by republicans until 1940, had paradoxical effects. An effective electoral tactic, it substituted for the Left's lack of a common ideology. As one observer rightly notes, in itself the Left "did not exist, but was composed of tendencies and families afflicted with insurmountable contradictions, except on the defensive terrain of the republican cause."[17]

In practice, the end of the monarchist Right as a serious political threat left the republicans, no longer threatened from the Right, at liberty to turn on one another. The siren call of ideological purity, which would always bedevil French politics,

quickly led to schism. Gambetta, through his willingness to embrace the opportunities in 1875, gave rise to the Opportunists, an alliance of moderate and conservative
republicans who were firmly republican and anti-clerical but leery of calls for greater
social and economic equality. Such willingness to compromise alienated another
group of republicans who never accepted the constitutional compromises of 1875
and who eventually organized as the Radicals. With their pugnacious politics
embodied by Georges Clemenceau, the Radicals held fast to such ideals as the full
separation of Church and State, as well as a system of government based exclusively
on a single-house legislature representing the nation. Radical demands reflected the
fading, but still potent, Jacobin ideal of direct democracy.

Given the division between a large monarchist minority on the Right and
slightly larger republican majority on the Left, itself divided between the
Opportunists and the Radicals, loose groups disciplined enough to win elections
but not to govern, the young Third Republic fell into a pattern that would last its
entire lifespan. Prime ministers came and went quickly, lasting six months to a
year, as did their fractious cabinets. Yet a fundamental political stability existed
behind the rounds of governmental musical chairs. The state fulfilled all vital functions on which all parties agreed: law and order, national defense, the creation of
schools, and imperial expansion. Divided by political issues, Radicals and
Opportunists and even conservatives shared in defense of a common class outlook.[18] None of the groups contending for power in the Third Republic supported
radical social or economic policies.

In the end, far from reconciling Left and Right, the events of 1877 further
reinforced the mutual distrust between monarchists and republicans. On one side
stood those Frenchmen who, to varying degrees, embraced the 1789 Revolution's
values of equality of opportunity, parliamentary government, secular education,
and a chastened Church. On the other side, the anti-Republican Right denied the
legitimacy of these same values, advocating instead monarchy, authority, hierarchy, and Catholicism. Nevertheless, for many Frenchmen once haunted by the
specter of the Reign of Terror, after 1877, the Revolution had been tamed.
According to Gambetta, the Republic could not be identified with any single
struggle. "We do not deny the misery and suffering of part of the nation," he
declared, but "we must also beware of the utopias proposed by those who believe
in a panacea or formula for the happiness of the world."[19]

Meanwhile, excluded from power but slowly reemerging after the bloody
repression of the Commune, at the far end of the Left were workers' organizations
and the socialist movement—or, rather, movements; French socialists proved to be
as prone to ideological fission as the republicans and monarchists. In the pages of
his paper *L'Egalité*, the patriarch of French socialism, Jules Guesde, damned republicans for having turned against the social ideals of the Commune, declared that
cooperation with the bourgeois Republic was tantamount to class betrayal, and
insisted upon the inevitable victory of the working class. With socialism's failure to
send any representatives to the National Assembly , a number of Guesde's followers
concluded that his ideological convictions were admirable, but also suicidal.

In 1882, the socialist movement split into unequal parts. The majority, composed of realists, or Possibilists, led by Paul Brousse, baptized themselves the Federation of Socialist Workers (Fédération des Travailleurs Socialistes). They believed they followed a French tradition of socialism in focusing on practical reforms to improve workers' lives at the local level, improved sanitation, public parks, and services. Such a position met only disapproval from the true believers under Guesde, who called themselves the Workers' Party (Parti Ouvrier or PO). This strict Marxist branch of socialism opposed working within the system for reforms that would only disguise the evils of capitalism. However, the PO did take part in elections, considered "schools of socialism" because they presented an opportunity to educate and win over workers to socialism's ultimate goal of revolution. In contrast, the budding labor movement refused to support any of the branches of the socialist movement. Such division and refusal of large sections of either the socialists or the workers to work within the system further limited the early Third Republic's attention to social issues.

THE REPUBLIC AND WOMEN'S RIGHTS

The hesitant appearance of the Republic changed everything and nothing for women. "Universal suffrage" applied to just half of the universe: Only men voted in the Third Republic. This is not as paradoxical as it may seem, The revolutionary values of liberty, equality, and fraternity are easily gendered. Fraternities, for example, are by definition exclusive male societies that are hostile to the presence of women. Similarly, there were republicans who defined equality so that certain groups, because of what they believed to be their very nature—determined by race, religion, or sex—forfeited their benefits.[20]

French republicanism defined itself in entirely masculine terms. Its ostensibly universal claims flowed from qualities like reason and rationality, thought to be the exclusive possession of men. As a result, male anxiety concerning women received an unexpected yet powerful boost from the revolutionary legacy. French republicans consistently held that the right to vote "derives from the principle of equality among individuals." Yet women, too closely tied to the stubborn particularity of their sex, fell short of the abstract status of the individual.[21] While the Third Republic's exclusion of women was not unusual from a comparative perspective—no nations in 1875 granted voting rights to women—it *is* unusual that a nation devoted to the ideals of liberty, equality, and fraternity excluded women until 1944, long after women had been granted the vote in most other countries.

The brutal repression of the Commune silenced feminism in the early 1870s. Later in the decade, however, a group of moderate, pro-republican feminists began gently to resume advocating for women's rights. France never generated a suffrage movement comparable to those that would roil political life in nineteenth-century Britain and the United States. During the early Third Republic, even some committed feminists like Maria Desraimes and Léon Richer, who founded the Association pour le droit des femmes (Association for Women's Rights) in 1871, argued against their enfranchisement—at least until they were freed from the influence of the Church. According to common republican wisdom, where the priest led, women were sure to follow, because the first attempt to create primary schools in nineteenth-century France had focused on boys, leaving girls to be educated almost exclusively by Catholic schools. Women were also considered to be more emotional and less rational and thus more easily swayed by religious authority figures—and those Catholic authorities barely concealed their contempt for the Republic. As a result, by making suffrage truly universal, the Republic would commit suicide, for women would vote not their own minds, but the Church's interest. Richer himself insisted that the vast majority of voting age women would "take their orders from the confessional."[22] This, at least, was the justification of the Senate each time it rejected the Chamber's proposed law to give women the vote.

Thus rather than advocate female suffrage, early French feminists adopted the tactic of chipping away at the wall of patriarchy. They fought to undo the many civil and legal disabilities that burdened women. They were, for example, unable to testify in court, unable to serve as guardians to their own children if widowed, and required to have permission from their husbands to work for wages. These all flowed from the Napoleonic Code's pronouncement that the "husband owes protection to his wife, the wife owes obedience to her husband." Family law rested on the assumptions of the double standard. A husband's adultery represented an unfortunate but understandable peccadillo. It only constituted a crime if committed in the conjugal residence. A wife's adultery, however, represented a mortal threat to the family and the law treated it harshly. Although it was a crime, courts often refused to convict husbands who killed their wives in the act of adultery.

Given how deeply ingrained such assumptions were, early French feminists did not demand reforms for women on the basis of equality. They preferred the term "equivalence." Rather than challenging the idea that men and women were fundamentally different and that women's special nature particularly suited them to home and family, moderate republican feminists used those ideas to argue in favor of improving women's status in the family. Making a direct political parallel between the family and the political system, Richer explained, "If we are to be a true nation, there can be no inconsistency between the political law that says *equality* and the civil law that says authority. . . . It is an inevitable fact that tyranny in the family gives birth to tyranny in the state."[23] Feminists succeeded in undoing a few of these disabilities over the course of the 1880s. In 1884 the Naquet Law legalized divorce but only on three grounds: conviction of one spouse for a serious offense, cruelty and abuse, or adultery, but for husbands only if it took place in the conjugal residence. Still under the Naquet Law, women could initiate a divorce. Most legal advances for women awaited the next century.

By 1878, moderate feminists Richer and Desraimes had gained enough support to host an international congress on women's rights. Representatives from nearly a dozen countries came to Paris, where they hailed the spirit of 1789 as their own. While the delegates covered topics as diverse as equal pay for equal work, the recognition of housework, and demands to end state regulation of prostitution, they passed over the thorny issue of female suffrage in silence. The conference thus excluded the woman who represented a new more radical variety of feminism, Hubertine Auclert.

France's militant pro-suffrage feminist Hubertine Auclert, who in fact coined the term "feminism" in 1882, had earlier broken with Desraimes and Richer. In contrast to their tactics of chipping away at the wall of patriarchy, Auclert announced a politics of assault. Auclert insisted that working for civil rights served no purpose. "Political rights are the keystone that . . . will guarantee all the other rights. As long as woman does not possess this weapon—the vote—she will be forced to submit to the system of patriarchy. All her efforts to conquer her civil and economic freedoms will be in vain."[24] In her lonely and quixotic career to win the vote for women, Auclert published a newspaper, *La Citoyenne,* and engaged in acts of civil disobedience. She refused, for example, to pay taxes since the constitutional phrase "all the French" ("tous les Français") could not include her when it came to taxation yet exclude her from the vote.[25] In the speech she wrote for the 1878 conference in Paris, but never gave, Auclert underscored the Republic's inherent contradiction: "Until you have recognized the complete right of women— civil and political rights—your struggle to obtain a greater liberty can appear to impartial witnesses and to us, the neglected half of humanity, only as a quarrel between despotisms."[26] By the time Auclert died in 1914, all French feminists had come around to advocating suffrage. Yet women were no closer to the vote than they had been in 1876.

Nevertheless, the Revolution's legacy eventually guaranteed both civic and political equality for women in France—in part because "the idea of the *patrie* issues less from national specificity than the universality of rights, so that to accept the exclusion of women necessarily places any patriot in contradiction with his own logic."[27] As a result, while the immediate impact of the Revolution on women's rights was negative, it nevertheless introduced certain expectations, based upon the core notions of progress, perfectibility, and equality, that ultimately proved liberating, particularly in the realm of public education.

CULT OF THE PUBLIC

Flush with their victory at the polls, yet still haunted by the memory of a hostile countryside in 1848 and 1871, republicans turned to the task of winning provincial and rural France over to republicanism. It was a vast task. As a concept, the Republic had inspired little loyalty among the peasants; instead, as with the Church or royal power, republicanism was refracted through the prism of local culture, local language, and local concerns.

Nevertheless, the Franco-Prussian War already had galvanized the rural population. The sheer number of men mobilized spurred the beginnings of a movement in which the nation took precedence over the local region (or *pays*). Equally important was the "revolution of city halls."[28] In 1877, towns and villages gained the right to elect their own mayors. Until then, the national government in Paris had appointed local administrators. (The city of Paris alone was still deprived of this right.) This momentous law brought many rural Frenchmen into politics for the first time, since they could now change policies that directly affected their lives. People were invited to think nationally, but act locally, and the state, which had always seemed an indifferent and oppressive force, became engaged and responsive.

By the end of the 1870s, the fledgling Republic had intentionally worked to create a "cult of the public."[29] Taking a page from the writings of Jean-Jacques Rousseau, French republicans sought to teach the lessons of patriotism. Public meetings, festivals, concerts, and contests were all orchestrated in order to teach the tenets of republicanism. In 1879, "La Marseillaise," banished during the Second Empire, once again became the national anthem. In 1880, Bastille Day (July 14) became the official national holiday, though only after much debate among the deputies over whether the violent taking of the Bastille should be honored or shunned. A similar evolution took place in 1880 with the cult of Marianne. The female personification of republican France, depicted by Eugène Delacroix with one breast fearlessly exposed as she strode over the bodies of fallen comrades, was recast in countless busts as a sedate and matronly figure. These images were installed in city halls across the country while above the doors artisans chiseled the trinity of revolutionary values—Liberty, Equality, Fraternity.

Republicans believed the classroom to be the most critical public space for forging a republican citizenry. More than in any other realm, schools triggered a fierce struggle between the State and Church. For the better part of the nineteenth century, the Church maintained a viselike grip on education.[30] Though the Church's position was weakened during the last decade of the Second Empire, it benefited in the early years of the Third Republic from the cautious policies of Thiers' minister of education, Jules Simon, and encouragement of the supporters of the Moral Order. Clarifying precisely what was at stake, Pope Pius IX, in his *Syllabus of Errors* of 1864, rejected the modern world and set many French Catholics on a collision course with the Third Republic, declaring that the great task of the schools was to give "the people religious instruction, bringing them to piety and to a truly Christian moral discipline."

With the eclipse of the monarchists in 1877, a newly confident Third Republic quickly acted to bring education under its control. Jules Ferry, who variously served as prime minister and minister of education from the mid-1870s to mid-1880s, understood the political and social stakes involved. In a series of laws passed under his guidance, he committed the Republic to the secular education of its children, slowly prying away the classroom from the Church's grip. He declared: "It goes to the very security of our future that the administration of the schools and the nature of the curriculum not be left to Catholic prelates who insist that the Revolution was tantamount to the murder of god . . . and that the principles of 1789 negate the concept of original sin."[31] By the mid-1880s, the National Assembly passed a series of laws associated with Ferry's name that dissolved the most active Catholic teaching orders, the Jesuits and Assumptionists, and introduced free, secular, and compulsory schooling for girls and boys from the ages of seven to thirteen.

Allegory of the Law on Education Passed, Jules Ferry, 1881. Bibliothèque Nationale, Paris/Archives Charmet/The Bridgeman Art Library.

In addition, the government created secondary schools for girls, although the curriculum included domestic instruction and failed to include the Latin required for advancing to university. To replace nuns, who made up the vast army of primary school teachers, the Republic also established teacher training schools, or *écoles normales*, in every department for both men and women. On the other hand, the Republic's efforts to educate girls were intentional. Girls and women represented a particular target of this massive republican effort. As Ferry declared, those republicans who thought women were neutral "fail to see the secret and persistent support they carry to this fading world."[32] The stakes were clear: As anticlerical and republican historian Jules Michelet had declared in the mid 1800s, "By whom are our daughters and our wives educated? By our enemies."[33] The Church's monopoly over girls' education justified, as we saw, the reluctance of even feminist republicans to give women the vote.

Ferry recognized that only by taking the classroom from the hands of the Church could girls—future wives and mothers—be pulled into the world their republican husbands and sons were bringing into being. While feminists like Auclert supported Ferry's reforms, they found little comfort in his rationale. Far from turning women into fully independent and equal citizens, Ferry instead wanted to create suitable companions for republican husbands and mothers who would instill republican values in their children. Ferry's education reforms were part of a broader effort to refashion French society, casting it in the new garb of republicanism. The Republic, to survive, could not repeat the perceived mistakes of its republican ancestors. In particular, there was no longer any place for the "decadent" woman of the Old Regime, embodied by the courtesan. A more austere and virtuous woman, worthy companion to her republican husband and educator of future republicans, would replace her. The great wave of paintings from this period depicting women reading books reflects this new republican morality. As one contemporary declared, "Every woman who opens a book exorcises a demon."[34]

Ultimately, Ferry and his fellow republicans contributed to the slow emancipation of women. In particular, the creation of *écoles normales* for women opened up a new and respectable career for young women. It was "within the teaching profession that the movement toward assimilation was most evident, creating a female workforce meeting the same criteria, subjected to the same forms of recruitment, examinations and inspection as their male colleagues."[35] Women thus slowly began the long climb to full political and social equality under the Republic's ambivalent gaze.

The embrace of the Republic's social and pedagogical reforms varied dramatically not only from men to women, but also from one region to the next.[36] The Church had deep roots in regions like Catholic and conservative Brittany. Breton novelist Pierre-Jakez Hélias, born into a republican family, recalls his father's admonition concerning the chasm between the "Reds" (republicans) and "Whites" (Catholics) in the village of Plozévet: "Education was the only possession that fathers did not bequeath to their sons. The Republic offered it to everybody. Anyone could take as much as he pleased. And the more he took, the more he could free himself from the Whites, who were in possession of nearly everything else."[37] Conversely, in large cities or Protestant strongholds such as Nîmes and southern department of the Gard, the Catholics, not republicans, were isolated and embattled. By the end of the 1880s, the Republic was nevertheless well on the way to laying the foundations for a republican citizenry.

The men and women given the task of defending the Republic's political ideals were the primary schoolteachers, called *instituteurs* and *institutrices* because their task was to "institute" the nation. The Third Republic's schoolteachers have long passed into myth as the "hussars" of the Republic. Yet, far from undertaking a merciless offensive against religion and local languages and customs, these men and women often turned a blind eye to the teaching of the catechism or use of the local *patois*, or language. Moreover, their lot was a difficult one. For example, an *instituteur* in southeastern France in the 1880s was caught between the distrust of the peasants, who mistakenly thought he was rich because he did not work the soil, and the hostility of the village priest who disapproved of his marriage to the local *institutrice*. As for the marriage, it was probably dictated as much by economic necessity as romantic desire since his wife, who received a smaller salary for the same workload, could not live alone on her meager earnings.[38]

When this schoolteacher voted against Napoleon III in 1870, he exclaimed: "O magic power of universal suffrage, which gives the humblest man the right . . . to count as much as the most powerful.[39] Clearly, the great majority of *instituteurs* were committed to a secular and republican France that spoke a single language and benefited from the rule of law and principle of equality. The spirit of rationalism permeated a syllabus that emphasized science, mathematics, literature, grammar, and spelling. Yet morality, defined in republican terms as civics, was hardly absent from the school day. As the Ministry of Education declared, the *instituteur*'s task was to guarantee that his students "served an effectual moral apprenticeship."[40]

The Republic's ambitions were also reflected in the widely adopted school text *The Tour of France by Two Children* (*Le tour de la France par deux enfants*). First published in 1877, the book recounts the adventures of two orphaned Alsatian boys who crisscross a nation filled with colorful peasants, artisans, and professionals, yet devoid of urban workers and factories, priests and pilgrimages. The boys' voyage seeks to reclaim all of France—an understandable desire in the wake of a military defeat that was partly due to the lack of maps and familiarity with terrain.[41] Through the children's rambles across France's many regions—a gray and severe north peopled with laconic types, a verdant Midi teeming with the stereotypically garrulous southerners—the author, a woman named Augustine Fouillée who published under the gender-neutral pseudonym G. Bruno, celebrates regional diversity, but more importantly praises national unity. Her characters make much ado in their disdain for dialects and regional languages, and their story is driven by the same republican faith often associated with the *instituteur*.

THE REPUBLIC FOUNDS A NEW EMPIRE

During the 1880s, as he created the public school system, Ferry directed an even more controversial project: the colonization of overseas territories and creation of a new, global empire. France had already begun the process in 1830 when Charles X ordered the invasion of Algeria in a futile effort to restore respect for his tottering throne. Algeria would remain the crown jewel, but republican France in 1881 would transform its administration compared to the Second Empire—in ways that hardly conformed to the march of democracy in France. In addition, the Third Republic embarked upon a series of dramatic conquests in other parts of the world. French missionaries had long been active in Tahiti, where a French Protectorate had been established in 1842. In 1880, the Third Republic annexed Tahiti and several neighboring Polynesian islands. In 1881, Ferry sent troops to secure a Protectorate in Tunisia, citing the security of Algeria's eastern border. Ferry would have liked to have done the same in Egypt, where French influence dated back to 1898. But he was briefly out of power in 1882, and the British—determined to protect India by securing control of the Suez Canal—established their own Protectorate instead. Back in office in 1883, Ferry compensated for this setback by completing a takeover of Cochinchina, Cambodia, Annam, and Tonkin (present-day Vietnam and Cambodia) begun in a half-hearted fashion two decades earlier by Napoleon III. The Chinese government fought French expansion, but eventually

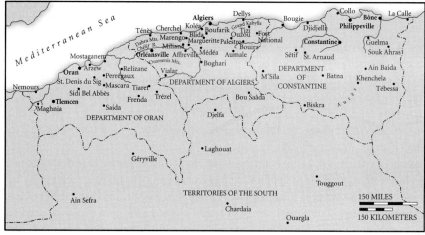

Map 3.1 The departments of France in the nineteenth century.

signed a treaty that recognized France's political and economic interests in what became known as Indochina. In 1885, the tiny colony of Djibouti in the Horn of Africa was founded to supply French ships on their way to these new Asian colonies. And throughout the 1880s, French troops began for the first time to push into the interior of West and Equatorial Africa in search of military glory and new peoples to conquer – before their British, German, Belgian and Italian imperialist rivals beat them at the same brutal game.

The government's 1881 reorganization of Algeria was the least controversial of the Third Republic's new colonial policies, at least among French legislators. Settlers in French Algeria, more of whom were arriving there all the time, were committed republicans, and they were determined to be treated as full citizens of France. They were equally determined to keep the majority Muslim population in Algeria deprived of any political rights. The settlers easily obtained satisfaction from Paris. The northern regions of Algeria, where most colonists lived, had been divided into three French departments in 1848. Under the Third Republic, each of these departments was given the right to elect two deputies to France's lower house, while the army continued to administer the southern territories. In 1881 another step toward integrating Algeria into France was taken when the territory was placed under the jurisdiction of the Ministry of the Interior, rather than under the Ministry of Foreign Affairs—which usually handled colonial affairs.[42]

In theory, the same laws were now to apply in Algeria as in France. In practice, only European settlers (and naturalized Jews) in Algeria enjoyed the full rights of citizenship. As noted in Chapter 1, the Arab and Berber populations were excluded from all political representation in 1865 on the grounds that their Muslim personal status made them ineligible for French citizenship. The Third Republic maintained this policy. To obtain citizenship, Algerians had to give up living under Muslim law, something very few (only 551 from 1899 to 1909) were willing to do.[43] As subjects rather than citizens, Muslim Algerians were subjected to a separate legal code, known as the *Indigénat,* which imposed harsh penalties for minor infractions. Assured in this manner of a monopoly on power in Algeria, the settlers soon began to see it as their new French homeland, and their homeland alone. To cite one telling example, Augustine Fouillée set *Les enfants de Marcel* (*Marcel's Children*), her sequel to *Le tour de la France,* in Algeria. The story recounts the resettling of an Alsatian family there. As the family's grandmother declares, "Blessed land, you have become almost as precious to me as the motherland. . . . When my time has come, I will take my final rest in your soil without regrets, my new Alsace."[44]

While the administrative assimilation of Algeria into metropolitan France went unopposed, both the Right and Left denounced Ferry's expansive imperialism in other parts of the globe. On the Right, Paul Déroulède, leader of the League of Patriots, a nationalist organization founded in 1882 and dedicated to *la revanche,* or revenge against Germany, demanded that the nation keep its eyes on Alsace and Lorraine, which Germany had torn from France at "the blue line of the Vosges." On the Left, Radical politician Georges Clemenceau agreed. The Republic's true interests were in Europe, countering an ascendant Germany. He charged Ferry with being duped by Bismarck's effort to channel the nation's energies beyond the Mediterranean. Furious also about the clandestine manner by which Ferry's government had taken the nation into war with China, Clemenceau, in a famous confrontation in the lower house, declared that Ferry's adventures had betrayed France's true interests and risked the lives of its soldiers in the name of foreign adventures. These are not, he snarled, "ministers I have in front of me, but criminals in the dock."[45]

Further to the Left, the socialist movement also opposed the policy of creeping colonization. According to socialist leader Jules Guesde, imperialism was no different from anti-clericalism: Both were efforts to distract workers from their true economic interests. Ferry's support came largely from Gambetta, who now declared that France "lies not just between the Atlantic and the Alps, the Vosges and the Mediterranean, but wherever there are French interests and wherever French industry and trade are active."[46]

Meanwhile the public in general remained indifferent to French imperial expansion. Unlike Germany and Britain, a rabid, populist pro-imperialist movement did not take root in France. This public indifference, together with Opportunist support, allowed Ferry to launch the Third Republic's colonial policy. No less important than the work of these politicians was the activity of soldiers in the field. Colonial officers like Bugeaud, Galliéni, and Lyautey, who would all play crucial roles in domestic politics, first established their reputations by creating "facts on the grounds" in Africa and Asia. Their approach was pungently summarized by one officer in western Africa: "Since the government was foolish enough to send me 500 men, I set out to accomplish on my own what it lacked the nerve to make me do. They will now be forced to carry on."[47]

While Ferry cited economic motives for extending the empire—insisting that France's economic survival depended on foreign markets and raw materials, especially given the blistering growth rates and colonizing activities of England and Germany—the debate still rages over the legitimacy of this argument. Economic historians have shown how the investment of money, men, and material failed to produce important economic dividends. Yet other historians argue that such studies are beside the point. What mattered was that such activity *appeared* to profit French business and trade. Beyond economics, a kind of bureaucratic fatalism was also at play. In a process begun by the acquisition of Algeria, successive French regimes concluded they were obliged to gain additional territories in order to maintain those already in France's possession. To some extent, competition with Germany and Britain became its own excuse for empire.

It may well be that economic reasons, from Ferry or Gambetta's perspective, were ultimately irrelevant. Imperialism was its own justification.[48] Its advocates believed it was a cure for social division, worker unrest, and national decadence. Moreover, of all European nations, republican France felt particularly compelled to build an empire. This explains the curious fact that monarchist leaders of the early Third Republic had not undertaken imperial expansion. Only after republicans gained control did the empire grow. Republicans insisted that France was uniquely endowed by its history and culture to undertake a *mission civilisatrice,* or "civilizing mission," to the rest of the world. In a measured reply to Clemenceau's attack in 1885, Ferry declared: "You cannot hold up before France an ideal that would be suitable for Belgium or Switzerland: France cannot merely be free; she must be great, exercising over the destinies of Europe all the influence which is rightly hers, and carrying it all over the world."[49] After 1885, the Republic would embark on further conquests in sub-Saharan Africa, Madagascar, and Polynesia; it would also face the daunting task of civilizing the 60 million inhabitants of these territories— most of whom would never set foot in metropolitan France.

THE REPUBLIC AND THE PROVINCES

Like her earlier book, Fouillée's *Les enfants de Marcel* became a standard text in the French schools. French educational and imperial ambitions in fact had much in common: The Republic's colonialism was its educational policies writ large.[50] France's overseas expansion in turn mirrored a much more advanced project at home—namely, that of acculturating other peoples in the language and values of republican France. In 1883, at the very same time that colonial politicians helped to create the Alliance Française to bring French to a tiny fraction of African and Arab peoples, a new generation of *instituteurs* was bringing the French language to virtually all young Bretons and Corsicans. Until the 1890s, however, the Republic also displayed a good deal of tolerance toward regional languages. Ferry never sought to make linguistic unity an element in his education reforms, and Gambetta always praised the nation's cultural diversity.

Yet there remained in this early phase an inevitable tension between republican tolerance and a republican conception of a unified and unitary France. Moreover, from Paris, the French provinces often appeared as wild as the deserts of North Africa. The rhetoric of the *mission civilisatrice* usually associated with France's overseas empire, also spilled into the reports of provincial republican officials. As one bureaucrat declared in 1891, the standard method for teaching French was "as applicable to little Flemings, little Basques, little Bretons, as to little Arabs and little Berbers."[51]

As it turned out, the "little people," whether north of the Pyrenees or south of the Atlas Mountains in Algeria and beyond, had much to say about this attitude. The process of acculturation was a two-way street, and the Third Republic negotiated a series of compromises, linguistic and cultural, with the various peoples it absorbed into the nation and empire. During the 1880s in the northeast, in French Flanders, the French language coexisted uneasily with the local Flemish tongue.[52] To the far south, in Languedoc, Parisian hostility to the local tradition of the *course camarguaise,* or running with the bulls, gave way not just to tolerance but to efforts to co-opt the symbolism on behalf of the Republic.[53] And to the west, in Brittany, republican *instituteurs* taught in Breton for the simple reason that their students would not otherwise understand them.[54]

However, in the 1890s attitudes on both sides began to change. The Republic increasingly defined itself against the Church and the values it represented, including the defense of regional traditions and languages. At the same time, local societies representing these same regional interests adopted a more pragmatic approach. Certain groups, like the Félibrige, founded by the poet Frédèric Mistral and devoted to the preservation (and, at times, reinvention) of the Provençal language and customs, were rightly suspected by Paris of reactionary politics. Other groups, however, emphasized both the importance of their cultural heritage and their attachment to republican France. In any case, the Third Republic began targeting local *patois,* or dialects, and languages for elimination in the public elementary schools. Children were punished for speaking anything other than French and were taught a unitary version of French history, starting, in the famous first line of one history text, with "Our ancestors, the Gauls." This process created a "schizophrenic existence" for many provincial Frenchmen and women who balanced an abstract Republic on the one hand and life in a concrete locality on the other. One historian, Mona Ozouf, notes about her own Breton childhood, "Our ancestors the Gauls were unquestioned in the classroom, but mocked at home, where we referred to our ancestors the Gallois [a branch of Celtic civilization linked to Breton identity]."[55]

THE WORKING CLASS

Ambivalence also shot through the ties between the working class and the Republic. It is impossible to define precisely the nature and number of workers in the early Third Republic. Traditionally, French workers in the nineteenth century fell into three categories: rural workers who labored in mines and mills when not working the soil, urban craftsmen who constituted France's artisan elite, and industrial workers in France's relatively small industrial regions, who had neither farmland nor skill, but only their labor to offer. By the Opportunist Republic of the early 1880s, these three categories represented a quarter of the entire working population, numbering as many as 6 million men and women. While artisans had traditionally dominated labor movements up through the Commune, after the 1880s the industrial workers came to control the burgeoning labor movement.

Early labor historians long sought the origins of working-class consciousness. For some, it began in France with the repression that followed the 1830 Revolution, while others placed it with the events of 1848, and yet others believed the Commune finally and fully thrust workers on the stage of history. In any case, by the 1880s French workers were well aware they were both workers and French. While Napoleon III had legalized strikes in 1864, the Third Republic legalized trade unions in 1884. Worker militancy had been on the rise, from 30 or so strikes in 1870 to 121 strikes in 1881. In passing the 1884 law legalizing unions, the government was not motivated by a desire to improve the lot of the working class as much as by the hope that unions would provide more effective ways to control worker unrest. Yet striking workers increasingly turned to the state, especially after collective bargaining was established in 1892, to force concessions from recalcitrant employers who continued to ignore the unions.[56]

Through the first three-quarters of the century, French industry had little in common with either modern conceptions of the factory or the dramatic social and economic transformations that had already taken place in Britain. Most often, French industry was small scale, with manufacturing in workshops or small "factories" numbering 10 or fewer employees. While there were modern textile firms in northern France and foundries in Lorraine, French production standards were still governed by an artisanal elite who produced "high value-added" or luxury goods like clothing, china, perfume, toys, jewelry, and furniture. An earlier generation of historians argued that this reflected a more general backwardness of the French economy when compared to Britain. More recent historians, however, dismiss such comparisons. The persistence of the French economic model, they contend, reveals nothing more than a healthy response to the particularities of French social, demographic, geographic, and international opportunities and realities.[57]

Most historians, however, agree that by the 1880s the pressures of mechanization and rationalization began to carry the day. The increasingly proletarian nature of the working class entailed changes in their worldview and politics. The focus on independent workers' cooperatives in the work of Pierre-Joseph Proudhon, a mid-nineteenth-century socialist theorist who inspired earlier generations of skilled workers, gave way to Marx's claims, which better responded to a world where skill had been eclipsed by brute labor.

In 1880, the Third Republic issued a blanket amnesty for all Communards—a political as well as a humanitarian gesture made on the eve of the first official July 14 national holiday. Such concessions, however, seem to have had little effect on workers who had grown increasingly dubious about the benefits of the Opportunist Republic. This became clear in the workers' embrace of new symbols that challenged the traditional hallmarks of the Republic. "La Marseillaise," reborn in 1880 as the national anthem, lost ground amongst the working class to Eugène Pottier's "The Internationale." A Communard, Pottier wrote the text in 1871, but it was rescued from obscurity only in 1883. Unlike "La Marseillaise," in which Frenchmen are united by the love of liberty, "The Internationale" presents workers of all nations united against those who enslave them.[58] Moreover, the *Mur des fédérés*, or Wall of the Federals, at the Père Lachaise cemetery, the place of summary execution for hundreds of Communards in 1871, now became a symbol of working-class solidarity. The wall drew thousands of workers, committed to a "complete break with the bourgeoisie," who carried the red flag of the Commune and confronted the forces of order marching under the tricolor blue, white, and red flag of the Republic.[59]

In general, life for the urban worker in the late nineteenth century was most often precarious and grim. A deep economic depression that settled on Europe from the late 1870s to early 1890s only increased the hardship of the working-class' daily lot. Moreover the Republic, committed to its liberal ideology, was reluctant to introduce laws interfering with the workings of the marketplace. Men worked 12-hour days every day but Sunday, while women and children had slightly better hours, for much lower wages. In 1892 children younger than 13 were prohibited from factory work, while women could not work more than 11 hours a day. The Republic's social policies were equally primitive. An extremely limited disability plan was enacted only in 1898, while retirement and health insurance would not be introduced until the mid-twentieth century. The contrast with authoritarian Germany was sobering: Germany's Chancellor Bismarck, hardly a charitable soul, nevertheless in the 1880s created workers' health insurance, disability, and retirement funds in order to parry the rise of the German socialist movement.

Germany had also outstripped France in the realms of public health and hygiene. The Franco-Prussian War had unleashed a European-wide pandemic of smallpox that killed more than half a million people. Yet with vaccination mandatory in the German army, far fewer German soldiers and citizens died than their French counterparts, whose political leaders did not make smallpox vaccinations obligatory until 1883 for soldiers and 1893 for children.[60] Most provincial cities lagged behind the great improvements in water and sewage disposal imposed on Paris by Baron Haussmann during the Second Empire. Until the turn of the century, provincial cities like Rennes and Rouen were ill served by existing systems. A pedestrian's daily lot was dodging the avalanches of garbage from windows and the streams of sewage from emptied chamber pots and drained cesspits. These foul tributaries almost always leeched into rivers, which also most often served as the unique source of drinking water. Not surprisingly, until the end of the century, typhoid fever and cholera simmered and at times boiled over into full-blown epidemics.

For many French workers, *liberté* seemed to mean the freedom to drink oneself to death. Third Republican France led the world in the consumption of alcohol; according to one study, workers in Paris drank more than three liters of wine per day.[61] Alcoholism became a preoccupation of public authorities and intellectuals; while it had been earlier been associated with traditional forms of festivity, the austere and scientific atmosphere of republican France cast the practice in a new and sobering light.[62] Politicians like Jules Simon campaigned actively against drinking, while Zola's novel *L'Assommoir* reflected the grim ubiquity of wine and absinthe—once identified with artists, but now consumed mostly by workers—in poor neighborhoods. The very title, the French term for "knock senseless," had come to signify a "saloon" by 1876 when the novel was published. Thus while Zola cared about the misery of the working class, he completely accepted middle-class assumption of the era that workers were the victims of their own excess. When it was first serialized in the republican newspaper, *The Public Good* (*Le Bien Public*), Zola declared that *L'Assommoir* was meant to "educate the worker in order to elevate him morally; free him from the slums where air hangs thick and noxious; above all, curb drunkenness, which decimates the populace while ravaging its intelligence."[63]

Bathing remained a significant event for the poor in republican France. It required considerable material and financial means, which helps explain why the

The New Staircase in "Au Bon Marché," from *Le Monde Illustre*, circa 1875, Frederic Lix and August Deroy. Private Collection/Lauros/Giraudon/The Bridgeman Art Library.

act was thought to be fraught with great risks to the bather's health. The obstacles in the domestic use of water certainly contributed to a widespread urban belief among workers that water caused sterility in women, while many in the country-side believed that a layer of dirt benefited one's complexion. Ultimately, hygiene had less to do with cleanliness than with attractiveness. "It meant polishing crude manners, combing one's hair, occasionally washing one's hands (and beard) and . . . sprinkling oneself with eau de Cologne."[65]

In the end, incremental improvements in public health were due to better diets as much as to heroic medical breakthroughs or emphasis in republican schools on the virtues of using a comb rather than one's fingers. On the one hand, food remained precious and the great staple was bread. As Pierre-Jakez Hélias observed, for many poor wretches in Catholic Brittany the prayer "Give us this day our daily bread" came "from the heart, for bread was by no means guaranteed."[66] On the other hand, while bread accounted for nearly one-fifth of an average house-hold budget in 1850, it had dropped to less than one-tenth by the end of the century.[67] This shift reflects both improvements in the functioning of the market-place and a decline in the size of the average French family. Diets slowly became more diverse as the rail system connected cities and countryside; previously rare items like meat became more common.

The steady gait of the civilizing process also reflected the so-called democra-tization of luxury. This process was spurred by a French invention, the department store. Though the first stores were established in Paris during the waning years of the Second Empire, by the early 1880s they rivaled traditional historical sites like the Louvre and Notre Dame. Contemporaries described department stores such as Le Bon Marché and Le Printemps as cathedrals of the new religion of consumer-ism. Their monumental façades, great cupolas, and sweeping display windows mirrored the architectural logic of medieval cathedrals. At the same time, the the-atrical arrangement of goods—from sheets and umbrellas to delicacies, undergarments, and ready-made clothing, all of which had once been the reserve of artisans but now staggered the senses of visitors—transformed basic needs into flights of desire and imagination.

While workers were still initially untouched by this phenomenon—the stores were located in the bourgeois heart of the city and Haussmanization had forced workers to the outskirts— the growing lower middle classes, or petty bourgeoisie, were lastingly affected. Not only did the stores' vast bureaucracies help create a new class of white-collar workers, but the creation of affordable ready-made cloth-ing allowed the new social classes to dress the bourgeois roles they aspired to assume. As we will see in Chapter 4, the great Paris Expositions brought the prov-inces to Paris, where visitors became consumers of the Republic. But the department stores instead brought Paris to the provinces through the mailing of millions of catalogues and almanacs. Just as school texts taught the values of the Republic, store catalogues also conveyed a national culture. The illustrations seduced the reader not only to buy material goods, but also to identify them with social and political goods. The Bon Marché, no less than *Le tour de la France par deux enfants,* the *instituteur,* and the rail and postal systems, helped form a new national, middle-class, and republican culture.[68]

CHAPTER 4

The Imperial Republic
1885–1894

By 1885, Victor Hugo had been reduced to near silence by illness. Yet France's greatest writer had also become the living symbol of the Republic: a man whose life had spanned the better part of the century, a politician who had served as deputy and senator, a poet and novelist who had consecrated his art to the ideals of the revolution. His contradictions were no less symbolic. While his writings made him wealthy, Hugo bequeathed little of it to the working class whose lot he depicted so movingly in his books. The works themselves, monuments of high romanticism, were out of fashion by the time of his death on May 22, 1885, when realism, naturalism, and symbolism reigned.

The commemoration of Hugo's life rivaled the same romantic excesses of his writings. On May 31, Hugo's coffin was placed under the Arc de Triomphe. As night fell, great lights were turned on, illuminating the grand catafalque. A wave of humanity swept around the coffin, while souvenir stands did a brisk business in Hugo memorabilia.

The funeral cortege lurched early the next morning down the Champs-Elysées, across the Place de la Concorde and over the Seine to the Left Bank, an itinerary that avoided eastern and working-class Paris. Nearly eight hours after it started, the coffin—placed, as Hugo directed, in a pauper's hearse—reached its final resting place, the Pantheon, followed by a crowd that numbered 2 million. Scorned by Hugo as a "great sponge cake," the Pantheon was originally the Saint-Geneviève Church. Ever since the 1789 Revolution, the building's name and purpose had alternated between the Pantheon, symbol of a secular nation, and Saint-Geneviève, place of worship for a Catholic nation. With Hugo's death, the pendulum came to a rest. The Republic reclaimed the site for France as the Pantheon once again, and rededicated it to be the final resting place for the Republic's "great men." (The first and only woman honored with a place in the Pantheon for her own accomplishments was Marie Curie, and that only in 1995, 61 years after her death.) Hugo was the Third Republic's first official tenant.

The funeral's pageantry failed to conceal the many tensions that characterized France in this period referred to as the fin-de-siècle, or end-of-the-century—a term coined by contemporaries who experienced the period of the 1880s and 1890s as one of great transition and change. Always a double-edged phenomenon, change was a source of despair as well as hope. Frenchmen and Frenchwomen at the end of the nineteenth century celebrated dramatic material progress while also experiencing an elusive sense of anguish and uncertainty. Everything, the literary review *Fin-de-siècle* announced in 1891, "is mixed, confused, blurred, and reshuffled in a kaleidoscopic vision."[1] A sign of the hopes and uncertainty of the times was the birth of new political configurations on the Right and the Left, both of which challenged the increasingly complacent Opportunist Republic.

DEMOGRAPHIC AND ECONOMIC UPHEAVALS

As we saw in the previous chapter, one change starting in the middle of the nineteenth century became a source of widespread anxiety among elites by the 1870s: France's population growth rate began to slow. In the eighteenth century, France had a rapidly growing population, reaching about 26 million on the eve of the 1789 Revolution. But 25 years of bloodshed during the Revolutionary and Napoleonic wars had killed over 1 million men. The resulting drop in the birthrate proved temporary, however, and France's birthrate recovered quickly. By 1850 the French population stood at some 36 million.

Many French leaders associated a large and growing population with power and prosperity. Alarms were first raised when census data revealed that in 1854 and 1855, the total number of people who died exceeded the number of births. While this trend did not continue, France's population growth rate had slowed definitively. The ignominious defeat in 1870 only confirmed some observers' worst fears about the negative effects of the declining birthrate, or *dénatalité*. Adding to the anxiety, the defeat also resulted in a threatening, newly unified Germany whose population greatly exceeded that of France.[2] And things got worse. Between 1871 and 1911, France's population grew 8.6 percent, reaching about 39 million, while Germany's population increased 60 percent to a total of 65 million.[3]

In the 1880s, a growing number of people in France—especially political and religious leaders—continued to worry and to speculate about why the birthrate was slowing. One thing was clear: French people were having fewer babies, and everyone from doctors, scientists, and Catholic moralists to social reformers and even feminists began to advocate state policies to reverse the trend. In 1896, Jacques Bertillon, a statistician, together with several doctors and social scientists, founded the Alliance for the Growth of the French Population to push for such reforms.

In the short term, however, perhaps the most important consequence of *dénatalité* was a labor shortage; here, the easiest remedy for employers struggling to keep down their costs was to find workers outside of France. As a result, for the first time in modern history, immigration began to reshape France's political landscape.

On the issue of immigration, silence speaks louder than words. Until the last quarter of the nineteenth century, the very words "immigration" and "immigrant" did not figure in French sociological or legal studies.[4] Only after the shocks of 1870–1871, coupled with growing uneasiness over France's stagnant birthrate, did the phenomenon of "immigration" claim the nation's attention. Waves of foreign workers started arriving in France, particularly Paris and the industrialized regions in the north and east, to work on the development of urban, industrial, and railway infrastructure.

Immigration peaked between 1876 and 1886, when foreigners made up 2.96 percent of the total population and 7–8 percent of the working population. The main immigrant groups were Italians and Belgians, who alone accounted for 61 percent of the total immigrant workforce from 1872 to 1911.[5] Other groups included Germans and Spaniards, and there was an important influx of Central and Eastern European Jews as well after 1881, fleeing pogroms, anti-Jewish riots, in their homelands (1.7 percent in 1872, 4.5 percent in 1911).[6] These burgeoning "guest worker" populations, particularly those from Italy and Germany, bred anxiety and resentment, encouraging the growth of xenophobia, or hatred of outsiders, among French workers and small shopkeepers. At the same time and somewhat paradoxically, the growing preoccupation with immigration prodded the state in 1889 to revise the canons of citizenship. No longer willing to deny foreign workers' male offspring the "odious privilege" of military service, France shifted the basis of citizenship from the parent's nationality to the place where the child was born.[7] Henceforth immigrants' children born in metropolitan France could acquire French citizenship upon reaching adulthood.

Yet if France's new immigrants were looked down upon by French workers, it was not simply because of a traditional fear of "outsiders." The presence of foreign workers was symptomatic of larger structural changes in the economy that were deeply destabilizing to France's older skilled working class. For much of the nineteenth century, France's traditional skilled trades had developed alongside more industrialized economies like Great Britain's. Leather- and furniture-making, hat- and glove-making, silks and fine linens, glass-blowing, jewelry, and clothing remained vital not just for France's trade balance, but also for its self-identity. These so-called *articles de Paris* were, in a way, so many articles of faith in the abiding value of French craftsmanship.

By the early 1880s, though, technological innovations from abroad laid siege to this economic model based on luxury and hand-crafted goods. From across the Atlantic came mass-produced shoes made by Goodyear, while from across the Rhine German factories were now shipping new fabrics made from cheaper materials. A traditional culture based on well-built and long-lasting products increasingly gave way to one founded on quickly made and easily replaced goods. As much as French traditionalists on both sides of the ideological spectrum wrung their hands over these socioeconomic changes, the great majority of French consumers welcomed them. Just as French politicians had to adjust to the process of democratization, so too did French business have to adapt to a democratization of luxury.

Or, as was often the case, not adapt. For every French manufacturer who survived by rationalizing production—often through lowering costs by either mechanization or replacing male workers with unskilled women or foreign laborers— many more fell by the wayside. Just as the end of the twentieth century in America introduced vast changes in industry—as traditional blue-collar jobs disappeared and new kinds of white-collar skills appeared—so were there similar shocks in fin-de-siècle France as factory workers displaced skilled artisans producing *articles de Paris* . The export of luxury goods from France crashed during the 1880s. In just one year, from 1882 to 1883, the value of Parisian exports alone fell nearly one-third. The great economic churn left in its wake the wrecks of countless ateliers and small workshops, leading contemporary observers to write obituaries for the "end of an industrial era: the final decomposition of the independent atelier."[8]

BOULANGER'S RISE AND FALL

The "decomposition" of the small workshops had great political and cultural consequences. Many critics worried about the rise of impersonal factories, along with their anonymous, unskilled, and uprooted workers. In the crucible of these real changes and perceived threats, in the fin-de-siècle people became increasingly aware of and concerned about a social phenomenon: the crowd. Few observers better reflected this pervasive anxiety than Gustave Le Bon. Trained as a medical doctor, Le Bon lived through the Paris Commune and witnessed first-hand the collision between urban and rural France. In 1895, he published *The Psychology of Crowds,* baptizing his age as the "ERA OF CROWDS." When people are pulled from their rural roots and thrown into cities, he argued, the framework of traditional beliefs and social hierarchy collapses. Closely knit communities decompose into crowds, a mass galvanized by simple ideas. As a result, the "people"—the central republican item of faith—easily becomes the "crowd," the nation's greatest menace. The ultimate justification of a Republic, the people thus also potentially threatened the bourgeois social order.

Le Bon noted that charismatic leaders skilled at using the tools of modern public relations could manipulate crowds to achieve their own ends. Undoubtedly, he had in mind the political turmoil of the 1880s, which climaxed with the meteoric rise and fall of General Boulanger. Between 1879 and 1885, a succession of Opportunist ministries held power. A short-lived "Great Ministry," from November 1881 to January 1882, dominated by the man about whom few French felt neutral, Léon Gambetta, briefly interrupted the Opportunists' reign. However Gambetta's attempt to revise the electoral system failed and Gambetta resigned after two difficult months. His brief ministry aroused fear in his enemies both among moderate republicans on the Left and the extreme Right, but before he could return to the political fray, Gambetta died prematurely.

Some viewed Gambetta as the last of the great republican heroes. The decidedly unheroic Jules Ferry dominated the ministries during the first half of the

"Emperor Boulanger the First," caricature from the front cover of *Le Grelot,* May 29, 1887.
Private Collection/Archives Charmet/The Bridgeman Art Library.

1880s, either as prime minister or minister of national education. Dull and colorless, Ferry's methodical and prudent ways helped solidify many of the Republic's original gains. When Ferry stepped down for the last time in 1885, the Third Republic was as secure as the reputation of Hugo, who would be embalmed and immortalized scarcely two months later.

No sooner secured, the Republic found itself sorely tested in the late 1880s, in the form of a charismatic hero on horseback, General Georges Boulanger. Named minister of war in 1886, Boulanger represented all things to all people. Opportunists favored Boulanger because he had true republican credentials—or so it seemed; nationalists flocked to him because of his declarations of revenge against Germany for the loss of Alsace-Lorraine; and workers focused on his expressions of sympathy for the strikers at Decazeville. On the extreme Left, the former Communard Henri Rochefort's newspaper *L'Intransigeant* saw in Boulanger the return of Jacobin authority and purity. Yet many on the extreme Right embraced Boulanger's emphasis on military glory. This was especially the case with nationalists like Paul Déroulède, whose League of Patriots (La Ligue des Patriotes) founded in 1881 showcased the anti-liberal and violent tendencies that heralded twentieth-century fascist movements.

It so happened that Boulanger cut a brilliant figure. During the military parade at the Longchamp racetrack in Paris' Bois de Boulogne in 1886, the dashing general thrilled the crowd. Such popularity made many Opportunist republicans uneasy; the specter of Bonapartism seemed alive and well. Opportunists were so uneasy that they forced Prime Minister Freycinet, who had appointed Boulanger minister of war, to resign in May 1886. Boulanger was packed off to a provincial military command, but not without a frenzied send-off at the train station, where the crowd sang "La Marseillaise" and cheered "General Revenge."

At the end of 1887, a scandal enmeshed the government. President Jules Grévy's son-in-law, Daniel Wilson, was caught selling government decorations, including the Legion of Honor (Légion d'honneur), by law awarded only for "eminent merit," to the highest bidders from an office inside the presidential palace. The affair rocked the political establishment. Disenchanted voters turned to Boulanger, who had recently been forced to retire from the army, as a cure for the rash of corruption. Under Clemenceau's leadership, some so-called Radicals—the name taken by republicans just to the left of the Opportunists—distanced themselves from Boulanger, increasingly worried about the specter of military dictatorship. Yet other Radicals, as well as socialists and nationalists, hitched themselves to Boulanger's star. Apart from hostility to the perceived arrogance and corruption of republican politicians then in power, Boulanger's supporters had little in common.

Yet a debate still continues over the movement's nature and significance. One school of historians, led by René Remond, sees Boulangism as an expression of Bonapartism. Little distinguishes it, they claim, from this well-worn and fundamentally conservative ideological strand on the Right. Other historians, however, like Zeev Sternhell, insist that Boulangism was the symptom of a new and more menacing movement on the Right taking root in the wake of the 1870 defeat and made possible by the advent of mass politics and further industrialization. For example, the movement had anti-capitalist and anti-Semitic aspects that were alien to Bonapartism. No less importantly, Boulangism trumpeted a fervent nationalism that celebrated an irrational attachment to the nation (and, at the same time, scorned the role of reason in politics). All of these aspects point to an early form of fascism, making it a movement with little in common with the traditional Right.[9]

Another new element of Boulangism that fascists would later emulate was the use of elections to gain power. The Third Republic allowed politicians to run in more than one district. Starting in 1888, Boulanger's name was entered in a series of local elections across the country, all of which he easily won: Peasants, workers, and white-collar workers rallied to his banner. The most dramatic electoral victory was the January 1889 by-election in Paris. The government pulled out all the stops in support of the republican candidate, but Boulanger decisively defeated him on January 27. For French republicans and followers of Boulanger alike, this was the decisive moment. Would the ex-general try to overthrow the Republic?

The crowds milling in Paris soon had their answer. Whether restrained by republican scruples or sheer indecision, Boulanger did not take to the streets.

Instead, he decided to enter additional by-elections in the evident hope that he would be carried to power by a river of ballots, not blood. His decision proved fatal to his ambitions. The minister of the interior, announcing his intention to arrest Boulanger for treasonous activity, had taken the measure of his man. Rather than facing charges or attempting a coup, Boulanger crossed the Belgian border in flight from the warrant. The country seemed to forget him as quickly as it had discovered him, Two years later, when Boulanger committed suicide next to his mistress' grave in Brussels, he had become a comic figure. Still, at the time Boulanger seemed to pose a real threat to the new Republic, and the nationalist forces and sentiments that his brief ride to power unveiled were not so easily dispelled.

CULTURAL TRANSFORMATIONS

The years 1888–1889 marked not only the fall of Boulanger but also the rise of the Eiffel Tower, the great emblem of the World Exposition in Paris. During the previous Paris fair, in 1878, the Republic had just emerged from the May 16 crisis that ended MacMahon's presidency. By 1889, 11 years later, the Republic's political and social foundations were solid and it was prepared to throw itself a party. But the event would also be instructive. It was not accidental that the Exposition dovetailed with the centenary of the 1789 Revolution.

The 1889 Exposition perfectly reflected the republican credo of science and progress. The Gallery of Machines, a vast iron and glass exhibition hall housing 16,000 machines, was one sign of this secular faith, but the Eiffel Tower was, and remains, its most potent symbol. Chosen after a competition, the Eiffel Tower was controversial from the start. Given its tremendous height, some reviewers worried that a strong wing might topple the structure. Other observers had aesthetic objections. A committee of 300 artists and writers, led by Alexandre Dumas and Guy de Maupassant, scorned Gustave Eiffel's design, describing it as an "odious column of tin." Yet the tower was a great popular success.[10] Edouard Lockroy, the chairman of the organizing committee, compared the structure to the great Enlightenment project, the Encyclopedia: both served as monuments to intellectual ambition, technological skill, and collective effort—a noble sentiment, though one wonders how many of the more than 3 million tourists who visited the tower during the Exposition, gazing at the thousand-foot high elegant arc of iron lattice from below or the great maze of Paris from above, thought of their experience in these terms. Or perhaps they did marvel at the technology that would form the basis for the modern skyscraper, made possible by a metal frame undergirding the structure.

The 1889 Exposition aimed both to cultivate civil virtues and to entertain. One of the pavilions, a re-creation of the Bastille, the prison and armory destroyed in 1789, served as home to a rollercoaster, music hall, mock medieval souvenir shops, and a theater that staged a show called "Escape of the Prisoner from the Bastille." Equally impressive was "Cairo Street," a Disney-like Main Street lined with "authentic" Arab cafés, souks, and belly dancers where spectators could "see" the new empire up close. Although such exhibits pretended to a educational function, they blurred the lines between edification and titillation, between the virtues of the citizen and the desires of the consumer, like the wax figures at Musée Grevin, which had sensationalist tableaux of human sacrifice in Africa and state executions in France but also a scene of Eiffel and Lockroy inspecting the Eiffel Tower.[11] The exhibits were also a source of anxiety for conservative observers. Edmond de Goncourt worried that "While looking at the Exposition and on everyone's face the coarse bestial joy which twists up even the gray moustaches of old women, I think of the ennui of next year for these people who have taken the habit of partying, and I fear that from this ennui there will emerge a revolution."[12]

Goncourt need not have worried. The memory of revolution had turned, quite literally, into a souvenir. Fittingly, Montmartre, the revolutionary district that gave rise to the Commune, in the 1880s became a magnet for tourists seeking forms of popular and high art that mocked bourgeois virtues. Since 1881, the Chat Noir (Black Cat) cabaret had been the flagship of *fumisme*—the term given to the art of practiced disdain for bourgeois values. Failed painter Rodolphe Salis, who ran the Chat Noir café, claimed it had been founded under Julius Caesar and frequented by Charlemagne and Rabelais. Waiters dressed in the uniform of the Académie française—France's preeminent learned body whose forty elected lifetime members, known as the Immortals, were in charge of keeping the French language pure—served drinks while Salis lavished insults on his guests. The bourgeois clientele loved it.

One of the café's most famous performers, singer Aristide Bruant, opened his own café in 1885 called Le Mirliton. Like Salis, Bruant specialized in hurling scorn at his bourgeois fans—a remarkably profitable activity. Bruant's raillery, sharp but calculated, allowed his audience to shed their bourgeois identities for the night. And though he sang sympathetically of the working class, Bruant tended to idealize them as the "down and out." His true genius lay in using the *argot* of working-class Paris— he even published a dictionary of Paris slang—evoking a world that his bourgeois clientele had never experienced. Reflecting the trend in entertainment in fin-de-siècle Montmartre, Bruant packaged a safe form of slumming for middle-class consumption. At establishments like the Chat Noir and Le Mirliton, the goal was to provoke in its guests a "release of feelings and emotions that were repressed or restricted in everyday bourgeois life." Men and women found a space "where the increasingly organized and regulated life of the modern city could be left behind for an evening by those unable to escape it for longer."[13]

The transformation of Montmartre into a refuge from middle-class respectability was in part a legacy of Haussmann's rebuilding of Paris under the Second Empire, which had dramatically expanded the city's bourgeois neighborhoods in the first place. Haussmann's changes to Paris' urban landscape had another unintended effect. The new arcades, exhibition halls, cafés, squares, parks, and big boulevards that he created provided a venue for people to see and be seen. Paris in the fin-de-siècle became, in the words of German critic Walter Benjamin, the "capital of the nineteenth century." Its streets provided entertainment for many young middle- and working-class men, often referred to as bohemians or, from the verb *flâner,* which means to stroll, *flâneurs,* the term poet Charles Baudelaire preferred. No novel better evoked this world than Guy de Maupassant's *Bel Ami* (1885), set in the heart of Paris, which followed the rags-to-riches saga of Georges Duroy – a man on the make who receives his big break when he runs into an old schoolmate in a café on one of the city's teeming boulevards. This bohemian street culture also provided the context in which a homosexual subculture could and did develop. Gay men "used the urban spaces available to them to create for themselves a unique geography of sexual pleasures throughout the city."[14] As a result Paris became something of a haven for homosexuals, where Oscar Wilde, after his release from prison and fleeing the more repressive climate of Great Britain, spent the last years of his life.

Alongside the commercialized middle-class cafés and tourist establishments in places like Montmartre, Paris and other cities large and small also had authentic working-class cafés. Reflecting a democratization of leisure (if not luxury), such cafés became extensions of the home for many working men and a small but, as time went on, increasing number of women. Private lives were lived out in public, partly created by the endemic housing crisis in Paris and the cramped living quarters and lack of domestic privacy in all industrial centers. Cafés also functioned as extensions of the workplace. In the café, deals were made and jobs could be found. Artisans periodically broke off from their work in order to hoist a glass. Alcohol was widely believed to energize the body; no less importantly, through rounds and toasting, drinking represented a social rite for working-class men that underscored the virtues of equality.[15] In fact, one of the great bones of contention between employers and skilled workers was the issue of café breaks—an intolerable practice for employers who wanted both to maintain a 10 or 11 hour workday and to increase productivity.

While patterns of sociability changed in Paris and the large provincial cities with the development of new forms of consumption, slowly, rural France was also changing. Many of the traditions that marked village life were quietly disintegrating under the forces of modernization. Better communication and transportation systems and the didactic efforts of the Republic undermined the celebration of Carnival and midsummer bonfires, as well as annual religious events like the *pardon* in Brittany, in which great pilgrimages unfolded on the feast days of patron saints. By 1889, national celebrations encouraged by Paris, most importantly July 14, the national holiday, were pushing aside older local traditions. Efforts to outlaw cockfights and bearbaiting, led by the recently created Society for the Protection of Animals, were spurred as much by concern with the moral well-being of the spectators as the physical well-being of the animals. At the same time, the growth in literacy and domestic comforts assured the decline of communal practices like the *veillée,* a long-standing rural tradition of neighbors gathering during the long winter nights to share the warmth and light of a single hearth and pass the time with storytelling and songs. As with blood sports and Carnival, republican authorities considered the *veillée* a primitive activity unworthy of citizens.

Yet the impact of the Republic's continuing "civilizing mission" at home was more uneven and ambiguous than it might appear from the vantage point of Paris

Bretonnes au Pardon (Breton Women at a Pardon), Pascal Dagnan-Bouveret (1887).

and national policy. Far from being passive, regions responded in creative ways to the government's efforts to create a unified nation. For example, the Félibrige, a literary movement founded in 1854 to preserve the southern region's Provençal language and culture, and other similar regional associations mobilized against Paris pressures. Also, in Languedoc, a traditional southern province, a great groundswell of resistance emerged against Paris' attempts to outlaw the *corrida,* or bullfight. Even though the *corrida* was a recent import from Spain, Félibrige writers like Frédéric Mistral, Charles Maurras, and Léon Daudet defended it as a "native" tradition. In 1894, the Republic backed down from its efforts to suppress it. Still more local or regional "traditions" were tweaked to make them suitable, or quite simply invented. The *fête arlèsienne* in Provence was a "ritual" sprung directly from Mistral's imagination, in which women paraded in "time-honored" costumes. So, too, for the *Barzaz-Breiz,* a collection of what were claimed to be Breton folksongs. In fact, the song collector, Theodore de la Villemarqué, largely invented the *Barzaz-Breiz* to celebrate a way of life that never was.

In the realm of high culture, institutions like the Paris Opéra and Ecole des Beaux Arts lost their commanding presence in the face of serious attempts to make the traditional arts more democratic. Musical entrepreneurs like Jules Pasdeloup popularized "serious" music through Sunday concerts. In a telling sign of how much popular opinion had changed since the Franco-Prussian War, Pasdeloup also reintroduced Parisians to the work of Richard Wagner, so closely associated with German nationalism, yet who had already won over highbrow critics in France.[16]

The Impressionist movement reflected a similar process of popularization. From its beginnings in the early 1860s in the work of Edouard Manet through its official birth in 1874, when Edgar Degas, Claude Monet, Auguste Renoir, and Paul Cézanne exhibited their work together, the Impressionist movement scandalized the artistic establishment. Many critics found their emphasis on light, surface, and fleeting "impressions" dubious. Beyond that, established artistic elites were also bothered by their choice of subjects. Rather than treating mythology and history, the Impressionists instead depicted the everyday tasks and scenes of ordinary men and women, from middle-class families on a Sunday walk in the park to working men and barmaids in cafés and cabarets. However, from rebels the Impressionists eventually became the new establishment—an ironic shift, given their subject matter. Poet and critic Stéphane Mallarmé dwelt, with forgivable exaggeration, on the tremendous social and political implications of this change: Whereas the artist had previously been a recluse "to whom was given the genius of a dominion over an ignorant multitude . . . today the multitude demands to see with its own eyes."[17]

CHURCH VS. REPUBLIC? FEARS OF DEGENERACY

While Impressionists grew defiant toward the artistic establishment at the end of the century, relations that had earlier been strained between the French Catholic hierarchy, the Vatican, and the Republic initially grew more accommodating. In the 1890s, Pope Leo XIII moved the Church away from the reactionary policies of his predecessor Pius IX and prodded the French Catholic hierarchy to reach a truce with the Republic. He met with resistance, as several high members of the French clergy turned down the pope's request to serve as the French Church's public voice for this new policy. Finally, in late 1890, Cardinal Lavigerie, Archbishop of Algiers, launched a policy of reconciliation between the Church and the Republic known as the Ralliement (Rally to the Republic). Lavigerie declared that as long as the Republic did not pose a threat to Catholic principles, the Church should accept it. He urged the creation of a conservative party within the framework of the Republic.

Against this background, in 1892, Pope Leo XIII took the exceptional step of publishing an encyclical in French, titled *Au milieu des solicitudes* (*Among the Concerns*), that explicitly accepted the French Republic's legitimacy. This document represented a dramatic reversal of papal policy. Nevertheless, while the Ralliement initially caught the public's attention, it failed to create an enduring political movement. The Ralliement supporters hoped to create an electoral coalition of politicians who shared a desire to reconcile the Church and the Republic. But in the elections of 1898, only 38 representatives linked to the Ralliement won, while the socialists continued to grow in strength. The Ralliement itself represented an uneasy alliance of Catholics who shared a religion but varied greatly in their attitudes toward politics and social change. Some Catholic leaders, like the conservative Jacques Piou, were dedicated to preserving the established social order, while others, like the Legitimist Albert de Mun, wanted to address its inequalities. The latter maintained that they were following an encyclical the pope had issued in 1891, *Rerum novarum* (*Of New Things*), which recognized the existence of social injustice and exhorted Catholics to care for the underprivileged. The Ralliement also alienated some French Catholics who continued to oppose Ferry's Republic. Yet for many French Catholics, the debate about the Republic was academic: They had long since come to terms with the Republic while holding onto their religious faith.

It is difficult to generalize about the extent and significance of religious practice in fin-de-siècle France. In the southwest and Massif Central, as well as the Paris basin, church attendance had dropped to single digits. In western regions like Brittany and the Vendée, however, approximately half of the population still trooped to Sunday services. But it is not clear whether strong church attendance signified active faith or attachment to tradition. Attendance was also gendered. Most girls attended Catholic primary schools. Given gender norms that defined women's roles in terms of their domestic, educational, and nurturing roles, the Church and its charitable activities provided one of the few outlets for middle-class women wanting to expand their social horizons.[18] The Church continued to provide charitable assistance particularly for young working-class women down on their luck. Thus for cultural, social, and economic reasons, women were far more closely tied to the Church than were men. Married couples often reflected this divide. The anti-clerical socialist leader Jean Jaurès' wife was deeply devout. Claude Monet's mistress, Alice Hoschédé, waited until her husband, from whom she had long been separated, died before marrying the painter. The Provençal writer Alphonse Daudet had fierce debates with his observant wife, Julia, over the Republic's removal of crucifixes from classrooms.

Overly schematic accounts of Church-State divisions obscure a number of interests—or, more accurately, fears—the two institutions held in common. Most important, both Church and State worried over maintaining social order. The Church's hold over its flock reassured conservative republicans. Like Napoleon, they saw social control in the mystery of the Trinity—or, more prosaically, in the practices of communion and confession. Fears of Boulangism on the Right and socialism on the Left—in 1896 the socialists swept to victory in several cities—helped unite Catholics and conservative republicans who also shared fears about a perceived decay in public and private morals. This perception was reflected in a rash of articles and books expressing concern about France's physical and moral degeneration, which Catholics blamed on the decline of religion. Tellingly, republican freethinkers, who pointed to a different list of suspects—immigration, urbanization, industrialization—were as preoccupied with national decline as Catholic conservatives were. In his novel *Fecundity*, as well as a series of newspaper articles, staunch republican Emile Zola deplored France's anemic birthrate and lambasted an intellectual avant-garde "out to ruin our robust Gallic health, our good nature and fruitfulness."[19]

Zola was hardly concerned about restoring Catholicism. Secular rationalists shared the Church's concern about decay and decadence not for religious reasons but owing to new scientific theories, and in particular Darwinism. Even freethinkers not bothered by the notion that humans and apes might have descended from a common ancestor found causes for concern, not in Darwin's writings per se, but in theories that extrapolated from biological evolution and applied the idea of survival of the fittest to race, nation, and social class. Increasingly the conviction about the superiority of French civilization, which propelled France outward and justified its conquest of more "primitive" peoples, turned in on itself. What went up the evolutionary ladder might come back down. As France modernized, fewer men worked on the land and more people lived in cities, where it was believed that they no longer "struggled" to survive or contended with forces of nature. Observers worried that the ease of urban living could sap French men's vitality. Somewhat contradictorily, Zola's novel *Germinal* expresses clearly the fear that the harshness of the working-class environment was stunting and deforming an entire social class.

One possible remedy for such degeneration was the cultivation of sports, one of whose pioneers was Pierre de Coubertin. Scarcely eight years old at the time of the Franco-Prussian War, Coubertin was the scion of an aristocratic Parisian family tied to a world that died in 1789. Impatient with his family's nostalgic longings, the young man devoted his time to fencing, boxing, and horsemanship. These pastimes turned into Coubertin's vocation when he crossed the Channel in 1883 and toured Rugby, Eton, and the other sites of English sportsmanship. Coubertin returned to France with the mission of putting "color in the cheeks of a solitary and confined youth, [toughening] his body and character by sport, its risks and even its excesses."[20] However, the obvious breeding ground for organized sports, the *lycées* or high schools, lacked the space and interest for such activities. Moreover, school authorities were attached to the tradition of 11-hour class days and detected an unhealthy odor in physical exercise and competition.

Coubertin tried to stand this bias on its head. Physical activities, he claimed, were essential for preparing a national elite for the political and social challenges facing the nation. But the notion of an elite coexisted uneasily with republican values. As a result, Coubertin's pleas fell mostly on deaf or hostile ears. Yet Coubertin refused to concede defeat. In 1894, Coubertin called on the gathered representatives from 13 countries in the central amphitheater of the Sorbonne (part of the University of Paris) to revive the ancient Olympics. His motivations were complex; he hoped the resurrected Olympics would further the goals of a healthy population, peaceful coexistence among nations, and internationalism. But he also was driven by his fears of a new world dominated by mass pleasures, mass politics, and mass consumption. Improbably, he had better luck with re-creating the Olympics than with introducing educational reform in France. The Olympics were reborn in 1896, but only after World War II did the French school system take outdoor play seriously.

Elite observers' worries about the degeneration of French men were further magnified by another new development: the first appearance of what contemporaries called the "new woman," who seemingly rejected traditional bourgeois values. From the 1890s on, a small but visible group of middle-class women began to dress, behave, and live in ways that challenged gender norms. They remained single or entered nontraditional relationships; took up "male" professions like law, medicine, or journalism; and some became feminist activists. Many of the new women were associated with a journal Marguerite Durand created in 1897, *La Fronde,* which was entirely produced, written, edited, and even typeset by women. Unlike other journals directed at women, rather than clothing and homemaking *La Fronde* covered politics, international affairs, sports, and the stock market. Moderate feminists like Léon Richer and Maria Desraismes, who dominated the 1879 feminist congress, began to decline in the 1880s as the more radical Hubertine Auclert pressed demands for the vote in more militant and challenging ways. While very few women lived the new woman lifestyle much less joined feminist groups, the phenomenon attracted attention and aroused fear far beyond their numbers. Many of the major newspapers included daily articles on the new woman, who also become the subject of novels and plays. The new woman's unconventional lifestyle, along with feminists' demand for equal rights, linked up with broader social anxieties about the declining birthrate and degeneracy. The new woman, many believed, rejected maternity and further emasculated France's men.[21]

CIVILIZING OVERSEAS

Such concerns provided one impetus for continuing imperial expansion under the Third Republic. Many observers, hoping to counter the signs of degeneracy and lack of masculine vigor, advocated "manly" empire-building as essential for reinvigorating the nation. Yet as the Third Republic pursued further conquests beyond France's older colonies in the Caribbean, Algeria, the South Pacific, and coastal Senegal in the 1890s, its pro-imperial lobbyists and policy-makers soon confronted a dilemma. On the one hand, they invoked France's special republican *mission civilisatrice*—inherited from its revolutionary past—to help prod their ambivalent fellow citizens to support new colonies in Southeast Asia, Central and West Africa and Madagascar, and Polynesia. This mission, and the ostensible inability of the so-called inferior races to improve on their own, justified imperialism in the first place. On the other hand, no one in France wished to pay for programs to improve the livelihoods of the desperately poor native peoples inhabiting the colonies.

The government resolved this dilemma not by ignoring its promises (although there was plenty of that), but by often turning to the most convenient and inexpensive alternative available for implementing their civilizing programs: Catholic missionaries.[22] Indeed, France's empire seemed to be one project upon which

Postage stamp depicting Marianne, the official representation of the French Republic, ca. 1893. Bibliothèque des Arts Décoratifs, Paris/Archives Charmet/ The Bridgeman Art Library.

republicans and Catholics could agree from the outset. One of the most popular republican dictums of the 1880s—uttered by none other than Gambetta himself—was that "anticlericalism is not an item for export." Yet far from always getting along, secular administrators and missionaries routinely fought each other for "the hearts and minds" of their colonial subjects, in ways that echoed the divide in France between many Catholics devoted to their faith and anticlericals determined to cleanse the nation—and particularly its public schools—of the Church's influence.

By the early 1890s the era of new conquests was beginning to wind down, except in parts of sub-Saharan Africa, where the French had started later than in North Africa and Southeast Asia. In 1893, Laos was officially added to France's Indochinese territories. In 1893 French Colonel Louis Archinard captured and defeated the Sultan Ahmadu, heir to the Tukolor commercial state in West Africa. Further west, in Western Sudan (present-day Mali), the brilliant Muslim empire builder and rival of Ahmadu, Samori Touré—like the great Algerian Amir Abd el-Kader before him in the 1840s—successfully resisted the French military for thirteen years until his final capture in 1898. The Merina Kingdom of Madagascar, too, was only "pacified"—that is to say not only conquered but also dissolved—in the late 1890s under General Joseph Galliéni and his military collaborator, the young Louis Hubert Lyautey.

Wherever it could the French government began shifting from military to civil administration, in the hope that these territories would start yielding the promised economic dividends. Governments General were set up in Indochina (a federation eventually composed of five territories: Tonkin, Annam, Cochinchina, Cambodia, and Laos) in 1887, (see Map 10.1, p. 268), French West Africa (a federation made up of seven territories: Senegal, Ivory Coast, Dahomey, Guinea, the French Soudan, Mauritania, and Niger) in 1895, Madagascar in 1896, and French Equatorial Africa (a federation made up of four territories: Gabon, Middle Congo, Oubangui Chari, and Chad) in 1910. Imperial pro-consuls embarked upon ambitious programs of port and rail construction across the empire.

The Third Republic's new empire was ruled along very different lines than the tiny *vieilles colonies,* or old colonies, of Guadeloupe, Martinique, Réunion, and coastal Senegal, where the citizenship and the suffrage rights of all males regardless of race had been recognized in 1848, and then again in 1870. After 1900, all of France's new colonies were expected to be self-financing. Each territory was subdivided into districts headed by a French *commandant* (a civilian administrator despite the military ring of his name). *Commandants* were responsible in their districts for gathering taxes, building roads, overseeing the administration of justice, and providing—in theory at least—both a school for teaching local children French and a local clinic. In G. Bruno's *Le tour de la France par deux enfants,* children in what was now referred to as the metropole—that is to say France within its traditional European boundaries—could read about how free vaccinations were given in Indochina because "France, always generous, extends to all . . . its benefits and its aid."[23] Another part of France's *mission civilisatrice* was to eradicate "feudal" vestiges deemed incompatible with modern civilized behavior: slavery where it still existed, trial by ordeal, cannibalism, and superstition generally.

In the new colonies, the native populations were legally subjects of the Republic, rather than citizens; those few subjects who acquired French language and culture could apply to become citizens, but in practice few naturalizations were granted. *Commandants* had extraordinary powers at their disposal to keep their subjects in line. The special penal code known as the *Indigénat* already in force in Algeria was extended to Africans, Asians, and Pacific Islanders, allowing administrators to impose fines and jail individuals for up to 15 days without appeal for a whole host of infractions (including insufficient deference to French administrators). While in theory abolishing slavery and local forms of feudalism, French colonial administrators imposed on colonial populations a certain number of days of free labor working on local public works projects for the colonial administration, a system that easily lent itself to abuse. Both the crusading spirit of the new republican regime and the intensifying biological racism of the era infused all of these policies; for contemporaries it made perfect sense to bring liberty and fraternity at gun point, with equality and democracy postponed to some indefinite future when supposedly inferior colonial peoples were "mature enough" to deserve them. Meanwhile these same colonial subjects were expected to pay taxes and to serve under French colors should their new French fatherland—*la patrie*—need them.

With its expanded empire, republican France would become by 1914 a nation of close to 100 million French, of whom 60 million were colonial subjects. A corps of about 4,000 French administrators governed these subjects, with the help of numerous auxiliary personnel hired among the local populations: chiefs and traditional elites hoping to preserve some semblance of their former power, former slaves seeking to escape servile status, or ambitious French-educated "new" men and women who believed that their best career chances lay with the colonizers. Only Algeria—no longer a colony since its attachment to the Ministry of the Interior in 1881 made its three northern departments an integral part of France— attracted a significant numbers of settlers, or *pieds noirs* (black feet—presumably a reference to the black boots they wore) as they came to be called. With its Mediterranean climate and proximity to France, Algeria witnessed a virtual land grab between 1871 and 1898, as a vast new influx of colonists seized the richest territories and reduced the local Arab and Berber populations to landless laborers. By 1900, there were over 600,000 settlers living in Algeria, many of whom had arrived from other impoverished Mediterranean countries, especially Spain, Italy, Portugal, and Malta. French-born colonists who chose to move to Algeria, typically from the Midi or Alsace-Lorraine, looked down upon these poorer foreign settlers.

In 1889, the Republic granted access to citizenship to all settlers in Algeria of European descent regardless of origin, while the local Muslims remained subjects rather than citizens. Set apart by their superior rights and ostensibly superior civilization based on reason and technological prowess, almost all colonists—rich or poor—despised the native Algerians, deemed incapable by virtue of their Muslim religion of assimilation into French culture or of making their country prosper. By century's end, Algeria had "become a tale of two economies sitting side by side. On the one side were the rich settlers, whose huge enterprises comprising 2,350,000 hectares of the best land and using the latest agricultural techniques produced food and wine for export; on the other, the Algerian peasantry who were forced to maintain a subsistence economy with archaic techniques."[24] The six deputies elected by settlers from the three Algerian departments became vociferous supporters of a new colonial lobby in Paris, dedicated to protecting French financial interests throughout the empire. Led by the politically savvy deputy from the department of Oran, Eugène Etienne, this lobby made sure that any pro-Arab reform in Algeria never passed in the Chamber of Deputies.

Indochina was viewed as France's most promising new colony in the 1880s, in part because it was seen as a springboard to trade with China. The patchwork of regions that made up the new federation had long attracted French missionaries as well as traders. Episodic violence against republican authoritarian French rule in Indochina only really ended in 1897, at which point plantation owners, merchants and bankers, and petty traders of all sorts found their way to Southeast Asia. This European community always remained tiny relative to the native population and was concentrated in the French quarters of cities like Hanoi or Saigon, where even the most humble European was reputed to live in opulent "Oriental" splendor. Indochina held a special place in the late nineteenth-century public's imagination as a particularly exotic outpost, but the reality was more prosaic. The military, shopkeepers, businessmen, missionaries, and administrators who made up the French community were internally stratified according to occupation and income. Yet all colonists viewed the local populations through a prism of racial hierarchies, which traded on such stereotypes as the "passive yellow races."[25]

Sub-Saharan Africa, because of its inhospitable climate and poverty, attracted the fewest number of French. Traders and bureaucrats built up the port cities of Dakar—capital of French West Africa (Afrique Occidentale Française, or AOF)—and Abidjan in the Ivory Coast, which became entrepots for West Africa's main exports, such as peanuts (for oil), coffee, and cocoa, all cultivated by African peasants. In the vast tropical forests of French Equatorial Africa (Afrique Equatoriale Française or AEF), whose capital was Brazzaville, the French government leased most of the land to concessionary companies in search of timber, ivory, and rubber. These companies paid a nominal tax to the state to "develop" the colony, then routinely forced locals to work for them. Their scandalous treatment of Africans—similar to the atrocities occurring at the same time in the Belgian Congo—produced a humanitarian backlash in France at the turn of the century; the companies were not, however, dismantled until the interwar years.[26]

In contrast to the small number of public servants, planters, merchants, and traders traveling out to Indochina and sub-Saharan Africa at the end of the nineteenth century, approximately 58,000 Catholic religious workers lived abroad—most of them in the French empire (North Africa and parts of West Africa were the exception, since the Catholic Church had little success proselytizing in Muslim states). More than a million French women and children supported their efforts by donating money and prayers. These missionaries tended to live much closer to indigenous populations than the administrators the government sent or the merchants and settlers who came voluntarily. Missionaries might stay in the same village for years at a time, whereas administrators repeatedly moved all around the empire. Wherever they settled, religious workers set up churches, schools, orphanages, segregated colonies for people with leprosy, and hospitals. For many of the colonized, in other words, the first and sometimes only French person they saw was a representative of—at least in theory—the Third Republic's greatest enemy: a Catholic bent on converting them to the one "true" religion. The presence of so many missionaries in the empire was a boon to administrators looking for a cheap way to fulfill the civilizing directives emanating from the Ministry of Colonies in Paris. As a result, in most colonies the administration came to rely on missionaries to staff government schools and hospitals. But conflicts abounded in the empire between religious workers and their secular critics who believed the Catholic Church, allowed to flourish overseas, still posed a threat to the Republic back home.[27]

These conflicts could take a number of different forms. Some colonial administrators and colonists resented religious conversion's disruptive impact on the colonial populations, for it could turn neighbors against each other and split whole villages into feuding clans. They argued that the Church's divisive presence was preventing the colony from developing economically. In Paris, republican deputies excoriated Catholic missionaries in Indochina for teaching Latin in their schools rather than French and questioned whether any Catholic priest could be a good patriot. Petty disputes over material and labor were also the stuff of everyday life in the colonies. In Madagascar an administrator complained bitterly to his superior that a local Jesuit told his converts to steal telegraph poles belonging to the state to use in the construction of his chapel. These conflicts escalated even further by the end of the nineteenth century, when continued labor unrest and escalating nationalism in France destroyed the fragile truce between republicans and Catholics represented by the Ralliement.

By the first years of the twentieth century, republican antipathy toward the Catholic Church ran deeper than ever, leading to a renewal of the state's war against the Church that reverberated overseas. For example, in Tahiti in French Polynesia, the administration had long relied on a single order of religious sisters to carry the burden of educating the local population. Colonial administrators hoped that missionaries would stem the islands' catastrophic population decline by molding "depraved" Tahitian girls into good mothers trained in modern French child-rearing practices. By 1900, however, the government turned against its Catholic allies, now blaming the sisters for failing to stem population decline in a colony devastated by diseases that accompanied French colonization. The administration closed down missionary schools in the name of defending the Republic against theocracy, but then, hypocritically, failed to create secular ones to replace them.[28]

If fraught Church-State relations at home were often refracted overseas, the empire was also a place where some people experimented with new religious and gender identities not possible in France. The most infamous woman of the French empire at the turn of the century, the flamboyant Isabelle Eberhardt, was the illegitimate offspring of an Armenian Orthodox priest turned anarchist and an aristocratic German woman. Eberhardt was raised in a highly unorthodox manner outside of Geneva, Switzerland. Tutored at home, she learned classical and European languages as well as Arabic, history, geography, and philosophy. From an early age, she wore only men's clothes and learned to ride a horse as vigorously as any man; she also absorbed the ambient Orientalism of the era that portrayed all Muslim peoples as sensuous, lazy, and deeply mysterious. Hopelessly out of place in bourgeois society, Eberhardt cultivated ties with the Paris literary avant-garde, then fled Europe at the age of 20 for the French Algerian town of Bône. There she converted to Islam, took on a new name (Mahmoud Saadi), and scandalized colonial society by dressing as an Arab man, imbibing hashish, and wandering through the streets and markets at all hours of the night, either alone or with Algerian male companions. While drugs, alcohol, sexual digressions, and transvestism could be tolerated in fin-de-siècle Paris cabarets, in Algeria Europeans were expected to keep their distance from the *indigènes* (natives) in order to preserve the myth of French cultural and moral superiority.

By 1899, Eberhardt discovered that life in the Saharan desert was more to her liking than colonial Bône; she cast herself as a nomad, married an Algerian sergeant—who had exceptionally become a French citizen—and deepened her knowledge of Islam by joining a mystic sufi order, all the while writing about her experiences. As the French military under General Lyautey began encroaching upon southeastern Morocco from Algeria in 1903, Eberhardt agreed to conduct a delicate diplomatic mission for the army, only to die tragically in a flash flood upon her return in 1904. After she was buried in Algeria, her memoirs became a bestseller in France.[29]

Unified by a common reality of white privilege, the empire taking shape in the waning years of the nineteenth century was nevertheless always a space of many contradictions and fissures. For a handful of disaffected expatriates like Eberhardt seeking freedom from stifling conventions, Algeria represented a kind of theater for acting out fantasies of the Orient and transgressing boundaries. For all her radical behavior, however, only at the very end of her life did Eberhardt see Algerians in terms other than the stereotypes within which she had been raised. For the vast majority of French women, the empire was less a place to try on new identities than one where traditional gender hierarchies were, if anything, more exaggerated than at home. Colonial military and administrative service, as well as settler agriculture, were viewed as quintessentially man's work—the stuff of which real heroes were made in an increasingly bureaucratic age.[30] In contrast, French women who ventured overseas were expected to remain in their "proper" feminine places to better reflect the virility of their husbands and other male colonizers.

A European Woman in Algeria, 1910, Louis Rémy Sabattier. Private Collection/Archives Charmet/ The Bridgeman Art Library.

Missionaries and republicans shared yet another concept of empire, albeit one no less defined by gender or race than the quest of adventure and heroism that motivated so many young men to exile themselves to the far corners of the globe. For Catholics and the ardent sons and daughters of 1789 alike, the goal was to convert colonial "others" to their view of the world, even if it meant carrying their metropolitan quarrels with them. Other French people simply went to the colonies to make money. And despite the de facto segregation that obtained everywhere, sympathetic relationships between colonizer and colonized were sometimes possible. Certainly before World War I many French administrators and merchants lived with native women and fathered children whom these men occasionally legally recognized.[31]

Yet whatever their purpose overseas, their individual prejudices or lack thereof, their class or their status, all French people in the colonies had the weight of the imperial system behind them, often leaving colonial populations little choice but to tolerate their new bickering overlords. The same might be said of workers in France, also subjugated to the civilizing efforts of anxious fin-de-siècle industrialists and legislators. As citizens, however, male workers had the political means to fight back that were denied to the vast majority of France's colonial subjects.

THE LABOR MOVEMENT AND SOCIALISM

The French working class did not feel particularly privileged in 1880s France. The fear of unemployment, the weight of 12-hour days, and near-total absence of social security were the lot of most working men, women, and children. Only in 1892 did the National Assembly prohibit the employment of children under 13 and limit those under 16 years to no more than 10 hours a day. Despite—or because of—this lack of basic protection, a minority of workers and middle-class sympathizers began using their new rights to fight for improvements. In a country famous for its divisions among and between unionists and socialists, this movement to change the lot of workers achieved an unprecedented degree of organizational unity by the end of the century.

Even in cities, the family remained one of the most important institutions in the life of workers. Urban worker families, not surprisingly, were different from peasant ones; in the city, the nuclear family prevailed, characterized by the absence of the elders and by the early departure of children from home. The number of children tended also to be smaller, due both to space constraints and to the new industrial culture of efficiency being adopted by factory owners. Employers stressed the importance of domestic hygiene and aimed to create a work pool of healthy, sober, punctual workers with families only large enough to be an impetus, not a hindrance, to working long hours in a factory.[32]

In the face of the relentless pressures of employers upon them, at home and in the work-place, workers turned to trade unions and, increasingly, to a particular kind of labor organization known as Bourses du Travail or Labor Exchanges, for solidarity. Bourses du Travail were places where workers could meet and debate political issues, as well as find libraries and job centers. Labor exchanges multiplied during the last decade of the century, largely owing to the work of Fernand Pelloutier. Journalist by trade, Pelloutier sought—in keeping with certain anarchist ideals of self-government—to maintain the independence of the labor exchanges from political parties. In 1892, Pelloutier helped to create the Federation of Labor Exchanges, with the aim of coordinating strike action nationally. A strike a year earlier that turned, horrifically, to bloodshed, was one of the impetuses behind this move to federate. On May 1, 1891, soldiers fired on demonstrators in Fourmies, a grim textile and metal industrial town in northern France. Nine demonstrators were killed, including a two-year old child, and more than 30 others were wounded.

In the wake of this massacre, the Federation of Labor Exchanges decided to adopt a revolutionary new weapon in its struggle against employers: the general strike. Rather than agitating for specific improvements in wages, hours, or working conditions, all of which signified accepting the existing system and working to reform it from within, the general strike was a refusal to reform the system—and instead was meant to deal a death blow to the capitalist system. Support for the general strike carried forward to 1895, when a single unified trade union organization, the General Confederation of Labor (Confédération Générale du Travail or CGT),was born, marking the climax of a long effort to overcome divisions amongst stubbornly independent unions. In 1902 the final step unifying the French labor movement occurred when the CGT and the Federation of Labor Exchanges united under the name CGT.

Although the number of trade unionists remained relatively small—less than a half a million in 1895—their influence was significant. The CGT's aim was not to lobby for reform or lay the foundations for a mass political party, but "to build solidarity through practical actions and to increase the impact of the working class on French society."[33] The CGT adopted the new ideology of revolutionary syndicalism, which was less a doctrine or program than a hodgepodge of ideas and ideals. Revolutionary syndicalists rejected parliamentary politics as working within a system they preferred to overthrow via revolution. Thus rather than strikes aimed to bring about specific improvements, the CGT espoused action that expressed its rejection of capitalism, including boycotts, industrial sabotage, and, ultimately, the general strike, which, its partisans and theorists fervently believed, would bring society to a halt. The CGT's disdain for reformism meant that even the growing strength of the labor movement in France did not lead to social reforms through the political system that would have made life easier for the working class.

The socialist parties faced a similar dilemma. Not only did the state mistrust them, but the men they wished to recruit were also wary. Nevertheless, membership in the most important socialist party, Jules Guesde's Workers' Party (Parti Ouvrier or PO), grew at a relatively rapid pace, from 2,000 members in 1889 to 16,000 members 10 years later. While the labor movement looked to the writings of the French theorist Pierre-Joseph Proudhon for their inspiration, the PO socialists turned to Karl Marx—or, at least, a Marx translated and simplified in French. One of the party's leaders, Paul Lafargue, happened to be Marx's son-in-law. But the Guesdists' rigid organization and allergy to compromise long undermined attempts by other socialist individuals and groups to achieve unity. Not surprisingly, in 1893, more independent socialists—31—won seats to the National Assembly than did socialists attached to organized parties, who took only 18 seats.

These independent socialists included Jean Jaurès, whose name has been given to as many boulevards and squares in France as his hero and fellow southerner, Léon Gambetta. Born to a provincial and struggling middle-class family in southwestern France, Jaurès' life vindicated the Republic's belief in the power of education. He won a scholarship to the prestigious Ecole Normale Supérieure in Paris, the training ground for the Republic's vanguard of intellectuals. Graduating in 1881, Jaurès returned to the south, where he took the post of philosophy professor at a *lycée* in the town of Albi. As would be true for many other *normaliens* (graduates of the Ecole Normale Supérieure), Jaurès soon made his mark in politics. Taking up the cause of the mine workers in the town of Carmaux, he won the seat representing their district in the parliamentary elections of 1893. Though he had previously identified himself as an independent, Jaurès now announced that he was a socialist. But unlike that of Guesde, Jaurès' socialism was broad, flexible, and inclusive; it favored compromise over confrontation and sought to better the condition of the working class before the advent of revolution. Jaurès' idealism and eloquence quickly thrust him to the forefront of the socialist movement. In 1905, he succeeded in weaving the various strands into a unified party, which took the name "the French Section of the Workingmens' International" (Section Française de L'Internationale Ouvrière or SFIO). Though Jaurès and Guesde shared the leadership, the contrast remained stark between the two socialists. Whereas Guesde's politics were narrow and severe, Jaurès' worldview was humane, optimistic, and inspired less by Marx than by the values of 1789. The rank and file respected Guesde, but loved Jaurès.

The socialists faced opposition not just on the Right, but also on the extreme Left. For a brief and shattering moment between 1892 and 1894, a group of anarchists paralyzed France. For anarchist theorists, the desperate lot of the urban proletariat and indifferent attitude of the bourgeois Republic required radical measures. Working for reforms was useless. Government was not the answer—it was, to the contrary, the problem. Anarchists shared Rousseau's belief that man, fundamentally good, is corrupted by society. Once the shackles of the state were destroyed, men and women would associate with one another as independent and free individuals. Given their fundamental distrust of any form of government, anarchists were more hostile to Guesde's dogmatic Marxism than to Jaurès' humanism. As literary critic and practicing anarchist Félix Fénéon remarked, "It is well known that the goal of our Marxist functionaries would be a society where each citizen will bear a serial number. They prefer the complexity of a clock to that of a living body."[34]

Anarchist thought had simmered in Paris since the Commune, but had always remained abstract. In 1892, all of this changed. In March, a series of bombings rocked Paris; although no one was killed, an anarchist named Ravachol was arrested, convicted, and guillotined. His execution transformed him into a martyr and inspired a young student, Emile Henry, to follow Ravachol's example that same year. The bomb Henry planted at the Paris office of the Société des Mines de Carmaux killed an office boy and four policemen.

In 1893, a bomb was thrown from the gallery of the France's lower house, the Chamber of Deputies. Though no one was killed, the incident unnerved Paris by breaching the very center of republican power. The bomb thrower, an impoverished worker named Auguste Vaillant, was caught, convicted, and executed. A week after Vaillant's execution, Emile Henry (who had gone underground following his earlier "deed" in 1892) set off a bomb at the Café Terminus near the Saint Lazare train station in central Paris. One diner was killed, 20 others injured. An outraged crowd caught Henry and took him to the police. The artisans, white-collar workers, and merchants who frequented the Café Terminus, people who had been sympathetic to the anarchist cause, were stunned.

With fear mounting, in December 1893 the legislature responded to the anarchist attacks by passing a series of laws, known as the "scoundrel laws" (les lois scélérates), that outlawed the encouragement or even approval of past or future attacks and forbade association with individuals who "intended" to be "evildoers." Undeterred, anarchist intellectual Félix Fénéon explained his approval of such anarchist acts. Henry's bomb at the Café Terminus, he argued, rather than killing the innocent, was aimed at "a voting public" as guilty as anyone else for the Republic's crimes.

Alone among the theorists and intellectuals, Fénéon did not stop at the propaganda of the word. In 1894, he turned to practicing the deed. In April, he ignited a bomb in the restaurant of the fashionable Foyot Hotel. Ironically, the only diner injured was the critic Laurent Tailhade, who had declared after Vaillant's attack, "What matters the victims if the gesture is beautiful." Tailhade lost an eye, but not his fervor for the cause. Then, in June 1894 an Italian anarchist, Cesare Santo, to avenge the refusal to pardon Vaillant for his victimless attack of the Chamber of Deputies, murdered French President Sadi Carnot. The angry public attacked the local Italian Consulate in Lyon where the murder took place and sacked an Italian restaurant. In response, the Republic passed a third "scoundrel law," prohibiting all expressions of anarchist propaganda, in June 1894. In the subsequent police crackdown, Fénéon, although he had never been charged with his crime, was arrested. He was among 30 suspects brought to trial in the summer of 1894.

The "Trial of the Thirty" quickly became a cause célèbre. Fénéon's sharp wit turned the trial into a spectacle. For example, when the judge claimed that Fénéon was seen speaking to two other anarchists behind a lamppost, the urbane defendant replied "Can you tell me, your Honor, where behind a lamp-post is?"[35] Ultimately, the jury cleared Fénéon and his fellow defendants. The bombings waned and eventually stopped after the trial's conclusion, but they reflected the deepening divide between the bourgeois Republic and its critics and created an atmosphere of fear that was slow to dissipate. It is perhaps this fear that accounts for the overheated reaction of the nation to a new scandal that broke out in the fall of 1894, when a spy was discovered in the ranks of the army. An officer named Alfred Dreyfus was promptly arrested and court-martialed—launching what was eventually to become the Republic's greatest challenge to date: the Dreyfus Affair.

CHAPTER 5

The Republic Divided

1894–1914

Calm and courteous, Gaston Calmette welcomed Henriette Caillaux to his office at the Paris newspaper *Le Figaro* on March 16, 1914. The editor's demeanor was impressive: After all, for nearly three months, Calmette had led a vicious editorial campaign against his visitor's husband, Joseph Caillaux, the leading Radical politician of the day. Over the years, Caillaux had served as minister of finance, responsible for introducing the nation's first income tax law, as well as prime minister, intent on seeking peaceful relations with Germany. While neither of these policies sat well with the conservative and nationalist *Le Figaro,* the newspaper did not debate the issues; instead, under Calmette's guidance, it engaged in character assassination, revealing intimate letters Caillaux had written to a former mistress. Just the day before Madame Caillaux's visit, Calmette's paper reproduced a facsimile of one of these letters.

Before Calmette could invite his visitor to take a seat, she asked, "You know why I have come?" When Calmette replied he did not, Caillaux pulled a pistol from the folds of her fur coat and shot him dead. Grabbed by Calmette's employees, Caillaux was arrested, jailed, and charged with murder. By the time the sensational trial began, on July 20, the affair had so mesmerized the public and press that events elsewhere were largely ignored. Remarkably, this indifference extended to the series of events in central Europe that would trigger World War I just a couple of weeks later. "Instead of giving the diplomatic situation the attention it required, newspapers focused so intensely upon the Caillaux Affair as to create the illusion that virtually nothing else existed."[1]

The nineteenth century, most historians noted, came to an end in 1914. But in a sense, the curtain in France fell not in August, when Europe was pulled into the vortex of World War I, but several months earlier with the Caillaux Affair. The product of developments that characterized French society in the first decade of the new century, Caillaux Affair grew out of a fascination with psychology and its focus on the implacable power of the unconscious, a burgeoning nationalist fervor, ever more closely identified with the political Right, an embattled stereotype of women as domestic creatures governed by their emotions, not their intellects, a crisis of masculinity festering ever since France's defeat to Germany in 1870.

All these factors were compounded by an ever more influential mass press, which blurred the lines between the public and private, information and sensationalism. However, many of these threads, which grew fatally knotted by 1914, had been spun 20 years earlier.

THE DREYFUS AFFAIR

In 1894—the same year as the anarchist Trial of the Thirty—another "affair" and trial took place: the court-martial of a French army officer, Captain Alfred Dreyfus. All three trials shared common traits, especially in the ways they reflected the changing political and ideological challenges confronting the Republic. In 1894 as in 1914, mainstream leaders of the Third Republic stirred deepening hostility at both ends of the political spectrum. In fact, both the radical Left and the radical Right denied the Republic's legitimacy: It was the oppressor of the working class for the extreme Left, the unnatural product of abstract reason and cosmopolitan values for the extreme Right. Worlds apart on nearly every issue, anarchist theorists like Fénéon and ultra-right ideologues like Charles Maurras, the founder of the anti-republican, royalist movement Action Française, were joined by their hatred of *la gueuse,* or slut—the pejorative term her enemies gave to Marianne, the female allegory symbolizing the French Republic. While the Republic eventually prevailed—even emerged strengthened—the Dreyfus Affair posed a serious challenge to its stability.

In December 1894, Captain Dreyfus, assigned to the Army General Staff, was charged with passing military secrets to Germany. The damning piece of evidence was a memorandum, or *bordereau,* sent to the German military attaché in Paris. The *bordereau,* found in a trashcan at the German embassy by a French spy posing as a cleaning lady, listed for a German military officer a series of confidential French military documents. Although the *bordereau* was not signed, suspicions fell immediately on Dreyfus, partly because his family was Alsatian, a region ceded to Germany in 1871, and partly because he was the only Jew on the General Staff.

At his court-martial, several handwriting experts testified that Dreyfus' handwriting did not match that on the hand-written *bordereau.* In response, the prosecution called Alphonse Bertillon, who declared that Dreyfus had deliberately tried to disguise his handwriting. Bertillon illustrated his thesis with an array of charts and enlarged photographs—a performance that convinced most spectators that Bertillon himself was insane. Yet the army insisted on Dreyfus' guilt—so much so that to clinch its case, it introduced hearsay evidence and a secret dossier of incriminating reports, which eventually turned out to have been forged.

Within days, on December 22, 1894, Dreyfus was found guilty of treason and sentenced to life deportation. Two weeks later, in the courtyard of the Ecole Militaire, Dreyfus' epaulets were torn off and his sword broken—a military degradation watched by a crowd that included the right-wing nationalist Maurice Barrès, the great actress Sarah Bernhardt, and the future Zionist Theodore Herzl. On January 17, Dreyfus was bundled from his Paris prison in the dead of night, was bound in leg irons and handcuffs, and started his long journey to Devil's Island. For the next four and one-half years, Dreyfus was the lone prisoner on this heat-blasted and malarial rock off the South American coast of French Guiana, where his guards, forbidden to talk with him, were ordered to "blow his brains out" should an unidentified ship approach the island.[2]

The Affair revealed important ideological, social, and political forces at work in fin-de-siècle France. First, the army, after the humiliation of 1870, had become a critical source of national pride. As Maurice Barrès observed, "The choice is clear.... On the one hand, there is Dreyfus' honor; on the other, there is the honor of all the ministers and generals who have sworn to Dreyfus' guilt."[3] The only difference of public opinion in France when the Dreyfus case first became public concerned not Dreyfus' guilt, but his punishment. Some people criticized Dreyfus' sentence as too lenient. Even important figures on the republican Left, like Clemenceau and Jaurès, declared that Dreyfus had only escaped the firing squad thanks to his social connections, since he came from a well-to-do family. Indeed, at first few people beyond Dreyfus' immediate family, particularly his wife Lucie and brother Mathieu, believed in his innocence. In their efforts to reopen the case, the Dreyfus family met resistance everywhere, including the French Jewish community, which was worried that advocating a new trial for Dreyfus would be seen as confirmation that they cared more about their sectarian interests than about the good of the French nation.

Support for Dreyfus came from unlikely places. Anarchist sympathizer and literary critic Bernard Lazare joined forces with the Dreyfus family in 1895. Like Jaurès and Clemenceau, Lazare at first dismissed the trial and conviction of Dreyfus as a bourgeois affair of no interest to anyone beyond the Dreyfus family. But after a series of meetings with Mathieu Dreyfus, in which he learned about the nature of the court-martial, Lazare concluded that Dreyfus had been framed. The dangers posed by anti-Semitism and nationalism trumped Lazare's ideological indifference to the fate of a wealthy officer. In 1896 Lazare published *A Judicial Error: The Truth about the Dreyfus Affair,* a powerful critique of the trial that forced the case back into the public arena.

While the former anarchist was completing his pamphlet, an equally improbable figure joined the ranks of Dreyfus' defenders. In March 1896, the newly installed head of army intelligence, Lieutenant Colonel Georges Picquart, discovered documents that pointed to Commandant Esterhazy, a Hungarian émigré serving on the General Staff, as the author of the *bordereau*. An anti-Semite himself, Picquart nonetheless found himself appalled by the miscarriage of justice. However, his superior officers, not in the least concerned by the miscarriage of justice, were convinced that reopening the Dreyfus case would badly damage the army's reputation. When Picquart apprised his superiors of his discovery of evidence against Esterhazy, the army silenced and demoted Picquart with a transfer to a desert outpost in Tunisia.

Worried by Picquart's discovery, Colonel Joseph Henry, an army intelligence officer, fattened the "secret dossier" by forging documents that implicated Dreyfus.

Henry justified the forgeries on the grounds of patriotism. He firmly believed that preserving the honor of the military counted more than Dreyfus' actual innocence or guilt. Henry's anti-Semitism also colored his view of the case. After all, Dreyfus' "race" necessarily made him a traitor. While Henry was adding forged proof of guilt to Dreyfus' file, Picquart relayed his findings about Dreyfus' innocence to a fellow Alsatian, the vice president of the Senate, Auguste Scheurer-Kestner. In a letter to his colleagues, Senator Scheurer-Kestner declared that Dreyfus' court-martial was "unacceptable in the nineteenth century and that it dishonored the Republic."[4]

With great reluctance, the army opened an inquiry and eventually held a new court-martial to consider the charges leveled against Esterhazy, the likely author of the *bordereau*. In January 1889, the military judges, deliberating less than three minutes, returned a verdict of "not guilty" for Esterhazy. With their decision, the judges hoped to keep Dreyfus securely locked away on Devil's Island. But at this very moment the affair shifted from the narrow confines of the courtroom to the stage of public opinion. The affair, in a word, became *the* "Affair."[5]

THE "AFFAIR"

By the end of the nineteenth century, the popular press had become an important vehicle for public opinion. Galvanized by the liberal press law of 1881 that lifted the strict censorship rules imposed by the Second Empire and maintained during the "Moral Order" era, newspapers had already joined in the many political battles of the Third Republic. However, the lines between analysis and opinion, journalism and sensationalism, were at best blurred. Tellingly, many papers carried serialized novels on their front page. These popular novels blended a number of ingredients—innocent victims, improbable plot twists, and colorful characters— that also happened to shape the Dreyfus Affair.[6]

Among the most successful practitioners of the serialized novel was Emile Zola. Yet unlike many of his fellow novelists—or for that matter, many journalists—Zola was a dogged researcher whose works exposed the gap between republican rhetoric and the brutal social and economic realities of the era. By 1898, he was at the height of his fame. Liberals hailed his completed cycle of novels, the *Rougon-Macquart,* as a masterpiece, while many conservatives, shocked by Zola's open portrayal of drinking and sex in his novels, dismissed them as smut. Zola, skeptical of the army's case against Dreyfus, was stunned by Esterhazy's rapid acquittal. The court-martial's refusal to recognize the real culprit left Dreyfus' family and supporters deeply depressed and demoralized. Yet rather than giving up, Zola went on the attack, publishing an astonishing letter in Clemenceau's newspaper *L'Aurore*. Addressed to the president of France, Félix Faure, Zola's letter, provocatively titled "I Accuse!" ("J'Accuse!"), dismantled the case against Dreyfus point by point, identifying by name the officers responsible for committing this "stain" against the Republic. Lucid and incendiary, the letter transformed the affair.

"Truth is on the march." Zola's stirring declaration electrified Dreyfus' supporters, known as Dreyfusards. For the Dreyfusards, individual rights, including
the right to a fair trial, were paramount, and no damage to the army's reputation
could justify imprisoning an innocent man. They also began to suspect not just
that people within the military had concocted evidence to convict Dreyfus and
then covered up their actions, but that the army as a whole, in conjunction with
other nefarious, anti-republican forces like the Catholic Church and royalists, had
joined together in a vast conspiracy. Thus the person of Dreyfus mattered less to
many Dreyfusards than the principles they defended and the enemies they believed
they struggled against.

In the short term, Zola's letter failed to change Dreyfus' situation. In 1898,
Zola was hauled into court by the former minister of war, General Mercier, and
found guilty of libel. Facing a jail sentence and threatened by anti-Dreyfusard
mobs, the novelist fled to Britain. But anti-Dreyfusards were not yet satisfied. The
army imprisoned Colonel Picquart for revealing military secrets to the press, and
Scheurer-Kestner was forced to step down as vice president of the Senate. On what
basis did Dreyfus' enemies discount the mounting evidence of his innocence?
Military officers, mostly old aristocratic elites vaguely anti-Semitic in orientation
and unreconciled to a republican government, clearly believed that the army's
honor was at stake and took every measure they could to prevent Dreyfus' conviction

"J'Accuse!," letter by Emile Zola, published in *L'Aurore*, January 13, 1898. Private Collection/
Archives Charmet/The Bridgeman Art Library.

from being overturned. To monarchists and extreme right-wing nationalists, Dreyfus and his supporters threatened the army and therefore the nation.

This emphasis on the nation by the anti-Dreyfusards revealed just how much the Right had changed by the 1890s. For much of the nineteenth century, conservatives on the Right remained principally attached to the monarchy and the Catholic Church—leaving nationalism to the Left. From the 1789 Revolution on, the republican Left created, used, and owned nationalism as a way of empowering the people against those seeking to dominate and oppress. For republicans, France embodied the abstract values of the Revolution and the Enlightenment. The declaration of the French League for the Defense of the Rights of Man and Citizen, the world's first human rights organization founded in 1898 in response to the Dreyfus Affair, underscored this paternity: "Each of us has a great mission to accomplish. We must make known and loved the ideas of Justice, Truth and Liberty."[7] By the nineteenth century's end, however, the Right began to redefine and claim nationalism for itself.

Right-wing, anti-Dreyfusard nationalists had a different idea of France from that of the Left. Rather than the vehicle of abstract, Enlightened values, the French nation was, according to Barrès' famous formula, formed by "*la terre et les morts*"—"the soil and the dead." This organic, even racial form of nationalism—hardly surprising in an imperialist age—distinguished, in the writer Charles Maurras' phrase, between the "legal" France and "real" France. The 1789 Revolution had led to the notion that a constitution created a nation of laws, "legal" France. Maurras rejected that notion, arguing instead that the nation rests on a people linked by ancestry to a particular territory. Some right-wing nationalists, like Barrès, favored a populist, plebiscitary, or Bonapartist regime that occasionally would cement popular support by inviting the public to vote its approval. In this way, through mass actions with little choice, the "individual is absorbed by the family, race and nation."[8] Others, like Maurras, insisted upon natural social hierarchies. Natural elites would rule a hierarchical society that required the restoration of the monarchy. In both cases, this new right-wing, "integral" nationalism promoted a vision of the nation as an organic entity, a people determined by ancestry, tied to the soil, and opposed to external and internal foes threatening its purity.

These nationalists despised the Third Republic and everything it stood for. To this degree, they made common cause with the old monarchist Right. And yet, the old and new Rights shared little apart from a common enemy. The new Right was, in many respects, an avatar of the fascist movements that would scar European history in the twentieth century. During the last years of the nineteenth century, a number of "leagues" appeared in Paris. Rather than traditional parties that accepted the rules and values of the republican system, the leagues contested the system from without. The most notable movements were the Anti-Semitic League, founded in 1897 by Jules Guérin; the Committee of the Action Française, created in 1898 by Maurras and Maurice Pujo; and the Federation of Yellows, established by Pierre Biétry in 1902. While each of these movements took on the character of its particular leader, they were nevertheless marked by three common traits: the idealization of violence (practiced in the street no less than in the press), the rejection of existing political principles (most often they defined themselves by what they opposed; i.e., they were anti-parliamentarian, anti-democratic, anti-liberal), and, perhaps most important, the effort to find a "third way" between Right and Left, capitalism and socialism, liberalism and conservatism.[9]

Linked to the new, anti-republican nationalism, the Dreyfus Affair also served as the crucible for the creation of a new kind of racial anti-Semitism. No longer the preserve of the Catholic Church, anti-Semitism had achieved the status of an ideology: a bundle of contradictory ideas that supposedly offered a key to the mysteries of the modern age. Jews were not merely outsiders because they were not Christians, but they were also outsiders by ancestry. From a religious minority, Jews now represented a biological threat to the purity of the French nation. The most notorious purveyor of this new form of French anti-Semitism was Edouard Drumont. In 1886, he penned *La France Juive* (*Jewish France*) a two-volume denunciation of what he viewed as the corrosive presence of Jews in French politics and culture. The book quickly sold more than 100,000 copies, exploiting widespread anxiety and fears spurred by a rapidly changing economy and society.

In the phantasmagoric world portrayed by Drumont and his peers, the Jew was transformed into a mythical and mutually contradictory being. He was both the wealthy banker who crushed small shopkeepers and workers and the socialist militant who exploited these very same victims. As the Catholic newspaper *La Croix* put it, "Don't these 'revolutionaries' and 'financiers' pursue the same goal? Namely, the ruination of small owners, small shopkeepers, small farmers: in a word, the real France?"[10] The great upheavals convulsing French society, according to Drumont, issued from the "savage energy of Jewish invaders" that would forever remain a foreign body within France. In 1889, Drumont founded the Anti-Semitic League to militate against Jews; in 1892, he capitalized on his earlier successes by launching the anti-Semitic newspaper *La Libre Parole* (*Free Speech*).

Drumont viewed Dreyfus as symptomatic of the threat Jews posed to France. Under his and the Anti-Semitic League's impetus, the streets began to throb. During the Dreyfus Affair, the League organized anti-Semitic demonstrations; crowds chanted: "Throw the kikes in the water" and "Death to the Jews." Popular unrest and violence occurred even in cities with little or no Jewish presence, like Rennes and Saint Malo in Brittany. The danger was greatest in the city of Algiers, which the settler community in Algeria had made their capital. Home to a relatively large Jewish community, Algiers became a critical arena for anti-Semitic French politicians who stirred the volatile *pied-noir* community—many of whose members had long resented the citizenship granted to Algerian Jews by the 1870 Crémieux decree—to bursts of violence. In response to the Dreyfus Affair, waves of rioting, pillaging, and killing of Jewish residents swept the city of Algiers. In the elections of May 1898, Algiers elected Edouard Drumont as its deputy.

Anti-Semitism, the new right-wing nationalism, and fierce defense of the army against any and all critics—all were intensified by the era's pervasive fears about French masculinity. A familiar anti-Semitic trope represented Jews as effeminate, fearful cowards, a characterization frequently used against Dreyfus himself. The Affair itself spawned a huge number of duels, signaling the underlying gender anxiety. Surprisingly, bourgeois men, lawyers, judges, and journalists took up this old, aristocratic practice, quick to defend their honor against any and all assaults, which was how they interpreted any questioning of their roles in the Dreyfus case. Dueling, which was, strictly speaking, illegal, also surprisingly rarely resulted in death. The real man had to be willing to face death in defense of his honor. Radical leader Clemenceau alone engaged in over 20 duels. French nationalists on both the Left and the Right supported dueling as a way of reinforcing masculine honor and courage.[11]

Nationalist fervor, racism, and pro-army sentiment were also stoked in the spring and summer of 1898 by a dangerous new development on the colonial front. In an abandoned fort on the Upper Nile in a remote corner of the Sudan in Africa, a tiny column of French and African soldiers led by Captain Jean Louis Marchand faced a much larger and better-armed English force under the command of Lord Kitchener. Both were there to claim this particular piece of the continent for their respective countries, and the question was whether war—a real possibility in an increasingly belligerent age—with Britain could be averted. For this to happen, one side would have to swallow its pride and accept the humiliation of withdrawal. The obvious candidate was Marchand: Not only were his forces outnumbered, but the French claim to the Upper Nile was considerably more tenuous than Britain's. For the latter, control of the Upper Nile was essential to

The "Mission Marchand," which left Loango, in the Congo, and reached Fashoda, Sudan, 1897–1898. Archives du Ministère des Affaires Etrangères, Paris/Archives Charmet/The Bridgeman Art Library.

safeguarding the British protectorate in Egypt, established in 1882 at the expense of French influence there.

But Marchand, and more importantly the mass media and colonial lobby who lionized him, was not so easily persuaded. It was a symptom of the era that ever since the mid-1890s, an aggressive demand for "revenge" against Britain's "odious spoliation" of Egypt had arisen even among traditionally Germanophobe politicians and publicists on both sides of the political spectrum.[12] Parliament had overwhelming voted for the expedition headed by Marchand, a highly popular hero of the earlier French military campaigns against Ahmadu and Samori in West Africa. Marchand's mission was very clearly to cross Africa from west to east and claim the Upper Nile for France. Marchand had set out in May 1898, and in late September 1898, news reached Paris that he had safely arrived in Fashoda. Kitchener and Marchand, it turned out, met on September 19, and Kitchener had demanded that the French evacuate the fort and abandon any claim to the region. Refusal, he intimated, could mean war. Back in France, right-wing nationalists and their newspapers suddenly saw in Marchand a potential new Boulanger, and insisted that he stay put at Fashoda. The army's, and the nation's, honor—now more than ever—required standing firm. If the government backed down, the Right added, this would be further proof that the Dreyfusards and, behind them, the Jews were secretly the allies of Britain.[13]

THE DÉNOUEMENT

Yet just as Marchand mania, Anglophobia, and war-mongering reached new heights in late summer 1898, the army's case against Dreyfus began to come undone. In August 1898, Colonel Henry, confronted by a fellow officer, confessed to having forged the secret documents in the Dreyfus file. Arrested and placed in the prison of Mont Valérien in a western suburb of Paris on August 30, Henry committed suicide that same night. A rash of resignations, led by the army chief of staff and minister of war, followed. At the same time, Esterhazy, by then living safely in exile in England, admitted that he had indeed written the *bordereau* and was the real culprit. Obstacles remained. Drumont led a successful campaign to raise money to commemorate Henry's suicide as a "patriotic sacrifice": The 25,000 contributors to the "Henry Monument" were clearly unprepared to accept a retrial. Many government leaders, including the Opportunists in power when Dreyfus was first convicted, repeatedly raised institutional obstacles to revisiting the Dreyfus trial. President Faure consistently opposed revision of the Dreyfus trial, while successive prime ministers were either hostile to Dreyfusards or feckless in the face of fierce army stonewalling. The only initiative managed by France's paralyzed government in the fall of 1898 was to order Marchand, on November 4, to abandon Fashoda. War had been avoided, but at the cost of France's complete humiliation, which only served to harden the anti-Dreyfusards' resolve to topple the Republic.

Time, however, was not on the side of the nationalists. In early 1899, President Faure's tenure came to a sudden end—he died of a stroke while in his mistress' arms at the presidential Elysée Palace. With Radical support, the moderate Emile Loubet replaced Faure. President Loubet, a man of few ideals, did have courage. During a visit to the elegant racetrack at Auteuil, a nationalist dandy brought his cane down on Loubet's head. Though his top hat was mashed, the president announced with great aplomb that the "Republic is more difficult to rumple."[14] More importantly, René Waldeck-Rousseau became prime minister in June 1899. One of France's most prominent lawyers, Waldeck-Rousseau was no more an idealist than Loubet; in 1894, he had prudently turned down the opportunity to defend Dreyfus. But Waldeck-Rousseau, recognizing the dangers that the anti-Dreyfusard forces posed for the Republic, was determined to bring them to heel.

As a result, the Dreyfusards had good reason to be optimistic when, in June 1899, the Court of Appeals voided Dreyfus' 1894 sentence and scheduled a new trial for August in Rennes. Overnight, the Breton city was transformed from a dull provincial city to the stage for a political drama watched by the world. While Dreyfus, back from Devil's Island, prepared to see his family for the first time in five years, the right-wing nationalist movements organized massive protests. Groups like the Action Française, the Anti-Semitic League, and the League of Patriots sent trainloads of members to Rennes to protest the retrial, while the forces of republican order effectively locked down the city. On September 9, 1899, after several weeks of hearings, the court-martial delivered its verdict to a gaunt and malarial Dreyfus. By a 5-to-2 vote, once again, they found Dreyfus guilty. The army simply would not admit its error.

Ten days later, after complex political negotiations, President Loubet pardoned Dreyfus on September 19, 1899. Exhausted and in poor health, Dreyfus ignored the advice of supporters like Clemenceau and accepted the pardon. Many of his supporters urged Dreyfus to reject a pardon that implied guilt and to remain imprisoned and fight on for full exoneration. They cared more about the abstract causes Dreyfus represented than about the man himself. As one Dreyfusard, prominent intellectual Charles Péguy, recalled with unjustified bitterness, "We were ready to die for Dreyfus, but Dreyfus wasn't." Soon afterward, Waldeck-Rousseau declared to the Chamber of Deputies that the "Dreyfus Affair is over." In a narrow sense, the prime minister was right: The affair no longer threatened to break France in half. His government had arrested anti-Semitic agitators and amnestied those officers involved in Dreyfus' wrongful conviction, Dreyfus returned to his long-suffering family, and the press turned to other stories.

THE PUBLIC INTELLECTUAL

In addition to providing an arena for the new right-wing nationalism, rising populist and racist anti-Semitism, and the popular press, the Affair also served as midwife to the birth of the intellectuals. It is uncertain who first coined the term, which, moreover, was not always a badge of honor. Anti-Dreyfusards like Barrès used 'intellectual' as a term of scorn. Yet Barrès himself, a prominent novelist, journalist, and politician, qualified as an intellectual. Like those he lambasted,

Barrès held a position of "power and authority in the political and cultural establishment, and thus defined norms and values for the rest of society." In French
political and cultural discourse, anyone could exercise intellectual activity but not
everyone could be an intellectual.[15]

When Zola published "J'Accuse!", he did so less as France's preeminent novelist than as an agent of justice and truth. This applied equally to the dozens of
writers, artists, and professors who subsequently signed a public declaration, titled
"Manifesto of the Intellectuals," that called for a revision of Dreyfus' trial. In fact,
both texts reveal one of the critical traits of the French intellectual: the same preoccupation with the principles of truth and justice. They portrayed themselves as the
guardians of abstract values that transcended the nation. Yet intellectuals were also
entwined with the particular history of France—a history that began in 1789.
Intellectuals in France offered "not merely assistance to the cause of justice or support for the defenders of the Republic but a vision of society, of the ways in which
the inadequate present might be rendered into a better future."[16]

Inevitably, intellectuals on the Left took divergent approaches. Sociologist
Emile Durkheim, for example, based his political and ethical claims, and thus his
standing as an intellectual, on ostensibly scientific grounds. In works like *Suicide*
(1897) and *The Rules of Sociological Method* (1895), Durkheim proposed a science
of society that would reveal a shared code of ethics upon which government could
base its social policies. He introduced the concept of "collective conscience" in his
effort to depict the ways in which societies develop beliefs and values. This concept
also served as foil to modern phenomena like anomie. The rhythm of contemporary life, Durkheim argued, loosened the group bonds that previously defined our
lives, leaving many people uprooted and alienated.

Romantic rather than rationalist, though equally committed to the Republic
and the Dreyfusard cause, was Charles Péguy. A brilliant student at the Sorbonne,
Péguy's attachment to the Republic was emotional, nearly mystical. In early works
like his biography of Joan of Arc, *Jeanne d'Arc* (1897), Péguy wrote lyrically about
the medieval saint, portraying her as the embodiment not of Christian faith, but of
the French people. With the advent of the Dreyfus Affair, Péguy threw himself into
the fray. Although Péguy felt driven by the same patriotism that fueled the anti-
Dreyfusards, Péguy argued that the army, far from damaging itself by reconsidering
the case, had to be above all suspicion and, as a result, had to admit its errors. In the
wake of the Dreyfus Affair, Péguy founded a journal, the *Cahiers de la Quinzaine,*
whose influence reached far beyond its few hundred subscribers. In the journal's
pages, Péguy gave voice to a nearly visceral form of socialism that was far closer to
Jaurès than Guesde. In fact, for Péguy, Guesde was to socialism what the Jesuits
were to Christianity: an arid and stifling interpretation of a rich and liberating
philosophy.[17] Péguy applied the same parallelism to the ethos of the Opportunist
Republic: The only difference between secular and Catholic dogmatism was a
cloud of incense. In each case, imagination and instinct fell victim to logic and
bureaucratic routine—or, in Péguy's famous phrase, *mystique* was overtaken by
politique.

Not all intellectuals came from the Left. Barrès, one of the most notable intellectuals on the Right, like Péguy on the Left, developed a notion of nation based on affective and emotional rather than rational claims. Barrès' novel *Les Déracinés* (*The Uprooted*), published in 1897, portrays a group of provincial youths who have come to Paris for their education. They all fall under the spell of the Paul Boutellier, a professor of Kantian ethics. Boutellier serves as the emblematic figure of all that is rotten in the Republic. Under his influence, these young men, "uprooted" from their customs and communities, become drifters among abstract values, victims of the Republic's positivist education. In the novel, Boutellier is likened to a "drill sergeant pounding into his recruits the rules handed down from above."[18] Inevitably—for those who, like Barrès, decried the decline of tradition and community and rise of rationalism and individualism—nearly all the students come to a bad end.

While Barrès couched his ideology in fiction (as well as thousands of editorials), another leading right-wing intellectual, Charles Maurras, presented his thought in taut and nearly Cartesian reasoning. In the pages of his paper *Action française*, launched in 1908 and hawked by thuggish vendors recruited among university students known as the "king's camelots" (*camelots du roi*), Maurras offered a systematic demolition of the Republic and its values. To Maurras' mind the Republic, sordid spawn of the French Revolution, violated the very essence of the French nation. The Republic's embrace of reason and equality represented a disastrous detour off France's true path of faith and hierarchy—a path defined by the Catholic Church and French monarchy. Maurras labeled the agents of this decay the so-called anti-Frances—Protestants, Jews, and Freemasons guilty of undermining the foundations of the "true" France. The cure, the deaf and aloof Maurras argued, was loud and gritty: street battles and menacing marches against left-wing organizations or competing right-wing ones, led by his youthful "camelots." Although the *Action française* movement attracted relatively few members prior to 1914, its paper had many more readers; the *Action française*'s unrelenting critique of the bourgeois Republic made sense even to some people on the Left, where a group of disaffected theorists, including Georges Sorel, incorporated some of its elements into their thought.

Nearly as well known among contemporaries as Maurras and Barrès was the anti-Semitic novelist and journalist Sibylle-Gabrielle Marie-Antoinette de Riquetti de Mirabeau, known by her pen name Gyp. The daughter of a ruined Legitimist family, Gyp wrote countless articles and more than a hundred novels, most of which the popular press serialized. In fact, Gyp perfected the "anti-Semitic novel"—a literary genre that built on and in turn amplified right-wing nationalism in fin-de-siècle France. Drumont published several of Gyp's novels in *La Libre Parole,* effectively erasing the already blurred line between Drumont's incendiary journalism and Gyp's serialized novels, both replete with repulsive Jewish caricatures.

In important ways, Gyp embodied the era's contradictory tensions. On the one hand, she detested many aspects of modernity, condemning cars, electricity, and other symptoms of what she called the "age of fake." On the other hand, Gyp's embrace of anti-Semitism, Boulangism, and integral nationalism all placed her in the forefront of modernity. In her life as author and journalist, Gyp embodied the era's new woman, a character type also prominent in her novels. Yet it was an odd brand of what might be considered feminism. Her novels featured unconventional heroines, defined as much by their admirable independence as by their appalling attitude toward Jews and the Republic. In an age when women neither voted nor held political office, Gyp pursued a different path of political engagement, attaching her life and work to the aspirations of the anti-democratic forces on the Right. Ironically, Gyp's work supported an ideology and political movement that fiercely opposed women's freedom to choose Gyp's lifestyle.

As with Drumont's writings, a crude form of populism and hesitant identification with economically oppressed classes informed Gyp's anti-Semitism. However, Gyp's answer to the misery of the working poor was not to advocate laws establishing a more equitable society, but to propose emptying society of Jews, considered as agents of economic disparity, social dislocation, and intellectual disenchantment. The hero of her novel *Israel,* published in 1898 at the height of the Dreyfus Affair, warns, "When the parliamentary Republic cedes to a dictatorship, or to an empire, or to any other type of authoritarian regime, the liquidation . . . is going to be rather painful."[19]

STATE AND CHURCH GO THEIR SEPARATE WAYS

The Dreyfus Affair was largely an urban, particularly a Parisian, matter. Regional newspapers during the Affair reveal a provincial and rural France less fascinated by the issues and personalities surrounding Dreyfus. And yet, the Affair had a deep and lasting impact on the direction of national politics. By the time Dreyfus accepted the presidential pardon in 1899, Dreyfusard idealism and innocence had given way to republican coalition-building and pragmatism.

One key result of the Dreyfus Affair was the end of Opportunist dominance, as Radical Republicans assumed leadership of the Third Republic. Radical Prime Minister Waldeck-Rousseau described himself as "a republican moderate, but not moderately republican."[20] Waldeck-Rousseau's inspired blurring of categories also informed the creation of his government; for the first time ever, a socialist, Alexandre Millerand, was named to a cabinet position. The recent realignment of the socialists had anticipated this move. Prodded by Jaurès, the socialists, unlike the Confédération Générale du Travail or CGT, concluded that the dangers posed to the Republic by the anti-Dreyfusards eclipsed the issue of class struggle and increasingly chose to participate in the political process. Yet Waldeck also appealed to the republican Right, including in his cabinet General Gallifet, the republican officer who had overseen the repression of the Commune.

Waldeck-Rousseau's ministry emerged strengthened from the struggle over Dreyfus. Extreme elements on the nationalist Right found themselves, temporarily at least, isolated. Fringe figures like Jules Guérin, the leader of the Anti-Semitic League, and Paul Déroulède, who led a failed coup attempt, were either in prison or exile. Yet the right-wing revolutionary nationalism of Barrès and Maurras had not been defeated—on the contrary, it entered the political mainstream when nationalists swept to victory in the Paris municipal elections of 1898. Although many conservatives repudiated Maurras' continuing endorsement of street violence, they covertly sympathized with his hatred of democracy, Jews, and foreigners.

The conflicting currents of nationalism seemed less violent in the provinces, where the culture of Radical republicanism flourished. The Republic had successfully cast itself as the defender of private property, individual rights, and small business. By the turn of the century, the Radicals on the republican Left also became increasingly strident about the issue of secularism. Leading Radicals like Waldeck-Rousseau and Ferdinand Buisson had both sincere and pragmatic motives. Despite the Ralliement's tentative efforts to find a common ground, the Catholic Church remained uneasy with the Republic. After all, the Church had opposed reopening the Dreyfus case, supported the army, and was closely linked to nationalists and anti-Semitic forces. The division between Church and Republic had deep roots. An ancient institution like the Catholic Church, based on hierarchy and faith, could scarcely embrace a society informed by the revolutionary principles of liberty, equality, and fraternity. If the Left viewed the Dreyfus Affair as a conspiracy against the Republic and its values, by supporting the wrong side the Church again could be portrayed as a threat. Radicals were also eager to portray the Church as a clear and present danger to the Republic because galvanizing the forces of republicanism against the Church not only neutralized a traditional foe, but could also distract the working class, if only for a time, from bread-and-butter issues. Much as they relished a fight against the Right, Radicals were mostly reluctant to tackle and improve the grim economic realities of the working class.

Gambetta's cry—"Clericalism: There is the enemy!"— received a new lease on life in 1902 when Radicals, in alliance with 43 socialists, won an electoral victory. The tenaciousness that the new prime minister, Emile Combes, brought to his battle against the Church reflected the rigid education he received as a seminary student. Unlike his predecessor Waldeck-Rousseau, Combes had neither the desire nor the ability to limit the tensions between the Church and State. Instead, he pursued a policy of confrontation, methodically tearing away from the Church what it had long considered its rights and duties. In 1903, the government shut down more than 80 religious congregations, leading to a massive diaspora of nuns, priests, and monks from various orders. The following year, the government banned all religious orders from teaching, forcing the closure of 12,000 schools in France and many schools in the colonies. Ironically, at the very moment that the Radicals portrayed Catholicism as a monolithic and hostile force, dissident reformists within the Church were attempting to find a following. French Catholics like theologian Alfred Loisy sought to lessen the tensions between the Church and the Republic, and in 1902 social reformer Marc Sangnier founded a movement, the Sillon, committed to aiding the working class. These groups nevertheless found themselves on the defensive as much with their own Church as with republicans on the Left. The Catholic Church responded to the Republic's mounting anti-clericalism with a campaign of its own, and in 1910 a new combative pope, Pius X, banned Sangnier's Sillon movement.[21]

At the climax of the struggle, the Republic passed the law of December 9, 1905, formally separating Church and State. The event was both more and less significant than it first appeared. On the one hand, it marked the end of a relationship with its roots in the Old Regime, severely tested by the rigors of the Revolution and restored to an uneasy truce by Napoleon's Concordat. Since that 1804 agreement, the French government had in effect supported the Catholic Church, paying its clergy and funding its schools, hospitals, and charities. The 1905 law put an end to all that. For many republicans, the divorce seemed to herald the end of one era and the beginning of a new and happier one. Yet such optimism about the end of bitter partisan divisions overlooked the many other social and economic tensions that remained unaddressed. By the same token, many Catholics harbored fears that the 1905 law would lead to the decline and even death of the Church, fears that proved unfounded. Of course, the Church was sorely tried in the immediate wake of the separation. In essence privatized, the Church initially foundered, suffering from the loss of state funds and hemorrhaging the ranks of men entering the priesthood. However, the separation eventually benefited the Church in unforeseen ways.

Jean-Baptiste Bienvenu-Martin separating the State from the Church, caricature from *Le Rire* magazine, May 20, 1905, Charles Leandre. Private Collection/Archives Charmet/The Bridgeman Art Library.

Not only did the number of seminarians gradually rebound, but so too did their quality, commitment, and energy. At the same time, the 1905 law shifted the survival of the Church to the shoulders of the faithful, not the taxpayer. Last but not least, Catholics overseas fearful of discrimination redefined their goals to coincide more closely with the republican colonial project, thereby ending the quarrels that had divided missionaries and administrators throughout the empire.[22]

While the Radical-led governments were waging their final assault on the Church, a quieter but equally momentous realignment was taking place within the ranks of France's fractious and divided socialist camp. The Dreyfus Affair was the great impetus needed for the two rival leaders, the Marxist Jules Guesde and the reformist Jean Jaurès, to set aside their differences and to merge into a single unified party—although it was Jaurès's expansive humanism rather than Guesde's dry intellectualism that won over the rank and file. As noted in Chapter 4, this party took the name Section Française de l'Internationale Ouvrière (SFIO). Jaurès had been re-elected to the Chamber of Deputies in 1902, in the general mobilization of the Left unleashed by the Affair; in 1904 he assembled a team of enthusiastic young intellectuals and founded the socialist newspaper, *L'Humanité,* which quickly became one of France's leading dailies. With the anticlerical struggle behind them in 1905, socialists of all stripes optimistically believed that long overdue reforms for working men and women lay just around the corner.

In the short term, then, the balance sheet of the Dreyfus Affair was clear. The Church had been placed on the defensive and the Republic and the values of 1789 had triumphed. But the Republic's victory was soon threatened by a menace far more imposing than the supposedly "occult forces" of the Church. The fragile alliance formed during the Affair between conservative and reformist republicans, the middle class and working classes, was beginning to give way. From 1904 until 1914, the nation experienced a wave of labor militancy unparalleled in the history of the Third Republic. Workers and peasants alike gave notice that, with the Church defeated, they expected social reform and would take direct action to achieve it. Eventually, the Republic did begin to undertake some modest social reforms, but neither at the pace nor on the scale that workers, socialists, or feminists desired.

NEW CRISES

In 1905, the Combes government fell when the socialists withdrew their support. Veteran Radical republican Georges Clemenceau (1906–1909) and independent socialist Aristide Briand (1909–1910) led the major governments that followed. The 64-year-old Clemenceau came to power in a crisis atmosphere. As the Dreyfus Affair finally petered out, hundreds of workers began flocking into the national trade union federation, or CGT, founded in 1895. The CGT further exacerbated fears of social revolution by calling for a general strike in favor of the eight-hour workday on May 1, 1906. A horrific mining disaster at Courrières on March 10, 1906, where a gas explosion killed over a thousand miners, caused many miners to begin the strike early. First miners in the north, then workers across the country demonstrated in angry solidarity with those who had died. While the strikes did not produce the general insurrection some union leaders hoped for, they launched a pattern of strike actions by teachers, postmen, miners, metal workers, and construction workers that would be sustained up until the outbreak of World War I – despite repeated government repression.

And not only urban workers struck. The year 1907 saw protests by France's southern wine growers in the lower Languedoc, suffering from a crisis of overproduction. In the 1890s phylloxera had decimated France's vineyards; by the early 1900s most wine-growing peasants had replanted with American vines and were flooding the market with cheap wine. With their livelihood threatened by declining prices, wine growers sought protection against competition and fraud; as many as a half million supporters mobilized to pressure the government, threatening to withhold their taxes until they got help. Their willingness to protest was another sign that an older way of life was beginning to disappear in parts of rural France as a result of new market forces. From peasants working only for themselves, the men and women of the Languedoc had become modern "farmers" producing crops for sale, working larger farms, substituting machinery for labor, and organizing to defend their interests.

Confronted with this upsurge of working-class and agrarian militancy, Clemenceau mobilized the powers of the state. Already known as the Tiger (he deemed the name a compliment), he now earned a second nickname: "top cop of France." Clemenceau never hesitated to use the army and the police to put down strikers and protesters by force. The man who alternated in power with Clemenceau, Briand, although he started his political career as a socialist, followed the same policy; both men believed in maintaining the authority of the French state at all costs.

The subsequent rift that split the republican camp might have healed if Clemenceau and Briand had combined repression with even minimal reforms at a time of a widening gap between rich and poor. By the turn of the century, the so-called second industrial revolution was underway, created by the expansion of new, advanced sectors of the French economy, including chemical, electrical, and automobile manufacturers concentrated around Paris, Lyon, and Grenoble and the steel regions of Lorraine. After years of recession in the 1890s, the French economy recovered after 1900 and began a period of vigorous growth. Debate still continues over the role of government policy, particularly protectionist tariffs, in this recovery. At the end of the nineteenth century, in response to the recession, Jules Méline, who served variously as prime minister and—arguably a more important position for a rural nation—minister of agriculture, orchestrated punishing import tariffs. The walls of protectionism may have contributed to the recovery after 1900, allowing France to cultivate a diversified economy of small businesses and to remain largely self-sufficient.

On the other hand, France's recovery may well have happened despite Méline's tariffs. The French revival occurred in the context of a revitalized global economy. At the time, some critics argued that France's recovery would have been even more rapid and enduring had its economy not been fettered by self-defeating tariffs. Protectionist measures only propped up decaying and uncompetitive producers that would otherwise have disappeared in the free play of market forces. The debate about the efficacy of protective tariffs hinged "largely on the kind of society preferred by the two camps."[23] For defenders of *la douce France* (traditional France) the tariffs were a good and great thing; for advocates of a modern competitive France, the tariffs were a millstone fatally handicapping the country.

But only the very rich profited from the economic growth at the turn of the century. Meanwhile for most workers, the rising cost of living outpaced their wages. France also lagged desperately behind Britain and Germany in passing basic social legislation, such as restrictions on work hours, measures to improve safety, and disability and unemployment insurance. It was this long-simmering anger about inequities and lack of safety protections that triggered the strikes in the first place. Clemenceau himself well understood the need for reform alongside repression, but he was hamstrung by a conservative Senate's hostility to new taxes to fund social measures. As a result, the years between 1906 and 1910 saw only limited social redress. In 1900 a 10-hour workday had been passed and in 1905 compulsory military service had been cut from three years to two, a move that resulted more out of a desire to punish the army for Dreyfus than to improve the lot of workers; in 1906 workers were given a compulsory day of rest; in 1907 a married women's earnings law gave working wives control over their own wages, by law previously controlled entirely by their husbands; and in 1910 old-age pensions were created for workers and peasants (cynically called "pensions of the dead" by trade unionists because they kicked in at age 65, which was above the life expectancy of most citizens).

Between 1911 and 1914, when conservative republicans and Radicals again alternated in power, the only social measure passed was aid to large families and maternity leaves. Private industrialists in Nord and Paris basin had experimented with something called family allowances. This was a sum of money added to the paycheck of the father for each child born in wedlock. While the Catholic business owners who instituted these allowances hoped to reverse declining birthrates, the allowances allowed them to avoid across-the-board wage increases, by differentiating the salaries of workers to enable those with children to get by. The allowances were also meant to encourage working mothers to stay in the labor force, where they (along with the influx of over a million new foreign workers between 1896 and 1911) supplemented France's labor shortfall. Working fathers (the allowances were at first paid to the father) could only get the allowance at the end of the month if neither husband nor wife (nor working child) had missed a day of work; thus the allowances also were a tool of labor discipline. The government, increasingly anxious about population trends, viewed family allowances as a possible way to reverse *dénatalité*. Gingerly, the republican leadership began to adopt and expand those allowances.[24] Although the Radicals attempted repeatedly to pass a progressive income tax as well in these years, it was invariably defeated.

NEWS OF CYCLES, CYCLES OF NEWS

Tensions between the bourgeoisie and working class were also reflected in popular culture and sporting activity, and nowhere more so than in the rage for cycling. With the introduction of mass-production techniques, prices fell and the bicycle, formerly the pastime of the well-to-do, was within the reach of most white-collar and factory workers by 1900. Tellingly, as early as 1893, one bicycle manufacturer unveiled a new inexpensive line, the *démocratique* model, aimed at a blue-collar clientele.[25]

The democratization of the bicycle was a cause both for celebration and anxiety. As the bicycle's price plummeted and its dependability grew, distances between places shrank and the pace of life sped up. Not only were workers liberated by the advent of the bicycle, but so, too, were women. The blurring of traditional social and gender categories caused a great deal of debate over the benefits of cycling. One (male) expert warned that women who cycled were prone to "nymphomania and characterized hysteria," while others bemoaned the loss of feminine modesty. Needless to say, the source of despair for traditionalists was cause for joy for progressives: One feminist leader, Maria Pognon, praised the "egalitarian and leveling bicycle" that would help liberate her sex.[26]

The bicycle also intersected with another trend of the era, the invention of the mass press at the turn of the century. The continuing explosion of newspapers was ignited by the rise of mass literacy, improvements in printing technology, and, no less important, the creation of leisure time. Not only did sports fill this vacuum, but so too did newspapers reporting on sports. Similar to our own age of endless news cycles, where the media often generates the "events" it then covers, so too in turn-of-the-century France. The cycling press spawned dozens of races that were then followed by their own reporters. It was only a matter of time that one of these dailies, *L'Auto,* hatched the stunning idea of a bicycle race across the width and breadth of France.

In 1903, the Tour de France bicycle race debuted, stretching over more than two weeks and nearly 2,400 kilometers. The press relished the race's extreme demands and suffering of its contestants; journalists outdid one another in their descriptions of the cyclists' "ravaged" and "gaunt" faces. At the same time, cyclists were depicted as machines, mere extensions of their bicycles and of the factories where many of them had once worked. With legs that pumped liked pistons, cyclists became known as "pedal workers," even "convict workers of the road" (*les forçats de la route*). Not surprisingly, the event's organizers long denied cyclists the right to unionize. More astonishingly, the organizers also first resisted the introduction of gears, arguing that such technology would cheapen the cyclist's achievement. It would make cycling easier—another way of saying it would lessen the pain. Despite the endless repetition and stamina required to complete the race, the rewards were enormous. The Tour promised not just fame, but money, a prize of nearly 20,000 francs, a staggering sum of money given that the average worker's salary was just 5 francs a day. As a result, the finish line marked the divide between working-class woes and middle-class comfort.

But the race also unified. Cycling through various provinces of France expressed the notion of French identity as both national and regional, and the race even reached out to a region no longer part of the nation. Between 1906 and 1910, *L'Auto* persuaded the German authorities to allow the Tour de France to pass through Alsace-Lorraine. Though the event was billed as apolitical—"sport has no fatherland," trumpeted *L'Auto*—the emotional significance of the event was obvious. The newspaper boasted that its posters in Alsace were the first to be published exclusively in French since 1870, and "La Marseillaise" was actually heard as racers sped along Alsatian roads.[27] Franco-German cooperation around a sporting event would nevertheless prove short-lived. In 1911 the Alsatian leg of the Tour de France was cancelled, a sign that long simmering tensions among all the Great Powers were reaching a dangerous tipping point.

A DANGEROUS DIPLOMACY

The decade before World War I witnessed growing strains between France and Germany over continental and colonial issues. To understand these strains, it is necessary to return briefly to the evolution of French and German diplomacy since the early years of the Third Republic. Ever since its defeat in 1870, France had sought revenge for the loss of Alsace-Lorraine and a return to Great Power status, in part by expanding its overseas empire. Yet given Germany's far greater military, economic, and demographic resources, French diplomats were adamant that their nation should never again face Germany alone. This determination led France and Germany together into a complex set of competing alliances that increasingly divided Europe into two armed camps. Should any one of the Great Powers be attacked, a war involving all of them would inevitably follow.

After German unification, the kaiser's diplomats had cultivated their "natural" ally, the Austro-Hungarian Empire; by 1882 Italy had joined Germany and Austria-Hungary to form the Triple Alliance. In response, republican France felt it had no choice but to attempt to woo its own allies to "contain" Germany, starting with Russia. In 1892, the most democratic regime on the continent signed a treaty of friendship with its most autocratic ruler, commemorated with great pomp by the naming of a new Paris bridge after Tsar Alexander III, who made a state visit to France in 1896. In his moving autobiographical novel based on his French grandmother's account of this episode, Russian writer Andrei Makhine puzzles over this instance of Realpolitik. Learning that "La Marseillaise" was played at the ceremony, the young protagonist wonders: "And the tsar? Did he know what the song was about?"[29]

Germany retaliated by embarking on an all-out arms race, competing not only with France by land but also with Britain by sea, and by becoming more aggressively expansionist overseas. By the turn of the century Germany's growing military prowess and colonial ambitions prodded the French and British governments—six years after Fashoda—to resolve enough of their outstanding colonial disputes to sign an Entente Cordiale in 1904. France finally recognized the British Protectorate in Egypt (but forced the British to leave Egypt's archaeological services, which dated back to Napoleon's invasion of 1798–1801, in French hands), in exchange for British support of France in Morocco. Britain and Russia also moved closer after Russia's defeat in the Russo-Japanese War in 1905, so that by 1907 a "Triple Entente" of France, Britain, and Russia confronted the Triple Alliance of Germany, Austria-Hungary, and Italy.

The Triple Entente left no doubts that should war break out, France, Russia, and Britain could outman, outspend, and outproduce Germany and its weaker allies of Austria-Hungary and Italy. A frightened German General Staff had every incentive to believe that only a swift victory against France—which could mobilize more quickly than Russia—would preempt eventual defeat and redress the balance of power in Germany's favor. The Germans knew they could not fight a two-front war, both in the west and the east, and win. In 1906, General Alfred von Schlieffen, chief of the German General Staff and a keen student of military history, thus hatched a plan for knocking out France first should war break out with Russia. Schlieffen argued that the German army's right flank should make an immediate sweep through neutral Belgium and Luxembourg, bypassing French defenses and allowing German forces to march south, surround Paris, and envelop French armies from the west.[30] Caught from behind, as in 1870, individual French armies could be crushed before Russia completed its mobilization, which Schlieffen calculated would take six weeks. As he lay dying in 1913, Schlieffen's alleged last words were: "Strengthen the right flank! Strengthen the right flank!"—fateful words upon which Germany's entire war strategy rested.[31]

When Schlieffen came up with his plan in 1906, war among the Great Powers in Europe seemed increasingly likely. A year earlier another colonial dispute had threatened to escalate, this time between France and Germany in Morocco, still a sovereign nation. France sought to extend its "traditional" influence over the North African state, while Kaiser Wilhelm II was determined to block any such expansion of French power. While the situation was defused in 1906, an international crisis erupted again on July 1, 1911, when Germany went so far as to send a gunboat to the Moroccan port of Agadir. France and Germany, however, managed once again – after a tense six-month diplomatic standoff – to strike a deal. In return for making Morocco a "protectorate" France ceded a swath of its territory in equatorial Africa to Germany. On March 30, 1912, the Sultan of Morocco—his monarchy already heavily in debt and facing rebellion from within—signed a treaty accepting the French Protectorate.

Critics on the Left, most prominently Jean Jaurès, denounced the dangers of such escalating militarism and imperialism on both humanitarian and geopolitical grounds. Jaurès' book *L'Armée nouvelle* (*The New Army*), published in 1911, made clear that technological advances had made war unthinkably destructive. Yet this was precisely what the European powers risked in their continued race not just for more colonies, but also for arms, alliances, and influence in Europe itself. In a much-publicized speech given in Basel in 1912, Jaurès invoked the pealing of the city's church bells. Quoting from a poem by German poet Freidrich Schiller, Jaurès exhorted the assembled crowd of "the living to resist the monster [and] break the thunderbolts of war."[28] Although war between France and Germany over Morocco was narrowly averted in 1912, two years later France would not be so fortunate.

PREPARING FOR WAR

As tensions mounted in Europe between 1912 and 1914, French statesmen and military commanders took a variety of measures of their own to prepare for war. First, in 1913, the French legislature passed a law reversing its earlier measure against the army and extending obligatory military service from two back to three years. Military service had always been a defining attribute of (male) republican citizenship—a sacred duty that went along with the political rights of the citizen.

Jean Jaurès addressing a crowd, 1913. Private Collection/The Bridgeman Art Library.

Second, a consensus emerged that France could impose this same "blood tax" on their colonial subjects, even though the latter did not have the vote, as partial repayment for the benefits of France's civilizing mission. In 1910, General Mangin—who had made his career in the colonies—had hit on the idea of creating a "Force Noire" or "Black Army," recruited among its African subjects to help make up France's demographic deficit in the case of war. In 1914, the army called for volunteers throughout the empire and soon began to conscript them by force. Over the course of the war, about 500,000 colonial soldiers, or almost 7 percent of French troops, would fight for France, many involuntarily.[32]

A third important area of military planning was defining battlefield doctrine. The General Staff, led by General Joseph Joffre, believed that the safety of France required taking the war to the enemy. Known as the "all-out offensive," the idea was that well-trained French soldiers, imbued with patriotic fervor, could not be stopped.[33] Joffre enshrined this doctrine in the last of the many war plans drawn up before 1914, Plan XVII, which nevertheless gave the generals considerable operational flexibility to respond to whatever move the Germans made.[34]

Yet the army was never given the funds to provide its soldiers with the training or the leadership to implement such an offensive strategy. French soldiers spent much of their pre-war military service on garrison duty, instead of learning the discipline and organization under fire necessary to sustain an offensive in the age of the machine gun. The same inferiority affected materiel, although it should be kept in mind that Germany was preparing for two attacks (France then Russia) compared to only one by France. The French had 2,500 machine guns in August 1914 compared to the Germans' 4,500; 3,800 75mm artillery pieces compared to the Germans 6,000 77mm guns; and practically no heavy artillery. Perhaps the only place the army did not scrimp was on the soldiers' dashing red and blue uniforms, inherited from the nineteenth century. France's white-gloved commanders found red trousers to be more distinguished and patriotic than the khaki favored by the British. France, then, was both overconfident and underprepared in 1914. Although its army and navy were still widely feared in Europe, no one foresaw the kind of conflict they would have to fight.

The fragile peace in Europe finally came to an end in the summer of 1914, for reasons far beyond French control; the catalyst was not in fact competing imperialist claims overseas but long-simmering tensions in the Balkans. On June 28, a Serbian-backed Bosnian nationalist assassinated the heir to the Habsburg throne, Archduke Franz Ferdinand, in Sarajevo. A month later, on July 28, Austria, backed by its ally Germany, declared war on Serbia. On July 30–31 Austria mobilized, but so too did Russia despite French urgings to wait. As Serbia's ally, Russia was protecting its credibility in the Balkans, but it hoped that its mobilization against Austria would not lead Germany to reciprocate. The Triple Alliance made that option impossible—but in order to fight Russia, Germany had to activate the Schlieffen Plan and invade neutral Belgium and defeat France in the six-week window envisaged by Schlieffen before Russia could complete mobilization.

On July 31, Germany sent a final message to France, asking whether it would stay neutral in case of war between Germany and Russia. Here, the past dominated the present. France had spent the previous 34 years seeking to reclaim its Great Power status and take revenge on Germany for its earlier defeat. It could hardly respond to Germany's provocation by abandoning Russia, to whom it was tied by the treaty of 1892. Therefore on August 1, when Germany declared war on Russia, France began its own mobilization. On August 3, Germany formally declared war on France. Firmly convinced that they were victims of German aggression, the French people prepared to defend their national territory. The Great War that Jaurès had so feared, and warned repeatedly against, had begun.

CHAPTER 6

The Republic at War
1914–1919

On July 31, 1914, socialist leader and ardent pacifist Jean Jaurès was shot to death in a Paris café by a fanatical French nationalist. The next day, the bells of France rang to mobilize the nation for the very war that Jaurès had so long tried to prevent but others ardently desired. In Paris, the long silent bells of Notre Dame and other old churches suddenly transformed the city into a vast "bronze hallucination."[1] As novelist Roger Martin du Gard wrote of August 1, 1914:

> Suddenly . . . a deafening racket filled the space: the great bell of the church was loudly tolling a single note one after another, distinct, resonant, solemn. People, rooted to the spot, stared at each other for a moment, stupefied. Then they began to run off in all directions. . . . In the distance, other bells swung into action . . . everywhere resounding to the same insistent rhythm, sinister as a death knell.[2]

In an age when half of the French population lived in the countryside and when the radio was still used only for military purposes, when television was not yet invented and when cinema was still silent, France went to war in 1914 in the same way that it had done in centuries past. The old-fashioned sound of bells, however, had little to do with the horrors of the modern, mechanized war that was to come. On that fateful August day, the bells presaged both the deaths and the myths of the only successful war waged by France in the entire twentieth century.

The Great War, the name it was given by those who lived through it, which lasted from August 1914 to November 1918, deeply marked the character of modern France. Historians still do not understand all the consequences of this catastrophe and continue to debate its origins, but they agree that the subsequent history of France cannot be understood except in its bloody light. Of all the questions spawned by the war, perhaps none has remained more difficult to answer than that of how and why French soldiers and civilians were able to stay the course for over four years in the face of unimaginable suffering and cruelties. World War I on the Western Front was fought overwhelmingly on French soil. The French mobilized 8.4 million men and suffered proportionately more casualties than any other major power did. And although they may have won the war, they did so at such a cost that only a vindictive and thus unworkable peace would satisfy them. The great irony of World War I is that winning the war meant losing the peace, thereby creating the conditions for new domestic and international instability and crisis in the decades that followed.

1914: MASS MOBILIZATION

When France's bells began ringing on August 2, the initial mood among elites in the cities was optimistic. On August 2 in Paris, socialist Jean-Richard Bloch wrote to pacifist writer Romain Rolland: "The war of the Revolution against feudalism is reopening. Will the armies of the Republic assure the triumph of democracy in Europe and perfect the work of [17]93?"[3] Two days later, intellectual Charles Péguy noted: "We go to war as soldiers of the Republic, for the general disarmament and the war to end them all."[4] On August 6, writer André Gide wrote of "crushing Germany" and the beginning of a new era in which "the United States of Europe will be bound by a treaty limiting their armaments; Germany will be reduced or dissolved; Trieste will be given to Italy, Schleswig to Denmark, and above all Alsace to France."[5] Intellectuals on the Right like Léon Daudet and Charles Maurras hoped that the war would revive military, nationalist, and religious values. Forty thousand foreign-born Poles, Italians, Czechs, and Swiss immediately volunteered to fight for the France that had become their new *patrie*, or fatherland.[6]

Peasants were more reserved, for the new harvest was soon ready. Who, they asked, was going to work their fields? And, with so many horses commandeered by the army, how were old men, women, and children supposed to take care of the farms? According to the prefects of 26 departments, the mobilization order was received with "reserve" by 21 percent, with "coolness" by 27 percent, with "approval" by 52 percent.[7] A questionnaire sent by the minister of education to teachers from six departments revealed that the "popular mood" was 57 percent negative, 20 percent "calm and composed," and 23 percent "patriotic," with the most frequently mentioned reaction being "weeping" and "desolation."[8] But there were surprisingly few objectors. The army headquarters had expected as many as 13 percent, but only 1.5 percent of the population actively resisted the call to arms.[9]

On August 3, German troops crossed the Belgian frontier, violating its neutrality. Britain, an ally of Belgium, declared war on Germany a day later. France's military Plan XVII, while allowing for some operational flexibility, was oriented toward a French offensive attack through Alsace-Lorraine and the Ardennes. General Joffre decided to attempt that offensive, convinced that Germany would not be able to muster enough regular army troops both to invade through Belgium and to resist a broad French offensive in the east. He ignored evidence that Germany would use reserve units alongside its regular troops and invade with a numerical advantage of 3 to 1 (750,000 to 250,000).[10] By the last days of August, it looked like the crushing German victory over France of 1870 was repeating itself: The French offensives had gained nothing in the east, and German troops were pouring into northern France, reaching the Somme River on August 28. On September 3,

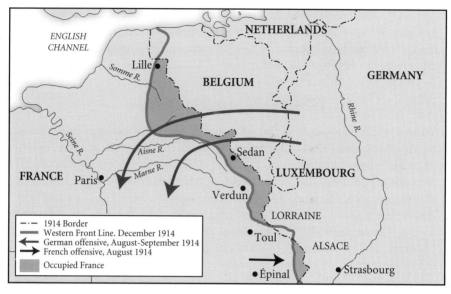

Map 6.1 The invasion of France and the Western Front, 1914.

just one month after Germany's declaration of war, a panicked French government transferred temporarily to Bordeaux, expecting that Paris would fall.

Yet, however bloodied, French troops and their British allies had the advantage of moving on home territory, while German supply lines became more and
more stretched. Joffre, imperturbable, ordered a retreat south across the Marne
River, and on September 6 French and British troops counter-attacked to the south
and west of the German armies. Every known motorized vehicle in Paris, even
taxis (who nevertheless haggled over their fares), was mobilized to transport
troops to the front. In the "miracle of the Marne," exhausted Allied troops finally
routed even more exhausted German ones.

On September 8, it was the Germans' turn to order a retreat. Moving fast and
far, the Germans had the time and the foresight to choose where to stop in a "race
to the sea" as they sought an opening in the French and British lines further to the
north. The French, British, and Belgian armies in the west held, as they also moved
north trying to outflank the enemy. The positions that both armies staked out in
mid-October, face to face in a line of trenches to protect their troops that ran from
Switzerland to the English Channel—the famous "Western Front"—would remain
fundamentally unbroken until 1918. Thousands of square kilometers of France's
most valuable territory—home to 50 percent of its coal production, 64 percent of
its iron, and 58 percent of its steel—was now under German occupation. In under
two months of fighting, 329,000 French soldiers had died and 600,000 more were
wounded. Such casualties made this period the most lethal of the entire war and
were a harbinger of the horrors yet to come. Still, as the war of movement now
settled into a war of attrition, jubilant Frenchmen and Frenchwomen saw only
evidence that final victory would surely be theirs.[11]

The jubilation after the "Marne Miracle" reveals the extraordinary sense of national feeling that suddenly bound the French together as never before. President Raymond Poincaré had given a name to that unity in August 1914, when war was first declared. He proclaimed a "sacred union," or *union sacrée,* of all French in the face of the enemy, and the country responded overwhelmingly in favor. All divisions—religious, political, class—disappeared in the face of Germany's aggression. In the Chamber of Deputies, Edouard Vaillant, a former Communard, shook hands for the first time with Albert de Mun, an officer in the Versaillais army that had suppressed the 1871 uprising. This gesture perfectly reflected the determination to bring everyone, including Catholics and socialists, into the leadership of the Republic as part of the war effort. Catholics rallied massively to the national cause, and priests volunteered to serve as regular soldiers rather than as chaplains. Poincaré repeatedly thanked religious organizations for their patriotic faith. Prime Minister Viviani brought two socialists into his war cabinet on August 26, and a third, Albert Thomas, would eventually run the Ministry of Munitions. As intellectual Julien Benda recalled years later, "I saw the totality of the French, nobles and common men, soldiers and merchants, urban people and peasants, democrats and absolutists, capitalists and workers, united in communion with the sentiment of belonging to the same group."[12] The civilian government now turned the power to make strategic decisions over to "Papa" Joffre, the victor of the Marne.

The first months produced another element that, along with the lethal casualty rate and the *union sacrée,* would differentiate this war from all others previously fought on metropolitan soil: an active propaganda machine that from the outset depicted the participants in racialized terms of French "civilization" versus German "beastliness." From the moment the Germans violated Belgian neutrality in a shocking breach of international law, stories circulated of atrocities; the *"Boche"*—a slur against German soldiers meaning "wooden head"—cut off the hands of youngsters, bayoneted infants, roasted children's feet, and assaulted women. Separating fact from fiction remains difficult even now. Certainly some Belgian civilians resisted the German invasion by sabotaging roads, blowing up railway tunnels and bridges, and sniping at the enemy. German soldiers responded by raping and pillaging, shooting large numbers of hostages, and bombarding tens of thousands of buildings. The priceless medieval manuscripts of the University of Louvain burned in one such attack. The French soon routinely depicted all Germans as more beast than human.[13] Republicans had long justified the conquest of colonies in terms of France's universal mission to civilize "African heathens" and "Oriental despots," and this dehumanizing imagery proved easy to transfer to the German "savage" again threatening France. The German army never shook this image, in part because of its harsh occupation of northern France, which, like Belgium, was to become a virtual colony of Germany until 1918.

World War I was, in all these ways, the first "total war" because it mobilized the entire French population, in occupied and non-occupied France and the empire. If France was to be made whole again, all of society would have to sacrifice on an unprecedented scale. In the case of occupied France and overseas France, the methods for securing civilian sacrifice were direct and brutal. The Germans treated civilians as prisoners of war, while French administrators in the colonies not only conscripted soldiers but also forced the impoverished local populations to produce foodstuffs and cash crops deemed essential to the war effort in Europe— even though much of the requisitioned raw materials rotted in colonial ports because of insufficient transport.[14] In the case of "free France," consent to total war could neither be taken for granted nor be forced. The French government would have to earn its citizens' consent, once it became clear that no further "miracles" were imminent.

TAKING THE OFFENSIVE 1915–1916

In 1914 all European armies confronted a technological revolution on the battle-field and outside of it, which transformed the face of battle in ways no one anticipated. The war was the first in which railways played an important role, mobilizing troops on the continent and from the colonies; transporting new recruits, munitions, and food to the front; evacuating the wounded; and ultimately moving to the front lines the American troops that began arriving in late 1917. Aviation was also now put to military purposes for the first time. The French still celebrate Georges Guynemer, who took part in more than 600 aerial combats, scored 53 victories against German pilots, and was killed in combat in Belgium in 1917, at the age of 23. Between 1912 and 1914, military strategists had projected aviation only for reconnaissance flights and for use against zeppelins and infantry. But by the end of 1914 both sides realized that this war would also be fought in the air, and fighters and bombers were developed.[15] Finally, European armies faced each other with unprecedented firepower in the form of machine guns, bolt-action rifles, and howitzers. "Modern weapons allowed armies to set up impregnable defensive positions, and neither the officer corps nor the general staffs worked out how to use modern technology, or evolved tactical concepts to break through such defenses, until 1918."[16] The only concession Joffre made to the appalling loss of life in the first months of fighting was to replace France's famous red and blue uni-forms for grey-blue ones that blended easily into the ubiquitous mud of the battlefield.

Despite the fact that both sides had now dug in along the Western front, the Allied commanders—Joffre and Sir Douglas Haig—continued to believe in the possibility of mobile warfare. They thus launched a number of offensives in 1915 against German lines, each more pointless than the last. The most important ones took place in the spring in the Artois and in the fall in Champagne. Each offensive began with artillery bombardments to saturate enemy defenses; attackers were then, in theory, to rush out of their trenches and rout the enemy. Bombardments before an attack, however, inevitably alerted the enemy to an impending offensive and allowed the Germans to move reserves to the targeted sector. In the course of 1915 over 1 million French were wounded or killed, with no significant break-through of German lines. When the Allies tried to open a new front in the

Dardenelles to distract Germany by attacking its ally, the Ottoman empire, the results were equally disastrous. Yet at the year's end Joffre insisted that the French were still winning, albeit with a different goal than in 1914. Rather than a *percée,* or breaching, of German lines, they were now pursuing a *grignotage,* or nibbling away, of the enemy through attrition.

Far from learning from the Allies' disastrous examples, the new chief of the German General Staff, Erich von Falkenhayn, decided in February 1916 to launch his own offensive against the isolated French outpost of Verdun. The principal lesson that both the German and Allied commands drew from the previous year was that the 1915 offensives had simply not been large enough, strong enough, or well-planned enough to succeed. Falkenhayn proposed to correct this mistake by attacking with unprecedented firepower a spot he felt sure the French would defend to the last man. Verdun and the series of small forts around it sat on a small piece of Lorraine that the French had kept after 1870 and that had been critical in stopping the German offensive in September 1914. France, Falkenhayn gambled, would never give up this particular piece of sacred soil, while the Germans—safe behind massed artillery pieces—would take few casualties. Victory in the west, he predicted, would at last be theirs.

Falkenhayn was right in at least one part of his gamble. After initially hesitating, the French General Staff accepted that Verdun had to be defended at all costs. The small town of Verdun had been stripped of its heavy artillery early in the war to shore up French armies to the north, and Joffre's first instinct was to abandon the sector, particularly once the main fort in its outer ring of defenses, Douaumont, fell easily on February 25 after only four days of fighting. But Prime Minister Aristide Briand immediately realized that to lose another piece of France to the Germans would prove catastrophic for both civilian and military morale. Joffre was ordered to defend Verdun or be sacked. Joffre changed his mind and turned the formidable task of saving Verdun over to General Philippe Pétain, the sector commander. Pétain had been passed over for promotion before the war for espousing the power of a defensive war in the modern age. After August 1914, however, his rise had been meteoric, although Joffre never did share Pétain's views on the virtue of defense over offense.

The epic battle of Verdun, which lasted from February to November 1916, would sear the collective French psyche for generations to come. No other battlefield in the Great War produced the same concentration of firepower or accumulated as many shattered human remains per square kilometer as Verdun. It was said at the time that if the dead of Verdun suddenly arose, they would not all have had room to stand. In preparation for the battle, the Germans built 10 new railroads to carry in their arsenal and the extra troops needed for the attack. Entire French villages in the occupied zone were evacuated to make room for the invading force. The few remaining French inhabitants could only watch "in helpless horror at the endless lines of men and material, at the great guns bringing death towards their own people."[17] For sheer concentration of firepower in a tiny space—an eight-mile sector—nothing like it had ever been seen: a total of 1,220 pieces of artillery, including 13 monstrous Big Berthas, the biggest guns ever used in the war. Two and a half million shells were also stocked for the first six days of the assault.

The result was slaughter on an unprecedented scale even for World War I, as the French swallowed the bait and threw most of its army into battle. Aviators flying over the Verdun battlefields called it a "strip of murdered nature" that seemed to belong to another world. "Every sign of humanity has been swept away. The woods and roads have vanished like chalk wiped from a blackboard; of the villages nothing remains but grey smears."[18] Shells fell like rain, and a pall of sickening poisonous smoke hung over the sector. Trenches packed full of troops were little more than muddy ditches; the stench of human putrefaction assaulted new arrivals because it was impossible to bury the dead. Corpses—too numerous and too dangerous to recover—floated in the gullies, quartered and requartered by the incessant German artillery. Every square foot of land contained some piece of decomposed flesh: "[Y]ou found the dead embedded in the walls of the trenches, heads, legs and half-bodies."[19] The sensation of being under bombardment was vividly captured by Paul Dubrulle, a 34-year-old Jesuit serving as an infantry sergeant: "To die from a bullet seems like nothing . . . but to be dismembered, torn to pieces, reduced to pulp, this is a fear that flesh cannot support."[20]

And yet, against all odds, the French army managed to hold on as a result, in part, of two critical innovations introduced by Pétain. He first organized a new line of defense, supplied by a constant stream of trucks making their way along a single road into the sector. This fragile artery, upon which the whole defense effort depended, was immortalized after the war as *la Voie Sacrée* (the Sacred Way) by Maurice Barrès. Second, Pétain rotated units in and out of the front lines every few days, before they could be damaged beyond repair. Over the course of the next 10 months, 70 out of the 85 divisions that made up the French army in 1916 would go through Verdun, forging a unique bond among those who survived and making it the one war experience almost all soldiers had in common.

Such determined French defense led the exhausted Germans to attempt a full-scale offensive along the whole Verdun front on April 9. Once again the French line held. Pétain, not known for his optimism, issued an Order of the Day that has remained legendary. "The ninth of April was a glorious day for our forces," he began, but it was his ending that stirs hearts still: "Courage, on les aura"—"Courage, we will have them." Yet the worst was hardly over. An impatient Joffre decided to "promote" the overly cautious Pétain out of Verdun and to turn command over to a younger general, Robert Nivelle. Nivelle was responsible for one failed offensive after the other in the late spring. In late April, the Germans repulsed their attempt to retake Fort Douaumont; in early June, Nivelle ordered six futile attacks in an attempt to relieve Fort Vaux, another principal buttress protecting Verdun. By now there were rumblings of discontent in the French legislature over how the war was being waged. Yet, in one of the many intangible turning points of this most incomprehensible of wars, just as civilian confidence in Joffre's command wavered, the Germans weakened. On June 23, a German offensive failed to break through French lines and Nivelle issued that evening the second legendary Order of the

Day associated with Verdun: "Ils ne passeront pas"—"They will not pass." On July 1, British troops relieved pressure on Verdun by opening a second front on the Somme, near the town of Péronne, where German troops were farthest from their base.

In the long run, although no one realized it yet, the tide of the war was turning against Germany. Its inferior manpower compared to the combined forces of France, Britain, and eventually the United States would force it to remain on the defensive until the spring of 1918. In the short run, however, there appeared little advantage yet to either side. The Somme offensive, like that at Verdun, ground on almost continuously through the summer and fall. Four million men fought over a 40-kilometer line at the Somme, making it the single largest battle of the war and the "largest engagement fought since the beginnings of civilization."[21] It has also earned its place in the annals of history as the single bloodiest one. The British under Haig took 60,000 casualties alone on the first day—a figure greater than total French casualties in the single worst month of Verdun. The 10 days of heavy bombardment in late June to "soften up the enemy" had left German machine guns—carried down to the safety of their deep dugouts—intact; they simply cut down orderly rows of British soldiers until the piled-up bodies made further movement impossible. By the time the guns stopped five months later, Britain had lost 420,000 men, France 340,000, and Germany 400,000.[22]

The Allied dead at the Somme and Verdun together fell just short of the million mark, an average of one soldier killed every five seconds.[23] Once again the senseless bloodletting had resulted in stalemate, and the new strategy of *grignotage* was in shambles. Although French counter-attacks at Verdun in October allowed them to regain the most critical parts of the French position lost to the Germans in the spring, their military value remained dubious. Late in 1916, the government transferred Joffre to a desk job in the War Ministry and cast about for a new military commander.

THE SOLDIERS' WAR

The numbingly large casualty figures that characterized the Western Front in 1915 and 1916 raise the question of how soldiers survived in the underground world of the trenches. It is here that the lowly French infantryman—the *poilu*, or hairy one, so called for his unkempt hair, beard, and mustache grown at the front—permanently lived. Along the Western Front, vast networks of Allied and German zig-zagging trenches faced each other. A no-man's land ranging from 50 to several hundred meters separated the protagonists' front trenches. Relentless artillery barrages transformed no-man's land into a denuded, muddy moonscape pocked with crater holes. By 1915 each side had three lines of trenches, and by the end of the war they would have as many as six. The rear trenches provided logistical support for the front "firing" lines; densely entangled barbed wire defended each line of trenches, and parapets of earth or sandbags ostensibly protected the front trench from enemy fire. Each combatant nation had its own style of trenches; in

Paul Fussell's words, "the French trenches were nasty, cynical, efficient and temporary"—for the French high command optimistically believed that battle would eventually return to open country. "The English were amateur, vague, ad hoc, and temporary. The German were efficient, clean, pedantic and permanent. Their occupants proposed to stay where they were."[24] In time, the Germans lined their trenches with cement.

Trenches were necessary in a war dominated by artillery fire that was 10 times more deadly in explosive power, range, and accuracy than at the beginning of the nineteenth century. "To speak of the horror of the trenches is to substitute hyperbole for common sense: the war would have been far more horrific if there had been no trenches. They protected flesh and blood from the worst effects of the firepower revolution of the late nineteenth century."[25] Yet while digging into the ground was the only defense against the shells and machine guns, it was partial protection at best. The terror of bombardment was particularly intense, since artillery caused two-thirds of all wounds inflicted. Shells fell intensively for several days and nights uninterruptedly before an offensive, and sporadically in between attacks. These bombardments destroyed all links between soldiers and their leaders, isolating individuals and cutting off supplies to the front lines. Bombs that burst into huge ragged chunks of crude iron disfigured and dismembered the soft human carapace beyond recognition. "Men squashed, cut in two, or divided top to bottom, blown into showers by an ordinary shell, bellies turned inside out and scattered anyhow, skulls forced bodily into the chest as if by a blow with a club," wrote Henri Barbusse, in his grim war account of 1916, *Under Fire*.[26] The huge number of head wounds sustained by soldiers inspired the French military to pioneer improved protection. In June 1915 the French army, in a move quickly copied across the battlefield, replaced the soldiers' soft cloth caps with modern steel helmets. With time soldiers developed the ability to "read a bombardment" by listening to it, identifying where a shell was headed, its caliber, and probable point of impact.

Yet however horrific the strain of steady artillery fire, it was worse when it ended, since next came a furious bayonet attack by enemy infantry. Even more terrifying was launching an attack of their own, when soldiers had to climb out of the trenches in the face of direct machine gun fire and attempt to cross no-man's land to dislodge the enemy. They thus prepared for "going over the top" as if for certain execution. Soldiers prayed, wrote letters to their families, and exchanged promises with their comrades about contacting their loved ones should they die. They all knew that death, when it came, would be anonymous and unheroic as they raced in a state of almost hyperawareness toward the mangled barbed wire of the enemy positions. Soldiers rarely knew who killed whom, even in no-man's land; one-on-one combat occurred sporadically, and many survivors could not bear to tell the details.

Almost as frightening as dying was being wounded. Anticipating clean bullet wounds, understaffed military services could not handle either the flood of men or the type of wounds they encountered. While disinfectants and anesthetics were soon adopted and new therapies such as blood transfusion, X-rays, and excision of

Morocco to France to Germany. Various types of French colonial soldiers in a German prison camp. Private Collection/The Stapleton Collection/The Bridgeman Art Library.

damage tissue emerged, the medical services never overcame the logistical problems of moving the wounded quickly out of the front, and then evacuating them to hospitals in the rear. Minor improvements in medical efficiency nevertheless allowed an astonishing number of soldiers with badly disfigured bodies and faces to survive. Soon referred to as the *gueules cassées* (broken faces) and *mutilés de guerre* (war mutilated), these men would serve as a constant reminder after the war of its brutality. Their ranks were swelled by those suffering mental trauma, or what the French called *commotion*—shellshock. Doctors who were initially convinced that shellshock was a form of cowardice soon developed an alternative diagnosis: involuntary physical resistance. These soldiers were treated close to the front, so as not to be separated from their comrades, and given rest.

Captured French soldiers were humiliated in traditional ways. French prisoners of war (POWs)—600,000 by 1917—were typically put to work in German mines and factories or as hard labor. The Germans, unlike the French and British, had only a few colonies from which to draw a non-European source of labor, and they thus relied more heavily on POWs. In addition to malnutrition and the loss of freedom, these prisoners suffered deeply from knowing that they were neither contributing to the war effort nor being remembered. These feelings also afflicted officers, although they were spared the hard labor that befell the enlisted men. A young captain named Charles de Gaulle, captured at Verdun in 1916, wrote to his parents the following in 1917 from his camp in Ingolstadt:

A sorrow that will end only with my life, and which I thought I could never encounter so deeply or so bitterly, afflicts me now more directly than ever. To be so totally and irremediably useless as I am in the times we are going through, when every bit of me wants to strike out. Moreover, to be in such a situation as I find myself, as a man and as a soldier, is the most cruel one you can imagine.[27]

De Gaulle was not alone in feeling that, as a man and as a soldier, this war had brought "unimaginable cruelty," particularly by removing him from the line of fire. In World War I, the only way of being a "man," according to propaganda, was through the sacrifice and courage of combat. De Gaulle attempted several escapes, but because of his exceptional height, six feet four inches, he was always recaptured.

The soldiers' life in the trenches was typically made up of 20 to 25 days under fire, followed by rest and then two to three months in a quiet sector before being sent on the offensive again. For all the terror of periodic bombardments and attacks, trench life thus produced long periods of boredom, when there seemed little to do but wait. Daytime hours were taken up with cleaning weapons or repairs; those tasks done, soldiers had time to read, write, try to delouse themselves, or sleep. Real work began with nightfall, when, under the cover of darkness, trenches could be improved, extended, or fortified; rations could be brought up from the supply lines; and messages could be delivered. Machine gun, artillery, and sniper fire remained constant threats. As all daylight activity could be observed and disrupted by planes, the soldiers had to work by night to repair the trenches, to bring supplies and relief: "Men were continually exhausted: they dozed by day and, paradoxically, as the nights became shorter the opportunities for sleep became greater."[28] Particularly disorienting was the fact of often never seeing the enemy, despite smelling his food or hearing snatches of his conversation. Despite the tendency to demonize the unseen enemy, occasionally soldiers on both sides called a tacit truce and stopped to fraternize. On Christmas Day 1914, the French and British troops and their German opponents sang carols, exchanged greetings and gifts, and even played soccer together. No subsequent fraternization ever went as far as that first Christmas, when memories of peacetime had not yet faded.

By 1917 the French war dead were approaching the 1 million mark. Yet still there were no signs that France was winning, or indeed that the war would ever end. Meanwhile, official bulletins were distributed daily in the trenches that fudged the war's casualty rates. Soldiers in the trenches nevertheless managed to preserve a sense of both purpose and hope. As historians struggle to understand the face of battle from the soldiers' perspective, an increasingly complex interpretation of this aspect of the war has emerged.

At one time it was tempting to portray the World War I trench experience as one of total dehumanization. According to this view, the *poilus* went like lambs to the slaughter, victims in every sense of a war that they had not asked for and could not control. More recently, however, scholarship has suggested that, without playing down the unprecedented physical and psychological strains of the Western front, many of the soldiers managed to retain their dignity and even to negotiate some of the terms of their own participation. For example, soldiers created intense solidarities in the trenches that helped to sustain them. Within these groups men supported each other, pooled resources, learned about each other's families, and mourned together when one of their own perished. New bonds of mutual dependence and fraternity diminished class and race differences among enlisted troops, even as the egotistical need to save oneself endured.

Primary group allegiances—operative in all wars, after all—were thus one form of holding on. Creating a counter-culture was another one. From the outset, French troops penned songs, carved images, published trench newspapers, wrote diaries and endless letters home, and created their own trench *argot,* or slang, that affirmed daily their humanity in the midst of terror. Soldiers never stopped expressing themselves at the front. In their letters home, in their newspapers, and in their songs, combatants also remained intensely interested in, and bound to, civilian life behind the lines, both critical of its comforts and illusions about how well the war was going and eager to influence it. Singing was particularly important for venting *poilu* frustration, but also for giving a sense of power when he mocked government propaganda. One early song caricatured a soldier's leave time as follows:

> *The civilian drinks what he wants*
> *The* poilu *drinks what he can. . . .*
> *The former says "we will hold!"*
> *And it's true that they hold well*
> *They all hold on to their skin,*
> *And [hold] their rear ends warm.*[29]

As this song suggests, "normalcy" was only a train ride away, and letters and packages from home arrived daily. Leaves were instituted in July 1915, and soldiers

Postcard from a French soldier to his family, with an allegorical depiction of Alsace as an Alsatian woman, World War I, 1918. Private Collection/Archives Charmet/The Bridgeman Art Library.

made the most of them. While at the front, husbands, fathers, and sons did their best to manage their financial affairs and jobs from afar, through regular correspondence. In the case of some Catholic soldiers, duty to defend the nation became fused with a duty to defend God, and the soldier's ordeal became that of Christ. Maintaining this intense connection to what they had known before being mobilized—whether family, profession, patriotic duty, or God—and to which they hoped one day to return, was another important way in which the *poilus* demonstrated their consent to a war that they could not control. Front soldier Louis Mairet, killed on April 16, 1917, at Craonne, aptly caught the mood—both defiant and resigned—of the trenches two years into the war when he wrote in his diary:

> Do they know why are they fighting? . . . The soldier of 1916 is fighting neither for Alsace, nor for Germany's destruction, nor for the fatherland. He is fighting because he is honest, because he has become used to it, and because he is forced to do it. He is fighting because he cannot do otherwise.[30]

THE CIVILIANS' WAR: OCCUPIED ZONES AND THE HOMEFRONT

Until recently, most histories of World War I have focused on the gruesome violence done to soldiers and its short- and long-term impact; and as we shall see, when the war finally ended, it was the soldier's suffering and extraordinary heroism that were remembered and officially commemorated. But total war had a devastating impact on civilians as well, whose courage and consent were equally critical to holding firm. Not having anticipated the kind of war it would become and buttressed by the moral certainties of the "long nineteenth century," when the idea of progress seemed unshakable, the French civilian population collectively made the decision over and over that they too had to go on, so that the devastating loss of soldiers' lives should not be in vain. From a material point of view, this may have been an easier decision for civilians in free France to make than it was for their counterparts living under German occupation. Yet the world of the homefront was also dramatically altered, particularly as women stepped into their men's shoes while being expected to maintain their traditional roles as virtuous mothers, ministering angels, and dutiful wives.

Nowhere was civilian morale more tested than in the occupied zone and the militarized zones directly behind the front lines. Germany's war aims against French civilians were the same as those against French soldiers—the destruction of the ability of France ever again to make war against Germany. In the occupied zone, the Germans imposed special arbitrary levies on cities and towns; dismantled industrial machinery and sent it to Germany; requisitioned food, labor, and materiel; and imposed reprisals if their demands went unmet. As the war dragged on, with more and more of their own men under arms, the Germans began deporting unemployed or indigent French civilians either to Germany or to occupied France and Belgium. Soon the occupied territories seemed little more than a vast prison, where—in a chilling prelude to what was to come during World War II—Germans "concentrated" civilians in labor camps or transported them in cattle cars to where they were most needed.

Faced with defeat, invasion, and humiliation, civilian France mobilized for war in many different ways: economically, socially, politically, and culturally, all of which were mutually reinforcing. When the mobilization orders came in August 1914, the men directly affected were convinced that they would be home by Christmas. Within weeks, a government that had planned for a short war began to confront the fact that its current industrial production would never be able to sustain a protracted conflict. One month of combat had depleted its supplies of armaments, while after mobilization most firms retained on average only about one-third of their workers. The French state's first challenge was shifting to a war economy, and doing so quickly, since so much of their coal, iron, and steel production was in occupied France. War Minister Alexandre Millerand assembled the nation's leading industrialists in September 1914 and announced two goals: a target production of 100,000 shells a day, with state subsidies for the building of new arms factories, and a vastly expanded production of heavy and light artillery pieces, to try to close the gap with Germany. By June 1915, the Dalbiez Law released 500,000 essential war workers from the front to try to meet the targeted goals. Industrialists also turned to other labor sources: foreigners and colonial subjects, some categories of prisoners, and also women, who now had access to highly paid jobs from which they had always been excluded. In metallurgy their gains were spectacular: Women went from 5 to 20 percent of the workforce. In most sectors, however, their presence only increased slightly, since women in France had long worked in factories.[31]

French wartime production was stunningly successful. Shell production increased tenfold from 1915 to 1918; powder and explosives production increased sixfold. By 1918, French industry was producing 1,000 artillery pieces per month and 261,000 shells and 6 million cartridges per day. French companies became the chief arms suppliers for the Allies, including the United States, from which they imported much of their primary materials as well as capital to finance expanded production. The key to this extraordinary turnaround, in a country known for its economic "backwardness," lay in a unique partnership forged between the state and private industry by socialist visionary Albert Thomas. In 1916 Thomas was appointed to head a new Armaments Ministry. He promptly broke with pre-war liberalism by combining market principles with centralized planning. The state assisted private initiative through guaranteed loans and outright grants, but demanded in return the right to control prices and implement production plans. At all times private industrialists had the right to accept or refuse state orders. Paris for the first time became a major center of large industry, as did the Loire Basin. By 1918 some 17,000 companies employed 1.7 million people in armaments manufacturing. In the coming years metal workers, usually just off the farm, would become the most radicalized of French workers, and future recruits to communism.

The second greatest challenge faced by the government was feeding and housing its civilian population despite the absence of the principal breadwinners in most families and the onset of massive inflation induced by a combination of war-time borrowing and increasing the money supply. Here rural France and urban France present very different pictures. In 1914, half of the French population still resided in the countryside. Military allowances paid to families for daily needs, instituted at the onset of hostilities, made an enormous difference; wartime inflation benefited those who had food to sell, and peasants never faced the food and fuel shortages that plagued urban-dwellers. One of the means devised by the government in order to help the farmers was to channel the refugees from the German-occupied zone toward the countryside. Even with this, the amount of uncultivated land increased. The wheat harvest diminished from 88 million quintals in 1913 to 77 million in 1914, 60 million in 1915, and 58 million in 1916. An extraordinarily wet summer in 1916 exacerbated this shortage. But in general, women, children, and the elderly managed each year to bring in the harvests in the absence of military-age men. Many peasants became richer, reflected in an upsurge in purchases of new farms, bicycles, and farm equipment, as well as women dressed in new clothes. In many communes, while the courage of women taking over farms was praised, their prosperity was also noted. As one police report put it, "they had taken advantage of the situation and amassed tidy sums."[32] The notion that women had stayed at home and benefited from the war while the men had gone to the front and suffered would make for strained gender relations in the 1920s.

In the cities, the departure of the head of family to war had more severe consequences. Industrial workers kept pace with inflation only in the armaments industry; in other sectors, they faced not only eroded incomes, but also, after 1917, fuel and food shortages and, most terrifyingly, sporadic aerial bombardment from zeppelins. Yet urbanites too experienced new forms of state support, in the form of a government employment office, pensions for men disabled by the war, and support for orphans. Under Albert Thomas, the state increasingly sought to mediate disputes between workers and factory owners and to make unions partners in the negotiations over production. By and large, even in cities, it appears that war morale held. One of the striking findings of government spies, who spent a good deal of effort trying to gauge whether support for the war effort was waning, was how little attention Parisians paid to the bad news from the front throughout 1915. Even the soldiers on leave in the city, these reports repeated over and over, showed no sign of war weariness, declaiming publicly in cafés and railway cars their belief in an Allied victory. The soldiers' confidence was infectious. While Parisians may have grumbled endlessly about wartime hardships, they continued to accept the necessity of war—and also to ignore, or at least not complain about, the lack of success.[33]

PRIVATE LIFE, CENSORSHIP, AND CONSENT

On the whole, the war did not challenge the conservative sexual mores of the Third Republic. Between 1914 and 1916, there were fewer trials for adultery than before the war. It is true that the penalty against adultery was raised, from a 50-franc fine to 45 days in prison. But it also appears that the war boosted many individuals' spirit of sacrifice and duty. Heroic cabaret singers shunned before 1914 "redeemed" themselves by taking care of wounded soldiers by day while working at night. At the other extreme, the war temporarily changed intimate relations within some bourgeois marriages. Jean-Marie Apostolidès told the following story about his grandfather, a medical captain, and his grandmother, a very austere Catholic woman who had kept her husband at a distance before the war:

> He was authorized to approach her only during the war, during his leaves. As he was risking his life for France, she accepted a similar sacrifice and abandoned herself to his caresses that otherwise disgusted her profoundly. This is how they had four children, all of them conceived between 1914 and 1919, after which they separated again.[34]

Yet the war changed French family life permanently in another way, as everyone faced early on the very real prospect of losing a loved one. In 1916, visiting Paris in the middle of the war, a foreign traveler commented on its silence and said that arriving in Paris was like "entering a cathedral."[35] "Never before had war caused so many deaths in France, particularly in so short a time." Half of the 1.3 million soldiers killed by the end of the war lost their lives in its first 17 months; in the last five months of 1914 alone, 2,000 soldiers died on average each day, or 1 every minute. The average fell to 935 per day in 1915, 677 in 1916, and 419 in 1917, but in 1918, when the war of attrition gave way once again a war of movement, the average surged to 800 a day.[36] Casualties among junior and noncommissioned officers were higher than among private soldiers, since they had to lead attacks and placed themselves at greater physical risk. In France as elsewhere, these officers were overwhelmingly from the ranks of the educated middle and upper classes and from the age cohort of 18 to 46. Death then touched these socioeconomic and age groups disproportionately. The cavalcade of death plunged the French nation into a collective mourning unprecedented in modern times. Equally stressful was the constant anxiety about possible news to come. Because most soldiers were assiduous correspondents, a break in letter delivery could only mean that an offensive had been launched. When still no letter arrived, the waiting became unbearable. Often it took weeks for official news that a soldier had been wounded or killed to reach those left behind.

Grief took many forms. Faced with a demographic reversal of the natural order of things—in the sense that the old were allowed to live while the young were cut down just as they reached adulthood—parents, wives, orphans, and siblings experienced survivors' guilt. Some parents yielded to despair and died themselves, apparently for psychosomatic causes. Most families were unable to retrieve their soldiers' bodies, which either were never recovered or were hastily buried in military cemeteries near the front. They thus had neither funerals nor tombs for enacting the traditional rites of mourning and focusing their grief. Families were haunted by the knowledge that their sons, brothers, and husbands had died alone, often in unimaginable agony. From letters exchanged between the bereaved and the dead soldiers' comrades, we know that over and over again, families sought to find out what final moments had been like, whether others had been with their loved ones, and where bodies had been placed. They thus sought to fill the terrible gaps in their knowledge that added to the excruciating suffering with which death had already burdened them.

Mourning on this collective scale raises the complicated question of how women as a group experienced the war compared with men. Certainly one of the dominant images handed down from the war—although it was rarely given form in war monuments built in the 1920s—was that of the grieving woman. A man's duty was to become a soldier and die heroically for the nation, a notion that postwar commemorations repeated over and over; woman's primary role was bravely and quietly to sacrifice the man she loved most, while sustaining the family.

Yet the reality of war was that in order to sustain their families, French women could not stay in their traditional roles. Many women exhibited uncommon courage, in ways that both reinforced and challenged stereotypes from the pre-war era, when "the ideal heroine was small, young, pretty, and, if possible, orphaned."[37] For example, Marcelle Semmer, 20 years old, blonde and frail, was lionized by the press because of her bravery—and because she offered an image of French female heroism that conformed to preexisting expectations. After the French army had retreated over the canal where she lived, in Picardy, she "opened the swing bridge and threw the key to the mechanism into the canal to prevent the Germans from crossing in pursuit. . . . Arrested by the Germans, she declared: 'I am an orphan. I have only one mother, France, and it does not bother me to die.'"[38] More typical yet less noticed was the matronly Mme. Macherez of Soissons, 64 years old and the widow of a senator. As a woman of means with great local authority, she successfully negotiated with the invading Germans, remained in charge of the nursing post that she had organized in Soissons, and stopped the Germans from burning the city by stoutly declaring: "You must shoot me first."[39]

Women—especially working-class women who had to support themselves—also worked in munitions factories, served as drivers in the Army Automobile Service, or worked as carpenters for the Army units. But although women took on many jobs that were traditionally associated with men, their most praised role was that of nurses. Nurses came overwhelmingly from the middle classes, since they were not paid. The French Red Cross was particularly proud of its war record, which included "more than twenty volunteer nurses killed at the front [and] nearly one thousand [who] received the Croix de Guerre," many of them for "bravery under fire."[40]

Prevailing gender norms nevertheless still viewed single women in public as needing protection. The absence of millions of men loosened such restrictions, but did not do away with them altogether. One result during the war was that writers, journalists, and soldiers often accused single women who traveled alone to the front as nurses or who ran farms or rented apartments on their own of—usually imagined—immoral behavior. The war thus placed all women in a double bind.

It offered them some new opportunities to take on roles previously open only to men, but it also led to heightened anxieties that women who assumed men's responsibilities were becoming either sexualized and immoral or too much like men. Over time, war propaganda increasingly promoted an idealized vision of French society that was worth dying for, in which men would return to find their beloved *patrie,* and the pre-war gender order, just the way they had left it.[41]

As this example suggests, World War I also marked the birth of modern propaganda targeted at every man, woman, and child; thus it is tempting to ask what role it played in securing this extraordinary consent behind the lines. Official wartime propaganda took many forms, but principally it consisted of press and postal censorship, designed to keep "unwanted facts" from the public, and official versions of events and depictions of the enemy, disseminated especially after 1915 through newsreels. The military authorities maintained a strong grip on cinematography. They produced more than 600 newsreels that were transported around the countryside and the front and were designed to channel public opinion and fuel martial ardor.[42] The result, as far as the press was concerned, was what the soldiers came to call *bourrage de crâne,* or skull torture – that is to say, a litany of fatuous statements that whitewashed the face of battle. All newspapers, from *L'Humanité* on the Left to the *Echo de Paris* on the militarist and Catholic Right, published such inane imaginary comments from or about combatants, as: "It's nothing to speak of, I'll be disabled that's all" (April 1915); "they all go into battle as to a fête [party]" (May 1915); "apart from about five minutes a month, the danger is minimal. . . . [C]asualties and death [are] the exception" (May 1915); "they looked forward to the offensive as to a holiday" (October 1915); "the very fact that he [the enemy] is not advancing is an outstanding success, and raises immense hopes" (February 1916, from Verdun); "the troops went through their maneuvers at Verdun as they might on a field exercise" (March 1916, from Verdun).[43]

From the outset, the government censored the press and letters to and from the front, in an effort to shape public opinion. The government considered its control over both media and personal correspondence vital to morale "by leaving [the nation] in ignorance of the gravity of certain military defeats, of diplomatic failures and of the horrors of the war."[44] Yet with the constant coming and going of soldiers, civilians learned about the war's horrific costs anyway—and they still wanted a fight to the finish. Such acquiescence can be explained by the fact that alongside the state, France's cultural elite—its schoolteachers, priests, professional classes, and especially intellectuals and artists—enthusiastically and continuously supported the war effort. And where these elites led, the majority of ordinary French men and women followed. We have already noted the bourgeoisie's spontaneous willingness to send its sons into battle. This same class massively mobilized its intellectual resources not to deceive the nation but to convince it of the justice of the war. Maurice Barrès wrote a column in the *Echo de Paris* every single day of the war. French university luminaries such as the famous sociologist

Emile Durkheim—who lost his only son in the war and died himself of grief in 1917—and his disciples Maurice Halbwachs and François Simiand published pamphlets on war issues and joined in planning the war economy. Poets Guillaume Apollinaire and Blaise Cendrars served in the military; the former lost his life, and the latter lost his right arm.

On a more prosaic level, throughout France schoolteachers were enjoined to incorporate patriotic themes and explain current events in their classes. They "should collect examples of heroic acts and hold them up to 'our little ones, so that they learn to admire France.'"[45] A new genre of children's literature flourished, in which France's heroic youths cheerfully killed Germans. The Catholic clergy was no less imbued with patriotism, in part because they saw in the war an occasion for reuniting the nation and restoring the Church to its rightful place after the anti-clerical struggles. Little matter the motive; the result was unequivocal support for the Republic's war effort. As a Paris bishop put it during a memorial service for the war dead in 1915, "And what is the song of those who have died in battle? It is 'La Marseillaise.' It is to the strains of 'La Marseillaise' that they knock at the door of this basilica. Open it for them, admit them to immortality."[46]

Not just in 1914, then, but in 1915 and 1916 as well, the war allowed republicans and Catholics to put aside their intense differences, in the service of a higher common cause: that of France and, more particularly, of French civilization against German barbarism. That the "*Boche*" remained a barbarian while the heroic French *poilu* was defending not only helpless women and innocent children but civilization itself was never left in doubt. The early German atrocities in Belgium gave government propagandists and educated commentators alike an arsenal of imagery to deploy and, as the war wore on, no one tried seriously to counter the same crude charges of cannibalism, infanticide, and sexual perversion first hurled at the Germans. Instead they were recycled. Meanwhile the notion that civilization itself lay in the balance appealed to both republicans and Catholics long used to thinking in messianic terms. War rhetoric also transformed the African colonial subjects forced to serve under French colors from "primitives" into valued "little French brothers."[47] In any balance sheet of how and why the homefront held for three straight years, propaganda—more than censorship—must figure prominently.

1917: BREAKING POINT

In October 1916, the first good news in a long time trickled back from Verdun. The new theater commander, General Nivelle, had retaken the French forts of Douaumont and Vaux with relatively few casualties. Nivelle attributed his successes to the adoption of new tactics, such as attacking in small groups under decentralized leadership and using rolling artillery fire in the place of a concentrated barrage. He then managed to convince the government to authorize a general offensive for the spring of 1917, based on his new doctrine. The French, Nivelle argued, could break through the German lines at the base of the great bulge formed by the enemy's position in France, which ran along a 150km salient from Arras to Craonne, and finally win the war. Far from securing victory, how-ever, the attempted *percée* of 1917 was in every sense a fiasco, and occasioned the first serious mutinies of the war as well as defeatism on the homefront. Worse still, it was a fiasco that could have been prevented. In the fall of 1916, the Germans, too, had reconsidered their tactics, in ways that Nivelle chose to ignore. The new German generals abandoned the packing of infantry in the front trenches, creating instead a series of deep defensive strong points. The bulk of the infantry would remain beyond the reach of enemy artillery, free to launch local and general counter-attacks. The decision to retreat, hold, or counter-attack would be left to lieutenants and captains on the scene.[48]

In the spring of 1917, as soon as they got wind of French plans for a major offensive, the Germans put these new tactics to their first brilliant test. They first withdrew German troops from the salient that Nivelle planned to attack, thus removing the offensive's rationale. When Nivelle went ahead on April 16 and attacked anyway along the Chemin des Dames, the new defense in depth undercut French offensive tactical innovations. The French, led by Senegalese troops on a day of mixed rain and snow, broke through the thin first German line, but the deeper they drove, the higher French casualties became. By the end of the second day, 120,000 soldiers lay dead or wounded. Nivelle, like his predecessors, refused to call off the attack. On April 22, he returned to the tactic of *grignotage.* As yet another offensive bogged down, the government lost confidence in Nivelle and on May 15 replaced him with Philippe Pétain. By that time, however, the unthinkable had happened for a nation at war. Soldiers in many divisions were now refusing orders and instead holding demonstrations to air their grievances.

The mutinies that broke out in April 1917 and lasted until October were less a refusal to continue the fight for France than to continue fighting in the same sense-less way that their generals had repeatedly required of them. In a deeper sense, citizen soldiers were exercising their democratic rights to appeal to their govern-ment directly. "For a brief moment in time, they were essentially free to decide what to do next."[49] The *poilus* who mutinied remained for the most part nonviolent and loyal, even as they disobeyed their commanders; no one deserted. Although exact numbers are hard to determine, perhaps 25,000–30,000 soldiers were involved over a four-month period.[50] By any measure, the French army was taking deplorable care of its soldiers in 1917. Its medical services were crude and inade-quate; its generals had refused to come to the front lines and see for themselves, coldly calculating that Allied superiority in manpower would make them victors in the long run; and the essential *pinard,* or wine ration, was now intermittent. For the most part the mutineers wanted decent treatment and the abandonment of tactics that were doomed ahead of time. A song from 1917 captured the bitterness toward the highest military leaders:

> de Nivelle has leveled us
> And Joffre gave us the war
> And Foch has flattened us . . .

And Petain has kneaded us . . .
And Mangin has eaten us.[51]

As another soldier wrote home, he wanted: "peace and the right to leaves, which are in arrears. No more butchery; we want liberty; no more injustice. . . . [W]e need peace to feed our wives and children and to be able to give bread to the women and orphans. We demand peace, peace."[52]

Peace, yes, but not at any price. It became clear in the tense summer months, as the command structure struggled to contain the mutinies, that these rebellious men remained committed to ejecting the German army from French soil. In other words, they used the opportunity afforded by the mutinies to rethink their roles as citizen soldiers, and ultimately to recommit to the war effort. Pétain appears to have understood what was at stake. In the end, repression was relatively light; although 3,427 soldiers were court-martialed and 554 condemned to death sentences, only 49 mutineers were shot. France could hardly do otherwise, given its depleted manpower. Pétain visited every division to hear complaints and made important reforms in food distribution and leave policy. Above all, he made clear that he would husband the lives of soldiers. In Pétain famous words: "[W]e will wait for tanks and the Americans." True to his word, Pétain spent the rest of 1917 building up French reserves rather than launching more attacks. But the mutinies had been a close call, leaving a bitter memory that would resurface in the difficult years of post-war reconstruction.

The year 1917 saw not only mutiny but also mounting pacifism and defeatism on the homefront, both real and imagined, fueled only partly by the disastrous Nivelle offensive. The overthrow of the Russian tsar in March would soon lead to Russia's withdrawal from the conflict, allowing Germany once again to fight a one-front war. Meanwhile the winter of 1916–1917 was an exceptionally long one; not only mutiny but also mounting pacifism and defeatism persisted through a cold winter that lingered into April. At home, long-simmering labor discontent in the key munitions industry erupted into strikes as wartime inflation reached new heights, as high as 100 percent between April and July 1917. As usual, peasants who had food to sell benefited, while the urban working population, who had already faced fuel shortages, now found bread prohibitively expensive as well.

There was, however, one piece of good news. The United States in April 1917 announced that it was joining the Allies, in response to Germany's declaration in January of unrestricted submarine warfare. But since the United States had neither an arms industry nor a standing army, in the short run France and Britain would have to supply it with armaments, thus exacerbating demands on an already war-weary working force. Fear that this really would be a war without end, and increasing doubts that total victory—even if achievable—could possibly be worth the price, further weakened national unity. Three years of total war had confused gender roles, increased class tensions, and introduced new racial and ethnic strains, pushing civilian forbearance, too, to the breaking point.

REVOLUTION?

One sign of the revolution—temporary as it turned out—that the war had wrought in labor relations was that women workers, rather than unionized French male laborers, decided now to protest against their employers. The war had witnessed an enormous expansion of the Confédération Générale du Travail (CGT), France's largest trade union, from 100,000 members in 1916 to 600,000 in 1918. Yet its leader, Léon Jouhaux, steadfastly adhered to the *union sacrée* and did his utmost to keep its members at their jobs. Male workers excused from conscription because of their industrial skills had every incentive to cooperate; they could be sent to the front if their employers deemed them troublesome. Women factory workers, in contrast, had less to lose by protesting, and much to gain.

Starting in late 1916, women workers in certain sectors struck for higher wages and shorter working hours, to better meet the new responsibilities imposed by the war on them at home. The biggest strike wave coincided with the mutinies, in the spring of 1917, although there is no direct evidence of coordination between the two. Also in 1917, the February Revolution in Russia, triggered by women demonstrating for bread, may have played a role. In France, 10,000 women in the textile industry kicked off the protests, and strikes soon spread to the metal-working and munitions factories in the Paris region. Some 75 percent of the strikers were women; in addition to higher wages, they demanded that men and women sacrifice equally. All workers, but especially female ones, were highly suspicious of *embusqués*, or shirkers—men who appeared to be avoiding their duty as soldiers by staying behind in the factories. During the strikes, women targeted harsh foremen and either arrogant or incompetent male co-workers as shirkers who should take their proper place alongside husbands, fathers, and sons in the trenches.

As in the mutinies, however, rarely did the strikers call for peace at any price, although they did intimate that the peace when it came would have to justify their sacrifices. The state stepped in and arbitrated minor wage hikes that ended the strikes, and women workers, like the front-line soldiers, agreed then to return to their jobs. Yet both forms of protest made clear that by 1917 the war had created new and possibly deeper fractures than had existed before 1914 and that other interests could at least temporarily prevail over the defense of the country, "something that had not hitherto happened."[53] Strikes would break out again in the munitions industry in the spring of 1918, this time among male workers who were more openly anti-war than the previous spring. But they too petered out in the face of their rank and file's unwillingness to jeopardize the continued prosecution of the war.

Workers—both female and male—and soldiers were not the only laborers to come out of the war more militant and determined to right wrongs occasioned by the war's totalization. World War I opened up a new chapter in French race relations by drafting not just colonial soldiers but colonial laborers, as well as low-wage Chinese workers, and bringing them to France. French colonial subjects had a very mixed record of treatment at the hands of the French. In French

West Africa, forcible conscription between 1914 and 1917 is remembered even to this day as a return to the worst horrors of the slave trade, as young men who had no desire to die for their colonial masters were hunted down and turned over to recruiting agents by the local French administration. Only in 1917, after serious revolts broke out in parts of French West Africa, were positive incentives—including the promise of easier access to citizenship—introduced in exchange for voluntary enlistment. Colonial troops nevertheless fought with a valor that finally convinced many politicians of the value of the empire. In combat, the trenches could be the great levelers, as *poilus* and the African troops found themselves in classic small group solidarity against artillery fire that did not discriminate on the basis of color.

No such leveling benefited the 220,000 colonial and foreign laborers drafted to replace French citizens in factories.[54] Compared to French citizen workers, foreign and colonial labor worked longer hours, with worse pay, and were subject to special surveillance and segregation by an increasingly stressed civilian population and local authorities. Resented for making possible the release of more loved ones to the front, Indochinese, Malagasy, and North and West Africans were also seen through the same racist lens present in the empire. Colonial authorities overseas had long tried to maintain a sense of superiority among much more numerous indigenous populations by proscribing contact between "pure" white women—usually the wives of administrators—and supposedly oversexed and degenerate "black" and "yellow" men. Anxieties about interracial relations now resurfaced in France, in soldiers' letters home but also in police reports. "We don't want the blacks in Paris and in other regions mistreating our wives," wrote one mutineer in 1917.[55] Foreign and colonial laborers faced daily discrimination made worse by their lack of rights. Repatriated immediately after the war's end, colonial labor and military conscripts returned home deeply embittered by their wartime experiences, but also much better informed about France's laws, French internal divisions, and traditions of dissent—lessons they would put to their own use in a new wave of post-war anti-colonialism.

Such a broad climate of dissent from the lowest ranks of society, whether civilian soldiers or colonial subjects, working-class women or foreign workers, terrified civilian and military authorities alike in 1917. More worrying still, members of the middle and upper classes of French society—whose support and leadership of the war effort had been so crucial—also momentarily wavered. Some were tempted, as socialist pacifists in all the belligerent nations argued for a negotiated peace with a return to the status quo ante. International peace conferences, led variously by women, trade unionists, and socialists, had already convened in 1915 and 1916. In the crisis atmosphere of 1917, the government refused passports to French delegates wishing to travel to the third international socialist meeting in Stockholm in May. Albert Thomas responded by withdrawing socialist support from the government. Defeatism among prominent Radicals was also on the rise. Charismatic Radical politician Joseph Caillaux, his political career recovering from pre-war scandal after his wife was acquitted of murdering the editor of *Le Figaro,* openly advocated extending peace feelers. More than one deputy and several journalists were discovered to be accepting bribes from Germany to sue for peace.

In this tense atmosphere, the aging "Tiger" Georges Clemenceau, since 1914 the most resolute defender in the Chamber of a war to the finish, emerged as the only leader capable of remobilizing the nation and purging it of its perceived internal enemies. From August 1914 on, Clemenceau had waged a relentless war of the pen against anyone suspected of war weariness or incompetence, and by 1917 he included President Poincaré in this group. Although Poincaré personally despised Clemenceau, the latter's uncompromising position on the need for a French victory offered the only way out of the growing paralysis that threatened the nation. On November 20, 1917, just days after the Bolshevik seizure of power in Russia added to a sense of impending catastrophe, Poincaré appointed Clemenceau prime minister—and France entered upon a kind of civilian dictatorship. Clemenceau promptly ordered the arrest of all suspected pacifists and compromised deputies. Several "spies" were tried and executed. Yet no one who heard Clemenceau's inaugural speech—including Winston Churchill, who was sitting in the gallery of the Chamber of Deputies—could fail to be moved by his appeal: The time had come, he insisted, for the nation "to be entirely French" and to fight a *guerre intégrale*—a total war—until Germany had been repulsed; the fate of humanity demanded nothing less.[56]

1918–1919: WAR'S END

Clemenceau's resolution injected a new and desperately needed spirit into the nation. As prime minister, and at great personal risk, he—unlike the generals or any previous political leader—visited the front weekly. In March 1918, Germany signed the Treaty of Brest-Litovsk with Lenin's new Soviet Russia, freeing troops up for a major new offensive in the West. Several months earlier, Germany's tactical experts had come up with a genuinely new offensive doctrine, one destined to mark the entire twentieth century. Elite storm troops were formed who could gain and maintain the initiative in battle by exploiting breaks in the enemy's line. Short intense artillery barrages would create the breaks, storm troops would rush in and destroy communications, and the infantry would follow and mop up any remaining resistance. On March 21, 1918, the Germans launched a million men against the Allies. They concentrated their attack at various points on the British line to the north, initially to devastating effect. As rapid German gains threatened to split the British army from the French and to open up a corridor for a German sweep to Paris, the Allied governments took the long overdue step of establishing a supreme command to control and coordinate the French, British, and American armies. The job went to the brilliant French General Ferdinand Foch, whose determination to fight and strategic grasp of German innovations made him, rather than the cautious Pétain, Clemenceau's first choice.

Both decisions proved critical in turning the tide against Germany, whose lightening successes that spring masked essential weaknesses: insufficient training, ever younger and ever fewer infantry, exhaustion, and overstretched lines. By the end of June the Germans were once again threatening Paris, but their offensive had cost them a staggering 915,000 casualties, and they could no longer defend their gains. On August 8, the Germans lost eight divisions in one day, and their army began to disintegrate as half a million German soldiers deserted. Allied strength, in contrast, increased daily with the arrival of hundreds of thousands of Americans. Their offensives around Verdun nevertheless incurred casualty rates similar to those of the Allies earlier in the war: a thousand a day. In the end 4.7 million Americans were mobilized; 116,000 died and 204,000 were wounded between August and November 1918.

On July 18, 1918, the Allies began a series of counter-attacks that would continue until November, when the Germans sued for peace despite not yet being pushed back to their own frontiers. Casualties on both sides in the final offensives remained as high as in the war of movement in the fall of 1914, but with America's resources now thrown into the balance and German morale at its nadir among troops and its starving civilian population, the German commanders in October let it be known that they now wished to hear Allied conditions for an armistice.

"Four Years in the Fight, The Women of France, We Owe Them Houses of Cheer," YWCA support for French women, post–World War I poster. Private Collection/Topham Picturepoint/ The Bridgeman Art Library.

At 11 o'clock on the eleventh day of the eleventh month of 1918, four and a half years of war came to an end. German delegates signed a cessation of hostilities in General Foch's personal railway car, parked in the Compiègne forest—a location one German footsoldier, Adolf Hitler, would not forget. The armistice's conditions were harsh, a prelude to the vindictive peace treaty that would soon follow. Among the many clauses, Germany agreed to withdraw from occupied France, Belgium, Luxembourg, and also from Alsace-Lorraine within 15 days. German troops would withdraw from both banks of the Rhine, which would become an Allied zone of occupation pending the signature of a final peace treaty. Germany had to hand over its navy, military equipment, and trains and trucks to the Allies as well. As the bells, this time of peace, pealed throughout France, everyone poured into the streets, weeping, singing, and embracing. The "incomprehensible" had finally ended, and the reckoning of its ultimate costs had not yet begun.

That there had to be a reckoning was not in doubt; but it took place in myriad ways, and at different tempos, depending on who lost what, individually and collectively. The official reckoning began in early 1919 as the representatives of the Allies assembled at Versailles to hammer out a peace treaty, led by the "Big Four": Lloyd George, Woodrow Wilson, Italian premier Vittorio Orlando, and Georges Clemenceau. Yet clashes emerged almost immediately at the peace conference over how to treat Germany. As an American entering the war late, Wilson had a very different vision of the possibilities of the future from Clemenceau and Lloyd George. In January 1918, President Wilson had outlined a series of 14 points for the future organization of the world, positing a utopian liberal order of free markets, free elections, and international cooperation. The right to self-determination would cause democratic nations to rise from the wreckage of the old empires; Germany, stripped of its ill-gotten gains and forced to be "liberal," would soon join the ranks of powerful but peaceful free states.

Lloyd George and Clemenceau had no such illusions. The Communist Revolution in Russia raised the specter of social revolution spreading westward to their own working classes; Clemenceau and Lloyd George thus gave priority to establishing bulwarks against radicalism, not democratic freedom. And the French people, Clemenceau knew, needed a settlement that appeared to confirm that their sacrifices had been worthwhile. They wanted a victor's peace—just as Germany had wished against France when it launched war in 1914—with provisions designed precisely to ensure that Germany could never be great again. Yet victory had been neither France's alone, nor total—an armistice was not an unconditional surrender. British and American aid had been crucial, and the latter had been secured not through brilliant French diplomacy but because of German blundering. However much they might wish it, the French could not dictate the peace terms alone. Nor could a German nation of 60 million, straddling the heart of Europe, be permanently repressed, regardless of the aggression of its generals. Expecting the impossible from Versailles, the French were bound to be disappointed by what they did get—a compromise peace that satisfied no one, yet whose ratification provided a golden opportunity for both old political divisions to reemerge and new ones to form.

MAKING PEACE

The Versailles Treaty, much scorned since the moment the ink dried as unworkable, cannot be understood without taking into account the contradictory objectives that it embodied. All the signatories agreed on at least one point: that Germany bore moral and financial responsibility for the war, and that it would have to pay for the damages it had inflicted. A war guilt clause assigned blame for the war exclusively to Germany and its allies. The treaty further stipulated that Germany would have to pay the entire war bill, including for damages caused by acts of war against civilians, as well as all military pensions. Such provisions bordered on the absurd, since Germany's own economy lay in ruins—as France's had not in 1871—and for it to pay reparations would require first a revival of its economy—exactly the kind of rebuilding that France most feared. The issue of reparations would haunt European relations for the next 10 years, as France clung stubbornly to its right to collect them, only setting itself up for disappointment when Germany proved incapable of paying. The Treaty also contained a variety of military and diplomatic provisions intended to ensure that Germany could not attack France again. Its army and navy were scaled back, no air force was allowed, and the imperial possessions of the defeated German and Ottoman empires were divided among the victors as League of Nations Mandates. France received Mandates in Lebanon, Syria, Cameroon, and Togo. Mandates differed from protectorates or colonies, in that they obliged the mandatory power to prepare the inhabitants for self-rule with the oversight of the League of Nations (whose founding charter formed the first 26 articles of the Treaty). Clemenceau demanded the creation of one or several buffer states along the Rhine, occupied by or linked to France. But the other Allies balked at any such dismemberment of Germany in the West, and France had to settle for a demilitarized Rhineland, enforced by a 15-year occupation.

These provisions were hotly contested in the French Chamber. For the Left, in solidarity with the new Weimar Republic founded in the wake of Germany's collapse, the treaty was too harsh. Opinion from the Center and Right, in contrast, lambasted Clemenceau for the treaty's lack of teeth. There was no real guarantee against German recovery or rearmament and no assurance that the Germans would ever pay reparations. While the signatories had made some gestures toward establishing collective security, both a Britain firmly tied to its global empire rather than to Europe and an isolationist United States refused any explicit long-term commitment to come to France's aid. Whereas France had begun World War I in alliance with both Russia and Britain, it now could only count on the fragile new states of central Europe—principally Poland and Czechoslovakia—and the new League of Nations to maintain its security. In the end the French legislature ratified the treaty, in part because it had little choice. The Versailles Treaty, signed in the Hall of Mirrors in Versailles where the German empire in 1871 had first been proclaimed, was a bad peace because it was a vengeful one. It avoided confronting head-on the problem of how to reintegrate the German nation into Europe on terms that, while justly punishing its military leaders, would allow democracy to take root among its people and thus obtain collective security for all Europeans. Yet in 1919 this was the only kind of peace the French could imagine.

For all its subsequent importance for the evolution of international relations, the peace negotiations were not uppermost in the minds of French in the months after the armistice. No sooner had the guns been silenced than the national community began its painful quest to find proper ways, collectively and individually, to mourn and reassure themselves that their loved ones had not suffered in vain. In addition to the 1.3 million dead, over 1 million were designated permanent invalids and 3 million "semi-invalid."[57] Nearly half of the entire metropolitan male French population had fought in the trenches, and of those, about two-thirds were either dead or injured. They left behind 600,000 widows and 760,000 orphans. France suffered more than any other major combatant nation. Of France's total population, 3.4 percent had been killed, compared to 3 percent for Germany, 1.6 percent for Britain, and 0.07 percent for the United States. Among colonial troops, black Africans sustained the highest losses: over 200,000 soldiers were conscripted; their dead made up over 50,000 of the 78,000 colonial subjects who died for France.

The mourning that had begun during the war continued much more publicly in its aftermath. On every piece of French soil where soldiers had fought, monuments to the *poilus* arose that the living might remember what had transpired there. A million French men lay buried in cemeteries adjacent to the great battlefields, in row upon row of gravestones that still bear silent witness to the magnitude of the catastrophe. Each of the 36,000 communes in France erected in its public square a monument that listed the names of the fallen, as well as an inscription thanking these men "morts pour la France" ("who died for France"). These monuments became sacred sites in their own right, reuniting the dead with the living in symbolic ceremonies that affirmed year in and year out that the preservation of the nation had been worth their sacrifice. Every year on November 11, every woman, man, and child in communities throughout France gathered to read out the names of the dead. United during the war in their will to hold on, the French remained partially united in peace through shared acts of commemoration that reminded them that everyone had been touched by tragedy.

Two spectacular acts of official commemoration occurred immediately after the war. These were the victory parade of July 14, 1919, and the decision to bury an unknown soldier under the Arc de Triomphe in 1920. Both represented an attempt by the state to shape how French citizens would remember the war. The victory march served principally to glorify the military, with Foch and Joffre riding side by side down Paris' Champs Elysées. Yet four horribly maimed men wheeled by nurses also led the parade. One thousand *mutilés de guerre* followed them—eliciting, presumably, horror at their scarred bodies as well as respect.

Fifteen months later, on November 11, 1920, the French inaugurated a new commemorative process that was soon emulated around the world, when they chose to bury an unknown soldier from Verdun in Paris. Since so many bodies had never been recovered or identified, the government decided to use the remains of one anonymous soldier to commemorate the general heroism of all. Every bereaved family could thus imagine this soldier as its own. In what has been called the last great public performance of the *union sacrée,* representatives from all faiths and all political parties participated in the ceremonies that culminated in the public display of the coffin on Armistice Day. Hundreds of thousands of weeping mourners poured into the streets in a paroxysm of grief.

The burial of the Unknown Soldier, however, had a political dimension as well. The year 1920 marked the fiftieth anniversary of the birth of the Third Republic. Born in the midst of another national tragedy, the government wished to emphasize that it was the Republic, as much as the French people, that had made the nation whole again. The inscription on the grave of the unknown soldier read: "Here lies a French soldier who died for *la patrie,* 1914–1918." Two plaques flanked the inscription. One read, "4 September, 1870, the Proclamation of the Republic"; the other, "11 November 1918, the Return of Alsace-Lorraine to France."[58] Whether the Republic had sacrificed too much to preserve the nation remained to be seen.

CHAPTER 7

The Deceptive Peace
1919–1929

In December 1927, Henriette Alquier, a 29-year-old village schoolteacher from southwest France and left-wing feminist, was accused of disseminating information about birth control—a punishable offense in France since 1920. With the return of peace, the National Assembly had also passed a harsher law against abortion, making any person involved in an abortion liable to imprisonment. While concerns about France's declining birthrate had been building from the end of the nineteenth century, the huge loss of life during World War I intensified fears about French depopulation, shifting the current of opinion known as "pro-natalism" to the mainstream. Equating national strength with a vigorously growing population, pro-natalists insisted that rebuilding France required increasing the birthrate by whatever means possible. Every political party was pro-natalist after the war, and the 1920 laws easily passed. Alquier, on the other hand, was less worried about the declining birthrate than about France's continuing high infant mortality rates, the lack of adequate welfare to address child poverty, and the class bias of the pro-natalist legislation. Bourgeois deputies, she claimed, had passed the 1920 laws to deprive working women of information that they needed. Meanwhile middle-class women could "limit the number of their children in the privacy of their boudoir or adulterous love-nest." In the end Alquier was acquitted, but not before a storm of controversy for promoting "immorality."[1]

The Alquier Affair, as it came to be known, illustrates in a variety of ways the great impact World War I had on French society in the 1920s, and that society's ambivalent response to the transformations thrust upon it. French men and women were caught between a sense that they must continue to "modernize" to remain competitive in a new international order that included the rise of the United States, and a desire to return to the pre-war status quo—including traditional gender roles—for which so many had died. Alquier herself was the product of these contradictory trends. She personally benefited from a 1920 law that gave equal pay to female and male schoolteachers. In another beneficial reform, after 1924 girls could follow the same curriculum as boys at the secondary school level, thereby gaining access to a university education. However, unlike women in Britain, Germany, and the United States, French women did not get the vote after World War I. The suffrage movement, which suspended its activities during the war, never recovered its strength. Many of the pre-war suffrage leaders had either died or shifted their energies to the growing international pacifist movement, and younger women had other priorities. The legislature also kept postponing the welfare legislation that would have better protected French children born after the war. France's indecisiveness about the proper place of women in society was typical of a decade that combined dynamism in many domains with deep resistance to change.

1919: FEARS OF REVOLUTION AND A SHIFT TO THE RIGHT

As soldiers began demobilizing, the French government faced the first of many crises that would erupt in the early 1920s: a major challenge from the ranks of the working class. The cooperation of workers had been essential to winning the war, and they were determined to win better working conditions and salaries with the return of peace. France did not experience the revolutionary turmoil of either wartime Russia or post-war Germany, but it did face major strikes in 1919 and 1920 that many thought might turn revolutionary. Men returned to jobs where wages lagged behind the cost of living; many joined France's major trade union, the Confédération Générale du Travail (CGT), whose membership tripled from 600,000 in 1914 to 1,800,000 in 1920. With the war over, there was nothing to restrain workers from protesting. The government attempted to head off discontent by passing the eight-hour workday in April 1919—which workers had been demanding for 30 years. The CGT nonetheless called a strike for May Day 1919, and some 500,000 demonstrators turned out.

In this militant climate, the November 1919 elections—France's first since 1914—returned the most conservative majority since the 1870s. Conservative republicans of all stripes had formed an electoral alliance known as the Bloc National, which preyed on ordinary people's desire to punish Germany for the war and fear of a Bolshevik-style revolution erupting in France. Socialists, women, and workers were the primary losers. Socialists, who had won 102 seats in 1914, dropped to 68 in part because they refused to ally with their traditional partners, the Radical Party. While they actually gained in number of votes cast, they were penalized by a new electoral system adopted in 1919 of voting for lists rather than single candidates. The Chamber of Deputies had overwhelmingly voted a motion supporting female suffrage in May 1919 to recompense women's war effort; but in the wake of the Bloc National's victory, this motion languished before the Senate until 1922, when it was rejected—and would continue to be rejected until after World War II.

A conservative majority also meant no new deal for France's workers. Dismayed by the Chamber's shift to the Right, 1.3 million workers launched a new strike wave after the November 1919 elections. The government of Alexandre Millerand reacted harshly by dismissing striking workers and sending in the army to quell any unrest. It became clear that neither the state nor employers were willing to continue the wartime policies of negotiating with workers. Thoroughly embittered by the strike failures, French workers quit their unions in droves; it would be another 10 years before organized labor recovered from its post-war defeat.

With the perceived threat of revolution quelled, parliamentary politics reverted to their pre-war pattern: the appearance of instability as governments came and went but considerable continuity in personnel as the same politicians shuffled in and out of the most important ministries. The extraordinary powers granted to the executive for waging war and saving the peace were rolled back, leaving the legislature once again supreme—and, as in the past, hardly ever able to act decisively. In the early 1920s the most pressing questions facing French governments were a combination of economic and foreign policy ones: how to collect reparations from Germany in order to rebuild France, and how best to preserve peace.

FOREIGN POLICY IN THE 1920s

In the early 1920s, economic questions dominated foreign policy as never before under the Third Republic, as statesmen attempted to come to grips with the enormous costs of World War I and to make Germany pay the bill. The war had hit no Western European country harder than France, in terms not only of the proportion of men killed, but also of material costs. In the northern departments occupied by the Germans, coal mines, houses, factories, public buildings, roads, bridges, and rail lines had all been destroyed, and millions of acres of farmland were out of production. France confronted the future 26 billion francs in debt, much of it borrowed from the United States, which now demanded repayment. The war debt in turn fuelled inflation, which shocked a nation whose currency had been stable for a century. For most men and women, it was an article of faith that peace would restore the franc to its 1914 value. Post-war governments thus remained committed to trying to prevent any further loss of value to the franc while also rebuilding, which meant borrowing more and more money while awaiting German reparations. France lurched from one fiscal crisis to another in the early 1920s, as conservative republicans and Radicals alike refused any new taxes, forcing succeeding governments to float new loans to cover escalating expenditures and the continuing deficit.

Much of the early post-war economic instability stemmed from the Bloc National's refusal to make hard economic choices out of the mistaken belief that German payment of war reparations would cover all costs. Hence the Bloc National remained determined to enforce all the clauses of the punitive Versailles treaty against Germany even if it meant that France would have to act alone. And, indeed, it soon became clear that when it came to the enforcing the peace, France would have to act without help from its wartime allies. In 1919, an isolationist U.S. Senate had refused to ratify the Versailles Treaty, thus nullifying an agreement that the United States and Britain would come to France's aid should it be attacked. Russia, now under the control of the Bolsheviks, was banned from the family of nations, and Britain chose to withdraw as well from European affairs. In its quest for security, the French government had little choice but to sign treaties with the weak and troubled nations of Eastern Europe: Poland, Czechoslovakia, Yugoslavia, and Romania. These security arrangements with unimpressive allies essentially left France on its own, should Germany's Weimar Republic violate the Versailles Treaty's harsh clauses. Given the treaty's extraordinary unpopularity in Germany, it was only a matter of time before such violations would occur.

One of the most contentious issues between France and Germany in the early 1920s was the occupation of the Rhineland (the area between the western border of France and the Rhine River), which was stipulated by the Versailles Treaty to last 15 years. German opposition to the French occupation forces was intense, and took a deeply racist and sexualized form reminiscent of World War I propaganda. The French troops sent to the Rhineland in 1920 included many colonial soldiers from sub-Saharan Africa. German war rhetoric had depicted these soldiers as bloodthirsty savages—whose presence in the French army proved how "de-civilized" France had itself become. These disturbing stereotypes resurfaced in the early 1920s. The young Adolph Hitler wrote in *Mein Kampf* that "the main artery of the German people flows through the playground of black African hordes"; however extreme, Hitler was hardly alone. In Britain and America campaigns were founded as well against the "Black Horror on the Rhine," as the French occupation was called, which "thrust barbarians . . . with tremendous sexual instincts into the heart of Europe."[2] Such language revealed deep insecurities internationally about the ability of Europeans to rebuild their countries and maintain their empires, after so much loss of life during four and a half years of total war.

Franco-German tensions—and the racist rhetoric—escalated even further in May 1921, when the reparations figure for Germany was set at a staggering figure of 132 billion marks, or "over twice the pre-war German national income."[3] This war bill further inflamed extreme nationalists in Germany, who were determined to terrorize their own government if it accepted such terms. Yet Poincaré's conservative government would tolerate nothing less from Germany's new Weimar Republic than full compliance. France in the early 1920s still suffered from a "war mentality [that] underscored French weakness and the potential for German resurgence."[4] The stage was thus set for a new showdown between the two formerly warring nations. The catalyst came, tragically, in June 1922, when two right-wing German officers assassinated German Foreign Minister Walther Rathenau—himself a strong advocate that Weimar should pay its reparations bill in full. Within months, the Weimar Republic defaulted on its payments to France. In January 1923, in keeping with the "make Germany pay" and "go-it-alone" nationalism that had brought the Bloc National to power, Poincaré retaliated by ordering French troops into the Ruhr industrial district in Germany to seize in kind—principally coal—the reparations that Germany owed France. When German miners protested the occupation by refusing to work, Poincaré replaced them with French ones, at an additional cost to the French taxpayer. In order to provide money to its striking workforce, the Weimar government then printed money until it became worthless—and produced the legendary hyperinflation that permanently alienated so many Germans from their young Republic.

The French occupation of the Ruhr had momentous consequences for the international post-war order, and for France's place in it. The imminent collapse of the German economy forced the United States and Britain back into European affairs, threatening to recall their loans to France, and refusing to consider requests for new loans, until the reparations question had been solved. France, in short, could no longer impose its will on the continent. The French franc fell a further 46 percent in value in 1924, and Poincaré ultimately withdrew French troops from Germany—with little to show for the occupation. An international commission, led by American banker Charles Dawes, was then convened to work out a new reparations regime, based this time on international loans, new taxes, revenues from railroads, and a realistic assessment of Germany's economic capability. Germany would pay less, in exchange for guarantees that the scaled-down scheme would be enforced. In 1925, reparations finally began trickling in to France, due in part to American loans to Germany. France's financial crisis was not yet over—it would only really end with Poincaré's stabilization of the franc in 1928. A major source of tension between Germany and France had nevertheless finally been removed.

Despite the humiliating way in which it had been achieved, the resolution of the reparations question ushered in a much more constructive era in Franco-German relations. Poincaré's retreat from the Ruhr briefly brought to power the only leftist government of the decade, the Cartel des Gauches, a coalition of Radicals and socialists led by Radical Edouard Herriot. The Cartel lasted just two years and was wrecked when French bankers sent their badly needed capital abroad on the grounds that any government supported by "reds" would jeopardize their wealth. But its Foreign Minister Aristide Briand would stay put for an unprecedented six years (1925–1931), with full support from Poincaré, who became prime minister again from 1926 to 1929. An early advocate of the political and economic federation of Europe, Briand embodied an important and idealistic new current of opinion that believed that international cooperation could prevent future war. Nationalism and even patriotism had emerged from the war tainted, especially on the Left, and pacifism and internationalism took their place. The cornerstones of international cooperation were the new League of Nations in Geneva and disarmament, both of which Briand ardently supported. He was fortunate in having an equally skilled, practical, and long-serving German "internationalist" counterpart: Gustav Stresemann, chancellor of Germany between August and November 1923 and foreign minister in all subsequent German cabinets until his death in 1929.

Together Briand and Stresemann forged what has come to be known as the "Locarno spirit," predicated on integrating Germany into the rest of Europe through a generous revision of the Versailles Treaty. In 1925, they negotiated a treaty between Germany and its Western neighbors guaranteeing their mutual frontiers, the Locarno Pact. In 1926 Germany was allowed to join the League of Nations. In August 1928 Briand helped to broker the Briand-Kellogg Pact, by which the major European powers, the United States, and Japan all agreed to renounce war as a means of settling international differences. Although unsuccessful, it would form the basis of the United Nations Charter after World War II. In 1929, again at Briand's urging, the Allies signed the Young Plan, which hastened the end of military occupation of the Rhineland in Germany; by 1930 the Allies had withdrawn all their troops from German soil five years ahead of schedule, and Germany had agreed to the Rhineland's continued demilitarization. A large number of French and German associations across the political spectrum, from teachers' unions to industrialists' and economists' groups, supported these hopeful initiatives to foster a permanent peace in Europe. In the realm of internationalism, an unusual consensus transcending the traditional Left-Right divide had been achieved by the end of the decade.

DOMESTIC POLITICS: REALIGNMENT ON THE LEFT

Despite certain continuities with pre-war patterns, there were several new developments in France's domestic politics in the 1920s. Perhaps the most radical change was the birth in 1920 of a communist party in France, in the wake of the Bolshevik Revolution of 1917, and the division of the Left that it caused. Indeed, such division was one of the reasons the center Right was able to dominate post-war politics. After his successful seizure of power, Lenin formed the Third International and invited all existing socialist parties in Europe to join it. Adhesion to the Third International, Lenin made clear, would mean complete subservience of French socialists to Moscow. At their annual conference in 1920, members of France's unified socialist party, the French Section of the Workingmen's International (Section Française de l'Internationale Ouvrière or SFIO), gathered in the city of Tours to consider Lenin's invitation. To join the International on Lenin's terms would be to repudiate the SFIO's time-honored tradition of democratic governance of their party. Yet at a time when details about mass starvation and the civil and class war unleashed by the Bolsheviks were still relatively unknown, Lenin's revolution also stood out as a beacon of hope in a dismal French post-war landscape of worker retrenchment.

At Tours, a majority of socialists voted to accept Soviet conditions and to form a new party, the French Communist Party (Parti Communiste or PC) loyal to the Third International; this majority took with it the SFIO's newspaper L'Humanité. However, a rump of socialists under the leadership of Léon Blum, successor to the murdered Jean Jaurès, proved unwilling to compromise their freedom and remained in the SFIO. The trade union movement also split, as its revolutionary members left the General Confederation of Labor (Confédération Générale du Travail or CGT) to form the pro-communist General Unified Confederation of Labor (Confédération Générale du Travail Unitaire or CGTU) in 1922. The schism

The Tours Congress, Ho Chi Minh (1890–1969), from *L'Humanité*, December 1920.
Bibliothèque Nationale, Paris/Archives Charmet/The Bridgeman Art Library.

at Tours meant that France now had two parties on the Left—a socialist one and a communist one—and a fragmented union movement, thus ending the unity that Jaurès had worked so hard to achieve in 1905.

Despite the schism, the SFIO soon recovered the ground that it had lost at Tours. Blum in 1920 had retained the allegiance of most of the deputies elected on the socialist ticket (54 out of 68), as well as France's socialist mayors and trade unions leaders and the majority of its regional newspapers and weeklies.[5] This committed hard core worked successfully throughout the 1920s to restore the party's appeal. By 1924 the SFIO had approximately 60,000 members and represented a far more important political force than the PC, whose membership had dropped to 40,000; by 1933 SFIO membership had climbed back to 131,000. The party's new newspaper, *Le Populaire,* also extended its readership, especially after Blum became its political director in 1927. The nucleus of SFIO support was the same industrial and agricultural workers as before the war, and the party gradually expanded to include civil service workers, white-collar employees, and various other groups from the lower middle classes.[6]

While still Marxist in theory, the SFIO in practice remained reformist rather than revolutionary, much as it had before the war. Under Blum's leadership, the SFIO hewed closely to the ideals embodied by Jaurès. Blum—an intellectual who like Jaurès had trained at the elite Ecole Normale Supérieure but who lacked the warmth and exuberance of his predecessor—was in every sense Jaurès' disciple. As Blum put it, socialism was "a morality, almost a religion, as well as a doctrine." To be a socialist one only had to follow the voice of one's "conscience," because socialism was "the product of justice and pity." For Blum socialism was to play the role in modern life that religion had played during the Middle Ages, and unite people in the name of "ideal purposes and the collective good."[7] Such humanist overtones remained incompatible with the orthodox Marxism and the tenets of violent class struggle that the new PC was embracing.

Yet while all French socialists shared certain fundamental values, they nevertheless divided on the best political tactics to adopt in 1920s, and it took all of Blum's formidable intellectual skills to keep the party intact. On the one hand, there was a left wing, which excluded any collaboration with a "bourgeois" government and reaffirmed the revolutionary orthodoxy of the party and its proletarian base. On the other hand, there was a reformist wing, which was ready to collaborate with governments led by Radicals in order to broaden their appeal to the middle classes and to work for reforms for workers. And there was a center, represented by Blum, who tried to preserve the unity of the party by forging a compromise that the SFIO would remain committed to the "conquest of power" and the revolutionary transformation of the existing order. But if the opportunity arose, it could "exercise power" in the existing system by forming a cabinet on its own. Meanwhile, the SFIO should not repeat its 1919 mistake of trying to go it alone in elections. Rather, it should enter into coalitions with other parties—principally the Radicals—while refusing to accept ministerial positions should the coalition win.[8] An alliance of Radicals and socialists, the Cartel des Gauches, successfully defeated the conservative Bloc National in 1924.

THE CENTER RIGHT: RADICALS AND CONSERVATIVES

The rise of the politically extreme PC affected France's other traditional party of the Left as well: the inaptly named Radical Party, which now lost its "radical" edge and moved to the center of the political spectrum. In the 1920s, the Radicals became the party of the republican establishment, with most of the same leaders as before the war. Their politics consisted principally of "letting sleeping dogs lie."[9] They were the party of backstage maneuvers, of political compromises and pragmatic solutions, not of long-term plans or far-reaching ideologies. Their support tended to come from the middle classes of France's many small towns. In certain respects, the Radicals had become another conservative party—but what they wished to "conserve" was France's revolutionary heritage and the republican ideals epitomized during the Dreyfus Affair. They thus continued to oppose state bureaucracy and stood for the individual, the virtues of self-help and voluntary associations, pro-natalism, internationalism, and peace. Anti-clericalism remained key to the Radicals, who continued to oppose what they viewed as the Catholic Church's "obscurantism." Such views led the Radical Party, for example to reject women's suffrage, on the by-then dubious grounds that women overwhelmingly would vote for parties closest to the Catholic Church. Given the Catholic Church's loyalty to the Republic throughout the war, Radical leaders' continued anti-clericalism grew increasingly out of touch with the concerns of ordinary citizens in the 1920s, who saw the volatile economy rather than the Church as the greatest threat.

Between 1920 and 1924, Edouard Herriot, a man of letters and president of the Radical Party, reorganized it to include 70,000 members grouped in 500 committees. The party structure nevertheless remained weak and left room for many indepen-dents who, although running on Radical lists, could then migrate toward other parties of the Left or to the Right. In the early 1920s, the Radicals allied with the moderate wing of the trade union movement, the CGT, and participated in the Bloc National conservative government (1919–1924). Between 1924 and 1926 Radicals led the Cartel des Gauches. In 1928 they chose to ally with the conserva-tives and became junior partners in a new government led by Raymond Poincaré. The Radicals would not win another election until 1932, when—at the height of the Depression—they again returned to power in alliance with the socialists.

In contrast to the Radicals, the conservative republicans who dominated in 1920s France were defined less by their membership in a particular party than by their origins and shared outlook. Their emblematic figure was Raymond Poincaré, whose political career spanned the period between 1887 and 1929. As president of the Republic from 1913 to 1920, Poincaré had played a decisive role in France's entry into the war, the creation of the *union sacrée,* and the peace settlement. In the 1920s he emerged as France's leading politician, serving as prime minister from May 1922 to June 1924 and again from July 1926 to July 1929. Poincaré drew his primary support from industrialists, large landowners, and moderate Catholics. This rallying of Catholics to the conservative Republic was partly due to the common experience of all French men in the trenches and partly due to legislation favorable to the Church passed by the Bloc National in the early 1920s. Religious orders were now tolerated; the 1905 law on the separation of Church and State was not extended to the recovered territories of Alsace-Lorraine; and in 1921 diplo-matic relations with the Vatican were restored.

Conservatives in the 1920s stood for many of the same bourgeois and repub-lican values as the Radicals: patriotism tempered by internationalism, economic liberalism, preservation of the unity, quantity and quality of the French population, and separation of Church and State.[10] Yet there remained key differences. Some conservatives endorsed female suffrage for the same reason that Radicals opposed it: They assumed women would vote for them. Conservatives were also more pre-pared than Radicals to expand the role of the state in the economy, the government, and the private lives of citizens. Poincaré was the first prime minister to introduce career civil servants into his cabinet, on the grounds that they were doers, rather than talkers.[11] And he successfully pushed for an increased role of the government at the expense of the legislature and made use of decree laws (not subject to parlia-mentary debate and thus not involving parliamentary responsibility)—a precedent that all governments would follow in the crisis-ridden 1930s.[12]

Under Poincaré's energetic leadership, the old Left-Right divisions in France seemed to recede in the second half of the 1920s. Parliament embarked upon a period of dynamic internal reform that paralleled its successful policy of Briandism abroad. One of Poincaré's principal accomplishments was to restore confidence in the franc, whose value had plummeted again in 1926. Through the use of decree laws, Poincaré cut spending and instituted higher taxes. In 1928 he abandoned once and for all the attempt to restore French currency to its pre-war level and devalued the franc. A monetary law set the franc's value at approximately 20 percent of the pre-war value. Currency devaluation was a bitter pill for many French to swallow, since it eroded their savings; it nevertheless boosted economic growth by making French goods cheaper on foreign markets and reducing debts incurred by investors.

With a stabilized franc at home, and a successful policy of reconciliation with Germany abroad, conservative republicans and Radicals found the political will to work together in two other areas: education and welfare reform. In 1924 girls' public *lycées,* or high schools, adopted the same curriculum as boys' schools; in 1930, *lycées* became tuition-free. And in 1928 and 1930, France's first safety net of medical insurance and pensions for workers finally passed, funded not only by deductions from earnings but also by contributions from employers. In 1932 family allowances, additional sums added to wages for employees with two or more children, pioneered by private industrialists in the North and the Paris basin at the turn of the century, became compulsory for urban and industrial employers. This contributory program, with employers, employees, and the state paying into a fund, was meant to ease the economic burden of raising children and thereby reverse France's declining birthrate.[13] All of these measures represented small but important steps in building the comprehensive welfare system that still exists in France today.

ECONOMIC MODERNIZATION

France by the mid-1920s was well on the road to economic recovery, and even prosperity. In 1923, French gross national product (GNP) returned to its 1913 level, and although it then remained stagnant, in part due to the continuing instability of the franc, between 1928 and 1930 the French economy surpassed its pre-war level by a dramatic 33 percent. As before the war, its technologically most advanced sectors led the way. Through continued economic concentration in its pioneering steel and automobile industries—accelerated during the war—France acquired second place worldwide in metallurgy. Electricity from hydroelectrical stations, chemical products, and the building and cement industries also boomed. These advanced sectors were based in huge factories that used new American methods for rationalizing production, including efficiency studies, scientific management, the assembly line, and payment by productivity, inaugurated by Henry Ford and Frederick Taylor. Many of these techniques, often referred to as "Taylorism," had been introduced in government-owned plants during the war to meet the extraordinary demand for munitions, transport, and other war materiel. Whereas textiles had accounted for half of all industrial work in the nineteenth century, by 1930 textiles and metal working each accounted for a quarter of the industrial workforce. Two symbols of industrial concentration and plant modernization in the 1920s were the giant Renault automobile plant in the Paris suburb of Boulogne-Billancourt, with a workforce of over 30,000, and the Citroën automobile factory at the former munitions plant on the Quai Javel, also on the outskirts of Paris. Both companies had converted to American-style mass production of munitions during the war, and their owners emerged as veritable apostles of rationalization.

Economic growth in the late 1920s physically altered France's landscape and transformed a portion of France's working class. New urban centers developed around key industries, while the spatial distance between rich and poor increased in large cities. Large concentrations of male and female workers, fresh off the farm or boat, were now relegated to "red belts" around cities such as Paris, Lyon, and Marseilles. Crammed into high-density suburban slum dwellings with little privacy or modern sanitation, these supposedly dangerous and left-leaning elements were segregated from the middle and wealthy classes inhabiting France's increasingly affluent urban downtowns. On the job, young rural women were segregated from men, both by the more menial tasks they were assigned and by their lower pay.

Male or female, a new type of factory worker was emerging, semi-skilled, tied to the mind-numbing grind of the assembly line, and much less autonomous than the craftsman of the nineteenth century. As Georges Navel, who moved from job to job in the 1920s, wrote later about life at the Citroën factory, "Even more than the urging or the bosses, it was the drum-beat of the machines that speeded your movements. . . . [W]hen I left the factory it had entered into me. In my dreams I was a machine. The whole earth was nothing but an immense factory."[14] In the 1920s, factory workers in huge plants represented 20 percent of the industrial workforce. At the other extreme, however, 34 percent of France's labor force worked for small firms with fewer than 10 employees. French industry thus continued to be a dramatic mix of traditional and modern, a pattern that would not change until after World War II.[15]

Continuing another trend of the war years, France's new industrial workers in the 1920s were often immigrants. France in the 1920s became Europe's foremost melting pot, in response to the desperate need for foreign workers to compensate for the 1.4 million war dead. By 1931 France was home to 2.7 million immigrants, or about 7 percent of the population. In that year it surpassed the U.S. rate of foreign population growth, "a demographic shift unknown in other European nations before the Second World War."[16] Immigrants, who were usually single males, came from Italy (perhaps a third), as well as Poland, Belgium, and Spain, and to a lesser extent from French North Africa. Armenians from Turkey and Russians fleeing persecution from the Soviets arrived as well, since republican France traditionally offered asylum to all refugees. France's Jewish population increased in these years from 150,000 to 200,000. By 1930, immigrants represented around 15 percent of the workforce, and in mining and heavy industry their numbers reached 40 percent. In many large factories, especially automobile plants, they outnumbered French nationals by the 1930s. Most immigrants were guaranteed social rights due to treaties worked out between their home governments and that of France; the one exception were colonial subjects from the French empire, who ironically—because they were not citizens—had no claim to rights of any kind while working in France.

The government initially assumed these "guest workers" would be temporary; but the recovering economy continued to require immigrant labor. As a result, the legislature passed a very liberal naturalization law in 1927 making it possible to become a French citizen after only 3 years of residency instead of 10, and encouraging immigrants to start families in France or to bring their families with them. With this decision, immigration became a permanent structural aspect of French society in the twentieth century. While the new arrivals caused periodic outbursts of xenophobia, there was no revival of the vicious anti-Semitism of the Dreyfus era, and the spirit of the 1920s was on balance one of tolerance at a time of full employment. Tolerance, however, did not mean integration or prosperity for those who migrated to cities. Cut off from their roots, whether in the provinces or abroad, and from the rest of society, most of France's new industrial class did not profit from the economic recovery of the late 1920s, when their wages barely rose; they exercised little political clout and suffered mostly in silence.

Rural France presents a markedly different picture from the modern industrial sector. Here traditional patterns persisted, despite a continuing rural exodus into the cities and gradual disappearance of the most precarious farms over the course of the decade. In 1914 half of France's population earned their living off the land or from the rural professions, a proportion far higher than in other industrialized nations; in 1931 for the first time there were more town-dwellers than farmers. Peasants in the 1920s did not necessarily mechanize; production returned to pre-war levels but did not exceed it, and farmers still consumed much of their own production. Yet rural France, far from being denigrated for its "traditionalism" in the 1920s, became an object of curiosity, affection, and protection among French literati, state policy-makers, and the bourgeoisie. In their new cars, many well-to-do city-dwellers devoted Sundays or holidays to exploring France's regional cultures and village rituals and celebrating this diversity as a key element of what made French civilization so unique.[17] Typically these observers showed no real understanding of most farmers' harsh existence.

WOMEN'S ROLES: THE ADVENT OF MODERNITY?

Economic restructuring in the modern sectors of the economy, based on American models of efficiency, was one of the war's many consequences. Americanization, as it came to be called, had a profound albeit uneven effect on French social life and cultural practices, depending on one's social class, gender, and age, and whether one lived in the city or the countryside. One cultural change often associated with

Americanization was the emergence in the 1920s of the French version of the modern woman known as the flapper—or *la garçonne* in French, which translates loosely as a woman looking and acting boyishly, in other words, independently. French women after the war changed their appearance and behavior in startling ways. They began bobbing their hair; wearing shorter skirts and trousers; smoking cigarettes; taking up sports, including—for the bourgeoisie—driving automobiles and flying airplanes; going to the cinema alone; and dancing to the tunes of the Charleston. Contemporaries, especially conservatives, were profoundly shocked: Women seemed to be not merely acting like men, but trying to look like them. French civilization, they argued in a massive outpouring of commentary on the subject, was threatened by this assault on the natural gender order. As war veteran and author Pierre Drieu la Rochelle angrily wrote, "this civilization no longer has clothes, no longer has churches, no longer has palaces, no longer has theatre, no longer has paintings, no longer has books, no longer has sexes."[18]

While hardly liberated, there is no question that some younger women, particularly in urban areas, were determined to secure new ways to have fun after the austerity of 1914–1918 and to build on the independence that many of them had gained after managing four and a half years without fathers, husbands, and brothers.

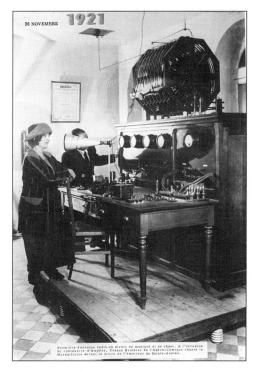

First French public radio broadcast from the radio station of Sainte-Assise on November 26, 1921. CNAM, Conservatoire Nationale des Arts et Metiers, Paris/Archives Charmet/ The Bridgeman Art Library.

And as these women rejected the authority and culture of their elders, society sometimes met them halfway. For example, new organized youth movements for girls, typically connected with religion, emerged in the 1920s. In 1927 the Young Christian Workers (Jeunesse Ouvrière Chrétienne or JOC), a social movement to rechristianize young working-class men, was founded, as was a separate branch for young women, the Young Christian Working Women (Jeunesse Ouvrière Chrétienne Féminine or JOCF). Similar groups formed for other segments of this age group, including the Young Christian Students (Jeunesse Etudiante Chrétienne or JEC) and the Young Agricultural Christians (Jeunesse Agricole Chrétienne or JAC) for rural youth, each of which had a sister organization for young women as well.

Keeping boys and girls, young men and young women separate was intended in part to prevent male domination within the groups and allow female leadership to emerge. These groups prized adventurousness and a can-do attitude and allowed girls to engage in a collective experience for the first time outside the home. Neither the male nor the female sections were overtly political; they principally sought to bring youth into contact with the Church by Christianizing the workplace, the village, or the university. But these organizations were radical in the sense of giving young girls in particular a new sense of worth and preparing them to take on more social responsibilities later in life outside the family.[19] As one young female working-class recruit put it: "The priest took the trouble to see me on my own. He got me to talk about the factory, my work, my problems. It was certainly the first time a priest had taken any interest in my work and listened to me."[20]

Given the number of male war casualties, interwar France had a surplus of women who had no choice but to support themselves; in addition the precarious economy for much of the 1920s meant that many less well-off women continued to work in factories or other menial jobs after marriage. Most middle-class married women entered sectors considered appropriate for women, since these jobs presumably required such "female" qualities as caring, nurturing, and educating the young: nursing, education, office work, and especially social services. France had a dense network of charities and social services going into the war, almost completely staffed by women. In the pro-natalist atmosphere of the post-war decade, public and private social services expanded even more dramatically. None of these sectors was perceived to threaten masculine identity or disrupt women's primary role as homemaker; in the case of office work, women always remained at the bottom of the career ladder. While increasing numbers of better-educated women joined the liberal professions, their numbers remained painfully low. In 1934, only 600 out of 25,000 doctors were female, and there were just five university professors.[21] Women intellectuals of the era were never as prominent as their male counterparts.

Among rural women, perhaps the most important change introduced by the war was the spread of urban medical practices to the countryside, particularly with respect to pregnancy, nutrition, childbirth, and childcare. Whereas their illiterate grandmothers and mothers had relied upon midwives and religion to see them through the complications of childbirth, younger rural women schooled by the Third Republic began seeking out the advice of doctors during the war years. They grasped the importance of modern hygiene and sterilizing against germs and also had the extra income—thanks to the wartime flow of cash into farmers' hands—to afford doctors' fees. First-time fathers serving in the trenches alongside older men from different parts of France often benefited from the child-rearing experiences of the latter, and some passed what they learned on to their wives in their many letters home. Aware of their own mortality, young soldiers then encouraged their wives to protect each precious child born during the hostilities—when the birthrate decreased by 40 percent—at any cost. Rural women's embrace of modern childcare methods became a national trend after 1915.[22] In 1911 infant mortality rates in France were 15.7 percent, in 1921 they had dropped to 11.6 percent.[23]

French feminists in the interwar years, while disappointed by the failure of women's suffrage and never able to recover the organizational strength they had achieved on the eve of the war, did not give up the struggle for the vote. A suffrage bill was put forward in the Chamber of Deputies almost every year between 1920 and 1936 with considerable support across the political spectrum, blocked each time by the Radical-dominated Senate.[24] As in the past, the feminist movement remained divided in ways that reflected larger fissures in French society. Feminists on the Left sought to improve the lives of female workers first and foremost. Mainstream republican feminism, led after the war by Radical party member Cécile Brunschwig (she joined the party despite its anti-suffrage stance) until her death in 1946, was pragmatic and reformist. A well-connected member of the Dreyfusard intelligentsia, Brunschwig hoped to render women's suffrage less threatening by proposing that the vote be granted in stages, starting at the local level. Republican feminists also sought to improve women's civil rights while waiting for the vote, for example, demanding equal opportunities for women in France's liberal professions. In the 1930s, internationalist-turned-feminist Louise Weiss challenged Brunschwig's gradual approach to the suffrage by turning to direct action—again to no avail. All feminists in the interwar years ran up against the fierce opposition of those who preferred to maintain women in their traditional role in reproduction and domesticity, and who worried that granting more rights would lead women to refuse marriage or motherhood or to abandon their families and homes.

FRANCE AND ITS EMPIRE

After World War I, France's governing elites agreed that the empire was more valuable and necessary than ever, for a combination of economic, diplomatic, and ideological reasons. Economically, the various colonies became an important source of raw materials, as well as a protected market for French manufactures; by 1939, 40 percent of French exports went to the empire, and the empire provided 37 percent of French imports.[25] Diplomatically, the empire shored up France's prestige as a global power, on a par with the British, particularly after the humiliating withdrawal from the Ruhr in 1924. Ideologically, committed republicans believed that France more than ever had an opportunity and an obligation to spread the material benefits of progress and civilization to what were still viewed as the "backward" peoples of the globe. The new League of Nations reinforced this belief; the French, Belgians, and British had been given their League Mandates over the former German colonies in the Middle East and Africa, on the understanding that the international community would enforce good imperial governance. Colonial subjects could report abuses directly to the League, and it was expected that all Europeans would become better colonizers than in the past.

The renewed emphasis on empire had direct implications for the peoples of the empire, positive in theory but mostly negative in practice. In the poor sub-Saharan colonies, where most French were either merchants or imperial administrators, the latter retreated from an earlier promise to extend citizenship to the minority of young Africans who had acquired a French education and were living in new imperial cities like Dakar and Brazzaville—a group designated paternalistically as *évolués* (the culturally evolved). The French claimed that these men were only "half-civilized" and thus not ready for modern political rights. In their place, the colonial government emphasized the need to preserve "authentic" African cultures and to ally itself with older conservative rural elites. Economically, the French adopted a new policy of agricultural *mise en valeur,* or rational economic development, predicated on building more railroads, more healthcare facilities, and more schools for their subjects and expanding cash crop production for export. France insisted that it owed the colonized these improvements as a reward for their wartime sacrifices, and planned to pay for them with reparations from Germany. When these reparations failed to materialize, administrators resorted to forced labor—usually facilitated by their new allies, the local chiefs—and abandoned their welfare projects.

In the richer overseas territories of Indochina and Algeria, the outcome was slightly different. In Indochina, rubber and rice exports rose spectacularly in the 1920s but failed to produce a significant increase in general prosperity; the profits went mostly to French plantation owners and a small Indochinese bourgeoisie, peasants were squeezed, and working conditions for rural and industrial laborers remained horrific. Here too a rigid and authoritarian colonial bureaucracy failed to alleviate the growing pauperization of workers or to meet the aspirations of French-educated younger people for better lives and greater autonomy. The successful modern nationalist movements in Japan and especially China in the early twentieth century had encouraged such aspirations among the Vietnamese earlier than anywhere else in the French empire. Yet rather than consider democratic reforms, French imperial authorities after the war continued to prop up the historic royal sovereigns in Cambodia, Laos, and Annam while divesting them of any real power and to staff their administration at the local level with pro-French Chinese-educated mandarins.

In the three French Algerian departments of Oran, Algiers, and Constantine, too, there was a dramatic expansion in agricultural output—principally in wine production—on modernized and large-scale farms concentrated in the hands of about 26,000 settlers, or *pieds noirs*. By 1930 Algeria's *pied noir* population had risen to 833,000, most of whom, however, had abandoned farming and moved into colonial coastal cities like Algiers, Constantine, and Bône to become modest tradesmen or civil servants. At the same time, better healthcare introduced by the French meant improved life expectancy for Muslim Algerians, and their numbers had grown close to 6 million in 1921. Throughout the interwar years the number of native Algerians continued to rise, while the European population remained stable.[26] The booming wine industry coupled with indigenous population growth had a mixed impact on the local Arab and Berber Muslims. On the one hand, continued land concentration in the hands of French capitalist farmers trans-formed ever larger numbers of Algerian peasants into landless proletarians. On the other hand, some new economic opportunities opened for Algerian workers in the cities and in France, at least until the Depression. Yet urbanization, mobility, and new job opportunities for younger French-educated Muslims only fed demands for more and better schools, jobs, and rights, all of which the French administra-tion failed to deliver.[27]

A small number of republicans on the Left who had traveled to the empire criticized this continued pattern of colonial exploitation, particularly in sub-Saharan Africa where there was no settler lobby to thwart reformers' efforts. Yet rather than challenge the right of a democracy to govern another people by force, these critics sought only to shame the French government to live up to its civilizing promises, convinced that colonialism would reform itself if the glare of negative publicity was strong enough. In 1921, France's most prestigious literary award, the Prix Goncourt, thus went to a black author from Martinique who had briefly served in the colonial administration in Africa, René Maran, for his novel *Batouala*. The novel combined a crude ethnography of the people of equatorial Africa with a vicious indictment of French rule there. One of the most celebrated foreign cor-respondents of the day, Albert Londres, also published a lurid and in-depth exposé of conditions in much of West Africa in 1928 in the popular Parisian daily news-paper *Le Petit Parisien*. Londres, who had spent four months traveling in Africa, concluded that slavery in the French colonies had only been abolished on paper. André Gide provided a scathing first-hand account of private rubber companies in Equatorial Africa in his memoir *Voyage to the Congo* (1927). These accounts kept the issue of colonial reform alive among the Radicals and socialists, who agitated for improved conditions for colonial workers and the extension of democratic freedoms to the empire. But with the conservatives monopolizing power in the 1920s, no such reforms materialized.

Also making reform unlikely was a flood of racist stereotypes in France throughout the 1920s—the same ones that surfaced in other countries when French African troops occupied the Rhineland. Popular and scientific literature warned in particular of the dangers of miscegenation between whites and blacks—"an ugly word" meaning the "interbreeding of people classified as belonging to different races."[28] Pulp novelists, doctors, and certain social scientists claimed that sex across the racial divide would lead to a further degeneration of the white French "race," already weakened by the bloodletting of the war. Louis Vignon, a lecturer at the Ecole Coloniale, the training school for French overseas administrators, wrote that "people of mixed race were infertile hybrids made unstable by the 'conflict of heredities.'"[29] Advertisers for many products played on racial stereotypes. One brand of soap, for example, purveyed images of Africans as dirty by virtue of their skin color, scrubbing themselves in the hope of becoming white.[30] These images in part reflected anxieties about whether colonial troops would return to their subordinate "place" in the empire, after their experience of serving on the Western Front. The fact that in the 1920s more French women were accompanying their administrator husbands, or traveling to the colonies alone, also seems to have encouraged the emergence of racialized and sexualized stereotypes. Images of dirty or dangerous Africans and Asians served subliminally to remind women that they had to preserve their distance from the colonized, in order to keep white French prestige in the empire intact.

Yet in other ways these racist images were the product of broader intellectual developments in post-war France. Whereas the Radicals and socialists remained committed to the republican view of the nation as a community of equal citizens open to all throughout the 1920s, including recently naturalized foreigners, many conservatives found a racial definition of the nation, reminiscent of that used by the Right during the Dreyfus Affair, increasingly compelling. For example, the professional ethnographer and deputy in the Chamber, Louis Marin, used his study of folklore in the interwar years to argue that France's civilization was the unique product of generations of ethnically pure French born on French soil. In the 1920s, such theories were the stuff of academic debates rather than the view of the government, whose immigration policies remained liberal; nevertheless Marin's racialized view of the nation had the stamp of scientific credibility, which would make it all the more seductive when tough economic times returned.[31]

Against this mixed backdrop of both reformism and racism, the French government launched its first-ever mass propaganda campaign in the 1920s to sell the idea of overseas France to its citizens. This campaign culminated in two separate but equally grandiose Expositions: first, a centenary celebration in Algiers in 1930, commemorating the conquest of Algeria and its incorporation into the nation due to the efforts of its white settler population; and second, a monumental Colonial Exposition in Paris in 1931 dedicated to displaying the "civilizing" efforts of France throughout its vast empire, which 8 million French attended.

Learned conferences on Algeria's past and the construction of new public buildings in Algiers formed part of the year-long commemoration of Algeria's conquest. The most vocal *pieds noirs* in Algeria wished to impress upon their fellow French, often traveling to Algiers for the first time at the time of the centenary, the achievements of this newest part of the national territory—l'Algérie Française— after 100 years of colonization. Organizers presented French Algeria as primordially modern and "Latin" in culture—that is to say, Mediterranean and Christian—just like any other southern French province. The official commemoration excluded

COMMISSARIAT DU MINISTÈRE DES COLONIES

PALAIS PERMANENT

SECTION DE SYNTHÈSE

LA
PLUS
GRANDE
FRANCE

EXPOSITION COLONIALE INTERNATIONALE 1931

Poster for the Paris Colonial Exposition, 1931. Bibliothèque Historique de la Ville de Paris, Paris / Archives Charmet/The Bridgeman Art Library.

any reference to Algeria's pre-1830 Ottoman past or Islamic culture. Buildings and monuments commissioned for the celebration reflected this exclusively "Latin" identity: They were resolutely high modern—a testament to French Algeria's supposed economic vitality—whitewashed, and devoid of any traces of the Islamic architecture that characterized the city before the arrival of the French.[32] Already marginalized economically and politically, Arab and Berber Algerians thus saw their cultural traditions erased at the centenary. The message, clearly, was that Algeria in 1930 was largely a French creation, which would always remain an integral part of the French nation.

The 1931 Colonial Exposition in Paris provided yet another showcase for empire. Here, too, according to Commissioner Marcel Olivier, the object was to place "before the eyes of its visitors an impressive summary of the results of colonization, its present realities, its future."[33] It projected a vision of a Greater France, in which the metropole and colonies were united as one; in this vision, however, the colonized were not effaced as in Algiers, but rather subordinated to the French. The Exposition took the form of a tour around a miniature empire. A separate pavilion represented each colony, and native craftsmen as well as their crafts were put on display. The central attraction was a full-scale reconstruction of the twelfth-century Cambodian temple of Angkor Wat, which the French administration had begun restoring. In this instance, the implicit message was that even the parts of the empire that had once had magnificent civilizations of their own were now so decadent that they needed modern French know-how to preserve their pasts. The overall image of the Exposition was that of an ethnically diverse but politically unified imperial nation-state, centralized under the guidance of the French, without whom the peoples of the empire would never advance. When exactly these "primitive" Africans and Pacific Islanders, "exotic" Indochinese, and "orientalised" Muslims from Tunisia and Morocco would be considered "mature enough" to rule themselves was left unaddressed.

While it is always difficult to know how such imperial propaganda was received, it appears that, particularly in the case of the very well-attended 1931 Colonial Exposition, a number of ordinary French men and women for the first time responded to the Republic's attempts to forge an emotional bond with the empire. Working-class boys, impoverished peasants, and middle-class women alike could imagine escaping their limited prospects at home for careers overseas. Some popular attitudes even challenged the racism of elite politicians, propagandists, and scientists embedded in the fair. A poll conducted by a new women's magazine in 1928 was revealing on this score. It asked its readers whether they accepted the idea of marrying a person of color. Of those responding, 1,060 out of 2,040 rejected the idea, worrying that children of mixed race would not be accepted or that blacks were "naturally savage"; as one put it, "I like *café au lait* [coffee with milk] but not in the cradle." Yet 980 respondents accepted the principle of mixed marriage—as long as the man in question was a good husband.[34]

A NEW COSMOPOLITANISM?

In the 1920s, a need to bury the painful memories of the war, the advent of Taylorized industries, the influx of foreigners, and the growing visibility of the empire created the conditions for a new cosmopolitan culture to begin to take root in France. People from all walks of life were exposed to—and willingly embraced—ideas, images, and technologies that expanded their horizons beyond those of rural or even urban France. The American loans that helped finance France's rebuilding introduced more pervasive and seductive advertising as well as new forms of mass entertainment, including the spread of movie theaters and radio broadcasting. Cinema was the most popular new form of mass entertainment. Residents of the working-class suburbs of Paris went to see French, American, German, and even Soviet movies. The biggest box-office hits in cities and small towns alike were historical epics like Abel Gance's *Napoléon* (1927), screen adaptations of classic or modern novels, and in the 1930s light-hearted comedies starring Fred Astaire and Ginger Rogers, the Marx Brothers, or Maurice Chevalier. The appearance of radio gave a further impetus to mass culture by broadcasting results of sporting events like soccer, tennis, and boxing. In 1921, Parisians gathered in the streets to await the result of the "match of the century," between American boxer Jack Dempsey and Frenchman Georges Carpentier.

While a newspaper for auto and cycling aficionados, *L'Auto-Vélo,* had created the Tour de France in 1903, by the 1920s radio broadcasts changed the public's experience of the event, allowing them to experience the Tour as it unfolded and to hear interviews with the racers immediately following each stage.[35] The radio also serialized mystery and adventure escapist novels, the most popular of which were *Fantomas* and *Arsène Lupin.* Singers Mistinguett and Maurice Chevalier became radio stars in the 1920s, and Tino Rossi in the 1930s.[36] In 1930 there were 500,000 radio receivers in France, and the French could tune into one state-owned station and many private ones. In 1932 there were more than 2 million registered radio owners, and in the 1930s radio became an important part of government or party propaganda.[37]

Radio and cinema did not, however, displace newspapers. Circulation increased after the war, and a new tabloid press was born—as significant in its impact as the earlier emergence of the penny press. In the mid-1920s the six major dailies in Paris had readership that fluctuated between 500,000 and 1.5 million each, while smaller papers—ranging from those associated with a specific political point of view and literary or religious weeklies to scurrilous scandal rags—also proliferated. This increase, too, was driven by rationalization and new technologies, such as the wirephoto, the commercial 35mm Leica camera, and the first flash bulbs. After the war, the rising cost of newsprint, the devaluation of the currency, and the vastly increased size of the printing runs led to new economies of scale for the big dailies. Papers had to maintain circulation or shut down, and the fact was that scandal and the *fait divers*—brief news stories, usually lurid—sold papers best. The introduction and popularity of photojournalism and newsreels also transformed how news was communicated. Sensational photographs splashed across the front pages told the story instantly, leaving less room for actual reporting.[38] News, in short, had become even more of a commodity, to be packaged in as alluring a way as possible. Overall, the post-war boom in radio, film, and photojournalism vastly expanded the opportunities to influence—for both better and worse—populations confronted for the first time with such extensive modern means of propaganda in peacetime.

Among the glittering avant-garde in Paris—which remained the cultural capital of the West in the 1920s—cosmopolitanism took a different form. A new generation of French intellectuals emerged from the senselessness of war more convinced than ever that bourgeois faith in reason and science was misplaced, and was determined to find more "authentic" experiences, art forms, and philosophies in unconventional and exotic places.[39] Their quest was helped by the flood of talented artists, poets, and writers who flocked to Paris from abroad in the 1920s, including from the United States. The most spectacular rejection of middle-class materialism and conventions came from a fringe group of artists and poets known as the Dadaists and their successors, the Surrealists. The Dadaist movement was initiated in 1916 in Zürich by Romanian expatriate Tristan Tzara, who then brought Dadaism to Paris in 1920. "Dada" could mean "yesyes" in Romanian, or a "hobby horse," or baby talk.[40] Tzara saw conventional literature as a "museum of words" that had to be destroyed in order to liberate human creativity. "Let every man cry: there's a great destructive, negative job to do . . . : Abolition of memory, DADA; abolition of archeology, DADA; abolition of prophets, DADA; abolition of the future, DADA . . . Liberty DADA, DADA, DADA," wrote Tzara in his *Dada Manifesto 1918*.[41] The sheer apparent meaninglessness of the term was intended to provoke the establishment; indeed Dada had as its only program a lack of program. More a "happening" than a literary movement, Dadaism tried to avoid becoming pinned down either aesthetically or politically.

Three young French poets, André Breton, Louis Aragon, and Philippe Soupault, enthusiastically joined Tzara's Dadaist movement in Paris in the early 1920s. However, they soon grew dissatisfied with Dadaism's pure negativity and in 1922 launched their own "Surrealist revolution." In the interwar years, almost every major French writer went through a Surrealist phase. Surrealists differed from Dadaists by drawing deeply upon the writings of Freud, seeing in the release of subconscious drives the key to producing true art.[42] In his 1924 *Manifesto of Surrealism* Breton called for an exploration of the unconscious, analysis of dreams, and "automatic writing . . . dictated by thought, without any control exercised by reason, without any aesthetic or moral concern."[43] Surrealism drew in painters, too, such as Giorgio de Chirico, Max Ernst, Juan Miró, Salvador Dali, and René Magritte; photographers, such as Man Ray; and sculptors, such as Jean Arp. Many of these writers and artists also turned to Oceanic and African artifacts—masks and sculptures in particular—and to American jazz music, and a craze for so-called primitive art and jazz together swept the capital. Intellectuals believed that both somehow provided access "to a more fundamental relationship to experience and emotion" than the cultural conventions of the West with which they had grown up.[44] This positive valuation by the avant-garde of the primitive was another voice combating the overt racism of the empire.

Along with painting and sculpture, cinema too became a popular medium of Surrealist artistic expression. The most famous Surrealist movie was the 1929 *An Andalusian Dog*, directed and produced by Luis Buñuel and based on a screenplay by Buñuel and Dali. The movie featured a Surrealist dream sequence involving such shocking scenes as a man slicing the eyeball of a young woman, a hermaphrodite playing with an amputated hand and then being run over by a car, a dead mule on a piano, and an ending shot of a young woman and her companion buried to the waist in the sand and devoured by insects under a hot sun. The movie had no "logic" or story line, but like primitive art it was supposed to shock the viewer's psyche and unleash the dreams and possibilities that had been stifled by reason's horrifying dominance in modern life. The premiere of the movie, recalled Buñuel, was a high society event whose "applause disarmed me."[45]

Another manifestation of post-war cosmopolitanism was the development of a new school of cultural anthropology devoted to preliterate societies and predicated on fundamentally different principles than the essentializing ethnography of

Louis Marin. Prominent Sorbonne philosopher Lucien Lévi-Bruhl published in 1922 a treatise on non-Western cultures entitled *Primitive Thought* in which he celebrated the ostensibly mystical, affective, and prelogical qualities of African and Oceanic cultures. The comparison with France was obvious: Were not the "civilized" and "logical" imperialist nations the true barbarians? Might not French civilization have something to learn from the "savages" inhabiting its empire? And were not all great civilizations the result of contacts and exchanges? While *Primitive Thought* was popular reading among the Surrealists, Lévy-Bruhl also attracted a dedicated following among French university students. The late 1920s and early 1930s witnessed the first serious academic study of the peoples beyond Eurasia by some of the most talented young thinkers of the interwar generation, including Claude Lévi-Strauss, Jacques Soustelle, and Germaine Tillion.

Yet the quest for meaning among intellectuals disillusioned with traditional French civilization after the war did not always lead to a positive evaluation of "other" cultures; post-war revulsion with the West could take the form of nihilistic despair. The most celebrated example of such despair was the brilliant writer Louis Ferdinand Céline. Céline, a medical doctor, was a wounded veteran of World War I who traveled widely and worked in rural public health clinics in the 1920s. His revolutionary use of popular *argot*, or slang, helped to express a deep loathing of the so-called civilized world that had produced the war in the first place. Peace, Céline made clear, was no different than war. Both were nightmares filled with millions of suffering and diseased human beings—whether soldiers or the poor. His pervasive nihilism found powerful expression in his famous first novel, *Voyage to the End of the Night,* published in 1932. In the words of his admiring contemporary, Drieu la Rochelle, Céline took the only path available to an honest writer, that "to spit, only to spit, on the condition that one produce a Niagara of spit."[46] Céline was also deeply misogynist, anti-Semitic, and racist, blaming the Jews for leading Europe into war in the first place and exalting the world of men. While the Surrealists and cultural anthropologists would mostly gravitate to the Left, Céline would provide intellectual fuel for the far Right in France—which began to revive in the mid-1920s.

CHALLENGES TO THE REPUBLIC

The combination of conservative rule at home; the pursuit of cooperation with, rather than revenge against, Germany; the consensus on empire; the return of prosperity for the middle classes; and Paris' innovative art scene gave the Third Republic every appearance of stability in the second half of the 1920s. Underneath its surface calm, however, France was home in these years to a number of new political currents that challenged the status quo. These included the development of extreme parties on both the Right and the Left and the development of anti-colonial nationalism overseas.

Before the war, the Action Française had alone occupied the far Right in France. In the early 1920s the Action Française still boasted some 20,000 members,

but its intellectualism and monarchism was too old-fashioned for a new generation nurtured on the violence and propaganda techniques of the Great War. In the
mid-1920s a small number of short-lived extra-parliamentary and paramilitary
leagues emerged in France to compete with the Action Française on the far Right;
these intensely nationalistic leagues were modeled on Mussolini's Black Shirts in
Italy, and like them attacked the perceived enemies of the middle classes—principally socialists and communists—through street violence. The victory of Herriot's
Cartel des Gauches in 1924 provided the immediate impetus for the formation of
such leagues in France.

Industrialists fearful of a communist takeover typically bankrolled these
leagues.[47] For example, millionaire Pierre Taittinger (of champagne fame) founded
the Jeunesses Patriotes in 1924, whose youthful members used direct action against
the communists in the name of national defense. Numbering as many as 65,000 in
1926, they wore a uniform of blue trench coats and Basque berets. George Valois
founded another league called the Faisceau in 1925, also to struggle against
Bolshevism and to offer a nationalist alternative to both it and the Third Republic;
underwritten by the perfume magnate René Coty, the Faisceau had some 60,000
members in 1926. Valois loathed Jews, foreigners, Protestants, and Freemasons—
and the Republic they ostensibly controlled—contrasting them with devout,
Catholic, hard-working French people by birth and blood.

Despite their rapid growth and impressive numbers, these groups proved
short-lived. Their followers tended to be unemployed youths, a small number of
veterans yearning for the masculinist ambiance and violence of the army, and
members of the lower middle classes hurt by inflation. Support for these leagues
diminished noticeably during Poincaré's second premiership from 1926 to 1929.
Industrialists and bankers were reassured with a conservative republican in charge,
and France once again enjoyed prosperity. Without massive economic dislocation,
the anti-democratic and ultra-nationalist spirit of the leagues had little chance of
taking root among the majority of French conservatives the way the Fascists had
in Italy. There were also too many of these fringe groups for any one of them to
gain momentum: The Faisceau collapsed in two years, and the Jeunesses Patriotes
abandoned much of its anti-parliamentary rhetoric while Poincaré was in power.
Finally, in France, most veterans—a key constituency for Mussolini's brand of fascism—would have little to do with the leagues and their taste for street action.
France's 3 million veterans formed their own associations after the war, making
theirs a far larger movement than any party or union. These veterans' associations
stood for pacifism above all else and rejected politics in general as divisive. Veterans
were overwhelmingly from the humbler ranks of the peasantry and smaller businessmen, the backbone of the Republic, groups that had prospered in France's
democratic society since 1870. Veterans' associations in the 1920s thus remained
loyal to the Republic, for which they had sacrificed so much and which reflected
their own values and interests.

The waning of the leagues' appeal coincided with a setback for the older
Action Française as well. In 1926 Pope Pius XI condemned the organization for

violating Christian values. The most conservative Catholics in France had long assumed that their religious faith was incompatible with the liberal values of the Republic, and many had supported the anti-democratic and anti-Semitic politics of the Action Française. The papal condemnation opened the way for some of these Catholics genuinely to reconcile with the Republic and to throw their energies into carrying the teachings of the Catholic Church into all aspects of society. Yet while the anti-republican extreme Right receded in the 1920s, it did not disappear; indeed its leaders remained only too ready to take to the streets against communism and France's republican institutions, should the need—in their estimation—again arise.

The evolution of the PC also posed a challenge to the Republic over the course of the post-war decade. In the early 1920s the PC had appeared to be the more dynamic and popular of the two parties on the Left in France. After the SFIO-PC split at Tours, membership in the SFIO stood at between 30,000 to 35,000 members, compared to an estimated 120,000 defections to the PC. Yet the communists' divisive political tactics had quickly cost them much of their initial popularity, except among a dedicated hardcore. In keeping with Soviet directives and strict Marxist orthodoxy, the communists had immediately turned their backs on traditional French patriotism, abandoning the republican anthem "La Marseillaise" for the communist "Internationale" and the French tricolor for the red flag of international worker solidarity. In 1923 the PC had urged French soldiers occupying the Ruhr to fraternize with the enemy. French communists also regularly denounced the vote and the press, central to the Republic, as mere "tools" of the ruling classes. In 1928, the PC went a step further and adopted a new Stalin-inspired line of "class against class" during elections. They began ordering communists to oppose all socialist candidates as greater class enemies than candidates on the Right because the socialists supported reform rather than the violent overthrow of capitalism. Communists hoped to convince rank-and-file socialists and workers in general that only the PC stood for their interests and that socialists in the National Assembly were in fact "bourgeois enemies." Only a truly proletarian revolution could emancipate workers and create a more just society.

These sectarian stances, along with the party's bureaucratic structure and silencing of all dissent, soon alienated a large percentage of those who had joined so precipitously in 1920. In 1933, the PC membership had dropped from its high of 120,000 a decade earlier to 28,000. But what it lost in numbers, it made up in commitment from those who remained. In the late 1920s the PC began organizing in the new working-class urban suburbs and impoverished rural communities ignored by every other party and promoting workers there to party leadership. The "red belt" of Paris—the suburbs around the new car factories where an estimated 1 million workers and their families lived in the interwar years and which represented the largest zone of working-class settlement in France—was the party's stronghold. The PC's organizing in the 1920s would pay rich dividends in the crisis-ridden 1930s, when a new generation of workers and peasants flocked to the PC. In 1931 31-year-old Maurice Thorez, a miner who had been won over first to socialism, then in 1920 to communism, and who had and rapidly risen through the ranks of the PC, became secretary general. The PC had a genuine worker at its head, which would add to the communists' prestige and credibility among France's working class when the Depression set in.

A third voice of radical dissent in the 1920s focused on the legitimacy of France's overseas empire. By the 1920s, Paris was home to a handful of young, often French-educated, anti-colonial leaders from different parts of the empire, who began to demand not only reform but also outright independence for their peoples. Several of these leaders had been radicalized by their participation in World War I, when they had experienced real equality with the *poilus* (infantry-men) in the trenches. Others had been recruited as laborers in France during the war and had discovered the political protests of the French working class. Still others had come to France as students. All were profoundly disillusioned by the refusal of colonial authorities to grant significant political freedoms either at the end of World War I or after, and they chose to stay in France because they could organize there politically more freely than in the colonies.

Some of these early nationalists discovered an invaluable ally in the new French PC. The PC, as part of its commitment to proletarian revolution everywhere, announced that it would work to emancipate colonized peoples, along with work-ers, from "bourgeois" European rule. The young Vietnamese activist and future revolutionary nationalist Nguyen Ai Quoc, who would soon change his name to Ho Chi Minh, was a founding member of the PC in Paris in the early 1920s, while a student. In 1930 Ho Chi Minh would help create the Indochinese Communist Party in Vietnam, which would be critical in leading the struggle for national indepen-dence. In 1926, the Algerian Messali Hadj drew upon help from the PC and support from fellow immigrants in Paris to found the Etoile Nord Africaine, the first Algerian nationalist organization. A small group of African workers in Paris seeking the con-tinued modernization of their homelands, rather than the conservatism and ruralism that the French colonial administration was embracing in the 1920s in West and Equatorial Africa and Madagascar, would also forge ties with the PC.

Yet not all anti-colonial nationalism in the 1920s took the form of political movements. Two distinctive cultural movements also emerged, one among black students in France, and a second one in Algeria among its religious doctors of law, or *ulama*. The first was the literary movement known as Négritude, founded by two brilliant students and poets, Léopold Sedar Senghor from Senegal and Aimé Césaire from Martinique. Négritude celebrated black cultural achievement, while still acknowledging the possibility of working with France. Also in the 1920s, Algeria's *ulama* (doctors of law) began articulating the notion that culturally, Algeria was a Muslim nation first and foremost—an idea decidedly at odds with the *pied-noir* notion of Algeria as an integral part of France, or, as they put it, Algérie Française. They too were disillusioned with French rule, and they encour-aged the birth throughout Algeria of cultural clubs to promote a purer form of Islam and pride in Algeria's own language—Arabic, own religion—Islam, and own Algerian nation.

The French government responded to the development of these anti-colonial movements by placing all foreigners, including colonial subjects, in France under surveillance—a fundamentally undemocratic practice previously reserved for suspected criminals.[48] And it ruthlessly suppressed any signs of political dissidence in the empire throughout the 1920s and 1930s. The French faced four major rebellions during these years, including the so-called Rif War in the Protectorate in Morocco (1925–1926) and a revolt in its mandate in Syria (1925–1926).[49] In 1930 a mutiny broke out in northern Indochina among Vietnamese soldiers serving in the colonial army at the garrison at Yen Bay in the Red River Delta, which lasted into 1931; and a three-year revolt in Equatorial Africa erupted in 1928. French authorities refused to believe that the masses mobilized in these uprisings had legitimate grievances against their imperial overlords or were capable of formulating political ideas such as a desire for self-rule. This repression, along with the shock of the Depression in the 1930s, would only serve to radicalize further the very anti-colonial resistance the French had hoped to contain.

In France, the colonial repression of the 1920s gave rise to one other form of protest. In 1931, the Surrealists mounted a French anti-colonial exhibit timed to coincide with the Colonial Exposition at Vincennes. Awakened to the abuses of colonialism by their new appreciation of African and Oceanic art, many Surrealists had joined the PC in the late 1920s, because of the party's anti-imperialism. They then began circulating manifestos for "the immediate evacuation of the colonies and the indictment of the generals and functionaries responsible for the massacres of Annam, Lebanon [sic], Morocco, and Central Africa."[50] In the same spirit, they decided that they had to organize a "Counter-Colonial Exposition" in 1931 in three small rooms in the heart of Paris—which is all they could afford. The exhibit was a modest affair compared to the grandiose architecture on display out at Vincennes, and had only some 4,000 visitors. But its message was radical for its time. The exhibitors placed European "fetishes" such as Catholic reliquaries alongside African and Oceanic sculptures, thereby proclaiming the equal value of the world's cultures, rather than ranking them—as at the official Colonial Exposition at Vincennes had—hierarchically.

CALLS FOR RENEWAL

For most of the 1920s, the common experience of memorializing the war dead continued to help bind the French nation together. "Pas d'oubli, non, pas d'oubli" ("No forgetting, no, no forgetting") was the unifying refrain uttered across the nation each year as November 11 approached.[51] But by the decade's end, the Great War's many unanticipated consequences were creating new divisions while perpetuating older ones. Between 1900 and 1939, France's population increased by only 3 percent, and that was largely the result of immigration, while that of Germany grew 36 percent. France also had more people over the age of 60 than any country in the world. The indirectly elected Senate continued to protect the interests of rural and small town France, and traditional party divisions guaranteed parliamentary paralysis. Socially, France remained a highly compartmentalized society, in which industrial workers and peasants had little contact with each other, much less with the more affluent bourgeois.[52] To many young men and women growing up under the influence of the new mass media and technologies, many imported from the dynamic and young United States, the Third Republic appeared to be in the grip of hidebound and unimaginative old men unable to change with the times.

Not surprisingly, then, in the late 1920s calls for political renewal began to emerge among all the republican parties. The Radicals' meager record of achievements in the post-war decade inspired criticism from within their own ranks. A group of "Young Turks," who included such younger deputies as Pierre Mendès-France, Pierre Cot, and Jean Zay, shared less a common program than a certain style and set of frustrations. They agreed that the nation needed a stronger more effective executive branch of government less dependent on the whims of a legislature unrepresentative of the country at large. A complex modern economy, they argued, required some kind of centralized planning and expert technicians to run it.

Among socialists, a new critical generation frustrated at Blum's policy of refusing participation in government emerged in the late 1920s: the so-called neo-socialists grouped around a prominent deputy from Paris, Marcel Déat. Like Blum, Déat was an intellectual. Yet his training had extended beyond philosophy to include sociology, and he used this training to criticize the party's reigning Marxist orthodoxy. The study of sociology had convinced Déat that socialists did not need to wait for the proletarian revolution, which would not happen anyway. Developing the notion that socialists should use the state to control capitalism to workers' benefit, Déat began to shift from far Left to far Right.[53] Eventually Déat completed the transition to fascism, arguing for strengthening the authority of the state in the name of a "national socialism" defined by "Order, Authority, Nation."[54]

Conservative republicans, too, cast about for new ways to govern France. When Poincaré finally resigned from politics in 1929, the energetic 54-year-old André Tardieu succeeded him. Tardieu was an unorthodox proponent of economic and political modernization, who became the dominant figure in French politics between 1929 and 1932. He expanded social insurance, raised the salaries of civil servants, and helped to extend electricity in the countryside, believing each of these public expenditures would enhance national prosperity. Tardieu also advocated uniting conservatives in a single party.

In a context of relative prosperity and peace these calls for renewal remained largely ineffective, and the Third Republic continued to drift. With the onset of a worldwide Depression, the rise of fascism internationally, and the threat of war in the 1930s, however, the demands for change became more strident and widespread. In particular, extremist elements on the Right began to profit from the escalating crisis and mounted a serious challenge to democracy itself. In the 1930s, the Third Republic would face a period of both economic downturn and political divisions far more severe than any it had previously known.

CHAPTER 8

The Republic in Peril
1929–1939

On February 13, 1936, the 64-year-old leader of the French socialist party (Section Française de l'Internationale Ouvrière or SFIO), Léon Blum, was returning home at midday in the car of his fellow socialist deputy Georges Monnet. Madame Monnet was also present. A crowd attending the funeral of Jacques Bainville—a journalist, historian, and one of the founders of the extreme right-wing movement Action Française—stopped the car as it arrived on the Boulevard Saint-Germain. Recognizing Blum, the onlookers besieged the car. Angry demonstrators first punched Monnet when he tried to reason with the mob, then turned on Blum as well as Madame Monnet. Seriously wounded and his face covered in blood, Blum decided that he and the Monnets should make a dash for safety. Protected by a few guards and workers from a nearby construction site, they found refuge in a building across the street as cries of "assassins," and "finish them" reverberated around them.

The attack was a sign of the times. By the early 1930s, French political life had again dramatically polarized and descended into street violence, in ways reminiscent of the Dreyfus Affair. This time, however, the divisions were not only between the Right and the Left but also among various factions on the Right and the Left, as each accused the other of betraying "the cause," or of being too moderate, or of selling out the nation. The hatred of nationalists from the Action Française for the Jewish socialist leader Léon Blum was often matched by that of the communists on the far Left, who believed that Blum was betraying the interests of the working class. In April 1935, far Right leader Charles Maurras wrote that Blum was a "naturalized German Jew" who deserved to be "shot in the back" for subverting France.[1] Communist Surrealist poet Louis Aragon was no less violent. In his 1931 poem "The Red Front" he wrote: "Fire on Léon Blum, / Fire on the performing bears of social democracy."[2] Meanwhile Blum saw the Radicals as proto-fascists, while Radical leader Edouard Herriot pointed out the hypocrisy of well-heeled socialists claiming to be for both democratic institutions and the dictatorship of the proletariat.[3]

Such political divisiveness reflected a new preference for ideological purity across French society in the 1930s and a growing taste for authoritarian over democratic political solutions to the Republic's many problems. The long-term roots of this radicalization lay in the brutalizing experiences of World War I, but the Great Depression that gripped the world after 1930 and the threat of another world war were the more proximate causes. As the economic prosperity of the late 1920s evaporated, groups on both the Right and the Left accused the established leaders of the Third Republic of being corrupt and ineffectual and cast about for radical alternatives to parliamentary politics as usual.

DEPRESSION

In 1932 the Depression arrived later in France than elsewhere, but it also lasted longer. As the Depression lingered, an economic and social crisis rapidly developed into a political and constitutional one. Economically, the nation did not recover from the Depression before the renewed outbreak of war in 1939, when its industrial production was still below the 1929 levels. The failure of recovery was due in part to the government's persistent refusal until 1936 to devalue the franc, despite devaluations of the pound sterling in 1931 and the dollar in 1933. As a result, French exports remained overvalued and noncompetitive, and by 1933 had fallen by two-thirds compared with 1928. Devaluation conjured up the inflation of the 1920s, which had left deep psychological scars among the millions of thrifty small property owners who had seen their savings evaporate. Bourgeois families living on fixed annuities had also seen their incomes, and thus their standard of living, decline. In the early 1930s, politicians compared the defense of the franc with the defense of Verdun.

Another peculiarity of the economic crisis in France reflected its dual economy, split between modern and rural sectors. The modern sector was unevenly affected. Among businessmen, the most modern enterprises—for example, car manufacturer Citroën—and the luxury export industries, such as French silk manufacturers, faced dramatic losses. Yet rather than imaginatively retooling to cater to the mass market in a time of falling prices, French car manufacturers continued to reject cheaper models in favor of expensive ones that were no longer selling. Unemployment at its peak affected 1 million workers, which although enormous, was significantly lower than in Germany, Britain, or the United States, in part because employers were able to send some foreign workers home. Indeed, one of the first anti-Depression measures was the passage of a law in 1932 designed to tighten up controls on immigration. Many other French workers returned to the farms that they had left 10 years earlier. Because prices fell, those who stayed on the job experienced an increase in real wages and so were comparatively better off than before.

In contrast peasants, shopkeepers, small businessmen, and artisans in the traditional sector—the very groups who made up the social base of the Republic—suffered from the beginning. The agricultural depression was particularly intense: Wheat prices fell by 40 percent and wine prices by 60 percent. Four out of six heads of rural households were out of work. Farmers tried to stock crops when they realized that they could not sell them without losing money, "but barns and silos ran over."[4] France's 2 million shopkeepers soon faced a new competitor, in the form of discount stores that promised low single prices, bought in bulk, and lured their customers in with rebates and free gifts. The proliferation of discount stores with names like Prisunic ("one price") and Monoprix ("the same price") threatened the very existence of small independent retailers. The government responded to deficits by tightening its belt and cutting the wages of middle-class public servants—another key constituency of the Third Republic. The crisis thus eventually affected important sections of the conservative and Radical electorate, without significantly weakening the strength of organized blue-collar workers. This outcome—unique to France—created the conditions for maximum social and political polarization, in which the Third Republic's "politics as usual" was the first casualty.[5] With democracies toppling across Europe in the 1930s, the Third Republic's ability to surmount this most recent series of crises was far from assured.

1932–1934: RADICALS IN POWER

For the governments dealing with the Depression, the most immediate impact was a drastic decline in tax revenues and the appearance of budget deficits, combined with rising social expenditures. Poincaré had led a conservative coalition to victory in 1928, but he himself retired due to illness in 1929; it was thus his conservative successors who dealt first with the crisis. They adhered to a policy of strict financial orthodoxy and deflation, raising tariffs to protect French goods and cutting spending. Both policies reduced consumption further, by raising prices while putting less money in the pocket of consumers. By 1932 voters were ready for a change; for the first time since 1924 the Radicals and socialists formed an electoral alliance that brought the Radical leader, Edouard Herriot, to power. But, again as in 1924, the left-leaning coalition failed to bring the economic crisis under control. Reflecting the Radical party's small-town and fiscally conservative base, Herriot also sought to cut government spending and reduce the deficit. The Radicals' coalition partners, the socialists, argued that this would only make the crisis worse, and they continued as in the past to refuse to take ministerial positions in a Radical-led cabinet. The result was deadlock. Six ministries rose and fell in 18 months, with no decisive action to address the crisis. Germany's dramatic election of Hitler in January 1933, in the midst of such government instability, only served to fuel a growing sense of panic among the French electorate.

Since the feuding political parties did nothing to solve the economic crisis, a power vacuum gradually opened in French politics. Soon the government faced a terrifying new threat, as competing groups of all kinds began to intervene directly into politics through street action. The year 1933 witnessed mass demonstrations, often violent, by new organizations representing such different constituencies as public employees, peasants, shopkeepers, and small businessmen. These were more than interest groups. In the crisis atmosphere of the Depression, they tapped into a growing sentiment of anti-parliamentarianism, anti-communism, nationalism, and anti-Semitism to become politically extreme. "We will converge on the lair which is called Parliament, and if necessary we will use whips and sticks" stated, for example, the National Federation of Taxpayers, an association that represented shopkeepers—a group which in the past had always supported the Radicals, and the Third Republic.[6]

Equally frightening were the anti-parliamentary and paramilitary leagues of the far Right. Although they had declined greatly in numbers and influence in the late 1920s, with the distress of the early 1930s the leagues revived and began to organize military-style demonstrations. These included the Jeunesses Patriotes, and especially the Croix de Feu, now under the leadership of World War I veteran Colonel de La Rocque. Smaller new groups also began to form in direct imitation of Hitler or Mussolini. Perfume manufacturer François Coty financed Solidarité Française, modeled on the Nazis, and Marcel Bucard founded the Francistes, which looked to Mussolini's fascism for inspiration.

One of the most debated questions in the history of interwar France is whether these groups on the far Right in the early 1930s (and their 1920s predecessors) can be called fascist, or are better described as quasi-fascist. Many scholars continue to see "the frontiers between authoritarianism and fascism [as] at best imprecise," especially in France where none of the competing groups on the far Right ever came to power.[7] Others typically identify multiple fascisms in Europe, with national variations each of which requires careful analysis.[8] But whether fascist or quasi-fascist, all extremist movements on the Right in Europe in the 1920s and 1930s shared certain similarities. These included "a dynamic stress on action and regeneration, the cult of leadership, and a populism which denounced parliament and political parties as out of touch with an imagined 'real' national community."[9] In their desire to overthrow the Republic and replace it with an authoritarian system, these extreme Right movements also always applied military values to civilian life, and blamed more harshly than traditional conservatives communists, socialists, Freemasons, internationalists, "and in many but not all cases Jews for most of the nation's ills."[10] In France, the Croix de Feu, the Francistes and Solidarité Française, and other similar groups consistently displayed these characteristics. And regardless of the labels historians choose to use in analyzing these movements, many people at the time, particularly on the Left, were convinced that these extremist groups posed a fascist threat to the Republic analogous to Mussolini and Hitler.

THE RIOTS OF FEBRUARY 6, 1934

Despite the warning signs that power in France was shifting to the streets in 1933, no one was prepared for what happened on the night of February 6, 1934 in the nation's capital. That evening, massed demonstrators erupted into violence in front of the French Chamber of Deputies in Paris. The police panicked and shot into the crowd. A pitched battle ensued for most of the night, in which hundreds of both rioters and policemen were injured. The demonstrators failed to breach the barriers protecting the Chamber, but a stunned nation awoke to the news that 14 people had been killed in the attempt and 1,500 wounded. Many assumed that the far Right had attempted a coup d'état and that the Republic was in imminent danger of collapsing.

The origins of the February 6 riots can be traced back to a parliamentary scandal that broke out in early January, known as the "Stavisky Affair." Alexandre Stavisky was an embezzler of Russian Jewish descent who in 1934 had used his connections with some minor Radical politicians to take control of the municipally owned bank in the small town of Bayonne. He had then issued millions of francs of fraudulent bonds in its name. Small-time savers had always favored investment in municipal credit, since towns had a reputation for investing cautiously. Ordinary citizens—who traditionally backed the Radicals—were thus Stavisky's chief victims, while certain Radical politicians were perceived to have made enormous profits. On January 9, Stavisky was found dead under mysterious circumstances, and the right-wing press reacted swiftly. Stavisky's "Jewish" friends in high places, they strongly suggested, had had him killed to avoid embarrassing revelations about their profiteering—proof that a cabal of Jews, Freemasons, and Radicals was ruling, and ruining, France. The communist daily, *L'Humanité*, drew a different but equally critical conclusion: This latest "Affair" proved that the whole bourgeois political system was bankrupt.

Poster on the bloody suppression of the demonstrations at the Place de la Concorde, Paris, February 6, 1934. Bibliothèque Nationale, Paris/Archives Charmet/The Bridgeman Art Library.

Influenced by this sensational reporting, public opinion took the bait, and pressure mounted for Radical Prime Minister Chautemps to resign. On January 27, 1934—after only two months in office—he stepped down, and two days later ambitious Radical politician Edouard Daladier replaced him. Daladier then dismissed Paris' conservative prefect of police, Jean Chiappe, known to be friendly to the right-wing organizations. This action triggered the February 6 riots. A broad but disorganized assortment of nationalist and authoritarian veterans' groups and leagues called for mass demonstrations to converge on the Chamber of Deputies. At the same time, the communists mobilized their own rank and file "to protest against the regime of profit and scandal," in the name of workers everywhere.[11] Far greater numbers than anticipated turned out on the night of February 6, and the uncoordinated marches soon escalated into a confused pitched battle with the police. Less than 24 hours later Daladier himself resigned, despite a vote of confidence from the Chamber. He believed that only a new and more "national," that is right-wing, government could restore order and confidence.

For the first time in the history of the Third Republic, street agitation had brought down a legally constituted government. For the moment, however, France avoided the complete collapse of democracy that had occurred in Italy and Germany at comparable moments of crisis. While the protests had been planned to dislodge the center Left from power, there was no right-wing leader waiting in the wings. With the Radical leadership thoroughly discredited, it fell to conservative republicans to try to restore confidence in the regime. They turned to a former president of the Republic (1924–1931), 71-year-old Gaston Doumergue, to form a new cabinet. Doumergue put together a "national union" cabinet in which traditional Radicals like Herriot sat side by side with visionary conservatives like Tardieu. Yet the return of a conservative government did not, as it had at a similar moment of economic and political crisis in 1926 under Poincaré, end either antiparliamentary agitation in the streets or France's economic problems. Conservatives would nevertheless remain in power for the next two years. During this time political divisions in France only deepened.

1934–1936: CONSERVATIVES IN POWER
AND RADICALIZATION OF THE RIGHT

Upon coming to power in the aftermath of February 6, 1934, the Doumergue government asked the legislature for and received the right to issue laws by decree to cut government spending and balance the budget. When the economy remained stalled six months later, he then proposed a constitutional reform to allow the president to dissolve the Chamber and hold new elections in the case of a vote of no confidence. According to Tardieu, "[N]either in the management of finances, the direction of the public mind, nor in the conduct of foreign affairs, is the elective regime, in its present form, sufficient to its task. . . Profound corrections are needed to save it."[12] For socialist leader Léon Blum, this measure sounded dangerously authoritarian, and he vigorously opposed it. Blum so alarmed the Radicals in

Doumergue's coalition that they withdrew their support from his "national union" government. Defeated on the question of constitutional reform, Doumergue stepped down, to be succeeded first by the conservative Pierre-Etienne Flandin (November 1934–May 1935) and then by the much-reviled and unpopular Pierre Laval (June 1935–January 1936)—a former Radical who had by now moved decisively to the Right.

On the economic front, Laval bypassed the legislature altogether, using emergency decree laws to continue Doumergue and Flandin's policy of deflation, cutting wages, raising taxes, reducing war pensions, and cutting the income on bonds by 10 percent, thereby drastically reducing public expenditures. France's civil servants experienced their first real pay cut since the start of the Depression. These measures, and the unemployment, small business foreclosures, and hardship they perpetuated, further alienated many people from the government. Under Laval's watch, the far Right that had erupted on the national scene on February 6, 1934, increased its numbers dramatically in the countryside and in the cities. In the summer of 1935 agitator Henri Dorgères founded a peasant Green Shirt movement, with the slogan "Believe, Serve, Obey," which grew from 35,000 members to 140,000 in its first few months. Dorgères was an advocate of a return to an "organic society" ruled by "natural elites" and a third way between capitalism and socialism, known as corporatism. Corporatism was based on class conciliation rather than class warfare and called for employers, managers, and workers, organized into "natural" economic groups by economic sector, to govern themselves and run the economy. Dorgères tapped in to the discontent of rural populations in the face of falling prices. His followers adopted the storm-trooper rituals, uniforms and emblems, and slogans and anthems reminiscent of the other fascist movements and leagues.[13]

By far the most dangerous development in the mid-1930s, however, was the expansion of Colonel de La Rocque's Croix de Feu. It grew from about 40,000 before February 6, 1934 to an all-time high of 400,000 and perhaps 500,000 members in early 1936.[14] The Croix de Feu was a nationalist and anti-democratic group originally made up of veterans, but which attracted many traditional conservatives after Doumergue failed to secure a strengthening of the executive in November 1934. It also had a wide following among French settlers, or *pieds noirs*, in Algeria. What was needed, these supporters claimed, was a new generation of "competent" men untainted by politics—men of action like the ex-army officer Colonel de La Rocque, an open admirer of Mussolini. The Croix de Feu fielded a paramilitary force that far exceeded any other organization and staged military-style parades and motorcades to intimidate workers in France's urban centers.[15] For an increasing number of French men and women frightened by the Depression and the February 6 riots, the authoritarianism of the Croix de Feu seemed the most promising way to rid the nation of its supposed enemies, restore order, and end the political and economic crisis.

From 1933 on, one such enemy whom it became more and more popular to blame was France's Jews. Since 1917, when the Bolsheviks had overthrown the

Russian tsars, overt anti-Semitism in France had been limited to the extreme Right, which identified the communists in France with the Jews and saw Jews as a foreign menace from whom the "true" French nation had to be protected. In 1933, however, the arrival of 25,000 Jewish refugees, mostly middle-class professionals, fleeing Hitler's Germany caused anti-Semitism to spread toward the center of the political spectrum. In a time of continuing economic crisis, these refugees were perceived as competition for French businessmen, lawyers, and doctors. French medical students began regularly to beat up foreign Jewish students at their universities. Fearful of alienating its middle-class constituencies if it did not agree to their demands, the National Assembly passed a law that limited the practice of medicine to French citizens. Conservative governments in 1934 and 1935 then signed legislation that barred even naturalized immigrants from these professions for 5–10 years following their naturalizations. These laws were of momentous significance; for the first time in the history of the Third Republic, a two-tiered system of citizenship had been created with regard to professional rights. Even though they bore the same obligations of citizenship, including military service, as all citizens, recently naturalized French citizens (usually Jewish) had fewer professional rights than citizens born in France.[16] Such overtly exclusionary public policies helped to make anti-Semitism more respectable in France and constituted one more sign that traditional republican values were under siege in the crisis atmosphere of the mid-1930s.

The escalating strength of leagues sympathetic to authoritarian solutions at home and abroad did not, however, go unanswered by France's major political and trade union leaders on the Left or by millions of ordinary French men and women who continued to defend republican ideals. Frightened by the violence of the February 6, 1934 riots and alarmed that France might go the way of Italy or Germany, the Radicals, the SFIO, and the PC put together an unprecedented electoral alliance whose goals were the preservation of peace and the reaffirmation of democracy at home and abroad. This alliance of the Left became known as the Popular Front. Against all odds, the Popular Front swept into power in May 1936, and Léon Blum, the leader of the SFIO almost beaten to death three months earlier, became the prime minister. While much of the rest of Europe was succumbing to Hitler's virulently anti-Semitic and racist brand of fascism, a majority, even if only a slim one, of Frenchmen voted into office the most broad-based liberal coalition of the entire history of the Third Republic, and placed a Jewish socialist at its helm. The Popular Front gave hope to many citizens in France that the Republic could be reinvigorated from below. But it also further terrified a broad segment of conservative French, who saw any alliance of socialists and communists as a threat to property and—especially when this alliance was headed by a Jew—as a further infiltration of France by "foreign" elements.

THE FORMATION OF THE POPULAR FRONT

The first inkling that a broad union of forces on the Left was possible came six days after the February 6 riots, when workers across France demonstrated against fascism.

The General Confederation of Labor (Confédération Générale du Travail or CGT) called for a general strike on February 12, 1934. Throughout France, all branches of the labor movement, along with the traditionally divided communists and socialists, marched together for the first time since 1920, to protest the leagues' attack on the Chamber of Deputies. Because of its unprecedented unity, February 12, 1934 instantly became one of the "great days" in the history of French labor. Yet despite this show of unity among the rank and file, deep divisions remained among the leaders of the two parties of the Left. The socialists remained suspicious of the communists, who since 1927 had been denouncing them as class enemies. And the communists for the very same reason were not sure they could trust the socialists.

Real progress toward forging an electoral alliance among the communists and socialists—and eventually the Radicals—to fight fascism only occurred after a revolutionary change in Stalin's politics in response to Hitler's rise to power in 1933. Hitler posed a dramatic new challenge to liberals and communists alike. The new German chancellor immediately eliminated his enemies, including the German Communist Party, and destroyed Germany's democratic institutions, before embarking upon a massive rearmament program. Most of Europe's liberal leaders failed in the short term to realize the full extent of Hitler's war plans. The Soviet dictator, Joseph Stalin, on the other hand, understood the need to contain Hitler, and so it was suddenly in the Soviet Union's interest to promote broad-based anti-fascist coalitions and to see all of the European democracies strengthen their armies. In a historic about-face in late May 1934, Stalin ordered communist parties throughout Europe to stop the destructive policy of attacking socialists who stood for election. Communists should instead unite with all the democratic parties and support policies of European national defense against fascism. In the wake of this dramatic decision, the leader of the French Communist Party (Parti Communiste or PC), Maurice Thorez, became one of France's most vociferous defenders of democracy against fascism, extending a hand not only to socialists, but to Radicals and Catholics as well. The popularity of anti-fascism among workers encouraged SFIO leader Blum to accept Maurice Thorez's new overtures, although with certain misgivings. After so many years of antagonism between the two parties, Blum questioned the motives of Thorez—and, behind him, Stalin. Despite these suspicions, on July 27, 1934 the SFIO signed a unity pact with the PC to present a common list of candidates in the next elections, scheduled for May 1936. Thorez next reached out to the Radicals, without whom the SFIO and PC could not win a majority. By dropping many of its traditional positions, such as hostility to military expenditures and economic provisions that antagonized the middle classes, and by couching their appeal in an unprecedented patriotism, the PC gradually won Radical support to the cause of an electoral pact as well. By the summer of 1935, former Radical premier Edouard Daladier was demanding a new left-leaning orientation for his party, as were Jean Zay and Pierre Cot, two younger Radical politicians deeply committed to republican renewal. With the Radicals actively cooperating, an organizing committee was set up in July to frame a common program and adopt a new slogan: "Bread, Peace, Liberty." Finally, in October 1935 the Radicals officially adhered to the Popular Front.

By January 1936, the organizing committee had hammered out the Popular Front program, which proved to be moderate in every sense. The common program called for a combination of political and economic actions. Under the heading "defense of liberty," the Popular Front promised to dissolve the paramilitary organizations, guarantee women's right to work and trade union rights, reform the press, provide equal access for all political organizations to government-run radio, and raise the school-leaving age. The Popular Front also urged a parliamentary investigation into the political, social, and economic conditions in France's colonies, particularly North Africa and Indochina. Under the "defense of peace" the Popular Front called for "international collaboration for collective security within the framework of the League of Nations" and for "automatic and unanimous application of sanctions in case of aggression."[17] At the same time and somewhat at odds with its previous clauses, it emphasized disarmament and the nationalization of all weapons industries. There was no call for constitutional reform—for the parties of the Left, the earlier efforts of conservatives to strengthen the executive seemed part of the fascist threat, not part of the solution to France's deep problems.

The economic provisions avoided any mention of social revolution; they focused instead on "the restoration of purchasing power destroyed or reduced by

"Le Front Populaire contre la Misère, le Fascisme, la Guerre, pour le pain, la paix, la liberté," cover of a brochure, 1936. Bibliothèque Nationale, Paris/Archives Charmet/ The Bridgeman Art Library.

the depression," a repeal of Laval's decree laws, a reduction of the workweek without a corresponding reduction in wages, adequate pensions, the establishment of a national unemployment insurance system, and a major program of public works. Although Blum believed that the nationalization of monopolies was essential to achieve political democracy and popular sovereignty, he agreed to leave any mention of them out of the program, so as not to alienate middle-class voters. Nevertheless, to protect the savings of ordinary people, the program stipulated that control of the privately held Bank of France would be removed from "the economic oligarchy"—a reference to the "200 families" who supposedly controlled the country's economic destiny.[18] And the Popular Front program promised not to devalue the overvalued franc, a campaign pledge that Blum would not be able to keep. In sum, the provisions of the common program made clear that the priority was preserving the Republic from fascism and preventing war, not substituting socialism for capitalism. In this sense it was, first and foremost, "a negative coalition."[19] It did, however, promise to introduce—if elected—immediate economic relief and long overdue social reforms, in order to give French workers and other unrepresented groups a stake in the Third Republic for the first time.

THE ROAD TO VICTORY 1935-1936

With this message of republican renewal, the Popular Front swept thousands of French people into politics between 1935 and 1936. Even constituencies without the vote, such as women, youth, and many anti-colonial nationalists in the empire, responded enthusiastically. The Popular Front also gained the support of groups unhappy with the government's deflationary politics and dedicated to peace. An early sign of this unprecedented unity and widening base of support was a massive Bastille Day parade on July 14, 1935, that the newly formed Popular Front organized to honor the Republic. Hundreds of thousands turned out in the name of bread, work, and peace, giving the Popular Front parties the appearance of an irreversible tide. Families brought their children, their presence a stark reminder of who would be the losers if the militaristic leagues were not stopped. It was a scene that was to be repeated over and over in the coming year, as peaceful pro-republican demonstrators reclaimed the streets of Paris and other urban centers from the paramilitary forces of the far Right. In yet another sign of cross-class and ideological solidarity, the red flag of militant labor commingled with the blue, white, and red tricolor of the Republic while columns of socialists and communists linked arms on their way to the *Mur des fédérés* in the Père Lachaise cemetery, symbol of the martyrdom of the Communards of 1871. At their head, Blum, Thorez, and Daladier marched side by side, raising clenched fists in salute to the gathered masses. The clenched fist would soon become the image of the newly united and confident Left in France.

The formation of the Popular Front coalition was not matched by a similar unity among the conservative parties on the parliamentary Right, who published no electoral program of their own. Instead they portrayed the Popular Font as the work of Moscow. And the anti-parliamentary extreme Right responded, predict-ably, with renewed street action and incitement to violence in its press. The Action Française intensified its anti-Semitism, whose virulence now surpassed that of the Dreyfus Affair. Léon Blum became the object of a particularly ferocious hate cam-paign, as the elections approached. It was on February 13, 1936 that the "king's camelots" (*camelots du roi*)—the Action Française's street gang—attacked and viciously beat Blum on the streets of Paris.

Yet by the spring of 1936, the Popular Front had become unstoppable, and in the second round of voting on May 3, the coalition scored an impressive victory at the polls. Since—against all predictions—the SFIO with 149 seats came in ahead of the Radicals with 116 seats, Léon Blum became the prime minister-designate. For the first time in the nation's history, the SFIO had become the leading party in the Chamber. Even more sensational was the rise of the communists, who took 15 percent of the vote and whose seats rose from 10 to 72. They made particular gains in industrial centers, while the socialists' gains came primarily from rural France, at the Radicals' expense. Settlers in Algeria elected 4 Popular Front depu-ties, out of a total 10 deputies. When all the Popular Front deputies were added up, they stood at 378 to 222 opponents. Among coalition members, only the communists refused to join Blum's government, but they pledged their full support.

Careful observers nevertheless pointed out that the rough division between Left and Right throughout the country had not changed much. If there was a uni-fied France of the Popular Front, it faced a second and very different France of equal strength, deeply hostile to the new government in power. Ominously, the stock market took a brief plunge after the elections. Despite the Popular Front's electoral triumph, it thus remained to be seen if it could stay together and lead, at a time of not only deep division within the country at large, but escalating threats from abroad.

MAY–AUGUST 1936: REFORM

A lawyer and an intellectual cautious by nature as well as by training, Blum was acutely aware of the limited mandate enjoyed by the Popular Front and of the need to reassure conservatives that he stood for democracy not revolution. His first move was to adhere to the constitutional procedure of waiting a month before the convening of the new legislature and the formation of a new government. Despite much urging from fellow socialists, Blum refused to take office during the month separating the May elections from the convocation of the new National Assembly. As he put it, the Popular Front government under the first socialist premier would take office "in the most normal, most legal way."[20]

Yet by waiting, he immediately lost the initiative to a militant social move-ment from below. Elated by the victory of the Left and determined to profit from a favorable political moment, the workers in the big new factories in Paris' and other cities' suburbs had spontaneously erupted into action. By June 1936, 1.8 million workers were on strike throughout France, in over 12,000 strike actions that constituted France's biggest strike wave ever. In a new tactic, workers joyfully occupied "their" factories and locked out their bosses, rather than simply staying home. The entire Renault factory at Billancourt, employing 30,000, was taken over by its workforce. Factory sit-ins gave the massive uprising a festival atmosphere reminiscent of the heady first days of the Paris Commune, as workers passed the days discussing, fraternizing, and singing. New members streamed into the unions. Photographers sensed that something new was afoot, and their riveting pictures of a work world turned upside down made instant headlines. The impact was seismic, and many on the Right assumed a Soviet-style revolution was imminent. Indeed, a minority of the strikers called for just such a revolution.

From the outset, however, the CGT leader, Léon Jouhaux, as well as PC leader Maurice Thorez rejected these calls outright. Neither wished for a revolution at this juncture, and both feared that the strike movement would go too far and compromise the Popular Front experiment before it had even begun. Blum too was adamant on this point: The socialists as well as the communists had pledged themselves to reform, to the exercise of power, not to its revolutionary conquest. "Our aim," he stated, "is not to transform the social system, it is not even to apply the specific programme of the socialist party, it is to execute the programme of the Popular Front."[21]

Mistinguett (1874–1956) singing for the strikers. Illustration from L'Illustré du Petit Journal, 1936.
Private Collection/Archives Charmet/The Bridgeman Art Library.

The strikes thus had to be brought to an end as quickly as possible. Blum was helped in the short term by employers, who, when faced with the unprecedented occupations of their factories, immediately capitulated, although they would never forgive the Popular Front for a strike wave that the government had done nothing to encourage. But in the heat of the moment they panicked and agreed to meet union representatives in the presence of Blum. On June 7, in a single afternoon, the two sides hammered out an unprecedented set of concessions, the Matignon Accords, named for the prime minister's residence where they were negotiated. For the first time ever in France, the Matignon Accords shifted significant power to organized labor. Workers were guaranteed two weeks of paid vacation, a 40-hour workweek, wage increases of 15–17 percent, recognition of collective bargaining and union rights, and no penalty for strike action. When the Assembly ratified the Accords later that month, labor returned to the workplace and the strikes ended.

With industrial peace temporarily restored, the government felt emboldened by the extraordinary scope of the Matignon Accords to push through another round of dramatic reforms. Never in peacetime had a Third Republic legislature ratified so many new measures as quickly as the Popular Front did from June to August 1936. While the Popular Front had earlier rejected the idea of a government-initiated economic plan, which CGT leader Léon Jouhaux had pushed for in emulation of the Soviet five-year plans, it went ahead and nationalized the Bank of France and the armaments industry and merged France's railroads into a mixed public-private enterprise. In another historic first, three women were made junior ministers in the cabinet: Radical feminist Cécile Brunschwig and Nobel Prize–winning chemist Irène Joliot-Curie, who was close to the PC, were attached to the Ministry of Education, and socialist militant and retired schoolteacher Suzanne Lacore joined the new Ministry of Public Health. Blum also dissolved the far Right leagues.

Also true to his electoral program, Blum convened a committee of experts and all of the high administrators from the colonies to explore how to end forced labor. He immediately supported the resurrection of a bill first introduced in 1931 by socialist deputy Maurice Viollette to allow the tiny minority of educated Algerians—a projected group of 21,000 out of a total North African Algerian population of 5 million—to apply for French citizenship without giving up their Muslim status.[22] Neither female suffrage nor decolonization was contemplated, and the Algerian settler lobby sank even this limited citizenship bill even before it could come to a vote, but the Popular Front had at least imagined a new deal for both women and colonial subjects. Blum also amnestied political prisoners across most of the empire, lifted press restrictions, authorized trade unions and political meeting, and launched surveys in West Africa and Indochina to collect data on living conditions, women's rights, and child labor. For many colonial subjects, too, the election of the Popular Front was a moment of hope.

Blum's minister of the interior, Roger Salengro, also took measures to ease the plight of a new wave of Jewish refugees seeking asylum in republican France, particularly after the passage of the Nuremburg racial laws in Germany in 1935.

In defiance of the hardening anti-Semitism of the right-wing press, the government endorsed the League of Nations' Geneva accords to issue identity certificates that protected refugees from expulsion; naturalizations of foreigners increased from 28,951 in 1936 to 48,630 in 1938.[23] As a British spokesman wanting to help refugees put it in February 1938, "when the Popular Front won its electoral victory, France regained her traditional mood of generosity to the victims of persecution."[24]

Equally impressive, the Popular Front developed youth, health, culture, leisure, and sport programs directed toward the masses. Both before and during the Popular Front, worker demonstrations became celebrations and family outings. The same "invisible" workers who had staged the factory "sit-ins" took to the streets of France's many downtowns with their wives and children, making politics a daily pageant. The Bastille Day parade of 1936 was, wrote the British journalist Alexander Werth, "the most immense procession Paris had ever seen."[25] Thanks to the 40-hour workweek and two-week paid vacations, workers had leisure time for the first time. Many working-class families had their first holidays ever and crowded onto France's beaches and other vacation spots that had previously been the exclusive province of the bourgeoisie.

Enthused by the worker élan of June, Blum demonstrated in his first months in office that a democratic state like the Third Republic could be as effective and as innovative as the fascist regimes of Germany and Italy, or the communist regime of the Soviets, in meeting the aspirations of ordinary people—especially young people—to participate in all aspects of the life of the nation, including high culture. The Popular Front created the position of undersecretary of the state for sport and leisure, and another one for scientific research. The minister of education, Jean Zay, vastly increased expenditure on the arts and education and raised the school-leaving age to 15. By promoting youth-hostel movements, workers' educational projects, and theater and film, the government hoped to break down artistic barriers between elites and popular audiences—a program many French intellectuals enthusiastically embraced. The films of Jean Renoir, who identified closely with the values of the Popular Front, are cases in point. His films *The Grand Illusion* (1937), a patriotic and hugely successful movie about World War I, and *The Rules of the Game* (1939), a scathing denunciation of upper-class moral disintegration, managed to combine a socialist commitment to celebrating the common man with high artistic values.

The Popular Front also wished to democratize France's long tradition of science and scientific discovery; to this end it opened two spectacular museums in conjunction with the 1937 World's Fair held in Paris: the Museum of Man, an anthropological museum that sought to teach an appreciation of non-Western cultures through the display of everyday artifacts, and the Palace of Discovery, devoted to astronomy, physics, and engineering. A third museum devoted to French folklore was created as well in 1937, with the explicit intent of reconciling republican universalism with regional particularism. Modern citizens were encouraged to come to know and value France's peasant heritage, not because it contained some mystical racial essence, but because disappearing rural folkways were understood to be a part of what had made French civilization unique in the first place.[26]

The dynamism of the Popular Front in its first few months proved that it had succeeded in integrating workers and youth into the Republic in ways that all previous regimes had failed. Yet the very breadth of popular support precipitated growing opposition to Blum's government. The far Right press began a vicious slander campaign against Roger Salengro, which drove him to suicide in November. After Blum banned the extreme Right's leagues, the latter reorganized into formal political parties. Late in 1936, Jacques Doriot, a former communist expelled from the party in 1934, founded the French Popular Party (Parti Populaire Français or PPF) explicitly to fight communism and promote fascism in France. Subsidized by a combination of bankers, steel magnates, and manufacturers from Paris, the North, Marseilles, and Algiers, the PPF recruited 70,000 mostly lower-middle class members within its first year. In late 1936, the older Croix de Feu ostensibly moderated its venom by transforming itself into a political party as well, the French Social Party (Parti Social Français or PSF). By 1937 it had an astounding 700,000 members. The PSF renounced violence, but it remained authoritarian and populist, ambivalent about democracy, and sympathetic to fascist Italy and Nazi Germany. In 1937 it had far more members than any other party in France, and it had become the largest party among the *pieds noirs* of Algeria.

ECONOMIC AND FOREIGN POLICY

Elected to defuse anti-parliamentary forces, the Popular Front within a year had only managed to increase the Republic's enemies. To understand this outcome, it is necessary to turn from Blum's domestic policies to his fiscal and diplomatic initiatives. In both cases Blum had less room to maneuver, having inherited a lingering Depression and a rapidly deteriorating international situation. The policies he adopted antagonized not only conservatives but also many members of his governing coalition.

Economically, Blum's greatest challenge was to deliver on his campaign promise of "bread and work" by ending the Depression; instead his policies perpetuated the crisis—although French businessmen and bankers were as much to blame for this outcome as the prime minister. As discussed previously, Blum chose initially to reverse the deflationary policies of previous governments and increase demand by raising wages through the Matignon Accords. And at first the Matignon Accords did stimulate the economy, by increasing industrial production, lowering unemployment, and giving people more money to spend. But this success did not last. Unfortunately, one plank of the Matignon Accords, the 40-hour workweek, undermined the success of its stimulus effects. It made no sense to increase demand and at the same time restrict the capacity of factories to meet that demand. In theory, the 40-hour workweek was to have provided jobs for the unemployed, but once an initial pool of about 70,000 workers had been hired, the rest of the unemployed remained out of work because they lacked the necessary skills.

Moreover, rather than pulling France out of the Depression, the increase in wages sparked inflation.

Blum then faced the difficult decision of whether to devalue the franc. At first he resisted devaluation, hoping to maintain business confidence. But in the fall of 1936, pressure on the franc and a rapid decline in gold reserves left him no choice but to devalue; the franc lost 25–30 percent of its previous value. Nervous French investors promptly sent their funds abroad, while continuing inflation ate away at savings and the pay gains workers had won in June. Strikes broke out in protest. Rather than imposing exchange controls to stop the capital flight, in March 1937, Blum announced a "pause" in the Popular Front's reform policies, hoping in this way to restore investors' faith in his government. The only tangible result of his pause was to disappoint his own followers further and fuel criticism from the communists, without winning over conservative republicans.

It was not only Blum's failure to end the Depression that increasingly disillu-sioned large swathes of opinion. Foreign policy developments beyond the control of any French government were also critical, and here too Blum's responses alienated right-wing sentiment and introduced deep divisions among the Popular Front parties. Hitler's escalating aggression in 1936–1937 presented the Popular Front with its most difficult challenge of all, in large part because the Radicals and socialists disagreed fundamentally with the communists on how to respond. Many Radicals and socialists believed, along with the British, that the best way to pre-serve peace was through accommodating Hitler rather than challenging him. This tendency first manifested itself before the elections that brought the Popular Front to power. In March 1936, in flagrant violation of the Versailles Treaty, Hitler had sent troops into the Rhineland, a demilitarized zone since France withdrew its soldiers in 1930. Although the communists had insisted on the need for decisive military action, French and British public opinion on both sides of the political spectrum had strongly opposed confronting Hitler for pacifist reasons, while the French general staff had argued that the army was not prepared to take the offen-sive. Prime Minister Sarraut had therefore deferred to the British, who refused any commitment to send troops and failed to confront Hitler's violation of the Versailles Treaty.

Allowing Hitler to remilitarize the Rhineland rendered any guarantee of French aid to its Eastern allies meaningless. In addition, the French government had set a dangerous precedent. Henceforth, France would refuse to make any major policy decision regarding Hitler without British consent, at a time when their British ally failed to understand the nature of Hitler's revolutionary fascism, ideological hatreds, and global territorial ambitions. Maintaining the Franco-British entente was considered the cornerstone of French foreign policy, even when Britain refused to commit to a formal military alliance. In Blum's own words, the Franco-British union of democracies "is and remains the primordial condition of European peace."[27]

The election of the Popular Front in France two months later initially seemed to promise a more resolute French stance against Hitler, now that the three parties of the Left were allied. Blum immediately launched an expensive rearmament program that in the short term brought no economic relief but in the long term would make France war-ready. Another international crisis in July 1936 over the fate of republican Spain, however, quickly revealed and exacerbated the pre-existing differences between a PC ready to stand up to fascism and their pacifist and internationalist Radical and socialist allies. A Left-oriented Popular Front government had been elected in Spain in February 1936, but the following July General Francisco Franco began a fascist revolt against it. The Spanish republican government sought arms from the Popular Front in France to fight Franco.

Blum faced a dilemma. Conservative republicans and most Radicals in France feared that aid to the Spanish would unleash an international war; the British opposed intervention as well. Surely, the argument went, if republican France came to the rescue of democracy in Spain, the fascist governments of Italy and Germany would intervene on the side of Franco. Many Radicals, in addition, found the Spanish republicans too leftist for their tastes. The large number of pacifists in the SFIO also preferred nonintervention. Only the PC uniformly argued for help to the Spanish republicans, as part of its policy to contain fascism everywhere before it was too late.

Leaving his fellow Spanish republicans in the lurch was deeply distasteful to Blum, but in the end he deferred to the Radicals and socialists in his government; in August 1936 he proclaimed a French policy of rigid nonintervention in Spain, hoping against hope that Mussolini and Hitler would do the same. Both dictators claimed to adhere to the policy, while covertly continuing to send arms and volunteers to aid Franco's forces. The Soviet Union, for its part, secretly intervened on the side of the republicans. Blum had hoped that his solution would preserve his coalition, but French communists opposed the policy of nonintervention and began to criticize Blum's government. Their willingness to risk war for Spain, in turn, only made many pacifists in the SFIO increasingly suspicious of the PC's intentions. Socialists feared that the communists might be using France to promote a war with Hitler that the Soviets secretly wanted. The Radicals, and especially the right wing of the party, were even more appalled by the stance of the communists. They already blamed them for the strike wave of June, which had sowed panic among the party's middle-class base, and now they too suspected the PC was trying to involve France in a European war. These mutual suspicions not only weakened the Popular Front during its first year in office but also meant that, outside of the PC, fewer and fewer voices in France were willing to stand up decisively to Nazi aggression.

DIVISION AND FAILURE

Less than a year after taking office, the Popular Front began to unravel under the divisive impact of the Spanish Civil War combined with monetary devaluation, resurgent strikes, and the loss of earnings. The changing mood became clear on March 16, 1937, when tragedy struck the streets of Paris. Colonel de La Rocque's right-wing Parti Social Français had announced a meeting in a cinema theater in

Clichy, in northern Paris. Communists and left-wing socialists decided to organize a counter-demonstration. When the counter-demonstration led to a clash between the supporters of the PSF and those of the Left, the police were called in. A pitched battle ensued between police and Popular Front supporters, with horrific results: 5 dead and perhaps as many as 200 wounded. Blum, who was at the opera, left his seat and hurried to the hospital as soon as he learned what had happened. Ironically, his midnight appearance, in tuxedo and tie, among the relatives of the wounded workers provoked only cries of indignation.[28] The next day the Left-leaning news-papers were full of photos of Blum with "the blood of workers" on his shirt.[29]

Three months later, Blum resigned from office when the Senate refused him new emergency powers to deal with the economy, despite the approval of the Chamber. The Senate's actions precipitated a constitutional crisis. Blum had three choices: He could resign; he could dissolve the Chamber, call for new elections, and hope for an even stronger majority that would have forced the Senate's hand; or he could have easily aroused the country to demonstrate en masse—workers were eager to defend the gains they had made under the Popular Front. The Radicals in Blum's cabinet were adamant that the best course was for him to resign. The legal-minded Blum then concluded that there was "no middle ground between yielding and fighting."[30] Fighting—that is, unleashing popular pressure against the government—would have caused the Radicals to desert the Popular Front. The coalition between the middle classes and the proletariat, essential in Blum's mind to the defense of republican institutions, would then have been destroyed. Better to resign and let the Radicals form a new government with continuing support from socialists and communists than risk a leap into the unknown. Like his deci-sion over the Spanish Civil War, this one was immensely painful for Blum. It was even more so to the members of his party, who had not imagined that the Popular Front—new in so many respects—"would fall, and accept its fall, in the traditional pattern" of other Third Republican governments.[31] When Blum resigned, there were no demonstrations in his favor; the messianic ambiance of a year earlier had evaporated, and the man who had been used to receiving hundreds of affectionate letters from workers found himself, once again, isolated.[32]

Blum was replaced by Radical leader Camille Chautemps, who nevertheless promised to continue the Popular Front's overall policies, and Blum joined Chautemps' cabinet. In March 1938, Blum formed a second cabinet. Within three months, however, the Popular Front coalition had disintegrated completely, para-lyzed by continuing worker unrest, further weakening of the franc and business confidence, and indecision over the best response to Hitler's growing aggression. Blum resigned a second time in June 1938, and the Popular Front experiment was over.

THE POLITICIZATION OF INTELLECTUALS

In an important change in French cultural life between 1930 and 1938, the rise of fascism and the formation of the Popular Front brought the nation's intellectuals back into politics. In the 1920s most writers and artists had spurned conventional political commitment, or *engagement* as they called it, turning inward in quest of alternative experiences that could help them make sense of the slaughter of World War I. The one exception had been André Breton and his fellow Surrealists, who had joined the PC in 1927 because of its anti-imperialist stance, only to be expelled in 1933 when they dared to criticize the Soviet Union. One of the most famous pamphlets of the 1920s, Julien Benda's 1927 *The Treason of the Intellectuals,* had warned writers against compromising their roles as defenders of supposedly eternal values by speaking out for interested material ones.

By the 1930s, however, being an intellectual in France meant tearing down the very barriers between thought and action that Benda had so passionately defended. Intellectuals abandoned their previous stance of art for art's sake, and like the rest of French society felt compelled by the continuing economic crisis and intensifying political polarization to identify with either the democratic values of the Left or the authoritarian values of the Right. At the same time, many were spurred on by the violence of the times to "overhaul the categories of French politics" by suggesting new philosophies altogether.[33]

One important new development in the early 1930s was the progressive Catholic philosophical movement known as personalism, led by Emmanuel Mounier. As we saw earlier, the pope's excommunication of the Action Française in 1926 had finally severed the older alliance between the Catholic Church and reactionary politics, allowing a more democratic and socially concerned Catholicism to emerge in France. Mounier was at the forefront of this trend. Like many of his generation, he believed that Western civilization and liberal capitalism were doomed; the question was what would replace them. In 1932, Mounier launched a new monthly journal entitled *Esprit,* which opposed unbridled individualism as well as fascist and communist collectivism in the name of a "personalist and communitarian revolution" that fostered community and a commitment to action. In 1936, *Esprit* went against the Catholic mainstream by opposing the fascist dictator Franco in the Spanish Civil War.[34]

Several other great Catholic writers also divorced themselves from the traditionally right-wing politics of the Church in this era to forge a more liberal path. These included François Mauriac and Georges Bernanos. Mauriac, a member of the French Academy and novelist, produced the bestselling *Life of Jesus* in 1936. That same year he commited himself to the Popular Front and the Spanish Republic.[35] Conservative novelist Bernanos was openly anti-Semitic and anti-American in 1931, denouncing the "half Saxon, half Jewish . . . future master of a standardized planet" and the cold, rational, mechanical man of "American" capitalism.[36] But by 1936 he had moved toward defending democracy, condemning Franco's massacres of republicans perpetrated in the name of Catholicism, and nationalism in general. Mounier's personalism and the Catholic humanism of Mauriac and Bernanos represented genuine alternatives for Catholics to the Action Française and its anti-Semitic politics of hatred, which became even more pronounced in France after the Popular Front's victory.

For secular intellectuals on the Left, political *engagement* took other forms. Like so many of his generation—too young to have fought in World War I yet forced to live in its stultifying shadow—writer André Malraux went abroad (to China and French Indochina) in the 1920s in search of adventure and to escape the dreariness of a supposedly decadent European civilization; his desire for action would lead him to idealize ideological struggle, heroism, and clear-cut solutions to complex problems in his 1930s writing. For example, he chose China as the setting for his 1933 masterpiece *Man's Fate,* which portrayed the military and philosophic vagaries of a group of (mainly) European intellectuals involved in the Chinese civil war at the end of 1920s. Malraux's heroes always saw revolutionary acts as liberating. In the mid-1930s, Malraux gravitated toward communism, whose sense of purpose he admired. Under the Popular Front, he glorified the bitter struggle of republicans in Spain against Franco.

For other writers on the Left, however, continued support for the communists became increasingly difficult. Eminent aging novelist André Gide, who had chronicled colonial abuses in the 1920s, also turned to communism in the early 1930s; but a trip to Stalin's Soviet Union in the 1936 thoroughly disillusioned him, and he henceforth became an outspoken critic of the Soviet regime—a position that inevitably put him at odds with other French leftist intellectuals and contributed to the internal political and ideological divisions that ultimately pulled the Popular Front apart.

Equally symptomatic of the *engagement* of the decade was the appearance in the late 1930s of the philosophy of existentialism. Existentialism would develop more fully during and immediately after World War II, but one of its primary movers, left-leaning Jean-Paul Sartre, published his first novel, *Nausea,* in 1938. *Nausea* chronicled the anguish of the human soul in a world devoid of meaning, at a time when the idealism of the Popular Front was collapsing and war with Hitler appeared inevitable. Yet the novel also contained the seeds of a more hopeful philosophy, predicated on the notion that the very realization of human misery and human frailty could give an impetus to action. Individuals were free to choose action—whether through art or through politics: This was the essence of existentialism. "What was so seductive from the very first glimpse of this new philosophy was the way it opened directly onto life," recalled sociologist Georges Bataille.[37] Existentialism captured the desire of many younger intellectuals in the 1930s to throw off the role of detached observer and to create a new world. As Sartre wrote later in his epic philosophical investigation *Being and Nothingness:* "Freedom coincides at its roots with the non-being which is at the heart of man. For a human being, to *be* is to choose himself."[38] Sartre and his fellow existentialist philosopher and lover Simone de Beauvoir did not choose to get involved in the Popular Front, but they would—like many other committed intellectuals of the 1930s—later support the Resistance.

In the polarized atmosphere of the 1930s, *engagement* also led some intellectuals to a strong identification with the values of the rapidly growing extreme Right. Two of the most disturbing examples were Pierre Drieu la Rochelle and

Robert Brasillach. Drieu la Rochelle, a war veteran, began his career as a Surrealist poet, then threw himself into extreme nationalist politics in the 1930s, whose cult of violence he celebrated. The hero of his eponymous novel *Gilles* (1939) was emblematic of a generation of men who—in the crisis-ridden 1930s—longed for the certitudes of the trenches and the intense immediacy of wartime existence. Gilles abandons France to fight in the Spanish civil war on Franco's side. Wounded in the middle of an enemy bombardment, he found what he was looking for: "What had he been in the last twenty years? Almost nothing. . . . Now he could be again. . . . He was regaining his lucidity, his irony. . . . This was it, he was himself again, he was himself more than ever. . . . He found a gun, went toward a loophole and began to shoot meticulously."[39]

Brasillach, too young to have fought in the war, was like Blum a brilliant graduate of France's elite Ecole Normale Supérieure, who became one of the most influential journalists and essayists of the 1930s. He disdained democratic practice and values and instead embraced in his writing the hypermasculinity and violence of post-war fascism. Brasillach looked to "Aryan" Germany to save France. A visceral opponent of the Popular Front and of the democratic culture that had brought it to power, he went so far as to call the Third Republic "an old syphilitic whore stinking of patchouli [a strong perfume derived from an herb] and yeast infection, still exhaling her bad odors, still standing on her sidewalk."[40] The ugliness of these sentiments is a telling reminder of how deeply divisive the political struggle was in France between 1932 and 1938, as much among France's intelligentsia as among the rest of its citizenry. Only after 1938 would these divisions begin to moderate; by then, however, it was too late to prevent another European war.

REPUBLICAN REACTION: 1938

The resignation of Blum in June 1938 freed the Radicals to form a new government. Disillusioned with their allies to the Left, the Radicals shifted rightward, in search of a leader who would roll back the 40-hour workweek, put France "back to work" on management's terms, and strengthen the state in the face of the increasingly menacing Nazi threat abroad and the far Right at home. They found such a leader in Edouard Daladier, who returned to power in April 1938, just after Hitler's *Anschluss* in Austria made war in Europe seem terrifyingly imminent.

During 1937 and the first months of 1938, Hitler had gone from one diplomatic triumph to another. He had continued to ship arms unimpeded to Franco's forces, which relentlessly gained the upper hand in Spain; then in March 1938 he had annexed Austria, thereby directly menacing France's ally Czechoslovakia. France and Britain had written off Austria in advance, but Czechoslovakia was a different matter. France had binding treaty commitments to the Czechs and if Czechoslovakia fell, there was little chance of stopping Nazi expansion further east. Daladier, unlike his pro-appeasement foreign minister, Georges Bonnet, hoped to convince the British prime minister, Neville Chamberlain, to stand by the Czechs; but he also believed that war must be avoided if France's economy was to be revived. When Chamberlain insisted that the Czechs accept a compromise satisfactory to Hitler, Daladier felt that France could not act alone. At a conference convened in Munich on September 30, 1938, Chamberlain and Daladier signed an agreement known as the Munich Accords that forced the Czechs to hand over their German-speaking Sudeten border provinces to Hitler.

Daladier was appalled by what he had agreed to, but he knew that much of French public opinion on the Left as well as on the Right remained profoundly anti-war—although not for the same reasons. Action Française, for example, believed that the many Jewish refugees in France were trying to drag the nation into a war of their own making against Germany: "[T]he French do not want to fight—neither for the Jews, the Russians, nor the Freemasons of Prague."[41] Many on the Left, in a pacifist reaction to the bloodletting of 1914–1918, wanted peace at any price. In 1938 the International League of Soldiers of Peace—one of France's most important pacifist organizations—published an appeal explaining that they were not prepared to fight and die over such a small matter as Czechoslovakia.[42] Paul Faure, general secretary of SFIO, warned in the newspaper *Le Socialiste* that a military response would represent the "antifascist mysticism that accepts the methods of fascism itself."[43] In this climate of virulent anti-war passion, Daladier received a triumphal reception from Parisians upon his return from Munich. In the National Assembly, only 75 communists and 2 independents voted against the Munich Accords. Many conservative republicans voted in favor of appeasement because they viewed Hitler as the only bulwark against communism. They hoped that France could now disengage from Eastern Europe altogether and fall back onto the resources of the French empire. Nevertheless, many of the socialist, Radical, and conservative republicans who approved ceding the Sudetenland to Hitler had considerable doubts about the course upon which they were embarking. All of these deputies drew the line here; for them there could, and would, be no more concessions to Hitler.

In this sense, like the Stavisky Riots and the election of the Popular Front, Munich was a decisive turning point in the fraught politics of the 1930s. The Munich Accords helped to inject a new sense of resolution into the Third Republic. Surrounding himself with some of France's most talented young civil servants as opposed to career politicians, Daladier began governing energetically, even autocratically, from the center Right. From October 1938 to September 1939, he ruled by decree for seven months. The previous August, at the height of the crisis over Czechoslovakia, Daladier had rescinded the 40-hour workweek, on the grounds that successful rearmament required longer hours in the factories. Unions were seen as the greatest impediment to stepping up production, and Daladier's finance minister, conservative Paul Reynaud, continued this frontal assault on the powerful labor movement. When a general strike was called in November 1938, Reynaud sent in the police; thousands were dismissed from their jobs, and union membership plummeted. Labor, so ebullient in 1936, now withdrew into sullen silence.

Daladier also dealt decisively with a new refugee crisis, and in the process hamstrung the far Right as effectively as he had the unions on the Left. The *Kristallnacht* pogroms in Germany on November 9, 1938 brought another wave of desperate Central European Jews into France fleeing for their lives. To these refugees were added nearly half a million Spanish refugees who crossed into France after Franco's final victory over republican forces in April 1939. Even the mainstream press referred to the arrival of these two groups of refugees as an "invasion." At first the government had tried to seal French borders by passing harsh decree laws that expelled illegal immigrants and rolled back the rights of recently naturalized citizens. In 1939, the government began to respond more pragmatically, as the refugee crisis showed no sign of abating and an influential sector of public opinion pressured for a return to more humanitarian policies. In April 1939, Daladier decided to require military service of all foreigners seeking asylum, thereby addressing France's perennial soldier deficit as war became more likely. He also passed the Marchandeau Law, banning religious and racial defamation in the press—a move aimed at the authoritarian and anti-Semitic leagues and parties. Professional interest groups nevertheless prevented any liberalization of the naturalization law that might have brought it in line with the new military service requirements.

Finally, Daladier further expanded the welfare policies of the late 1920s. In July 1939, he decreed France's most ambitious pro-natalist law to date, the Family Code, with generous new provisions to help families. As he put it when justifying the legislation, "[A] depopulated country cannot be a free country."[44] The Code subsidized marriages, provided a "first birth" bonus if a couple had their first baby within two years of marriage, lowered taxes for larger families, extended family allowances to all employees, increased the amounts for the third and subsequent children, and encouraged mothers to stay at home with the "mother in the home" allowance. The Code also introduced stricter penalties against abortion, pornography, and public immorality. Although the Family Code was the logical continuation of policies adopted a decade earlier, it was passed in a much more repressive and xenophobic context than the previous legislation. By the end of the 1930s, the protection of the French family and policing of women's sexuality went hand-in-hand with a crack-down on the far Right and the far Left and continuing discrimination against refugees and foreigners.

WAR-READY?

Under Daladier's firm hand, French rearmament began to take effect, although here much of the credit properly lies with the Popular Front. Blum had inaugurated France's first serious post-war rearmament program, when in 1936 the legislature voted 14 billion francs to be spent over four years. The backwardness of French factories as well as the 40-hour workweek had initially slowed down production, particularly in the aviation industry, but by 1938, the Popular Front's investment began to pay off. In addition, Daladier's actions against the unions created a whole new financial climate. Between 1938 and 1939 French military spending rose from 8.6 to 23 percent of national income, and a modern weapons industry was created almost from scratch. Unfortunately, French military doctrine at the end of the 1930s failed to develop in such a way to take full advantage of the new air force and tank capacity.

As soon as they withdrew their troops from German soil in 1924 (see Chapter 7), France's military leaders began to plan for the possibility of another war. Remembering how costly and completely ineffective France's pre-1914 obsession with the offensive had proved, how long the war had lasted, and how the death of 1.4 million soldiers in the Great War reduced the size of the "class" entering the army each year, France's military experts proposed a radically new national defense strategy. They saw the need to prepare for a long war, requiring the massive mobilization of resources and manpower, but they determined to make maximum use of machines and fortifications to minimize the loss of lives and proposed constructing a huge fortified barrier along France's entire border with its traditional enemy. In 1932, Minister of War André Maginot approved this plan, and construction began on what soon became known as "the Maginot Line."

The Maginot Line, which ran for almost 200 miles along the eastern border of Alsace and Lorraine, was designed to protect what were seen as the most vulnerable sections of the border. In case of a war with Germany, it was meant to absorb the first blow and provide a shield behind which France could assemble its reserves. But it did not extend along the frontier with Luxembourg or Belgium. These neutral countries presented a thorny dilemma for France's military planners. On the one hand, as officially neutral countries beyond France's northeast border, they could neither be included within France's defensive system, nor could they permit French soldiers on their soil unless their frontiers had already been violated. On the other hand, extending the Maginot Line just south of the Belgian border would make clear that Luxembourg and Belgium (and the Netherlands beyond) could expect no help in case of a German attack. France therefore reluctantly decided to leave its entire northern border with Belgium unprotected—but, given that gap, should war come again, a successful defense required France to launch an immediate and powerful counter-attack.

Early in the 1930s, the negative view that an offensive strategy posed unacceptable risks led both Britain and France to hesitate in building up their offensive forces. There was, however, one exception to that view inside the French military. Then-Colonel Charles de Gaulle pressed the French army to build its offensive capability and especially to expand mechanized divisions. His sensible arguments were nevertheless lost in the fights that erupted over de Gaulle's insistence that mechanization also required a highly trained, small, professional army. De Gaulle's proposal threatened the republican leadership's foundational belief in a national army of citizen-soldiers and aroused their fears of an anti-republican military. Republican leaders had good reason for suspicion. Military elites represented a remnant of the old aristocracy and tended to be right-wing in political orientation and contemptuous of politicians. As the Third Republic had reduced the term of universal military service from three years to one, the officer corps also had become increasingly disdainful of the common soldiers under its command, a factor that shaped military strategy and planning throughout the 1930s.

General Gamelin, head of the General Staff after 1935, and firmly loyal to the Republic, dutifully rejected de Gaulle's proposals. Yet Gamelin understood clearly the need both to rearm and to adopt new military technologies. He knew the Maginot Line would not solve all of France's problems. He was well aware of German doctrine on aviation and mechanized divisions and worked diligently, especially under Daladier, to modernize France's equipment, operations, and tactics. Gamelin nevertheless faced a number of disabling constraints. Not only did the air force fall outside his control, but he also failed to persuade Britain to concentrate on building mechanized divisions that could be coordinated with France's infantry and air resources. Most frustratingly, he could not coordinate defense plans with a Belgium reluctant to abandon its neutrality.

THE PATH TO WAR

Having proven to conservatives that he had no sympathy either for the domestic policies of the Radicals' erstwhile partners on the Left, the socialists and the communists, or for the violent tactics and rhetoric of the far Right, Daladier could afford to be more assertive toward Hitler. A new technique—public opinion polling—showed that by December 1938, 70 percent of those asked opposed any further concessions to Hitler, who was clearly intent upon invading the rest of Czechoslovakia, perhaps followed by Poland. Daladier revived France's time-honored strategy of seeking military cooperation with Russia against Germany, insisting that regardless of the issue of Bolshevism, overtures to the Soviet Union would preserve the peace. Yet neither side seemed committed to an agreement, in part because unbeknownst to France and Britain, Stalin had secretly contacted Hitler. Virtually no one in France, or indeed the world, predicted the Nazi-Soviet pact of nonaggression made public on August 23, 1939. News of the pact was a stunning blow for the French as well as the British because, as they understood too late, it meant imminent war with Hitler. French communists were thrown into disarray, and many chose to leave the party rather than drop their long-term commitment to fighting Hitler.

On September 1, 1939, the German army and air force invaded Poland, whose independence France and Britain had guaranteed six months earlier, on March 31, 1939. Daladier ordered the general mobilization of the French armed forces, and on September 2 he succeeded in getting a unanimous vote in the National Assembly for war credits. In a dramatic rupture with the mentality that had prevailed at Munich, on September 3 Britain and France sent out separate ultimatums, instructing Germany to withdraw from Poland by 11:00 a.m. When the deadline passed, first Britain and then France declared war.

Rather than immediately attempting to form a *union sacrée,* as in the summer of 1914, in the summer of 1939 the government undertook a further settling of ideological scores against perceived threats. When the Nazi-Soviet Pact was announced, Daladier immediately declared the PC illegal, banned the communist press, and arrested communists who had previously challenged the regime—regardless of their war stance. Daladier was pandering to the visceral anti-communism of conservative republicans, and his government's repression effectively drove French communists underground. They later emerged as key actors in the French Resistance, but they would not forget the persecution of 1939–1940. Throughout the empire, the government ordered the arrest of all known anti-colonial leaders, forcing these movements, too, into hiding, where they would further radicalize. And with the declaration of war in September 1939, "enemy aliens" were also interned, regardless of their previous refugee status.

Daladier's two years in office had gone a long way toward ending the institutional paralysis triggered first by the Depression, then by the polarization of politics in the wake of the Stavisky riots and the election of the Popular Front, and finally by the growing threat of war with Germany. Rule by decree had produced the economic recovery, military rebuilding, and resolute foreign policy that had eluded previous governments and had proven that the Third Republic's constitution was flexible enough to allow strong leadership to emerge in the midst of escalating domestic and international crisis.[45] Yet in providing decisive leadership, Daladier and Reynaud had further eroded the humane and democratic values that had so effectively mobilized large sectors of public opinion only two years earlier. It was thus a deeply disillusioned and still divided nation that faced its German enemy in 1939.

CHAPTER 9

The Dark Years
1939–1945

In his essay "The Republic of Silence," Jean-Paul Sartre presents a picture of the German Occupation of France during World War II as an era of stunning moral clarity. "Since the Nazi venom penetrated our very thoughts, every true thought was a victory. Since an all-powerful police tried to force us to be silent, each word became as precious as a declaration of principle. Since we were hounded, every one of our movements had the importance of commitment."[1] Director Henri-Georges Clouzot presents a much more ambiguous portrait in his 1942 film, *The Raven*, about a town torn apart by anonymous letters of denunciation. A character in the film, the psychiatrist, tells the town doctor, "You think that all people are good or evil [he grasps a hanging light which casts a pool of light in the otherwise dark room]. But where is darkness [he pushes the lamp and it begins to swing], where is light? Where is the border of evil? [The lamp illuminates different parts of the room as it swings.] Do you know which side you are on? Think about it and examine your conscience. You will perhaps be surprised."[2]

In some ways, both Sartre's vision of an era of good versus evil and Clouzot's suggestion of ever-shifting boundaries between darkness and light reflect aspects of the very complicated reality of what the French commonly refer to as the "dark years." This short but crucial period for France began with a shocking, traumatic, and rapid defeat similar in some ways to the blow that killed the Second Empire and gave birth to the Third Republic. Yet what happened to France after the moment of defeat differed profoundly between 1871 and 1940, largely owing to the vast difference between Bismarckian conservatism and Hitlerian totalitarianism. Whether they were fervently pro- or anti-fascist, people in France who were aware of Hitler's ideology agreed with Sartre that the period presented clear, stark choices. The vast majority of people in France, however, did not comprehend the difference between earlier Prussian militarism and Nazism. The reality for most people living in France was neither black nor white but shades of gray. For them the war represented an era of grinding hardship and trouble, punctuated by periods of extreme trauma. Nevertheless, after the war, a mythic picture of France under occupation emerged, one in which a nationwide, heroic resistance battled the Nazi conquerors and their small, unpopular, Nazi-imposed puppet regime.

Reality notwithstanding, post-war France chose Sartre's vision and rejected Clouzot's.

FROM PHONY WAR TO THE BATTLE OF FRANCE

After years of failing to stop German expansionism and a final attempt to appease Hitler in Munich in 1938, the German invasion of Poland on September 1, 1939 had finally spurred Britain and France to declare war on Germany on September 3. Millions of French families grimly faced the call-up of their husbands, fathers, brothers, which included all eligible men between 20 and 40 with fewer than four children. The public response in 1939 included none of the ostensible mood of excitement, none of the parades and public gatherings that greeted the outbreak of war across Europe in 1914.

Another difference with 1914 was that the declaration of war was not followed by immediate combat. In September 1939, France and Britain mobilized their armies and sent them to the front lines, where they sat and waited for war to come to them. Marc Bloch, a distinguished historian and father of five who served during the Battle of France and later died in the Resistance, described this period as an "interminable succession of days when, seemingly, nothing ever got done."[3] For nine months, from September until May, aside from occasional sorties, little actual fighting took place. England and France failed to use the opportunity to attack Germany's western front during the Battle of Poland. Rather than risking a direct attack against the German Siegfried Line and anticipating another long war of attrition, French leaders assumed that the Maginot Line would absorb the initial German blow. Not only did this decision leave Poland facing the unmitigated force of the German attack, against which it crumbled in a matter of weeks, but the nine months of inactivity, the so-called phony war, or *drôle de guerre,* also badly damaged troop morale. Sartre wrote in his diary from his military post, "All the men who left with me were raring to go at the outset." By November, he wrote, "[T]hey are dying of boredom."[4] The men, holed up in underground bunkers, could only wait for an attack.

In April 1940, Germany turned its attention west, attacking Norway. But for France the phony war finally ended on May 10, 1940, when Germany attacked Belgium and Holland. It looked like a repeat of Germany's 1914 offensive through Belgium, and the French military responded by advancing deeply into Belgium to meet the German attack. The result was a disaster for France, although one due to doctrinal errors, not to a lack of military preparedness. Contrary to a widely held belief, France had not failed to rearm in the 1930s. As we saw earlier, starting in 1936 it had rapidly built its air and mechanized forces. But as de Gaulle had foreseen, the French military had no coordinated plan for the offensive use of land and air power. French military planners had envisioned using tanks alongside infantry, meaning tanks would move no faster than the speed at which troops could advance on foot—quite the opposite of the German blitzkrieg with its coordinated use of infantry and airpower, spearheaded by rapidly moving tanks.

In addition, the military plan in place in 1939 was a counter-offensive plan. Relying on a strong defense in the initial phase, France had intended to take the first blow rather than launching an offensive, then to counter-attack by advancing deep into Belgium. The area critical to this plan's success was the hinge in between Belgium and the Maginot Line. Because the Ardennes Forest and the Meuse River made the hinge area difficult to penetrate, Gamelin had mistakenly assumed it was impregnable, and failed to fortify it against enemy attack. Rather than being deterred by the region's unfavorable geography, Germany directed the brunt of its forces at this vulnerable weak link in France's chain of defenses. Within five days of the start of the campaign, three key cities fell to Germany: Monthermé, Dinant, and Sedan, the same city whose fall in 1870 had presaged France's collapse. The French High Command, rather than using a Marnelike counter-attack, tried to hold a continuous defensive front line—without success. On May 26, the Germans completed their multipronged attack, demolishing the remaining armies and capturing a record number of French soldiers.

Yet, as German troops poured into France, the German tank column unexpectedly halted, short on gasoline, for a critical period. This brief window allowed the British to undertake a massive rescue of stranded soldiers across the Channel from the harbor of Dunkirk. Calling on all civilian and commercial ships to help in the effort, they rescued some 330,000 troops. Given their own needs, the British rescued their own troops first, unfortunately feeding French soldiers' perception that they were being abandoned on the beaches. Nevertheless, the British rescued some 130,000 French troops from Dunkirk as well. From there the German army continued west and south to take control of the Atlantic coast. The French Command, obsessed with defensive lines, delayed orders to pull their troops still stationed at the Maginot Line out, allowing the second wing of German troops to turn east and capture some 400,000 French troops from the rear. This total military fiasco set the scene for the Third Republic's demise.

EXODUS AND ARMISTICE

As the German armies advanced, retreating French armies were joined by millions of civilian refugees from Belgium and Holland, as well as from northern and eastern France. On June 2, the government ordered civilians to evacuate the Marne Department, but in general evacuation orders were inconsistent and belated. Often local civilian authorities left without organizing an orderly evacuation; entire towns packed up and left, while neighboring towns stayed put. One woman from Bernaville, a small village in the north, followed the orders to gather her belongings and her two small children and leave town, terrified by popular memories of the horrors of German occupation in that area during the previous war. But when she found that German armies were already ahead of her, she turned around and went home. "What was the point?" she asked.

The French government was no longer in Paris to answer her questions. Daladier's last government had fallen in March 1940, and Paul Reynaud had replaced him as prime minister. On June 10, the ministries, with hastily packed files, fled to Bordeaux on the Atlantic coast. In the resulting vacuum, panic swept into the capital, causing some 2 million Parisians to flee the city. The French expression for this period, "the exodus," highlights its cataclysmic nature to them. Raymond Ruffin, aged 11 in 1940, described refugees from the Battle of France passing through his small village: "Long columns of refugees flood into town, hanging on to ill-assorted and eccentric harnesses. Behind the heavy wagons pulled by big red horses with long blond manes, led by Belgians or people from the north of France, follow convoys of every sort of vehicle; from carriages and carts to asthmatic jalopies, the whole accompanied by bikes, baby carriages, hand carts, wheelbarrows, trailing behind or pushed by worn-out, panting, tattered pedestrians. The crowd seethed with shouts, curses, insults, crying babies."[5] For the 8 million civilians who left home, the exodus proved agonizing, slow, potentially fatal, and ultimately futile. Safety was an elusive goal in a country whose army and institutions were collapsing. While some people responded with solidarity, providing food or a place to sleep to desperate people, others exploited the misery of their fleeing countrymen, price-gouging for a drink of tap water.[6] Once the fighting had ended, getting home proved equally difficult. People from what became the "forbidden zone" in the far northeast corner of France were not allowed to return there.

French political leaders, faced with the rapid crumbling of France's army and its inability to regroup, had an unpalatable set of choices. An all-out military stand in France, questionable in its ability to stave off the German advance, would have required mobilizing the population, raising the specter of another Commune-style populist reaction. Only Prime Minister Reynaud advocated that course of action. Other leaders wanted to keep France in the war but recognized that the military campaign in France was over, and pressed the government to go into exile and continue the war from North Africa or even London. Finally, one group believed that France had lost the war and Britain would not hold out for long. Led by Marshal Philippe Pétain, Adrien Marquet, and Pierre Laval, this group wanted to end the fighting and seek terms from Germany.

The defeatist group gained the upper hand, forcing Reynaud to resign. Pétain became prime minister and initiated armistice negotiations. Given the traumatic conditions for millions of French people, Pétain 's promise to end the exodus helped legitimize France's new government.[7] On June 17, 1940, Pétain announced to the country over the radio, "The fighting must stop," a puzzling order, since an armistice would not be signed until June 22. When the Armistice entered into effect on June 25, 1940, the French government packed up and moved again, this time to town of Vichy in the unoccupied zone. Vichy's attraction was less the mineral waters, renowned for their curative powers, than the ample hotel space available for government offices. Vichy also lay in the district of the politician whose star was again rising, Pierre Laval. Meanwhile, the gap between Pétain's June 17 announcement and the start of the Armistice, on June 25, left French soldiers, still in the midst of battle, confused. Some regiments continued to fight, while others did not. Pétain had said the fighting must stop, and soldiers in the field hesitated to risk their lives for a lost cause. That confusion led to the capture of close to 1 million more French soldiers.

Given both the rapidity of the French collapse and the magnitude of the loss, the year 1940 replaced the year 1870 in French imaginations as the "debacle." Yet an admission of complete defeat and signing of an armistice was not inevitable, and not everyone accepted Pétain's decision. First, in June 1940, the French government could have gone to North Africa and carried on the fight from there, albeit with scant military resources. A second option would have been to form a government in exile in London as Holland, Poland, and other European countries did. A good number of French political leaders preferred either of those options, and 26 deputies embarked on June 21 for North Africa. One member of the government, Charles de Gaulle, whom Prime Minister Reynaud had named under-secretary of state for war, disobeyed his commanders and left for London. On June 18, the day after Pétain announced that the fighting must stop, de Gaulle addressed his fellow French over the British Broadcasting Corporation (BBC) with a very different plea.

Unfortunately, because the BBC did not record his address, no exact transcript of de Gaulle's speech exists. In the version published in his memoirs, de Gaulle claims to have insisted that the war was not over and called on all who agreed with him to join him in London to carry on the fight. As he eloquently put it,

General Charles de Gaulle (1890–1970), London, 1941. Institut Charles de Gaulle, Paris/Archives Charmet/The Bridgeman Art Library.

"The flame of French resistance must not and shall not die."[8] About 7,000 French soldiers joined de Gaulle, a remarkably courageous decision in light of military discipline and the political situation. Perhaps the most extraordinary act of collective resistance was when every adult male—124 men altogether—on Ile de Sein, a small island off the coast of Brittany, left for England to join de Gaulle's movement. No other community in France gave rise to anything like this island's unified rejection of the Armistice.

In another BBC broadcast in August 1940 de Gaulle warned that the Armistice would lead to the "disaffection and probable revolt of the natives of the empire." However, in the end only the governor of Chad, Félix Eboué—France's sole black governor and a native of the old colony of Guadeloupe—officially rallied to de Gaulle on August 26, 1940, although by the autumn French officials in New Caledonia and Tahiti had also joined the movement. Most colonial administrators from the rest of the empire remained loyal to Pétain, viewed as the legitimate leader of France. Several of them also shared his ideological orientation and were angry at Britain.[9] Eboué's decision to join de Gaulle nevertheless allowed the latter to gain control of the remainder of French Equatorial Africa in November 1940 and gave de Gaulle a base of operations there that would later prove decisive.

Inside France, a few exceptional civilians, like anthropologists Germaine Tillion and Jacques Soustelle and writer Jean Guéhenno, also rejected Pétain's declaration. The day Pétain spoke on the radio, Guéhenno wrote, "An old man who doesn't even have a man's voice but speaks like a little old lady, told us at 12:30 he had sued for peace. I think about our youth. It was cruel to see it part for war. But is it less cruel to force it to live in a dishonored country? I will never believe that men are made for war. But I know that they are also not made for servitude."[10] Impugning Pétain's masculinity, Guéhenno linked honor with rejecting the Armistice. Still, most people in France reacted with relief, saddened by the defeat but hoping that the war would soon be over. In the six weeks of fighting, some 92,000 men had been killed and another 1.8 million prisoners of war captured. Unfortunately, although the Armistice stopped the fighting and temporarily ended air raids, it did not mean a return to normalcy. Given its location and strategic resources and future Nazi war plans, France could not possibly hope to extract itself from World War II.

The terms of the Armistice were harsh. Germany was to occupy three-fifths of France, including the entire North Sea and Atlantic coasts. Seven different zones were created. A demarcation line divided the northern occupied zone from the unoccupied or free southern zone, establishing a frontier that French citizens (including public officials) could only cross with a special pass. The Armistice required France to turn all war materials over to Germany and restricted France to an Armistice army of 100,000 troops. French soldiers captured in June 1940 would remain POWs in Germany until the conclusion of a peace treaty. France also agreed, in a provision many found shocking, to surrender on demand any exiles from the Nazis who had found safe haven in France in the 1930s. Finally, France was to pay occupation costs of 20 million marks a day at the artificially inflated

Map 9.1 The seven zones of the German Occupation during World War II, with North Africa.

Annexed by Germany

Areas administered from
Belgium (de facto German rule)

German occupation from 1940

Occupied by Italian forces, 1940

Occupied by Italian forces, 1942

"Free zone" or Vichy France (occupied
by German troops, 11 November 1942)

- - - Boundary of "Forbidden zones"

UNITED
KINGDOM

La Manche
(English Channel)

Lille
Arras
La Havre
Rouen
Paris
Metz
Strasbourg

FRANCE

Tours
Poitiers

Bay
of
Biscay

Vichy
Lyon

Bordeaux

Avignon

Marseilles

SPAIN

CORSICA

BALEARIC ISLANDS

SARDINIA

Mediterranean Sea

500 MILES

500 KILOMETERS

Mers-el-Kébir
Oran
Algiers
Tunis
French North Africa
(Under Vichy until Nov 1942)

rate of 20 francs per mark.[11] The expectation of a quick treaty had motivated many political leaders at Vichy to opt for an Armistice rather than continued hostilities. Nazi leaders nevertheless left little doubt, to those paying careful attention, that their plans for France differed radically from anything Bismarck could have imagined 70 years earlier.

Meanwhile the British decided not to leave to chance the possibility of the French navy falling into the hands of the Nazis. In a move that bitterly turned many French even further against their erstwhile allies, on July 3, 1940, the British Royal Navy demanded the French to either turn over or scuttle the squadron of French warships anchored off the coast of Algeria at the narrow harbor of Mers el Kébir. When the French admiral refused, the Royal Navy sank the squadron, and 1,270 French sailors lost their lives. The remainder of the French fleet was still in Toulon, but the attack at Mers el Kébir psychologically caused many French temporarily to see Britain rather than Germany as the greater enemy.

VICHY: REVENGE OF THE MINORITIES

Leaders like Pétain and Laval had what seemed at the time powerful reasons for signing the Armistice. Given the speed of France's fall, they firmly believed that Britain would not hold out for long. Indeed, many in France thought Germany would ultimately rule the continent. Thus, they felt France could best wring concessions from Germany, a reduction in the burden of occupation costs, for example, or the return of its POWs, if it accepted the defeat and acknowledged the two governments' mutual interests through voluntary collaboration. Despite defeat and German occupation, Vichy leaders in June 1940 believed that France held several critical assets in its negotiations with Germany. First, much of its naval fleet at that point remained intact and still under French control. Second, France's large colonial empire stretching from Africa to the Middle East to Southeast Asia could also surely serve as a bargaining chip, given Germany's continuing hostilities with Britain. France's final asset was the threat of taking those assets and joining the Allies, resuming hostilities against Germany. But bargaining chips only work if the negotiator is willing to play them, something French leaders at Vichy in the long run proved unwilling to do. In effect they conceded the hand before they ever tried to play it, in part because they had other priorities on their mind, including a "National Revolution" to remake France politically, socially, and economically.

Once he became prime minister in June 1940, Pétain took advantage of the crisis that brought him to power to reshape France's political structure according to his own deeply held convictions. On July 10, 1940, the legislature voted 569 to 80 to grant Pétain full powers to revise the constitution. Pétain, despite his long service to the government, made it abundantly clear he intended to destroy the Third Republic and replace it with a more conservative, indeed authoritarian regime. While he had never been active in overtly anti-republican movements, Pétain had long shared the values of the traditional groups on the far Right like the Action Française. To Pétain and his circle, the defeat confirmed their opinion that the Third Republic rested on false assumptions and represented the culmination of all the evils that the 1789 revolutionaries had first foisted onto the nation: egalitarianism, liberalism, and anti-clericalism.

Thus in July, Pétain passed four Constitutional Acts ending the Third Republic and establishing a new government, *l'Etat Français,* or the French State, with its capital in Vichy. Pétain became the head of state (*chef de l'état*), a role akin to that of a president or monarch. Given the deep attachment of many people in France to Pétain, still revered as the Victor of Verdun, his leadership of the new French State gave it credibility. Initially Pierre Laval was made head of the government, in a role similar to that of prime minister. In a clear divergence from republican practice, however, Laval was also designated Pétain's successor. While Germany occupied only the northern three-fifths of France, Vichy's laws applied to both zones (except Alsace-Lorraine, which Germany again annexed) unless contradicted by the German authorities. The French State maintained some offices in Paris, where the government hoped eventually to return. Most importantly, French civil servants continued to function throughout France and the empire, with the Germans intervening only in matters of military, political, or ideological importance to them.

A leading scholar of this era, Stanley Hoffmann, has aptly called the new Vichy regime "the revenge of the minorities" because the people who came to power at Vichy had been outsiders to the Republic prior to the war. There were, loosely speaking, four such minorities, each of whom played some role in decision-making although not necessarily in consultation with each other. First and foremost were the so-called traditionalists. They included monarchists such as Charles Maurras of Action Française and conservative authoritarians more generally, who believed that a single, powerful leader should rule the country with the help of a natural hierarchy of elites. As the term "traditionalist" suggests, they were fundamentally anti-democratic and anti-modern, since their true desire was to turn the clock back to the years prior to 1789, not just in terms of having an absolute monarch, but also in promoting Catholicism as the religion of state. They also wished do away with large cities, factories, and industrial plants, restoring a France composed entirely of small family farms and small family-run shops led by an aristocracy and monarchy. Marshal Pétain, from an old family with a long military background, was their symbolic leader; indeed, Maurras called Pétain's rise to power in 1940 a "divine surprise." With his striking white-haired appearance, his heroic role in the Great War, and his background, the 84-year-old Pétain seemed a king, a father figure, and a national grandfather all wrapped up in one. Over the next two years, his coterie made savvy use of the Marshal's appeal, pumping out his image on posters, book covers, and postcards. Pétain was to become Vichy's public face, its emblem, the embodiment of the regime's stated values.

Vichy also attracted a very different kind of outsider, opportunists and politicians who had lost power in the 1930s and saw Vichy as an occasion to take revenge on their political enemies. Such opportunists were the second "minority" at Vichy, and no single figure better represents this group than the slippery politician Pierre Laval, Vichy's first and last prime minister. Laval had served twice as prime minister under the Third Republic as well as in the Senate, but was eclipsed by the Popular Front. Bitterly resentful toward those he blamed for his fall, Laval took advantage of France's defeat to further his own goals, regain power, and plot the downfall of his perceived enemies, primarily politicians on the Left formerly associated with the Popular Front. His previous predilection for trying to work with Germany in the 1930s to avoid war, his pacifism, and his staunch anti-communism lined up with Vichy's ideology, making him all the more willing to seize the opportunity that he in part had created by pressing to end the fighting in June 1940.

The third most important group of outsiders attracted to Vichy was that of the so-called experts—technocrats, engineers, and bureaucrats trained at France's elite schools of public administration or engineering, high-ranking civil servants, and industrial leaders. These men had long been frustrated by the meddling and incompetence of republican politicians, especially during the crisis-ridden 1930s. Products of France's urban upper middle classes, they were also prejudiced against many of the Third Republic's elected officials because the latter came from the provinces and humbler origins than themselves. Such class differences were compounded by the experts' sense of their own superior knowledge and training, which convinced them that they alone could guarantee the efficient running of the state and economic systems. These experts had been asked to serve in cabinets in previous moments of republican crisis, when civil rights had also been curtailed—for example, during World War I, under Poincaré in the late 1920s, and then again under Daladier in 1938.

An example of this kind of expert at Vichy was François Darlan, the admiral responsible for building up the French navy in the 1930s. From 1941 to 1942, Darlan served as head of the government and brought in many like-minded men, such as Pierre Pucheu, sales director for the French steel industry, who served as minister of industrial production and minister of interior; Yves Bouthillier, as minister of finance; and François Lehideux, as minister of industrial production. Ironically, these experts cared little about Pétain and his circle's goals of returning France to a simpler, more agrarian past, and they worked hard instead to modernize French industry. They diverted scarce resources to the most efficient producers and undercut the old-fashioned, small-scale operations that traditionalists favored. Their decisions in the extreme situation of war and foreign occupation reshaped the French economy in ways that would not become immediately apparent, speeding up the processes of concentration and rationalization—in short, the exact opposite of the traditionalists' goals.

The fourth group of outsiders that assembled at Vichy in 1940 was the loudest but also the least influential, at least initially; these were the fascists. While they were divided between intellectuals, like Drieu la Rochelle, Brasillach, and Céline, and actual leaders of movements in the 1930s, like the ex-communist Jacques Doriot or the ex-socialist Marcel Déat, they all viewed the situation in 1940 as charged with opportunity. Some of them went so far as to applaud France's defeat by the Nazis they admired. They pressed leaders at Vichy to mold the new state along fascist lines, arguing for the creation of a single party with its own paramilitary, a party takeover of state functions and a wide variety of social movements, and a compulsory, unitary national youth movement for boys. However, fascists quickly grew disillusioned with the traditionalists at Vichy, whose anti-republicanism was not nearly radical enough for them. Most fascists quit the sleepy town of Vichy and returned to Paris, where they published articles denouncing Vichy, the Resistance, and Jews. No fascist was given a position of power by Vichy in 1940.

Over time, some were brought into the government, in particular Joseph Darnand, a garage owner and World War I veteran who never adjusted to peace after 1918 and had developed his own fascist following. After the 1940 defeat, Darnand joined the Légion des Combattants, a veterans' group created by Vichy, but found it far too moderate. He thus left the Légion and created the Service d'Ordre Légionnaire, which in January 1942 gained official recognition; a year later it was renamed the Militia (la Milice) and became a French-style Gestapo that hunted down and killed Resistance fighters and others wanted by the German authorities. In August 1943, Darnand took a personal oath of loyalty to Hitler and joined the Waffen SS, which supplied the Militia with money and arms. Widely despised by the French public, the Militia never attracted more than 25,000–30,000 men. Darnand, however, proved to be the exception to Vichy's overall diffidence toward fascist elements. During its first two years, the new French State kept fascists away from the inner circles of power and exhibited few of the extreme characteristics of a fascist regime.

COLLABORATION

In France, a cynical joke made the rounds during the war: "The definition of collaboration: Give me your watch and I'll tell you the time." Germany's Hermann Göring seconded that view in a statement to Reich Commisssioners for Occupied Territories, "Collaboration for Messieurs les Français. . . . That they deliver everything they possibly can until they cannot do more; if they do it voluntarily, I'll say I'm collaborating; if they gobble it all up themselves, then they are not collaborating."[12]

The decision of the legally established Vichy regime to collaborate with the Nazi occupiers during World War II has been one of the most painful memories in modern French history. Indeed, it has been so painful that only in the 1960s and the 1970s did the French nation begin to confront this reality. Up until then, most citizens preferred a version of history proclaimed by Vichy officials at their post-war trials: that Germany had forced collaboration on them and that they had done their best to stave off endless German demands. But there is no question that collaboration was a Vichy initiative from the very first. The most notorious example was a meeting on October 24, 1940, at Montoire, a town in the Loire valley where, for the first and only time, Pétain and Hitler met for a brief series of talks. Shortly after the meetings, Pétain, in a speech on October 30, announced that France was "entering the path of collaboration."[13] Pétain hinted that France's POWs would shortly return and even that the demarcation line would be lifted.[14] Despite the meetings, French POWs remained captive in Germany and the demarcation line remained in place. Indeed, as local prefects from across France reported back to Vichy, much of the population responded to the news about Montoire with alarm.[15]

Within two months after Montoire, on December 13, 1940, Pétain fired Laval as head of the government. Many people interpreted Laval's dismissal as a renunciation of the very policy of collaboration that the Montoire meeting and Pétain's speech had announced. German leader Otto Abetz informed Pétain that Hitler himself considered Laval's treatment a personal insult. In fact, Pétain had not fired Laval in an attempt to reverse the policy of collaboration, but because he intensely disliked Laval's secretive style and tendency to go behind his back. Furthermore, the leaders who replaced Laval continued to work for collaboration with Germany. While Pierre Laval may have been the first architect of collaboration, his successor after December 13, François Darlan, continued along the same lines, exceeding Laval's proposals in some cases. On May 27, 1941, Darlan signed the Protocols of Paris, giving Germany access to French airfields in Syria and port and submarine facilities in Tunisia and Dakar in the fight against Britain.[16] Darlan also wanted to bomb the British in Gibraltar to retaliate for an Anglo-Gaullist raid on Dakar, hoping that Germany would see this as a sign of France's earnestness.

French saber-rattling against Britain in the end served no purpose, for the simple reason that German leaders were not interested in French military assistance. Hitler wanted to keep France's empire out of British hands and was pleased that French military forces across the empire, loyal to Vichy, proved willing to repel British advances. Germany nevertheless neither trusted France nor valued French military cooperation. The Germans were happy to use whatever France might offer, as long as the cash, food, and industrial production kept flowing—which they did thanks in part to Vichy's experts. But the real benefits France gained from collaboration were dubious, especially given the huge costs of complicity with the Nazi regime.

THE NATIONAL REVOLUTION

One sign that Vichy was more than a puppet regime of the Nazis was its decision to launch immediately an extensive set of domestic policy initiatives at home and overseas, known as the "National Revolution." The Vichy regime committed the cardinal sin of taking advantage of a foreign occupation to impose its own agenda upon the nation—one that conservatives had never managed to get voter approval for in peacetime. Politically, the National Revolution's goal was to restore to France an authoritarian system with, if not a monarch, at least a regal leader, Pétain, as its central figure—hence the four constitutional acts of July 1940 establishing the new French State that made Pétain the head of state. Vichy officials believed that a single, powerful leader would rule more effectively than the bickering and ineffective National Assembly of the Third Republic. In keeping with this anti-republicanism, another one of the National Revolution's earliest decisions was to replace the Third Republic's motto, "Liberty, Equality, Fraternity," with one more in keeping with Vichy's conservative values: "Work, Family, Fatherland."

On the economic front, the National Revolution espoused a particular program that had long been popular with traditionalists and fascists alike—corporatism—and which like so many of Vichy's policies was essentially backward-looking, at least in theory. Vichy's corporatism harked back to old regime corporate bodies, such as guilds, which had served as the fundamental productive unit in a pre-industrial economy. In a modern economy, corporatism ostensibly sought to restore something of an older guild mentality that, rather than seeing capital and labor in opposition, would inspire them to work together in the best interests of their businesses. Corporatism thus rejected both Marxist-inspired notions of class struggle and liberal capitalism's embrace of competition, preferring cooperation to protect the interests of the sector as a whole. To encourage cooperation, the economy was to be organized into branches and each branch was to be run by a corporation, which Vichy called Organization Committees (Comités d'Organisation, or COs). Vichy created a series of COs, one for each major branch of the economy. In a CO, three groups—employers, managers, and workers—were supposed to come together. Forced to see beyond their narrow self or class interests, they would presumably work for the best interests of the entire sector. Meanwhile, a Labor Charter, passed in October 1941, destroyed independent labor unions, which Vichy criticized for defending the narrow interests of workers, and outlawed strikes. The problem, of course, was that the working class lost the independent voice of its unions in exchange for a few seats on a CO where they were consistently outvoted and ignored.[17]

Yet another element of the National Revolution, "Return to the Soil," sought to reverse what the French called the "rural exodus" or movement of population from rural to urban areas, which had become more pronounced with the Depression. Vichy promoted regionalization and rural repopulation, creating bonuses for families who brought abandoned farms back into cultivation and providing loans to couples when they married if they agreed to live on a farm. Ironically, the risks of air raids and constant food shortages faced by urban residents did more than Vichy's incentives to slow the movement away from the land, and the farm population of France remained constant during the war.

As the second term—"Family"—of its new motto indicated, the National Revolution aimed also to reinforce Catholicism and traditional morality in France, including sexual morality. Leaders at Vichy partly attributed France's defeat in 1940 to the decline of religion and the weakness of the French family, which, in their view, explained the long decline in France's birthrate. Conservatives at Vichy intended to halt the breakdown of traditional family life, linked to what they considered the "excessive liberation of women" and lax morality more generally. Central to Vichy's domestic policy was a highly publicized effort to "restore" the French family through a combination of policies directed primarily against women, but also homosexuals. These included financial inducements to leave the labor force and have babies, restrictive legislation on divorce and on married

women's employment in the public sector, stringent enforcement of laws prohibiting abortion and contraception, and a massive propaganda campaign. Vichy also
established fines and prison sentences of six months to three years for anyone who
"commits one or several shameless or unnatural acts with a minor of his own sex
under the age of twenty-one," thus restoring notions of "natural" and "unnatural"
to the realm of sexuality.[18] Although Vichy leaders berated the Third Republic for
"destroying" the traditional family, in this area, as in many others, Vichy policies
built on policies pioneered by the Republic, including the family allowances that
increased salaries based on the number of children. Still, there were differences.
The Third Republic had sought to provide incentives for having large families.
Vichy policy was more coercive, aimed at reinforcing patriarchy, limiting the
employment of married women, policing sexuality more directly, reducing the
number of divorces, and inspiring, if not indirectly compelling, couples to have
more babies.[19]

Front cover of "Voyage officiel du Maréchal Pétain on 18–19 November 1940." Published by
Le Nouvelliste de Lyon, 1940. Private Collection/Archives Charmet/The Bridgeman Art Library.

Any government hoping to bring about a moral renewal would naturally turn its attention to children. Impressionable children and adolescents represented the best hope for reshaping national values. Catholic conservatives believed the Third Republic had created a population rendered soft by too easy a life, accustomed to too much leisure, debilitated by drink and dissolute activities like dancing, jazz, and films, and that this indolence too explained the debacle of 1940. As Pétain affirmed in a radio message addressed to the nation's youth, "The unwholesome atmosphere your elders grew up in slackened their energies, weakened their courage. . . . You who have committed yourselves from the youngest age to take the steep paths, you will learn to prefer the joy of difficulties overcome to easy pleasures."[20]

One way that Vichy sought to reform French youth was through overhauling public schools, which conservative educational thinkers held particularly responsible for corrupting France's youth. Vichy leaders blamed schoolteachers for instilling such values as secularism, a cult of science, republicanism, and pacifism, all of which supposedly also laid the groundwork for the 1940 defeat. Vichy thus passed a law in July 1940 allowing it to fire any civil servant considered to be an "element of disorder."[21] Primary schoolteachers bore the brunt of that purge.

In addition to removing "undesirables" from the classroom, the regime reintroduced the teaching of traditional morality and obedience, in the hope of restoring the Catholic Church's influence and inspiring reverence for Pétain. Across France, schoolchildren were obliged to sing the quasi-official anthem, "Maréchal, nous voilà," whose lines, "Before you, savior of France, we, your boys, swear to serve and to follow in your footsteps," expressed the regime's heavy-handed promotion of a cult of the leader.[22] Jacques Chevalier, minister of national education from December 1940 until February 1941, added "duties to God" to the moral instruction required in public elementary schools, while Chevalier's successor set aside time during the school day for religious instruction.[23] French texts directed at children celebrated the glories of the French race, while anti-Semitism not only surged in frequency in school texts but also became more explicit and even violent.[24] Vichy also undertook a short-lived experiment of its own to create future leaders. In the Alpine village of Uriage, the new French State permitted the founding of a leadership school for young men based on the personalist philosophy of Catholic intellectual Emmanuel Mounier.

As the preceding description suggests, most of Vichy's National Revolution legislation was passed in the first two years of the Occupation, 1940 and 1941. On balance, the program proved of limited effectiveness. Where the National Revolution dovetailed with a broader trend, such as people deciding to remain on their farms where at least they would have enough to eat, it worked. Elsewhere it produced entirely unintended consequences. For example, despite the regime's nostalgic rhetoric, the harsh economic realities of the Occupation meant that the experts empowered by Vichy were able to rationalize the French economy under Vichy to a much greater degree than before the war. Vichy's educational reforms directed at youth were belied by a dramatic increase in juvenile crime rates.[25]

The new leadership school at Uriage at first supported many of the National Revolution's goals, but eventually veered toward resistance activities—among its most illustrious graduates were the post-war left-wing intellectuals Hubert Beuve-Méry and Jean-Pierre Domenach. It thus had to be shut down by the authorities.[26] Most people in France were not fooled by the National Revolution's rhetoric, demonstrating in private correspondence their keen awareness of the gaps between what Vichy advocated and what it could in fact provide. As one correspondent denouncing the gulf between the regime's pro-natalist propaganda and the actual conditions faced by mothers trying to feed their children put it: "It's a disgrace, a scandal! Children are deprived of milk . . . and the government that preaches about the birthrate is doing nothing, absolutely nothing to ease the problem!" Another writer wondered, "[T]hey tell us: 'have children' but what are we supposed to feed them since we cannot even buy any milk?"[27]

DAILY LIFE IN FRANCE UNDER THE OCCUPATION

Although many people in France were relieved about the Armistice and admired Pétain, a hero of the Great War, they did not necessarily support collaboration, a term that requires us to pause. Vichy's top leaders willingly collaborated, going beyond the requirements of the Armistice to work with Germany. Then there was "collaborationism," the ideological support for Nazi Germany that inspired various far-Right individuals, authors and intellectuals like Drieu la Rochelle and Brasillach, fascist movements, and newspapers such as the notoriously anti-Semitic *Je Suis Partout*.

Yet the shades of grey multiplied at the lower levels of the government. Some French police officers enforced Nazi policies, arresting Jews and resisters. But most police officers carried on with their usual duties, patrolling traffic, investigating crime, and so on. Were they collaborators? What about postal workers, or railway workers? In all occupied countries, local administrators continued to fulfill their duties, deliver mail, and run trains. What truly set France apart was not low-level administrative work, but high-level collaboration. As for the general public, most historians agree that there was little enthusiasm for collaboration. Even people who started out supporting Vichy and collaboration began to turn away from Vichy over time. Rather than collaboration, perhaps a better word to describe the behavior of most low-level civil servants, and many ordinary people, is "accommodation," the term that historian Philippe Burrin uses in his book on daily life in France. Accommodation was hardly resistance, but neither did it indicate active support or acquiescence with Vichy.[28]

By far the vast majority of French people simply struggled, as most people usually do, to survive from day to day under conditions that varied depending on location, occupation, resources, and ethnicity. After the initial extreme trauma of the Battle of France and exodus, conditions stabilized by the end of the summer and early fall of 1940. From there, they steadily got worse over time, becoming extreme again at the end of the Occupation as fighting resumed on French soil.

For everyone, however, shortages defined life during the Occupation. Germany fully intended to prevent shortages at home by taking as much as possible from the occupied countries. Quickly Germany began siphoning off huge quantities of French agricultural production, wheat, milk, meat, and other food staples. In addition, France lost access to overseas sources of products like sugar, coffee, and tobacco. To avoid urban starvation, in September 1940 France instituted a rationing system. Each person in a household was assigned to a rationing category, and individuals fell into one of nine categories based on age, work status, or pregnancy. The category determined the quantity of each good a person was entitled to purchase. Tickets were issued and had to be turned in to the shopkeeper to purchase the goods, but even having a ticket was no guarantee of finding the food.

As with any system facing severe shortages, long lines became a constant feature outside every food shop, and often the shop ran out before serving everyone in the line. In every city, an active black market developed for food, cigarettes, wine, and just about everything else. Items were traded without tickets, under the table, at inflated prices, and having money to spare and the right connections always made a difference. Despite efforts to ensure that everyone met minimal food needs, French caloric intake during the war was the lowest in Western Europe except Italy—a dramatic change for a nation that had been Western Europe's richest agricultural producer. The situation varied: City people were worse off than those in rural areas; people in the north fared better than those in the south; rich people, as always, suffered less than the poor. Also better off were people who had relatives in the countryside willing to send them food, or people wealthy enough to purchase or trade goods on the black market. Yet even with access to the black market, caloric intake in France averaged 1,500 calories a day (most adults need about 2,000 calories a day); in the winter of 1942–1943, official rations dropped below 1,200 calories a day. Bread rations varied from 275 to 350 grams a day, and meat rations declined in January 1942 to an average of 4 to 6 ounces a week.[29]

On an individual basis, farming families often sent food packages to their urban friends and relatives.[30] The food did not always arrive in good shape, but a number of women who lived through the war describe how they learned to deal with this. Simone Martin-Chauffier, a woman whose Resistance connections placed her in constant danger, claimed to have been much more unnerved by her inability to feed her family. She writes about taking a ham her friend was about to throw away because it had maggots. But, she figured, "fire purifies" so she and her daughter cooked it. Her daughter's appetite waned over the next several days, and her husband puzzled over her insistence on serving the ham hot. But, she closed, "The dead maggots did not do anyone any harm."[31]

To make matters worse, Germany required all clocks in the Occupied Zone be set an hour ahead, on German time, for Berlin's convenience. Combined with a curfew, this meant that French people lost valuable daylight time. To prevent Allied air raids, a strict blackout required all windows to be covered to prevent any light from seeping out. As in 1870, the city of light went dark. Fuel for heating was also in extremely short supply. By chance, the winter of 1940–1941 was particularly harsh.

In Paris apartment buildings, heat was turned on only for a few hours every day during the winter to conserve fuel, and hot water was only available two or three days a week.[32] People gathered sticks from the parks to burn in fireplaces to stay warm.

As for clothing, people were issued textile points entitling them to limited quantities of new clothing. They could also exchange old clothes for textile points. The old clothing would then be repaired and resold. Women made blouses from old bed sheets or tablecloths and unraveled old sweaters to knit new ones. *Marie-Claire* even suggested that poodle fur clippings made nice sweaters.[33] This advice overlooked the fact that, unable even to feed themselves, many urban-dwellers got rid of their pets. The shortage of silk and nylon led to the development of new products. *Filpas* could be painted on legs to resemble stockings, and some women even carefully drew seams up the back. The purchase of new shoes required permission from city hall. With both rubber and leather virtually unobtainable, shoe soles were made of wood. Making virtue of necessity, the French fashion world designed outrageous wooden soled shoes for women.[34]

The psychological consequences of all these forms of deprivation were great. Middle-class women in particular found their inability to cook good meals or keep up with fashion changes hard on morale. For all housewives, survival demanded patience, hard work, flexibility, and, at times ingenuity. For the most part, those who escaped these conditions were elites and high-level collaborators; wealthy people willing to trade could find what they needed. In most rural areas, extreme labor shortages made life difficult, but rural families usually had enough food. One exception to that rule was that families living in wine-growing regions of southern France or other monocultural areas suffered hunger if the local product was of limited use in keeping people fed.

For some people, normal hardships intensified. For example, women whose husbands were POWs in Germany faced all of these problems without help from their spouses. Many prisoners' wives had children, adding the pressure of single parenting. With their greatly reduced income, most prisoners' wives worked outside the home, which created childcare issues; took in work; or relied on parents or in-laws for help. Finally, prisoners' wives dealt with the psychological pressures of separation from their spouses, a separation whose length they could not determine.

People living in Alsace-Lorraine faced a unique situation. As in 1871, Germany annexed the territories and attempted to "germanize" its people. The region's Gauleiter (administrator), Robert Wagner, required street names, signage, even personal names to be Germanized; all men named Jacques would have to be called Jacob. French was forbidden in public. To avoid speaking German, many locals switched to Alsatian, a Germanic dialect frowned upon but not prohibited. Schools were also required to teach in German and about German history and culture, and even the beret was outlawed. Starting in August 1942, the German army conscripted local men of eligible age into the Wehrmacht (130,000 soldiers called the "*malgré nous*" or "despite ourselves").[35]

Those people living in northeastern France also faced acute difficulties. While Germany did not annex them, the regions of the Nord and the Pas-de-Calais became the "forbidden zone," placed under the German military command in Belgium, not Paris. People in the forbidden zone were cut off from rest of France, and workers there were conscripted almost immediately for German factories. For many in the forbidden zone, this was not the first German occupation. Some individuals had personally experienced two previous German occupations, one in 1870–1871 and one from 1914 to 1918. The Nord was the region "most impenetrable" to Vichy persuasion, since the Vichy regime's policies had little impact there.[36] Those residing in the region also tended to be more anti-German and pro-British.[37]

People living in areas of combat or air raids suffered their own particular traumas. Allied air raids in France started early in 1942. On March 3, the Royal Air Force (RAF) conducted a massive air raid on the Renault factories in the Parisian suburb of Boulogne-Billancourt, which were manufacturing tanks for Germany. In that attack, 367 civilians were killed and 1,500 wounded. Air raids intensified in 1943, targeting industrial and strategic assets, train depots, and bridges. The period leading up to the Normandy landing on June 6, 1944 saw concentrated bombing in particular regions. The Mediterranean coast, site of a secondary Allied landing on August 15, 1944, also experienced very heavy bombing. In some cases civilians thought to be in high-risk zones were evacuated from their homes. But the Allies often confounded French and German expectations and attacked in unexpected areas. In the end, 60,000 French civilians died in Allied air raids during the war.

The French public's response to Allied attacks varied, shaped by location and by political orientation. Some, likely resisters or Resistance supporters, quoted the French saying, "You can't make an omelet without breaking some eggs." Others, from the opposite end of the political spectrum, railed against the criminal Anglo-Americans for attacking a supposedly neutral France. Many fell in between, terrified and anxious about their own survival and that of their loved ones, wanting it all to end.

Beyond the hardships and difficulties nearly everyone faced during the war, both the German and Vichy authorities intentionally targeted some people for harsh measures. Vichy singled out not only communists but also Freemasons because the Masons had long been ardent republicans. Masons were purged from the civil service, and schoolteachers were required to sign a pledge that they were not members of a Masonic Lodge. Lists of Freemasons were published in the press to inspire other employers to fire them as well. Many Gypsies were rounded up and sent to a camp in Saliers, in the south of France.[38] But the single largest group of "undesirables" deliberately targeted by Vichy policies were France's Jews.

ANTI-SEMITISM

Vichy intended to resolve what had long been described in interwar France as "the Jewish problem." The massive wave of Jewish immigration to France following the

Nazi takeover in Germany, then Czechoslovakia and Austria, made the question more urgent in the eyes of many. As we have seen, faced with mounting economic malaise in the 1930s, the Third Republic had passed a restrictive immigration law in 1932 and curtailed refugees' ability to work, and then interned "enemy aliens" in September 1939. Vichy's policies built on these precedents, but went considerably further both in their racial definitions and in their exclusionary drive. Most importantly and contrary to what Vichy leaders claimed after the war, Vichy persecution of Jews did not result from German pressure, but from Vichy's own impulses.

Four months after it was established, Vichy, on October 3, 1940, passed a comprehensive Jewish Statute, usually referred to as the Alibert Law. The Alibert Law, followed by 50 additional laws and decrees over the next year, defined a person as Jewish if three of four grandparents had been Jewish. Vichy's anti-Semitic legislation established quotas on lawyers, doctors, university students, architects, and pharmacists and revoked the French citizenship of Jews who had been naturalized under the 1927 law. Jews were banned from public parks, cinemas, swimming pools, restaurants, and libraries. In August 1941 Jews were prohibited from owing bicycles or radios. Jewish civil servants and teachers were fired, and remaining teachers had to swear an oath that they were not Jewish. Over time, Jewish businesses and other assets were "aryanized," or stolen.

Starting in 1940, 40,000 foreign Jews were forced to leave their homes and live in one of seven camps in conditions many described as atrocious. About 3,000 detainees died owing to lack of hygiene, cold, poor diet, vermin, and disease.[39] In June 1942, Germany required Jews in the occupied zone to wear the yellow Star of David and to register at their local city hall where lists were compiled. In December 1942, Vichy required Jews to have the word "Jew" stamped on identification and ration cards. The anti-Semitic laws thus created a system of identification, segregation, expropriation, and exclusion in varying degrees (in segregated camps or from the public sphere). While Vichy policy stopped short of extermination, the identification and segregation of Jews had fatal consequences for many Jews in the crucible of World War II.

Uninterested at first in France's "Jewish question," Germany eventually turned its attention to the Jews residing there, where it was immeasurably aided by Vichy's anti-Semitic enterprise. Starting in 1942, Germany began to demand Jewish deportations from France, with quotas making clear how many Jews they expected. A series of deportations of Jews to the east was signaled by a massive round-up in Paris on July 16, 1942. The Germans demanded 28,000 Jews from Paris. In two days, French police arrested 12,884 Jews in Paris, including women and children, and warehoused them in a massive sports arena, the Vélodrome d'Hiver (Vel d'Hiv). The inadequate facilities were quickly overwhelmed, creating appalling conditions. The Vel d'Hiv round-up was followed by arrests outside Paris, for a total of 36,802 arrests by the end of 1942. The round-ups proved to be a key factor in turning public opinion against Vichy. Many non-Jews who witnessed the events found these massive arrests of innocent people, children crying and clinging to their mothers, extremely disturbing. Many Jews who escaped arrest owed their survival to warnings, concierges lying to police, and neighbors hiding them from the authorities. In one of the war's more inspiring episodes, the mountain town, Le Chambon, nestled in the Auvergne, managed to hide 2,000 Jews under the noses of German soldiers.

On the other hand, Vichy, which was determined to maintain the appearance of French sovereignty and autonomy, ordered its police to carry out the raids and arrests of Jews. Such a concern produced new levels of barbarism on the part of Vichy officials. For example, while Germany did not require Jewish children, Laval included them to push the numbers up. He bargained with Germany, trading the lives of "French" Jews by asking that they be spared as long as he delivered more "foreign" Jews. France had a pre-war Jewish population of about 300,000. Of those, some 75,000 were deported, of whom only 2,500 survived. Over 200,000 Jews survived the war in France, something Vichy's leaders were quick to take credit for after the war. Yet, they survived despite, not because of, Vichy's actions, relying on their own wits, their own resources, and, often, the support of rescue organizations and ordinary non-Jewish French people.[40]

VICHY AND THE EMPIRE

For Pétain, the empire was important not only as a bargaining chip to be used—or so he hoped—against German demands. Like the National Revolution and the cleansing of "foreigners" from French soil, the empire had a privileged role to play in Vichy's plans for rejuvenating the French nation and "race" that had ostensibly degenerated under the Third Republic. Indeed, Pétain arguably paid more attention to colonial affairs than had his republican predecessors, and certainly more than the Free French resistance that opposed him.[41] Moreover, Vichy had a much freer hand to experiment with new policies in the empire than it did in occupied France, since all colonies except Equatorial Africa initially went over to Pétain, and the empire remained unoccupied. Only Indochina had been invaded in 1940 by Japan, and the Japanese quickly came to an agreement with French officials that left Vichy in charge of the colony as long as it guaranteed Japanese troops free passage through it and integrated its economy into that of Japan. Given such freedom of action, Vichy developed a colonial policy of its own that was simultaneously racist and traditionalist, much like the French State at home. With no pressure from the Germans, this policy was applied in most of the empire from 1940 to 1942.

Racism per se was of course nothing new in France or its empire—it had always underpinned the republican civilizing mission. But under Vichy, this racism became more outspoken and took a different form. Under the Third Republic, colonial subjects had been viewed as inferior, but capable at least in theory of eventually becoming equal citizens in republics of their own. Pétain, on the other hand, celebrated the natural and permanent superiority of the virile colonizing white French race—an attitude that had come to be shared by increasing numbers of

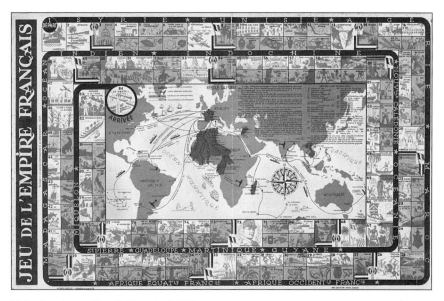

Vichy Boardgame "Jeu de L'Empire," 1941.   Research Library, The Getty Research Institute, Los Angeles (970031).

overseas administrators, merchants, and planters during political and economic crises of the 1930s, and especially after France's defeat in 1940. Vichy's racism (like its anti-Semitism, to which it was related) had a direct impact upon policy-making. Forced labor, taxation, and economic expropriation—all colonial policies that had been practiced under the Third Republic—became even more brutal in the 1940s, as a new cadre of governors general loyal to Pétain was appointed, and the empire was made to deliver raw materials to Nazi Germany. Jews in the colonies were also purged from the civil service on racial grounds.

Along with its own exclusionary brand of racism, however, the traditionalists at Vichy also decided to export the National Revolution to France's colonies. Most of the National Revolution's policies, such as corporatism, the "Return to the Soil," the revival of "traditional" customs and morality, the cult of Pétain, and a celebration of fitness and youth, had their counterparts overseas. Indeed no sooner had Vichy come to power than overseas officials set about re-creating the "authentic" political and social hierarchies that had been in place among the colonized before the arrival of the French republican administration—on the assumption that traditional authorities were always the best possible ones. Some administrators sought not only to restore traditional institutions but also to graft a cult of Pétain upon them. This policy was most evident in territories such as Madagascar and Indochina, which had strong pre-colonial traditions of monarchy. As one official wrote from Madagascar in 1941, comparing the situation under Vichy in the colony to that under the Third Republic, "From now on, [the local Malagasy] envision the Marshal in the image of their former *Mpanjaka,* who embodied absolute power. Things are much better so."[42]

Driving nostalgia for a "golden past" when traditional morality and customs ruled was the belief that such elites would naturally share the conservative goals of Vichy's National Revolution, and thus prove a strong counter to the growing nationalist movements France faced everywhere in the empire by the late 1930s. Ironically, the opposite was true. Vichy's attempt to revive traditional hierarchies and customs only served to foster a new sense of national resistance among the very peoples that Vichy had hoped would support the new French State. The Vietnamese, for example, now began to discover in their own history and folklore a "glorious" past that they could use to reclaim their liberty from the colonizer. As journalist Tao Trang wrote in 1940, the Vichy motto "Work, Family, Fatherland" "summarizes for [the children of Vietnam] all of our own program of reconstruction."[43] When the war finally ended, France would face a much more militant national liberation movement there than anything that had existed in the 1930s, one that effectively fused communism with nationalism.

In France's older Caribbean colonies such as Guadeloupe and Martinique, which had been much more republicanized than the African, Southeast Asian, and Oceanian colonies conquered at the end of the nineteenth century, the advent of Vichy would have a different outcome. Here it was not the revival of "tradition" that spearheaded anti-colonialism but the rescinding of long established republican rights, as well as outrage at the new discrimination leveled by Vichy at Jews, Freemasons, and communists. Males from Guadeloupe and Martinique had been able to vote for representatives to the local assemblies since the mid-nineteenth century, and they sent representatives to the National Assembly. When Vichy rescinded these rights, many Guadaloupeans fought these changes in the name of liberty. Their resistance movement would help end Vichy rule on their island in 1943.

Algeria presents yet a third case. The settlers there for the most part welcomed the Vichy regime, which immediately cracked down on the Algerian nationalist movement. Pétain sentenced the prominent pro-independence leader, Messali Hadj, to 16 years hard labor; he also repealed the Crémieux decree, thus disenfranchising Algeria's Jews. For French-educated Algerians, however, the defeat and occupation of France was a time of confusion about where political allegiances lay, at least until the arrival of the Americans in North Africa in November 1942. At that point, many rallied to the Free French, demanding in return recognition of Algeria's right to self-determination at the war's end. Muslim soldiers would make up a large percent of Free French forces that eventually landed in southern France in 1944, fully anticipating that with the liberation of France the democratic principles of 1789 would finally be extended to them.[44]

RESISTANCE

After the war, a myth developed that nearly everyone in France and many French overseas hated the German Occupation and had resisted it in some way, creating a nation of 40 million resisters carrying secret messages or hiding downed Allied airmen or Jews. In fact, it would have been extremely surprising had there been 40 million resisters in France during World War II, since no other country's population resisted on that scale. Moreover, unlike most other Western European nations occupied by Germany, France had a supposedly autonomous French State that not only spoke out against resisting the occupying authorities but also targeted resistance itself. Under these circumstances, resisting would have required exceptional courage and moral clarity. It would have meant not just opposing Germany, but also defying France's own government, which had come to power through legal means and which insisted that it was a legitimate authority. Early resisters would have had to challenge this legitimacy, something only a few people did.

Evaluating the extent of resistance requires a definition of the term. Some scholars define resistance in narrow, military terms. Resisting meant taking direct action against the German occupiers, military action such as combat, sabotage, assassination, bombing, or the dangerous activities of publishing and distributing Resistance newspapers, flyers, and posters. That definition would include the 7,000 or so French soldiers who joined de Gaulle's Free French movement in London in 1940. Not surprisingly, Vichy and the Germans labeled such people terrorists and traitors. A slightly wider definition would also include people who collected and passed along information to the Allies or to de Gaulle in London. Resisters needed shelter, cash, ration tickets, food, and liaison agents to carry critical messages to other resisters or to deliver weapons or other materiel used in combat actions. Very often women were involved in these kinds of activities, which allowed them to make use of their traditional domestic roles. Being a woman provided some level of "invisibility," since the authorities' mental picture of a resister was of a man. Women could escape notice, using an empty baby carriage to hide weapons, for example. Women often adopted masculine code names that further threw the authorities off the scent, and some women engaged in active combat.[45]

Only certain kinds of people would normally, in any society, be able to commit themselves to organized resistance, given the huge risks to their own and their families' lives. Resisters had to be willing to cut themselves off from friends and family and go underground. Young people without children were best able to make that choice, or military men who saw through Pétain and were prepared to risk their lives for their country. Communists were another group involved in the Resistance, but only as official party policy after Hitler violated the Nazi-Soviet Pact and invaded the U.S.S.R. on June 21, 1941. After the war, they called themselves the first party of the Resistance, the "party of the 75,000 martyrs," overlooking the party's official pre June-1941 refusal to oppose the Occupation.[46]

A broader definition of resistance would include not just those who published resistance newspapers, but also those who regularly read them and listened to the BBC's French broadcasts, some 2 million people.[47] "Resistance" could, in this sense, extend as far as including people who only temporarily provided shelter or food or who lied to the police searching an apartment, telling them the family had moved away. In fact, a successful resistance movement cannot survive without such widespread, unorganized popular support. The French Resistance, particularly once it developed armed units in the countryside, was really a guerrilla movement. Community support is integral to such movements, allowing the fighters to melt away. Yet since such resistance was transitory and often unrecognized, we will never know how many people it would include. A fairer view would include many of these temporary activities as well, because the Germans defined all such activity as criminal. A person caught hiding a resister, or with Resistance newsletters, could be jailed, deported, even executed.

Related to resistance, but more elusive and perhaps impossible to grasp fully, is the idea of dissidence. People not willing to join a resistance movement and risk their lives expressed in other ways their rejection of Vichy, its leaders, its ideology, the German Occupation, or all of these. Dissidence was apparent in the public response to the required showing of German-made newsreels before all feature films. By September 1940, film audiences in Paris routinely whistled, coughed, and sneezed loudly during the screening of the pro-German newsreels, titled "Actualités mondiales"("World News"), to the extent that German military authorities threatened to close down all Paris cinemas if such provocations continued. The situation got so bad that by January 1941 the screening rooms were not entirely darkened during the newsreels so that unruly spectators could be identified and arrested.[48]

The courts also provide a sense of this broader dissidence. Cases from district courts, which did not handle serious resistance charges, warn us not to take the small numbers in the organized Resistance to mean that the French people in general simply resigned themselves to being defeated, occupied, and run by an anti-democratic, collaborationist regime. For example, one June evening in 1942 in the Paris suburb of Montrouge, two French policemen, who had been working on a traffic checkpoint with the German police, heard a woman's voice yelling from an open window, "Pigs!" The police located the apartment and knocked on the door. A man opened the door. When asked if his wife had yelled out the window, he responded, "Certainly, the pigs are you. I'm not for collaboration, I'm French," and he slammed the door on them. Apparently, after they left, the wife once again yelled more "disagreeable words" out the window. In the end, however, the court levied a 100 franc fine on the husband for insulting French police officers to their faces.[49]

Perhaps a final case of what we can call dissidence is offered by young admirers of swing jazz, who developed a collective identity and a designation, the *zazous*, under the Occupation. In interwar Paris, jazz had developed a small but important following of fans, critics, and musicians.[50] After France's defeat in 1940, the small audience for jazz in France underwent explosive growth, as reflected in the rising number of jazz concerts and growing number of hours of jazz carried weekly on the radio.[51] The term *zazou* came from Cab Calloway and the Cotton Club Orchestra's 1933 hit, "Zag Zuh Zag." In his 1939 hit, "Je suis swing" ("I am swing") French swing star Johnny Hess united the terms swing and *zazou* with the lyrics: "Je suis swing/Je suis swing/Za-zou, za-zou, za-zou, za-zouzé."[52] Hess and other French swing musicians, including the internationally renowned Hot Club of

France with Django Reinhardt and Stéphane Grappelli, produced many hits and in June 1942 the Richard Pottier film, *Mademoiselle Swing,* opened.

The *zazous* rejected Vichy's moral order through their clothing and general appearance. Contrary to the clean-cut look favored in Vichy propaganda, the young men grew thin mustaches and wore long jackets and short pants with big baggy knees tapering to narrow ankles over white socks, an outfit that flaunted the textile industry stipulation that clothing should use the least fabric possible. Young French men clearly adopted the American zoot suit, described by its self-proclaimed creator, Chicago clothier and jazz trumpet player Howard C. Fox, as having the "reet pleat, the reave sleeve, the ripe stripe, the stuff cuff and the drape shape that was the stage rage during the boogie-woogie rhyme time of the early 1940s."[53]

Young women, in defiance of the era's conservative, feminine, maternal look, also had their own style that included short pleated skirts; blouses or jackets with large padded shoulders; heavy, flat shoes; died blond hair; and heavy make-up. For both sexes, dark sunglasses and a "Chamberlain umbrella," nicknamed after former British Prime Minister Neville Chamberlain, functioned as the ultimate trademark.[54] The rebellious youth also listened to jazz, music associated with degenerate American culture, and spent time in cafés in the Latin Quarter or along the Champs-Elysées. *Zazous* developed their own ironic language, for example, calling the Paris Metropolitain subway system the "*Pétain mollit trop,*" which translates as, "Pétain is getting too soft." *Zazou* culture clearly repudiated both the moralism of Vichy and the austerity of the era.[55]

Although the *zazous'* cultural rejection of Vichy did not represent a clear resistance stance, they did attract the ire of the authorities. In part the *zazous* constituted an easy target because they so visibly thumbed their noses at Vichy's values. The French government's frustration led to at least one police raid on a Paris café known as a *zazou* hangout, where they arrested young men under the drinking age of 20 or with no verifiable occupation. About a dozen of them were sent to rural areas, courtesy of a program that dispatched "idle" urban youth to the countryside to help bring in the harvest. Not content, the right-wing press continued to press for action against the *zazous,* leading to an incident in June 1942 in which a number of members of a fascist youth group reported in its paper, *Jeunesse,* that they had "scalped" several *zazous,* shaving off all their long, irritating hair.[56] After the Germans demanded that Jews in France wear the yellow Star of David, a number of *zazous* added political content to their rebelliousness, devising their own yellow star inscribed with the word "Swing." One *zazou* arrested in conjunction with that act of defiance was reportedly deported to Auschwitz.[57]

The *zazou* phenomenon ended abruptly early in 1943 with the introduction in France of forced labor in Germany, a time when calling attention to themselves could land young men in a labor convoy to Germany. While the *zazous* both drew on interwar jazz culture and foreshadowed post-war youth counter-cultures of the 1950s and 1960s, the context of war, foreign occupation, and a conservative government with an ambitious agenda for youth placed the *zazous* in a unique context that leaves us with many questions about who they were and what they intended.

TURNING POINT: 1942

By early 1942, conditions had considerably worsened in France, repression had increased, and Vichy's slogans rang increasingly hollow. As a result, popular support for the Vichy government began to wane. Already in August 1941, a frustrated Pétain spoke of the growing distance between his government and the people. "I have been conscious of an evil wind arising . . . in France. Minds are falling prey to anxiety, doubt is gaining hold."[58] However, growing dislike of Vichy would not necessarily have propelled more people into the organized resistance had not a combination of political events conspired to further disenchant the public. In April 1942 Pierre Laval, already deeply unpopular, returned to head the government. At the same moment Germany decided to impose forced labor on France. These developments together would create the conditions for the first time in France for large numbers of people to cross the line from dissidence to resistance.

At first, Laval tried to avoid German demands for forced labor by using France's POWs, over a million still in captivity in Germany, as bargaining chips. In a June 1942 speech, Laval proclaimed "I desire the victory of Germany" ("Je souhaite la victoire de l'Allemagne") and announced a program whereby French workers who volunteered to go work in Germany would allow French POWs to be

Workers in Germany, World War II poster, 1942. Bibliothèque Nationale, Paris/Archives Charmet/ The Bridgeman Art Library.

repatriated, a program called *la relève,* the term used when one military unit replaces another on the front lines. The press was instructed to bury the fact that it took three skilled workers to free one POW. Not surprisingly, the *relève* failed to supply enough labor to meet German quotas. The hoped-for figure was 250,000 workers, but despite a massive propaganda effort, by the end of the summer of 1942 only 17,000 French workers had signed up. Putting an end to the voluntary nature of the program, in September 1942 the French government required all workers ages 18 to 35 to register for labor service, the Service du Travail Obligatoire, or STO. Many of these workers were designated to "volunteer" for Germany, and they did all they could to avoid the duty. In one factory in Nîmes, for example, some 700 workers stopped work for three hours in solidarity with their 60 co-workers designated for the *relève.*[59]

Finally, on February 16, 1943, Germany imposed compulsory labor on all men born between 1920 and 1922, with exceptions for workers in critical sectors like mining, farming, or law enforcement. Hundreds of thousands of men then faced the stark choice of being deported to Germany to work in factories, live in a labor camp and likely face Allied air raids, or going into hiding. In its first three months 250,000 workers were sent to Germany, but the STO was so unpopular that over the next two months the numbers dwindled to 37,000.[60] In the end, some 700,000 French workers left on the STO. We may never know how many people went into hiding, a group called *refractaires* (dodgers); but for those young men who were already living outside the law, it was a short step into joining a resistance movement. At this point the *maquis,* a rural resistance army whose troops hid in forests and remote mountain areas, grew rapidly. These irregular military groups organized into units with commanders and conducted small military operations, such as the sabotaging of rail lines. By the end of the Occupation, the *maquis* was capable of conducting more serious military actions and engaged in a number of battles with German troops. Many historians believe that the psychological value of these efforts outweighed their strategic importance.[61]

Another key turning point, a military one, also came in 1942. After much disagreement and discussion, Britain and the United States decided to attack the German army in Africa, rather than opening a second front on the European continent as they had promised the U.S.S.R. French North Africa would provide a launching pad for what Churchill called the "soft underbelly" of Europe, Italy. Although there was some resistance on the part of French and colonial troops still under the control of Vichy, in November 1942 Allied troops quickly succeeded in taking over North Africa. French West Africa now joined de Gaulle's Free French alongside French Equatorial Africa, thus giving the Resistance control of the entire African empire. Former Vichy premier François Darlan, who happened to be in North Africa to visit his ailing son, at first refused an offer to join with the Allies, but eventually signed an agreement. Furious, on the symbolic date of November 11 (Armistice Day), Hitler ordered German soldiers to cross the demarcation line and occupy all of France. On November 28, as German soldiers approached the port of Toulon where French naval ships were stationed, the French navy scuttled its remaining fleet rather than allowing Germany to take it. In response to this act of defiance, Germany completely disbanded France's small Armistice army.

Leaders like Laval, Darlan, and others had operated on the assumption that France had key assets that gave it bargaining leverage with Germany. By the end of 1942, the French State no longer controlled its empire, had seen its navy scuttled, and had been forced to disband the only military force that Vichy had, the Armistice army. With the loss of its unoccupied territory on November 11, would Vichy leaders play their last card, resign, and disband the French government? Pétain never seriously considered it, proving that the French State's implied threat of rejoining the Allies had always been an idle one. Vichy had no chips left, and German demands became relentless.

From the end of 1942 forward, Germany began demanding higher quotas of Jews to deport. They intensified police action in France. Voluntary labor service became forced labor. All of Vichy's grand plans for the regeneration of France withered. Both Laval and Darlan were targets of attempted assassinations, and Darlan was eventually killed. Sabotage increased, and Allied air raids intensified. Vichy lost nearly all of its legitimacy, hanging on by the tattered shreds of Pétain's personal popularity. Leaders like Pétain had created the Vichy regime in 1940 to restore order, hoping to prevent the chaos of total war in France. Instead, it revived the demon of civil war in the form of the French Resistance, which pitted French against French as much as French against Germans.

CIVIL WAR: RESISTANCE, LIBERATION, AND THE PURGE

While the *maquis* became significant only after 1942, resistance to the Occupation had begun, if only on a very small scale, immediately after the Armistice was signed in June 1940. Given the risk of arrest and torture, resisters usually used false code names and only knew the few people in their circle or cell to prevent exposing large numbers of fellow resisters to arrest should one resister break under torture. Slowly a variety of more formal organizations developed, Défense de la France and Libération Nord in the occupied northern zone, Combat and Libération-Sud in the unoccupied southern zone, and the Organisation Civile et Militaire, which included career civil servants and military men. The Francs-Tireurs et Partisans were the military wing of the outlawed Communist Party(Parti Communiste or PC), which also organized resistance groups for immigrants and women. Most resistance groups also published papers. These groups came into being from the ground up, and some of them eventually made contact with de Gaulle's Free French in London—but de Gaulle did not create these groups in the first place.

Among resisters, an early dispute revolved around the appropriate tactics for the Resistance. Some groups advocated using violence and assassination, and in August and October 1941 two German soldiers and one civilian German official were killed in separate assassinations in Paris (on the Metro), Nantes, and Bordeaux. The Germans responded with ferocious repression. They rounded up hostages, mostly petty criminals and communists from the local jails, 50 in Nantes and another 50 in Bordeaux, and threatened to execute them unless the assassins were turned in. When no one came forward, all 100 hostages were executed, and another 50 were arrested and threatened with execution. With the horror mounting, Pétain finally stepped forward and offered himself as a hostage in exchange, ending the executions. No one ever turned in the people responsible for the assassinations, but at this point de Gaulle from London urged resisters in France not to use assassinations and direct attacks because the price was too high for the purpose it served. Thus resisters in France concentrated, especially in the first two years, on propaganda; on information gathering; on helping downed Allied airmen, Jews, and other people targeted by the Nazis to escape; and on sabotage.

As the tide of the war began to turn against Germany in 1942, de Gaulle increasingly focused on the internal Resistance. He felt that there needed to be some unity and coordination between it and his forces in London. In January 1942 de Gaulle sent a representative, Jean Moulin, to the unoccupied zone to persuade southern Resistance movements to recognize de Gaulle and coordinate their efforts under the Free French. In exchange, they would receive money and arms from London. After the Allied take-over of North Africa in November 1942, de Gaulle moved his headquarters to Algiers and in effect created a shadow government with all the usual ministries. Moulin persuaded the internal Resistance movements to form the United Resistance Movement (Mouvements Unis de la Résistance or MUR) on January 27, 1943. By late May 1943 he persuaded them to accept the leadership of a National Resistance Council (Conseil National de la Résistance or CNR), but three weeks later Moulin was arrested, tortured, and killed by the Gestapo (under agent Klaus Barbie). The CNR nevertheless survived with a new leader, Georges Bidault, and the resulting coordination with de Gaulle allowed internal Resistance groups to launch diversionary moves against German forces on D-Day. They also worked with de Gaulle's shadow government in Algiers to formulate France's post-Liberation plans.

Despite its growing strength and militancy, the French Resistance could not liberate France on its own. By the turn of 1944, nearly everyone expected the Allies to attempt a continental invasion. Germany had built a formidable line of defenses, Fortress Europe, along the English Channel coast, and ordered evacuations of civilians from many coastal regions as Allied air raids intensified in the spring of 1944. The Allies' Operation Overlord planned the landing much further east on the coast than Germany expected, on beaches code-named Omaha, Utah, and Juno. Even though the Allies succeeded in establishing the beachhead on D-Day on June 6, 1944, it was not until July 31 that they broke out of Normandy.

On August 15 the Allies, including seven French divisions, launched a second landing on the Mediterranean coast. As the Germans withdrew, Dwight Eisenhower, the Allied supreme commander, insisted at first that Allied armies by-pass Paris, which he considered a diversion. However, on August 18, Resistance movements in Paris called on the people of Paris to launch their own uprising; on August 22, barricades, the traditional symbol of revolutionary resistance, went up in the city.

Eisenhower relented, and General Jacques Philippe Leclerc and his Second Armored Division entered Paris. The German commander surrendered on August 24, and Paris was liberated. By then Germany had begun to pull its forces back to concentrate on planning an offensive against the Allies in eastern France, ironically where they had first invaded, in the Ardennes. They launched this battle, known as the Battle of the Bulge, in the winter of 1944–1945. Allied success in the Bulge signaled the end of German offensive operations in the west, but final victory would come only on May 8, 1945.

Although fighting continued through the winter and spring of 1944–1945, most of France was liberated by early September 1944. On August 26, de Gaulle and Leclerc led a victory parade down the Champs-Elysées to throngs of cheering crowds. No doubt most people in Paris, even if they had not actively resisted, were relieved that the ordeal was nearly over. Nearly a million French POWs neverthe-less remained in Germany, where German commanders held them as potential bargaining chips in future negotiations. When retreating, rather than leaving the camps to be liberated, some camp commanders forced the prisoners to march into the center of Germany under the extreme battle conditions of war's end. Many POWs lost their lives in these final months. In addition to the POWs, there were about 700,000 forced laborers in Germany; another 240,000 people had been deported from France to Germany, of whom 75,000 were Jews and the rest mostly resisters. The Provisional Government estimated nearly 2 million French nationals were in Germany in 1945. France was stunned to discover that only 38,000 of the 240,000 deportees—and just 2,500 of 75,000 Jews—were still alive at the end of the war.

Some people expected the hardships to melt away with the German army, but they were soon proven wrong. After the Liberation, the French economy was in shambles. Allied air raids had targeted rail lines, roads, and bridges. The summer 1944 harvest was badly disrupted by fighting, and the transportation and distribu-tion networks were hard hit. Thus scarcity, shortages, and rationing continued, and even worsened. And to the threat of insufficient food, another was immedi-ately added: that of bloody civil war. As the Germans retreated, a variety of people directly affected by the political struggles of the last four years—families or friends of resisters betrayed, deported, or executed—began taking their revenge against collaborators in a wave of reprisals known as the purge. Many cases of unsolved homicides appeared in court dockets, as authority figures turned a blind eye to this settling of scores.[62]

Reprisals taken against women accused of sleeping with German soldiers were one of the more unsettling aspects of the purge. After the Liberation, in towns across France, women accused of sleeping with Germans were targeted; their heads were shaved, swastikas were painted on them, and they were paraded in front of jeering crowds. Popularly labeled "horizontal collaborators," some of these women were prostitutes. In interviews, several people claimed they were POW wives who had slept with Germans. In fact, most shorn women faced accusations not just of having intimate relations with the German occupiers, but also of denunciation. Yet only women so accused faced this shaming ordeal in addition to official legal procedures. Clearly, women's perceived violation of sexual norms served as a metaphor for the Vichy leaders' political collaboration.[63] A secondary wave of reprisals followed the return of deportees in the spring months of 1945, when people became aware of the full horrors of the concentration camps. Some have claimed that as many as 100,000 people were killed in reprisals, but the actual number is closer to 10,000.

TURNING THE PAGE: THE MYTH OF THE GAULLIST RESISTANCE

The cycle of violence and reprisals against collaborators, real and imagined, came to a halt in part because of an idea that Charles de Gaulle expressed best on June 16, 1946. In a major speech in Bayeux, Normandy—the part of France first liberated—he told the people assembled there,

> First there came an elite, which sprang forth spontaneously from the depths of the nation and which, disdaining considerations of party or class, had dedicated itself to the struggle for the liberation, the grandeur and the renewal of France. . . . [T]his elite . . . despite heavy losses, was to carry the entire Empire and the whole of France along behind it. But it could never have done so without the assent of the vast mass of the French people. . . . While many had no choice but to bow to circumstances, the number of those that accepted those circumstances in their spirit and in their heart was literally infinitesimal. Never did France believe that the enemy was anything but the enemy, or that salvation lay elsewhere than the weapons of freedom. As the veils were ripped asunder, the deep-seated sentiment of the country manifested itself in its true colors.[64]

This speech articulated what can be called the myth of France as a nation of "40 million resisters." The Gaullist myth quickly took root, nourished by accounts written just after the war as well as by films, popular culture, and high school essay contests. In this version, aside from the tiny clique at Vichy, nearly everyone in France resisted the German Occupation; even people who were not official members of an organized resistance network or movement or militia had contributed by passing along messages, misleading Germans by reversing traffic signs, warning families in danger when police came to arrest them, and so on. This myth helped heal France's shame about its humiliating defeat, allowed France to save face, and move on, but it never really fooled most people, who knew full well who had resisted and who had collaborated. Furthermore, the notion of 40 million resisters both detracted from the real heroism of resisters and downplayed the significance of collaboration.

The Gaullist myth, by masking Vichy France's active contribution to the Nazi war effort and the Final Solution, also unintentionally provided a defense for Vichy leaders arrested and charged with treason. At their post-war trials, these men insinuated themselves into the idea of a nation of resisters, claiming, for example, that Vichy had served as a protective shield against the Nazi invader, sparing France the worst, softening the blows. Some Vichy leaders even claimed that they had collaborated in public all the while secretly supporting the Resistance behind the scenes. Overall, collaborationists represented a small but significant portion of the French population, many in high positions, who had supported Vichy and applauded its ideology, a continuation of the long-standing Right-Left divide in France. After the Liberation, France charged 124,750 people with treason; of those 38,000 were convicted and served time. The primary targets were public figures and notorious collaborators. Some prominent leaders were executed, including Pierre Laval, while de Gaulle commuted Pétain's death sentence to life.

The legal purge did not extend down far into the ranks of bureaucrats, industrial leaders, and civil servants, who mostly had stayed on the job. Leaving most public servants alone served the useful purpose of keeping the trains running, mail delivered, streets swept, and garbage collected. With much of its infrastructure in ruins, France could ill afford to let many qualified public servants go. As for economic elites, only a few business leaders faced arrest or trial. However, the state did confiscate the company of one of the most notorious industrial collaborators, Louis Renault, whose factories had produced tanks for Germany. Similarly, the post-war newspaper *Le Monde* was created when the provisional government handed the physical plant of the newspaper *Le Temps*, which had continued to publish during the Occupation until the end of November 1942, to a team of Resistance intellectuals, led by Hubert Beuve-Méry. Intellectuals who had written in support of collaboration, fascists like Brasillach and Drieu la Rochelle, were arrested and tried. Rather than face trial, Drieu la Rochelle committed suicide; Brasillach was convicted and executed for treason. Charles Maurras was also tried and convicted of treason. As he left the courtroom, he cried: "It's the revenge of Dreyfus!" To a large extent, Maurras was right. The Liberation restored France's republican, democratic, human rights traditions and silenced the staunchly antirepublican, monarchist, and fascist factions that had supported Vichy. Only in the 1950s would the far Right reappear in France, in a new nationalist, authoritarian, and xenophobic guise triggered by economic restructuring, the onset of the Cold War, and decolonization.

When de Gaulle had moved his operation to Algiers in May 1943, he had created, through the French Committee of National Liberation (Comité Française de Libération Nationale or CFLN), a shadow government for France, with contacts throughout the Resistance inside France. The CFLN, which in May 1944 became, per Eisenhower's order, the Provisional Government of French Republic, drew up plans for post-Liberation France, even deciding which local prefects had to be removed and who should replace them. The existence of a French organization ready to take over spared France much of the turmoil that might have followed the Liberation.

Quickly in the summer of 1944, the Provisional Government took over active day-to-day administration and, despite the existence of a collaborationist regime during the war, the Allies did not occupy France. While nearly all resisters were firmly committed to democracy, de Gaulle himself came from the political Right and was an immensely popular military general, whom many republicans distrusted. Working out what kind of government would replace the Provisional Government would take another two years, in which de Gaulle himself would prove the most visible casualty.

CHAPTER 10

Reconstruction at Home and Overseas
1945–1958

The final victory over Hitler on May 8, 1945, inspired celebrations in the United States and across many parts of Europe. In France, in contrast, V-Day was met with only muted public enthusiasm. By the spring of 1945, the happy memories of the previous August, when Paris had been liberated, had already faded in the face of continuing hardships and shortages. And across the Mediterranean, in France's most important overseas territory, Algeria, May 8 proved a trigger to a horrifying explosion of violence in the town of Sétif. During the town's official parade to celebrate the victory over Hitler, with thousands watching, certain indigenous participants raised nationalist flags as they shouted anti-colonial slogans calling for the liberation of Algeria. When the police tried to tear down the banners, a riot broke out and quickly turned bloody as angry Algerians went on a rampage against the local settlers.

Over the next five days, some 80 to 100 European *pieds noirs* (settlers) and their families were massacred and another hundred wounded. The French authorities responded with unprecedented ferocity—even for Algeria. General Duval, with Charles de Gaulle's full support, ordered a fierce crackdown on the Algerian population, including raids on suspected ringleaders, many of whom were killed, and the bombing and shelling of villages across Algeria. According to the French military, some 10,000 to 15,000 Algerians died in the reprisals, while the Algerians estimated the total deaths at 45,000. The brutal repression of Algerian desires for liberation followed France's liberation from German occupation by less than a year. Yet most people in France failed to recognize the hypocrisy of the nation's position in Algeria or anywhere else in the empire, and imagined that the empire would continue much as before. The memory of Sétif in France disappeared from public discourse until the very end of the twentieth century. Across the Mediterranean, however, the dreadful events of May 1945 only redoubled the conviction of many Muslim Algerians—especially the young—that their country would be freed from France only by force.

The events of May 8—waning jubilation in France, cruel blindness to the aspirations of Algerians for independence—were an early sign of the difficulties and contradictions that would attend the transition from Liberation to rebuilding. The Resistance leaders who formed the Provisional Government had hoped for a new political beginning for France that would break with the bad habits of the past. Instead, the birth of the Fourth Republic in 1946 was a messy affair, followed by a return to the political instability of short-lived governments characteristic of the Third Republic's later years. The link between the reestablishment of a Republic and the disproportionate repression of the Sétif uprising, moreover, foreshadowed a fundamental and ultimately fatal flaw: The Fourth Republic would collapse in 1958 because it could neither win nor end a war against Algerian independence. Yet despite the many political failures, the Provisional Government managed to prevent the nation from succumbing to civil war in 1944–1945, and the new Fourth Republic laid the foundations for impressive economic, social, and cultural changes for decades to follow.

THE PROVISIONAL GOVERNMENT IN CHARGE

As historian Robert Paxton has noted, France in August 1944 stood on the brink of civil war. Fewer people were killed during World War II than had been killed during the Great War, but many more civilians died in this conflict. And aside from those who died in air raids or fighting, many of those civilians were killed for political reasons. France was more divided by World War II than any other country with the exception of Yugoslavia, and an estimated 10,000 French people were killed in summary executions and other settling of scores during the Liberation.[1]

In the end, however, France avoided civil war and balkanization. In part this turn of events can be attributed to de Gaulle's success, as leader of the Provisional Government, in taking charge of the fraught transition from war to peace. De Gaulle used the bureaucracy, the military, and public ceremony to reassert state authority. During the fall of 1944, following a stop in Paris, de Gaulle visited the major cities of nearly every region of France, where he burnished his version of the "royal entry" of kings, following a script that started with a public greeting of the key state officials, meeting at the prefecture with invited guests, and culminating in a processional and public address from city hall, to the public acclaim of enthusiastic crowds. In this way de Gaulle both consolidated his control over local authorities across France and created an image of universal popular acclamation.[2] In addition to securing support for himself and his representatives as legitimate authorities, de Gaulle managed to channel the popular violence and anger against collaborators that accompanied the Liberation into legal procedures and court cases. Furthermore, despite rumors to that effect, the French Communist Party (Parti Communiste or PC) did not attempt to launch an uprising to take power but continued to work within the system. Finally, the creation of the Gaullist Resistance myth allowed the French to turn their backs on the recent past and concentrate on the future.

Despite France's complex internal problems in 1944–1945, de Gaulle felt that the nation had to play a military role in the defeat of Germany, if it was to once again be a major power. For that reason, and also to avoid it becoming a rival military force that might contest his power, the internal Resistance army was incorporated into the resurrected French army on September 23, 1944. By 1945, France had mobilized 18 divisions, or about 500,000 French troops, to take part in the final campaigns on the western front of Germany. The French units recaptured Strasburg, in the Alsace region, in November 1944, and fought alongside U.S. troops to capture Colmar in February 1945.

Significantly, the reconstituted French army that took part in the final campaigns included large numbers of colonial troops. As many as 250,000 indigenous soldiers from North Africa, West Africa, and Indochina took part in various campaigns between 1939 and 1945, including approximately 50,000 of the 240,000 French troops that landed in southern France in August 1944. De Gaulle had begun to consider the future of the empire as early as 1943, when he granted citizenship to tens of thousands of Muslims in Algeria, without forcing them to give up their personal status. At the beginning of 1944 he convened a first-ever conference of colonial administrators from North Africa, sub-Saharan Africa, and Madagascar in Brazzaville in Equatorial Africa, hosted by Félix Eboué, whom de Gaulle had promoted to the rank of governor general. The purpose of the conference was to draw up significant reforms to be implemented after the return of peace. As de Gaulle put it, there could be no question of decolonization, only greater assimilation of the colonies to France. These promises helped justify the use of colonial troops in defense of an ostensibly shared *patrie,* that of Greater France, in 1944–1945. Nevertheless, the individual colonial soldiers who served in World War II nearly disappeared from French collective memory. Only in 2006 were the 80,000 still-living colonial veterans' pensions equalized to those of white French soldiers, clearly in response to a moving film, *Indigènes (Days of Glory),* released that year, which focused on five North African soldiers who took part in the Liberation of France.

Although France contributed, at least in a limited way, to the Allied victory in May 1945, the "Big Three," Roosevelt, Churchill, and Stalin, excluded de Gaulle's Provisional Government from their critical meetings at Yalta (February 1945) and Potsdam (July 1945), which laid out the shape of the post-war occupation of Germany and addressed colonial regions across the globe. Yet relations between the United States and the U.S.S.R soon became strained, and the Americans began using France to counter-balance the Soviet Union. France's military contribution to Allied victory, combined with early Cold War tensions, thus worked in the end to France's advantage. The Big Three had already allocated France a permanent seat on the projected United Nations' Security Council in the summer of 1944; after May 8, 1945, France was given an occupation zone in Germany.

In contrast to his success at restoring internal order and France's military prestige, de Gaulle could do nothing to ease the nation's dire economic straits in 1944–1945. Four years of foreign occupation and air raids, first German and then

Allied, had left France badly scarred. The Allies had naturally targeted industrial areas, rail lines and depots, roads, and bridges, and the damage had affected 74 out of 90 departments. Over 2.6 million buildings had been destroyed, and 1 million people were left homeless.[3] Coastal areas of Normandy, the Atlantic, and the Mediterranean were hard hit, as were manufacturing and mining regions. In some cases entire cities were wiped out by bombing raids, including Le Havre, a critical port on the English Channel; the medieval town of Saint-Malo in Brittany; and Caen in Normandy, where only 400 of 18,000 homes were left undamaged after a 78-day siege.[4] In addition to the damage inflicted on infrastructure, buildings, and cities, air raids destroyed about 50,000 farms and 60,000 industrial businesses.[5] Food production had also been damaged by the 1944 fighting in France that largely took place during the summer growing and harvest seasons. Although German requisitions came to an end, raw materials remained scarce. For the ordinary person, basic necessities remained in short supply, and the Provisional Government had no choice but to continue rationing and price controls.

The extremely unpopular bread ration was lifted briefly at the very end of 1945 but was reimposed in January 1946 at 300 grams a day. Rationing, as always, led to black markets, where people who had money or goods to trade evaded restrictions by selling or bartering under the table. In the spring of 1945 prices rose some 39 percent and remained high through the end of the decade, making it even more difficult to make ends meet.[6] The food situation in 1946, already catastrophic, got even worse. In April 1947, the bread ration was reduced to 250 grams a day and was further reduced to 200 grams a day between September 1947 and May 1948. Rationing for some goods lasted until 1949.[7] In 1961, shortly after John F. Kennedy took office as president of the United States, the magazine *Marie-Claire* published a photograph of the ration card issued to then Jacqueline Bouvier for the study-abroad year she spent in France in 1949–1950.[8]

It was against this backdrop of extreme economic deprivation that de Gaulle and the Provisional Government turned to its last major challenge: rebuilding France politically. Although the wartime Resistance in France had primarily focused its efforts on ridding France of the Nazi occupiers, there was no lack of ideas among many resisters about what kind of government France should have after Liberation.

First and foremost, France would have to restore a Republic and preserve the empire. In addition to being democratic, this Republic would have to be ethical and socially progressive, and the empire more representative. Second, in contrast to the constant political instability and immobility of the Third Republic, resisters insisted that the new government should be "effective." Third and last, to avoid the Third Republic's "sterile" disputes, rather than bringing back previous leaders, most resisters advocated renewing the nation's elites by drawing on the Resistance's democratic, progressive, action-oriented leadership. In other words, resisters intended to play a major role in post-war society and politics, not just because they had "earned" this right by risking their lives in the Resistance, but also as a way of injecting action, morality, and integrity into the system.[9]

During the Provisional Government period, de Gaulle acknowledged these aspirations without really acting upon them, by creating a Consultative Assembly, which included representatives of all the Resistance movements and groups. Officially the Consultative Assembly advised de Gaulle, but in reality it had no real or legislative power. This solution, with the Provisional Government under de Gaulle more or less running things, clearly was unacceptable in the long run. France needed to create a new democratic government, write a new constitution, and eventually hold elections; it would take another year to complete these tasks.

THE NEW POLITICAL LANDSCAPE

One constitutional issue that had caused no end of conflict, debate, and division prior to the war had been resolved by fiat even before the war ended: women's suffrage. On April 21, 1944, de Gaulle had issued an ordinance granting women the right to vote. His move provoked little controversy, although after the Liberation many newspapers and magazines addressed the novelty of women voting, which they did for the first time in a series of regional and local elections held in April 1945.

The next major step toward creating a new legitimate government for France was a referendum held on October 21, 1945. The French people elected an assembly and voted on whether or not to restore the constitution of 1875, which would have reinstated the Third Republic, and if not, whether it reserved the right to approve a new constitution. A resounding 96 percent voted against restoring the Third Republic, signaling clearly that the public agreed with the Resistance leaders that France needed change. The results also endorsed an eventual national referendum to approve a new constitution; the people of France would have the final say.

The Constituent Assembly elected in October 1945 revealed how profoundly the war had changed France's political configuration. In a truly radical break with the past, the old, anti-republican Right no longer appeared to exist. For the previous 150 years, each French Republic had faced serious challenges from various groups on the far Right often united by little other than their fundamental rejection of republicanism and its liberal, democratic, egalitarian values. But the association with Vichy collaborationism had caused this anti-democratic Right— whether monarchist, authoritarian, anti-Semitic, fascist, or otherwise—to lose all legitimacy in 1945. Of course, the people and their ideas hardly disappeared. They simply kept quiet, closing down their organizational and media outlets, choosing not to express their views publicly for the time being. On the republican side, even moderate conservatives lost power just after the war. The Radical Party was also weakened, winning only 9.3 percent of the vote in 1945. While individual Radicals would play key roles after the war, the Radical Party ceased to be a critical player and never again matched the influence it had exerted throughout the Third Republic.

In place of the old Left-Right division, three roughly equal parties dominated the Constituent Assembly, ushering in what is known as the era of "tripartite rule."

First—in yet another extraordinary break with the past—the PC won the largest percentage of the vote, 26 percent, a reflection of its leading role in the Resistance. This vote, however, was also a personal vindication for the leader of the PC, Maurice Thorez, and his wife, Jeannette Vermeersch, despite a complicated wartime record. When the French government outlawed the PC in September 1939, Thorez had deserted from the French army, made his way to Moscow in November 1939, and lived there throughout the war. When de Gaulle's Free French subsequently sent a delegation to Moscow, Thorez denied that he had deserted, insisting that he left France for Moscow in 1943 (a fiction that official PC sources maintained until after Thorez's death in 1964).

After the Liberation, Thorez, convicted of desertion in absentia, asked for permission to return to France, which, with hard lobbying from two communist ministers in the Provisional Government, he received in November 1944. Thorez then resumed leadership of the PC and adhered strictly to the Communist International's dictates. Despite its authoritarian leadership, the party built an extremely loyal following at the grassroots level and among intellectuals. Many intellectuals saw capitalism as "American imperialism." To them, big American

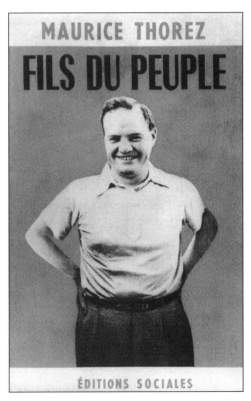

Cover of *Fils du Peuple*, by Maurice Thorez (1900–1964). Published 1949, Editions Sociales.
Private Collection/Archives Charmet/The Bridgeman Art Library.

corporations and the dehumanizing alienation of the production line resulted in nominal democracies that, rather than responding to the people, were under the sway of the "tyranny of international finance." These intellectuals viewed communism as an "ethical idea" and were lured by the PC's promise to defend "the civilizing values of the USSR against the American threat."[10] As a large and disciplined party, the PC had played an active role in the Provisional Government, joining ministries and taking responsibilities, which further explains its electoral success in 1945. Many people on the non-communist Left nevertheless remained extremely wary of the party, owing to the PC's lack of honesty about its role early in the Occupation and its strict Stalinism.

The second party of the three, the socialist SFIO (French Section of the Workingmen's International or Section Française de l'Internationale Ouvrière), won 24.6 percent of the vote in 1945. In 1940, the socialists had taken a principled stand, voting against granting Philippe Pétain full powers. While a few individual socialists had then worked in the Vichy regime, most had opposed it. After the war, the SFIO led a brief attempt to create a unified party of the Left, the Democratic and Socialist Union of the Resistance (Union Démocratique et Socialiste de la Résistance or UDSR), but the effort fizzled out quickly. The socialists proved a critical central element in tripartite rule, suspicious of the PC but bridging the gap between it and the newly created third party in the government, the Popular Republican Movement (Mouvement Républicain Populaire or MRP), which won 25.6 percent of the vote.

With the creation of the MRP, France for the first time had a Christian Democratic party, something that had proved impossible before the war owing to the deep divisions and mistrust between many Catholic and republican leaders. Founded in November 1944, the MRP's principal goals were first to reconcile the working class and the Catholic Church and second to reconcile the Church and Republic. The MRP's roots stretched back to the Christian social movements founded in the 1920s, such as the Young Christian Workers (Jeunesse Ouvrière Chrétienne or JOC), the Young Christian Farmers (Jeunesse Agricole Chrétienne or JAC), and the Young Christian Students (Jeunesse Etudiante Chrétienne or JEC). In 1935, these groups had expanded to include married couples. Their experiences in these movements had inspired many people to join the Resistance by organizing POW wives or writing or distributing a key Resistance news organ, the *Cahiers de Témoignage Chrétien* (*Christian Witness Notebooks*).[11] After the war, the MRP built on this framework to create a party that crossed class lines and that, while firmly Christian, remained equally committed to democratic pluralism.

Most of the original founders and leaders in 1944–1946 came from Left-leaning Catholic intellectual circles. Not surprisingly, however, many of the people who voted for the MRP just after the war came from the Right. With the traditional parties discredited, the most conservative voters turned to the MRP as the lesser of evils, the party that best represented their interests. Some observers claimed as many as three-fourths of the MRP's votes came from the old far Right, leading cynics to nickname the MRP "the Machine to Regroup Pétainists" ("La machine pour ramasser les Pétainistes").[12] Assuaging any fears of anti-republicanism, the MRP was led by a man with impeccable resistance credentials, Georges Bidault, who had replaced Jean Moulin in unifying the internal Resistance during the Occupation. The MRP also unusually opened itself to Protestants, refusing to be an exclusively Catholic party; most of the leaders, however, were Catholic.

By October 1945 then, the MRP, the PC, and the socialists had clearly emerged as the three leading parties in France. Meanwhile, the leader of the Provisional Government, Charles de Gaulle, refused to join any party, declaring that he was above politics. This was in keeping with the persona that he had created as the leader of the Free French. In presenting himself as an alternative to Pétain and defeatism, de Gaulle had denied Pétain's legitimacy in 1940, claiming instead that only his own fighting stance embodied true France. Once the war ended, the very existence of the Free French had saved French honor, and de Gaulle felt that aligning himself with a mere political party would tarnish that honor. What France really needed, de Gaulle argued, was an entirely new political system led by a powerful president who would be elected from outside the legislature, rather than a prime minister who led the majority party. The chief executive could then remain above party politics and counter-balance the political parties in the Assembly.

THE BIRTH OF THE FOURTH REPUBLIC AND THE FRENCH UNION

Clearly de Gaulle envisioned himself as the powerful president France needed, but none of the three leading parties supported the kind of presidential system he had in mind. Unfortunately they did not agree on much beyond that. The communists demanded a one-house legislature, arguing that an upper house would serve as a reactionary restraint of popular sovereignty. The socialists agreed with the communists on a single house, but then remained suspicious that the PC intended to absorb them. The MRP, on the other hand, insisted on a two-house legislature, afraid that the communists would dominate a single house and use it to take power.

As the three parties sparred over these issues with no resolution in sight, an angry and frustrated de Gaulle resigned as leader of the Provisional Government in January 1946. De Gaulle imagined that the people of France, devastated by his departure and disgusted at the political squabbling so reminiscent of the late Third Republic, would force the Assembly to beg him to return. In that case, de Gaulle planned to dictate his own terms—a presidential system. But many leaders in the Assembly were quietly relieved that he was gone, and had no intention of recalling him; as a result of his miscalculation, de Gaulle would remain out of power for the next 12 years.

By May 1946, the Assembly had managed to finish its work; the constitution it unveiled set up a single house assembly and a parliamentary system. Now, however, it was the voters' turn to worry that an assembly without the countervailing power of either a second house or a president would overly empower the communists. On May 5, 1946, the public rejected the new constitution in a divided vote,

10.5 million opposed to 9.5 million in favor, with 6 million abstentions. In June 1946, a second Constituent Assembly was then elected with a slightly altered political balance. The MRP gained votes, becoming the largest party. The PC also gained votes, increasing the mistrust of the socialists, who decided to ally with the MRP in support of a bicameral legislature. The end result was a constitution establishing a system almost identical to the Third Republic. A second referendum was held October 13, 1946, and this time the constitution was approved, 9 million to 8 million, with another 8 million, or 31 percent, abstaining. Both votes signaled that France remained deeply divided, with a large segment unsure or apathetic about the proper system for governing their nation.[13]

The new regime, the Fourth Republic, born in 1946 without much fanfare, thus included an upper house, the Council of the Republic, and a lower house, the National Assembly, elected by truly universal suffrage. The leader of the majority party or coalition in the Assembly served as prime minister. Like the Third Republic, the combined houses elected a president whose powers were limited. And just as the Fourth Republic was nearly identical in structure to the Third Republic, so its operation followed a similar pattern. As in the past, the executive branch remained weak, and governments rose and fell rapidly, with 26 different cabinets formed between 1946 and 1958.[14]

The drafters of the final 1946 constitution were somewhat more innovative on the imperial front, especially with respect to sub-Saharan Africa, making partially good on the promises of Brazzaville that colonized peoples deserved to have a greater say in their own affairs. Deputies from all the colonies had been elected to the Constituent Assembly, and they formed an important enough group to make their voices heard. Most French policy-makers realized that, in the face of intensifying nationalist sentiments and the post-Holocaust international reaction against institutionalized forms of racism, they had little choice but to rethink the terms of colonial rule, if they wanted to hold on to the colonies that remained. Indeed, World War II had already cost France two mandate territories—Syria and Lebanon—to whom the Free French had granted independence late in 1941 to ensure that they did not fall into the hands of the Germans. The Provisional Government had recognized this independence in 1943. And by 1946 the continued French status of a third colony, Indochina (Cambodia, Laos and Vietnam), also looked precarious: In Vietnam an extremely well-organized nationalist movement under communist Ho Chi Minh, the Viet Minh, had emerged in the north during the war, determined to both unify the northern and southern parts of the country and secure independence.

As the Sétif massacre had made clear, post-war authorities would not hesitate to use the stick against any and all "terrorists" and "rebels"—the terms they routinely used to refer to nationalists who sought to win immediate autonomy from France. But in 1946 the French government also proffered a carrot. The constitution that created the Fourth Republic instituted a new French Union in the place of the old empire, and the word "colony" was now generally erased from French legal terminology.[15] The old colonies of Martinique, Guadeloupe, Guiana, Réunion, and

St. Pierre et Miquelon became departments, with the same status as metropolitan departments, and the newer colonies, principally in sub-Saharan Africa and the South Pacific, were designated "overseas territories," while Tunisia and Morocco became associated states. All colonial subjects were granted Union citizenship, which expanded their legal and social rights—principally the right to vote in regional assemblies. The much-hated native penal and forced labor codes were abolished throughout the French Union. A minority of the French-educated elites, the so-called *évolués* in each territory, were also given the same political rights as French metropolitan citizens, and elected deputies to the French National Assembly. Finally, a government fund known as the Investment Fund for Economic and Social Development (Fonds d'Investissement et de Développement Economique et Sociale or FIDES) was set up in 1946 to channel capital for infrastructure into the desperately poor sub-Saharan territories. These were not meaningless reforms. Between 1947 and 1959 historian Jacques Marseille estimates that more capital was invested in Africa than during the 65 previous years. But France's "new deal" fell far short of the aspirations of the colonized. Tellingly, Union citizens were not even invited to vote in the referendum creating the Fourth Republic and French Union.

In Algeria as well, reforms were also passed, but these too failed to satisfy nationalists. In Algeria as usual the settler lobby in Paris made sure that their own interests were protected. In 1947 a newly created Algerian Assembly was given extensive financial powers for the first time, made up of two colleges each with 60 delegates. The system was nevertheless deeply skewed in favor of the minority of Europeans compared to the Muslim majority in Algeria. The first college represented 464,000 French and 58,000 Muslim citizens; the second represented about 1.5 million Muslims over the age of 21. By this point, however, most Muslim Algerian leaders had given up on the idea of reform anyway, although they remained too divided internally to coordinate a plan for forcing the French out. After the war, the older generation of nationalists in Algeria remained split among the radical supporters of Messali Hadj, the followers of the more moderate leader Ferhat Abbas, and various Islamic reform movements.[16] Meanwhile a new wave of landless and increasingly desperate Algerians further swelled the slums of Algeria's coastal cities in the late 1940s and early 1950s, in search of jobs that did not exist. The failure of the new Fourth Republic to ameliorate this growing poverty, combined with Algerians' memory of Sétif and the continuing division of Algeria's older nationalists, would provide the perfect conditions for a new generation of hardened young Algerian militants to emerge, committed to armed struggle against France at any cost.

POLITICS AS USUAL? THE EVOLUTION OF THE FOURTH REPUBLIC

Two years after the Liberation, then, France finally had a new, democratically created Republic and a new French Union. In the November 1946 elections, power shifted further in favor of the PC and the MRP (28 and 26, percent respectively) and away from the socialists (down to 18 percent). The new government that took office in January 1947 saw a number of critical developments. Most importantly, tripartite rule quickly came to an end. Although the communists won the largest number of seats in the November 1946 elections, they found themselves literally out in the cold, forced out of the cabinet by the onset of the Cold War.

Early in 1947, the American wartime alliance with the U.S.S.R. had not officially broken down yet, but it was badly strained. In what became known as the Truman Doctrine, the United States stated its intention to help all countries struggling against totalitarianism, which by then meant communism. Key French leaders from the newly elected government, led by Léon Blum, traveled in May 1946 to Washington, DC, to inquire about American assistance in rebuilding. They soon realized that the American government would be more favorable to assisting France if there were no communists in the cabinet, and France's prime minister, socialist Paul Ramadier, got the message. He had already clashed with the PC over his insistence on attempting to tame inflation with a series of deflationary policies, including wage freezes, tough medicine at a time of continuing shortages and hardship.

France also experienced a wave of strikes in the spring of 1947 that put pressure on the PC from below. A massive strike broke out at the state-owned Renault plant in May 1947, followed by a rail strike, both backed by the communist-led labor union, the CGT. These strikes gave Prime Minister Ramadier the reason he needed to expel communists from the governing coalition. Accusing them of plotting to overthrow the state, in May 1947 Ramadier fired the communist ministers. The PC would not have a cabinet seat again until 1981. French political leaders quickly felt the material benefits of lining up with the United States. In June 1947, U.S. Secretary of State George C. Marshall announced that the United States would make financial assistance available to rebuild Europe. Great Britain received the largest portion of Marshall Plan aid, but France was second in line, receiving 20 percent of the money disbursed. The communists joked that they had been persecuted under Marshal Pétain, and now were exiled under Marshall Aid.[17]

With the demise of tripartism, the Fourth Republic fell into a familiar pattern of operation. Since the PC was off limits in coalitions, the two leading parties, the MRP and SFIO, together always fell just short of a majority, which forced them either to turn to the tiny, moribund Radical party or to new parties. One such party, after April 1947, was created by de Gaulle, although he preferred to call it a movement, continuing to insist that he was above party politics: the Rally of the French People (Rassemblement du Peuple Français or RPF). The RPF immediately became popular among conservative voters, even former supporters of Vichy, and thus siphoned votes from the MRP, which lost some of its influence. Western-educated deputies from the colonies formed other new groupings; they often constituted a key swing vote that gave them power disproportionate to their actual numbers—2 percent of the deputies—in the Assembly. Due to the increasing proliferation of political parties, the Fourth Republic began to experience a series of unstable coalitions very reminiscent of the Third Republic.

Equally symptomatic of the return of previous political patterns was the appearance on the far Right in the early 1950s of a new movement known as Poujadism, named after its leader Pierre Poujade. The owner of a small shop that sold newspapers and stationery in the town of Saint-Ceré in the department of Lot, Poujade led a highly successful tax revolt against the state. Prime Minister Antoine Pinay, during his short stay in office in March–December 1952, had attempted to reduce inflation by borrowing and cutting government spending. Eventually Pinay resorted to price controls, angering many shop owners. Taxes hit hard, and Poujade's business had been struggling. When he learned that a delegation of tax inspectors planned to visit his town in July 1953, Poujade organized his fellow small business owners to resist them. Expanding his efforts, in November 1953 Poujade created the Union to Defend Business Owners and Artisans (Union de Défense des Commerçants et Artisans, or UDCA), which quickly gained national strength.

In 1954 France had some 1.3 million small businesses employing 2.3 million people, all of whom felt threatened by changes in the economy that reconstruction—fueled in part by American Marshall aid—were introducing. Small business owners in towns across France worried in particular about the arrival of the first wave of "Americanized" businesses, chain stores that could drive them out of business at a time when there was already reduced demand for their wares. By the early 1950s, many small-town merchants viewed national economic policies such as Pinay's anti-inflationary ones as nothing less than a conspiracy to promote the "American-inspired modernization" of France. In classic far-Right language,

Cover of *J'ai Choisi le Combat*, by Pierre Poujade (1920–2003), 1955. Private Collection/Archives Charmet/The Bridgeman Art Library.

Poujade's movement loudly blamed foreigners, including Americans, for their problems; revived old anti-Semitic tropes; and even used the pejorative term favored by Charles Maurras, "*les métèques.*" In short, Poujadism, which had begun as a populist, anti-tax, and anti-modernization movement, had become a racist nationalist movement reminiscent of Vichy. The Poujadist movement culminated in the 1956 elections, when their political party, the Union et Fraternité Française, won 52 seats (2.5 million votes) on a platform that also included a militant defense of French Algeria. It soon became clear, however, that the party had no real program, and slowly the Poujadist deputies either switched to more mainstream conservative parties or dropped out. One Poujadist deputy, Jean-Marie Le Pen, temporarily resigned his seat and enlisted as a paratrooper to serve in Algeria. In the 1970s, Le Pen would go on to found a new manifestation of this populist far Right, the National Front.[18]

THE GREAT DIVIDE BETWEEN INTELLECTUALS

While Poujadism represented the first attempt to revive the far Right, on the Left, changing political alignments in the wake of the Cold War created new ideological cleavages. These changes were most forcefully expressed in the dramatic quarrel between the era's two greatest intellectuals, Albert Camus and Jean-Paul Sartre. After the war, the two men, along with Sartre's lifelong partner Simone de Beauvoir, had emerged as leading figures of French existentialism, a philosophy focusing on the absurd condition of human existence. Sartre and Camus, longtime friends, journalists, and best-selling authors of novels and plays, had become intellectual superstars by the late 1940s. Thus the public row between the two that erupted in 1952 captured the attention of the world. It also reflected the ways in which left-leaning French thinkers were forced to assess their nation's relationship with the United States and the Soviet Union.

By the end of World War II, Camus had emerged as France's great voice of resistance—a voice that carried across the globe with the publication in 1947 of his novel *The Plague.* The account of a small group of men confronting the threatened epidemic of a dreaded disease, a metaphor for capricious evil posing an impossible choice, became an immediate bestseller in France and the United States. In 1951, Camus followed the novel with an essay, *The Rebel,* which was a harsh critique of totalitarian ideology, particularly communism. Some praised the book, others criticized it, but the book review all of Paris awaited, from *Les Temps Modernes,* was a long time coming. Founded by Sartre shortly after the war, this literary monthly had quickly become the platform for the nation's intellectual elite. Its board of editors, including Sartre, Simone de Beauvoir, and Maurice Merleau-Ponty, all promoted the post-war imperative of political commitment: The journal, in their eyes, must be the advocate for the oppressed workers at home and colonized peoples abroad.

Though critical of Soviet Union, the journal's intellectuals still viewed communism as preferable to American-style capitalism. For *Les Temps Modernes,* the exalted ends of communism ultimately justified the means, no matter how appalling those means might be. Sartre and his colleagues attempted to depict as honestly as possible the horrors of communism, yet framed them so as "to be left with an experience and a project worthy of their dreams and defensible in their own philosophical and ethical language."[19] While ambivalent about the Soviet system, by 1952, Sartre had firmly sided with Moscow. "Like it or not," he wrote, "the construction of socialism is privileged in that to understand it one must espouse the movement and adopt its goals."[20] And he continued, "an anticommunist is a rat. I couldn't see any way out of that one, and I never will. . . ."[21]

In the context of Sartre's declaration, *Les Temps Modernes* took on Camus. Its editor, Francis Jeanson, penned a remarkably fierce review even by Parisian standards. Jeanson dismissed Camus' essay as a superficial pastiche of Marxist thought. More devastatingly, he belittled Camus as a "beautiful soul," someone who thought he could keep his hands clean in the messy unfolding of history. To believe such nonsense, Jeanson declared, was nothing less than an "objectively reactionary" choice.[22] In a word, he told Camus, if you are not with us, you must be against us.

The review stunned Camus, who was given the opportunity to draft a reply for the same issue. Camus claimed the reviewer misrepresented his literary work and, most important, charged *Les Temps Modernes* with failing to respond to his fundamental question: Did the historical goals of Marxist theory require its followers also to accept the existence of political tyranny such as existed in the Soviet Union? For Camus the reality of labor camps and show trials and mass purges in the Soviet Union could only mean the answer was no. But for Sartre, who now entered the fray in the same issue, the answer remained yes. In a letter whose virulence eclipsed Jeanson's review, Sartre mocked not just his former friend's efforts as philosophizing, but ridiculed his intellectual pretensions. "A mixture of somber self-conceit and vulnerability has always discouraged anyone from telling you whole truths," Sartre sighed. "Sooner or later someone would have told you; let it be me."

When the August issue of *Les Temps Modernes* carrying the Sartre/Camus quarrel hit the newsstands, the clash of two literary titans fueled widespread public fascination. Even a popular tabloid, *Samedi-Soir,* better known for lurid images and scurrilous gossip, published, alongside its usual fare of racy photos, the screaming headline: "The Sartre-Camus Break is consummated."[23] While the breakdown of a longstanding friendship made this dispute particularly compelling, the intellectual issues at the core foreshadowed struggles that played out in the following decades amongst left-leaning intellectuals, repelled by the materialism of the West but also increasingly troubled by the Soviet Union's often brutal practices.

Thus during the Fourth Republic, vigorous intellectual debates continued in France. However, unlike during the Third Republic when such debates often displaced political action and left real economic or social problems unresolved, the Fourth Republic managed to deal with the serious economic problems it faced.

LAUNCHING AN ECONOMIC MIRACLE

Unstable and politically uninspiring as it was, the Fourth Republic nevertheless managed to set the stage for profound and long-lasting economic and social changes in France. Chapter 9 already hinted at the ways in which the backward-looking, reactionary Vichy regime nevertheless unintentionally promoted French economic modernization. By the mid-1960s, France's gross national product (GNP) surpassed that of Britain, and by the mid-1970s it was lower only than Germany's GNP among the 10 wealthiest European countries. From a largely rural economy based primarily on small family-operated farms, manufacturing companies, and commercial establishments, France became an urban, industrial nation. This structural transformation would have been barely discernable to the average French person in the late 1940s, but it was under the Fourth Republic that the key decisions fueling post-war France's "economic miracle" were taken.

The economic growth of the 1950s and 1960s was largely based on an unprecedented increase in productivity after the war. France's labor productivity grew at nearly 5 percent a year, a rate double that of the United States from 1949 to 1969. One major factor in France's rising productivity was the cooperation of labor unions, which did not oppose increasing the workweek from 40 to 45 and even 48 hours in the late 1940s. Marshall Plan money, too, was an essential factor in French economic success in these years. The influx of American dollars provided France with the resources to invest heavily in key sectors and to rebuild its infrastructure using the newest technologies. However, Marshall Plan money was contingent on establishing certain standards of efficiency and long-term strategies. To meet U.S. standards, France also created a new planning system for its economy, the General Planning Commission (Commissariat Général du Plan or CGP). Similar in many ways, including very often the same people, to Vichy's Organization Committees, the CGP included high-level government bureaucrats trained in economics and management, high-level industrialists, and business managers.[24] Unlike Vichy, the post-war CGP included representatives as well from the labor movement, who had a real voice. Such inclusion in part explains why labor supported the plans that emerged, even though the plans imposed real hardships on working people.

The CGP's First Plan in 1947 is often called the Monnet Plan, after the leading figure and first planning commissioner, Jean Monnet. This plan clearly set France's number one priority as rebuilding its infrastructure. Planning and investment focused on transportation and heavy industry, in particular energy and agricultural equipment. Some key industries in the energy sectors, such as coal, gas, and electricity, were nationalized. In part this decision reflected an idea many Resistance movements had expressed, which de Gaulle himself seconded on September 12, 1944, when he insisted that France would return its major sources of wealth to the "collectivity." The Bank of France, which despite its public role in French fiscal policy had been in the hands of 200 private shareholders (the so-called 200 families), was also nationalized, along with several other large banks and insurance companies. Owing to Louis Renault's ardent collaboration during the war, the Provisional

Government had nationalized Renault on November 15, 1944. The French rail system had been nationalized prior to the war, in 1937 with the creation of the National Railroad Society (Société Nationale des Chemins de Fer or SNCF). France nationalized an airplane engine company in May 1945 and created its national airline, Air France, in June 1945. But most of the economy remained in private hands. Post-war governments created a mixed, not a socialist, economy.

Although it was a five-year plan, the Monnet Plan differed significantly from Stalin's Five Year Plans, where private ownership was abolished, or even Nazi Five Year Plans, where the party had imposed itself on private owners. In France, the General Planning Commission studied the economy, drew up a master plan, and then facilitated negotiations between industry and labor. These negotiations resulted in a series of production targets for each branch of industry. Not only were production targets negotiated rather than dictated, but meeting them was voluntary. In fact, this kind of planning did not differ much from the planning regularly done in capitalist economies by large companies, except that the CGP plan coordinated entire sectors of the economy. Many sectors achieved or came close to the Monnet Plan's targets. For example, France managed to increase coal production from 50 million tons in 1946 to 57 million by 1952, just shy of its 60 million ton target. Crude steel, having dropped from 9.7 million tons annually in 1929 to 4.4 million in 1946, rose to 10.9 million tons, short of the 12.5 million ton target but an impressive rebound.[25]

Such successes bred a new sense of confidence and optimism among France's business elites. The optimistic psychological climate in turn produced another significant change: French investors were finally inspired to invest their capital in France. The so-called flight of capital had been a major economic and even political problem for the Third Republic. After 1945, French capital stayed home.

For the average French person, however, the Monnet Plan represented a brutal, if necessary, dismissal of anything that might make their lives easier. The laserlike focus on infrastructure and basic industry came at the expense of the average person's standard of living. Shortages of food, clothing, and consumer goods of all kinds continued. Rebuilding the many buildings and homes destroyed by the war was secondary. Many people were forced to double up with family and/ or live in marginal, decrepit buildings. In Normandy people with lodging were required to house a homeless family. In a number of cities, large groups of squatters took up residence in bombed-out buildings. By 1945, squatters in Marseilles, Anger, Lyons, Nancy, Caen, Roubaix, and even Paris organized a variety of squatters' movements demanding public action and articulating the new idea of a right to housing (*droit au logement*).[26]

France's material misery, which lasted into the 1950s, fed a widespread sense abroad that France's general economic development continued to lag. In his book *Village in the Vaucluse,* American sociologist Lawrence Wylie undertook a study of Roussillon, a French village in Provence, spending a year there in 1951–1952 with his family. Wylie was struck not only by the "ruins of the past, but also by the shabbiness of the present. There were none of the external signs of modernity, no chrome, no enamel, no electric ice boxes, no deep freezes, no television, no white kitchens, no glamorous bathrooms." These were available only to the middle classes. The farm equipment resembled an American automobile graveyard, and families were still driving 1923 Renaults. Wylie, as an American, could not help but feel the contrast with the contemporary American atmosphere for the white majority, with its booming economy, expanding prosperity, and exploding middle class, much of which rested on the generous GI Bill, which made university education and home ownership accessible to a much broader population after the war.[27]

In France, the CGP's second plan for 1952–1957 finally addressed the problems of food production, housing, and regional development. In particular, it undertook massive new construction of low-cost public housing (Habitations à Loyer Modéré, or HLM), and by the end of the decade, the government was building some 300,000 housing units a year. This construction boom was, however, a mixed blessing. While the housing was badly needed, it was usually built where land was cheapest, far from city centers, and builders paid little heed either to existing transportation links to nearby cities or to the availability of schools, shops, parks, public services, or other amenities. Contractors encouraged to cut costs used shoddy materials that degraded quickly, and they adopted a modernist style of reinforced concrete "towers and bars" that was deeply alienating. Bidding also encouraged builders to include more studio and one-bedroom apartments in the complexes, to provide as many units as possible. Unfortunately, ever-smaller floor plans were built just as France was undergoing a baby boom, leading families to cram into one- and two-room apartments that often had no sound-proofing. In the end, the HLMs mitigated the housing crisis and provided working families with a minimal level of amenities, but in such a way that would only contribute to future social problems.[28]

WELFARE, REPOPULATION, AND IMMIGRATION

Vichy had enacted some critical welfare measures long debated but never implemented under the Third Republic. After the war, former resisters insisted on proving that a democracy could do better in the social realm than Vichy had; the Provisional Government and the Fourth Republic would thus preside over a vast expansion of France's welfare system compared to the pre-war era. Yet in turning to welfare reform, the post-war reformers were not only trying to introduce social justice and outdo their predecessors. Improved social measures were also understood to be critical to national regeneration, and more especially to repopulation, without which France could not prosper once again. As a result of all these considerations, between 1945 and 1946 policy-makers knit their plans together with a combination of unrealized Popular Front plans and Vichy measures to create France's first truly comprehensive social security system, which incorporated health, disability, old age, death benefits, workplace compensation, and family allowances.[29] While the Provisional Government passed all of these measures, the Fourth Republic extended them in June 1948 to "non-earners" and in July 1952 to farmers.[30]

Two of the most significant aspects of post-war social security legislation were the creation of national health insurance that covered both medical care and prescription medications and the expansion of family allowances. Building on an interwar requirement that all employees enroll in a health insurance fund with state contribution to the funds, laws passed on October 4 and 10, 1945 created a single fund to cover all salaried employees and a separate fund for agricultural workers. Eventually health insurance covered students, writers, the self-employed, and small business owners as well. Policy-makers also continued France's long tradition of child-centered welfare by updating the family allowances contained in the 1939 Family Code. The Code had created a "stay-at-home mother" allowance paid to families with one income, presumably the father's income. During the war this allowance was renamed the "single salary allowance" since many POW wives earned the family's sole income. Whereas family allowances had originally been paid to the "head of household," usually the husband, the law of August 22, 1946, stipulated that they be paid to the person having "effective and permanent care of the children." The same law removed the requirement that the children be "legitimate" and included maternity and housing allowances. Children had to attend school and receive regular medical check-ups for their parents to be eligible for family allowances.[31] The Law of September 1948 added new financial benefits for parents of large families, for example, it reduced train and urban transit fares.

Family allowances redistributed the cost of raising children, and they have, since 1945, constituted a much higher proportion of social benefits in France than in any other Western European country. The hope was that France, through such redistribution, could with time expand its population by increasing the number of births. As it turned out, the demographers need not have worried so about France's birthrate. For reasons that still remain obscure, families began having more babies in the darkest year of the war (1942), and continued to do so through the lean years that followed. From a pre-war level of about 15 births per 1,000 population, by 1946–1950 France's birthrate had risen dramatically to 21 births per 1,000, where it remained through the 1950s.

Part of the baby boom in the mid-1940s can be attributed to the return home by June 1945 of nearly 1 million POWs, after five years of absence. In the former POW community, the huge number of birth announcements in the post-war years earned these babies a nickname: "children of the return" (*les enfants du retour*). Still, it seems clear that by the late 1940s family allowances were playing the very role for which they had been designed. The fact that family allowances started only with a second child and increased dramatically with the third child explains to some extent why more families were now having three children.[32] Depending on the salary and the number of dependent children, family allowances could exceed earned income. For example, in 1953, one father with seven children received family allowances that more than doubled his monthly salary.[33]

The obsession with French population size and the drive to increase birthrates that continued after the war would also affect the post-war government's view of abortion. Both Vichy's prohibition of divorce during the first three years of marriage and its draconian law of February 15, 1942, making abortion a crime against the French race, were annulled. On April 13, 1946, the government ended state regulation of prostitution, the subject of a long campaign. However, abortion remained illegal, as did contraception, and the number of people charged in abortion cases actually increased after the war. Before the war, about 200 cases were prosecuted a year, and under Vichy the number had peaked at 1,995 in 1943. After the war, the number of abortion prosecutions peaked at 2,232 in 1946.[34] Although less coercive than Vichy, post-war France was still unwilling to countenance free choice in matters of family planning.

Political concerns about the family, the birthrate, and the protection of children also resulted in a continuing intolerant atmosphere for homosexuality. While the post-war government condemned and explicitly rejected most of Vichy's moral provisions, on February 8, 1945, it reaffirmed the 1942 Ordinance criminalizing sex between an adult and a minor "of his own sex under the age of 21," on the grounds that the Vichy legislation legitimately sought to prevent the corruption of minors. A July 2, 1945 ordinance set the age of consent for heterosexual relations at age 15, whereas the February 8, 1945 law left that age at 21 for homosexual relations . This created what was referred to as the crime of homosexuality (*délit d'homosexualité*) for sexual relations between an adult and a minor aged 15 to 21.[35]

Conservative post-war family policies went hand-in-hand with new legislation on immigration, as France turned massively to its empire and other European nations to satisfy its immediate need for laborers to rebuild. Here, too, there was continuity with the past. Post-war immigration policies selected immigrants based on policy-makers' notions of who would provide maximum benefit to France, in particular considering whether the individual was from a group deemed capable of integrating into the nation.[36] To that end, a new 1945 Code of Nationality established categories of foreigners designated as either temporary, ordinary, or privileged residents of France. The Code, with unpleasant Vichy echoes, excluded non-French people from a variety of professions, including architecture, law, accounting, and pharmacy. Foreigners required permission from the government to practice medicine, dentistry, optometry, veterinary science, or massage and were encouraged to "gallicize" their surnames to lose a "foreign sound or look." They were evaluated on their degree of assimilation, as measured by language, schooling, and social activities.[37] In 1946, some 1.7 million foreigners (4.3 percent of the total population) resided in France, nearly all of them from other European nations (Italy and Poland led the way, with 25 percent each; Belgium and Spain followed).[38] In 1947, the government established unrestricted freedom of movement between Algeria and the mainland, with no requirement of employment to live in France, which paved the way for more North African workers to start arriving as well.

WOMEN'S LIVES AND CHANGING GENDER NORMS

Women voted for the first time in the spring of 1945, and their labor was needed for economic recovery. But at the same time post-war governments stressed the importance of women's domestic roles, and women played a major role in the baby boom. On balance, the era of the 1940s and 1950s was one in which women began to lay claim to new activities and rights in response to the many contradictory pressures placed on them by post-war reconstruction.

Although attaining the vote was surely a victory for women, two sources of disappointment were the small number of women either elected to office or joining the ranks of the political elite and the failure of women to change "politics as usual." Even in the immediate enthusiasm of voting for the first time, women only won a little over 6 percent of the seats in the National Assembly in 1946. From then on, the percentages declined, down to 3.5 percent in 1951 and 1.3 percent in 1958.[39] From 1947 to 1948, lawyer and Marseilles politician Germaine Poinso-Chapuis served as minister of health, the first woman ever to become a minister. For years feminists like Poinso-Chapuis had argued that when women won the vote, they would bring "the resources of their hearts to the solution of social problems; their good sense and domestic practicality to the problems of the national economy."[40] Instead, women's voting patterns turned out to be very close to those of men. Gender gaps, as elsewhere, were rare and usually fairly small.

The Fourth Republic's constitution guaranteed equal rights, including equal wages for equal work, and in the 1940s and 1950s the government actively encouraged women to join the labor force. To make it possible even for mothers of young children to do so, the state promised to build a network of childcare centers and preschools. However, given the government's lack of resources, it could not keep that promise. Life histories of women in the Paris region from the post-war decade make clear that working women with young children still usually left the labor force, if only temporarily, or sent their children to live with a grandmother or aunt if possible, or with a nanny.[41] And while the new national health insurance program included pre-natal and post-natal care, the fundamental legal inequality of married women, dating to the Napoleonic Code, remained in effect. Some provisions had been reformed, but a full overhaul of the Civil Code's provisions on women and marriage would not take place until 1965.

The post-war years were also an era, as in the United States, of a romanticized revival of domesticity for women, although at a much lower level of material comfort. France was poorer; therefore its cult of domesticity was much less linked to new consumption patterns than was true across the Atlantic. The gleaming kitchens of 1950s' America were rare in France. Rather, a number of psychological factors contributed to the domestic longings many women and families felt. Many POW wives who had worked outside the home and taken on new responsibilities during the absence of their husbands now wished to hand those responsibilities back to their spouses.[42] In addition, a great number of families had experienced the war as either a real or metaphorical attack on their homes. The Gestapo had tracked its enemies into the home, as had the French Militia, and Jews were often arrested at home. Air raids killed thousands and destroyed approximately 1 million housing units, both homes and apartments. Millions of people had been captured, deported, interned, displaced, or forced to move, share lodging, and move back with parents during the war. After such experiences it made sense for men and women to idealize the home as a symbol of peace, security, and stability. Finally, for many families, the single salary allowance monetarized and thereby valorized women's domestic labor in such a way that made women staying home a real option.[43]

Although the government, the media, and the schools continued to encourage domesticity and children for women, the war experience and its validation of women's skills also meant that domesticity was envisioned in new ways in the 1940s and 1950s. Post-war domesticity was not so much about a return to tradition, which had been such an important theme during the Vichy years, but about how hoped-for improvements would be a path to modernism. New domestic technologies would introduce science, rationalism, and efficiency into what had been viewed as a traditional art handed down by mothers to daughters. Science, education specialist Roger Cousinet wrote, had penetrated the home to such an extent that, to do a good job, housewives needed to educate themselves.[44]

Paulette Bernège had been France's leading expert on home economics since the 1920s. Even before the war she advocated that housewives not insist on doing things the way their mothers had, but make the home more efficient. In the 1950s, Bernège wanted housewives to apply the same Taylorist principles used in industry to the organization of domestic time and space, increasing productivity and reducing unnecessary effort and movement. Her books recommended improving workflow with the careful placement of appliances so as to avoid having to retrace steps and included model timetables for housewives—allocating, for example, 15 minutes in the morning to prepare and consume coffee.[45] Still, while many women may have wanted to modernize their homes in 1947, very few would have had the means to do so. In 1954, only 7 percent of all households had refrigerators (only 3.3 percent of which would be found in working-class homes, as opposed to 42 percent in middle-class families), and 8.5 percent had washing machines. As late as 1958, a survey of 25 working-class families in the Paris region found that 9 families were still without running water and 2 were without electricity.[46]

Another new arena where women arguably challenged traditional understandings of feminism was in a variety of consumers' organizations. Women played a key role in driving the development of consumer industries and consumer lending. Female-led groups exhorted women to be savvy consumers as a way of contributing to the renewal of France. Rather than a diversion of women's activism into a nonpolitical, domestic realm, this was a new kind of political activism, justified in terms of women's domestic roles.[47] More conventionally "feminist" was an emerging struggle to make contraception available to women. In 1946, Jenny Leclercq published a book arguing for legal contraception.[48] Other birth control advocates included Dr. Marie-Andrée Lagroua-Weill-Hallé and Jacques Derogy; Lagroua wrote the preface to Derogy's 1956 book *Children in Spite of Ourselves,* which was frank and explicit in advocating contraception and legalized abortion.[49] Derogy's book received wide attention and helped change social ideas about birth control in France.[50]

"I'm Kitting Out My Kitchen," special edition of *La Maison Française* magazine, 1950.
Bibliothèque des Arts Decoratifs, Paris/Archives Charmet/The Bridgeman Art Library.

But the most influential feminist of the early post-war era was Simone de Beauvoir—philosophy professor, novelist, and companion of Jean-Paul Sartre. Before the war Beauvoir lived the life of an intellectual, doing virtually no domestic work herself. During the war, however, she had had no choice, as she explained in her path-breaking book of 1949, *The Second Sex*. The experience was transformative. Having no knack for domesticity, Beauvoir had thrown herself into it with mania, keeping track of every food ticket; hoarding her stash of cabbages, rutabagas, and noodles; and thinking for hours about what she would prepare. One evening, while working at her desk, Beauvoir came to a realization. Noticing the pleasant aroma of the vegetable soup that she had prepared, she wrote, "I did not share the condition of housewives, but I did gain a good idea of their joys."[51] For the first time in her life, Beauvoir began to think seriously about the condition of women. The result was *The Second Sex*, a startlingly innovative work that has become a classic feminist text.

Beauvoir, after posing in her introduction a simple question—"What is a woman?"—argued that the ability to pose this as a question was in itself an answer to the question. Beauvoir pointed out that no one would think to ask a similar question about men, nor had books been written addressing the topic of the human male. Masculine and feminine, Beauvoir noted, were not symmetrical poles, since only women were defined by limiting criteria. In other words, according to Beauvoir, the absolute human type was masculine, leaving women imprisoned by their biological peculiarities. "Humanity is male and men define woman not in herself but as relative to him. . . . He is the Subject, he is the Absolute, she is the Other."[52] Beauvoir denied the biological foundation of the cultural and social differences between men and women, arguing, "in human society, nothing is natural. . . . [W]oman, like much else, is a product elaborated by civilization."[53] By insisting that "one is not born, but rather becomes a woman," Beauvoir took on conservative Christian views, claiming that monogamy, marriage, faithfulness, and sex for procreation alienated women.[54] She also challenged the left-wing circles she came from, denying that sexual oppression was secondary to class oppression.

Few followed Beauvoir's lead in the early 1950s. The Catholic Church put *The Second Sex* on its index of forbidden books, and some reviewers found her frank discussions of women's bodies and sexuality shocking. Most male intellectuals sharply rejected her analysis, and even most feminists at the time criticized Beauvoir's more radical arguments, although her text would eventually serve as a foundation for the generation of feminists active in the late 1960s.[55] Yet the very publication of the book in the late 1940s coupled with the various other new roles with which many women were experimenting in their daily lives suggests that, for matters of personal life, sexual mores, and gender roles, the superficially conservative Fourth Republic was a period of ongoing small but significant changes at the grassroots level. From the personal to the political, French people found themselves gingerly exploring new possibilities in their relationships. The same can be said of France's relationship with the rest of Europe.

REIMAGINING EUROPE: FRANCO-GERMAN COOPERATION

After World War I, finance expert Etienne Clementel had proposed a radical notion. Rather than punishing or demilitarizing Germany to neutralize its threat, France should instead harness Germany's economy to the rest of Europe where everyone could benefit from German economic might. Once it became economically dependent on its neighbors, Germany would be less prone to attacking them. Nearly everyone in France rejected Clementel's ideas in 1918, but Jean Monnet picked up the thread after World War II. The same man who inspired the French economic planning system, Monnet was a key leader pushing European economic integration. Germany's crushing defeat facilitated his task, as did memories of the catastrophic results of Germany's harsh treatment after World War I. And with the Cold War looming, France worried increasingly about being part of a badly decimated Europe seemingly at the mercy of the United States and the U.S.S.R. An obvious solution was to make Europe as a whole more united.

Monnet insisted that no one country in Europe could hope to compete economically with the powerful U.S. economy, nor could they compete militarily with either the United States or the U.S.S.R. However, if the various European countries integrated their economies into a single, larger economic unit, they could act to counter-balance the superpowers and retain some independence. European integration, from 1945 on, rested on the axis of French and German cooperation, which worked most successfully in the economic realm. The Organization for European Economic Cooperation (OEEC), created in 1947, coordinated money from the Marshall Plan for reconstructing Europe. The OEEC was renamed the Organization for Economic Cooperation and Development (OECD) in 1961. Another fruitful avenue of French-German cooperation opened in 1950 when French foreign minister Robert Schuman proposed a plan, inspired by Monnet's ideas, to put French and German coal and steel production under a single, shared authority. Schuman's initiative led to the birth in 1951 of the European Coal and Steel Community (ECSC), which included, in addition to France and West Germany, Italy, Belgium, Luxembourg, and the Netherlands.

Also in 1950, France proposed a unified European Defense Community (EDC). By the time the negotiations resulted in a proposed treaty, however, the French had shifted their attention to other matters; they no longer saw joint defense as the best way to contain Germany and feared the EDC might encourage German rearmament. The French Assembly voted against ratification in 1954, killing the idea. The United States nevertheless did succeed in appeasing France's security concerns by bringing West Germany into the North Atlantic Treaty Organization (NATO) in 1955, thus tying its rearmament to the Western alliance system.

By far the most significant development for the integration of Europe was the signing in 1957 of the Treaty of Rome between France, Germany, Belgium, Holland, Italy, and Luxembourg. Britain initially resisted joining, ambivalent in part about whether it was a part of Europe. The Treaty created the European Economic Community (EEC), renamed after 1992 the European Union, or EU, which established a customs' union or "Common Market" and committed the member states to develop common economic policies. The 1957 treaty also created the European Atomic Energy Agency. The EEC created a single free trade zone comparable in size and population to the United States. By agreement, tariffs within the EEC were gradually reduced to zero over the following 15 years. The EEC also committed members to coordinating economic and social policies across Western Europe, although coordination of six different economies proved a challenge from the start. The inevitable political tensions often intensified differences based on divergent economic interests. Yet there is no doubt that economic cooperation and free trade across Western Europe were enormously beneficial to all involved, helping to fuel an economic explosion in France in the 1960s–1970s.

THE FOURTH REPUBLIC REFUSES DECOLONIZATION

A global phenomenon after World War II was the end of the era of European imperialism in Africa and Asia, a process whose length, difficulty, and violence varied from place to place. The leaders of the Fourth Republic, like many other European colonial powers, were not the least bit prepared to relinquish their empire, convinced that overseas territories were necessary to retaining Great Power status and rebuilding France's economy, that no colonial peoples were yet capable of self-government, and that the creation of the French Union had answered all legitimate aspirations for change. Colonial questions in the 1940s and 1950s also became entangled with Cold War politics, as the United States at first supported French efforts to retain territories that might otherwise become—or so they feared—satellites of the U.S.S.R. For all these reasons, French policy-makers chose to meet with force the many nationalist challenges that erupted throughout the empire after the war. This policy led to the violent repression of radical movements, for example, in Madagascar between March 1947 and December 1948—where perhaps as many as 100,000 Malagasy died—and in Cameroon in 1950 and 1951; it also produced two significantly longer wars against nationalist revolutions in Indochina (1946–1954) and Algeria (1954–1962).

Indochina's independence movement had begun prior to World War II. By the outbreak of war in 1939, Ho Chi Minh had become its leader, and in 1941 he created the Viet Minh as an umbrella for all anti-colonial resistance movements. Ho Chi Minh had been educated in French schools, then eventually, as a young man, ended up in Paris, where he was exposed to the ideas of Marx and other communist thinkers. He returned to Vietnam in the mid-1920s, where he soon fused the liberationist, anti-capitalist, and anti-imperialist threads of Marxism with Vietnamese nationalism.

In 1940, in the wake of Germany's defeat of France, the Japanese army had threatened to invade Indochina. At that point the French governor general, Rear-Admiral Paul Decoux, with the support of Vichy's foreign minister, had negotiated two treaties that integrated the Indochinese economy into Japan's economic sphere and guaranteed French sovereignty, while allowing Japanese troops to be stationed in, and have free passage through, the colony. Despite the Japanese presence, Vichy thus had had a relatively free hand to adopt its own harsh measures during the war, imposing, as we have seen, its "National Revolution" and racial policies with great vigor. Ironically, Vichy's celebration of traditional Indochinese culture, values, art, and music may have inspired Ho Chi Minh to shift his emphasis from communist internationalism to a more nationalist message. The Viet Minh spent much of the war waging guerrilla attacks from the jungles on the Japanese, which helped win it public support.

The easy relations between local French authorities and the Japanese ended on March 9, 1945, when—to the complete surprise of the French—Japanese forces in a matter of hours overthrew the entire French colonial regime, arresting government leaders and killing any who resisted. Japan's quick rout of the French colonial government and army, which had governed Indochina for 60 years, effectively destroyed the illusion of superior French power in the eyes of the Vietnamese. During the war, de Gaulle and the United States had discussed the possibility of establishing an independent Vietnam, although no firm commitment had emerged. With Japan's surrender in August 1945, Ho Chi Minh created a Provisional

Government and began negotiations with the Allies for what he hoped would be full independence. Yet while Ho effectively controlled the north, he did not have the south under his authority, and by the fall of 1945 the Allies had reinstated the French in the southern half of the country. New negotiations ensued, this time between the French and Ho for some kind of Vietnamese autonomy within the French Union acceptable to both parties—but in June 1946 the talks were suspended with no resolution in sight. At this point local French military authorities decided to try to retake the north by force. In November 1946, High Commissioner D'Argenlieu bombed the port of Haiphong in the north, killing 6,000 Vietnamese civilians and virtually impelling the Viet Minh into armed resistance against the French.

Thus began the Indochina war between France and Ho Chi Minh's Viet Minh, which lasted eight years. Fearing the popular reaction that sending regular French troops to Indochina would arouse so quickly after the end of World War II, French leaders relied instead on career military men, colonial troops, and the Foreign Legion. By thus reducing the direct impact of the Indochina war on the lives of most French people, the government curbed the strength of anti-war sentiment at a time when most French were focused on rebuilding their lives. But there was also little pro-war sentiment: Only the MRP, which feared Ho Chi Minh's communism, and a small pro-colonial lobby in Paris, nicknamed the Saigon Clique, actively supported the Indochina war. Most people in France remained indifferent.

The French army managed to clear the Viet Minh from towns through massive aerial bombings, but they fatally underestimated Viet Minh strength in the countryside, where the Vietnamese now formed their own *maquis*. As the conflict dragged on, it became internationalized thanks to the Cold War, with communist China in 1950 supporting the Viet Minh and the United States supporting France; in the last four years of fighting, the United States paid 80 percent of France's military and development costs, and even then the war ate up 40 percent of the French defense budget.[56] The key turning point was the battle of Dien Bien Phu, a strategic valley in an isolated corner of northwestern Vietnam taken by elite French paratroopers in 1953. The French commander, General Navarre, had reinforced the position with 30,000 French troops. On March 15, 1954, Viet Minh General Giap surreptitiously surrounded Dien Bien Phu, cutting off all land routes and, most critically, access to the landing strip. Caught by surprise, France struggled to resupply its forces with airlifts, but on May 7, two months after the siege began, General Giap succeeded in taking Dien Bien Phu. Some 3,000 French troops were killed, another 4,000 wounded, and 10,000 taken prisoner; these were still considerably lower than the 20,000–30,000 Viet Minh casualties of this battle, but the Viet Minh, fighting to liberate their homeland, was willing to tolerate much higher losses than the French were.

With the humiliating loss of Dien Bien Phu, France faced the choice of either sending a much larger military force to Indochina or acknowledging a second military defeat within 14 years and withdrawing. In 1954, Pierre Mendès-France,

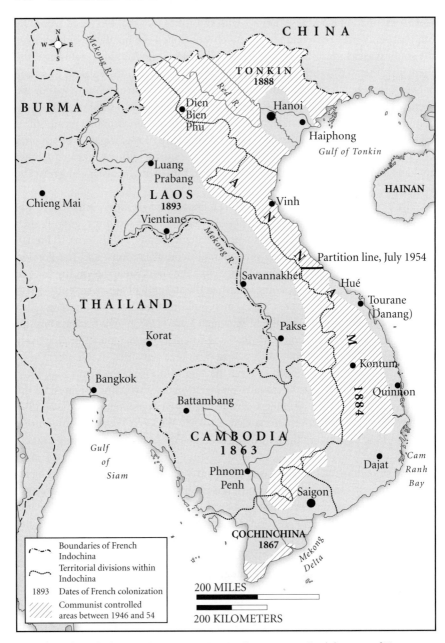

Map 10.1 The Indochina war, 1946-1954. In 1946 France recognized the state of Vietnam (Cochinchina, Annam, and Tonkin) as part of the French Union. In July 1954 Vietnam, Cambodia, and Laos won their full independence.

a Radical who had come to accept that France's days of empire were in fact over, promised if he became prime minister either to settle the conflict in Indochina in one month or resign. On taking office, Mendès-France immediately opened negotiations in Geneva to end the war; amazingly, he was able to keep his promise. The Geneva Accords, signed July 20, 1954, created two new independent countries, Laos and Cambodia. France agreed to withdraw all troops from Vietnam, which was divided at the 17th parallel; the north was placed under the authority of Viet Minh leader Ho Chi Minh. A prominent Catholic, Ngo Dinh Diem, became president of South Vietnam.

The Geneva Accords also called for nationwide elections in 1956 in Vietnam to determine its ultimate fate. Meanwhile, for 300 days following July 22, 1956, the day the Geneva Accords went into effect, anyone wishing to cross was allowed free passage north or south of the 17th parallel. While accurate figures are difficult to ascertain, about 800,000 mostly Catholic people from the North crossed over to the South, and about 150,000–200,000 mostly Viet Minh fighters crossed in the opposite direction.[57] In the end the United States, fearful that Ho Chi Minh's communist forces would win the elections scheduled for 1956, canceled them. Thus began the American military involvement against the so-called Vietcong, or Vietnamese communists. Over 92,000 French troops, nearly all of them colonial or legionnaires, died between 1946 and 1954, while 300,000 Vietnamese are estimated to have lost their lives. In France, those most bitter about the end of the war were the military, convinced that they could have defeated the Viet Minh if the civilian government had not pulled the rug out from under them.

THE ALGERIAN QUAGMIRE

The broker of the Geneva Accords, Pierre Mendès-France, proved to be one of the bright lights of Fourth Republic, who worked hard to overcome the old politics of paralysis. He firmly believed that France needed to look forward, which meant letting go of its empire, modernizing its economy, raising its standard of living, and reducing social inequality.[58] After successfully negotiating the Geneva Accords, Mendès-France quickly shifted his attention to North Africa. Although his government fell in 1955, under Mendès-France's successor, Guy Mollet, France granted independence to Tunisia and Morocco in March 1956 in a largely peaceful manner.

The next logical step in dismantling France's empire would have been granting independence to Algeria. However, because of its unique legal status and the presence of almost a million settlers, Algeria presented considerably more complicated issues, making even those opposed to colonialism in theory, like Mendès-France, unwilling to countenance leaving Algeria. All French governments continued to insist that Algeria was a part of France and willfully ignored the fact that dividing it into departments and offering citizenship under conditions unacceptable to the vast majority of the population had decidedly not made Algeria "French" in the eyes of most Muslims. As Mendès-France himself put it to

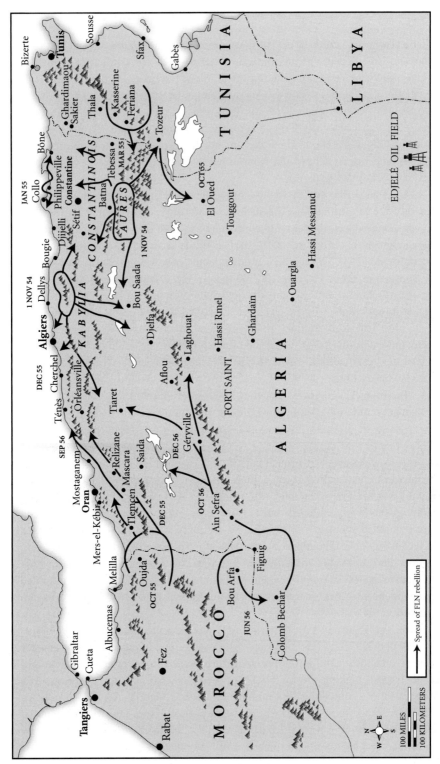

Map 10.2 The first phase of the FLN Rebellion against the French in Algeria, Nov. 1, 1954 through Dec. 1956.

the National Assembly in November 1954, shortly after signing the Geneva accords for Indochina:

> One does not compromise when it comes to defending the internal peace of the nation, the unity and integrity of the Republic. The Algerian departments are part of the French Republic. They have been French for a long time, and they are irrevocably French. . . . Between them and metropolitan France there can be no conceivable secession.

His minister of interior (and future president), François Mitterrand, agreed: "the only negotiation," he replied, "is war."[59]

And so war it would be, because by the end of World War II, key groups among Algeria's Muslims had become equally sure that an Algerian nation existed that owed nothing to France. Internal disputes, however, had prevented this nationalist movement from either uniting or agreeing on whether to resort to violence to oust the French; then the news of the defeat at Dien Bien Phu arrived in Algiers, galvanizing a new underground group—soon to be known to the world as the FLN (Front de Libération Nationale or National Liberation Front)—to take military action. On All-Saints Day, November 1, 1954, a core group of six young militants launched a series of 30 attacks across Algeria against the French and any Algerians who sympathized with them. Fires were set, bombs exploded in Algiers, and, in an incident that infuriated many in France, two French teachers, Guy Monnerot and his wife Jeanine, were taken off a bus and killed while the other

Pamphlet designed for recruiting young Muslims into the French army, ca. 1960. Musée d'Histoire Contemporaine, B.D.I.C., Paris/Archives Charmet/The Bridgeman Art Library.

passengers watched. The attacks were not meant to target only those of European descent, and the rest of the seven who died that day were Muslims. Nevertheless, France responded by sending in troops to punish the perpetrators and squelch, or so they hoped, any move toward independence. This "Toussaint Rouge," or "Red All-Saints Day" marked the start of the Algerian war.

Shortly after that, a new Algerian leader, Ahmed Ben Bella, emerged who managed to bring all the various nationalist groups, including Messali Hadj's many supporters, under the umbrella of the FLN; yet the FLN continued to struggle internally over tactics. Echoing an argument that had taken place within the French Resistance during the German Occupation, debate raged within the ranks of the FLN in late 1954 over whether to resort systematically to violence. The faction favoring force won that struggle and gained control of the FLN, and then unleashed a bloody and brutal campaign aimed not only at settlers but also at uncommitted Algerians. In 1955, FLN fighters brutally attacked European settlers in the town of Philippeville, again killing and mutilating women and children. France declared a state of emergency in April 1955 and took even more brutal reprisals against the local Arab population, labeling all FLN fighters "terrorists."

By 1956 France had truly committed itself to conquering the FLN, sending nearly 400,000 French troops. But it refused to call the undertaking a war, insisting that Algeria was French and therefore that the government was legitimately "maintaining order on French territory."[60] Nevertheless, these so-called police operations required such large numbers of soldiers that France could not, as in Indochina, rely solely on career military, colonial, or Foreign Legion soldiers. Most of the troops in this undeclared war were regular French army and Algerians loyal to France. With universal military service required of nearly all French men when they turned 20, the possibility of service in Algeria hit every sector of society. French public opinion thus quickly became aware of the costs of this campaign, both in money and in lives, and citizens began to have doubts about its wisdom.

The Battle of Algiers, waged between January and October 1957, proved to be a key turning point. The French won the battle, but at an enormous cost in terms of morale and support back home. Public confidence had already been badly shaken by revelations that the French army was using torture against the FLN and local populations, a particularly disturbing development in a country that had so recently been occupied by the Nazis. In 1957 and 1958, the use of torture became a major topic of debate in France, dividing those for whom social justice was paramount against partisans of the defense of the integrity of the nation above all else. Former members of the Resistance could be found in each camp.

Although the French government always denied that it had authorized the use of torture, the truth was murkier. In the mid-1950s the International Red Cross had tried in vain to gain access to detainees. France had replied that since this was not a war, detained Algerians were not POWs. Rather, they were being held in special "military internment centers" because they had been "taken captive in possession of weapons." Prime Minister Mendès-France finally gave the International Red Cross permission to visit these internment centers in 1955, but only under the condition that the Red Cross not make its work public. Then in March 1956, Prime Minister Guy Mollet, leader of the SFIO and head of a social-democratic coalition government, sent a proposal, which the National Assembly supported, to set aside individual freedoms in Algeria and to permit the police and French soldiers to use "extended questioning," "coercive measures," or "special treatment." Many years later, a key French commander, General Aussaresses, confirmed that underneath the euphemisms, "[the military was] given a free hand to do what we considered necessary." Accounts by survivors make it clear that ignoring the rules of the Geneva Convention and French law proved a slippery slope to abuse and torture. The tactics included stripping the victim, beatings combined with hanging by the feet or hands, electric shock, what today is called "waterboarding," and rape. Electric shock was the most commonly used, both because it allowed for increasing levels of pain and because it distanced the "questioners," merely pushing a button, from the direct infliction of pain.[61]

It was only in February 1958, however, that French public opinion became fully aware of the extent to which torture had become a systematic part of the war effort. At that time a journalist name Henri Alleg, member of the Algerian Communist Party and editor of *Alger Républicain* until it was banned in 1955 for its communist and anti-colonial point of view, published a damning account of his own arrest and torture at the hands of the French military, entitled *La Question*. Les Editions de Minuit, a publishing house born during the German Occupation to publish French Resistance texts, published Alleg's account, which he smuggled out of prison. Although the book itself was not banned at the start, the French press was prohibited from publishing commentary or reviews of Alleg's book. Nevertheless, by March the book had sold 60,000 copies. At that point the government banned it and seized the remaining copies, but failed to prevent it from circulating in large numbers. Alleg's graphic descriptions shocked the public as no other account to date had.[62] Despite the government's denials, Alleg's account was later seconded by the Red Cross report on its seventh mission to Algeria, summarized on January 5, 1960, by *Le Monde*. "Numerous cases of ill-treatment and torture are still being reported," the article disclosed. A colonel in the French police force had told the Red Cross delegates, "The struggle against terrorism makes it necessary to resort to certain questioning techniques as the only way of saving human life and avoiding new attacks."[63]

As anti-war sentiment grew in the wake of Alleg's revelations, the government became more and more paralyzed. The problem was not only divisions in the metropole; military-civilian relations, already tense, began to sour as the army became increasingly worried that the government might once again "sell it out"—an outcome that the army was determined to prevent at any cost. A separate military humiliation in Egypt in 1956 only strengthened this conviction. In November France had joined Britain and Israel to launch an invasion of Egypt, hoping to regain control of the Suez Canal that the Egyptian leader, Gamal Abdel Nasser, had just nationalized, and also to punish Nasser for furnishing weapons to the FLN. In the end, both the United States and the U.S.S.R. opposed the operation and forced its cancellation—making clear who was now calling the shots internationally. Yet however humiliating for the French and British governments, the aborted Suez mission proved even more frustrating to the French army; in its wake, the military's determination to win in Algeria—despite the politicians if necessary—only intensified.

The army's discontent reached a tipping point in the spring of 1958. On May 13, 1958, a newly formed French cabinet was rumored to be ready to negotiate a French pullout with the FLN. When the news reached Algeria, a group of French generals, together with support from right-wing settlers, revolted in the capital city of Algiers, seizing control of the local government and demanding the formation of an emergency government in Paris. The revolt proved to be the death knell of the already deeply compromised Fourth Republic, whose institutions no longer seemed capable—or so it appeared to the majority of French—of resolving the crisis. France, yet again, appeared to be on the brink of revolution, but whose?

Some of the people involved in the Algiers uprising were Gaullist agents; Charles de Gaulle, however, refused to take leadership of this group. After 12 years of political exile, he had no intention of rising to power via a military coup that would not be seen as legitimate and that would leave him at the mercy of French army units. But he was willing to seize the opportunity that his supporters had played a role in creating. On May 15, 1958, de Gaulle spoke to the French public. If the National Assembly invited him, de Gaulle offered to head a new cabinet in Paris, but only if he were empowered to draft a new constitution for France. The National Assembly hesitated, suspicious that de Gaulle's true goals were authoritarian. Questioned about his motives, he was said to have replied "Who honestly believes that, at age 67, I would start a career as a dictator?" Meanwhile, the real threat of a military coup grew. Disloyal units of the French army in Algeria landed paratroopers in Corsica and threatened to use Corsica as a stepping stone to launch a landing in France and overthrow the Republic.

On May 29, 1958, the Assembly finally gave in and invited de Gaulle to form a new cabinet. Officially de Gaulle did not overthrow the Fourth Republic. The National Assembly handed him power on June 1, 1958, voting full powers to de Gaulle to draw up a new constitution. A small committee of experts drafted a new constitution, which was submitted to a consultative committee and approved by the Council of Ministers in September. As he had in 1944–1946, de Gaulle insisted on a presidential system with a powerful executive branch. This time, fed up by the bickering and ineffectiveness of the Fourth Republic, the public supported de Gaulle. It remained to see what he would do with his power, both in Algeria and in France.

CHAPTER 11

De Gaulle Founds a New Republic

1958–1969

On August 22, 1962, a group of fanatical partisans of Algérie Française, known as the Secret Army Organization (Organisation de l'Armée Secrète or OAS), ambushed President Charles de Gaulle's motorcade at Petit-Clamart on the outskirts of Paris. This group bitterly opposed his recent recognition of Algerian independence and had been trying to assassinate him for over a month now. Fourteen bullets penetrated de Gaulle's vehicle and came within a hair's breadth of killing him. Miraculously the four occupants—the 72-year-old General, his wife Yvonne, his son-in-law, and his chauffeur—emerged unscathed. Yvonne de Gaulle, whose imperturbability perhaps exceeded that of her husband, jumped out to see whether the chicken in the trunk that she was taking home for dinner had been hurt.[1] De Gaulle had refused to crouch down during the attack, which, paradoxically, may have saved his life. He then insisted, as after all previous attempts on his life, on continuing exactly with the planned schedule. In this case he reviewed the military guard at a nearby airport before proceeding on by plane to his family residence.

De Gaulle's brush with death in August 1962 at the hands of the OAS signaled a turning point in the history of the young Fifth Republic. A month earlier, the French flag had been lowered in Algeria, after eight years of bloody conflict. A month later, in September 1962, the general would go to the nation with a new constitutional referendum, designed to strengthen the Fifth Republic by doing away with the electoral college and making the president directly elected. De Gaulle feared that without a popular mandate, future presidents might not have the authority to prevent a return to a system of parliamentary supremacy and the dreaded immobilism of the Third and Fourth Republics. At 72, de Gaulle was also worried about his "succession." The near-miss of the OAS so shocked the country that a majority proved willing to pass a measure that many had long resisted as a form of "Bonapartism" or "Pétainism" incompatible with French republican traditions.

The return to peace in 1962 thus coincided with the consolidation of what some historians have called the Monarchy of the Republic, a regime in which "the

275

"La Voix de Son Maître," advertising campaign against General Charles de Gaulle, **May 1968.** Private Collection/Archives Charmet/The Bridgeman Art Library.

indivisible authority of the State is entrusted completely to the President by the people who elected him. . . . [T]here is no other authority, either ministerial, civilian, military or judicial, which is not entrusted and maintained by him."[2] Four years after returning to power and founding the Fifth Republic, de Gaulle had completed his dream of endowing France with the strong executive that he believed was necessary for the nation to return to its former *grandeur*. He had also distanced himself from older republican ideology, with its emphasis upon reason, secularism, and revolutionary heroes and heroines. For de Gaulle, the new Republic was the nation first and foremost.[3]

Yet without the continuing trauma of the Algerian emergency to justify it, de Gaulle's singular style of presidential rule would gradually prove out of step with the political aspirations of a rapidly changing French society. In the 1960s the nation was finally reaping the material dividends of intensive post-war rebuilding. Under de Gaulle's decisive leadership, the French economy became one of the world's fastest growing and most technologically sophisticated. For most of the decade the electorate seemed satisfied with France's dizzying new affluence. But then, out of the blue, came a hurricane. In May 1968, ten years after de Gaulle's return, students and workers erupted onto the streets, shouting "dix ans ça suffit" ("10 years, that's enough") and, more enigmatically, "sous les pavés, la plage" ("beneath the cobblestones, the beach"). These "events," too, would escalate into a national emergency like the "events" in Algeria that had brought de Gaulle to power. This time, however, de Gaulle emerged less the savior than part of the problem.

THE REPUBLIC TRANSFORMED

When de Gaulle unveiled his new constitution on September 4, 1958—on that same date 88 years earlier the Second Empire had given way to the Third Republic—he claimed that his role as president would be to see fair play between the different branches of the government.[4] Yet from the moment he came to power, suspicions arose on the Left that de Gaulle was an aspiring dictator. In his youth, de Gaulle had been drawn not to Jean Jaurès and the republican Left, but to the rising star of the new Right, Charles Maurras. Maurras had claimed that the only way to reproduce past French greatness was through restoring the monarchy. By 1958, de Gaulle had long accepted that France would have to remain a Republic, and he never departed from republican legality while in office. But he was determined to create a highly personal regime that would subordinate the National Assembly and political parties to the executive, in order to overcome the political paralysis that had plagued France's last two republics and to endow the Fifth Republic with a new set of symbols to rally people to it.

The new constitution provided for a president elected every seven years by an electoral college of 70,000. As in the Third and Fourth Republics, the legislature was made up of a Senate chosen indirectly, balanced by a directly elected National Assembly. Should a conflict arise between the president and the legislature, the president could go to the people by calling a referendum, thus bypassing parliamentary authority altogether. De Gaulle frequently exercised this radical option, thus nurturing the myth that the French people and president were united. The president, and not the National Assembly, appointed a prime minister and Cabinet who set the government's agenda. Ministers could no longer be deputies, and in practice de Gaulle picked Cabinet members who were either skilled technocrats or loyal followers from his Resistance days—rather than the small town lawyers and doctors who had predominated in the past and who were beholden to their local constituencies. His first prime minister, Michel Debré (1959–1962), was a legal scholar who had helped draft the constitution; Georges Pompidou (1962–1968), his second prime minister, who served an astounding six consecutive years, was a banker with no political experience. Under de Gaulle, experts in the Cabinet had the upper hand in drafting legislation.

Although de Gaulle viewed excessive party spirit as one of the many reasons for France's decline in the twentieth century, he did not attempt to destroy party politics altogether; the government was still expected to have a majority to stay in power. He did, however, succeed in considerably reducing party influence, particularly during his first four years in office. In 1958 Jacques Soustelle, a loyalist from World War II, founded a new Gaullist Party, the Union for the New Republic (Union pour la Nouvelle République or UNR). It garnered 20 percent of the vote in November 1958 to become the single largest group in the Assembly. France's other conservative parties, centrists, and a portion of those voters traditionally on the Left but ready for change also rallied to de Gaulle, giving him an impressive 80 percent majority in the first legislative elections. The same voters resoundingly rejected the Fourth Republic by returning only 131 out of 537 sitting deputies. The communists, socialists, Radicals, and Poujadists had simply collapsed. When civil war threatened from Algeria, this largely Gaullist Assembly granted the president the right to rule by decree for a year, bringing political life to a full halt.[5]

After the Algerian war ended, the revived parties on the Left as well as moderates began to agitate for a return to more traditional parliamentary rule. Once again, de Gaulle found a means to upstage his opponents and keep power in his own hands. The show of force came in the wake of the Petit Clamart attempt on his life, when de Gaulle decided to revise the constitution to make the president elected by universal suffrage. Article 89 required prior approval from the National Assembly for any such change. De Gaulle instead took his proposed revision directly to the people in a referendum. Outraged socialists, communists, and members of the MRP (Mouvement Républicain Populaire or Popular Republican Movement) censured his government on October 5, 1962. A furious de Gaulle dissolved the assembly and called for new elections. In the constitutional referendum the "*ouis*" carried the day by 62 percent. The November elections were a sweep for the Gaullists as well, with the UNR winning 35 percent of the vote and 233 seats. Henceforth the parties would have to play politics by de Gaulle's new rules or not at all.[6]

For the remainder of his presidency, the parties chose the former, but this did not mean that political life stagnated completely. Between 1962 and 1968, the opposition parties gradually regained confidence and updated themselves. By the 1960s many people in France were looking for a new form of participatory politics that both broke with de Gaulle's heavy-handed paternalism and spoke to the problems of rapid social change created by the modernization of the economy. Symptomatic of this desire was the appearance of two new weeklies consciously inspired by *Time* magazine, *L'Express* and *Le Nouvel Observateur*. They reflected a yearning for younger more modern political leaders—ideally, a French JFK. This desire for real political participation came out vividly in the first direct presidential elections, scheduled for 1965. For the first time, the president and the opposition parties received equal airtime on France's state-controlled TV (see Chapter 12), allowing millions of ordinary citizens to discover "the face of the opposition."[7] The parties of the Left united behind an independent candidate, François Mitterrand, who ran an "American-style" media campaign and promised legalization of contraception, equalization of salaries and educational opportunities, and greater participation for women. De Gaulle, ever above politics, refused to campaign beyond his TV appearances. The race was uncomfortably close for the president, with de Gaulle receiving 55 percent and Mitterrand 45 percent of the vote in the second round. Opposition politics under de Gaulle would continue to evolve toward a more open system, until the surprise uprising of spring 1968—for two months—transformed the meaning of politics altogether.

To anchor his new presidential version of the Republic and rally the French to it, de Gaulle also innovated symbolically. The Third and Fourth Republics had drawn their legitimacy principally from the French Revolution, whose values they claimed to incarnate. The Third and Fourth Republics had adopted a panoply of images that celebrated this heritage: the tricolor flag; the slogan "Liberty, Fraternity, Equality"; Marianne; and "La Marseillaise"—not to mention republican heroes buried in the Pantheon. The Fifth Republic did not abandon any of these symbols; but in keeping with the moral legitimacy he had acquired during the war, de Gaulle tended to celebrate France as a nation of resisters rather than revolutionary republicans. De Gaulle's favorite heroes were Vercingétorix, who had long ago led the Gauls against the Romans, and Clovis, the French king who had founded the great Merovingian dynasty of the fifth century. Resistance, in other words, was what the entire and eternal French nation had always done best. De Gaulle delivered this message perhaps most forcefully on December 19, 1964, when he and his brilliant minister of culture, André Malraux, presided over the transfer of Jean Moulin's ashes to the Pantheon.[8] Jean Moulin had been de Gaulle's personal emissary to Occupied France in 1942, where he later died under torture at the hands of the Gestapo head in Lyons, Klaus Barbie. Respected by Gaullists and communists alike, Moulin's "canonization" gave the new Fifth Republic a Resistance pedigree and a martyr that everyone who had lived through the Occupation could embrace. What exactly Moulin offered to the post-war baby boomers was decidedly less clear.

THE ALGERIAN WAR

Historians have long posed the question of whether de Gaulle knew already in June 1958 that France would have to give up control of Algeria. The evidence suggests that he never had a clear plan for resolving the conflict; rather, he responded to developments pragmatically in ways that perpetuated—however unintentionally—this most brutal of wars for another four years.[9] At least initially, de Gaulle was willing to authorize an expansion of military operations in Algeria, as long as the officers in charge remained loyal to the Fifth Republic. Immediately upon coming to power, de Gaulle flew to Algiers to convince the settlers and dissident generals to end their revolt; "I have understood you," he told them. The declaration's ambiguity was revealed only much later. At the end of the same trip he proclaimed (but only once), "Vive l'Algérie Française" and announced a vast new program of economic and social reforms directed at the Muslim population. At that point "everything indicated that de Gaulle would seek to integrate Algeria through a combination of military action and economic concessions, and his supporters were sure that he would succeed where the Fourth Republic had failed."[10]

Yet by the end of 1958 the FLN (Front de Libération Nationale or National Liberation Front) had seized the initiative in the conflict, leaving de Gaulle to react rather than lead. Although losing militarily, the FLN rebuffed a French offer for an honorable cease-fire. Instead it garnered international support for an independent

Algerian republic, by creating a government-in-exile and putting its case for full independence before the United Nations.[11] Around the world one colony after another achieved national independence between 1958 and 1962, making continued French intransigence in Algeria embarrassing. French public opinion was also growing increasingly appalled at the army's use of torture. By 1959 polls showed that 71 percent of French favored negotiations with the FLN. Meanwhile, the war's costs were spiraling out of control and imperiling France's surging economic growth, which in turn threatened de Gaulle's projects to enhance France's international stature.

This combination of factors impelled de Gaulle within a year of coming to office to contemplate withdrawal from Algeria. Yet he insisted on doing so from a position of strength, which meant both continuing the military struggle against the FLN and persuading the die-hard partisans of French Algeria to accept the inevitable. The former proved easier than the latter. De Gaulle in fact continued to face two conflicts in Algeria: the war on the ground, which he authorized General Challe to expand further in 1959; and a growing anti-Gaullist insurgency among an extremist, or "*ultra*," group of French officers, settlers, and his own political backers determined to keep this "integral" part of the national territory French.

Revolt from within army ranks threatened again most seriously in January 1960. A few months earlier, on September 16, 1959, de Gaulle for the first time publicly endorsed the right of the predominantly Muslim population of Algeria to determine its own future once the fighting had ended. The effects of this announcement on the partisans of Algérie Française were nothing short of seismic. General Massu, one of the leaders of the May 13, 1958, movement and still in command of French troops, declared that he would arm the *pieds noirs* (settlers) if they organized against Paris. De Gaulle instantly recalled Massu, but the gunpowder had been prepared. On January 24, 1960, a hard core of dissident professional troops and settler sympathizers erected barricades in the streets of Algiers to protest Massu's demotion. Defiance then turned to violence when these troops shot dead 14 of the policemen sent to clear the streets, dredging up the dreadful specter of military dictatorship and another fratricidal civil war if the insurgents were not brought to heel.[12]

For five long days between January 24 and 29, the French people waited to see if this new revolt would escalate. But then de Gaulle "lanced the abscess" by going on national television and pleading for obedience from the troops.[13] His speech remains legendary in the annals of modern communication. Appearing in his general's uniform—so familiar to many officers in Algeria from their years together in the Resistance—he reiterated his September decision: "Self-determination is the only policy that is worthy of France. It is the only possible outcome." He then called the army to order: "It is I who bear the country's destiny. I must therefore be obeyed. . . . No soldier . . . may associate himself at any time, even passively, with the insurrection."[14] He closed by condemning both the FLN and the French dissidents, but also promising that the links between Algeria and France would not

Semaines des Barricades (Barricades Week). Algiers, January 24–31, 1960.

be severed. Within 48 hours of the broadcast, the insurrection had fizzled. Without granting any concessions, de Gaulle had purged the rebellious leaders and restored order in Algiers.

A variety of reasons explain why certain settlers and army officers were willing to risk all to keep Algeria French. International opinion tended to depict the *pieds noirs* as racial supremacists and greedy landlords determined to resort to violence to protect their ill-gotten privileges. While there was certainly some truth to this stereotype, it does not tell the whole story. In 1957, ethnologist Germaine Tillion estimated that only 12,000 out of Algeria's European community of 1,042,409 were rich landowners. This tiny minority owned most of the best agricultural land, ran the country's industries, and controlled the press, and their views exerted a disproportionate influence on the government in Paris.[15] But the vast majority of Algeria's settlers were small traders, urban workers, junior civil servants, or teachers; they too, however, lived better—and certainly apart from—the country's 9 million impoverished Muslims.[16] Some of these poorer Europeans had been prepared at first to reform French Algeria along more egalitarian lines. One of the most famous of these liberals was Algerian-born French writer Albert Camus—whose deep attachment to Algeria and anguish over the war became legendary. As Camus wrote in his journal, "What luck to have been brought into the world on the hills of Tipasa [in Algeria] and not in Saint Etienne or Roubaix [industrial cities in the north of France]. I appreciated my good fortune and accepted it with gratitude."[17]

Yet even liberals within the *pied-noir* community could not bring themselves to accept the legitimacy of Algerian independence. Indeed, after over a century of French occupation of Algeria, all settlers believed that they had built a new French society on the other side of the Mediterranean. For them Algérie Française was a frontier society in the image of the American West, in which "virile heroes ... with bloodied hands had created wealth from a harsh and unforgiving land."[18] Brought into existence by the French, Algeria was indissolubly part of France, to be defended to the death. As the war intensified, this version of the past hardened. As Camus declared in an interview shortly after receiving the Nobel Prize in 1957 (and just three years before his tragic death in a car accident), "I believe in justice, but I would defend my mother [i.e., Algérie Française] before justice."[19]

Professional officers—particularly from the elite paratrooper ranks of the Foreign Legion—were prepared to defy Paris for other reasons. Having been defeated in 1940, then humiliated at Dien Bien Phu and Suez, the army top brass was determined to smash the Algerian rebellion in order to restore their reputation. In Indochina and Egypt, they insisted, victory could have been theirs if the politicians had not gotten cold feet. Now the civilians appeared to be on the verge of pulling the plug once again on the army. The oldest officers wished also to preserve the "civilizing" empire of France's colonial commanders, under whom they had served. Last but not least, several of the officers had fought in the Resistance in North Africa in the name of eternal France. To them it was inconceivable that the same de Gaulle who had stood up to Nazi Germany would ever yield an inch of national soil. When he committed himself to self-determination, their sense of betrayal was that much more acute.[20]

"Barricades Week," as the army revolt in January became known, only strengthened de Gaulle's resolve to pull France from the Algerian quagmire. He had been holding out for a ceasefire, followed by a compromise settlement—a policy which the FLN consistently rejected. A visit to Algeria in December 1960, however, finally convinced him that the Muslim population would never settle for less than full independence. He returned to France and officially accepted this principle as the basis for all future negotiations. A majority of 75 percent of French voters approved his decision by referendum on January 8, 1961.[21] Yet while the metropole endorsed separation, the desperate defenders of French Algeria had reached no such conclusion. Before talks even opened between de Gaulle's government and the FLN, four generals—Challe, Jouhaud, Zeller, and Salan, backed by a group of *ultra*, or extreme, settlers—seized power in Algiers on April 22, 1961. They now called themselves the Secret Army Organization (OAS), in conscious emulation of the Secret Army of the Resistance that had formed against the German occupiers during World War II.

The next day in Paris, tanks rolled into the Place de la Concorde in anticipation of an airborne attack from the OAS. A somber de Gaulle donned his military uniform for the second time in less than a year to address once again a shaken nation on radio and television. In perhaps his most brilliant performance of the whole war, he placed all the blame for the rebellion on the four generals who had led the putsch—dismissively referring to them as "the little band of retired generals"; he then forbade "any Frenchman, and first of all any soldier, to execute any of their orders."[22] Conscripts and reservists in Algeria, huddled around their transistor radios, immediately rallied and the rebellion soon dissipated. It could easily have gone the other way: 14,000 officers and men were implicated, and by the end of April five generals and 200 other officers had been arrested.[23] The revolt only cemented French public support for a resumption of talks with the FLN. In May 1961 a new phase of negotiations began at the town of Evian on Lake Geneva.

The Evian negotiations did not end violence in either Algeria or France, as all parties tried to influence their outcome. The OAS vowed to continue the fight for Algérie Française by underground techniques of terrorism, and in 1961 inaugurated a reign of terror against the Muslim population and any French supporter of a pullout. The army of the FLN, the ALN, also increased its attacks against Europeans and any Algerians recruited by them. And the French state continued to harass, arrest, and intern Algerians living in France who supported independence. In his landmark work *The Wretched of the Earth*, Frantz Fanon, a psychoanalyst from Martinique, both theorized and justified this pattern of escalating "mirror violence." Fanon had treated torture victims in Algeria throughout the war, and deeply identified with the FLN's struggle. He argued that only violent revolution could liberate black subjects from the inherent violence of white colonial rule. Published in 1961, *The Wretched of the Earth* "became the classic vindication of the Algerian cause and a permanent indictment of colonialism," much admired by France's intellectual Left.[24] Fanon, however, had at least one eloquent critic in well-known Algerian novelist Mouloud Feraoun. Feraoun wrote in French, but he condemned all forms of violence unleashed by this most brutal of colonial wars, whose greatest number of victims were innocent civilians. Tragically, just days before the conclusion of the Evian Accords, the OAS murdered Feraoun.

One of the most gruesome episodes of French state violence against Algerians occurred on the night of October 17, 1961. Tens of thousands of impoverished Algerians living in shantytowns on the edge of Paris had decided to defy peacefully curfew controls that banned them from the city's center after dark. Dressed in their Sunday best, women and men of all ages gathered to demonstrate in favor of peace and an Algerian Algeria. The police chief, Maurice Papon—a former Vichy-era administrator responsible for deporting Jews from Bordeaux—orchestrated a savage repression. Some 11,538 were arrested, and historians estimate that somewhere between 120 and 200 were beaten to death and thrown into the Seine River. Incredibly, the massacre was covered up and few Parisians asked questions, even though anti-war sentiment now spanned the political spectrum. After seven years of war and media distortions of the conflict, many in France had unconsciously absorbed settler fears that all Algerians posed a danger to the nation.[25]

Public indifference to police brutality against Algerians in Paris became even clearer five months later. On February 8, 1962, French communist trade unions and parties of the Left led a demonstration against OAS violence and in favor of peace.

The police again responded viciously; eight people, including three women and a young child, died, and hundreds were injured at the entrance to the Charonne metro station. But because the victims were French citizens, not poor Algerian immigrants, public opinion massively condemned the incident and hundreds of thousands of Parisians attended their burial.

In this tense atmosphere, the FLN and de Gaulle inched toward agreement. Only after the French government in October 1960 gave up its claims to the Saharan territories—where oil reserves had been discovered and France had just detonated its first nuclear device—was real progress made. On March 18, 1962, de Gaulle and the Algerian government-in-exile signed the Evian Accords granting Algeria independence. Ninety percent of French voters approved the Accords in a referendum on April 8, 1962, and 99 percent of Algerians approved them on July 1, 1962. The Accords provided on paper for an orderly transfer of power, guarantees for French settler life and property in Algeria, and the preservation of French commercial and strategic interests. De Gaulle took it for granted that the *pied-noir* community would stay put; no one in France wished their return. The government was thus confounded by what happened next. Between mid-April and September, a flood of close to 1 million desperate settlers poured into southern France, leaving all their possessions behind. The final year of struggle had solidified two central truths for the *pieds noirs:* that they wished to remain French and that this was only possible on French soil.[26] Unwanted, destitute, and filled with hatred for the Parisian political elite, the settlers were one of the many bitter legacies of the Algerian war of independence. Another was the shadowy presence of the OAS on French soil, which continued for another year to attempt to assassinate de Gaulle despite the arrest and exile of their leaders.

In all, 24,614 French soldiers and perhaps 4,000 French civilians had died in the Algerian "troubles"—the government never would call them a war.[27] There were no war memorials and no accolades for any of them. In 1964 and 1968, de Gaulle extended amnesties to all convicted of treason during the conflict, and the memory of another civil war was quickly buried. Also forgotten were the estimated 200,000 Muslim loyalists or *harkis* who had served with the French. The government was adamant in 1962 that these men were not "repatriates"—the legal term extended to the *pieds noirs,* whose French citizenship was recognized. Rather, the *harkis* were designated "Muslim refugees" and were abandoned to their fate. About half made it to France on their own, where they continued to be denied social and political rights; many of those who remained in Algeria perished at the hands of the FLN.[28] The total number of Algerians who died will never be known, but they numbered at least 300,000 men, women, and children out of a population of 9 million.[29]

FROM EMPIRE TO NEO-COLONY

Despite the tortuous path he took to extricate France from Algeria, de Gaulle showed genuine skill in formally withdrawing from several other parts of France's empire in 1958, principally the territories of French West and Equatorial Africa, and Madagascar. International opinion could no longer tolerate holding any peoples in a colonial yoke, while the Cold War offered opportunities for France to lead the rapidly decolonizing "Third World" nations if it granted them independence on the right terms. Perhaps victory could be seized from the wreckage of empire, in the form of a new world role for France, especially in sub-Saharan Africa, where nationalism had been slower to organize politically than in Indochina or North Africa.

Since the creation of the Union Française in 1946, the African deputies in the Assembly had cultivated close ties with leading French politicians, sometimes even serving in the government. Both Félix Houphouët-Boigny of the Ivory Coast and Léopold Sedar Senghor of Senegal had risen to ministerial posts in France during the Fourth Republic. But they had also established their own political parties in West Africa and had begun pressing for greater autonomy rather than further assimilation. In response, the minister for overseas territories, Gaston Defferre, had pushed through a series of new reforms in 1956 (known as the Loi Cadre) that created elected local institutions in all of the African territories and increased local African recruitment into the civil service. France here went further than any other country in decolonizing its African possessions without granting independence. Developments in other parts of Africa nevertheless almost immediately outpaced Defferre's initiatives, especially in the British colony of Ghana, which became independent in 1957.[30]

When de Gaulle came to power, he initially hoped to offer enough economic and political incentives to keep the African territories French. As part of the Constitution of the Fifth Republic, the remaining colonies were given three choices in the referendum of September 28, 1958: total assimilation with France as departments, internal autonomy and democratic self-government in what was now to be called the Community rather than Union, and complete independence. De Gaulle announced these choices in a highly symbolic trip to Brazzaville in August 1958. There he declared, "When one is a man and a free man, one has no right to conceal it. . . . I have spoken. You have heard me. Africans will choose."[31] If any colony "freely" chose independence, however, France would cut off all financial aid immediately. Only Guinea exercised this option. True to their word, the French in their rush to exit from Guinea took everything with them including their telephones. Yet within two years the remaining French African territories were asking for formal independence without severing relations with France (the only exception was Djibouti, which became independent in 1977). De Gaulle persuaded the French to accept this outcome, realizing that French influence in the African continent could now take more advantageous forms. In 1960 the Community was formally dissolved, and the French empire—long a symbol of French greatness—ended.

Yet the dissolution was not quite complete, especially in the South Pacific and the Indian Ocean. The far-flung islands of Polynesia, New Caledonia, and the Comoros remained overseas territories, with indirect representation in the French National Assembly. The atolls of Mururoa and Fangataufa in French Polynesia would become favorite nuclear testing sites in the mid-1960s. And in its former territories in Africa, French informal control continued in a neocolonial guise. In 1960, the Fifth Republic established a monetary zone of the franc that included all of the former colonies in Africa. French investment and commerce were given privileged access there to areas rich in valuable mineral resources, in return for substantial ongoing economic and behind-the-scene military aid. In this way de Gaulle created client states in francophone Africa, whose votes he could then corral in the United Nations to defend French interests around the globe—or so he hoped—at the expense of those of Britain, the United States, and the U.S.S.R.

THE POLITICS OF GRANDEUR

Maintaining a francophone area while shedding the empire was critical to a larger foreign policy goal: securing France's independence of action in a bipolar world dominated by the United States and the Soviet Union. De Gaulle is probably most famous for his conviction that France was destined to rise again. The nation's fortunes had declined, first under Vichy, then under the morass of parliamentary politics created by the Fourth Republic. The challenge was how to restore a medium-sized power like France to great nation status in the era of the superpowers. De Gaulle's hope was that France could free Europe and other parts of the world from either American or Soviet hegemony by carving an independent third way across the Cold War divide. In seeking this path he repeatedly antagonized the United States, where his intentions were often misinterpreted. Yet at no time did he show any sympathy for Soviet communism; indeed, during the 1962 Cuban Missile Crisis he openly supported American actions. Once that threat passed, however, de Gaulle was persuaded that the United States was the more dominating force, so it became the superpower that he sought to counter most.

One of de Gaulle's first foreign policy objectives was to ensure French membership in the nuclear club by continuing the development of France's nuclear capacity begun under the Fourth Republic. Having its own *force de frappe* (strike force) would guarantee French sovereignty and allow the government to assert its own interests, and also protect its permanent seat on the UN Security Council. The French exploded their first atom bomb in the Sahara in February 1960, in the midst of the Algerian war. The missiles carrying nuclear warheads could, de Gaulle liked to remind both superpowers, be pointed in any direction. Kennedy responded in 1962 by selling Polaris missiles to Britain, thus tightening the Anglo-American alliance. Subsequent nuclear tests were carried out in Polynesia, with little concern for the environment or the peoples living there.

Before coming to power, de Gaulle had been very critical of the Common Market, as the EEC was more popularly known, because he feared it might limit France's freedom of action. Once in power, de Gaulle kept France in the Common Market, which was inaugurated on January 1, 1958; it was too important for his plans to modernize France's economy to abandon it. He also realized that the EEC offered yet another stage where France could carve out an independent world role.

In this spirit, he quickly sought to convert the EEC into a confederation of sovereign nations under French leadership. Achieving this goal, however, meant keeping out Britain. De Gaulle was suspicious that if the British were allowed in, the Americans would use their close alliance with Britain as a kind of Trojan Horse to insinuate themselves directly into European affairs. First in 1963 and then in 1967, de Gaulle vetoed Britain's bid to join the EEC.

De Gaulle distrusted NATO for similar reasons: It gave the United States too much influence in internal European affairs and endangered French autonomy. Set up after the war by the United States to counter the threat of Soviet aggression, NATO committed its members to fight if any one of them was attacked without provocation. Quarrels arose as early as 1959, when de Gaulle suggested to Eisenhower that decisions on the use of nuclear force within NATO should not be taken by the Americans alone, but rather by a directorate of France, Britain, and the United States. When Eisenhower politely refused, de Gaulle removed the French Mediterranean fleet from NATO, claiming that NATO did not cover the Southern Mediterranean, where France had vital interests (particularly in North Africa). In February 1966 de Gaulle announced that France was withdrawing from the integrated command structure of NATO. America was asked to remove its 30 bases and 27,000 troops from French soil. In de Gaulle's words, "[T]here is no longer any actual or possible subordination of our forces to a foreign power. In six months there will be no Allied command, unit, base or army on our soil. We will restore their wholly national character to our army, navy, airforce in matters of command, operations and training."[32]

De Gaulle's policies toward Germany revealed a similar pattern. De Gaulle very much believed in a United Europe as a counter to the Soviet Union in Europe, just not a dilution of state sovereignty within a federal structure. He felt, moreover, that the logical partner for France was West Germany—divided and weakened after 1961—not Britain; de Gaulle never forgot France's fatal dependence on its British ally in the 1930s. During his presidency, de Gaulle assiduously and successfully cultivated the German chancellor, Konrad Adenauer, thereby building on the legacy of Schumann and Monnet. In 1963 the elderly leaders signed a historic friendship treaty, ending a century of Franco-German conflict. Together, de Gaulle grandly claimed, the two nations would constitute "a bastion of power and prosperity of the same order as that constituted by the United States in the New World."[33] De Gaulle would gradually discover that Germany's dependence on the United States for support against the Soviet Union prevented Adenauer from truly embracing the concept of an independent Europe. The Franco-German alliance nevertheless became the dominant factor in European politics and ensured that Europe was constructed, at least initially, in the image of France.

De Gaulle also wooed nonaligned and newly independent nations, again in ways that sought to counter U.S. hegemony and that inevitably provoked Washington. In 1964 he chose to recognize communist China, without warning the Americans or his new German allies. The United States "sent Paris one of the briefest diplomatic notes on record, a curt, 150-word message that deplored the

French maneuver as "unwise and untimely."[34] In 1966, de Gaulle visited Cambodia during the Vietnamese war, posing outrageously as the liberator of Algeria and condemning President Johnson's escalation of the conflict. Was it not detestable, he noted, for "a great nation to ravage a small one?"[35] In 1967 he famously visited Montreal, where the francophone population was threatening secession, and proclaimed "Vive le Québec libre." And after years of supporting U.S. ally Israel, de Gaulle switched sides to build up French client states among the Arab powers.

This shift became fully evident during the 1967 Six Day War between Israel and Egypt; defying the rest of Western opinion, de Gaulle imposed a French arms embargo on Israel and called for the Israelis to leave their captured territories. In a news conference in November 1967, he went as far as to remark that the Jews were "an elite people, sure of themselves and domineering." Given recent history, these words were particularly insensitive, and one of de Gaulle's supporters, prominent intellectual Raymond Aron, promptly denounced them. De Gaulle was once again trying to preserve one of France's historic roles—this time as an arbiter in the Middle East, a part of the world where it and Britain had dominated before World War II. Israel's actions, de Gaulle felt sure, would compromise any long-term possibilities for peace in the region.

MARRYING THE CENTURY

One of de Gaulle's most remembered quips, made in 1960, was that France had to marry its century if it wished to be great again. Such a "marriage" required catching up economically with other industrial powerhouses—by adopting new technology and rational management—and ensuring French citizens the same level of material well-being that other advanced economies enjoyed. A further transformation of the economy, like a strong foreign policy, would instill the determination and self-confidence the nation needed to maintain its independence. To that end, de Gaulle not only put "experts" in power, but also relied on the system of planners inaugurated by the Fourth Republic and encouraged them to make even further reforms.

The Fifth Republic planners were extremely successful in meeting the goal of continued economic renewal—so much so that it has become commonplace to talk about a New France emerging in these years. Government and private investment in the French economy, already at 4.9 percent per annum between 1949 and 1959, grew to 7.6 percent in 1959–1973.[36] Much of this growth stemmed from de Gaulle's decision to press ahead with the Common Market. After January 1, 1958, French business and agriculture could no longer hide behind protectionist tariffs. To prepare its citizens psychologically for the brave new world of free market competition—and to sharpen national competitiveness—Finance Minister Antoine Pinay and economic expert Jacques Rueff devalued the franc by 17.5 percent. They then created a "new franc" for a "new France" equal to 100 old ones, increased taxes, and cut government expenditures.

Planners also used their control of financial incentives and access to industrial materials to encourage major companies to merge. Between 1966 and 1972, 136 firms merged annually.[37] Larger firms, de Gaulle believed, could be run more efficiently, especially if they used modern management techniques—which he insisted upon. Farms, too, were further consolidated into fewer and larger units, and the number of small grocers and independent businessmen declined precipitously. Finally, state-led modernization helped nurture an advanced sector that benefited particularly from government largesse and "expert" input: computers, aeronautics, space, armaments, and nuclear energy. Here the flashiest (but never lucrative) symbol of de Gaulle's modernizing ambitions was the government-sponsored development of the Concorde with Britain. This supersonic jet, which married French engineering and sleek design with British capital, was conceived to put France on the map as an international pace-setter in innovative technology.

The pay-off for these reforms, coming on the heels of those of the Fourth Republic, was dramatic. The volume of French foreign trade grew 10.8 percent between 1959 and 1974. Exports rose from 10 percent of gross domestic product (GDP) in 1959 to 17 percent by 1970, much of it to other countries within the EEC—who now replaced the former colonies as France's largest trading partners. High investment and expanding trade translated into remarkable economic growth overall in the first decade of the Fifth Republic. While economic growth in the other economic powerhouses slowed (United States, Germany, Britain) compared to that of the previous decade, the French economy grew 5.8 percent per annum between 1959 and 1970, second only to Japan's 11 percent. Unemployment remained at 1–2 percent where it had been since 1950, while real wages increased by two and a half times between 1954 and 1968. This was a full employment economy whose one cloud was 4 percent inflation through 1969.[38]

Economic growth in this decade was also reflected in a significant increase— for the first time ever—in the sale of durable commodities. Full employment, cradle to grave welfare, and the buoyant economy and birthrate meant there was less pressure to save for a rainy day. In the 1960s many middle-class French were finally able to afford the consumer goods whose manufacture earlier plans had deliberately postponed. The big-ticket items of choice were televisions, refrigerators, washing machines, and automobiles, all purchased on credit. Acquiring the confidence to buy on credit was itself a minor revolution in most households, and the media of the era encouraged married women at home to lead the way. Articles might show women, for example, carefully calculating the difference between buying a washing machine on credit and using a Laundromat until a couple had saved enough to buy one outright.[39] Not only were readers told that buying on credit was cheaper, housewives would "wash their sheets more often" if they had a machine at home. The tourist industry also mushroomed as more and more French could afford to travel.

Lurking beneath these rosy statistics was a more complicated picture of clear winners and losers in France's continuing post-war modernization. The number of farmers, already a target of restructuring in the late 1940s, shrank from 26.7 percent of the population in 1950, many already marginal, to just under 10 percent in 1975. These disappearing farmers either retired or migrated out. Those who stayed on the land were either already highly industrialized and commercialized, such as the capitalist wheat farmers in the north or the Paris basin, or they were younger and better educated farmers in areas like Brittany, Normandy, the Rhone Valley, and the Languedoc who adapted to the new market conditions by specializing in cash crops such as dairy products or wine. In another fundamental change, these younger farmers became highly politicized. From the 1960s on they developed militant tactics—for example, blockading major thoroughfares or public buildings by dumping their produce—to try to gain subsidies from the state or to protect their farms from being bought out.[40] They also showed much more optimism in the future and a concomitant willingness to take risks, which translated most concretely in purchasing on credit. American sociologist Laurence Wylie returned to the small village of Roussillon 10 years after his first visit in 1950. Then he had found it desolate, if not dying. By 1960 one of his informants, Jacques Baudot, reported that he now had "a new car, a tractor, and a television set, all of them bought on the installment plan."[41]

While the rural sector shrank, the number of blue-collar workers rose from 32 percent in 1945 to reach an all-time high of 39 percent in 1970. Here, too, there were important transformations, but ones that on balance made French workers the relative losers in the boom economy of the 1960s. Changes included the decline of France's old heavily unionized working class of coal miners and textile, iron, and steel workers; the movement of many of these workers into the new engineering, electronics, aircraft, automobile and chemical industries; the relocation of industry away from Paris to the provinces; and the expansion of a largely deskilled and semi-skilled labor force made up of more and more women and foreigners. The modern sector of the economy became more competitive by adopting the latest American labor-saving technologies in their factories, thus decreasing the demand for skilled labor. Many manufacturers relocated to the countryside in search of the cheapest labor, which often was female. Employers also hired increasing numbers of foreigners, who were brought to France by the government for just this purpose; by the 1970s one-fourth of the unskilled labor force was female and 14 percent foreign.[42]

French workers did see some material gains after the war, but these were offset by other losses. The gap between the prosperous and the underprivileged elements in French society became wider under de Gaulle than it had been in the 1940s and 1950s. Only in the 1970s would workers be able to afford the appliances already available to the middle classes. The government repeatedly gave preference to the latter in such measures as housing, taxes, and social benefits. Factory workers logged longer hours than any other European workforce for less pay and had no voice in management since trade unions were kept out of the workplace. Many had long given up hope in the main trade union, the CGT, which to them appeared part of the system. The PC meanwhile remained in the opposition under de Gaulle, leaving workers with no political channel. For younger workers, better educated than their parents, the rigid hierarchy and dehumanizing work of the rationalized assembly line became increasingly intolerable.

For foreign workers, conditions were even worse. In the post-war years, state planners realized that economic rebuilding would require an abundant labor source which the French themselves could not immediately provide. In 1945, a National Immigration Office had been set up to recruit foreign workers who were to come as much desired guests of the state and industry. Originally 89 percent came from other European countries with less dynamic economies—Belgium, Italy, Spain, Portugal, and Poland—many of whom were skilled; for them, work in France represented a better life. Most of the others came from France's colonies, especially the North African ones. With the simultaneous devastating impact of the war upon Algeria's economy, and the increased demand in France for unskilled labor, the portion of immigrants from North Africa surged, from 2.3 percent of the immigrant labor force in 1946 to 32.3 percent in 1975.[43] Unskilled immigrants ended up working heavy machines or on the assembly line or taking the menial service jobs that no one else wanted. In the gigantic and highly automated factories of Renault in Billancourt, two out of five workers by 1969 were immigrants.

For North African immigrants in particular, working in France meant being pushed to the margins of French society. Most were either young single males or married middle-aged men who arrived alone and later brought their families. They did not speak French—there had been no serious attempt to educate the Muslim population of Algeria during a century and a half of French rule—and there were few opportunities for learning the language once in France because of de facto segregation. In the workplace, immigrants tended to be relegated to spaces where other immigrants also worked. Isolation in the factory was compounded by segregated housing. Newly arrived North African immigrants lived either in slums in the inner cities, such as the Goutte d'Or in the 18th arrondissement in Paris, or in shanty towns hastily erected on the edges of already overcrowded working-class suburbs in the provinces or Paris. Families crammed together in hastily thrown-together shacks of wooden planks and corrugated tin, for which workers might pay half their salary in rent. There was no running water and no sewers, no access to schools or to other public services.

The existence of these *bidonvilles*—literally, towns made of jerry cans, as they came to be called—was the result of both insufficient low-income housing in France generally and systematic discrimination against North African Muslims during the Algerian war and after. When the French government had undertaken the massive construction of Low-Cost Public Housing (Habitations à Loyer Modéré or HLM) starting in the 1950s, few Algerian families gained access to it. Not only were rents too high for their wages and apartments too small for their families, but many French housing administrators believed, based on racial stereotyping, that Algerians could not manage living in Western-style housing with modern amenities without training. Still, French authorities worried during the Algerian war about the FLN's influence over Algerian workers in the shanty towns. Thus in 1956 the French government financed an agency, the National Society to

Construct Housing for Algerian Workers, which was to provide hostels and temporary housing. Most such housing involved prefabricated camps that were run by former policemen or soldiers who kept the residents under close surveillance, hardly an appealing option and one that did nothing to favor integration.[44] Even when public housing opened to North Africans, French police noted the phenomenon that Americans called "white flight." As North Africans moved in to public housing estates, French workers moved out.[45]

THE AFFLUENT SOCIETY

The final and most visible social transformation in the 1960s was the emergence of new salaried middle classes in France. By 1970, the percentage of all working people employed in the rapidly growing white-collar sector known as "services" had increased from 32 percent in 1946 to 50 percent.[46] At the higher end of the socioeconomic scale, this restructuring of the French economy gave rise to a hierarchy of senior and middle managers called *cadres,* whose responsibilities included supervising people and organizing work in private business or government. Senior managers, or *cadres supérieurs,* were typically graduates of France's elite and ultra-selective public schools for training high-level civil servants and future CEOs, known as the *grandes écoles.* In addition to such older *grandes écoles* as the Ecole Polytechnique (created by Napoleon), de Gaulle's Provisional Government had created a new one in 1945, the National Administration School (Ecole Nationale d'Administration or ENA), with the specific purpose of training the post-war generation of leaders. Entrance to one of these was determined by a system of national exams for which anyone in theory could sit; in reality only those already part of the bourgeoisie could afford to prepare for them. Skilled in mathematics and enthusiastic devotees of the American science of management, *cadres supérieurs* quickly acquired the same high status and salaries as secondary and university teachers, members of the liberal professions, and engineers. Middle-level managers, in contrast, usually attended the less prestigious public universities and found themselves stuck in highly bureaucratized enterprises, mostly pushing paper.

The generous welfare state and more technologically oriented economy triggered, in addition to new managerial positions, a vast expansion of lower-level clerical and technical jobs in health and education services, office work, banking and insurance, administration, and transport and commerce. These jobs, too, required a better-educated workforce than in the past. In 1959 the state thus raised the minimum school leaving age from 14 to 16, and in 1963 it created a new type of middle school, known as the *collège,* which all children ages 11–16 were required to attend. Thanks to these reforms, the French educational system democratized somewhat in the 1960s and provided the children of ambitious industrial workers, shopkeepers, and farmers with the academic skills to move into the lower levels of the service sector, and a better life than their parents. But the coveted exit exam from high school, the *baccalauréat,* or *"bac,"* as it was known, required for entry into either a *grande école* or university, remained largely the preserve of the upper middle class.

The changing profile of France's of growing middle classes marked a transformation in the bourgeoisie, who had previously owed their social prominence to the businesses they owned and to the wealth they then passed to their children, rather than to their education and intellectual acumen. The change was evident not just in the kind of work that the new breed of managers and white-color workers did, but in how they defined themselves outside of work. Increasingly, in the affluent new society, this was through consumption. *Cadres,* and especially the *cadres supérieurs,* had the means, the leisure time, and the energy to consume in more innovative ways than ever before. They emerged as trendsetters for the rest of France, determined to throw off the stuffy ways of their parents. And where they led, the rest of society would soon follow.

Heavy gastronomy and luxury couture were thus traded in for lean cuisine, the sports jacket, the mini skirt, and the bikini: The fast-paced times required eating and wearing less. Old-fashioned French words and concepts were jettisoned for more trendy American ones. "*Le week-end*" in a country house and holidays at the beach became practically obligatory. By 1963, the government had yielded to worker demands for a fourth week of paid vacation for all. As these examples suggest, the new bourgeoisie did not abandon hedonism per se, but reinvented its norms and forms. Nowhere was the transformation in middle class lifestyle more visible than in Paris, whose form was literally recast in the 1960s to make way for the young technicians of New France. Older working-class neighborhoods were razed and replaced with high-rise apartments that only the middle classes could afford. A ring highway known as the *periphérique,* designed to move traffic in and out of the city efficiently, also served as a kind of *cordon sanitaire*—separating the bourgeois heart of Paris from the working poor consigned to the ugly high rises of the outer belt.[47] Minister of Culture Malraux decreed that the façades of all buildings be sandblasted, and decades of soot and grime now began to come off. Bright advertising billboards too went up everywhere, another signifier of the new urbanism.

The creation and evolution of the new vacation conglomerate known as Club Med was among the most lasting signs of the new affluence. Club Med was the brainchild of Gérard Blitz and his wife, Claudine Coindeau. Blitz, an amateur athlete before the war, was an assimilated Jew who had joined the Resistance late and then worked with survivors from the camps when they returned to France. These returnees were taken to the Alps to recover their physical health through exercise and fresh air. Coindeau had spent the war living in a French colony—Tahiti. She introduced Blitz to Eastern mysticism and yoga and described to Blitz the physical beauty of the Tahitians, who supposedly lived without artifice. The "discovery" of both of these alternative lifestyles gave Blitz an idea. In 1950 he put an ad in a paper for recruits to a vacation on the island of Majorca, where participants would stay in U.S. army surplus tents, play sports all day, and dance all night under the stars. Hundreds of people signed up, and by end of the year Club Med had its slogan: Its vacations were "the antidote to civilization." Soon Blitz and his partner were building more permanent Club Med vacation villages up and down the Mediterranean and Adriatic coasts.

For Blitz, the rise of the consumer and technocratic society was disrupting an older world of sociability, replacing time spent with people with the acquisition of things. The newly bureaucratized and hierarchical workplace was already producing alienation. Club Med thus had to detoxify the body and revivify the soul. The accommodations of Club Med villages were kept simple. The staff played and danced alongside their guests, creating the illusion that no one was working. Talking about one's job was taboo. Locations were always sunny and exotic, reflecting the new desire to be outdoors. Villagers had to shed their clothes for sarongs and bathing suits, and no money could be in evidence. Everything was paid for with beads, purchased upon arrival. Meals were communal and social distinctions were supposed to vanish, and there was a clear undercurrent of sensuality and sexual liberation.

The irony of Club Med is that as it evolved, it became less an antidote to consumer civilization than its fullest expression. The villages were located in sites where labor was cheap, often in France's former colonies; North Africans were never part of the vacationing class, they were always among the service class. Vacationers could indulge their taste for colonial exoticism even though France was losing these regions politically. These contradictions became even more pronounced when Blitz brought in a new partner and Club Med became an openly commodified vacation package for the affluent. The beads were kept, but vacationers could now opt for luxury villages complete with staged entertainment. In 1969 Blitz bailed out, feeling his original notion of Club Med as an egalitarian escape from everyday life had been turned into one more commodity in the consumer-oriented New France.[48]

In sum, by the mid-1960s, de Gaulle's goal of modernizing France had certainly created new opportunities across French society. Yet it had also produced new tensions and new forms of alienation, for those who cared to pay attention. Ironically, at the forefront of those most troubled by modernization were its—seemingly—greatest beneficiaries: the post-war generation. By the late 1960s, baby boomers were coming of age. Unlike their parents, however, this generation had no memories of the deprivations of the war years; for middle-class youth, a stultifying desk job with little scope for initiative and a house in the suburbs represented an adult lifestyle that they were not sure they wanted. As for young workers stuck on the assembly line, the sight of older workers scrimping on their lunches to save enough to buy a long-dreamt-of automobile was equally demoralizing. As these two examples suggest, the critical attitudes of a vast new group of idealistic youths was perhaps the most dramatic and least planned for social change of the early 1960s.

EXPLOSION: MAY 1968

Every explosion needs tinder and a catalyst. In the spring of 1968, tinder was provided by the especially harsh conditions that prevailed at one Parisian university located in the soulless industrial suburb of Nanterre. Nanterre was a neglected arts and sciences faculty hastily built in 1964 on land still occupied in part by *bidon-villes*. Designed for 4,000 students, in 1967 some 12,000 were crowding into its classrooms and dormitories. Unlike the Sorbonne's Latin Quarter campus, Nanterre had no cafés, no bookstores, no restaurants. Bourgeois students faced daily reminders of poverty that they had not known existed. A distant and pater-nalistic administration supervised students closely while allowing them no real mechanism for expressing their grievances. In contrast, the sociology department at Nanterre had a number of younger professors keenly interested in analyzing France's recent social changes. Since the mid-1960s Nanterre was home as well to a core of dedicated revolutionaries who were already provoking clashes with the administration over university policy, including sexual segregation. They hoped to use generalized student discontent to launch a revolt that could bring down the government—and they almost succeeded.

If conditions at Nanterre were the tinder, a world event provided the catalyst for the events of May. In January 1968, the Vietcong launched the Tet Offensive against U.S. troops, signaling the end of any possible U.S. victory there. On March 18, the moment seemed right to a small group of radical Leftists to show their solidar-ity with the Vietnamese by bombing the American Express Office in Paris. When the police arrested a student from Nanterre on suspicion of involvement, a charis-matic sociology student of German Jewish origin named Daniel Cohn-Bendit, soon known by the moniker Danny the Red, and his comrades occupied the uni-versity's administrative block. On March 22, protests erupted in the classrooms, and lectures were called to a halt so that students could "discuss" the situation. The month of April was a highly politicized one at Nanterre, and on May 3 the minister of education decided to close the campus.

At this point student agitation moved to the Sorbonne, the most prestigious campus of the University of Paris. In a panic, the authorities suspended lectures and seminars there too on May 3, and then called in the police to arrest the student leaders even though the latter had promised to leave peacefully. Hundreds of out-raged students rallied to protest the police invasion of their campus; the police in the past had kept away from universities, which students considered their sacro-sanct space. As more and more students began taunting the police, the latter retaliated with tear gas and beatings that culminated in some 500 indiscriminate arrests. The battle lines were now fatally drawn, and demonstrations soon spread beyond the university to France's high schools. For a week, tens of thousands of students and the riot police known as the Republican Security Units (Compagnies Républicaines de Sécurité or CRS) remained locked in a series of street battles, whose images were caught on camera and filled the dailies. Then, on the night of May 10, the call went out to occupy the Latin Quarter in response to the continuing police occupation of the Sorbonne. [49] In conscious imitation of past Parisian revo-lutions, students started gathering up cobblestones, felling trees, and overturning cars to build barricades for the first time since the Liberation. This time the CRS responded with an almost military repression, complete with baton charges and water cannon turned on the students. Innocent by-standers sitting in nearby cafés were caught up in the dragnet. Scenes of indiscriminate police brutality during "barricades night" flashed across French television screens. Provincial campuses were also on the move, and a wave of sympathy swept across the nation for the students.

At the start of the troubles Prime Minister Pompidou refused to cancel a trip to Iran and Afghanistan, assuming the police had everything in hand. A week later he finally cut short his visit abroad. Although de Gaulle wished to send in the army, Pompidou decided on May 12 that the best way to restore order would be to back down and reopen the Sorbonne. The decision only served to widen the movement. Feeling their power, the students began to organize a kind of joyous self-government of their "recaptured" universities that echoed the early days of the Paris Commune. Street demonstrations continued, but they occurred against a backdrop of what would prove to be the real business of the 1968 uprising—at least for the students: mocking all forms of authority and liberating themselves and society momentarily in the process, principally through talking.

At the Sorbonne students hoisted red flags, occupied the biggest amphitheater, and began a prolonged sit-in open to all. They also took over the Fine Arts Faculty and the Odeon theater a few blocks away. For a month after May 13, students around the country debated a range of issues that they had hitherto never discussed: feminism, the built and natural environment, gay rights, the nature of democracy and revolution, alienation, commodity culture. The mood was infectious. Actors occupied theaters and took art into the streets; library and museum staffs formed collectives. Everyone marched. All barriers appeared to come down as students and faculty, staff and managers, sat as equals discussing the future of society and the world. Much of the festive spirit of that heady month was caught in the witty and subversive posters with which students plastered Paris, along with the graffiti they scribbled on walls. Some equated sex with freedom: "The more I make love, the more I want to make revolution"; others exposed empty conventions and materialism: "See Nanterre and live. Go to Naples with Club Med and die"; "Be realistic: demand the impossible"; "Art is dead, let's liberate everyday life"; "You will end up dying of comfort." Still others subverted traditional political discourse and attacked constraints in any guise: "Power to the imagination"; "No forbidding allowed"; "Don't get caught up in the spectacle of opposition, oppose the spectacle"; "I suspect God of being a leftist intellectual"; "I'm a Groucho Marxist." A new radical politics of tolerance emerged: "We are all German Jews" and "We are all undesirables" (a reference to immigrants). All insisted on genuine participation: "Long live communication. Down with telecommunication"; "Are you a consumer or a participant?"; "The walls have ears; your ears have walls."[50]

Student protest and revolt was one aspect of May, but there was another component to the uprising. The student movement eventually attracted the attention of vast numbers of workers, especially those who had never joined unions, principally the young and unskilled. For a moment in May worker and student protests converged, without ever melding. On May 11, the major unions decided to call a

"French and Immigrant Workers United," street poster of the student revolt, Paris, May 1968. Private Collection/Lauros /Giraudon/The Bridgeman Art Library.

general 24-hour strike for May 13—the day, 10 years earlier, that had opened the way for de Gaulle to come to power. Union leadership was at first against the students: They viewed them as bourgeois youth, and thus the class enemy, and union officials had no desire to lose a potentially revolutionary initiative to them. But the workers themselves did not need to be asked twice, since they knew all too well what it was like to bear the brunt of police brutality. A brief surge in unemployment since 1967—500,000, the highest since 1945—also made workers ready to protest. On May 13, mass demonstrations occurred in Paris and many other cities. This day of solidarity was followed by a wave of spontaneous strikes and factory occupations and sit-ins, in which the youngest workers led the way. Soon workers from the nationalized aviation industry and the huge Renault factories, railway and postal personnel, even the professional white-collar sector joined in. At its height, on May 23 and 24, the strike wave swept up somewhere between 7 and 11 million, out of a total workforce of 14 million. The country was paralyzed, store shelves were emptying, and gasoline supplies were running out. The students and the strikers were delighted.

With French commercial life grinding to a halt, Danny "the Red" by now a virtual media star, and students across the nation chanting "Adieu, de Gaulle," all eyes turned to the president. On May 14, de Gaulle had ignored the combined worker-student demonstration of the previous day to fly off to Romania. He returned four days later, and finally on the May 24 addressed the nation, promising a referendum on the issue of participation in universities and industry for June 13.

The nationally televised speech, uncharacteristically, had little effect, and the demonstrations and sit-ins continued. Pompidou then decided, in a conscious replay of tactics that had worked in June 1936, to call union and employer representatives to the negotiating table. Concessions to the workers, he believed, would defuse the crisis. The resulting Grenelle Accords were much more generous than the Matignon Accords of 1936: a 35 percent increase in the minimum wage, an across-the-board wage hike of at least 10 percent, a return to the 40-hour workweek, an improvement in working conditions and family allowances, and the promise of union representation at the workplace. They were signed on May 27, and Pompidou was confident that this time he had the situation back in hand.

He was wrong. When the secretary general of the CGT (Confédération Générale du Travail or General Confederation of Labor) met with 10,000 Renault workers, the rank and file jeered at him and voted the deal down, calling instead for "a government of the people." Like the students, the workers appeared to be holding out for more autonomy and greater participation in the decision-making processes affecting them. It was the turn of the leaders of the opposition on the Left—as surprised as the Gaullists by the magnitude of the strikes in a time of affluence—to try to turn the situation to their advantage. On May 28, socialist François Mitterrand and veteran Radical politician Pierre Mendès-France announced that they stood ready to form a provisional government. It seemed that de Gaulle, who in his television broadcast four days earlier had sounded tired and overwhelmed by the turn of events, would not weather the crisis. Pompidou put the armed forces on standby.

But despite his initial disorientation, de Gaulle eventually displayed the political acumen and icy determination that had served him so well in the past. On May 29, he suddenly canceled a cabinet meeting and headed off for an unknown destination. It was widely believed that he was going to his country residence to resign. This could not have been further from his intentions. He sensed that after four weeks of disorder and chaos, there were some in the country who had had enough. So he began lining up pro-regime forces and preparing for the *coup de théâtre* that would save his presidency and perhaps the Fifth Republic as well. His destination was Baden-Baden in Germany: He went there to consult with the head of French forces, General Massu, and to have 20,000 soldiers moved to the border. Massu assured him of his support, in exchange for the pardoning of the generals who had rebelled in Algeria. Feeling more secure, de Gaulle returned to France visibly strengthened and immediately went on television; this time he captured the nation's attention. France, he declared, faced two alternatives: de Gaulle or civil war. "I shall not step down; I have a mandate from the people. . . . If this situation continues I shall have to . . . use other methods than immediate national elections."[51] Workers and students would have to fight the army if they wanted to keep "imagination in power." He then quite wrongly accused the communists of plotting to take power and announced the dissolution of the National Assembly, with new elections to be held at once. The effect was dramatic. That evening a huge march of conservative supporters, estimated at over half a million, took place on the Champs-Elysées. The Gaullists had stolen a page from the students' own May script and mounted a demonstration that outdid any that had taken place so far that month. Conservatives were finally taking the threat of revolution seriously, and letting the "revolutionaries" know it.[52]

The ploy worked. The strikes tapered off and were over by mid-June and students, remembering their exams, drifted back into the classroom. Tragically three deaths—one high school student and two workers—occurred in final confrontations with the police. While some of the more militant student leaders on the extreme Left might have been tempted to take up arms, the majority of students and workers had no stomach for fighting. Armed conflict would have been the very antithesis of the spirit of the May uprising. More surprising, however, were the results of the June elections, held on June 23 and 30 and orchestrated principally by Pompidou rather than de Gaulle. In a political turnaround reminiscent of what had happened in February 1871, when the country at large had feared a militant movement in Paris, the voters returned an overwhelming conservative majority. Out of 400 deputies, over 300 were Gaullists now united into a single party, the Union of Democrats for the Republic (Union des Démocrates pour la République or UDR). The political atmosphere had lurched to the Right as dramatically as it had lurched toward rebellion two months earlier. In this new context, the country began to return to normal.

YOUTH, INTELLECTUALS, AND CULTURE
UNDER THE FIFTH REPUBLIC

What was "1968" all about? A landmark 1960 documentary, *Chronicle of a Summer*, provides some early clues. That summer a French ethnographic filmmaker, Jean Rouch, teamed up with a sociologist, Edgar Morin, to send two women out on the streets of Paris to interview passers-by. Are you happy, they asked? The answers—brief, and amusing or pathetic—provided the opening scenes for a movie that was to make film history. Rouch and Morin were among the first to use hand-held equipment and the urban landscape to capture a slice of reality. The point of their film was to focus on the moods and emotions of a group of Parisians—some average citizens, some highly individual types—during the Algerian War. The movie quickly moved from the opening random encounters to scheduled interviews with four main characters, all young: Marceline, a Holocaust survivor; Angelo, who worked grueling shifts in Renault's Billancourt factory; Landry, a student from the Ivory Coast, just arrived and keen on observing the French in France; and Marilou, a young, beautiful and deeply depressed Italian immigrant working as a secretary. The characters simply talked, gradually telling more and more of their random life experiences. Frustration with their jobs or studies was one common theme.

About halfway through, the talk switched to politics; gathered around a table, the group now hotly debated "the situation" in Algeria, Belgium's brutal decolonization of the Congo, class struggle, anti-Semitism, and racism. In a moving sequence Marceline described her life in a Nazi camp, where her father died. Some of the group then traveled to St. Tropez, on the Mediterranean coast, where they continued to talk; here Landry quipped that he had become an "African explorer of holidays in France." The film ended with Rouch and Morin walking in the halls of the Musée de l'Homme, France's ethnographic museum devoted to non-Western cultures. We see them assessing whether they have succeeded in capturing truthfully the experiences of those interviewed. What exactly have they documented? An objective slice of life? Or did their subjects "stage" their answers because of the camera? What is true experience?

Chronicle of a Summer reflected many of the developments and concerns that erupted in the student and worker protests of 1968. First was the youth and diversity of those interviewed in the film—only Marceline was born before the war, and several were foreigners. By 1964, there were 5 million French between the ages of 16 and 24, and 33 percent of the population was under the age of 20. Second was the movie's opening question: Are you happy? Many of those who revolted in 1968 believed that a technical and highly commercialized society that worshiped efficiency could never provide happiness. Third was their eagerness to talk politics of a certain kind—personal, those of the emerging Third World, and the problems of exclusion and inequality in France. Official Gaullist politics, as well as a bureaucratic and rigid PC, had had nothing to say on these subjects; these concerns too would spill out again later in the decade. Finally, the fact that it was an ethnographer and a sociologist who chose to explore the states of mind of average young people and the status of "truth" anticipated the key role certain intellectuals, and particularly sociologists, would play before, during, and after 1968.

May 1968 was many things at once: a revolt of youth against their elders, a libertarian wave of student protest, a carnivalesque inversion of all of society's rules, a new Paris Commune without the bloodshed, and a fairly conventional strike wave of epic proportions. It appeared out of the blue and was so unfamiliar and so innovative that historians still cannot agree on what it meant or why it happened. But there is no doubt that in France, the long-term roots of the events of May began with the post-war baby boom. Eight hundred thousand new births annually after 1950, coupled with immigration and the repatriation of 800,000 *pieds noirs* and 100,000 *harkis,* meant that within a generation the population had expanded from 40 million to 50 million. The problem facing French political leaders was how to integrate this vast new generation into the fabric of French society. For de Gaulle and his advisors the answer seemed self-evident: education. In the early 1960s the government not only extended the age of obligatory schooling but also expanded France's public university system. More years of education would, they believed, keep young people off the streets and prepare them for productive roles in France's high-tech economy. In 1967 there were over 500,000 university students in France, twice the number there had been in 1960. But the few new facilities built to accommodate the increase in students were not nearly enough to prevent overcrowding. In addition they were ugly, cheaply made, and run along authoritarian lines that echoed de Gaulle's top-down political style.

A second assumption also guided the government when it came to youth: that graduates would happily accept technical and managerial jobs in the growing service sector. On the surface, the assumption appeared sound. Like all Western countries rebuilding after the war, France saw a new youth culture emerge—but one less provocative and angry than its counterpart in Britain and the United States. Teenagers, who had more leisure and pocket money than ever before, sought to claim an identity separate from that of children or adults. They were able to do so due to certain new commodity durables, cheaply marketed and available to all, through which they withdrew into their own worlds. First came the transistor radio—critical as we have seen among the conscripts in Algeria, listening to de Gaulle; then came the Vespas, or motor scooters, soon the very symbol of freedom and imagination. New cultural forms followed, the most visible, or the loudest, of which was the arrival of rock music. France soon had its own homegrown pop rock icons in Françoise Hardy and Johnny Hallyday. An innovative combination jazz/rock and roll program on the radio, known as "Salut les copains" and the brainchild of a popular disc jockey and brilliant entrepreneur, Daniel Filapacci, made both into instant teen idols. Filapacci launched a fanzine by the same name in 1962, which reached a circulation over a million. Hallyday became the most photographed man after de Gaulle, and by 1963 Hardy had sold 2 million copies of her 1962 recording "All the Boys and Girls."[53] To some extent, the new culture blurred social distinctions and made adults, not the rich, the common adversary.

This culture was not consciously political, which was yet another reason de Gaulle and his prime ministers worried so little about it. But the fact that the young now felt a certain solidarity and autonomy meant that, under the right conditions, they might become politicized. And as middle-class teens moved from listening to their radios at home to attending classes at university, many students did become more openly critical of the status quo, first on French campuses and then in society more generally. Going to a university in France in the 1960s was a demoralizing experience. Education seemed to be modeled more after the assembly line in a factory than an ideal of the pursuit of knowledge for the betterment of society. At the same time students worried about whether their degrees would actually secure them jobs. Classes were enormous, with hundreds crowded into huge auditoriums. The relationship between students and faculty was often nonexistent. Professors for the most part were distant authority figures, and there was no student government on campuses. Students were expected to listen to lectures for an entire year in different subjects, and then be examined once at the end. Fully half of all students regularly failed their exams.

To the demoralization of the classroom were added other frustrations, on campus and off. One of the most striking themes of May 1968 was a demand for the sexual rights of adults and an end to the strict segregation of the sexes in dormitories. The 1950s had witnessed the beginnings of a new openness about sexuality and new forms of sexual expression. The pill was introduced in 1961 and legalized in 1967. Popular culture encouraged men to see themselves as "playboys" who could pursue pleasure outside the confines of the family and home. Women's clothing changed—bikinis became the most popular beach wear—to emphasize their sexuality. Women's right to sexual pleasure separate from reproduction was acknowledged, although preferably within the bonds of either marriage or a stable monogamous relationship.

A vibrant gay subculture also reemerged in Paris. The chic Left Bank neighborhood of St.-Germain-des-Près was known in the 1950s for its "folles," or effeminate, often cross-dressing gay male culture. Independently of the "folles," a new gay newspaper, *Arcadie,* was founded in 1954, and its affiliated private club opened in 1957. Repressive legislation passed in November 1960, doubling the penalties for offenses against public decency when they involved homosexuals, drove France's gay subculture again underground, but both *Arcadie* and its club continued to function.[54] *Arcadie* promoted what it labeled "homophilia" and distanced itself from any whiff of effeminacy, insisting that a true homosexual man would only be attracted to a virile man. In defense of blending in, *Arcadie* referred to Alfred Kinsey's landmark study of sexuality and claimed that except for his love of men, a homosexual was just like other men. Neither the paper nor the club included explicit references to homosexuality in their names. Both were symptomatic of a new exploration of traditional gender roles that attended rebuilding post-war France.[55]

Given these larger cultural developments around issues of gender and sexuality, students experienced university restrictions on the free expression of desire as particularly repressive. Less easy to chart was student dissatisfaction with the rapidity and impact of the state's embrace of modernization and commercialism. One sign was their enthusiasm for the avant-garde movies of Jean-Luc Godard, one the most controversial and prescient film makers of the 1960s. Godard was part of a group of young innovative "author-directors" who launched a cinematic "New Wave." Operating on slim budgets with small crews and hand-held cameras, New Wave directors adopted techniques such as flashbacks and stream of consciousness to produce movies with no story line, almost always set in Paris. Here Godard and others were influenced by *Chronicle of a Summer.* Godard's early movies tended to explore rather than criticize France's "Americanizing" society. But by 1967 Godard had moved from fascination to estrangement, as two different movies from that year make clear. His apocalyptic *Weekend* follows a young bourgeois couple on a visit to her mother and ends with a 10-minute tracking of stalled and wrecked automobiles that satirizes the cult of the weekend and the cult of the car (not to mention the bourgeois couple). *Two or Three Things I Know about Her* centered on a young suburban housewife prostituting herself to make ends meet in a Paris disfigured by new construction. Through her meanderings, Godard mocked a society cheapened by mass advertising and dulled to the threat of the bomb and America's presence in Vietnam.

A vanguard of students, however, did not wait until 1968 to discover left-wing politics. The Algerian war was their wake up call. At first students determined to protest the war had turned to the PC, only to learn—much to their disgust—that it had no real commitment to ending the conflict. The National Union of Students

Jean-Paul Sartre (1905–1980) selling the Maoist newspaper *La Cause du Peuple*, May 1968.
Private Collection/Archives Charmet/The Bridgeman Art Library.

(Union Nationale des Etudiants Français or UNEF) decided to organize its own demonstrations. After the signing of the Evian Accords, most students drifted away from the UNEF, but a core of militants remained who would play a leading role in 1968. They identified passionately with the armed struggles continuing in other parts of the world and organized themselves into a variety of sects. Some saw in Algeria the beginning of a general Third World Revolution; others identified with Mao's Cultural Revolution in China or the communist Vietcong fighting American imperialism in Vietnam; others still were inspired by Fidel Castro's and Che Guevara's Cuba and the civil rights movement in America. Thanks to television, radicals on campuses throughout Europe followed these struggles. By 1967 not only a generalized milieu of student discontent had emerged in France, but also a nucleus of hardened student revolutionaries in contact with fellow dissidents internationally.

In a country that worships its intellectuals, a final inspiration for the student revolt was a heady brew of new theoretical currents on the Left competing for acolytes. By the late 1950s, the post-war humanist and existentialist philosophies of Sartre, Beauvoir, Maurice Merleau-Ponty, and Camus as well as orthodox Marxism were already ceding ground to another school of thought, known as structuralism. Structuralism quickly entrenched itself in the university, and by the late 1960s was part of what students were trying to overthrow. The most famous structuralists—a group that included Jacques Lacan, Roland Barthes, and Claude Lévi-Strauss—were not philosophers at all; their ideas emerged from the newer social sciences of linguistics, sociology, anthropology, psychiatry, and psychoanalysis. Where Sartre and Camus had been concerned with establishing the moral responsibilities of the individual human in an absurd world, the structuralists denied that the creative individual even existed. Their study of linguistics convinced them that language did not reflect reality, but created it. All language, and thus all reality, was structured by rules that operated independently of human volition. The structuralist's task was to unmask these rules, which were universal. Lévi-Strauss, an anthropologist, reached this conclusion after comparing the myths of societies everywhere. These myths shared, he insisted, certain fundamental structures for apprehending reality, and human agency had no part in their fabrication.

Intellectually rigorous and profoundly innovative, structuralism won its practitioners many of the new teaching jobs that accompanied the expansion of the university system in the 1960s. Yet to some on the Left Bank, Barthes', Lacan's, and Lévi-Strauss' structuralist methods and "demotion of man" felt as cold and arid as de Gaulle's authoritarian and technocratic regime.[56] The decade thus witnessed a surge of other intellectual currents, which in keeping with the 1930s and 1940s tradition of *engagement* (intellectual commitment) offered trenchant critiques of the advent of contemporary social ills. Some of these critiques came from Marxists within France. Sociologist Henri Lefebvre at Nanterre developed an innovative theory of everyday life that stressed the total alienation of humans in advanced capitalist society. Lefebvre updated Marx by insisting that for humans to be genuinely free, social and sexual as well as economic relations would have to be transformed. Other more global critiques emerged from the nationalist struggles to end colonialism. In the closing pages of *The Wretched of the Earth,* Fanon encouraged colonized and ex-colonized peoples everywhere to rise up against their racist and imperialist masters and forge a new humanity independently and outside of the West:

> That same Europe where they were never done talking of Man, and where they never stopped proclaiming that they were only anxious for the welfare of Man: today we know with what sufferings humanity has paid for every one of their triumphs of the mind. . . . Come, then, comrades, the European game has finally ended; we must find something different. We today can do everything, so long as we do not imitate Europe, so long as we are not obsessed by the desire to catch up with Europe.[57]

For much of the 1960s, these radical calls to arms remained theoretical, at least as far as French students were concerned. But when revolt did break out, these various theories found a much broader audience.

Many analysts of the student protests of 1968, at the time and since, have seen in the "events" little more than children of privilege pursuing not class revolution but personal liberation in the wake of the new affluence. This assessment is not entirely fair. Certainly not all authority was challenged: Men expected women to fetch their coffee during the sit-ins. Yet the euphoric solidarity and massive taking over of public space did make clear that the Fifth Republic's existing institutions failed to meet many younger French citizens' changing "desires" in a rapidly modernizing economy and dramatically polarizing international arena. The events of 1968 left many complex legacies in France. But in the short term the most visible one was a permanent change in the relations between all youth and their elders.[58] The old barriers of authority were gone for good. Young people in France won their freedom at a much later date and in a much more transformative manner than their counterparts in America did.

Perhaps de Gaulle sensed this change. He dismissed Pompidou as prime minister on May 30, 1968, and set about preparing a broad set of reforms that, he hoped, would address the demand for greater political participation. Seeking as always to gauge public confidence in him, a year later he submitted a complicated document on decentralization to popular referendum. De Gaulle made clear that if the public rejected his referendum, he would resign immediately. The proposals failed when 53.7 percent voted against them. He left office on April 28, 1969, and never made a public statement again. He died a year and half later, on November 9, 1970. While the state funeral was attended by heads of state the world over, the burial ceremony took place, according to de Gaulle's instructions, at his country home in Colombey-les-Deux-Eglises in northeastern France, attended only by family, close friends, and military comrades. Historian Maurice Agulhon suggests that even in death he could not imagine sharing the limelight with France's other modern heroes resting in the Pantheon.[59] In any case, this was the proper ending for a man who had, maddeningly and from on high, fought for "a certain idea of France."

CHAPTER 12

A New France in a New Europe
1969–1981

Roy Jenkins, the first British president of the European Commission (1977–1981), remembered that during European Council meetings he would see German Chancellor Helmut Schmidt (1974–1982) change seats with his foreign minister so that he and the French President Valéry Giscard d'Estaing (1974–1981) "could always be next to each other, like two 'best friends' who insisted on sharing the same double school desk."[1] This close friendship between the two political leaders, both former finance ministers, both fiscal conservatives, and both interested in furthering European integration, had led to the creation in 1974 of the European Council in the first place, a group of nine heads of EEC member states who agreed to meet at least three times a year to discuss important matters on the EEC agenda. The European Council in turn launched in 1979 another key financial institution that further bound Western European nations together: the European Monetary System linking the currencies of the member states to prevent large price fluctuations.

For the technocratic and slightly right-of-center Giscard, the creation of the European Monetary System was a necessary measure of fiscal discipline, since France "could not hope to maintain stable trade flows within the Common Market with prices that fluctuate as much as the currencies."[2] Yet many on France's fractured Left as well as on the Gaullist Right viewed with alarm this Franco-German engine pushing for further European integration. The Left denounced a "Giscard-Schmidt plot" and warned that a France more integrated into Europe would embrace "Anglo-Saxon," neoliberal, free market, and thus by definition "American imperialist," policies. It also feared that France would adopt Germany's hard-line policy against far Left groups.[3] Gaullist adversaries of Giscard, while in theory favorable to the Franco-German entente, argued that further integration might limit France's sovereignty and dilute French national identity within a supranational European one. And would not, they worried, the interests of French farmers be sacrificed for the benefit of Italian and soon Greek, Spanish, and Portuguese farmers? As an exasperated Alexandre Sanguinetti, one of de Gaulle's veteran supporters and most devoted keepers of the flame, put it: "What is Giscard? He is Guizot, he represents a liberal Protestant bourgeois mentality in a Catholic country. He wishes to govern the nation as if it were English or German. This is a mistake that could prove costly to France."[4]

Giscard's "liberalism" reflected a new turn taken by France's leadership in the 1970s. Both of de Gaulle's successors as president, Georges Pompidou (1969–1974) and Giscard, believed in what Giscard would call in 1974 "change without risk"[5]— that is to say, a French version of a market economy that aimed at reducing social inequalities and creating a more modern and pluralistic society. Between 1969 and 1981, administratively France moved internally toward decentralization and externally toward greater European integration. Economically, it moved toward the creation, with the government's help, of companies big and powerful enough to compete on an international level. French workers—except for many of recent immigrant origin—finally saw their standard of living rise. Socially and culturally, educational opportunities expanded, and the mass media, women's bodies, and sexual minorities escaped the control of the state. If de Gaulle's paternalistic aim had been to put back together again a country that had lost its prestige, overseas territories, and innocence during and after World War II, principally by creating a presidential monarchy and a myth of Resistance, Pompidou and Giscard proved that the Fifth Republic was mature enough by the 1970s to become a different kind of democracy—one shaped in part by the continuing demands of a new generation of French citizens for more control over their own lives, more truth about their past, and more transparent governance in the aftermath of 1968.

RECONFIGURATION ON THE RIGHT

One major repercussion of 1968 was the disappearance of Charles de Gaulle from the political scene. Yet the presidential election held in April 1969 to replace de Gaulle also revealed the weakness of the post-1968 organized political Left. The communist and non-communist Left remained too divided to rally behind a single candidate. The Communist Party (Parti Communiste or PC) fielded its own candidate, Jacques Duclos, while the socialists further divided among themselves. Some socialists supported the non-socialist centrist candidate Alain Poher, while the remaining socialists divided their support between two presidential candidates, Gaston Defferre and Michel Rocard. In the first round, Alain Poher came in second with 23 percent, the communist candidate Duclos won a respectable 22 percent, but the socialists collapsed; together the two socialist candidates polled less than 10 percent of the vote. First place in round one went easily to Gaullist Georges Pompidou, with 45 percent of the vote. Many people credited Pompidou, de Gaulle's prime minister in May 1968, for having helped de Gaulle recover from these events. Yet de Gaulle had unceremoniously dumped Pompidou as prime minister before resigning himself. Thus while Pompidou represented the Gaullist party, he was able to separate himself from de Gaulle, articulating less hard-line, more centrist positions. In round two, Pompidou easily defeated Poher.[6]

Notwithstanding his willingness to make concessions to rioting students and striking workers in 1968 and his centrist electoral positioning, Pompidou maintained strong presidential power, often handling matters on his own without consulting his prime ministers. To prevent renewed upheaval after May 1968, Pompidou also favored vigorous policing. He opposed the university reforms de Gaulle set in motion, and he strongly objected to any attempt to institute workers' self-governance (*auto-gestion*) in industry. Still, Pompidou was less enamored of grand ideas and more pragmatic than de Gaulle, a manager rather than an idealist. He saw himself as the "Director of France Incorporated," and, like a corporate CEO, he built a team of faithful collaborators. Together they drew up a list of five basic objectives for his presidency: contribute to the advancement of Europe, improve industrial competitiveness within a European framework, modify the role of the state in an overly centralized system, rejuvenate social relations in both public and private enterprise, and keep citizens better informed.[7]

Inflation, oil crises, structural changes, and mounting unemployment nevertheless presented a serious challenge to Pompidou. The worthy goals of his 1971 Economic Plan would take time to change the economy, in part because worldwide oil crises in 1973 left the public uneasy and worried about economic stagnation. When, in April 1974, Pompidou died unexpectedly, after a secretive two-year struggle with leukemia, the public's anger about economic problems fell on the Gaullist candidate hoping to succeed him as president, former Prime Minister Jacques Chaban-Delmas.[8] For the first time since the creation of the Fifth Republic, in the 1974 presidential election a resurgent Left contested a divided Right. On the Right, the Gaullist candidate, Chaban-Delmas, found himself unexpectedly challenged from within his own camp, by center-Right candidate Valéry Giscard d'Estaing, who had served under de Gaulle as minister of finance from 1962 to 1966. A graduate of the prestigious Ecole Polytechnique and Ecole Nationale d'Administration (ENA), Giscard had served as a high-level civil servant in the General Inspection of Finances before entering politics in the mid-1950s. Giscard disliked the Gaullist, state-directed economy with its heavy central planning, advocating instead a strong dose of economic liberalism. He argued that free markets, lifting the regulatory burden on the French economy, would restore French prosperity.

Giscard gained the support of a younger generation of voters on the Right and defeated Chaban-Delmas in the first round of the elections. He then faced socialist François Mitterrand. The second round was a close and contested election, unusual after years of virtually uncontested Gaullist presidents. Giscard, who won the election not by harking back to Gaullism but by promising radical reforms, became the Fifth Republic's youngest president at the age of 48. Thus the Right retained power in 1974, but the vote indicated a readiness for change. Since 1958, France had been virtually a single-party state, with the executive, the legislature, and the courts all controlled by de Gaulle or the Gaullist party. Opposition groups and parties were entirely shut out, with no recourse, no way of making their voices heard or of influencing decisions over huge swaths of life short of public demonstrations or the print media.

In his first public speech on May 27, 1974, Giscard highlighted his desire to bring about change. Giscard intended to loosen the reins and to make the system more democratic and liberal by lifting some of the controls and opening up areas for greater input. His 1976 book, *French Democracy,* provided a detailed outline of his vision for France. He acknowledged that despite its liberal political structure, there had been a nearly unbridgeable gap between elites and ordinary citizens in French society prior to World War II. Institutions like schools, the family, and the Catholic Church had placed "powerful constraints" on the individual. Since 1950, what Giscard described as a hurricane had struck France, profoundly changing its society. The winds were unprecedented economic growth, the spread of education, and the "permanent eruption" of audiovisual media into everyone's life.[9] Despite the hurricane metaphor, Giscard viewed the changes primarily as positive and insisted that French society had made enormous progress. Yet the changes had created new problems, and Giscard insisted that to solve those problems, France needed to go beyond the outdated choice of either Marxism or classical liberalism. They represented powerful models of analysis and each had its appeal, but they belonged to the nineteenth century.

Giscard articulated three clear goals for late twentieth-century France: unity through justice, a constitutional community of free and responsible citizens, and a society of communication and participation.[10] To achieve these goals, Giscard intended to promote pluralism in all of its guises. Politically, breaking the monopoly of the highly centralized state meant empowering regions and local governments, including the city of Paris. Similarly, mass communication and economic structures would thrive with less state direction and more competition. Deregulated, competitive private enterprise could be counter-balanced by strong trade unions and consumer groups.[11]

In action, Giscard proved surprisingly true to at least some of his political manifesto. To start with, he lowered the voting age to 18. Giscard made monthly visits to "ordinary" people's homes, an awkward gesture, given his elite background, technocratic orientation, and somewhat stiff personality, but one he had hoped would symbolize his desire to connect with the average person. Whereas the constitution only allowed the president, the prime minister, or the head of either the Senate or the Assembly to appeal laws to the Constitutional Council for review, Giscard amended the constitution to allow a group of 60 representatives from either the Assembly or the Senate to appeal laws to the Constitutional Council.

Despite his liberal intentions to grant the regions more political autonomy, Giscard did not prove much of a decentralizer. Paris remained for Giscard the final arbiter of what was in the best interests of France—an attitude starkly revealed in his confrontations with the anti-nuclear movement (see later in this chapter) and various regionalist groups. Perhaps the most notable example of this tension took place in the Breton village of Plogoff. In 1979, the residents of this coastal town, supported by Breton regionalists, refused to allow the construction of a nuclear power plant in their town. The last years of Giscard's term were marked by repeated and violent confrontations between the protestors and police.

Yet at the same time that Giscard refused to devolve power to the provinces, he made city government in Paris much more democratic. As the capital of France, Paris was the largest city in France, with 2 million people in the city limits by 1974. Citizens of Paris, however, had no electoral control over the political, administrative, or police authorities that governed their city. This situation dated back to the French Revolution, when the Reign of Terror taught moderate political leaders to fear the radicalism of the people of Paris. To limit the threat that Paris' political independence posed to national leaders, the office of the mayor was abolished in 1799. Until Giscard's presidency, a prefect appointed by the national government had administered Paris, and order had been maintained by the National Police rather than a local, municipal police force. In 1977, Giscard restored to Parisians the power to elect their own mayor. Ironically, a former Giscard supporter, Jacques Chirac, was elected the first mayor of Paris and would use his position to challenge Giscard, eventually parlaying it to the presidency. Ambitious and relentless—his nickname was the "Bulldozer"—Chirac created his own Gaullist party, the Rally for the Republic (Rassemblement pour la République or RPR), in 1976 to advance his presidential ambitions.

The changes introduced by first Pompidou and then Giscard's neo-liberalism did not go unopposed even on the Right, particularly as the phenomenal economic growth of the 1960s began to slow. Economic insecurity and rising unemployment in the early 1970s, combined with anxieties linked to immigration, served in particular to revitalize the far Right in France for the first time since the early 1950s. At its second congress in 1972, a small movement called the New Order (Ordre Nouveau) decided to create a political party, the National Front (Front National or FN), to run in the 1973 legislative elections. The FN's leader was Jean-Marie Le Pen, who had briefly served as a Poujadist deputy in the 1950s before enlisting as a paratrooper with the French army in Algeria. Linking the early 1970s' problems of economic insecurity, unemployment, poverty, and crime in the suburbs to immigration, Le Pen argued that immigrants cost France valuable resources that should be spent on what he called *"les français de souche"* ("true French stock"). The FN attempted to arouse public anxieties about the "flood" of nonwhite, often Muslim, immigrants. Maintaining that North Africans, Africans, and Muslims could not be assimilated and represented a threat to the French race, culture, and identity, Le Pen called for closing France's borders, restricting asylum, "repatriating" (i.e., deporting) the 3 million non-European immigrants in France, stricter policing, and a reduction of social benefits for those immigrants remaining in France. In a similar nativist vein, the FN also played on fears that the external integration of France into European structures like the EEC would lead to the end of France as a sovereign nation.

This FN rhetoric echoed that of the old, anti-republican, far Right represented earlier in the century by the Action Française, authoritarianism, fascism, and Poujadism. Like the Vichy regime, the FN celebrated the "traditional family" with wage-earner father and stay-at-home mother. While not explicitly anti-democratic (and here, much like Poujadism, it did differ from the far Right's earlier incarnations), the FN ridiculed France's four main parties, deriding the PC, the PS, the Union for French Democracy (Union pour la Démocratie Française or UDF, Giscard's party) and the RPR (Chirac's party) as the "gang of four." Through the end of the 1970s, the FN failed to attract many voters, winning less than 1 percent of the vote. While it never represented the threat to the survival of a Republic that the pre-1940 far Right had in the 1890s and 1930s, the FN built its structure in the 1970s, and by the 1980s, its numbers rose enough to make it a significant and potentially more dangerous force in French politics certainly than Poujadism had been.[12] The FN's anti-immigrant message would hold particular appeal for France's shrinking class of industrial workers, in the face of a dramatic decline in blue-collar jobs and the increasing marginalization of their traditional party, the communists.

OLD AND NEW LEFT

The events of May 1968 bubbled up from below. This kind of bottom-up protest from a leftist, but not strictly orthodox Marxist, position came to be referred to as "*gauchisme*" (the word for "left" in French is *gauche*). *Gauchisme* rested on the 1968 notion of liberation through spontaneity and revolt; it celebrated action for its own sake.[13] While the ideas of those involved in the various protests, strikes, and riots were leftist in orientation, the organized Left's national leadership had found itself in disarray. In May 1968, the PC, the socialists, both major unions— the communist CGT (Confédération Générale du Travail) and the CFDT (Confédération Générale du Travail Unitaire)—and the secular reincarnation of the Christian trade union movement or CFTC (Confédération Française des Travailleurs Chrétiens), had all scrambled to play a role. Yet the reinvigorated grassroots activism unleashed by the student revolts proved to some extent short-lived. After the excitement of 1968, many of the rank and file people involved in the events grew increasingly disillusioned, wearied of activism, and eventually returned to their previous lives and routines. Still, some of the groups and movements born in 1968 survived, continuing to publish newspapers and convene meetings. Rather than evolving into national, well-organized bureaucratic movements or parties, what continued after 1968 was an ever-present willingness of people to take to the streets in protest.

In the early 1970s, periodic agitation broke out in a variety of places, such as banks, the post office, and more traditional industrial sites. In 1970, Renault workers in Le Mans protested against Taylorism's "scientific management practices" such as the assembly line; protests shut down an aluminum plant near Pau in 1973.[14] In 1973 workers launched a most unusual action at the Lip watch factory near Besançon. Rather than stopping work, they insisted on continuing to work. The company, which had about 1,200 workers, found itself in financial difficulties in the early 1970s as a result of a series of sales and mergers. Unable to get new financing, the firm declared bankruptcy in April 1973. Lip workers, angry about secret restructuring plans that came to light and convinced that the company was viable, seized and hid 65,000 watches and occupied the factory.

While nearly half of the Lip workers were members of the CFDT or the CGT, neither union initiated this action and both hesitated before supporting it. Within days the workers had sold enough watches to raise the capital to keep the factory in operation. They decided to continue working, producing, and marketing watches, which they did until they were evicted by the police in August. In response, striking workers opened a workshop in a nearby gym, negotiated with mediators, gained growing national attention, and sent delegates to appear at meetings across France. Responding to the Lip workers' call, on September 29, 1973, some 100,000 supporters marched in Besançon. Although the worker's action ultimately failed, it functioned in France as a symbol of what workers could accomplish in the face of business hostility to labor.[15]

In the 1970s, this new style of spontaneous protest forced the existing left-wing political parties to reassess their structures, tactics, and ideologies. The formerly formidable French PC, which throughout the 1960s could count on 25 percent of the vote in national elections, waned in the 1970s. In many ways, the French PC had long been much more than a party. Some historians have described the PC in the Paris suburbs as an "ethno-class" where, it was said, "one is born, not made, a Communist."[16] Communist voting strength derived overwhelmingly from the industrial working class that lived almost exclusively in certain neighborhoods, Paris suburbs, and regions.[17] In Bobigny, a Paris suburb and communist strong-hold, communist-backed demonstrations and protests, mutual aid activities, streets named for communist heroes, and cultural events like festivals, musical societies, drama groups, sports, and even film societies created and sustained a communist-infused local identity, lifestyle, and values.[18]

While the French PC's electoral strength rested on this working-class foundation, the party also had long attracted quite a few influential intellectuals, authors, university scholars, and leading cultural figures. Camus' intellectual trajectory, resulting in his painful public break with Sartre in 1952, nevertheless presaged a broader trend among this group. The Soviet military intervention in Hungary in 1956 and again in Prague, Czechoslovakia, in 1968 had led many leftist intellectuals to break with the party.[19] Alexander Solzhenitsyn, a dissident who had been imprisoned in a Soviet Gulag, or labor camp, dealt the final blow to communism's appeal for French intellectuals. *The Gulag Archipelago*, Solzhenitsyn's book that was smuggled out of the Soviet Union and first appeared in Paris in 1974, provided an especially shocking exposé of the Soviet system's repressiveness and cruelties. Since Solzhenitsyn's experiences dated to the post-Stalin era, fellow travelers could no longer insist that the worst excesses of Soviet communist rule had ended after the Great Purges of the 1930s, or even with Stalin's death. Even the extremely popular singer and film star Yves Montand, known for his left-wing sympathies, broke publicly with the PC in 1980.[20]

With intellectual support in rapid decline and an authoritarian leadership that insisted on a rigid pro-Soviet ideology and positions, the PC fell back on its base, the industrial working-class—just at the time that the economic changes of the 1970s were shrinking this class. With the death in 1964 of the man who had led the

PC since the end of the war, Maurice Thorez, the new leader Waldeck Rochet opened the door to some changes. Rochet was slightly less authoritarian than Thorez had been. Still, it took the shock of May 1968, during which many people on the Left felt betrayed by the PC, to provoke the PC to undertake real reforms in the hope of regaining support. In 1972, Georges Marchais, who had taken over as Secretary General, toned down the PC's strict Stalinism. Born in 1920, Marchais first worked as a mechanic at an aviation company. In 1942, during the war, either by force or by choice, a matter of some dispute, Marchais worked in Nazi Germany for Messerschmidt. After the war he was active in his local union and joined the PC in 1947. While he reversed course in the late 1970s, in his early years as secretary general Marchais advocated reforming the party and began to shift, gently, away from strict adherence to Moscow's dictates.

The challenge of maintaining electoral strength with a diminishing class base led Marchais to pursue an alliance with the socialists. Marchais hoped to keep the socialists from forming a coalition with centrist parties, as some socialists advocated. He assumed that the PC, which at the time was much larger, more tightly organized, and more disciplined than the fractious socialists, would naturally dominate any alliance with socialists and eventually gain power. But by end of the 1970s, Marchais had reverted to strict alignment with U.S.S.R., and the PC continued to shrink. In the end, the socialists proved more successful at building a broad electoral base that appealed to white-collar and middle-class voters and gained the upper hand in national elections.

For their part, the socialists had been in complete disarray throughout de Gaulle's presidency. The bungling of the 1969 presidential elections, when competing socialist candidates together had polled an embarrassing 8.7 percent of the vote, motivated a drive to reunify socialists into a single party. At a congress in June 1971 at Epinay, after an internal struggle among the various groups and their competing leaders, Mitterrand finally took leadership of what became, in 1971, the Socialist Party (Parti Socialiste or PS).

Having overcome internal divisions, Mitterrand realized the socialists still needed an external alliance to win the presidency and gain power. The timing was right; at that moment the PC had reached the same conclusion. The ensuing negotiations resulted in the 1972 Common Program of the Left.[21] Reformist rather than revolutionary, the Common Program called for the nationalization of nine of France's large industrial sectors, a communist demand to which Mitterrand acceded to prove his leftist credentials. Although it remained a revolutionary party in theory, the PC agreed to respect the democratic system and abide by electoral results. The Common Program also included an increase in the minimum wage, an anti-nuclear weapons policy, and the "promotion of women" with planks prohibiting discrimination, legalizing abortion, expanding child care, providing for school lunches and longer maternity leaves, and requiring that women hold 10 percent of the seats the alliance won in any election.[22]

Thus, despite its absence at the critical moment of 1968, the organized political Left unexpectedly revived in the 1970s. As it revived, *gauchisme* declined.[23]

However, rather than disappearing, *gauchiste* activism may simply have shifted to new groups. The habit of taking to the streets in protest spread beyond students and workers. The middle classes increasingly proved willing to engage in similar protests by the turn of the twenty-first century, often to protect their interests in narrower ways than original street activists ever envisioned. In any case, after 1968 a reinvigorated Left, in the form of either *gauchisme* or grassroots activism and organized oppositional parties, played an increasingly important role in French politics.

FOREIGN POLICY

France's foreign policy in the 1970s represented in many ways a continuation of Gaullist strategies—especially with regard to the United States, the Third World, and Europe—but with some key innovations. One important change of the early 1970s was a shift away from the anti-British orientation that had fundamentally governed de Gaulle's approach to Europe. Where de Gaulle had twice used France's veto to prevent Britain from joining the EEC, Pompidou was convinced that Britain should become a member, and negotiations on this point quickly resumed in 1970. By 1972 an agreement was reached to expand the EEC to include not only Britain but also Ireland and Denmark.

Further integrating Europe in tandem with Germany was undoubtedly France's greatest foreign policy success in the later 1970s, and here Giscard led the way. Like Pompidou, Giscard was truly committed to European integration, advocating annual meetings of European Community members and pressing further to expand the EEC to Greece, Spain, and Portugal. As we saw at the outset, he strongly supported a unified monetary system linking the various currencies, a policy that eventually led to the creation of a single currency for Europe, the euro. Giscard also promoted greater coordination of member states' economic policies, which he believed would increase and facilitate trade. In 1975, he thus invited the leaders of the seven largest capitalist economies in the world, Canada, West Germany, Italy, Japan, Britain, and the United States, to meet in the town of Rambouillet. That group continued to meet annually as the so-called G-7; with the fall of communism in 1989 it expanded to include Russia as the G-8, which still meets today. Giscard even managed to get Schmidt to agree that France and Germany would have an equal number of representatives in the European Parliament, even though Germany's population was larger than France's. In response to that concession, in 1979 France finally approved direct elections to the European Parliament.

The expanded EEC of the 1970s seemed to offer France a way to compete globally with the United States; yet here France's hand was not as strong as it liked to think. For one thing, despite Giscard's close working relationship with Helmut Schmidt, chancellor of Germany, the French and Germans approached relations with the United States from somewhat conflicting positions—literally and figuratively. West Germany was stuck between the East and the West, and thus was forced to rely on American power to balance potential military threats from the

Eastern Bloc. In the end, France's attempts to forge its own way independently of the United States only produced new antagonisms between the two after a brief "thaw" early in the early 1970s—especially with regard to the Middle East.

French relations with the United States had seemed to be to improving on the eve of de Gaulle's resignation, in part because the new U.S. President Richard Nixon and Secretary of State Henry Kissinger held the French World War II hero in high esteem. Soviet military intervention in Czechoslovakia in 1968, moreover, had forced de Gaulle to recognize that even limiting American influence in Western Europe would not lead the U.S.S.R. to loosen control over Eastern Europe. U.S. negotiations with North Vietnam, and the beginning of détente with U.S.S.R., further mollified de Gaulle, who had even promised to visit the United States in 1970. After de Gaulle stepped down in 1969, Pompidou fulfilled the presidential visit in February 1970. Yet while Pompidou and Nixon publicly presented their meeting as friendly, behind the scenes Nixon and Kissinger challenged Pompidou over French arms sales in the Middle East and over France's support of Arab powers there more generally rather than of America's principal ally in the region, Israel.

While the United States continued to support Israel in the early 1970s, France put an embargo on arms sales to Israel in response to Israeli land seizures resulting from the 1967 war. At the same time, France supplied weapons to Algeria and Iraq and agreed to sell fighter jets to Libya. Differences between France and the United States over relations with Israel and the Arab world in part reflected France's greater dependence on Middle Eastern oil supplies. Imported oil represented only 14 percent of U.S. energy consumption but 77 percent of French energy consumption. Beyond direct economic interests, the longstanding pro-Arab orientation of nearly everyone in the French Foreign Ministry (Quai d'Orsay) also continued to influence France's position on Middle Eastern questions.

These differences climaxed in 1973, when French leaders were infuriated to discover, only after the fact, that the United States and the Soviet Union had narrowly averted a nuclear confrontation in response to the 1973 Yom Kippur war between Israel and the Arab states. Washington leaders notified Western European leaders, who were after all in the potential line of nuclear fire, about the diplomatic skirmish only when it was nearly over. France, determined to maintain relations with Arab oil suppliers and angry at being out of the loop, refused to allow U.S. planes to fly over France to supply Israel and continued to sell arms to Libya and Saudi Arabia.[24] Thus, while relations between France and the United States had seemed to be improving under Pompidou, they quickly degenerated over France's desire to assert an independent foreign policy and America's sense that France was an unreliable ally at best.

Giscard, too, maintained the Gaullist precedent of independence from the United States in his foreign policy, particularly when it came to the so-called Third World. Like de Gaulle, Giscard insisted that France could be the voice and advocate for developing countries. However, this policy, which sounded altruistic, usually translated into either selling arms to these countries—propelling France to become the second largest arms exporter in the West, after the United States—or directly intervening in the internal affairs of its former colonies, particularly in sub-Saharan Africa. Under de Gaulle and Pompidou, France had refrained from any such open interference, while keeping the economies of the newly indepen-dent African nations tied to that of France. Giscard changed this earlier policy drastically, intervening militarily in Africa several times and expanding France's zone of operation into all francophone countries (including the resource-rich cen-tral African nations of Zaire and Rwanda, which had been under Belgian rule). In Zaire (now the Republic of the Congo), France stepped in to prop up notorious dictator Mobutu Sese Seko in 1975. In 1978, France sent troops and fighter plans to Chad in response to the kidnapping of French ethnologist Françoise Claustre, who was freed after the French government paid a ransom. International pressure, however, forced France to withdraw from Chad in 1980, proving that the French government could no longer act unilaterally in what it liked to consider its sphere of influence.[25]

Another embarrassing episode of neo-colonialism was linked to Giscard's long support of Emperor Jean-Bedel Bokassa, who took power in the Central African Republic in 1965. France provided Bokassa with significant financial and military support; Giscard made a state visit to the Central African Republic in 1975 and even sent a representative to Bokassa's coronation ceremony in 1977. Bokassa used his impoverished nation's resources to support his lavish personal lifestyle, and his rule was notoriously brutal and violent. When groups of students protested a rule requiring them to purchase expensive school uniforms produced by one of his wives, soldiers rounded up and killed about 100 school-age children, an event so horrifying that French troops helped overthrow Bokassa in 1979. Bokassa nevertheless survived the coup and fled first to France then to the Ivory Coast with his ill-gotten gains from the country's treasury. Once in the Ivory Coast, he revealed that he had given Giscard expensive personal gifts, including dia-monds, on several different occasions. While Giscard's spokesman insisted that the diamonds were worthless, industrial-grade gems, the problem was that they were given and received as personal gifts, rather than official gifts, which would have become government property. The satirical left-wing daily *Le Canard Enchaîné* broke the story in October 1979 and kept it front and center for a long time, tarnishing Giscard's reputation.[26]

Giscard's foreign policy in Eastern Europe attracted criticism as well, this time from the Right as well as the Left. While Giscard proclaimed neutrality in the Cold War, he aroused anger from conservatives by meeting with Soviet leader Leonid Brezhnev in May 1980 shortly after the December 1979 Soviet invasion of Afghanistan.[27] Giscard then antagonized supporters of human rights on the Left by refusing to come out firmly in support of the Solidarity movement that erupted in Poland in 1981, which challenged communist rule and Soviet influence. In short, compared to the impressive leadership he displayed in furthering European integration, Giscard's policies were clumsy and unappealing in Africa and insuffi-ciently critical of the Soviet Union.

ECONOMIC POLICY

European integration, by forcing French producers to become more competitive, hastened the economic development and modernization of the French economy, two goals that both Pompidou and Giscard explicitly embraced. Broadly speaking, Pompidou continued the economic policies of his predecessors, that is to say, the planning system that gave the government a central role in setting broad scope, priorities, and direction. In inaugurating the Sixth Plan in 1971, he nevertheless articulated two new guiding principles: first, that within the context of a market economy, the state would play a critical role in promoting economic development, and second, that industrialization should help France to master its future and satisfy the public's desire for a better life. Pompidou encouraged economic concentration, promoting such strategic sectors as information technology and telecommunications, modern transportation and urban renewal, and aeronautics and nuclear energy.[28] Under Pompidou telecommunications expanded, with the number of homes equipped with a telephone growing from one in seven in 1968 to three out of four by 1982, the year France launched the first successful, pre-Internet, videotext online service available over the telephone lines, the Minitel.

Pompidou also developed France's transportation system nationally and in Paris. He built several new highways and inaugurated the first bullet train, the Train à Grande Vitesse, or TGV, which operated between Paris and Lyons. In Paris, Pompidou continued to pursue de Gaulle's policies of cleaning things up and updating the city's infrastructure. In a tradition dating back to Napoleon III, French presidents of the Fifth Republic focused their attention on Paris, both France's capital and its largest city. Pompidou, like de Gaulle, sought to relieve the severe congestion stifling the capital. Roads and public transit urgently needed improvements to meet the needs of a burgeoning population and expanding economy. During the post-war economic expansion, the increasing desire and financial means of middle-class families to purchase their own homes had led to the explosive growth of bedroom suburbs outside the inner, working-class ring of suburbs. Many residents of the new suburbs commuted to Paris for work. Traffic congestion soared, leading Pompidou to inaugurate a new suburban transit system. The RER (Réseau Express Régional or Regional Express Network) extended the inner Paris Metro system to carry commuters in and out of the suburbs that continued to ripple from the city's center.

The need for industrial and financial corporate office space inspired something brand new to Paris in the 1970s—and yet another sign of Pompidou's commitment to modernization. A skyscraper, the Montparnasse tower and transit center, right in the center of the city, cast its shadow over a neighborhood famous as a gathering place for bohemian artists. To this day the only skyscraper inside the city of Paris, the Montparnasse tower's destruction of an old neighborhood and its uninspiring design did have the virtue of galvanizing groups in Paris concerned about landmark preservation.

They eventually stopped the razing of old neighborhoods under the guise of urban renewal, but not before Giscard completed, in 1977, another jarringly modern edifice, initiated by Pompidou to bring culture to the people. The Pompidou Center, designed by renowned architects Renzo Piano and Richard Rogers, destroyed a wide swath of the existing inner-city neighborhood, Le Marais, which had fallen on hard times. Fortunately however, rather than creating a sterile space unfriendly to pedestrians, the Pompidou Center blended high and popular culture in original ways that has functioned as a magnet for locals, tourists, and street performers ever since. The building, which houses the Museum of Contemporary Art and space for a wide array of educational and cultural programs, was designed to be "inside out," with much of the structure, color-coded heating, and electrical and ventilation ducts, normally hidden inside walls, forming the external skeleton of the building. Despite the violent juxtaposition of the factory style steel and glass building with the surrounding neighborhood, the Pompidou Center proved to be an urban renewal project from the 1970s that worked.

Despite that success, by 1977 Giscard halted the construction of skyscrapers, motorways, and modern buildings in Paris.[29] Thus another of Pompidou's planned ultra-modern office/commercial developments, La Défense, was built outside and just west of the city limits. A cluster of office and commercial towers, eventually La Défense included a third arch in a line starting with the small arch, the Arc du Carrousel, in front of the Louvre and continuing up the Champs-Elysées to the Arc de Triomphe. The biggest of the three, the Grande Arche de la Défense, sits at the end of the line of arches, unornamented and squarely of the twentieth century.

In addition to urban renewal projects and new commercial space, the 1970s governments nurtured provincial economic development, creating industrial regions focused on a particular, critical industry, aerospace in Toulouse, for example, and oil refining in Fos on the Mediterranean coast. By 2007 Fos was the world's third busiest petroleum port. In keeping with Pompidou's positive view of the EEC, France also began several new cooperative ventures, such as the Concorde, a supersonic jet developed with Britain, and Airbus, a joint aircraft design/manufacturing venture with Britain and Germany. Airbus quickly mounted significant competition with American-based Boeing and McDonnell-Douglas.

France was already committed to the development of nuclear energy when the 1973 oil crisis prodded Giscard to step up its investment in nuclear technology. France's interest in nuclear power as an alternative energy source had begun immediately after World War II. French leaders viewed the development of nuclear power as a way of regaining international respect and showcasing the strengths of French engineering and technology. In December 1948, the public reacted enthusiastically to the news that Zoé, France's experimental nuclear reactor, had a successful chain reaction, an achievement that then President Vincent Auriol insisted "will add to the radiance of France."[30] The first nuclear plants, Marcoule in the Gard (1955) and Chinon in Indre-et-Loire (1957), were heavily promoted to the local regions as a way of revitalizing the regions, bringing in jobs and even tourists as they updated and modernized local economies that had been on the losing end of French economic change.[31]

The 1973 oil crisis added new urgency to the development of nuclear power. In the wake of the October 1973 Yom Kippur war, in which the United States supported Israel, the oil-producing Arab nations formed a cartel, the Organization of Petroleum Exporting Countries, or OPEC, to control the region's oil exports. To hit back at the United States and drive up prices, OPEC nations agreed to reduce oil production, cutting supplies drastically. Prices quickly jumped four times higher. Without any oil reserves of its own, France was hard hit by the high oil prices. By 1974, inflation in France rose to over 10 percent.[32] In response, Giscard launched the construction of the Superphénix nuclear power plant in 1974. A second oil shock in 1979 only strengthened Giscard's conviction about the necessity for nuclear power.

Little resistance to building nuclear plants developed at first, and those who found fault, from Catholic moralist, communist anti-capitalist, or Poujadist anti-government perspectives, remained marginal.[33] Protests against either nuclear weapons or nuclear power plants never gained much traction on the French Left in comparison to the powerful anti-nuclear movements that developed in both the United States and West Germany. On the political Left, the socialists never adopted a forceful anti-nuclear position since many of them considered nuclear power critical to French economic growth. The pro-nuclear faction eventually dominated the party. As for *gauchiste,* extra-party pressure from below, in the 1970s, the "Greens" joined forces with more experienced veterans of older protest movements. But the veteran protesters, from radical anarchist factions, rather than aiming to stop a particular nuclear plant, used anti-nuclear protests to try to "smash the state apparatus," adopting confrontational tactics such as site occupation, sabotage, and pitched battles with the police. Thus the anti-nuclear movement found itself "hijacked by an extremist minority who were all too ready to engage in violence" and who turned off the larger public. [34] After a showdown in Malville in 1977, the anti-nuclear movement fizzled out in France, never gaining much support in public opinion. One result of this free hand that the government had with the development of nuclear power is that by 1990, nuclear power plants generated some 76 percent of France's electrical power.[35] Meanwhile the broader environmental movement would slowly rebuild and remerge in future decades in a more moderate guise.[36]

In addition to marking a new phase of industrial modernization, the 1970s represented a turning point for France economically in another sense: In that decade the rising standard of living finally reached most of the working class, allowing them to share in the consumer revolution that had already benefitted the middle classes in the 1960s. Rising income combined with new economies of scale that reduced prices made consumer durables widely available at prices that even working-class families could afford. Another element in democratizing the consumer revolution was the effort to link all households to public water and electrical systems, a task nearly completed by 1973, when 97 percent of all households had running water. By 1969, the number of French families with a refrigerator, which only 10 percent could afford in the 1950s, had jumped to 75 percent. As the accompanying table shows, over half of all households had an automobile by 1970, two-thirds had a washing machine, and 78 percent had a television.[37]

1950s to 1970s, Home Amenities in French Households

Washing Machines	10% (1958)
	66% (1973)
Automobiles	21% (1953)
	57% (1970)
Televisions	23% (1960)
	78% (1973)

For some social critics, these changes inspired anxieties about the brave new world of across-the-board consumerism and new concerns about American cultural hegemony destroying French culture and civilization. Popular author Christiane Rochefort had mocked these concerns as early as 1961 in her novel *Les petits enfants du siècle*.[38] Noting the common use of the birth bonuses paid by the state to encourage families to have children, a character refers to her neighbors' children as "Television Mauvin, Car Mauvin, Frigidaire Mauvin, Washing Machine Mauvin." Refrigerators, washing machines and automobiles might seem mundane today, but at the time many observers denounced them as encouraging shallow consumerist materialism. Yet household appliances had an enormous impact on many women's lives. One study of consumer society in France points out that French women's new self-identity as consumers drove many of these changes in the first place.[39]

THE SECULARIZATION OF FRENCH SOCIETY

The increasingly visible affluence at *all* levels of French society, combined with such successful modern technological advances as the Concorde, the TGV, the Airbus, and the Superphénix, led to the publication in 1979 of an important work of sociology whose catchy title immediately became—and has remained—a shorthand for the entire period of post-war economic growth: Jean Fourastié's *Les Trente Glorieuses* or *The Thirty Glorious Years*. Fourastié was referring to France's counterpart to Germany's post-war "economic miracle," the 30 years between the late 1940s and the late 1970s. Yet perhaps the most interesting part of Fourastié's book was not the visible revolution he chronicled—that is, the improved material standard of living in France in 1979 compared to 1949—but the invisible revolution, as he put it, that accompanied this increasing prosperity, particularly with regard to religious practice.

In his book, Fourastié compared two villages with which he claimed to be intimately familiar, having not only done research in the local archives but also spent time in each one for over 50 years. Madère, an underdeveloped village, had 534 residents, every one of whom had been baptized and attended mass regularly. Four-fifths of the people had been born in or very near the village. Infant mortality was high, at over 30 percent; hardly any children went beyond primary school, and only 1.2 percent of the children passed the *baccaularéat*. Three-quarters of the people made their living on farms, all of which were small. The town only boasted two tractors and a few small shops. About 7 percent of the people were salaried employees. Most people in Madère were relatively poor, with much of their income going to satisfy basic needs like food. Many townspeople could only afford meat once a week. Hardly anyone had money for leisure activities or travel.

Fourastié contrasted Madère with a town of similar size, Cessac, where only one in four people were farmers or farm workers, the farms were three times larger, all of them used tractors, and productivity was 12 times higher than in Madère. Nearly half of the Cessac's residents were employees, office workers, bankers, administrators, civil servants, and teachers. Nearly every household (95 percent) had such modern amenities as refrigerators, freezers, washing machines, indoor plumbing, and toilets. While only 5 households in Madère had telephones or an automobile, 110 households in Cessac had telephones, and the town's residents owned a total of 280 automobiles. Few of Cessac's residents attended church regularly (20 percent), and many residents were born elsewhere. Cessac residents could afford to travel out of town and even out of France for business or leisure.

After outlining the vast differences between the two villages, Fourastié surprises the reader by admitting that both descriptions actually apply to the same village, the town of Douelle, but in two different years; Madère represented 1946, Cessac 1975.[40] Douelle's story, while it highlights France's huge improvement in standard of living, also signals another dramatic change experienced during those years, the precipitous drop in Catholic practice. This drop mirrored a national change with profound implications for French society. In the 1970s, the vast majority of the French public, well over 90 percent, continued to identify itself as Catholic, with small Protestant and Jewish minorities and a growing Muslim one. The Catholic Church still provided schooling to large numbers of children. But the Church itself had undergone critical changes with the Second Vatican Council of 1962–1965, and over the 1960s the number of people who attended Church regularly began a precipitous decline. By the end of the 1960s, the number of adults reporting weekly communion had declined to less than 15 percent.[41] Religious practice continued to plummet in the 1970s, declining most rapidly among the youngest cohort. By 2005, 80 to 85 percent of people ages 18 to 24 reported never attending church. Even in the group with the highest percentage (over 90 percent) reporting themselves as Catholic—people aged 65 to 79—68 percent of men and 55 percent of women reported that they never attended a religious service.[42]

Until the 1960s in France, religious practice had predicted political orientation and voting behavior even more strongly than social class, occupation, schooling, or region.[43] That too changed completely as France secularized, resulting in the decline of the Christian Democratic Party founded after the war, the

Popular Republican Movement (Mouvement Républicain Populaire or MRP). There was no longer a strong Catholic voting *bloc* in the 1970s. Religious Catholics tended to remain politically conservative, but large numbers of people who identified themselves as Catholic shifted to the Left.[44] The Catholic Church's influence over morality and family life also declined in tandem with the drop in church attendance, as indicated by an increasing number of couples cohabiting, contraceptive use, extramarital births, and divorce.[45] Responding already to these changes in the early 1970s, first Pompidou and then Giscard adopted a number of social reforms that tried to meet French citizens' aspirations for a more open and modern society.

MAKING FRANCE MORE EGALITARIAN: THE REFORM OF EDUCATION

As part of their project to liberalize and modernize society across the board, Pompidou and Giscard took on the overhaul of certain traditionally conservative institutions in France, beginning with that of education. Widespread frustration with an educational system that was rigid, controlled from the top, out of touch with real-world needs, and elitist had provided one of the catalysts of the May 1968 upheaval; as a result, the student revolts brought many changes in the way education was perceived in France. The value of the classics, so important for the traditional French education system, was questioned. Latin and Greek were sacrificed for the study of modern languages, and students started being encouraged to "participate" and to "express themselves." From an institution whose primordial role was to pass on France's grand cultural tradition, the school began to be a place where children were helped to "open to life."[46] A key mover in post-1968 reform in France was Giscard, whose 1977 book *French Democracy* clearly articulated the importance of equal educational opportunities at all levels of society if France wished to modernize.

Educational reforms for primary, middle, and secondary schools were an essential first step in the further democratization of French society. For all school-age students, one dramatic change took place shortly after 1968. Public schools had been strictly segregated by sex, in part because well into the twentieth century, they offered boys and girls a very different curriculum. After May 1968, co-education was allowed in primary schools; in 1976 Giscard made co-education mandatory.[47] Nevertheless it was Giscard's educational reform of middle schools, or *collèges,* that had the most profound impact, not just on the schools, but arguably on French society. The middle school system instituted in 1963 had maintained two separate tracks—Colleges of Superior Education that tracked elite students who would go on to *lycée* (high school) and new Colleges of General Education that served the masses and directed them to occupational degrees. Giscard's key reform, the Haby Law of 1975, merged the two kinds of *collèges,* ending the tracking of students at age 11 and giving public primary school students the preparation needed to advance to a *lycée.* The impact of this reform on many people's lives is hard to exaggerate. Talented children from working-class or lower middle-class families could finally aspire to a higher status in life via education.

Within five years of the reforms, by 1980, about 40 percent of 16-year-olds still left school for work. Yet a phenomenal 60 percent continued on to high school, completing two to four more years. Of that 60 percent, about half went to technical *lycées* for vocational training and the rest to academic *lycées,* where they prepared to take the baccalaureate examination required for leaving with a high school diploma. Any student who passes the *baccalauréat,* or *bac* as it is usually called, can attend any university in France. Early in the twentieth century, the vast majority of French people only attended school to the age of 12. Only 2.5 percent of the age cohort passed the *bac* in 1931. The school-leaving age increased slowly to 14 by the 1930s. The fact that over half of France's young people went on to secondary education by 1980, with close to 40 percent getting a *bac,* a figure that had risen to over 60 percent by 2000, contributed greatly to the opening up of the French educational system and eventually French society.

The ultimate impact of this change on social mobility and class identity/division remains unclear. Prominent French sociologist Pierre Bourdieu conducted a study in the mid-1960s, first published just prior to May 1968. Bourdieu argued that educational systems both transmit knowledge and perpetuate class distinctions. The requisite cultural capital favors children of the dominant class. The notion of a meritocracy is an illusion, Bourdieu argued, denying that students of talent would naturally rise. He noted that working-class children simply did not have the cultural capital, the habits that middle-class children absorb daily in their families and social milieu that enable them to succeed. Bourdieu did not think changing the educational system's structure, opening it to new groups, would have much of an effect. Dominant classes, he pointed out, have ways of perpetuating their dominance. If more students were able to obtain a *bac* or a university diploma, then the social value of each of these degrees would decline. Other achievements inaccessible to the working class would function as new entry passes to middle-class status. As it happens, Bourdieu was at least partly correct. A degree from one of France's few elite *grandes écoles* replaced the *bac* as a barrier to elite status. While they are public institutions, the *grandes écoles* require expensive private preparatory courses to gain entry. Yet only degrees from the *grandes écoles* guarantee access to high-level jobs in public administration or business. Thus a university diploma, while conferring middle-class status, has not become a ticket to a high-paying job.

While Giscard's educational reforms may not have guaranteed greater access to the upper echelons of French society, their impact on the lives of young people is incontestable. One sign of that impact, the number of boys and girls ages 15 to 19 in the labor force, dropped precipitously from the mid-1970s to the early 1980s, making clear that it was really only in this era that true adolescence as we know it in the United States came to exist in France. Giscard's second highly significant educational reform was the expansion of publicly funded, optional but free *écoles maternelles,* or nursery schools, for children ages three to five. *Ecoles maternelles* had been a part of the public educational system since 1881. However, unlike elementary schools, municipalities were not required to provide an *école maternelle* until Giscard mandated it in 1975. Every child who turns three has the right to attend a free *école maternelle,* which falls under the auspices of National Education, indicating clearly that rather than child care, they are meant to be educational, combining play with pre-academic preparation. Attending an *école maternelle* was not compulsory, but with the increased availability and their reputation for providing high-quality preparation for primary school, the *écoles maternelles* quickly became extremely popular, highly valued by many families as a critical aspect in the socialization of children and their preparation for the rigors of primary school. Without a doubt, these preschools, which run all day long, also ease the problems for mothers of young children wanting to return to the workforce.[48]

MEDIA AND THE FREE MARKET OF IDEAS

In 1969, after the fall of de Gaulle, commercial advertising made its appearance on the French state TV channel programming. The "new society" touted in 1969 by Prime Minister Chaban-Delmas saw the beginning of liberalizing TV programming by creating two autonomous channels. Yet while Pompidou directed considerable attention to modernizing the economy and the infrastructure, in 1972 he was still convinced that "television is the voice of France" and that it had to be controlled and filtered as such.[49] In 1974, Giscard won the elections by running a very American-style political campaign that focused on his TV performance.[50] His presidency thus signaled the advent of a new age in French audiovisual communication, in which media would be used not only for its propaganda potential but also for its competitive possibilities.

Until Giscard, radio and television broadcasting had been entirely state-controlled. The programming remained elitist, intent on improving popular culture by broadcasting mostly classical music on radio and high-brow talk shows or French classical movies on TV. Paris completely dominated state-owned mass media, which presented little on regional life, no local interest/events/news, and no programming aimed at youth or immigrant subcultures. State control also meant that French radio refrained from all critical political commentary.[51] Eventually, private radio stations began to bypass this control by transmitting from just outside France, from Monaco or Luxembourg, for example. The private stations provided the public with more alternatives, favoring popular programming, variety and game shows, popular music, and uncensored news. In the 1960s even more alternative stations, so-called pirate radio, began broadcasting from the North Sea, and after 1968 more of those stations directed their programming to appeal to young listeners.[52]

France had only one, state-controlled, station broadcasting television programming until 1963, when a second state-controlled one was created. Television broadcasting had been added to radio in 1949 to become Radiodiffusion-Télévision Française, renamed the ORTF (Office de Radiodiffusion-Télévision Française) in 1964.

By 1960, only about one in four homes in France had a television. Anyone owning a television was (and still is) required to pay an annual television tax, with the funds going to support programming by the state-run channels. Over the 1970s, however, as prices came down and the French standard of living rose, a rapid expansion in television ownership took place. Even with continued government restrictions on radio and only two television stations after 1963, television ownership rose to nearly 80 percent of all households by 1973.

Although the state retained control over broadcasting, in 1974 Giscard divided the state-run Office of Radio and Television into seven separate offices: four for radio (Radio France, SFP, INA, TDF) and three for television (TF1, A2, FR3). Giscard thus made clear that radio and TV were "not the voice of France," but journalistic enterprises like any other. With these innovations in administration came changes in programming; entertainment, sports, and American serials gained a substantial percent of programming, and Anglo-American popular music came to dominate in France.[53] Yet at the same time, the liberalization of the media paved the way for innovative "high-culture" French programs to emerge. One of the most influential was journalist Bernard Pivot's wildly successful *Apostrophes,* a weekly talk show dedicated exclusively to writers, who were invited to come discuss their latest books and debate politics. Each week, 2.5 million people watched the show each week, and sometimes the television audience numbered 5 million.

Pivot's success both helped to create, and was created by, a new kind of intellectual in France. The declining fortunes of the PC (and, more generally, Marxist theory) and the growing power of the new electronic media, in particular television, were together giving rise in the early 1970s to a phenomenon popularly known as *les nouveaux philosophes.* The catchy, but slightly misleading label reflected changes not just in the trajectory of French intellectuals, but also broader changes in French society. The leading lights of this movement—most notably, Bernard-Henri Lévy and André Glucksmann—were not academic philosophers writing for an audience of specialists. Instead, much like their eighteenth-century ancestors, they were pamphleteers writing for the general public. Moreover, there was little that was terribly new in what they were writing—at least when set alongside the writings of public thinkers in the Anglo-American world or even earlier in France. For example, their "discovery" of liberal values and their skepticism of ideological absolutes had already been expressed by Raymond Aron in *The Opium of Intellectuals* (1955) and Camus in *The Rebel* (1951).

What was new, at least in France, was the eagerness with which these young Turks rejected their earlier generation's communist tendencies. Just one year after the 1974 publication of the French translation of *The Gulag Archipelago,* Glucksmann channeled the growing popular revulsion over the attitude of French intellectuals toward the Soviet Union. In broad, but largely justified, strokes, his book *La cuisinière et le mangeur d'hommes* (*The Cook and the Cannibal*) lashed out at the French Left, whose utopian blinders led it to justify the horrors of Soviet rule. With the literary panache that typified their approach, Glucksmann asked: "How many common graves must we dig in the name of false Communes?"[54]

Two years later, in 1977, Lévy followed up Glucksmann's success with his own *Barbarism with a Human Face,* which sold more than 100,000 copies. Like Glucksmann, Lévy attacked the catastrophic illusions long held in regard to the Soviet Union by the French Left, but he also lambasted the fatal attraction that utopian thought held for earlier generations of intellectuals. Both thinkers targeted not only the "calamitous Marxist detour in Western thought," but also the "dominant figures of post-war intellectual life, in France and elsewhere, who had peered across the touchlines of History, cheering on the winners and politely averting their eyes from their victims."[55] The first and greatest casualty was Sartre.

Equally new with the new philosophers was the medium through which they communicated. They were young, attractive, and attracted to the lights and cameras of television studios. Lévy cut a dashing figure with his mane of dark hair and open-necked shirt, while Glucksmann became one of the regulars on *Apostrophes.* While this was a cause of dismay for yet other intellectuals—Régis Débray denounced the death of the French tradition of intellectuals at the hands of these new media stars in his *Le pouvoir intellectuel en France* (1979)—most intellectuals came to terms with it. By 1981, of France's 42 most prominent intellectuals—listed in a poll undertaken by the French literary monthly *Lire*—28 had already appeared on Pivot's show.[56]

THE POLITICS OF MEMORY: DE GAULLE'S RESISTANCE MYTH QUESTIONED

As the baby boom generation came of age in the 1970s, the French public not only grew more open to outside trends thanks to greater European integration, educational reform, and deregulation of the media. It also showed a new willingness to undertake serious self-examination. In particular, the French began to break with the spell that de Gaulle had cast over France's past. Since the Liberation in 1944, the portrayal of occupied France had been profoundly colored by the "Gaullist myth," which held that aside from a minority of collaborators, the French people had been united in resisting the German Occupation. By the early 1970s this version of the past no longer satisfied the post-war generation, who began asking uncomfortable questions of its parents.

The May 1968 challenge to de Gaulle's political power may have paved the way for questioning other aspects of his mystique, but two more events in 1971–1972 helped break the taboo. An American historian, Robert Paxton, denied access to French archives for the war years, found ample material in the form of letters and memos sent by French authorities to Germany, stashed in archives the United States seized from Germany at the end of the war. On that basis, Paxton's book, *Vichy France: Old Guard and New Order,* published in 1972, argued that collaboration originated in France rather than representing a response to German demands. Translated into French in 1973, the book provoked painful outcries.[57] Yet a prominent French historian, Jean-Pierre Azéma, worked to have the translation published and within a few years, nearly all serious historians in France and elsewhere came to accept the broad outlines of Paxton's arguments, while modifying and refining some of his assertions.

Also in 1972, Marcel Ophuls completed a documentary, funded by the French government television station, entitled *The Sorrow and the Pity,* which took a pitiless look at the ugly side of life under the German Occupation. The film included some inspiring moments such as an interview with Alexis and Louis Grave, brothers from a rural region who described their experiences in the Resistance. But the film refused to paper over either the full extent of collaboration or the racist attitudes of many French and included interviews with schoolteachers who failed to object when a Jewish colleague lost his job, a woman whose head was shaved for collaboration, and a charismatic aristocrat seduced by fascism who had joined a French unit that fought alongside the German army on the Eastern Front. While a careful count reveals that the film includes as many interviews with resisters as with collaborators, many people were shocked by the unvarnished portrayal of at least a portion of the French public as cowardly at best, complicit at worst. State-owned French television, which had sponsored its production, refused to broadcast the documentary, which initially found its way into a single Paris cinema. Despite the more limited distribution, the documentary attracted a good deal of attention, inspiring both angry outcries and awkward soul-searching.

Some blind spots nevertheless remained. Ophuls only interviewed one woman, Madame Solange, an admitted supporter of Pétain who denied having denounced anyone to the Gestapo, the crime for which she was sentenced to 15 years.[58] It would take another 20 years for a similar national self-examination to begin to take place about the Algerian war, how it was fought in Algeria, the use of torture, how Algerians in France were treated, and the killing of Algerian protesters in Paris in October 1961. The two national shames were linked in the person of Maurice Papon, who as prefect during the war had helped deport Jews in the Gironde region and as Paris prefect in 1961 had directed the police action against Algerian protestors that led to over 100 deaths. Papon was finally brought to trial in 1997. Both Vichy and the Algerian war raised serious questions about the behavior of France's elite military leaders and civil servants and about France's real commitment to its republican ideals of equality as opposed to the reality of racism, both in the past and in the present.

THE REVIVAL OF FEMINISM

After years of retrenchment during the post-war era, feminism revived in the wake of 1968 *gauchisme* and contributed decisively to new legal, political, and cultural gains for women in the 1970s—including, most radically, the right to abortion. Many young women had been involved in the events of May 1968 but had found themselves frustrated by the way male activists treated them. Similar to what happened in the United States, French women active in 1968 came to resent their marginalization, the movement's refusal to include them in decisions, and the

dismissal of women's concerns as secondary. In response, an active feminist political movement revived, signaled by the birth in 1969 of the Movement for the
Liberation of Women (Mouvement de Libération des Femmes or MLF). With the
new movement, feminists finally regained visibility in the mainstream press. Early
on, rather than using the "essentialist" idea of women's special nature and role in
the family as the basis on which it pressed for change, the MLF based its demands
on strict equality, insisting that women were equal individuals and deserved equal
treatment as human beings, not because of their special nature.

On April 5, 1971, the left-wing magazine *Le Nouvel Observateur* published
"The Manifesto of 343," which came to be called "The Manifesto of the Sluts" ("Le
Manifeste des Salopes"). This document stated simply, "One million women have
abortions every year in France in dangerous conditions owing to the need for
secrecy. Yet the operation is simple. Millions of women have been silenced.
I declare I am one of them. I have had an abortion. We demand free access to contraception. We demand the right to abortion." The Manifesto, signed by 343 highly
prominent women, including philosopher Simone de Beauvoir, author Marguerite
Duras, and actress Catherine Deneuve, launched a campaign to legalize abortion
in France. One signatory of the Manifesto, attorney Giselle Halimi, went on
to represent a minor tried for having had an abortion after she was raped. The
so-called Bobigny Trial of 1972 attracted widespread media attention and helped
define the progressive spirit embraced by the neo-liberal France.

Poster supporting free contraception and abortion, ca. 1970.   Bibliothèque Marguerite Durand,
Paris/Archives Charmet/The Bridgeman Art Library.

In *French Democracy,* Giscard had argued that promoting unity through justice required recognizing and fighting discrimination, first and foremost through improving the position of women. "A true democracy must fight to eliminate [sex discrimination] in as many ways as the discrimination is exercised, in all walks of family, professional, and political life."[59] True to his word, under Giscard, feminists achieved many highly significant reforms. Giscard appointed six women to his cabinet, naming pioneering journalist and co-founder in 1946 of *Elle* magazine, Françoise Giroud, state secretary on the condition of women. While conservative in political orientation, Giroud firmly believed that women should be free to compete on equal terms with men. Giroud worked to "further the integration of women, their autonomy and individual rights"; to expand training for women for predominantly male professions; and to improve the condition of widows, divorcees and single mothers.[60]

Giroud nevertheless did not play a central role in one key feminist battle of the era, the legalization of abortion. Giscard worried that Giroud's open support of the pro-choice movement and its avowedly feminist rhetoric could arouse even more fierce opposition than they already expected in the Assembly. Thus the task fell to another key figure, Simone Veil, an attorney long committed to reforming France and promoting human rights. She and her family, with the exception of a sister who had gone underground into the Resistance, had been arrested and deported to Auschwitz-Birkenau in March 1944; Simone was the only one in her family still alive when the camp was liberated in January 1945. Veil resumed her studies in law and political science after the war and married in 1946. She joined the government and worked to reform prison conditions and to update adoption law and laws pertaining to children born out of wedlock, who were finally given equal rights.

Giscard appointed Veil minister of health. When she presented the law, she advocated for it in measured, logical rhetoric. First, Veil insisted that experience had proven "it is not possible to prevent clandestine abortions." Nor was it possible to apply criminal law to every woman who had an abortion, or even to doctors, who agree to the procedure because they know from experience that women turn to unsafe alternatives if they refuse. When laws are routinely ignored, Veil noted, disorder and anarchy result. Veil explicitly remarked on the fact that she was speaking from a woman's point of view "to this Assembly almost entirely made up of men." No woman, she argued, sought an abortion happily. It had always been and would always be "a drama." Legalizing the process would give society an opportunity to intervene and present other options. She reassured the Assembly that legalizing abortion would not slow France's population growth because legal abortions would simply replace the 300,000 illegal abortions performed annually. Veil insisted that the government intended to increase public support for families and provide better assistance to children of unwed mothers. She noted that the law was reasonable, limited, and moderate, but ultimately left the decision to the woman. Finally, the law had a five-year limit at which point it would require reauthorization.[61]

While Veil's argument was measured, and completely sidestepped the feminist demand that women be given control over their bodies, the Assembly's response was brutal, particularly from conservative deputies who were, after all, on her side of the aisle. While the Catholic Church's power had declined dramatically after World War II, and religious practice was in a freefall, the Church still remained a critical force, particularly important to conservatives. Measures restricting abortion had also long been linked to fears about declining French birthrates. Those fears had abated. But strong, Catholic, moral opposition to abortion remained, and conservative deputies expressed it in their heated responses to Veil's proposal. Albert Liogier insisted the bill would open the door to pornography and that for Satan, "contraception and abortion are nothing more than two chapters in the book of sexuality." Pierre Bas referred to abortion as "euthanasia for pleasure," and Jacques Médecin called it "barbarism organized and covered by law like under the Nazis."[62]

Veil expected resistance but expressed shock at what she felt was the hatred and incivility directed at her personally. In an interview marking the fortieth anniversary of her speech, Veil recalled particularly the comments of Jean-Marie Daillet, who asked if she personally would agree to throw the embryos into a crematory oven, a clear reference to the Nazi extermination camps she herself had survived.[63] She did, however, manage to work with deputies from the Left, who supported the bill, which passed on January 17, 1975. The law legalized abortion, but only in the first 10 weeks of pregnancy for healthy mothers and fetuses and only after a psychological evaluation of the pregnant woman. It also did not allow for national medical insurance to reimburse the costs, a policy that changed in the 1980s.

The relaxation of laws limiting contraception, the passage of laws allowing abortion, and, last but not least, the law of July 1975, which establishied divorce by mutual consent, reflected a society less obsessed with population size and pronatalism, a society more secure in its population after a long baby boom. It indicated the declining influence of the Catholic Church in areas of family life. Finally, it represented the culmination of years of slow and steady changes within family life, the slow acceptance of more egalitarian ideas about women even within traditional-looking structures of family, marriage, and childhood. Giscard's firm support of legal reforms that profoundly influenced women's lives was also a critical element.

SEXUAL MINORITIES DEMAND RIGHTS

Social legislation endorsed by Giscard, while ushering in a more egalitarian educational, legal, and political system that freed individual men and women from the strict morality of the Catholic Church, still essentially rested on the assumption of heterosexuality. If gays and lesbians garnered little official attention, their grassroots activism increased during the Pompidou and Giscard years. In 1970, a group of lesbians strongly influenced by the MLF tried to set up a feminist group within the homosexual Arcadie movement that had been founded in the 1950s. Expelled for being too explicitly political, they burst into public view on March 10, 1971, when they disrupted a radio talk show interview on the topic "Homosexuality, That Painful Problem," whose guest was none other than Arcadie's leader André Baudry. That same day, the first explicit, political gay rights movement, the Homosexual Front for Revolutionary Action (Front Homosexuel d'Action Révolutionnaire or FHAR) was born.

While lesbians had been inspired by women's liberation, many of the gay men drew their inspiration from the American gay movement.[64] Unlike Arcadie, the 1970s movement was willing to identify itself as homosexual and to place the emphasis on sexuality and not just love/desire. And where Arcadie had sought to remain respectable, FHAR's tactics were confrontational and its goals revolutionary. However, like Arcadie, the people involved in FHAR still refused to view themselves as a homosexual minority that needed to agitate for civil rights. One of the founders, Guy Hocquenghem, in his 1972 book *Le désir homosexuel,* echoed Arcadie's position that homosexual desire was fundamentally no different than any other desire.[65] They rejected the notion of what they called the "gay ghetto" of identity politics.[66]

FHAR did not last long. According to former activist Jean Le Bitoux, FHAR fell apart owing to internal dissension about how homosexuals should present themselves to the greater public and how best to protest social injustice. FHAR, a movement opposed to all authority, including so-called micro fascisms, never developed effective leadership. On the other hand, many of the lesbians who had been instrumental in creating FHAR found themselves dismayed with what they viewed as the gay men's increasing promiscuity, sexism, male chauvinism—even misogyny—and growing male domination of FHAR. While many members found it a dynamic and liberating experience, FHAR meetings quickly gave way to chaos, and the movement fell apart by 1973.[67] Yet that same year also saw new developments. The new *gauchiste* newspaper, *Libération,* founded by prominent intellectual leaders Serge July, Philippe Gavi, and Jean-Paul Sartre, took a pro–gay rights position and provided national coverage of the issue during what Le Bitoux labels the "dark years." Various groups began to organize and meet, including the Homosexual Liberation Group (GLH), a pragmatic group that rejected FHAR's confrontational and revolutionary tactics.

The first Gay Pride celebration, a march through central Paris, took place on June 25, 1977. Adopting the term "gay" like "our big American brothers," French marchers even denounced American anti–gay rights crusader Anita Bryant. The parade attracted several hundred marchers and was covered, in a sober fashion, by *Le Monde.* Also in 1977, nearly 5,000 people attended a highly successful festival of gay/lesbian films. Such events in the 1970s laid important foundations for future gay activism.[68] Jean Le Bitoux, with support from Michel Foucault, a prominent philosopher-historian and openly gay man, founded a new paper, *Gai Pied,* in 1978. The paper promoted gay lifestyle, clubs, bars, fashion, travel, and tourism. Finally, gay activists succeeded in overturning the 1960 laws against homosexuality in 1982.[69] Yet the debate within the gay community remained unsettled because it paralleled similar discussions across French culture having to do with the identity politics that challenge the supposedly blind universalism of the French Republic.

IMMIGRANTS' PLACE IN THE NATION

The discomfort about recognizing diverse subcultures and identities such as that of "gay rights" in French republican culture directly affected the situation of immigrants in France, a group that had changed dramatically in size and origins by the 1970s. Facing severe labor shortages just after World War II, France had encouraged immigration. Two more large influxes of immigrants arrived following the Indochina war in 1954 and the Algerian war in 1962. By 1975, 3.4 million foreigners resided in France, constituting 6.5 percent of the total population (compared to 4.3 percent in 1947). Sixty-seven percent came from other European countries (principally Spain, Portugal, and Italy), while 28 percent came from the African continent (14.3 percent Algerians and 6.6 percent Moroccans), 3.6 percent from Asia, and 1.9 percent from Turkey.[70]

Regardless of origins, most of the recent immigrants in France were either forced to live in shanty towns without such basic amenities as clean water, sanitation, and paved streets or were warehoused in grim housing projects. In 1970 two major scandals involving these immigrants and their horrific living conditions hit the media. In January 1970, five African immigrants died of asphyxiation in the Paris suburb of Aubervilliers because they lit a makeshift fire when their landlord cut off the heat. In response, 200–300 protestors occupied the headquarters of the organization representing business owners, accusing them of being "slave owners." Among the protesters, police arrested prominent authors Jean Genet and Marguerite Duras along with 114 others.[71] Ten days later, a Portuguese family of 10 died of fumes in their single room apartment in Grenoble. The nation was appalled when confronted with the extreme squalor, poverty, exploitation, and misery of immigrants in the midst of an increasingly affluent society. Prime Minister Chaban-Delmas visited Aubervilliers and declared that he too was shocked by the conditions, promising to put an end to *bidonvilles*.[72]

One solution was to continue to build large-scale public housing estates, using inexpensive land available outside the cities. Yet both the location and the structure of the public housing, huge towers set in suburbs far from most cities' amenities, created a new set of problems. By the 1970s, many of public housing's original residents, mostly working-class French families, had moved out, as more and more low-income immigrant families moved in. Unlike the first generation of French-born working-class families to inhabit the suburban public housing estates, immigrant families—especially those from the former empire—found themselves unable to make a comparable move up the social ladder. For one thing, the shock and humiliation many French people experienced with the "loss" of Algeria in 1962 left bitter feelings. North African immigrants thus represented a visible reminder of that loss, adding resentment to already existing, strongly negative racial stereotypes of "Arabs" as primitive and violent.[73]

Following the loss of parliamentary seats by the Gaullists in the 1973 elections, the Pompidou government recognized that building this huge, crowded low-income housing had not gained it popular support. From 1973 on, the scale of all new public housing projects was limited to no more than 1,000 units in small towns and cities and no more than 2,000 units in the Paris region and other large urban areas.[74] Nevertheless, the massive apartment buildings built in the 1950s and 1960s were allowed to remain standing and were new suburban ghettoes in the making.

The lack of mobility for immigrants living in the suburban public housing projects extended to their second- and third-generation descendants, people often referred to as immigrants, or, in a French locution, "second-generation immigrants" who were, in fact, French. The physical isolation, compounded by cultural and ethnic divisions, created a two-way sense of alienation. The people living in the suburbs felt isolated and started rejecting the broader society, which, they felt, feared and mistrusted the people living in the suburbs, "*les banlieusards*," as they came to be derisively called. While the urban geography inverts that often found in the United States, the basic dynamic is the same: Poor nonwhites are segregated into particular areas that have few amenities, bad schools, and high crime rates, which perpetuate the problems of poverty. The majority population grows distant and fearful, making mobility more difficult for minorities.[75]

By the end of the 1970s, the economic, structural, and social changes of the "Thirty Glorious Years," together with Pompidou and Giscard's commitment to making France more open and more competitive economically, had dispelled the once widespread view of France as the "sick man" of Europe. It had become a secular, urban, industrial, and affluent society, its family life centered on children and consumption. A generous welfare state, initially inspired by pro-natalist goals, ensured prenatal care, maternity leaves, day care, preschool, and public education, including a system that, after Giscard, opened the door to higher education to most students at virtually no cost. Workers received health care, unemployment, disability, and retirement benefits. France had created a truly "cradle to grave" system and had relegated religious practice—to the extent that it still existed—to a strictly private sphere outside of politics, as befitted, or so many thought, a Republic in the first place.

Rising prosperity, full employment, generous incentives, and a greater sense of optimism also helped to sustain the baby boom that had begun during the war. France's population rose to nearly 60 million in the 1970s, reducing fears of demographic weakness and its possible impact on France's global standing. And those babies experienced, as they grew up, the kind of childhood we have come to know and expect, focused on play and schooling in the early years, requiring a long period of dependence on family, with state protection from abusive or neglectful parents, treatment and reeducation for children who stray rather than prison and punishment. Women gained personal freedom, becoming more equal partners within marriage, able to control decisions about bearing children, with greater access to education and wider career options. And because, thanks to the *gauchiste* politics of the decade, these transformations were not simply imposed from on high, but negotiated by at least part of France's citizenry, the new affluent society met with the approval of the majority. Some of course still worried about the invasion of American culture—the "coca-colonization" of France—but on balance the nation appeared to have preserved its sense of self in the face of the two superpowers.

This said, the oil crises of 1973 and 1979 were also about to usher in a painful new 30-year transitional period to a post-industrial economy, in which inequalities—and with them xenophobia and racism, anti-Americanism, and, increasingly, anti-European sentiment—would grow.[76] The industrial sector in France, as measured by the number of workers in manufacturing, peaked in 1975, but French industry was already beginning to age.[77] The production of heavy industrial goods like coal, steel, and automobiles lagged as France found it more difficult to compete on the global market despite help from the state. Like other advanced economies of the West, France was shifting from a primary economy, with wealth generated by producing heavy industrial products, coal, steel, and automobiles, to a secondary economy centered on services, finance, and high technology. This "third industrial revolution," as historians call it, would be fully evident by the year 2000, but in the late 1970s France was just entering its first phase. As elsewhere, the shift caused the loss of jobs and threatened an entire way of life for many people whose families had long been the backbone of industrial labor force. They would bear the brunt of the move to a post-industrial economy as unemployment and inflation began to climb after 1973.

CHAPTER 13

The Republic of the Center
1981–1995

More than 20,000 men and women overwhelmed the Montparnasse Cemetery on April 18, 1980, to mark the burial of Jean-Paul Sartre. The small, wall-eyed man with a cigarette perpetually dangling from his lip was the totemic figure of post-war French intellectuals. He embodied the era's great philosophy, existentialism, and its political corollary, *engagement*. As a result, many interpreted Sartre's passing as the passing of a generation, even an age. Serge July, the editor of *Libération*—a newspaper Sartre helped found in 1973—announced that his mentor "occupied his century as Voltaire and Hugo did theirs."[1] Just as Hugo's funeral in 1885 marked the ascendancy of the Third Republic, Sartre's burial heralded the maturing of the Fifth Republic.

A double irony presents itself with Sartre's passing. Not only had Sartre ardently opposed the Fifth Republic, but the Left's electoral victory the following year confirmed the death of the rigid Marxist politics that Sartre had long embodied. By the early 1980s a rejuvenated Socialist Party swept into power, unleashing quasi-millenarian hopes on the Left of a new dawn in French politics and society. The economic and geopolitical realities of that same decade would nevertheless quickly undermine such outsized expectations. By the end of the decade, the Fifth Republic, first pulled toward the Right, then the Left, became the Republic of the Center.

SOCIALISM'S LAST HURRAH

Forty-five years after the Popular Front victory of May 1936, and greeted with similar euphoria, history appeared to repeat itself in May 1981. That month, the socialists were swept to power to the delight (and eventual despair) of the Left and the despair (and eventual delight) of the Right. The Left's victory was partly a result of the Right's inability to overcome internal squabbles. Jacques Chirac refused to rally to his nemesis Giscard, who nevertheless had finished well ahead of him, and more than 3 percentage points ahead of Mitterrand, in the initial round. For the

Left, however, the reflex of republican discipline had kicked in after the first round of the presidential vote, when communist leader Georges Marchais, who registered an anemic 15 percent, called upon the rank-and-file to vote for Mitterrand, who had finished second. By early evening of May 10, the unthinkable had happened: The Socialist Party (Parti Socialiste or PS), which a decade earlier seemed condemned to a splintered and impotent opposition, was now victorious. No less shocking, François Mitterrand, the socialist leader who had spent more than two decades opposing the institutions of the Fifth Republic, had become its president. Paris erupted in celebration, as did other strongholds of the Left. Less than two weeks later, Mitterrand led an official procession to the Panthéon. Clutching a red rose, the symbol of the PS since its creation in 1971, Mitterrand entered the cavernous interior alone in order to pay homage at the tombs of Jean Jaurès, Jean Moulin, and Victor Schoelcher (the unjustly neglected republican who in 1848 helped abolish slavery in the French colonies). Not surprisingly, mounting popular enthusiasm translated into a sweeping victory for the Left in legislative elections held three weeks later. The legislative elections on June 14, 1981, gave the socialists an absolute majority in the Assembly—288 seats—draining votes from both the Communist Party (Parti Communiste or PC) on the Left (the PC lost half of its former 88 seats) and the Rally for the Republic (Rassemblement pour la République or RPR) and Union for French Democracy (Union pour la Démocratie Française or UDF) on the Center and Right, now reduced to a 157 seats.

Mitterrand's opening salvo of decisions reflected the nation's hopes (and fears) for political, social, economic, and cultural change. While his prime minister, Pierre Mauroy, was a congenial and consensual figure, Mitterrand also appointed four communists to his cabinet, both as a gesture of noblesse oblige, since the socialists had won an outright majority and didn't require communist support, and as an important symbolic gesture. The communist presence in the new government seemed to confirm the electoral pledge to bring about a "rupture with capitalism."

Mitterrand quickly followed, in September 1981, with a raft of legislation that broke with the liberal economic policies of Giscard and instead approached the interventionist policies of both the Popular Front in 1936 and, equally important, de Gaulle's Provisional Government in 1945 (which had legislated the nationalization of Renault, the Banque Nationale de Paris and Crédit Lyonnais). The government announced the nationalization of financially sound industries like Rhône-Poulenc, a chemical /pharmaceutical company, and Saint-Gobain, which manufactures construction materials, along with faltering steel producers like Usinor, 36 banks (including Rothschild), and the investment companies Suez and Paribas. Minister of the Economy and Finance Jacques Delors directed a massive infusion of money into state benefits programs, including family allowances, pension, and housing benefits. Delors also raised the minimum wage in the expectation that the rising tide of state monies would revive the struggling economy. To finance these policies, a form of "redistributive Keynesianism" in which higher wages and social transfers would spur domestic demand, the government relied not just on deficit spending, but also on a new tax aimed at the nation's wealthiest citizens.[2]

The Mitterrand government also signaled a new era for women in politics. In important respects, the 1981 legislative elections marked a dismaying continuity with earlier elections. Women won only a small fraction of the seats (16 out of 269). As a result, like Giscard, Mitterrand sought to impose greater gender equality from above. Giscard had created the state secretariat of women's affairs, but Mitterrand went a step further with a Ministry of Women's Rights—reflecting the new government's intentions in both the administrative and symbolic realms—entrusted to the feminist activist Yvette Roudy. Five other women, including Edith Cresson at the Ministry of Agriculture and Nicole Questiaux at the Ministry of Social Security, also joined the cabinet. Ironically, to do so, Mitterrand exploited a Gaullist innovation he had previously lambasted as undemocratic: the presidential prerogative to name ministers who had not also won election as deputies. In another important gesture of the government's first months in power, Mitterrand abolished the death penalty, a practice closely identified with both monarchic and revolutionary France, which had increasingly isolated France from the rest of Europe.

REGIONALISM

Mitterrand also reduced some aspects of French administrative centralization. In part, Mitterrand was responding to increasing calls for local freedoms, particularly in the peripheral regions of Brittany, Corsica, and the Basque country. (Alsace-Lorraine, a case apart, was granted special exemptions after France reclaimed it in 1918). During Giscard's presidency (see Chapter 12), expressions of local resistance to Paris had broken out in Larzac in 1972, where farmers whose sheep supplied milk for Roquefort cheese makers protested plans to extend a military camp on their pastures, and Plogoff, where Breton peasants, fishermen, and students mobilized against plans to build a nuclear energy plant.

Both of these movements were still lodged like thorns in the side of the French state when the socialists came to power. In their respective ways, these regions were resisting the historical tendency toward "internal colonization"—namely, the colonization of the peripheral regions by Paris, which used them as sources of materials, manpower, and markets. The romance of regionalism was so compelling that certain areas, like Languedoc, largely invented a past as a basis for political claims against Paris. Robert Lafont, novelist and intellectual, founded the Occitan Study and Action Committee (Comité Occitan d'Etudes et d'Action) in 1962, which cast events as disparate as the medieval Albigensian Crusade in the 1200s and the repression of a 1907 wine growers strike in the region as instances of French internal imperialism. Lafont's critique was echoed in other regions. Brittany, on the north coast, for example, witnessed limited but persistent expressions of Breton nationalism, dating at least to the 1920s and the creation of the Breton Autonomist Party (Parti Autonomiste Breton). Both the Breton Democratic Union (Union Démocratique Breton or UDB) and the Brittany Liberation Front (Front de Libération de Bretagne or FLB) came into being during the twilight years of

Map 13.1 French regions and principal towns since 1982.

de Gaulle's presidency. A pale imitation of the Irish Republican Army (IRA), the FLB carried out a handful of relatively harmless bombings, while the UDB's performance in legal political activities was equally insignificant. It never won more than 4 percent of the vote in regional elections.[3]

Corsica, incorporated into France far later than Brittany and long neglected by Paris, proved a much greater threat. The Corsican Regional Action (Action Régionaliste Corse), created by the Simeoni brothers in 1967, was overtaken by a militant movement committed to achieving independence through violence, the National Liberation Front of Corsica (Front de Libération Nationale de Corse or FNLC) in 1976. Similar to the IRA, the FLNC had an above-ground, officially recognized movement, the Corsican Self-Determination Movement, whose campaign for independence was embodied in the slogan "Out with the French" ("I francesi fora").

But the FLNC's terrorism grew increasingly indistinguishable from the island's more traditional forms of clan violence and vendetta. In 1982, more than 700 bombings shook the island, sparking the slow exodus to the mainland of "French" islanders—many of whom were *pied-noir* families who had settled in Corsica after leaving Algeria in 1962.

Following in the tradition of the centralized French nation-state, both the Gaullist and Giscardian regimes responded in a rigid and unforgiving way to all of these regional separatist movements. Police actions in Brittany in the late 1960s and early 1970s suppressed the anemic FLB, but they helped radicalize the regionalist movement in Corsica. Upon taking power, the socialists decided to send a list of concessions rather than riot police to the Corsicans. In 1981, Interior Minister Gaston Defferre proposed a "special status" for Corsica, providing the island with its own regional assembly, its own executive office, and official designation as the "Corsican people," albeit one that is a "constituent part" of the French nation. Predictably, both the Gaullists and hard-liners on the Left denounced the gesture as undermining the historical unity of the French nation. At the same time, Defferre's gesture was too little for Corsican militants, who dismissed the offer as mere window-dressing: The local assembly was purely consultative and Corsicans were not recognized as a distinct ethnic group within France. As it turned out, even the limited recognition granted by the Defferre legislation was too much for the Constitutional Council, which ruled that it violated the Constitution's underlying principle of national unity.

The new government nevertheless pursued its policy of decentralization. The socialists had long criticized the Gaullist Republic for its isolation from the people and fulfilled their electoral promise of creating institutions more responsive to local concerns. In 1982, Defferre introduced a battery of laws easing the pressure of Paris on the regions. Regions now elected their own councils to manage local budgets and take responsibility for regional and town planning. Defferre's legislation led to a long, silent, but important shift in national governance, with the balance of power moving away from the centrally appointed prefects, formerly in control of all local initiatives, and toward locally elected authorities. While the national parties maintained their influence through regional representatives, the socialists' new institutions indeed reflected their affirmation of the *droit à la différence:* the right of the French to express their regional, ethnic, and linguistic differences.

CULTURE FROM ABOVE

The Socialist Party in power, like its mid-1930s Popular Front predecessor, was committed to using the state to make culture more accessible and popular, a policy that led to mixed results. While de Gaulle had invented the Ministry of Culture and turned it over to the novelist André Malraux, the Gaullist conception of culture was rooted in a high-culture, Paris-centric worldview. Malraux had created *maisons de la culture* (cultural centers) to serve as regional venues for productions of French classics like Racine and Corneille, aimed at bringing civilization to deprived provincials. The socialists sought to turn Malraux's approach upside down. Jack Lang took over as minister of culture. An energetic socialist deputy from the city of Nancy, Lang had earlier been involved in regional avant-garde theater, then served as the government's impresario and pageant master. He choreographed Mitterrand's post-victory visit to the Panthéon in May and celebrated the Left's sweeping legislative victory in June with a new event, the Festival of Music (Fête de la musique), when for one night French musicians of every ethnic and regional stripe claimed a street corner on cities throughout France and played music. Though initially dismissed by some critics as a "Lang-est day" of trifling and insignificant noise, the Fête was a great popular success and has become an annual June tradition across France. Though paradoxical, the Fête reveals Paris' ability to inspire diversity from above.

The socialists also further liberated important facets of the electronic media. Giscard's Television of France (Télévision de France or TDF), which had replaced the Gaullist Office of French Radio and Television (Office de Radiodiffusion-Télévision Française or ORTF) and transformed the three state channels into independent companies, was in turn dissolved. Mitterrand replaced it with the High Authority on Audiovisual Communication (Haute Autorité de la Communication Audiovisuelle), a public broadcasting authority largely independent of state control. At the same time, the government authorized the creation of four new television stations: The Five (La Cinq); M6; Canal Plus, a subscription channel; and Arte, a joint Franco-German channel. But the socialists, intent on overseeing the quality and "Frenchness" of television programming—given the overwhelming challenge presented by American media exports—refused to surrender complete control of the stations. The fate of The Five in this regard was exemplary: Unable to straddle the commercial demands of the marketplace and cultural imperatives of the government, the station went bankrupt in 1992.

The contradictions inherent to the socialist cultural agenda—the government cultivating popular art forms which by their nature seek to escape government control—soon became manifest. One glaring example was the Bastille Opera House, opened in 1990 and dwarfing the lush Garnier Opera House on the Right Bank. The new site was the Place de la Bastille, heavy with revolutionary memories, and thus a fitting background to a new "people's opera house." However, the building's structural flaws—the façade soon began to fissure while the design was universally criticized as empty and bloated—reflected the central conceptual problem. Opera was no longer a popular art form, and certainly would not become one given the high price of tickets at the new house.

Ironically, like Malraux, Lang often promoted high culture, despite massive evidence that the vast majority of the French public rarely, if ever, took advantage of the cultural venues created by the state.[4] Public indifference persisted despite the massive amounts of money; the budget of Lang's ministry doubled when the socialists came to power.[5] In particular, for cinema, although direct and indirect state subsidies helped the industry win international acclaim and remain distinctly

"French," the socialist attempt to expand this success in so-called heritage films largely fizzled. Under Lang's reign, the French film industry undertook a series of high-minded and high-budget films, frequently based on great works of French literature, most notably Claude Berri's adaptations of Marcel Pagnol's *Jean de Florette* (1985) and *Manon des Sources* (1986). While the Pagnol films were a critical and popular success, Berri's production of Emile Zola's novel *Germinal* revealed the limits of socialist cultural politics. In 1993, the same year that *Germinal*, the most costly film in French history, was released, *Les Visiteurs*, a low-budget Franco-Belgian comedy, also appeared. More than three times as many French went to see the free-spirited (and low-minded) comedy than Berri's mummification of Zola's novel.[6] Clearly, the French wanted to be entertained, not enlightened, at the cinema.

CULTURE FROM BELOW

Germinal's box office failure revealed the difficulty of controlling cultural activities from above. Cultural practices in France in the 1980s reflected more often the growth of regional and ethnic awareness, as well as the pressures of the commercial marketplace, than the heavy hand of the state. A constant concern for the film industry was the presence of American imports. During the first years of socialist government, the French film industry steadily lost ground at the box office to American movies. Along with infusing the national industry with subsidies, the socialists also responded at the diplomatic level. In 1981, Lang snubbed the festival of American cinema at Deauville; more usefully, the French delegation at the General Agreement on Tariffs and Trade (GATT) negotiations struggled to protect the nation's cultural products from the onslaught of globalization. This effort climaxed in 1993, when the treaty codified the famous "cultural exemption" from deregulated trade among nations: Films remained subject to strict quota requirements. Tellingly, French films managed to retain about 35 percent of the national market, and France is the world's third largest producer of films.[7]

At the same time, French filmmakers incorporated elements from American cinema in order to create a specifically French product that had little to do with either heritage films or slapstick comedies. The emblematic film of this new genre, called the *cinema du look*, was Jean-Jacques Beineix's *Diva*. Reaching the screen in 1981, the film was a stunning pastiche of musical and cinematic models. Though categorized as postmodern, the film's sensibility also reflects traditional French traits: One character engages in a motorscooter chase in the Paris Metro while another delivers a sublimely silly lesson in the art of buttering a baguette.

Diva also spoke to the general anxiety on both the Left and Right over the impact of a new global economic and political order on French culture. For liberal critics like Alain Finkielkraut, France had strayed too far from its universalist mission. In his diatribe *The Defeat of Thought* (*La Défaite de la Pensée*), published in 1987, Finkielkraut denounced the decline of a single standard for political and cultural values, which he naturally identified with Enlightenment France.

Multiculturalism was another word for cultural decline: "We are warned: if you insist on a strict hierarchy of values . . . and find it impossible to consider on the same cultural footing the author of the [Montaigne] *Essays* and a television celebrity [or] between Beethoven and Bob Marley, it is because you belong to the camp of reactionaries and killjoys."[8]

Despite such warnings that the end was nigh, French artists and audiences alike quickly adapted to a new world order that placed Bob Marley and Beethoven on equal cultural footing. The 1980s witnessed a vibrant renewal of linguistic, cultural,and national forms in the arts. In music, one era of the French *chanson* (the popular musical tradition dating back to the mid-nineteenth century, most often combining poignant lyricism with social or political commentary) came to an end with the deaths of Jacques Brel (1978) and Georges Brassens (1981). Yet a new era had already begun: Serge Gainsbourg, who had established himself in the 1960s, continued to perform, write, and scandalize (as with his reggae version of "La Marseillaise"), while younger contemporaries like Renaud, Jean-Jacques Goldman, Francis Cabrel, and Patricia Kass revealed the *chanson*'s durability. (According to recent studies, while two-thirds of baby boomers continue to listen to *chansons*, even in the younger 20 to 24 age group, a respectable one-third listen on a regular basis to *chansons*.)[9]

But the *chansonnier* found the stage increasingly crowded with a great array of newcomers, reflecting a powerful resurgence of regional traditions from below. In Brittany, harpist Alan Stivell and guitarist Dan Ar Braz reinvented Celtic music. Though at times spilling into New Age vapidity, the vitality of the Breton folk move-ment has revived a distinct, once nearly extinct, musical culture. In Corsica, the musical revival also found its voice with groups like I Murivini and Les Nouvelles Polyphonies Corses, which mix Corsican texts and traditional chants with modern instruments and a postmodern sensibility, seen in collaboration of artists like Patti Smith and John Cale. In a more playful spirit, Les Fabulous Trobadors, based in Toulouse, merged the medieval troubadour tradition with modern hip-hop.

The audiences for these various schools of music, however, are relatively small, urban, educated, and bourgeois. As with the nineteenth-century revival of regional languages and history, "the people" this music celebrates had long ago adopted Anglo-American pop and rock music. For example, *le rap* began to reach France in the early 1980s, broadcast by "pirate radio stations" like Radio Nova and finding an eager audience among the children of sub-Saharan immigrants living in the desolate *banlieues* (suburbs). France's most famous rapper, MC Solaar, was born in Senegal to parents from Chad and grew up in a Parisian suburb. Children of North African descent, on the other hand, rallied to *raï*. Born in the poor quarters of Oran and Algiers, *raï* melds repetitive and mesmerizing chants (based on old song traditions) against an electronic beat. As with rap, *raï* gave voice to a generation divorced from traditional political and social institutions not just in France, but also in Algeria, where both political and religious figures had long denounced its purportedly unwholesome influence. By the early 1980s, stations like Radio Beur were broadcasting *raï*, but as with rap in the United States, the music eventually won over a young, white, and bourgeois audience. In 1992, Khaled's single "*Didi*" rose to the top of the French music charts.[10]

IMMIGRATION AND FRENCHNESS

The audiences for *raï* and rap reflected a renewal of the perennial French debate over the nature of national identity. As the twentieth century neared its end, what role should immigrants play in France political life? Both the 1.5 million recent immigrants who came from Algeria, Tunisia, and Morocco by 1990 and their French-born children were often referred to as "immigrants." Furthermore, the line between religion and ethnicity grew blurred in the public imagination. Earlier waves of European immigrants had eventually subordinated their religious beliefs—Catholic, Protestant, or Jewish—to the Republic's secular ideals. However, as with Jewish immigrants in the early twentieth century, politicians across the ideological spectrum worried over the Republic's capacity to assimilate the most recent immigrants and their descendants. Unhappily, public debates more frequently confused than clarified the complex issue of immigration. Immigrants to France, rather than forming a single, monolithic community, varied dramatically. Thus, a small elite arrived in France from francophone countries just after decolonization to pursue an education. Much more numerous were economic immigrants, poorly educated and largely rural, from North Africa and sub-Saharan Africa seeking a better life in France. At the same time, France also attracted an important community of political exiles, ranging from the *harkis* after 1962 to the "boat people" fleeing Vietnam in the 1970s.

Most importantly, the *beurs*—French slang for "Arab"—uneasily straddled very different sets of cultures and languages. Born on French soil to North African immigrants, the *beurs* were French citizens. A critical element of French republicanism was the juridical principle of *jus soli*. Birth on French soil bestows citizenship to those who reach adulthood in France. Yet these second-generation French citizens of North African descent did not feel accepted by the French nation, nor did they identify with the countries their parents left for France. Novelist Azouz Begag neatly captured the cultural confusion of growing up *beur*:

> The bearded wonder, old Father Christmas and Co., never visited us . . . all because our boss is Mohammed. There's nothing in his little book about Christmas trees and presents on December 25. An oversight like that isn't easy to forgive. It makes you feel like finding a new boss, one who's more on top of his job. . . . So, not wanting to stand out from his friends, my father refused to have anything to do with Christmas. . . . Fortunately, the works committee in the factory where my father worked remembered us each year. . . . It was the highlight of the year, the moment when my brothers and sisters and I felt really close to the French—or, at least, close to the right side of them.[11]

Begag's use of the phrase "the right side" of the French hinted at an important development in French politics in the early 1980s, on the "wrong side" for Begag, the growing popularity of the extreme right-wing, xenophobic National Front (Front

National or FN) founded a decade earlier by Jean-Marie Le Pen. The FN slowly began to attract voters from both the Gaullist RPR and the PC. Working-class voters felt increasingly anxious about immigrants who seemed to threaten their job security and neighborhoods. The FN slogan, "France for the French," appealed to these economically insecure voters. Tellingly, the FN's first electoral success was in Dreux, a small city in western France whose economy was staggering under the weight of bankrupt industries and unemployed workers. In 1983, Dreux elected to the post of assistant mayor the FN candidate, Jean-Pierre Stirbois. The following year brought even more unsettling news. In the 1984 elections to the European Parliament, the FN won 11 percent of the vote, translating into 10 seats. The irony of the party's presence in the European Parliament, given its anti-Europe rhetoric, was largely lost in the sound and fury of commentary that followed the elections.

The FN's growth generated a powerful response in the immigrant community. Soon after the 1983 Dreux election, community leaders organized the "march of the beurs," a kind of multicultural Tour de France in which demonstrators marched peacefully across France for six weeks. In December 1983, Mitterrand officially welcomed the marchers, who by then numbered more than 100,000, when they reached Paris. The march's success led to the creation of SOS-Racisme in 1984, a media-savvy organization fronted by a charismatic young man of color and evocative name, Harlem Désir, who coined the celebrated slogan "Touche pas à mon pote" ("Hands off my pal"). SOS-Racisme was, however, less substance than surface effect. Politicians reluctant to address the underlying issues and anxieties of the electorate were happy to embrace the movement's vague appeals. As a result, beurs increasingly snubbed SOS-Racisme, concluding that the movement's moralizing and photo-ops with political and entertainment celebrities were at best irrelevant, and at worst worked against their actual interests.

While the Right's dislike of SOS-Racisme was hardly surprising, SOS-Racisme also unsettled many on the Left. Given their shared belief in the primacy of the unitary nation-state (the French Republic), a single language (French), and a single set of secular values (inspired by the French Revolution), many socialists and Gaullists were disturbed by a "multicultural" France. Rather than celebrating a multicultural society of distinct ethnic communities and ethnic politics, as in America, French policy, they thought, should assimilate these communities into French society. The conservative Figaro Magazine announced in a 1984 headline: "France Is Afraid" ("La France a peur").[12] In 1985, the same magazine portrayed Marianne, the female symbol of the French Republic, with her head covered in an Islamic headscarf and the revolutionary trinity—Liberty, Equality, Fraternity—replaced by a question: "Will we still be French in 30 years?" While the article was no less sensational than the cover art—claiming, through statistical sleight-of-hand, that the birthrate of "non-Europeans" would eventually overwhelm France—it reflected both popular anxieties and the willingness of the media to exploit these fears.[13]

In 1981, the socialist government granted immigrants the right to assemble freely and supported granting them the right to vote in local elections. At the same time, a critical development in the Left's emphasis on human rights was a new, if hesitant refrain: the right to be different (*droit à la différence*). This notion was conceived in reference to regional identities in France but was increasingly aimed at immigrants as well. The government declared an amnesty for nearly 150,000 undocumented immigrants living in France. But these generous impulses suffered under the impact of a declining franc and rising unemployment. After 1983, the mainstream political parties responded to the public's growing disillusion with the socialist program; even sympathetic socialist leaders like Defferre, who was both government minister and mayor of racially diverse Marseilles, announced that "in France, we don't have the same habits of living" as North African immigrants.[14]

While a nationalist backlash grew against immigrant communities across Europe, France was especially vulnerable. The Algerian war had a great impact on national attitudes toward Arab and Berber immigrants—public discourse tended to depict all "Arabs" as fundamentalists or National Liberation Front (Front de Libération Nationale or FLN) terrorists—as well as on *pieds noirs,* portrayed as racist overlords and reactionaries. It seemed to some observers that the principle of *jus soli,* so central to the French republican tradition, had "transformed large numbers of second-generation immigrants—particularly North Africans—into French citizens, but citizens indifferent, sometimes antagonistic, to that citizenship."[15] By 1983, the debate over immigration reflected a deeper malaise in France—a malaise that led commentators, influenced by the work of Michel Foucault and Pierre Bourdieu, to replace the term "*les immigrés*" with "*les exclus*" (the excluded). Foucault's historical studies traced the ways in which societies across time and space create structures and categories of exclusion, while Bourdieu argued that there were yet other paths to poverty than being an immigrant from the Maghreb. There were also the "internally excluded" (*exclus de l'intérieur*): native-born Frenchmen and Frenchwomen who, lacking the "cultural capital" needed to succeed in a given society—formal and informal education, cultural references, professional and social status—are condemned to marginal lives. At this level, Bourdieu affirmed in *La Misère du Monde* (*The Misery of the World*), a person's skin color hardly mattered. At the bottom of the social ladder, everyone experienced entrenched, institutionalized forms of discrimination.[16] To an important degree, social exclusion and disempowerment were not the exclusive burden of North African immigrants.

THE REINVENTION OF "LA PAUSE"

By mid-1983, Mitterrand's "redistributive Keynesianism" had clearly proven unable to dam the tidal forces of the global economy: Unemployment increased to more than 2 million, from 6.3 to 8.6 percent of the labor force. The socialist government's economic, monetary, and industrial policies had, at best, redistributed unemployment among various social and age categories. The trade deficit fared no better; French workers, flush with money provided by the government trying to prime the pump, bought imported goods while stagnating demand for French exports failed to offset those imports. With inflation approaching 14 percent and deepening financial instability, Delors devalued the franc three times and, in early 1983, imposed a wage and price freeze.[17]

Part of the problem was the solution offered by economists like Delors: a unified European market. Not only was France constrained by global economic realities, but also by the commitments made to the European Monetary System. France had entered the system in 1979, in the belief that it would maintain a strong franc. The inherent contradictions between the desire to reignite an inert national economy, on the one hand, and to maintain the franc within a transnational system that included the strong German mark, on the other, were too great to overcome. The socialists had to choose between France and Europe. Despite the stubborn resistance of many in the PS concerned about the threat European integration posed to France's "universal" Republic, Mitterrand and Delors—following here in the footsteps of Giscard—ultimately chose Europe.

The morning after the municipal elections of March 1983, politicians read the handwriting on the wall. The conservative parties won handily in nearly every city with the notable exception of Marseilles. In Paris, the list led by Jacques Chirac swept all 20 *arrondissements,* including the working-class neighborhoods in eastern Paris. Mitterrand's response was immediate. Rather than call for a "pause," as Blum did in 1936, Mitterrand called for an end to the government's policies. Delors reaffirmed France's commitment to the European Monetary System, dramatically reduced public spending, suspended the process of nationalizations, and began reprivatization. Moreover, the socialists restructured industries, like coal, steel, and shipbuilding, which were unable to compete in the global economy. Tens of thousands of workers were laid off. The French "Red Belt," industrial areas on the outskirts of Paris with a strong communist identity and politics, turned into the Rust Belt, a zone of political resentment. Disillusioned with the Left, many of laid-off industrial workers, rather than rallying again to a communist party embalmed in its Stalinist worldview, instead "migrated" to the other extreme, giving their vote to the FN.

While Mitterrand's new austerity policy reduced both inflation and the balance of payments deficit, it failed to promote economic growth, which remained at an anemic 1.9 percent, or job growth, with unemployment rising above 10 percent. Among both middle-class professionals and blue-collar workers there was growing anxiety concerning unemployment. This unease was deepened by dramatic changes in employment relations. Throughout the "Thirty Glorious Years" from 1946 to 1976, both blue- and white-collar workers in France grew accustomed to full employment, long-lasting contracts, and generous benefits. Yet these conditions began to fray; by the time the socialists came to power, there was a new world of short-term contracts and greater market volatility, with unhappy consequences for the cohesion of French society.[18]

While the government staggered under the weight of currency devaluations and budget austerity, it tried to prove its left-wing ideological purity in other realms, most explosively in education. In a concession to its militant wing, the socialist minister of education, Alain Savary, introduced legislation in late 1983 to halt all public funding of religious schools (which de Gaulle had partly revived in 1959). The reaction was volcanic: On June 24, 1983, more than 1 million French protesters gathered in Paris to defend the *école libre* (religious schools that followed the state-dictated curriculum). They formed a great river of humanity that, due to shrewd planning by Catholic groups, spilled into the Place de la Bastille, the traditional gathering place of the French Left. Conservative Catholics and opposition parties were joined by a range of organizations not usually associated with religious or political movements, but mobilized by their concerns over the faltering state of public education and angry at the government's overreach. Rather than a revival of clericalism, the protest movement revealed that parents "were fundamentally attached to the principle of freedom of choice in educational matters."[19]

Mitterrand quickly withdrew Savary's school funding legislation, accepted the resignations of Savary and Mauroy, and appointed Laurent Fabius prime minister. Scarcely 37 years old, armed with the intellectual tools and technocratic confidence of having attended France's most prestigious *grande école*, the Ecole Nationale d'Administration, Fabius was indifferent to the traditions of French socialism and beholden to a president determined to tack toward the center. Emptying his government of communist ministers and placing Pierre Bérèrogoy in the Ministry of Finance, Fabius undertook a program of "modernizing and uniting." It soon became apparent, however, that the new socialist concept of "modernization" differed little from the neo-liberalism of the parties of the Right, the UDF or the RPR, which did little to mollify Fabius' allies on the Left. A Marxist wing of the Left alliance led by Jean Pierre Chevènement and socialist leader Lionel Jospin criticized Fabius' economic policies. Retreating from the traditional interventionism (*dirigisme*) of both the socialist Left and Gaullist Right, Fabius reduced spending, reversed the policy of nationalization, and committed the government to a strong franc. While this new agenda did little for a besieged working class, it tamed the inflation rate and increased the buying power of the middle class, which had now become the socialists' principal constituency. Along with this constituency, Fabius found firm support in Mitterrand: The so-called Fabius effect, it seemed, might stave off a complete socialist rout.

FOREIGN POLICY

While they began to distance the state from economic matters, the socialists elsewhere reemphasized the primacy of the state. In foreign policy, Mitterrand was nearly more Gaullist than de Gaulle in following an independent foreign policy, particularly in relation to the United States. Both socialists and Gaullists distrusted American economic, political, and cultural power. Yet Mitterrand broke with Gaullist policy by thawing ties with Israel, becoming the first French president to visit Israel in 1982, and by recognizing the strategic imperatives France shared with NATO. Most significantly, Mitterrand braved domestic resistance in 1983 by supporting NATO's decision to place Pershing II nuclear missiles in West Germany as a necessary response to the Soviet decision to base short-range missiles on its western border.

Notably, Mitterrand never questioned the Gaullist justification for France's nuclear strike force (*force de frappe*), considering an independent nuclear force to be a diplomatic and national imperative. He ordered the resumption of nuclear tests in the South Pacific, leading to the tragic-comedic Rainbow Warrior Affair. In 1985, the environmental organization Greenpeace had sent the Rainbow Warrior to the area in order to protest the tests; while in harbor in New Zealand, the ship was sunk by the French intelligence services in a bungled affair that cost the life of a photographer. However, while it garnered intense media coverage, the Rainbow Warrior Affair had no important repercussions for French policy. While anti–nuclear weapons and energy galvanized opposition parties and public opinion in the United States and elsewhere in Western Europe, the resumption of nuclear weapons testing led to hardly a ripple of protest in France, and nuclear tests continued until 1992.

The continued relative absence of popular protest to nuclear testing reflected a long-standing national consensus on maintaining France's rank among nations. While he had criticized the Republic's nuclear strategy prior to 1981, Mitterrand insisted upon the necessity of the strike force once he assumed office. In fact, he tweaked certain tactical aspects of the force to strengthen the same strategic considerations held by de Gaulle—namely, that the threat of triggering a nuclear holocaust would dissuade any potential enemy from invading France. Continuity in foreign policy extended, at least until 1986, to other aspects of foreign policy. The socialists, like their predecessors, tried to keep equal distance between the United States and the U.S.S.R. and insisted on remaining outside of NATO's military structure while upholding its commitment to the integrity of Western Europe. Mitterrand's adoption of a Gaullist worldview changed, however, when the world itself changed, signaled by the collapse of the Berlin Wall in 1989.

ODD BEDFELLOWS: THE EVOLUTION OF COHABITATION

The "Fabius effect," it turned out, proved too little and too late to save the PS in the March 1986 legislative elections. The centrist and Gaullist alliance, led by Chirac from his mayoral office in Paris, won a majority of seats, even though the PS succeeded in remaining the largest single party in the Assembly. At the same time, because of the socialists' revision of the electoral system, the FN won 35 seats, the same number that an exhausted and ideologically destitute PC managed to salvage.

The redistribution of seats created a situation commonplace in American politics but unprecedented in the history of the Fifth Republic: A sitting president now shared power with a legislature controlled by the opposition. Since the birth of the Fifth Republic in 1958, the same party had always held the presidency and the legislature. Until 1974, both de Gaulle and Pompidou worked with a Gaullist majority in the Assembly. Giscard may have broken with the Gaullists, but he nevertheless had a right-wing majority in the legislature. Mitterrand's victory in 1981 represented a dramatic shift of power to the Left, but like his conservative predecessors, he had a friendly legislative majority.

Since the Fifth Republic's Constitution did not address this state of affairs, the political parties had entered unchartered waters. Prior to the 1986 election, as the trends became apparent, pundits worried what would happen in the event that the Right won the legislative elections. Could this prove the fatal flaw in France's fifth attempt at republican government? Would "cohabitation" work? If the Right won, should President Mitterrand resign? Could France operate with a socialist president and a Gaullist prime minister? The answers depended on whom one asked. While some opposition figures, like Raymond Barre, insisted that the Constitution prevented them from serving if asked by Mitterrand, yet others, like the ambitious Jacques Chirac, loudly contradicted Barre. As a result, when his old socialist nemesis called upon him to form a government, Chirac gladly accepted. It quickly became clear that the socialist president and Gaullist prime minister were condemned to live together. Neither could pull too far in one direction or another, yet each one was happy to undermine the other's efforts when the occasion presented itself. At the same time, both men knew they could not be seen as simple obstructionists since each planned to run for president in 1988. Thus Mitterrand and Chirac felt equally obliged to show restraint and flexibility.

The two men began to circle around one another almost immediately. Chirac submitted an ordinance to fully reprivatize the banks and industries still in the government's hands—a continuation, in fact, of the liberalizing economic policies of his socialist predecessor. Though Mitterrand denounced the proposal, the conservative Assembly promptly enacted it. In fact, the difference between the conservative and socialist governments' economic policies was mostly rhetorical. As a result, the most significant clashes occurred in arenas with room enough for ideological posturing, including women's rights and immigration. For example, Chirac abolished the ministerial portfolio for women's rights, reversing a process first begun by Giscard and pursued by Mitterrand. Then, in October 1986, Chirac's interior minister, Charles Pasqua, ordered the roundup of more than a hundred undocumented Malian immigrants in Paris. As the news stations filmed the Malians dragged onto a plane with a one-way ticket to their native country, many recalled the round-ups of Jews during the German occupation of World War II.

Yet Pasqua was unmoved; indeed, he went a step further and sought to revise French citizenship criteria. Rather than automatically receiving citizenship, children born in France to non-French parents would have to file papers for citizenship upon reaching majority. The proposed law sparked a firestorm. In an increasingly polarized nation, the extreme Right declared that it did not go far enough, and the Left asserted that Pasqua's proposed law negated a founding principle of the Republic. Mitterrand declared his opposition to Pasqua's effort; it was, he declared, "inspired by a philosophy he did not share."[20] The knockout blow to the law, though, was delivered by an initially unrelated event. During the fall of 1986, university and *lycée* students were mobilizing against another proposed law, authored by Chirac's minister of education, Alain Devaquet. Universities were still free and admission was open to all students who had passed the baccalaureate exam. Devaquet sought to "Americanize" the system by introducing tuition and admissions criteria. The proposal galvanized student organizations, already on edge over the sluggish economy and tight job market. Driven by professional anxiety and republican conviction, they launched a series of mass protests across France in the late fall. In early December 1986, one of the protestors, Malik Oussekine, died after being beaten by the police in Paris. Confronted by the wrath of student, union, and immigrant organizations, along with a public increasingly alarmed at state violence, Chirac shelved both the nationality and the university reform bills a few days later.

MITTERRAND'S SECOND TERM

In fact, many people began to rally to a status quo where neither the Left nor Right could step beyond certain limits without being brought to heel by public opinion. Whether the issue was education or immigration, the majority of the French people were ill at ease with measures seen as extreme or redolent of ideological claims that echoed the Vichy years. Both socialists and Gaullists were punished, in the streets and voting booths, for efforts to repeat past confrontations. This centrism marked a sea change in French political life. The political actors disliked cohabitation, but the French public made it clear that they wanted the parties to govern together. This demand seemed all the more reasonable since the main parties fundamentally agreed on such vital national interests as foreign policy, nuclear energy, the nuclear strike force, the constitution of the Fifth Republic, and the state's historical responsibility to guarantee the social well-being of its citizens.

As the 1988 presidential elections made clear, Mitterrand absorbed this lesson better than Chirac. During the series of clashes with his conservative prime minister, the socialist president transformed the constitutional constraints of his office into political virtue. He presented himself to the nation not as a force of change or rupture but as one of continuity and unity—from "change life" ("Changer la vie") in 1981, the Mitterrand campaign coined a new slogan, "France United"("La France unie"). To be sure, Chirac was vulnerable to Mitterrand's charge that he was courting the voters attracted to the FN, which had won more than 14 percent of the vote in the first round of the presidential election. The PC reached yet another nadir, winning less than half of Le Pen's vote.

When Mitterrand decisively defeated Chirac in the second round on May 8, 1988, winning a second term in office, there was no repeat of the fears and frenzied celebrations in 1981. Even the French Stock Exchange welcomed the news, rising slightly the day after the election results were announced. An influential book declared that same year that the Republic was now committed to the center of the political spectrum. According to François Furet, the iconoclastic historian of the French Revolution and leading author of La République du centre (The Republic of *the Center*), French political life had matured to the point where it no longer struggled over the claims of the 1789 Revolution, but instead accepted the consensual politics found elsewhere in the West. The election results of 1988 certainly seemed to confirm Furet's subtitle, "The End of the French Exception."[21]

FUROR OVER THE *FOULARD*

But as the rest of the decade revealed, the French had not completely renounced their exceptionalist reflexes. The bicentennial celebration of the French Revolution played on the theme of unity, but other events emphasized new agents of discord. Most significantly, the "headscarf affair" (*affaire du foulard*) started in 1989 when local authorities at a *lycée* in the Paris suburb of Creil forbade a few Muslim female students to wear their headscarves inside the school. The local leaders argued that displaying religious affiliation in the neutral space of the public school violated separation of Church and State and expressed sectarianism rather than republican universalism. Although it involved just one town, Creil's headscarf policy sparked a national debate that revealed acute anxiety over republican values, national identity, and the apparent threat posed to one and the other by the North African immigrant and minority community. While many public figures, including Danièle Mitterrand, the president's wife, and the minister of education, Lionel Jospin, rallied to the young women, defending their "right to difference," others supported the school authorities' vision of neutrality, with both camps citing France's historical attachment to the universal principles of human rights.

The decision made in 1989 by the Council of State (Conseil d'Etat), a body that determines constitutionality, was a model of jurisprudential tact. While it declared that ostentatious symbols of religious affiliation must be banned in public schools, the display of modest signs—including the headscarf—was deemed permissible. Rather than dampening the ideological flames, the ruling simply stoked them. The supporters of the ban insisted that the headscarf was a sign of religious servitude, while its critics claimed that the ban violated the girls' right to free expression. With little evidence but much passion, the ban's advocates declared that the *foulard* was imposed on Muslim girls by their fathers or by religious leaders—a violation of the republican guarantee of freedom of conscience. Ironically, the Muslim girls were thus cast in the same role as Catholic women had been by republicans at the end of the nineteenth century. In both instances, women and girls were viewed as not knowing their own minds or desires and in need of protection from the influence of their priests or imams.

As a result, although only a very small minority of Muslim girls wore the headscarves, the issue refused to disappear, particularly against the background of rising Islamic violence. A series of terrorist attacks associated with extreme Arab and Islamist groups in France riddled the decades spanning the 1980s and 1990s. A murderous shooting rampage in the old Jewish quarter of Paris, on the rue des Rosiers in 1982; a bomb explosion at the railway station of Marseilles in 1983; bombings in Paris of several department stores and bookshops in 1986; and ten years later,

Paris metro bombings in 1995—all of which were the the work of extremist Arab organizations—roiled a public debate that was already edgy and emotional.[22]

THE PARADOXES OF PARITY

Just as the headscarf affair divided traditional allies on the Left, so too did another issue—gender parity. French women gained the vote in 1944, but their presence in politics remained exceptional. Between 1945 and 1993, the percentage of women in the National Assembly never rose above 7 percent, and most often barely hovered at about 4 percent. As late as 1993, with just 35 female representatives in the 577-member legislature, France ranked with Greece as the EU member nation with the lowest percentage of women in political positions. Republicans agreed that this was an unfortunate state of affairs, but differed on how to repair it.

Shortly after taking power, the socialists passed a bill imposing a gender quota in city elections: Women had to constitute at least 25 percent of electoral lists. The Constitutional Council struck down the law as a violation of both Article 3 of the 1958 Constitution and Article 6 of the 1789 Declaration of the Rights of Man and of the Citizen guaranteeing the full equality of citizens before the law, which forbids "any kind of division by category of the voters and those eligible for election."[23] In the 1990s, the advocates of electoral parity regrouped, galvanized by a 1992 book, *Au pouvoir citoyennes! Liberté, égalité, parité* (*Power to Female Citizens: Liberty, Equality, Parity*). The authors, Françoise Gaspard, Claude Servan-Schreiber, and Anne le Gall, argued that full sexual equality was central to French republican ideals. The following year, France's leading newspaper, *Le Monde,* published a manifesto signed by 288 men and 289 women (the total number of deputies in the Assembly), ranging from feminist activists like Gisèle Halimi to the conservative Simone Veil, calling for absolute parity in representation between men and women. While opinion polls showed that a significant majority of men as well as women supported the idea, important dissenting voices on the Left worried. Political theorist Elisabeth Badinter argued that parity, far from a step forward, was a "regression" based on sexual differences. Any such "quota" would undermine the universalism of republican ideals—ideals no less dear to women than men.[24] In any case, parity would have to wait.

A SECOND ACT FOR THE SOCIALISTS

With his victory in 1988, Mitterrand named Michel Rocard as his prime minister. Short of an outright majority in the 1988 legislative elections, Rocard looked to the center to find allies. But he was also forced toward the center in response to the persistently high unemployment rate and Finance Minister Pierre Bérègovoy's insistence on maintaining a strong franc. Nevertheless, in 1988 Rocard managed to introduce the Minimum Insertion Income (Revenu Minimum d'Insertion or RMI), which guaranteed a minimum income for the nation's poorest families (including immigrants). The RMI not only provided income support but also sought to overcome the structural barriers of "exclusion" by addressing the recipient's needs for "reinsertion" through job training, drug rehabilitation, general education, and the like. As one advocate, Pierre Rosanvallon, declared, the RMI is based not just "on the right to live, but the right to live in society."[25]

But Rocard's second year as prime minister was marked by a series of strikes from a staggering array of unions, ranging from nurses and postal workers to the police, angry at the government's refusal to increase state spending. With France swinging between paralysis and confusion, the public grew increasingly disillusioned with Rocard's apparent lack of leadership. And so, having squeezed his prime minister for all he was worth, Mitterrand forced Rocard from office in late 1991, replacing him with Edith Cresson. The first woman ever named as prime minister, Cresson was a political veteran, having earlier served as minister of agriculture. Unfortunately, a combination of elements turned this historic event into a soap opera. First, there was an institutional flaw. The Republic in part compensated for the paucity of women in the National Assembly through ministerial appointment. De Gaulle had created this opportunity in 1958: In his desire to free his government from the influence of the Assembly, he dropped the requirement of earlier Republics that only elected representatives could serve as cabinet ministers. A perverse result is that women became unusually dependent on presidential (and, invariably, male) patronage. This mechanism, familiar to Americans but counter to France's republican tradition, partly explains the widely hostile response to Cresson's short tenure. Critics on the Left, in particular, portrayed her as little more than Mitterrand's puppet. In the end, "citizenship may indeed have a gendered content; . . . the interests of men and women may not always be identical, and . . . the rules, ideas, culture and imagery of the Republic have always been those of its male citizens."[26]

By April 1992, Mitterrand concluded that Cresson, hounded mercilessly by the opposition and her own party, as well as weakened by a number of controversial remarks and policies, had to go. He replaced Cresson with Bérègovoy, closely identified with the socialists' policy of economic rigor. Yet Bérègovoy, like Cresson, found himself battered by political attacks from both ends of the ideological spectrum and powerless to prevent the socialist collapse. In the legislative elections of March 1993, the party lost more than 200 seats and seemed condemned to a long stretch of wandering in the political desert.

FRANCE AND THE WORLD

Competing with the various domestic crises during this period were events unfolding beyond France's borders. Certain of these had been designed and implemented with France's participation, like the painstaking construction of the European Union; others were unforeseen, like the collapse of the Soviet Union, reunification of the two Germanys, and break-up of Yugoslavia. Mitterrand was no less surprised than other Western statesmen when, in November 1989, the Berlin Wall came down. While his initial reaction has often been criticized as guarded and uncertain, Mitterrand nevertheless accepted the inevitability of reunification. His great concern was that Germany be reborn within a unified Europe. Mitterrand's efforts led European leaders to sign the Maastricht Treaty on February 7, 1992, which officially created the European Union. The Treaty committed signatories to a common foreign and security policy, the creation of Union citizenship above and beyond national citizenship, and—most controversially—the adoption of a single European currency no later than January 1, 1999.

Like his predecessors, Mitterrand believed that France could maintain its global rank and influence only from within a united Europe; the appointment of dedicated Europeanists like Jacques Delors signaled this European orientation. At the same time, Mitterrand understood the deep ambivalence the French felt over the prospect of subordinating France's foreign and economic policy to European institutions in Brussels and the planned extinction of the franc to make room for the "euro," as the new currency was to be called. As a result, Mitterrand decided to submit the Maastricht Treaty to a referendum, set for September 1992. Editorials, debates, and polls monopolized the media, with public opinion seriously divided over Maastricht.[27] Both pro- and anti-Maastricht voices, which cut across traditional party lines, wanted France to salvage what it could in a globalizing economy but disagreed over the means to do so. The pro-Maastricht camp argued that a unified European market would enhance demand for French commercial, even cultural products, while the anti-Maastricht side worried over the fate of France's independence. The slim margin of victory for the pro-Maastricht forces—scarcely more than 51 percent—reflected a nation divided on means, but united by common aspirations and fears.

In a post–Cold War world dominated by America, Mitterrand found much less room to maneuver than de Gaulle, Pompidou, or even Giscard. One significant challenge facing Mitterrand was the build-up to the first Gulf War in 1990. When Mitterrand came to office, he assumed a complicated legacy from previous governments in regard to Middle East policy. More sympathetic than his predecessors to Israel's security concerns, Mitterrand also reassured the Arab states that French foreign policy—most notably arms sales and technical assistance—would not change. Like the United States, France under Mitterrand sided with Iraq in the bloody and prolonged Iran-Iraq War, generously supplying Saddam Hussein's regime with military hardware.

In the end, though, France was too generous. Iraq eventually reneged on its payments to France, souring ties between the two nations. Nevertheless, when Iraq invaded Kuwait in 1990, Mitterrand was of two minds over the wisdom of joining the American-led coalition. Domestically, many in the North African community sympathized with Iraq's cause, while both the Left and the Right blamed American imperialism for the gathering storm. Mitterrand methodically pursued diplomatic means to force Iraq's withdrawal from Kuwait. By the end, French public opinion tired of Saddam's intransigence and supported Mitterrand in his decision to add 10,000 French troops to the coalition. When hostilities began, important fissures appeared in French society. Both North African and

Jewish radio stations turned into 24-hour talk radio outlets so that listeners could unburden themselves.[28] The rapid success of Operation Desert Storm resolved, if only temporarily, the fears it had originally provoked.

France was again forced to question its diplomatic clout during the crisis in the Balkans. While Yugoslavia broke apart and descended into civil war in the mid-1990s, Mitterrand made a surprise visit to besieged and battered Sarajevo, promising French logistical aid. The trip caught the world's attention, but did little to promote European unity. Ultimately, neither France nor Europe proved capable of responding to the crisis, which ended only when American-led NATO air strikes forced the Serbs to back down.

Finally, in his dealings with France's overseas territories and its former empire, Mitterand showed progressive statesmanship in some instances while continuing neo-colonial behavior in others. The South Pacific territory of New Caledonia had erupted into violence in the early 1980s and then again more seriously in 1988. The Melanesians, or Kanak, (43 percent of the population) wanted independence, while the settlers of French origin (37 percent) did not. On June 26, 1988, Rocard helped to broker an agreement that dissipated tensions by postponing a referendum on independence until 1998 and giving the Kanak virtual autonomy in three mineral-rich provinces and the Europeans control of the capital, Nouméa. In contrast, in Africa Mitterrand cynically maintained preexisting close ties with francophone dictators, intervening militarily to prop them up in the name of a special French African relationship. In 1994, France failed to prevent the Hutu extremists in power in Rwanda (formerly a Belgian colony, thus francophone) from carrying out a genocide against the minority Tutsi. The horror of the genocide led to a new Africa policy. Mitterrand began slashing French subsidies to African governments, realizing that the nation could no longer afford such independent policies; in the late 1990s, France began favoring military cooperation with international forces and African regional bodies rather than going it alone on the continent.[29]

THE AUTUMN OF THE PATRIARCH

During the last years of Mitterrand's second term, France had several occasions to reassess its past. One of the reasons was the resurfacing of Mitterrand's own past. In 1994, journalist Pierre Péan's Mitterrand biography, *Une Jeunesse Française: François Mitterrand 1934-1947,* created a sensation. Péan portrayed a young Mitterrand who dallied with extreme Right movements and served in the Vichy regime. Mitterrand eventually quit Vichy and went underground, joining the Resistance. Nevertheless, the public was astonished by the contradiction between a socialist president who began his first term by paying homage to Jaurès and Moulin and his younger self, follower of a Right-wing Catholic movement who had briefly served Pétain's Vichy regime (and had been awarded the regime's medal, the *francisque*). Further confusing the public imagination was the revelation by the satirical weekly, *Le Canard Enchaîné,* that Mitterrand had sent flowers every Armistice Day to the tomb of Marshal Pétain.

There were other echoes from the "dark years" of World War II—a recurring process of "discovery" and renunciation that historian Henry Rousso has labeled the "Vichy Syndrome." Details soon surfaced about Mitterrand's friendship with René Bousquet, the police official who oversaw the massive round-up of Jews in Paris in 1942. Tried after the war and forbidden to hold public office, Bousquet nevertheless flourished, becoming director of the Bank of Indochina and intimate of political figures across the spectrum, including the young and ambitious Mitterrand. Only in 1986, when revelations about Bousquet's past and friendships became public, did Mitterrand break off relations with him.

Also in the early 1990s, France prepared for the trial of Maurice Papon. As prefect of Gironde under Vichy, he sent hundreds of Jews to Drancy for deportation. He was not seriously troubled after the war for his actions and, in fact, served as Paris' prefect of police under de Gaulle. In this capacity, Papon was ultimately responsible for the events of October 17, 1961, when the police had crushed a peaceful demonstration of thousands of Algerians, killing over a hundred participants. For many observers, Papon's trial on charges of crimes against humanity—a marathon trial that ended in 1998—served as a judgment of France's treatment of its Algerian immigrants no less than of its Jewish citizens and refugees during World War II.[30]

Ironically, while Péan's biography revealed details of Mitterrand's youth, the public remained ignorant about his current state. By 1994 Mitterrand was in the late stages of prostate cancer. As his health waned, so too did the fortunes of the PS. The party's inability to challenge the economic liberalism of its opponents on the Right, to reduce the unemployment rate, to rally its traditional constituents to its banner, or to avoid the moral rot that afflicts any party in power too long spelled, if not disaster, at least another period of cohabitation. In the 1994 legislative elections, the socialists again lost their majority and Mitterrand appointed conservative Edouard Balladur to form a government. The new prime minister offered a sharp contrast to Chirac: Whereas the Paris mayor was all angles and ambition, Balladur, who had been a voice of moderation as minister of finance in the earlier Chirac government, was all curves and willing to work with Mitterrand.

In fact, Balladur found that his most serious opposition came not from the Left but instead from the resurgent Right. Once again, Pasqua was given the keys to the Ministry of the Interior, where he quickly resurrected the proposed reform to the nationality code he had been forced to shelve a decade earlier. At the same time, the new minister of education, François Bayrou, fanned the embers of the headscarf affair. Reinterpreting the deliberately vague 1989 constitutional ruling, Bayrou banned headscarves inside all public schools. The debate over religion, secularism, and national identity reignited, this time against the background of an ascendant National Front and rising Islamic fundamentalism, particularly among Algerians on both sides of the Mediterranean. By then, racial tensions in France were heightened by an appallingly bloody war in Algeria between the FLN, which had run Algeria since independence, and the Islamic Salvation Front (Front Islamique du Salut, or FIS), a party of Muslim fundamentalists. The French government supported Algeria's decision to nullify the FIS's stunning electoral victory in 1992, alienating many *beurs*.

As the debate over the headscarf and France's support of the corrupt and anti-democratic FLN continued, the film *La Haine* (*Hatred*) appeared in 1995. Directed by Matthieu Kassovitz, the movie traces the lives in an impoverished *banlieue* of three young men— a *beur*, a Jew, and a black man—whose friendship is based on their common alienation from French society. The film's most memorable image— one character's dream of falling from the roof of a public low-income high rise, telling himself as he fell past each floor, "So far, so good"—captured the tragic situation of life in these quarters rich in unemployment, drugs, and despair.

Religious tensions were playing out in a familiar register as well. Education Minister Bayrou undermined his republican credentials at the end of 1993 when he reintroduced a bill to provide full state financing for religious schools. As it had with the socialists' earlier effort in the opposite direction—an end to even partial state financing of private schools—the public pushed back. More than a million people marched along the streets of Paris in January 1994 on behalf of the republican principle of secularism (*laïcité*), forcing the government to withdraw the bill.

The FN tried to exploit the growing unease about immigration in particular. Le Pen's brutally xenophobic language struck a deep chord among voters worried that their jobs, physical security, or, more vaguely, way of life was threatened by the influx of "foreigners." The French were not alone to be drawn to such demagoguery; across Europe extreme right-wing organizations were sprouting like toxic mushrooms

June 1995 demonstration of French anti-racist Groups, Place du Trocadéro, Paris. Photograph courtesy of Paul Silverstein.

in the swamp created by relentless media coverage and public anxiety. Yet, more so than anywhere else, in France the FN maintained its hold on a significant propor-tion of voters—varying from 10 to 15 percent—and also stood out for its historical pedigree. Observers noted important continuities between the FN, Boulangism, the interwar fascist leagues, the Vichy regime, and post-war Poujadism. Moreover, the FN continued to attract an increasing number of voters from the working class, which had traditionally supported the PC or the socialists. Such working-class support gave the FN, despite superficial similarities to other extreme right-wing parties in Europe, "a Franco-French specificity."[31]

The FN's success pushed national political debates to the Right. Positions that a few years before had been judged extreme now appeared reasonable. For example in 1993, Pasqua turned into law the same nationality code, with slight modifications, that had sparked such a firestorm in 1986: Children born in France to non-French parents would have to request, instead of receive automatically, citizenship upon reaching their majority. Remarkably, a *beur* organization, France Plus, noted that law-abiding immigrant children had nothing to fear from the pro-posed revisions, while even socialists like Chevènement supported the measure. As in the United States, immigration and national identity now cut across tradi-tional Right/Left political lines in France.

These tensions played out during the twilight of Mitterrand's presidency. There was a good deal of sound and fury over his accomplishments: Mitterrand had clearly left his mark, but what was its nature and lasting impact? During

I. M. Pei's pyramid at the Louvre, 1981–1989. Louvre, Paris /The Bridgeman Art Library.

Mitterrand's 14 years, Paris had loosened its bureaucratic stranglehold on the provinces; from Toulouse to Montpellier, Strasbourg to Rennes, there was a genuine flowering of regional politics, economies, and cultures. In Paris, the cultivation of culture was even more pronounced; not only was the Ministry of Culture seeding a dizzying array of theatrical, cinematic, artistic, and musical projects, but architects were equally busy erecting enormous monuments to the Mitterrand era. Just as the harvest in the arts was of mixed quality, so too were these *grands travaux,* the name given to vast buildings inspired by Mitterrand's architectural ambitions. Perhaps here more than in any other domain Mitterrand was intimately involved. On the one hand, he oversaw elegant postmodernist buildings, like I. M. Pei's Pyramid at the Louvre and Jean Nouvel's Institute of the Arab World; on the other hand, there were less fortunate constructions, like the Bastille Opera and the oppressive, if functional, National Library.

Mitterrand's most important accomplishments were, in a sense, inadvertent. First, his embrace of the Gaullist institutions he had formerly denounced helped "normalize" French politics, pulling it toward the center. Second, with the collapse of a bipolar world in international politics, Mitterrand had little choice but to align France with American interests. At certain moments France saw itself as a European David defeating the American Goliath. But, by and large, Mitterrand guided foreign and economic policies that obeyed the dictates of reality. Third, Mitterrand's presidency revealed the limits of the state, particularly in the realm of economic affairs. Despite 14 years of intermittent efforts to redress the nation's unemployment rate, more than 12 percent of the French labor force was out of work when Mitterrand left office. The invisible hand of an increasingly global market had bested the weakened hand of socialist policy-making.

In the end, perhaps Mitterrand was even more Machiavellian than either his admirers or critics believed. The editor of *Libération,* Serge July, argued that by imposing the socialist financial and monetary agenda in 1981 and pushing France into an economic crisis, Mitterrand both justified his revolutionary credentials and demonstrated the impossibility of revolution. The political rhetoric of 1981–1983 revealed itself to be as utopian as the Paris Commune's language a century before. France simply could no longer afford to maintain its "exceptional" character in a growing global economy and shrinking Europe. Completing the story started in 1870, in which an earlier convert to republicanism from the Right, Adolphe Thiers, played a crucial role, François Mitterrand helped make France, in July's phrase, "ordinary."[32] While France would continue to resist the American model of an unfettered marketplace and insist upon a generous network of social welfare and public services, the earlier socialist model had revealed itself too idealistic in a world that had grown too interdependent.

CHAPTER 14

France since 1995

"France had committed the irreparable." This curt phrase delivered on July 16, 1995, by the newly elected French president, on the subject of Vichy's role in the deportation of Jews, electrified France. By placing responsibility for the deportation of French and foreign Jews squarely on the shoulders of the French nation, President Jacques Chirac broke with the Gaullist myth of a nation of resisters. He also broke with the refusal of responsibility by all post-war presidents, from Pompidou to Mitterrand, to accept France's responsibility for the role it played in the Final Solution. On that day, marking the forty-third anniversary of round-up of Jews by French authorities, Chirac apologized on behalf of the French nation.

Equally important, his words began to redeem his presidential campaign promise to heal the country's *fracture sociale* or "social fracture"—a term designating the growing divide between those integrated socially in France, and the impoverished residents of suburban slums, often of African or North African heritage, known as *les exclus.* By directly addressing an issue that had long divided the nation—an act, moreover, earning the praise of most French citizens—Chirac seemed to be equal to his rhetoric of compassionate conservatism. But this moment quickly passed: By the end of the year, Chirac's government proved to be no less a victim of its own ideological hubris than the socialists had been 14 years earlier.

Mitterrand may well have been a Third Republic Radical transposed to the Fifth Republic. Like his predecessors, he shifted between two impulses. On the one hand, he firmly believed in republican values like the nation and social justice. On the other hand, he was a skilled politician who often played the game without much thought for ideological principles.[1] Much the same could be said of Jacques Chirac. While he admired the Gaullist heritage, he was also capable of tacking with the political winds. In the end, while Mitterrand exposed the impracticality of socialism, Chirac revealed the limits of Gaullism for France in a global age. Yet, while Mitterrand and Chirac's attachment to the ideological imperatives of their respective parties was dubious, their attachment to power was never in doubt.

FROM "SOCIAL FRACTURE" TO "SOCIAL DEMAND"

Ever since 1976, when he created the Rally for the Republic (Rassemblement pour la République or RPR), Chirac claimed the Gaullist mantle. He believed that the state had to respect the self-regulating character of the economy, promote business, and encourage economic development. But Chirac also committed the RPR to working toward a more equitable distribution of benefits among all French people—an aspect of *dirigisme,* the belief held by those on the Right as well as Left that the state must play a role in the nation's economy that belonged to the Gaullist legacy. During the 1995 presidential campaign, Chirac criticized Balladur's laissez-faire approach to the economy and instead argued for a "third way" between unregulated capitalism and socialism. An energetic Gaullist, Chirac seemed poised to redress the persistent anxiety of the electorate over unemployment, exclusion, and violence.

Chirac's rhetoric was successful. In the first round of voting, Chirac won 21 percent, second only to socialist Lionel Jospin's 25 percent. Balladur tallied just 18 percent, while the National Front (Front National or FN) under Le Pen won 15 percent and the Communist Party (Parti Communiste or PC), under the good-natured and ineffective Robert Hue, continued its slow mutation into a historical curiosity item, with less than 9 percent of the vote. Remarkably, the perennial Arlette Laguiller, who had been running as the Trotskyist candidate ever since 1965, won nearly 6 percent of the vote, while the Greens, under Dominique Voynet, a doctor who had begun her career in Doctors without Borders (Médecins sans Frontières), failed to pass the 5 percent threshold. The results of the second round, which pitted Jospin against Chirac, ended with the latter's victory, thanks to the support of moderate voters attracted to his campaign promises. The Right followed with a convincing victory in the legislative elections, and Chirac named Alain Juppé as his prime minister. A Chirac protégé and graduate of the National Administration School (Ecole Nationale d'Administration or ENA), France's elite school of administration, Juppé's technocratic background also represented a retreat from earlier ideological battles. In forming his government, Juppé further confirmed the new government's inclusiveness with his appointment of 12 women to ministerial positions, whom the French media labeled "*les jupettes*" (France's word for the mini skirt), an amusing but dismissive play on Juppé's name.

These early steps were soon reversed, however. Like the socialists in 1983, Juppé's ministry collided with the realities of a European and global market. While the government's initial economic policies carried a strong whiff of Gaullist state intervention, the effort to stimulate the stalled economy and staunch the persistent hemorrhage of joblessness fizzled. By the end of the year, a reorganized cabinet—one with far fewer women ministers—fully embraced the reigning liberal wisdom of deregulation and decreased state spending. Juppé adopted an austere budget to meet the economic criteria required by the Maastricht Treaty—a budget containing cutbacks to the nation's generous social security system, particularly in health benefits and retirement pensions. The public responded to the proposed changes with a crippling series of strikes in October 1995 that first began in the public sector. Civil servants from the post office and transportation sectors were soon joined in their protest marches by university students, angered over reductions in state spending on education. By December, the paralysis that gripped France recalled the events of 1968. By Christmas, Chirac and Juppé were forced to withdraw the more controversial aspects of their legislation.

For many participants, the strikes represented a popular protest against the sea change in the world economy. The strikers rebelled against the impression of the French state's impotence in the face of trans-national economic realities. Whether labeled globalization, neo-liberalization, or Americanization, this economic trend, to which Chirac's government had surrendered, represented the protesters' great nemesis. Pierre Bourdieu, leading intellectual on the barricades, reminded the strikers they had taken to the streets to defend a "civilization of republican equality of rights: rights to education, to health, culture, research, art and, above all, work."[2] Novelist Viviane Forrester doubled down on Bourdieu's all-or-nothing rhetoric in 1996 with her bestseller *The Economic Horror*. Forrester denounced the state's refusal to maintain, in the face of globalization's marauding capitalism, the republican values of national independence, social solidarity, and economic justice.

While Forrester spoke for the Left, many on the Right shared her anger over France's predicament. Nationalism once again cut across traditional ideological divisions. But so, too, did support for the government's effort at modernization. Intellectuals like Pierre Rosanvallon, a prominent historian and theoretician of republicanism, and sociologist and former 1968 activist Alain Touraine argued that France still lacked the intermediary bodies to resolve such disputes and resisted the necessary steps that would modernize social and state relationships. Rather than an inspiring example of national resistance to the forces of modernization, the strikes were symptomatic of a society incapable of renewing itself. The strikers represented not those at the bottom of the social ladder, those known as the *banlieusards,* warehoused in grim suburbs (*banlieues*) with few services and poor public schools, finding their access to decent jobs blocked by unacknowledged racial prejudice. Rather, they were the relatively privileged—students and workers—seeking to protect their status. This signaled a mutation of the "*gauchiste*" reflex of grassroots activism, seeking protection in the guise of leftist rhetoric of acquired rights at the expense of expanding opportunities.

A NATION IN SEARCH OF A DEFINITION

While not *banlieusards* themselves, strikers nevertheless may have been inspired at least in part to act by the social and economic deprivation of France's poorest inhabitants. The protests, seemingly protective of privilege, did also reflect a deeper malaise—an unease that, in certain respects, resembled the same state of mind in France after 1871. "What is a nation?" was the question famously asked by Ernst Renan in the wake of France's defeat in the Franco-Prussian War. Similarly, toward the end of the twentieth century, the great issue confronting France, for Alain Touraine, was no longer social, but national.[3] What did it mean to be French, particularly in a world increasingly dominated by a single economy and media? The dilemma that now confronted the Fifth Republic was reconciling its ostensibly global vocation with a new global economic system whose influence reached deep into France itself. During the 1990s, many people struggled with this dilemma in a number of cultural domains.

Particularly newsworthy was the battle over the French language. From its former claim as the universal language of reason, diplomacy, and art, French had become increasingly marginalized. Invariably, the foe was American English. In 1964, the essayist and China scholar known as Etiemble expressed this fear in his witty book *Parlez-vous franglais?* According to the author, the growing use of Anglicisms in French was a symptom of "yankee imperialism." If you are what you speak, then the French had to make a vigorous effort to purge their language of such corruptions.

Forty years later, Etiemble's spirit was alive and well in the person of Chirac's minister of culture, Jacques Toubon. His ministry proposed a law imposing the use of French in all official matters, as well as in radio and TV advertisements. The law quickly became the butt of jokes. As *Le Monde* announced (in French-inflected English), "Mr. Minister, you've committed an idiocy." The Constitutional Council mostly agreed, ruling that the state could not dictate the use of language to private citizens. The law's final version, far narrower in scope than Toubon's original proposal, led to the publication of a guide for French equivalents to commonly used American words and phrases, such as "*la remue-méninge*" for "brainstorming," "*micro coupé*" for "off the record," and "*restauration rapide*" for "fast food. " The guide was quickly dubbed *Le Toubon*.

As with the strikes, the issue of language made for odd political bedfellows. The leftist newspaper *Le Monde Diplomatique* sympathized with Toubon's concern, insisting that France had to stem the spread of *franglais*, which was little more than the stalking horse for American cultural imperialism. In fact, with the partial exception of television and films, very little American English had seeped into French. Moreover, as French linguists observed, seepage in itself was perfectly natural (given how much French seeped into English post 1066). New developments and technologies required new vocabulary. While the official term for email, *courriel*—an "el" for electronic was added to the end of *courier*, the French word for mail—was a reasonable neologism, most French people instead adapted the English word "email," but with a French twist based on their pronunciation. Called *mel*, it is a good example of the natural history of language. Nevertheless, like the miner's proverbial canary in the cage, the well-being of France's language, for many observers, reflected the well-being of its people.[4]

Chirac also chose to do battle on behalf of preserving French language outside of France by becoming a vocal supporter of the international movement known as *la francophonie*. The term "*francophonie*" was first coined by a French geographer, Onésisme Reclus (1837–1916), in 1880 to designate all countries and peoples where the French language was spoken. *La francophonie's* official organization, however, was founded on March 20, 1970, in Niamey, the capital of Niger, when the representatives of 21 francophone countries, under the leadership of four heads of states of formerly French colonies—Léopold Sédar Senghor of Senegal, Habib Bourguiba of Tunisia, Hamani Diori of Niger, and Prince Norodom Sihanouk of Cambodia—signed a Convention creating the Cultural and Technical Cooperation Agency. The Agency's aim was to promote and diffuse the cultures of its francophone members and to "intensify cultural and technical cooperation amongst them." At a time when the formal bonds of empire had dissolved, francophone African leaders were interested in continuing cultural and educational exchanges with France and each other, and France was determined to maintain cultural as well as economic influence in its former colonies. In subsequent decades, the movement shifted orientation, taking as one of its slogans "Unity in diversity" and standing for democracy and human rights as well as the promotion of the French language worldwide.[5] Since 1986 the heads of all member states have met biannually to promote the use and spread of the French language and francophone cultural pluralism, as an alternative to the domination of English and the global spread of American mass culture. In 2009 the International Organization of La Francophonie (Organisation Internationale de la Francophonie or OIF) had 56 member states, some of whom had only tiny—or indeed no—communities of French speakers. The OIF claims to represent 2 million French speakers worldwide.

While support for *la francophonie* was already important under Mitterrand, Chirac moved responsibility for it from the Ministry of Culture to the Ministry of Foreign Affairs, thus making defense of the French language a critical part of his foreign policy. Although fluent in English himself, having lived as a student in the United States, Chirac began refusing to speak anything but French while abroad, including during official visits to America, and France regularly began providing two-thirds of the OIF's budget.[6] Active state support of *la francophonie* was (and is still) accepted by the majority of French as a self-evident need to protect their language and identity in a world that threatens to be taken over by English.

Yet another example of fear about the future of a specifically French identity surfaced in the panic over *la vache folle,* or mad cow disease (BSE, or bovine spongiform encephaly). In early 1996, the British government announced that several deaths in Britain were attributable to a previously unknown disease contracted by eating tainted beef. Barely controlled panic ensued—after all, the disease had infected nearly 200,000 British cattle—and the European Union banned all British meat exports. As with *franglais,* the popular perception in France of *la vache folle* in French bore little relation to reality: Only 30 infected French cows were found.

Still, the revelation that French farmers had used tainted grain feed set ablaze the gathering tinder of confusion and fear. *Le Canard Enchaîné* pounced at the chance to tie the issues of language and food purity. On the front page, the editors appropriately misquoted Hamlet: "Tout beef or not tout beef?"[7] French farmers were not amused. Cattle herds were slaughtered in many regions as the consumption of beef dropped drastically. The state responded with full compensation for farmers forced to slaughter their herds, a reminder of the reflexive attachment the French still felt for their countryside. Meanwhile, the feared epidemic hinted darkly at the implications of a united Europe and the cost of merging national traditions and practices into a global system.

But if there were costs to European integration, there were also new opportunities. Just as the siege of Paris in 1870–1871 led to the invention of the tradition of the neighborhood horse-butcher, so too did this new "biological" siege of France in 1996 lead to the reaffirmation, and at times reinvention, of another tradition: the gastronomic *retour au pays,* or return to the land. The food scares reinvigorated rural policy in France and reinforced the practice and allure of local products certified with the label AOC or Controlled Regional Appellation (Appellation d'Origine Contrôlée).[8] The dairy and beef sectors began the practice of certifying products that had previously been associated only with French wine and cheese. There was a similar movement among bakers. In 1990, an outspoken baker, Raymond Calvel, declared that the baguette "is not as appreciated as much as it should be. If bakers do not react, we shall find ourselves facing the following paradox: a French baguette sold in Tokyo will be better than the one sold in Paris." Confronted by the rise of industrial baking practices and wholesalers, militant artisans like Calvel reemphasized regional baking traditions and alternative grains that can be traced to their soil.[9] While the baguette itself was a recently invented tradition, artisans, not industrial firms, were responsible for its creation. Calvel's use of France's iconic bread points to the central role bread has played in French social life.

La malbouffe, a neologism for bad food and bad eating habits, was coined to reflect the preoccupation with the threat to French cuisine of hormone-inflated beef and tasteless bread. Though not always made explicit, denunciations of corrupted foods and farming practices went hand in hand with denunciations of America. The most striking instance of French militancy occurred in August 1999, when José Bové, who had played a leading role in the sheep farmers' protests at Larzac 20 years before, led a group of commandos into Millau, a small city in the Aveyron. They swarmed over a half-completed McDonald's restaurant, literally dismantled it, and dumped the pieces in the city square. "It was a beautiful day," Bové recalls, "everyone was having a good time and many people ended up on the terraces of Millau's restaurants."[10] When the police arrested Bové, he won worldwide notoriety, his thick moustache briefly as notorious as the golden arches of the McDonald's he had just demolished.

Though not related to food, Chirac's decision to end mandatory military service in 2001 also turned on the question of nation and citizenship. Up until then, every young, able-bodied French man had to decide whether to fulfill his one year of required military service or waive it by choosing a lengthier public service alternative. Universal military service had been fundamental to republicanism ever since the 1792 *levée en masse* (mass conscription) and was a constant source of friction between republican leaders and the more elite, conservative, even anti-republican officer corps. But by the turn of the twenty-first century, new military technology rendered useless a citizen's army strong in numbers but weak in training. Chirac's decision to end universal military service did not generate much attention, since most families were relieved, but it profoundly changed the life pattern of most young men. Chirac's move was thus not only a nod to de Gaulle's controversial interwar proposal for a professional army—one that the general decided not to implement when he became president in 1958—but also a gesture to public opinion, long weary of the military service. But for many it deepened, rather than answered, the question of what it meant to be French.

THE LEFT(S) STRIKE BACK

To the relief of serious bread-lovers, Juppé's government eventually established legal criteria for *boulangeries* (bakeries). (According to the law, an authentic bakery is where the baker oversees every step of the process of bread making.) It was not as easy, however, to address France's economic woes. In power for two years, the Juppé government by spring 1997 was caught in a web of union strikes, political corruption scandals—one involving the mayor of Paris, Jean Tiberi, that seemed to implicate both the prime minister and president—and widespread disillusionment over the state's inability to improve employment figures. Given this turn of events, observers expected the government to hunker down and try to weather the storm.

Instead, Chirac stunned France when, in early spring of 1997, he dissolved the National Assembly and called for new elections. His motivations were mysterious, but the consequences were disastrous for the Right, which lost nearly half of its 465 seats. At the same time, the Left returned to power with a majority of 320 seats. Yet the Left was far from unified. It was dominated by a resurgent Socialist Party (Parti Socialiste or PS), led by Lionel Jospin, the party secretary who had begun his professional career as a professor of economics and capitalized on an aura of simplicity, honesty, and decency—qualities that the fallen Juppé government hardly seemed to represent. But a gaggle of other parties, including the Greens, headed by Dominique Voynet, and a splinter party, formed by Jean-Pierre Chévènement, called the Citizen's Movement, allied with the PS, forming the so-called *gauche plurielle* (plural Left), and were now expected to share power.

On the Right, there was equal confusion. As the mainstream Gaullist RPR collapsed, the FN maintained its strength. Le Pen's party won nearly 15 percent, repeating its strong showing in 1994. Its success led to a divisive debate among the mainstream politicians on the Right over whether, and to what degree, they should cooperate with Le Pen. Refusing any kind of rapprochement with Le Pen, Chirac was left with no choice but to cooperate with the victorious Left. In the same position he had forced Mitterrand into 10 years before, Chirac asked the leader of the opposition, Lionel Jospin, to form a government. In a firm nod to gender equality, eight women ministers were brought on board, including Elizabeth Guigou as attorney general, Dominique Voynet at Environment, and Martine Aubry at Employment. Aubry's appointment was perhaps the most significant. The daughter of Jacques Delors and graduate of the ENA, Aubry had quickly climbed the ranks of the state hierarchy, serving in the ill-starred Cresson and Bérègovoy cabinets. A highly visible and eloquent opponent of the FN, Aubry cared deeply about the plight of *les exclus*. In 1993, Aubry founded the Foundation to Act against Exclusion (Fondation pour Agir contre l'Exclusion). While she acknowledged the limits of traditional forms of interventionism, Aubry faulted the Republic for falling short in its duties to its poorest citizens.[11]

Aubry's determination to modernize socialist politics and governance— coined as "politics in a new key"—reflected Jospin's own temperament. In a sense, the 60-year-old socialist was the accidental prime minister; not only did the elections come as a surprise, but Jospin's lack of charisma did not promise a brilliant political career. Yet this very lack of flair, combined with his intellectual gifts and aura of decency, counted for a great deal with an electorate thoroughly dispirited by the raft of corruption scandals, the persistence of high unemployment, and the growing divide between the haves and have-nots. Jospin set out to become a "conscious creator of post-socialism," determined to build upon Mitterrand's successes and correct his mistakes.[12]

With Aubry at his side, Jospin revived strategic elements of the discredited socialist program of 1981. This was not surprising, given the Right's lackluster laissez-faire approach, as well as Jospin's conviction that the state must play a central role in the nation's economic life. Yet he insisted that France's economic problems could not be solved at the national level, but only in a European context. To the relief of his fellow European leaders, Jospin announced his intention to abide by the economic and financial dictates of the European Monetary System; since all of Europe shared France's unemployment woes, European-wide solutions were necessary. Yet Jospin jiggled the details and mobilized the French state's hefty resources. Led by Aubry's ministry, the government introduced a program with a goal, only partly realized, of creating 150,000 temporary jobs for unemployed youths. In his most controversial and dramatic policy, in 1997 Jospin, again working closely with Aubry, reduced the workweek to 35 hours.

Jospin hoped that the shorter workweek would create new job opportunities; his critics feared that it would hobble French industry in the global economy. In the 35-hour rule's most controversial aspect, a worker's pay would not be reduced along with her hours. In this regard, Jospin found himself caught between a rock— the unions, which refused to accept a salary reduction—and a hard place—the employers, who were hostile to the notion of paying for hours not worked. This dilemma resulted in a series of negotiations that made the law impossibly complex for most workers or employers. In the end, both sides claimed vindication. The government estimated that during the course of five years more than 350,000 jobs were created as the result of the 35-hour workweek. Conservative critics both dismissed these claims as exaggerated and, more importantly, argued that the law not only undermined economic growth, but also cost taxpayers billions of francs in various subsidies to employers to compensate their losses.[13] Perhaps the only issue both sides agreed on was Jospin's happy timing. The early months of his government corresponded to an upturn in the French economy, fueled by rising levels of exports and foreign investment in French industries.

Like his conservative predecessor, Jospin also confronted issues that posed the questions of what it meant to be French, and what it meant to be France, at the approach of the new millennium. The 1993 Pasqua Law's changes to citizenship for children of immigrants were revoked in 1998, making citizenship automatic again. Also in 1998, Elisabeth Guigou proposed legislation creating the Civil Solidarity Pact (Pacte Civil de Solidarité or PACS), a form of civil union providing unmarried couples with many of the rights, ranging from tax breaks to pension benefits, enjoyed by married heterosexual couples. Though the bill applied to unmarried heterosexual couples, attention focused on homosexual couples who would also benefit from the law. Just two years before, in 1996, the annual Lesbian and Gay Pride march in Paris, which attracted more than 100,000 participants, marked an important stage in public recognition. Religious and family organizations mobilized against the law, taking to the streets in counter-marches, while conservatives held up the bill in the Assembly. In 1999, however, the socialist majority finally passed a modified bill that was duly signed into law.

Parity, the term that refers to required gender parity in wages and political representation, proved equally contentious. Like the PACS, parity reopened the traditional schism between religious and lay groups; it also sparked objections from some on the Left worried about the republican principles of universality, indivisibility, and equality among all citizens. Again led by Guigou, the government plunged into the struggle for gender parity. Her ministry revised those constitutional articles the Constitutional Council had cited in earlier ruling against the parity law; it was now specified that men *and* women must have equal access to elected office. The revised parity law gained bipartisan support in the Assembly. Women on the Right, like Simone Veil, and the Left, like Edith Cresson—both veterans of earlier gender battles—applauded the proposed law. Yet other women raised hard questions. Prominent intellectual Elisabeth Badinter—married to Robert Badinter, former minister of justice under Mitterrand—maintained her earlier opposition: "[T]he ideology of quotas," she wrote, "creates sordid and humiliating calculations." Reminiscent of "affirmative action," parity represented, in the end, yet one more victory for Americanization. At the same time, Lionel Jospin's partner, philosopher Sylviane Agacinski, argued that a rigid interpretation of the republican credo of universalism blind to gender or racial differences was a mystification, a sham. Pretending that discrimination did not exist and refusing to acknowledge it only perpetuated existing inequalities.

In the end, the overwhelming majority that favored the law passed it in 1999. While the parity law's immediate effects were mixed—the number of women mayors remained disappointingly low even if the number of women councilors at the level of commune reached nearly 50 percent in 2001—the vote for parity has rightly been described as "transformative."[14] Not only did France become the first

European country to legislate equal political access, but the law also revealed a new and broader understanding of France's traditional universalist ideology. Parity and the PACS did not undermine the Republic, but instead shaped a new consensus on republican ideals.

ABROAD AT HOME

France's willingness to recognize the "right to difference" started not with reference to personal identity but to France's regions. Thus a big disappointment was the continuation of violent regional politics, in particular in Corsica. During the Mitterrand era, France had been the target of sporadic but persistent terrorist attacks, most often the work of Islamic extremists, as well as fringe revolutionary groups like Direct Action. These bombings intensified the debate over immigration and assimilation. But Corsican terrorists who demanded independence from France were the greatest source of violence on the island. The unrelenting bombings and shootings had created an exodus of "French" residents from the economically and politically troubled island. The troubles reached a crescendo soon after Jospin took office, when in February 1998, Corsican militants assassinated the republican prefect, Claude Erignac. The murder galvanized the state. Chevènement, serving as interior minister, again mobilized the rhetoric of the indivisible Republic to suppress the Corsican threat to a unitary France.

Yet police actions alone could not repair the situation. On the one hand, Chevènement cited overwhelming public support on the mainland, as well as in Corsica, for his actions. While 25 percent of the island's electorate had voted for nationalist parties or the secessionist Corsica Nazione in the 1999 elections, the remaining 75 percent gave their votes to parties that wished to keep Corsica within France. On the other hand, a minority, if bloody-minded and determined enough, often carries the day. It was clear that only a political solution would reconcile the opposing tendencies. In a series of moves, including a controversial announcement that he favored the 1992 European charter that promoted the use of regional languages (like Corsican), Jospin worked to find common ground among the various factions. At the end of 1999, he convened a summit with all the political factions, with the expectation that the discussions would lead to an enhanced form of autonomy for Corsica.

Perhaps inevitably, this prospect outraged not just many on the Right, who preferred the example of Spain's refusal to deal with its own Basque terrorists, but also a significant number of those within the plural Left. Chevènement resigned in protest, while commentators like Jacques Attali, who had served as Mitterrand's spokesperson, warned about the "Europeanization" of traditional nation-states like France, which now seemed in the process of becoming "a large Belgium, or worse still, a small Russia."[15] Historian Emmanuel LeRoy Ladurie, whose book *Montaillou* had inadvertently fueled the romance of Provençal regionalism in the 1970s, shared these fears. How can the supporters of Corsican independence cite the Declaration of the Rights of Man, he wondered, when their goal would trample on the rights of the overwhelming majority of Corsicans who wanted to remain a part of France?

While France remained in some ways unsure how to reconcile its unitary vision of itself as a Republic with its increasingly multicultural population, one event suggested a world of new possibilities. Surprisingly, it was a sporting event that pointed to a new understanding of a Republic united. France hosted the soccer World Cup in 1998, but few people expected much of the home team, *les bleus* (the blues). The media expressed the widespread skepticism over the players' desire to win—a critique that sometimes carried racist undertones. Many of the players hailed from francophone Africa and the Caribbean, while the team's star, Zinédine Zidane, was born into a family of Algerian Berber immigrants living in a *banlieue* of Marseilles. Yet *les bleus* hurdled one obstacle after another, making it to the final game against the heavily favored Brazilian team. In a remarkable match at a new stadium built just for this event, the Stadium of France (Stade de France) just outside Paris, *les bleus* defeated Brazil 3-0 to win the title.

The nation immediately erupted in celebration and, France being France, intellectuals and politicians presented the team as a metaphor for a new plural France. For a moment, the nation had seen one possible future: a multicultural one that worked in new hues. In a play on the national colors of blue-white-red, as the French refer to their tricolored flag (and which were emblazoned on *les bleus'* jerseys), team members and columnists alike embraced the slogan *black-blanc-beur* (black-white-Arab) after the 1998 victory. A similar vision of plural identity was echoed five years later in a pioneering July 2003 exposition in honor of Bastille Day. Fourteen gigantic portraits of French women, from varied ethnic backgrounds but all adorned with the symbols of the French Republic, appeared on the pillars of the National Assembly—an exposition tellingly called "The Mariannes of Today."[16]

INTELLECTUALS: THE REASON FOR THE CLERKS?

By the twentieth century's end, French intellectuals wondered if France's future reserved a place for a new Zola, Barrès, or Maurras, their ancestors who had burst onto the national stage at the beginning of the same century. Did this new fin-de-siècle, marked by the rise of a global economy and decline of traditional ideologies and perhaps even the nation-state, signal the end of the intellectual? Already, during the first years of the Mitterrand era, French intellectuals had seemed to reach an impasse. On the one hand, there was dissatisfaction over the political status quo—a situation that, for critics, reflected *la pensée unique* (one-track thinking), the derogatory term they gave to the sway that a free market and laissez-faire economics seemed to hold over the humbled French state. In an editorial in *Le Monde* in 1983, a government spokesperson, Max Gallo, decried the "silence of the intellectuals of the Left." Gallo was not hard of hearing; support among intellectuals for the increasingly embattled socialists was tepid. The many responses ignited by Gallo's appeal revealed that intellectuals had grown dubious about traditional ideals on the Left, as well as the desirability or ability of the state to influence economic or cultural issues.

The dilemma can be stated as follows. For the first three quarters of the century, Left and Right "were the terms in which intellectuals defined themselves. . . . The very idea of an intellectual who did not think in these terms . . . seemed a contradiction in terms."[17] But many intellectuals found themselves unsure what to do when, under the weight of historical events like the collapse of the Berlin Wall, the unraveling of the Soviet Empire, and communist China's love affair with the free market, these categories disintegrated. To some intellectuals, the era marked the end of ideologies, if not history itself. Emblematic of this confusion was the publication in 1997 of *Le livre noir du communisme* (*The Black Book of Communism*). A collection of rich but uncontroversial historical essays on communism, the book's editor, historian Stéphane Courtois, caused a sensation with his introduction. He argued not only that Leninism and Stalinism were two peas in an ideological pod—a notion that the Left had more or less already accepted—but that communism was indistinguishable from Nazism. Both ideologies, he stated, were genocidal and totalitarian. This claim, of course, was more difficult to accept by a generation who had either fought Nazism because they were committed communists or had long been attracted to the utopian ideals of communism. The book became a bestseller in France, and the subsequent storm of controversy it created among intellectuals indicated that, though confused about their status, their confusion was at least able to command the public's attention.

Not surprisingly, Courtois appeared on French television personality Bernard Pivot's weekly show devoted to books and ideas, *Bouillon de culture,* which loosely translated means "cultural soup" (the term *bouillon* also has a slang meaning, "a mouthful"). Like Pivot's earlier television show *Apostrophes,* which ran from 1975 to 1990, *Bouillon de culture* was tremendously successful, pulling in an audience of 11 million viewers.[18] Yet this very success was part of the problem. Watching artists and intellectuals chat had become more popular than reading their books. In a sense, Pivot's show was symptomatic of another cause of the decline of the intellectual. By the century's end, television and, increasingly, the Internet, had overwhelmed the traditional bastion of intellectual activity, the print media, and in the process undermined the older ways of legitimating and maintaining a clearly defined category of intellectuals.

Pierre Bourdieu, the era's most powerful critic of the distorting power of the electronic media, nevertheless conquered it. Until his death in 2002, he was France's last great intellectual. Bourdieu weighed the consequences of a "mediatized" culture that confers power on those with the best ratings, not the best analysis. Though a maverick, Bourdieu was also a throwback of sorts. Intellectuals alone, he argued, could legitimate themselves. Public opinion, manipulated by the electronic media, must play no role. At the same time, Bourdieu became increasingly active on behalf of society's *exclus;* he supported, as we have seen, the 1995 strikes against Juppé's efforts at modernization, and in 1998 became the public voice for the newly created Movement of the Unemployed. When in 1998 protestors took over the elite Ecole Normale Supérieure—the alma mater of many leading socialists—Bourdieu hailed them as a "social miracle." In a speech he gave at the school, he praised their actions, which had pulled "the unemployed, and with them all insecure workers, whose numbers increase daily, out of invisibility, isolation, silence, in short, out of non-existence."[19]

THE REPUBLIC IN DANGER

Bourdieu's death in early 2002 deprived France of his badly needed critical voice as it experienced a series of difficult political events. President Chirac had successfully changed the constitution, reducing the president's term of office, meaning his own term, from seven to five years. Thus France went to the polls in the spring of 2002 to elect a new president. In the first round of voting in April, France shocked itself and the world when the incumbent president, Jacques Chirac, came in first, but won scarcely 20 percent of the vote. While this was a dismal approval rating, even more sobering for many French citizens, socialist Lionel Jospin, whom most people expected to contest Chirac in the second round, was knocked out of the running by Jean Marie Le Pen, leader of the far Right FN, who won nearly 17 percent of the vote. Le Pen's second place finish launched an avalanche of analyses and soul-searching. French commentators sought to understand how France's radical Right candidate found his way into the final round of the presidential elections. Some thought Jospin's dry personality, and the mistaken belief of many socialist supporters that his victory was inevitable, led many socialist voters to stay at home that day—voter turnout was relatively low—or cast a protest vote for clearly marginal candidates like Noël Mamère of the Greens. Others concluded that Jospin's efforts to straddle the political and economic tensions between a liberal Europe and socialist France disillusioned too many voters on the Left. Yet others argued that the system, far from failing, worked all too well: The function of the first round of voting, after all, was to allow the voters to express their preferences.

In the end, Le Pen's second place finish clearly revealed that the mainstream political parties had failed to respond to a stubborn belief on the part of nearly one-fifth of the French people that forces from within, like the Muslim community, and without, like the European Union, threatened their country. As with the Dreyfus Affair, France's dramatic economic, demographic, and social transformations stirred anxiety as well as anticipation. The FN picked up several of the themes of earlier xenophobic and reactionary movements and found an audience eager for a firewall against these "anti-French" forces. Just as Barrès and Maurras in the previous fin-de-siècle had identified the Jews as a "nation within a nation" incapable of assimilation, Le Pen insisted that Muslims were equally resistant to integration and endangered "the essential nature of the French people."[20]

The choice left many of the electorate in a quandary. On the one hand, a sitting president suspected of violating campaign fundraising laws while mayor of Paris and despised by the Left, and an increasing number on the Right, now faced off against a racist, rabble-rousing populist. What to do? Chirac deliberately invoked the politics of republican defense, and the public responded in kind. From across the ideological spectrum, political parties, student organizations, professional unions, intellectuals, and the media concluded that the Republic was in danger. Leading figures warned that *not* voting, that refusing to choose between the two men was the worst choice of all. The public agreed. With grim determination, an overwhelming majority of French rallied to Chirac. In the second round of voting, in early May, more than four-fifths of the electorate cast their vote for the sitting president. In many cases, a vote for Chirac really represented a vote against Le Pen, even for some voters who had flirted with the FN. The Republic had survived, but it did not triumph.

Nevertheless, Le Pen had his revenge. During the second round of campaigning, most mainstream political parties had rallied to Chirac, leaving the veteran politician free from having to define his platform and detail the goals of his second term. But once elected, Chirac, forced to acknowledge the contrary currents in public opinion that the election made clear, created a cabinet at odds with itself. On the one hand, Chirac asked Jean-Pierre Raffarin to form a new government. Low-key and reassuring—Raffarin had helped lead the battle for authentic French bread—he promised a gentler and kinder Republic. On the other hand, Chirac appointed Nicholas Sarkozy as minister of the interior.

While he himself was the son of immigrants—his father was Hungarian, his mother was a Greek Jew—Sarkozy represented the republican Right. His appointment satisfied those on the Right who called for a strong, if not authoritarian, Republic that would guarantee security and respect. A number of critics claimed that Sarkozy, even more than the earlier minister who had pushed through changes to nationality law, Charles Pasqua, pandered to the FN voter. Certainly, like Le Pen, Sarkozy ran against the political establishment. Instead of graduating from the elite administration school (ENA), Sarkozy scrambled up the ladder of the RPR by virtue of sheer energy, skill, and ambition. He also employed, though to a lesser degree than Le Pen, language that smacked of racism. For example, Sarkozy opposed Turkey's joining the EU, citing the incompatibility of its Muslim population with European values. Sarkozy also argued that the French census, which famously did not use racial and religious criteria, should begin including such factors as race. Finally, in 2007, he called for the creation of a Ministry of Immigration and National Identity—a title that had unfortunate echoes of the Vichy regime.

It must be noted, however, that Sarkozy balanced such provocations with equally energetic efforts to give France's "visible minorities" greater institutional voice. He established the French Council for the Muslim Religion, insisted upon the appointment of the first Muslim prefect, and declared that France would be well served by adopting elements of the American practice of "positive discrimination," the French term for affirmative action, to improve the lot of French ethnic minorities. This openness to affirmative action was the principal reason behind Sarkozy's desire to include the category of race in the French census. Sarkozy underscored his rejection of the FN, affirmed his Gaullist identity, and argued that his own family background was evidence of the Republic's ability to turn immigrants

Librairie Sana, Islamic bookstore in Paris, 2009. Photograph courtesy of Paul Silverstein.

into Frenchmen and Frenchwomen. Sarkozy cited as his heroes Jean Jaurès and Léon Blum—two names that have never been uttered, except in scorn, by Le Pen.[21]

By May 2007, Sarkozy had parlayed his notoriety as Chirac's minister of interior to the presidency, winning the election against France's first ever female presidential candidate, Ségolène Royale. Thus the 2007 presidential election, pitting the half-Jewish son of immigrants against a woman, signified that France's gender and ethnicity-blind republican universalism in fact had space for multiculturalism. Once in office, Sarkozy continued to cross left-right boundaries in his own form of triangulation, balancing conservative economic and public order policies with the appointment of people like Bernard Kouchner, leader of Doctors without Borders, as foreign minister and Fadela Amara, feminist activist and advocate for impoverished women living in the *banlieues*, as secretary of state for urban policies.

FREEDOM FRIES

Even prior to his presidency, Sarkozy came in for a great deal of criticism for his unabashed admiration for the United States—yet another position foreign to the French populist tradition. Yet he had fully supported the position of Jacques Chirac and his Foreign Minister Dominique de Villepin—as well as the great majority of French—opposing the American effort beginning in 2002 to mobilize its allies for the war in Iraq. France's position, at the outset, was clear, since it insisted that all international discussions and actions had to proceed under the auspices of the United Nations (UN), which had passed a resolution sending arms inspector Hans Blix to Iraq in November 2002. With equal consistency, France insisted during the spring of 2003 that strong evidence for Saddam Hussein's weapons of mass destruction had to exist in order for the UN to pass a second resolution authorizing war against Iraq. This evidence never materialized, nor did French support for U.S. President George W. Bush's decision to invade Iraq.

In the end, France's position illustrated its obstinate tendency to maintain its "exceptional" status in global diplomacy. While time revealed the wisdom of Chirac's position—his motivations may have been complex, but he rightly and repeatedly pointed out that war, always the worst answer to a crisis, inevitably leads to unforeseen and possibly worse consequences—it also unleashed a reflexive anti-French sentiment in the United States. France's reaction to yet another instance of American domination in world affairs was no less reflexive, however. American disdain for France's perceived grandstanding and U.S. Defense Secretary Donald Rumsfeld's dismissal of France as "old Europe" was matched by the French conviction that it had to lead a European stand against American "hyperpower." Still, while Chirac's position was supported by more than 90 percent of the French, his position did not truly represent a serious revival of Gaullist independence in foreign policy. In the end, internal divisions over Iraq paralyzed the EU. At the same time, France's inability to dissuade the United States from going to war emphasized the imperative of acting in concert with the rest of Europe.[22]

Less inspiring was Chirac's handling of the Treaty on the European Constitution. Signed by the 25 members of the EU in 2004, the draft presented a closer integration of member states and required ratification in each and every state. As with his dissolution of parliament in 1997, Chirac miscalculated. Rather than submitting the treaty to Parliament, he instead decided to ask the French electorate to ratify it. Far from the easy "yes" vote he anticipated—which, in the Gaullist tradition, would also serve as symbol of personal popularity—the referendum quickly became controversial. It attracted a growing number of critics who, not surprisingly, cut across party and ideological lines, ranging from the far Left—which considered the treaty a capitalist instrument—to the extreme Right, which denounced the dilution of national sovereignty. Between these extremes were a good number of republicans, moderates, and socialists who worried over the constitution's complexity and what had come to be known as the "democratic deficit": the lack of popular accountability for the institutions and bureaucrats the treaty would establish and empower in Brussels.

On May 25, 2005, nearly 55 percent of French voters rejected the treaty. The results sent tremors across the continent. Other member states of the EU postponed their own referendums, forcing many political leaders to review their options. In France, the consequences were equally dramatic. Chirac's diminished standing was further battered; according to a poll in *Le Figaro,* only 18 percent supported Chirac's policies. Though Chirac shuffled his cabinet, replacing Raffarin with Villepin, the final 18 months of his presidency unfolded under the shadow of this defeat. Cast as the Republic's last hope in 2002, Chirac now seemed doomed to be remembered as little more than the puppet caricaturing him on one of France's most popular television shows, *Les guignols de l'info* (literally, *The Marionette Evening News*), in which ridiculous puppets parody various current political leaders. From the clueless but energetic and vaguely nice character he had been a few years before, the Chirac puppet now often appeared in a Superman costume with "SM," for *Super Menteur*, or Super Liar, splashed across his chest. There was a growing chorus of "Ten years is enough"—which had last echoed along Paris streets in 1968, aimed at Charles de Gaulle. In the summer of 2005, the socialist weekly *Le Nouvel Observateur* seemed to speak for men and women across the political spectrum: "What will remain of the Chirac years? Nothing or almost nothing! Neither grand design as with de Gaulle, nor grand projects as with Mitterrand. We will only take note of his resistance to Bush during the Iraq war and the controversial recognition . . . of the French State's responsibility during the Occupation. It doesn't amount to much."[23]

FRANCE TODAY

Historians will, of course, debate this harsh epitaph. At the time, though, grim assessments seemed justified. At the climax of the World Cup between Italy and France in July 2006, *les bleus*—who had failed to win a single game in the 2002 tournament—stumbled badly as the game drew to a close. With the score tied, Zinédine Zidane, the hero of France's victory in the same event in 1998, deliberately drove his skull into the chest of a defending Italian played who had provoked him with insults. Zidane was ejected from the game, which France went on to lose in overtime.

This time around, there was no outpouring of pride in the national media, much less claims for *les bleus* as a model for French society—at least, a model to be emulated. The team's collapse seemed to mirror not only the country's disillusionment with Chirac but also a brutal eruption of violence in the social arena. In the summer of 2006, France was still reeling from riots that had engulfed its forsaken suburbs in 2005. These riots were sparked by the accidental death of two youths in the desolate Paris suburb of Clichy-sous-Bois. Fleeing the police, Zyed Benna and Bouna Traoré climbed into a power substation and electrocuted themselves. For the next several weeks, the housing projects for the poor that surround Paris and other major cities became battlefields between protesting youths and French security forces.

In November 2005, with the government unable to master events, the National Assembly gave extraordinary powers to Sarkozy's Ministry of Interior to search, question, and arrest citizens, as well as impose curfews and press censorship. The law, as many critics noted, had first been enacted in 1955 to deal with the growing unrest in Algeria, and had since been used just twice before in metropolitan France (both occasions during the Algerian War) and once in New Caledonia in the wake of the 1984 uprising. For many commentators, these actions seem to point to a

Low income housing in Aubervilliers. Photograph courtesy of Paul Silverstein.

continuing logic of colonial rule within post-colonial France. Perhaps equally telling was Sarkozy's language. During a visit to suburban Argenteuil, which had been
swept by the violence, the minister declared his determination to rid France of
"*la racaille*," or "rabble," which had claimed the streets. The remark—instantly
broadcast around the world and unanimously condemned—was a far cry from the
black-blanc-beur vision of a tolerant France that had seemed genuinely possible in
1998. Sarkozy's revealing slip was part of a confusing set of discourses vis-à-vis
France's "others" that emerged in 2005.

On the other side, in an indication that perhaps France was ready to include
the "excluded," the Académie Française, long a conservative bastion of French
males, welcomed its newest "immortal," francophone Algerian historian and novelist Assia Djebar. In her official address, Djebar dwelt on the significance of the
Academy's decision to welcome an Algerian woman into its ranks. She did not
mince her words. For her ancestors, the experience of colonialism had left an
"immense wound," and she expressed her stupor over a law recently sponsored by
a small group of conservative deputies, requiring high schools to teach the "positive role" of French colonialism. An "inattentive" National Assembly had passed
the law in 2005, but repealed it the following year in the wake of a public outcry.
Djebar noted France's destructive impact not just on Algeria's native peoples, Arab
and Berber, but also on their languages, "devalued" and excluded from the official
curriculum.

Yet, at the same time, she confessed, the "French language became my own."
Adopting a phrase from the Enlightenment thinker Denis Diderot, Djebar declared
that French—and, by extension, France—places her "à la fois au-dehors et au-dedans":

Paris, Seine River at dusk, 2008. Photograph by Sarah Fishman.

"simultaneously outside and inside." On the one hand, Djebar bears the scars of a tangled and violent history; on the other hand, she has benefited from its presence. Decrying the blindness and inhumanity of the colonial enterprise, she also praised the many French teachers and thinkers who, along with her Algerian mentors, shaped her intellect and character: from her grade school teacher who recited Baudelaire, to a university professor who taught Descartes, to the ethnographer of Algeria and legendary member of the Resistance, Germaine Tillion, whose professional research and personal ethics underscored the necessity of dialogue among peoples. So many French individuals, she concluded, have helped to create this "space for my meditation and dreams . . . my utopia, perhaps."[24]

Utopia does not exist; by definition, it is "no place." Republics, however, have and continue to exist; by definition, they are "the public thing." The five French Republics have all represented complex and contradictory struggles to create societies based on universal and humane values. That these efforts have never been fully successful is clear; perhaps they never will be. Yet many individuals and movements inspired by these same ideals have struggled to make them real. The history of modern France, from one Republic to another, and from imperial practice to post-imperial soul-searching, is a history of women and men living their lives according to a certain understanding of France. The task of historians of modern France is to follow Djebar and Tillion and to consider matters from outside and inside of the Republic's many—and still shifting—boundaries.

Abbreviations

AEF Afrique Equatoriale Française/French Equatorial Africa

AOF Afrique Occidentale Française/French West Africa

CFDT Confédération Française Démocratique du Travail/French Democratic Confederation of Labor

CFLN Comité Français de Libération Nationale/French Committee of National Liberation

CFTC Confédération Française des Travailleurs Chrétiens/French Confederation of Christian Workers

CGP Commissariat Général du Plan

CGT Confédération Générale du Travail/General Confederation of Labor

CGTU Confédération Générale du Travail Unitaire/General Unified Confederation of Labor

CNPF Conseil National du Patronat Français/National Council of French Employers

CNR Conseil National de la Résistance/National Resistance Council

CO Comité d'Organisation/Organization Committee

CRS Compagnies Républicaines de Sécurité/Republican Security Units

ECSC European Coal and Steel Community

EDC European Defense Community

EEC European Economic Community

ENA Ecole Nationale d'Administration/National Administration School

EU European Union

FHAR Front Homosexuel d'Action Révolutionnaire/Homosexual Front for Revolutionary Action

FIS Front Islamique du Salut/Islamic Salvation Front

FLB Front de Libération de Bretagne/Brittany Liberation Front

FLN Front de Libération Nationale/National Liberation Front

FLNC Front de Libération Nationale de Corse/Corsican National Liberation Front

FN Front National/National Front

FTS Fédération des Travailleurs Socialistes/Federation of Socialist Workers

GND Government of National Defense

HLM Habitations à Loyer Modéré/Low-Cost Public Housing

JAC Jeunesse Agricole Chrétienne/Young Christian Farmers

JEC Jeunesse Etudiante Chrétienne/Young Christian Students

JOC Jeunesse Ouvrière Chrétienne/Young Christian Workers

JOCF Jeunesse Ouvrière Chrétienne Féminine/Young Christian Working Women

MLF Mouvement de Libération des Femmes/Movement for the Liberation of Women

MRP Mouvement Républicain Populaire/Popular Republican Movement

MUR Mouvements Unis de la Résistance/United Resistance Movement

NATO North Atlantic Treaty Organization

OAS Organisation de l'Armée Secrète/Secret Army Organization

OECD Organization for Economic Cooperation and Development

OIF Organisation Internationale de la Francophonie/International Organization of La Francophonie

ORTF Office de Radio-Diffusion-Télévision Française/Office of French Radio and Television Broadcasting

PACS Pacte Civile de Solidarité/Civil Solidarity Pact

PC Parti Communiste/Communist Party

PO Parti Ouvrier/Workers' Party

PPF Parti Populaire Français/French Popular Party

PS Parti Socialiste/Socialist Party

PSF Parti Social Français/French Social Party

RMI Revenu Minimum d'Insertion/Minimum Insertion Income

RPF Rassemblement du Peuple Français/Rally of the French People

RPR Rassemblement pour la République/Rally for the Republic

SFIO Section Française de l'Internationale Ouvrière/French Section of the Workingmen's International

SNCF Société Nationale des Chemins de Fer/National Railway Society

STO Service du Travail Obligatoire/Compulsory Work Service

TDF Télévision de France Television of France

UDB Union Démocratique Breton/Breton Democratic Union

UDCA Union de Défense des Commerçants et Artisans/Union to Defend Business Owners and Artisans

UDF Union pour la Démocratie Française/Union for French Democracy

UDR Union des Démocrates pour la République/Union of Democrats for the Republic

UNEF Union Nationale des Etudiants Français/National Union of French Students

UNR Union pour la Nouvelle République/Union for the New Republic

Notes

CHAPTER 1 THE EMBATTLED REPUBLICAN TRADITION: 1792–1870

1. Translation found at http://old.marseillaise.org/francais/english.html.
2. http://www.elysee.fr/elysee/anglais/the_institutions/founding_texts/the_declaration_of_the_human_rights/the_declaration_of_the_human_rights.20240.html.
3. Roderick Phillips, *Untying the Knot: A Short History of Divorce* (Cambridge, England: Cambridge University Press, 1991), pp. 58–62.
4. Linda S. Frey and Marsha L. Frey, *The French Revolution* (Westport, CT: Greenwood, 2004), pp. 52, 53.
5. Quoted in "Review" by Peter McPhee, Suzanne Desan, *The Family on Trial in Revolutionary France* (Berkeley: University of California Press, 2004), *H-France Review*, Vol. 5, no. 98 (Sept. 2005).
6. John Ruedy, *Modern Algeria: The Origins and Development of a Nation* (Bloomington: Indiana University Press, 1992), p. 52.
7. Karl Marx, *The Eighteenth of Brumaire,* http://www.archive.org/stream/theeighteenth-bru00marxuoft/theeighteenthbru00marxuoft_djvu.txt.
8. Alain Corbin, *The Village of Cannibals: Rage and Murder in France, 1870,* trans. Arthur Goldhammer (Cambridge, MA: Harvard University Press, 1992), pp. 35–36.
9. Raymond Huard, *La préhistoire des partis, le mouvement républicain en Bas-Languedoc* (Paris: Fondation Nationales des Sciences Politiques, 1982), pp. 143–145.
10. See Eugen Weber's "Who Sang the Marseillaise?" in *My France* (Cambridge, MA: Harvard University Press, 1992), p. 93.
11. Quoted in Ibid., p. 70.
12. T. J. Clark, *Image of the People: Gustave Courbet and the 1848 Revolution* (Berkeley: University of California Press, 1973).
13. Quoted from Edmond Goblot, *La barrière et le niveau. Etude sociologique de la bourgeoisie française moderne,* in Theodore Zeldin, *France 1848–1945: Ambition and Love* (Oxford: Oxford, 1979), pp. 15–16.
14. Norma Evenson, *Paris, A Century of Change: 1878–1978* (London and New Haven, CT: Yale University Press, 1979).

15. David Jordan, *Transforming Paris: The Life and Labors of Baron Haussmann* (Chicago: University of Chicago Press, 1995), p. 188.

16. Christophe Charle, *Histoire sociale de la France au XIXème siècle* (Paris: Seuil, 1991), p. 121.

17. See Theodore Zeldin, *France 1848–1945: Taste and Corruption* (Oxford: Oxford University Press, 1980), pp. 151–154.

18. Quoted in Alastair Horne, *The Fall of Paris: The Siege and the Commune 1870–1871* (London: Penguin, 1965), p. 46.

19. Ruedy, *Modern Algeria,* pp. 75–76.

20. Geoffrey Wawro, *The Franco-Prussian War: The German Conquest of France in 1870–1871* (Cambridge, England: Cambridge University Press, 2003), p. 22.

21. Quoted in Ibid., p. 17.

22. Quoted in Ibid., p. 19.

CHAPTER 2 L'ANNÉE TERRIBLE: 1870–1871

1. Gay Gullickson puts the number of volunteers at 1,500, while Alistair Horne writes that 15,000 women were said to have applied. See Gullickson, *Unruly Women of Paris* (Ithaca, NY: Cornell University Press, 1996), p. 100; and Horne, *The Fall of Paris* (New York: Penguin, 1965), p. 171.

2. Gullickson, *Unruly Women of Paris,* p. 149.

3. Ibid., p. 104.

4. Quoted in Carolyn Eichner, *Surmounting the Barricades: Women in the Paris Commune* (Bloomington: Indiana University Press, 2004), p. 36.

5. J. M. Thompson, *Louis Napoleon and the Second Empire* (New York: Noonday, 1955), p. 300.

6. See J. P. T. Bury and R. P. Tombs, *Thiers: 1797–1877* (London: Allen and Unwin, 1986).

7. Quoted in Geoffrey Wawro, *The Franco-Prussian War: The German Conquest of France in 1870–1871* (Cambridge, England: Cambridge University Press, 2003), p. 39.

8. Wolfgang Schivelbusch, *The Culture of Defeat,* trans. Jefferson Chase (New York, Henry Holt, 2003), pp. 102–104.

9. For the history of the anthem, see Michelle Vovelle, "La Marseillaise," in Pierre Nora, *Les Lieux de mémoire,* Vol. 1 (Paris: Gallimard, 1997).

10. Rupert Christiansen, *Paris Babylon* (New York: Viking, 1994), p. 140.

11. Quoted in Herbert Lottman, *Flaubert: A Biography* (New York: Fromm, 1989), p. 227.

12. Stéphane Audoin-Rouzeau, *1870: La France dans la guerre* (Paris: Armand Colin, 1989), p. 39.

13. Ibid., p. 23.

14. Eugen Weber, *Peasants into Frenchmen: The Modernization of Rural France* (Stanford, CA: Stanford University Press, 1976), p. 101.

15. Audoin-Rouzeau, *1870,* pp. 45–56; Weber, *Peasants into Frenchmen,* p. 103.

16. Michael Howard, *The Franco-Prussian War,* 2d ed. (London: Routledge, 2001), p. 3.

17. Ibid., p. 68.

18. Wawro, *The Franco-Prussian War,* p. 42.

19. Howard, *The Franco-Prussian War,* p. 33

20. See William Serman, "Les généraux français de 1870," in *Revue de défense nationale* (Août–Septembre 1970), pp. 1319–1330.
21. See Ibid., pp. 1319–1330.
22. Quoted in Howard, *The Franco-Prussian War*, pp. 133–134.
23. Emile Zola, *The Debacle* (London: Penguin Classics, 1973), p. 281.
24. *Paris under Siege, 1870–1871: From the Goncourt Journal*, ed. and trans. George Becker (Ithaca, NY: Cornell University Press, 1969), pp. 52–53.
25. René Rémond, *La vie politique en France* (Paris: Armand Colin, 1969), pp. 245–246.
26. See Schivelbusch, *Culture of Defeat*, pp. 109ff.
27. Audoin-Rouzeau, *1870*, p. 140.
28. Howard, *The Franco-Prussian War*, p. 285.
29. Ibid., p. 232.
30. *Goncourt Journal*, entry for August 28, 1870.
31. *Goncourt Journal*, entries for November 7, December 31, November 23, and December 8, 1870.
32. Bertrand Taithe, *Defeated Flesh: Medicine, Welfare, and Warfare in the Making of Modern France* (Lanham, MD: Rowman and Littlefied, 1999), p. 107.
33. *Goncourt Journal*, entry for January 13, 1871.
34. This is, in turn, the ingenious interpretation of Hollis Clayson in *Paris in Despair: Art and Everyday Life under Siege (1870–1871)* (Chicago: University of Chicago Press, 2002), p. 175.
35. For this interpretation, see the works of Gay Gullickson, Hollis Clayson, and Carolyn Eichner.
36. *Goncourt Journal*, entries for October 28, October 15, and December 10, 1870.
37. See Clayson, *Paris in Despair*, pp. 53ff.
38. Quoted in Ibid., p. 160.
39. Colmar von der Goltz, *The People under Arms*, quoted in Schivelbusch, *Culture of Defeat*, p. 9.
40. Robert Tombs, *The Paris Commune 1871* (London: Longman, 1999), p. 46.
41. Quoted in Wawro, *The Franco-Prussian War*, p. 279.
42. Quoted in Audoin-Rouzeau, *1870*, p. 295.
43. Quoted in Jean-Marie Mayeur and Madeleine Rebérioux, *The Third Republic from its Origins to the Great War*, trans. J. R. Foster (Cambridge, England: Cambridge University Press, 1987), p. 6.
44. Quoted in Bury and Tombs, *Thiers*, p. 197.
45. C. Allain, "Les conséquences de la défaite française de 1870 sur les relations inter-européenes," in *La guerre de 1870–1871 et ses conséquences* (Colloque Paris 1984–1985), quoted in Audoin-Rouzeau, *1870*, p. 316.
46. Quoted in Schivelbusch, *Culture of Defeat*, p. 114.
47. Vicomte de Meaux, quoted in Frederick Brown, *Zola: A Life* (New York: Farrar, Straus and Giroux, 1995), p. 211
48. The phrase is Michel Winock's. See *La fièvre hexagonale* (Paris: Seuil, 1986), p. 15.
49. Martin Phillip Johnson, *The Paradise of Association: Political Culture and Popular Organization in the Paris Commune of 1871* (Ann Arbor: University of Michigan Press, 1996), p. 83.
50. Quoted in Brown, *Zola*, p. 215.
51. Quoted in Ibid., p. 214.

52. *Goncourt Journal,* entry for March 20, 1871.
53. Henri Lefebvre, *La Proclamation de la Commune* (Paris: Gallimard, 1965), p. 390.
54. Roger Gould, quoted in Tombs, *The Paris Commune,* p. 27.
55. Quoted in Ibid., p. 2.
56. Karl Marx, *The Civil War in France* (International Publishers Co., 1988), p. 66.
57. Tombs, *The Paris Commune,* pp. 90–98.
58. Stewart Edwards, ed. *The Communards of Paris* (Ithaca, NY: Cornell University Press, 1973), p. 169.
59. *Goncourt Journal,* entry for May 28, 171.
60. Quoted in Brown, *Zola,* p. 221.
61. Tombs, *The Paris Commune,* p. 179.
62. Edith Thomas, *Les pétroleuses* (Paris: Gallimard, 1963); Eichner, *Barricades.*
63. *Goncourt Journal,* entry for May 24, 1871.
64. *Goncourt Journal,* entry for May 31, 1871.
65. Bury and Tombs, *Thiers,* p. 207.
66. Tombs, *The Paris Commune,* pp. 173–175.

CHAPTER 3 THE RETURN OF THE REPUBLIC: 1871–1885

1. T. J. Clark, *The Painting of Modern Life* (Princeton, NJ: Princeton University Press, 1984), p. 24.
2. John House, *Impressionism: Paint and Politics* (New Haven, CT: Yale University Press, 2004), pp. 110–111.
3. See Sudhir Hazareesingh's discussion in *Political Traditions in Modern France* (Oxford: Oxford University Press, 1994), pp. 65–96.
4. Philip Nord, *The Republican Moment* (Cambridge, MA: Harvard University Press, 1995), p. 7.
5. François Furet, quoted in Robert Tombs, *France: 1814–1914* (London: Longman, 1996), p. 437.
6. John Ruedy, *Modern Algeria: The Origins and Development of a Nation* (Bloomington: Indiana University Press, 1992), pp. 76–79.
7. Quoted in Raoul Girardet, "Les trois couleurs," in Pierre Nora, ed., *Les Lieux de mémoire,* Vol. 1 (Paris: Gallimard, 1997) p. 56.
8. Quoted in Jean-Marie Mayeur and Madeleine Rebérioux, *The Third Republic from Its Origins to the Great War, 1871–1914,* trans. J. R. Foster (Cambridge, England: Cambridge University Press, 1984), p. 18.
9. See Robert Nye, *Masculinity and Male Codes of Honors in Modern France* (Berkeley: University of California Press, 1998), p. 77.
10. Quoted in Tombs, *France: 1814–1914,* p. 139.
11. J. P. T. Bury, *Gambetta and the Making of the Third Republic* (London: Longman, 1973), p. 273.
12. James Lehning, *To Be a Citizen: The Political Culture of the Early French Third Republic* (Ithaca, NY: Cornell University Press, 2001), p. 28.
13. Tombs, *France: 1814–1914,* p. 439.
14. Quoted in Michel Winock, *La fièvre hexagonale* (Paris: Calman-Lévy, 1986), p. 77.
15. Charles Dupont-White, quoted in Pierre Rosanvallon, *Le Sacre du citoyen: Histoire du suffrage universel en France* (Paris: Gallimard, 1992), p. 411.

16. Odile Rudelle, *La République absolue, 1870–1884* (Paris: Publications de la Sorbonne, 1984).
17. Winock, *La fièvre hexagonale*, p. 88.
18. Sanford Elwitt, *The Making of the Third Republic* (Baton Rouge: LSU Press, 1975); and *The Third Republic Defended* (Baton Rouge: LSU Press, 1986).
19. Quoted in Winock, *La fièvre hexagonale*, p. 86.
20. See Siân Reynolds, "Outsiders by Birth? Women, the Republic and Political History," in Martin Alexander, ed., *French History since Napoleon* (London: Arnold, 1999).
21. Pierre Rosanvallon, *Le Sacre du citoyen. Histoire du suffrage universel en France* (Paris: Gallimard, 1992), pp. 522–523.
22. Claire Goldberg Moses, *French Feminism in the 19th Century* (Albany, New York: SUNY Press, 1985), p. 219.
23. Ibid., p. 201.
24. Ibid., p. 213.
25. See the chapter devoted to Auclert in Mona Ozouf, *Les mots des femmes* (Paris: Fayard, 1995), pp. 201–233.
26. Quoted in Karen Offen, *European Feminisms 1700–1950* (Stanford, CA: Stanford University Press, 2000), p. 152.
27. Ozouf, *Les mots des femmes*, p. 211.
28. Phrase from Daniel Halévy, *La République des ducs* (Paris: Grasset, 1937).
29. Nord, *The Republican Moment*, p. 216.
30. Quoted in Theodore Zeldin, *France 1848–1945: Intelligence and Pride* (Oxford: Oxford University Press, 1980), p. 148.
31. Quoted in Antoine Prost, *L'enseignement en France 1800–1967* (Paris: Armand Colin, 1968), p. 195.
32. Quoted in Ozouf, *Les mots des femmes*, p. 365.
33. Tombs, *France: 1814–1914*, p. 168.
34. Camille Pelletan, quoted in Nord, *The Republican Moment*, p. 226.
35. Ozouf, *Les mots des femmes*, p. 370.
36. Robert Gildea, *Education in Provincial France 1870–1914* (Oxford: Oxford University Press, 1983).
37. Pierre-Jakez Hélias, *The Horse of Pride: Life in a Breton Village*, trans. June Guicharnaud (New Haven, CT: Yale University Press, 1978), p. 134.
38. See Theodore Zeldin's chapter devoted to education in *France 1848–1945: Intelligence and Pride* (Oxford: Oxford University Press, 1980).
39. Quoted in Ibid., p. 168.
40. Quoted in Ibid., p. 178.
41. See Jacques and Mona Ozouf, " 'Le tour de la France par deux enfants,' " in *Les Lieux de mémoire*, Vol. 1, p. 280.
42. Martin Evans, John Phillips, *Algeria: Anger of the Dispossessed* (New Haven, CT: Yale University Press, 2007), p. 32.
43. Ruedy, *Modern Algeria*, p. 86.
44. Quoted in Raoul Girardet, *L'idée coloniale en France de 1871 à 1962* (Paris: Plon, 1972), p. 66.
45. Quoted in D. R. Watson, *Georges Clemenceau: A Political Biography* (London: Eyre Methuen, 1974), p. 94.
46. Quoted in Wolfgang Schivelbusch, *The Culture of Defeat*, trans. Jefferson Chase (New York: Henry Holt, 2003), p. 179.

47. Quoted in Tombs, *France 1814–1914*, p. 206.

48. Ibid., p. 202.

49. Quoted in Watson, *Georges Clemenceau*, p. 95.

50. Girardet, *L'idée coloniale*, p. 88.

51. Quoted in Eugen Weber, *France: Fin de Siècle* (Cambridge, MA: Harvard University Press, 1984), pp. 489–490.

52. Timothy Baycroft, *Culture, Identity and Nationalism: French Flanders in the Nineteenth and Twentieth Centuries* (London: Royal Historical Society, 2004).

53. Robert Zaretsky, *Cock and Bull Stories: Folco de Baroncelli and the Invention of the Camargue* (Lincoln: University of Nebraska, 2004).

54. Caroline Ford, *Creating the Nation in Provincial France: Religion and Political Identity in Brittany* (Princeton, NJ: Princeton University Press, 1993), p. 25.

55. Quoted in Jean-Yves Guiomar, "Le 'Barzaz-Breiz,'" in *Les Lieux de mémoire*, Vol. 3, p. 3506.

56. See the useful survey in Susan Milner, "What About the Workers?," in Alexander, ed., *French History since Napoleon*, pp. 314–320.

57. See Roger Magraw, "'Not Backward but Different?': The Debate on French 'Economic Retardation,'" in Alexander, ed., *French History since Napoleon*, pp. 336–363.

58. Michel Vovelle, "La Marseillaise," in *Les Lieux de mémoire*, Vol. 1, pp. 139–140. See also Marc Ferro, *L'Internationale: Historie d'un chant de Pottier et Degeyter* (Paris: Editions Noêsis, 1996).

59. Cited in Madeleine Rebérioux, "Le mur des fédérées," in *Les Lieux de mémoire*, Vol. 1, p. 539.

60. Weber, *France: Fin de Siècle*, p. 63.

61. Ibid., p. 28.

62. See W. Scott Haine, *The World of the Paris Café* (Baltimore: Johns Hopkins Press, 1996), pp. 107–117.

63. Quoted in Frederick Brown, *Zola: A Life* (New York: Farrar Strauss and Giroux, 1995), p. 365.

64. Kathleen Kete, *The Beast in the Boudoir: Petkeeping in Nineteenth-Century Paris* (Berkeley: University of California Press, 1995).

65. Alain Corbin, "The Secret of the Individual," in Michelle Perrot, ed., *A History of Private Life*, trans. Arthur Goldhammer, Vol. 4 (Cambridge, MA: Harvard University Press, 1995), pp. 484–485.

66. Hélias, *The Horse of Pride*, p. 226.

67. Weber, *France: Fin de Siècle*, p. 64.

68. See Michael Miller, *The Bon Marché* (Princeton, NJ: Princeton University Press, 1981).

CHAPTER 4 THE IMPERIAL REPUBLIC: 1885–1894

1. Eugene Weber, *France: Fin-de-siècle* (Cambridge, MA: Harvard University Press, 1986), p. 10.

2. Joshua Cole, *The Power of Large Numbers: Politics and Gender in Nineteenth-Century France* (Ithaca, NY: Cornell University Press, 2000); Karen Offen, "Depopulation, Nationalism and Feminism in Fin-de-Siècle France," *American Historical Review*, Vol. 89 (June 1984): 648–676.

3. Susan Pedersen, *Family, Dependence and the Origins of the Welfare State: Britain and France 1914–1945* (Cambridge, England: Cambridge University Press, 1993), p. 60.

4. Gérard Noiriel, *Le creuset français* (Paris: Seuil, 1988), p. 78.

5. Michelle Perrot, "Les classes populaires urbaines," in Fernand Braudel and Ernest Labrousse, eds., *Histoire économique et sociale de la France* vol. 4 :1 (Paris : Presses universitaires de France, 1979), p. 459.

6. Pierre Birnbaum, *La France aux Français: Histoire des haines nationalistes* (Paris: Seuil, 1993), pp. 29–117.

7. Rogers Brubaker, *Citizenship and Nationhood in France and Germany* (Cambridge, MA: Harvard University Press, 1992), pp. 106–107.

8. Philip Nord, *Paris Shopkeepers and the Politics of Resentment* (Princeton, NJ: Princeton University Press, 1986), esp. chap. 4.

9. See René Rémond, *Les Droites en France* (Paris: Aubier, 1982); Zeev Sternhell, *La Droite révolutionnaire* (Paris: Seuil, 1978).

10. Norma Evanson, *Paris: A Century of Change, 1878–1978* (New Haven, CT: Yale University Press, 1979), p. 132.

11. Vanessa Schwartz, *Spectacular Realities: Early Mass Culture in Fin-de-siècle Paris* (Berkeley: University of California Press, 1998).

12. Charles Rearick, *Pleasures of the Belle Epoque* (New Haven, CT: Yale University Press, 1985), p. 146.

13. Jerrold Seigel, *Bohemian Paris: Culture, Politics, and the Boundaries of Bourgeois Life, 1830–1930* (New York: Penguin, 1986), pp. 239–240.

14. William A. Peniston, *Pederasts and Others: Urban Culture and Sexual Identity in Nineteenth-Century Paris* (New York: Harrington Park Press, 2004), p. 9; thanks to John Goins for his help.

15. W. Scott Haine, *The World of the Paris Café: Sociability among the French Working Class 1789–1914* (Baltimore: Johns Hopkins University Press, 1998).

16. Weber, *France: Fin-de-siècle,* pp. 144–145.

17. Quoted in T. J. Clark, *The Painting of Modern Life* (Princeton, NJ: Princeton University Press, 1984), pp. 267–268.

18. Bonnie Smith, *Ladies of the Liesure Class: The Bourgeoises of Northern France in the Nineteenth Century* (Princeton, NJ: Princeton University Press, 1981).

19. Frederick Brown, *Zola: A Life* (New York: Farrar, Strauss and Giroux, 1995), p. 781.

20. Weber, *France: Fin-de-siècle,* p. 208.

21. Mary Louise Roberts, *Disruptive Acts: The New Woman in Fin-de-Siècle France* (Chicago: University of Chicago Press, 2002), pp. 3–6.

22. J. P. Daughton, *An Empire Divided: Religion, Republicanism, and the Making of French Colonialism, 1880–1914* (Oxford: Oxford University Press, 2006), p. 6.

23. Quoted in Alice L. Conklin, *A Mission to Civilize: The Republican Idea of Empire in France and West Africa 1895–1930* (Stanford, CA: Stanford University Press, 1997), p. 61.

24. Martin Evans and John Phillips, *Algeria, Anger and the Dispossessed* (New Haven, CT: Yale University Press, 2007), p. 38.

25. Eric T. Jennings, *Vichy in the Tropics: Pétain's National Revolution in Madagascar, Guadeloupe and Indochina, 1940–1944* (Stanford, CA: Stanford University Press, 2001), pp. 133–137; Pierre Brocheux and Daniel Hémery, *Indochine: la colonisation ambiguë, 1858–1954* (Paris: Editions de la Découverte, 2001), pp. 187–191.

26. Robert Aldrich, *Greater France: A History of French Overseas Expansion* (New York: St. Martin's Press, 1996), chap. 4.
27. Daughton, *An Empire Divided,* p. 11.
28. Ibid., chaps. 4 and 5.
29. Julia Clancy-Smith, "The 'Passionate Nomad' Reconsidered: A European Woman in L'Algérie Française (Isabelle Eberhardt, 1877–1904)," in Nupur Chaudhuri, *Western Women and Imperialism: Complicity and Resistance* (Bloomington: Indiana University Press, 1992), pp. 61–79.
30. On gendered concepts of colonial heroism, see Edward Berenson, *Colonial Heroes: Masculinity, the Mass Media and Charisma in France* (Berkeley: University of California Press, 2010).
31. Owen White, *Children of the French Empire: Miscegenation and Colonial Society in French West Africa, 1900–1960* (Oxford: Oxford University Press, 2001); Emmanuelle Saada, *Les enfants de la colonie. Les métis de l'Empire français entre sujétion et citoyenneté* (Paris: La Découverte, 2007).
32. Perrot, "Les classes populaires urbaines," pp. 517, 512.
33. Susan Milner, "What About the Workers? The Trade Unions' 'Short Century,'" in Martin Alexander, ed., *French History Since Napoleon* (New York: Arnold and Oxford University Press, 1999), p. 318.
34. Joan Halperin, *Félix Fénéon: Aesthete and Anarchist in Fin-de-siècle Paris* (New Haven, CT: Yale University Press, 1988), p. 241.
35. Ibid., p. 289.

CHAPTER 5 THE REPUBLIC DIVIDED: 1894–1914

1. Edward Berenson, *The Trial of Madame Caillaux* (Berkeley: University of California Press, 1992), p. 3.
2. Michael Burns, *Dreyfus: A Family Affair, 1789–1945* (New York: Harper, 1992), p. 167.
3. Ibid., p. 256.
4. Ibid., p. 191.
5. Ibid., p. 228.
6. Michel Winock, *Le Siècle des intellectuels* (Paris: Seuil, 1997), pp. 150–151.
7. Ibid., p. 164.
8. Quoted in Zeev Sternhell, *La Droite révolutionnaire, 1885-1914: Les origines françaises du fascisme* (Paris: Seuil, 1978), p. 161.
9. For a succinct summary, see Gilles Le Béguec and Jacques Prévotat, "L'éveil à la modernité politique," in Jean-François Sirinelli, *Histoire des droites en France*, Tome 1, Politique (Paris: Gallimard, 1992), pp. 213–289.
10. Quoted in Béatrice Philippe, *Etre juif dans la société française* (Paris: Editions Montalba, 1979), p. 230.
11. Robert Nye, *Masculinity and Male Codes of Honor in Modern France* (Berkeley: University of California Press, 1992), esp. chaps. 8 and 9.
12. Quoted from the *Petit Parisien,* in Edward Berenson, *Heroes of Empire: Manliness, Media and Charisma in Europe's Conquest of Africa* (Berkeley: University of California Press, 2010), chap. 5 (forthcoming).
13. Quoted from *L'Intransigeant,* October 1898, in Ibid., chap. 5.
14. Willa Silverman, *The Notorious Life of Gyp* (Oxford: Oxford University Press, 1995), p. 154.

15. Sudhir Hazareesingh, *Political Traditions in Modern France* (Oxford: Oxford University Press, 1994), p. 36.

16. Tony Judt, *Past Imperfect: French Intellectuals 1944–1956* (Berkeley: University of California Press, 1992), p. 251.

17. See Winock, *Le Siècle,* p. 86.

18. Quoted in Ibid., p. 100.

19. Silverman, *The Notorious Life of Gyp,* p. 131.

20. Winock, *Le Siècle,* p. 62.

21. Rod Kedward, *France and the French* (New York: Overlook Press, 2006), p. 27.

22. J. P. Daughton, *An Empire Divided: Religion, Republicanism, and the Making of French Colonialism, 1880-1914* (New York: Oxford University Press, 2006), p. 18.

23. Robert Tombs, *France 1814–1915* (London: Longman, 1996).

24. Susan Pedersen, *Family, Dependence, and the Origins of the Welfare State: Britain and France, 1914–1945* (Cambridge, England: Cambridge University Press, 1995).

25. Christopher Thompson, *The Tour de France* (Berkeley: University of California Press, 2006), p. 11.

26. Eugen Weber, *France: Fin de Siècle* (Cambridge, MA: Harvard University Press, 1986), pp. 201–203.

27. Thompson, *Tour de France,* pp. 68–69.

28. Quoted in Charles Sowerwine, *France since 1870: Culture, Society, and the Making of the Republic,* 2d ed. (New York: Palgrave Macmillan, 2009), p. 86.

29. Andrei Makhine, *Dreams of My Russian Summers,* trans. Geoffrey Strachan (New York: Simon & Schuster, 1997), p. 27.

30. Williamson Murray, "The West at War," in Geoffrey Parker, ed., *The Cambridge History of Warfare* (Cambridge, England: Cambridge University Press, 2005), p. 279. Schlieffen favored violating the neutrality of Belgium and Luxembourg at the outset to prevent the kaiser from pulling back at the last moment. In the end, Kaiser Wilhelm vetoed the invasion of Luxembourg.

31. Jean-Baptiste Duroselle, *La Grande Guerre des Français, 1914–1918* (Paris: Perrin, 1994), p. 46.

32. Richard S. Fogarty, *Race and War in France: Colonial Subjects in the French Army* (Baltimore: Johns Hopkins University Press, 2008), pp. 26–27.

33. Leonard V. Smith, *Between Mutiny and Obedience: The Case of the French Fifth Infantry Division during World War I* (Princeton, NJ: Princeton University Press, 1994).

34. Robert Doughty, *Pyrrhic Victory: French Strategy and Operations in the Great War* (Cambridge, MA: Harvard University Press, 2005), pp. 37–38.

CHAPTER 6 THE REPUBLIC AT WAR: 1914–1919

1. Joseh Delteil, *Les poilus,* quoted in Pierre Miquel, *Les poilus* (Paris: Plon, 2000), p. 62.

2. Roger Martin Du Gard, *Les Thibault,* quoted in Richard D. E. Burton, *Blood in the City: Violence and Revelation in Paris 1789–1945* (Ithaca, NY: Cornell University Press, 2001), p. 205.

3. "Correspondance entre Romain Rolland et Jean-Richard Bloch 1914–1919," quoted in Hew Strachan, *The First World War* (London: Viking, 2004), p. 59.

4. André Ducasse, Jacques Meyer, and Gabriel Perreux, *Vie et mort des Français 1914-1918. Simple histoire de la Grande Guerre* (Paris: Hachette, 1959), p. 26.

5. André Gide, *Journal*, I, 1887–1925, ed. Éric Marty (Paris: Gallimard, 1996), p. 830.

6. Ducasse et al., *Vie et mort*, pp. 26–27.

7. Jean-Baptiste Duroselle, *La Grande Guerre des Français, 1914–1918* (Paris: Perrin, 1994), p. 63.

8. Quoted in Niall Ferguson, *The Pity of War: Explaining World War I* (New York: Basic Books, 1999), p. 187.

9. Ducasse et al., *Vie et mort*, p. 24.

10. Leonard V. Smith, Stéphane Audoin-Rouzeau, and Annette Becker, *France and the Great War, 1914–1918* (Cambridge, England: Cambridge University Press, 2003), pp. 34–35.

11. Ibid., p. 40.

12. Julien Benda, *Esquisse d'une histoire des Français dans leur volonté d'être une nation* (Paris: Gallimard, 1932), p. 101.

13. Smith et al., *France*, pp. 46, 111.

14. Marc Michel, *Les Africains et la Grande Guerre: L' appel à L' afrique, 1914–1919*, 2d ed. (Paris: Karthala, 2003), pp. 211–231.

15. Duroselle, *La Grande Guerre*, p. 212.

16. Williamson A. Murray, "The West at War 1914–1918," in Geoffrey Parker, ed., *Cambridge Illustrated History of Warfare: the Triumph of the West* (Cambridge, England: Cambridge University Press, 1995), p. 266.

17. Alistair Horne, *The Price of Glory, Verdun 1916* (London: Penguin, 1962), p. 41.

18. Quoted in Ibid., p. 174.

19. Quoted in Ibid., p. 176.

20. Quoted in Ibid., p. 177.

21. Paul Fussell, *The Great War and Modern Memory* (New York: Oxford University Press, 1975), p. 12.

22. Smith et al., *France*, p. 83.

23. Martin Gilbert, quoted in Charles Sowerwine, *France since 1870: Politics, Culture, Society*, 2d ed. (London: Palgrave, 2009), p. 106.

24. Fussell, *Great War*, p. 45.

25. Strachan, *The First World War*, pp. 163–164.

26. Quoted in Horne, *Price of Glory*, p. 65.

27. Quoted in Smith et al., *France*, p. 52.

28. Strachan, *The First World War*, p. 167.

29. Our translation. Quoted in Regina Sweeney, *Singing Our Way to Victory* (Middletown, CT: Wesleyan University Press, 2001), p. 227.

30. Louis Mairet, *Carnet d'un combattant* (Paris: Crès, 1919), p. 174.

31. Laura Lee Downs, *Manufacturing Inequality: Gender Division in the French and British Metalworking Industries, 1914–1939* (Ithaca, NY: Cornell University Press, 1995), p. 7.

32. Quoted in Jean-Jacques Becker, *The Great War and the French People*, trans. Arnold Pomerans (Dover, NH: Berg, 1985), p. 121.

33. Ibid., p. 139.

34. Jean-Marie Apostolidès, *L'audience* (Paris: Exils, 2001), p. 55.

35. Jean Bernard, *La vie à Paris* (Paris: Lemerre, 1916), p. 629.

36. Smith et al., *France*, p. 69.

37. Margaret H. Darrow, *French Women and the First World War: War Stories of the Home Front* (Oxford: Berg, 2000), p. 109.

38. Ibid., p. 108.
39. Ibid., p. 108.
40. Ibid., p. 142.
41. Susan R. Grayzel, *Women and the First World War* (Harlow: Longman, 2002), p. 62.
42. Smith et al., *France*, p. 53.
43. Quoted in Becker, *Great War*, pp. 31–32.
44. Ibid., p. 63.
45. Quoted in Ibid., p. 156.
46. Quoted in Ibid., p. 179.
47. Dana Hale, *Races on Display: French Representations of Colonized Peoples* (Bloomington: Indiana University Press, 2008), pp. 91–117.
48. Murray, "The West at War," p. 281.
49. Smith et al., *France*, p. 124.
50. Ibid., p. 122.
51. Quoted in Sweeney, *Singing Our Way*, p. 231.
52. Quoted in Smith et al., *France*, p. 124.
53. Becker, *The Great War*, p. 211.
54. Tyler Stovall, "Colour-Blind France? Colonial Workers during the First World War," *Race and Class*, Vol. 35, no. 2 (April 1993): 36.
55. Quoted in Smith et al., *France*, p. 124.
56. Quoted in Ibid., p. 114.
57. Sowerwine, *France since 1870*, pp. 111–112.
58. Smith et al., *France*, pp. 174–175.

CHAPTER 7 THE DECEPTIVE PEACE: 1919–1929

1. Siân Reynolds, *France between the Wars: Gender and Politics* (London and New York: Routledge, 1996), p. 19.
2. Owen White, "Miscegenation and the Popular Imagination," in Tony Chafer and Amanda Sackur, eds., *Promoting the Colonial Idea: Propaganda and Visions of Empire in France* (London: Palgrave, 2002), p. 135.
3. Robert Paxton, *Europe in the Twentieth Century* (New York: Wadsworth, 2002), p. 171.
4. Christopher Fischer, "Review," Michael E. Nolan, *Mythologizing the Enemy in France and Germany, 1898-1914* (New York, Bergahn Books, 2005), *H-France Review*, Vol. 8, no. 29 (February 2008).
5. Jean-Jacques Becker and Serge Bernstein, *Victoire et frustrations 1914–1929* (Paris: Seuil, 1990), pp. 230, 234.
6. Joel Colton, *Léon Blum: Humanist in Politics* (Durham, NC: Duke University Press, 1987), p. 59.
7. Ilan Greilsammer, *Blum* (Paris: Flammarion, 1996), pp. 249–250.
8. Colton, *Léon Blum*, pp. 56–77.
9. Eugen Weber, *The Hollow Years* (New York: Norton, 1996), p. 115.
10. John F. V. Keiger, *Raymond Poincaré* (Cambridge, England: Cambridge University Press, 1997), pp. 342–344.
11. René Rémond, *Le siècle dernier de 1918 à 2002* (Paris: Fayard, 2003), pp. 64, 122.
12. Ibid., pp. 63–64.

13. Susan Pedersen, *Family, Dependence, and the Origins of the Welfare State: Britain and France, 1914–1945* (Cambridge, England: Cambridge University Press, 1995), p. 75ff.

14. Quoted in Julian Jackson, *The Popular Front in France: Defending Democracy, 1943–1938* (Cambridge, England: Cambridge University Press, 1988), p. 85.

15. H. R. Kedward, *France and the French: A Modern History* (New York: Overlook Press, 2005), p. 124.

16. Mary Dewhurst Lewis, *The Boundaries of the Republic* (Stanford, CA: Stanford University Press, 2007), p. 1.

17. Kedward, *France and the French*, p. 144; Jean-François Chanet, *L'école républicaine et les petites patries* (Paris: Aubier, 1996), pp. 314–318.

18. Quoted in Mary Louise Roberts, *Civilization without Sexes: Reconstructing Gender in Postwar France, 1917–1927* (Chicago: University of Chicago Press, 1994), p. 2.

19. Reynolds, *France between the Wars,* pp. 51–53.

20. Ibid., p. 55.

21. Linda L. Clark, *The Rise of Professional Women in France: Gender and Public Administration since 1830* (Cambridge, England: Cambridge University Press, 2006); Reynolds, *France between the Wars,* p. 96.

22. Martha Hanna, *Your Death Would Be Mine: Paul and Marie Pireaud in the Great War* (Cambridge, MA: Harvard University Press, 2006), pp. 171–175.

23. Ibid., p. 294.

24. Reynolds, *France between the Wars,* p. 210.

25. Martin Thomas, Bob Moore, and L. J. Butler, *Crises of Empire: Decolonization and Europe's Imperial States, 1918–1975* (London: Hodder Education, 2008), p. 133.

26. Benjamin Stora, *Algeria 1830–2000. A Short History,* trans. Jane Marie Todd (Ithaca, NY: Cornell University Press, 2001), p. 14.

27. Thomas et al., *Crises of Empire,* p. 132.

28. White, "Miscegenation and the Popular Imagination," p. 133.

29. Quoted in Ibid., p. 136.

30. Dana S. Hale, "French Images of Race on Product Trademarks during the Third Republic," in Sue Peabody and Tyler Stovall, eds., *The Color of Liberty: Histories of Race in France* (Durham, NC: Duke University Press, 2003), p. 131.

31. Herman Lebovics, *True France: The Wars over Cultural Identity 1900–1945* (Ithaca, NY: Cornell University Press, 1992).

32. Nabila Oulebsir, *Les usages du patrimoine. Monuments, musées, et politique coloniale en Algérie (1830–1890)* (Paris: Editions de la Maison des sciences de l'homme, 2004), 261–291; Patricia Lorcin, *Imperial Identities: Stereotyping, Prejudice and Race in Colonial Algeria* (London: Taurus, 1995).

33. Quoted in Patricia Morton, *Hybrid Modernities: Architecture and Representation at the 1931 Colonial Exposition, Paris* (Cambridge: Massachusetts Institute of Technology, 2000), p. 70.

34. White, "Miscegenation," pp. 134–136.

35. Christopher Thompson, *The Tour de France: A Cultural History* (Berkeley: University of California Press, 2006), pp. 42–43.

36. Becker and Bernstein, *Victoire et frustrations,* pp. 382–383.

37. Rebecca Scales, "Radio Broadcasting, Disabled Veterans, and the Politics of National Recovery in Interwar France," *French Historical Studies,* Vol. 31, no. 4 (Fall 2008): 644.

38. Paul F. Jankowski, *Stavisky, A Confidence Man in the Republic of Virtue* (Ithaca, NY: Cornell University Press, 2003), pp. 4, 38; Michael Miller, *Shanghai on the Metro: Spies,*

Intrigue and the French Between the Wars (Berkeley: University of California Press, 1994), pp. 226–228.

39. Antoine Prost, Jay Winter, and Helen McPhail, *Republican Identities in War and Peace: Representations of France in the 19th and 20th Centuries* (Oxford: Berg, 2002), pp. 228–229.

40. Robert Short, "Dada and Surrealism," in Malcolm Bradbury and James McFarlane, eds., *Modernism: A Guide to European Literature 1890–1930* (London: Penguin, 1991), p. 294.

41. Quoted in Charles Sowerwine, *France since 1870: Culture, Society and the Making of the Republic,* 2d ed. (London: Palgrave, 2009), p. 156.

42. Short, "Dada and Surrealism," p. 302.

43. Quoted in Becker and Bernstein, *Victoire et frustrations,* p. 380.

44. Morton, *Hybrid Modernities,* p. 106.

45. José de la Colina and Tomás Pérez Turrent, *Objects of Desire: Conversations with Luis Buñuel,* trans. Paul Lenti (New York: Marsilio Publishers, 1992), p. 19.

46. Pierre Drieu la Rochelle, *Gilles,* quoted in Douglas Collins, "Terrorists Ask No Questions," in Dennis Hollier, ed., *A New History of French Literature* (Cambridge, MA: Harvard University Press, 1989), p. 914.

47. Robert Soucy, *French Fascism: The First Wave, 1924–1933* (New Haven, CT: Yale University Press).

48. Clifford Rosenberg, *Policing Paris: The Origins of Modern Immigration Control Between the Wars* (Ithaca, NY: Cornell University Press, 2006), p. 5.

49. Martin Thomas, *The French Empire between the Wars: Imperialism, Politics and Society* (Manchester, England: Manchester University Press, 2005), p. 211.

50. Quoted in Morton, *Hybrid Modernities,* p. 100.

51. From *L'Avenir de la Meuse,* September 8, 1927, quoted in Daniel J. Sherman, *The Construction of Memory in Interwar France* (Chicago: University of Chicago Press, 1999), p. 306.

52. Julian Jackson, *The Popular Front,* pp. 18–19.

53. Serge Bernstein, *Léon Blum* (Paris: Fayard, 2006), p. 355.

54. Dominique Borne and Henri Dubief, *La crise des années trente (1928–1939)* (Paris: Seuil, 1989), pp. 84–85.

CHAPTER 8 THE REPUBLIC IN PERIL: 1929–1939

1. Serge Bernstein, *Léon Blum* (Paris: Fayard, 2006), pp. 428–429.

2. Quoted in Eugen Weber, *The Hollow Years: France in the 1930s* (New York: W. W. Norton, 1994), p. 148.

3. Ibid., p. 149.

4. Ibid., p. 39.

5. Julian Jackson, "1940 and the Crisis of Interwar Democracy," in Martin S. Alexander, ed., *French History since Napoleon* (London: Arnold, 1999), p. 226.

6. Quoted in Vicki Caron, "The Path to Vichy: Antisemitism in France in the 1930s," U.S. Holocaust Memorial Museum, Center for Advanced Holocaust Studies, Occasional Paper, 2005, p. 3.

7. Robert Paxton, *French Peasant Fascism: Henri Dorgères' Green Shirts and the Crises of French Agriculture 1929–1939* (Oxford: Oxford University Press, 1997), p. 158.

8. Robert Soucy, *French Fascism: The First Wave 1924–1933* (New Haven, CT: Yale University Press, 1886); and *French Fascism: The Second Wave 1933–1939* (New Haven, CT: Yale University Press, 1995).

9. H. R. Kedward, *France and the French. A Modern History* (New York: Overlook Press, 2005), p. 174.

10. Robert Soucy, "Problematising the Immunity Thesis," in Brian Jenkins, *France in the Era of Fascism: Essays on the Authoritarian Right* (New York: Bergahn Books, 2005), p. 90.

11. Quoted in Charles Sowerwine, *France since 1870. Culture, Society, and the Making of the Republic*, 2d ed. (London: Palgrave, 2009), p. 139.

12. A. Tardieu, *L'heure de crise*, quoted in Jenkins, *France in the Era of Fascism*, p. 152.

13. Paxton, *Peasant Fascism*, pp. 65, 156–159.

14. Brian Jenkins, "Introduction: Contextualizing the Immunity Thesis," in Jenkins, *France in the Era of Fascism*, p. 15.

15. Kevin Passmore, "The Construction of Crisis in Interwar France," in Ibid., p. 192.

16. Caron, "The Path to Vichy," p. 6.

17. Quoted in Colton, *Léon Blum*, p. 112.

18. Quoted in Ibid., p. 112.

19. Jackson, *Popular Front*, p. 46.

20. Quoted in Colton, *Léon Blum*, p. 132.

21. Quoted in Jackson, *Popular Front*, p. 60.

22. France Tostain, "The Popular Front and the Blum-Violette Plan," in Tony Chafer and Amanda Sackur, eds., *French Colonial Empire and the Popular Front, Hope and Disillusion* (London and New York: Macmillan and Saint Martin's Press, 1999), p. 222.

23. Vicki Caron, *Uneasy Asylum: France and the Jewish Refugee Crisis, 1933–1942* (Stanford, CA: Stanford University Press, 1999), p. 136.

24. Quoted in Caron, *Uneasy Asylum*, p. 141.

25. Quoted in Dudley Andrew and Steven Ungar, *The Popular Front and the Poetics of Culture* (Cambridge, MA: Harvard University Press, 2005), p. 144.

26. Shanny Peer, *France on Display: Peasants, Provincials, and Folklore in the 1937 Paris World's Fair* (Albany: State University of New York Press, 1998).

27. Quoted in Jackson, *Popular Front*, p. 192.

28. Bernstein, *Léon Blum*, p. 508.

29. Quoted in Sowerwine, *France since 1870*, p. 153.

30. Quoted in Colton, *Léon Blum*, p. 275.

31. Ibid., p. 277.

32. Kevin Passmore, "The Republic in Crisis: Politics 1914–1945," in James McMillan, ed., *Modern France 1880–2002* (Oxford: Oxford University Press, 2003), p. 64.

33. Jackson, *Popular Front*, p. 259.

34. John Cowburn, S.J., *Personalism and Scholasticism* (Milwaukee: Marquette University Press, 2005), p. 68.

35. Sowerwine, *France since 1870*, p. 163.

36. George Bernanos, *La grande peur des bien-pensants*, quoted in Richard D. E. Burton, *Blood in the City: Violence and Revelation in the City, 1789–1945* (Ithaca, NY: Cornell University Press, 2001), p. 268.

37. Quoted by Denis Hollier, "Plenty of Nothing," in Hollier, ed., *A New History*, p. 895.

38. Quoted in Gabriel Marcel, *The Philosophy of Existentialism* (New York: Citadel Press: 1971), p. 79.

39. Pierre Drieu la Rochelle, *Gilles* (Paris: Gallimard, 2000), pp. 685–686.

40. Quoted in Alice Kaplan, *The Collaborator: The Trial and Execution of Robert Brasillach* (Chicago: University of Chicago Press, 2000), p. 81.

41. Quoted in Caron, "The Path to Vichy," p. 11.

42. Michel Leymarie, *Les intellectuels et la politique en France* (Paris: Presses Universitaires de France, 2001), p. 53.

43. *Le Socialiste*, September 15, 1938.

44. Quoted in Kristin Stromberg Childers, *Fathers, Families and the State, 1914–1945* (Ithaca, NY: Cornell University Press, 2003), p. 40.

45. Philip Nord, "La IIIe République," in Jean-François Chanet, Vincent Duclert, and Christophe Prochasson, eds., *Dictionnaire critique de la république* (Paris: Flammarion, 2002), p. 61.

CHAPTER 9 THE DARK YEARS 1939–1945

1. Jean-Paul Sartre, "La République du silence," *Situations III* (Paris: Gallimard, 1949), pp. 11–14.

2. Quoted in Julian Jackson, *France: The Dark Years, 1940–1944* (Oxford: Oxford University Press, 2001), p. 326.

3. Marc Bloch, *Strange Defeat: A Statement of Evidence Written in 1940,* trans. Gerard Hopkins (New York: Norton, 1968), p. 6.

4. Jackson, *The Dark Years,* p. 117.

5. Raymond Ruffin, *Journal d'un J3* (Paris: Presses de la Cité, 1979), p. 28.

6. Dominique Veillon, *Vivre et survivre en France 1939–1946* (Paris: Payot, 1995), p. 56.

7. Hanna Diamond, *Fleeing Hitler: France 1940* (Oxford: Oxford University Press, 2007).

8. Charles de Gaulle, *Complete War Memoirs,* trans. Richard Howard (New York: Simon and Schuster, 1968), p. 85.

9. Eric Jennings, *Vichy in the Tropics: Pétain's National Revolution in Madagascar, Guadeloupe, and Indochina, 1940–1944* (Stanford, CA: Stanford University Press, 2001), pp. 10–11.

10. Jean Guéhenno, *Journal des années noires* (Paris: Gallimard, 1947), p. 11.

11. Robert Paxton, *Vichy France: Old Guard and New Order* (New York: Norton, 1972), pp. 52–54, 143–144; Jean-Pierre Azéma, *From Munich to the Liberation,* trans. Janet Lloyd (New York: Cambridge University Press, 1984), pp. 45–46.

12. Quoted in Michel Cépède, *Agriculture et alimentation en France durant la deuxième guerre mondiale* (Paris: Génin, 1961), p. 161.

13. Jackson, *The Dark Years,* p. 173.

14. Christian Delage and Vincent Guigueno, "Montoire, une mémoire en représentations," *Vertigo,* Vol. 16 (1997): 47, 56.

15. Brett Bowles, "Newsreels, Ideology and Public Opinion under Vichy: The Case of La France en Marche," *French Historical Studies,* Vol. 27, no. 3 (Spring 2004): 428.

16. Jackson, *The Dark Years,* p. 179.

17. Henry Rousso, "L'activité industrielle en France de 1940 à 1944. Economie 'nouvelle' et Occupation allemande," *Bulletin de l'Institut d'histoire du temps présent,* Vol. 38 (December 1989): 25–68; Adrian Jones, "Illusions of Sovereignty: Business and the Organization Committees of Vichy France," *Social History,* Vol. 11, no. 1 (January 1986): 1–31.

18. Micahel Sibalis, "Homophobia, Vichy France, and the 'Crime of Homosexuality': The Origins of the Ordinance of 6 August 1942," *GLQ: A Journal of Lesbian and Gay Studies*, Vol. 8, no. 3 (2002): 302.

19. Miranda Pollard, *Reign of Virtue: Mobilizing Gender in Vichy France* (Chicago: University of Chicago Press, 1998); Francine Muël-Dreyfus, *Vichy and the Eternal Feminine*, trans. Kathleen A. Johnson (Durham, NC: Duke University Press, 2001).

20. Quoted in Veillon, *Vivre et survivre,* p. 223.

21. W. D. Halls, *Youth of Vichy France* (Oxford: Oxford University Press, 1981), p. 113ff.; Pierre Giolitto, *Histoire de la jeunesse sous Vichy* (Paris: Perrin, 1991), p. 129.

22. Jean-Michel Barreau, "Vichy, idéologue de l'école," *Revue d'histoire moderne et contemporaine,* Vol. 38 (1991): 592.

23. Halls, *Youth of Vichy,* pp. 20–32; Giolitto, *Histoire,* pp. 97–123; Stéphane Corcy-Debray, "Jérôme Carcopino, du triomphe à la roche Tarpéienne," *Vingtième Siècle,* Vol. 58 (April–June 1998): 70–82.

24. Giles Ragache, *Les enfants de la guerre. Vivre, survivre, lire et jouer en France 1939–1949* (Paris: Perrin, 1997), pp. 114–118, 122–133.

25. Sarah Fishman, *The Battle for Children: World War II, Youth Crime and Juvenile Justice in Twentieth-Century France* (Cambridge, MA: Harvard University Press, 2002).

26. John Hellman, *The Knight Monks of Uriage* (Montreal: McGill-Queens University Press, 1997).

27. Contrôles techniques, Archives Nationales, F7: 14927, February 24–March 2, 1944; February 17–23, 1944; January 20–27, 1944.

28. Philippe Burrin, *France under the Germans: Collaboration and Compromise,* trans. Janet Lloyd (New York: The New Press, 1996).

29. Michel Cépède, *Agriculture et alimentation,* p. 151; Paxton, *Vichy France,* p. 360; Arthur Marwick, *War and Social Change in the Twentieth Century* (New York: St. Martins, 1974), p. 193; Henri Amouroux, *La vie des Français sous l'Occupation* (Paris: Fayard, 1961), pp. 131–151; Azéma, *From Munich to the Liberation,* p. 234; Yves Durand, *La France dans la deuxième guerre mondiale 1939–1945* (Paris: Armand Colin, 1989), p. 77.

30. Cépède, *Agriculture et alimentation,* p. 331.

31. Simone Martin-Chauffier, *A bientôt quand même* (Paris: Calmann-Lévy, 1976), p. 180.

32. Veillon, *Vivre et survivre,* p. 134.

33. *Marie-Claire,* May 10, 1943.

34. Dominique Veillon, *La mode sous l'Occupation* (Paris: Payot, 1990).

35. Samuel H. Goodfellow, *Between the Swastika and the Cross of Lorraine* (DeKalb: Northern Illinois University Press, 1999).

36. Jackson, *Dark Years,* p. 247; Richard Cobb, *French and Germans, Germans and French: A Personal Interpretation of France under Two Occupations, 1914–1918/1940–1944* (Hanover, NH: University Press of New England, 1983), p. 41.

37. Lynne Taylor, *Between Resistance and Collaboration: Popular Protest in Northern France, 1940–45,* Studies in Modern History (London: Palgrave, 1999).

38. Robert Zaretsky, *Cock and Bull Stories: Folco de Baroncelli and the Invention of the Camargue* (Lincoln: University of Nebraska Press, 2004), p. 135.

39. Donna Ryan, *The Holocaust and Jews of Marseille: The Enforcement of Anti-Semitic Policies in Vichy France* (Dekalb: University of Illinois Press, 1996), pp. 79–126.

40. Michael Marrus and Robert Paxton, *Vichy France and the Jews* (New York: Basic, 1981); Susan Zuccotti, *The Holocaust, the French, and the Jews* (Lincoln: University of Nebraska Press, 1999).

41. Ruth Ginio, *French Colonialism Unmasked: The Vichy Years in French West Africa* (Lincoln: University of Nebraska Press, 2006).

42. Quoted in Jennings, *Vichy in the Tropics,* p. 66.

43. Quoted in Ibid., p. 157.

44. Martin Evans and John Philips, *Algeria, Anger of the Dispossessed* (New Haven, CT: Yale University Press, 2007), pp. 50–51.

45. Paula Schwartz, "Partisanes and Gender Politics in Vichy France," *French Historical Studies* Vol. 16, no. 1 (Spring 1989): 126–151.

46. Jackson, *Dark Years,* p. 601; H. R. Kedward, *Resistance in Vichy France: A Study of Ideas and Motivation in the Southern Zone, 1940–1942* (Oxford: Oxford University Press, 1978).

47. Paxton, *Vichy France,* p. 295.

48. Bowles, "Newsreels," p. 436–437; Brett Bowles, "German Newsreel Propaganda in France, 1940–1944," *Film, Radio and Television,* Vol. 24, no. 1 (March 2004): 45–67.

49. Archives Départementales, Paris 221/73/1/10.

50. See Jeffrey H. Jackson, *Making Jazz French: Music and Modern Life in Interwar Paris* (Durham, NC: Duke University Press, 2003).

51. Emmanuelle Rioux, "Les zazous: un phénomène socio-culturel pendant l'Occupation" (Mémoire de maîtrise, Université de Paris X, 1987), pp. 56, 52.

52. Ibid., pp. 13, 29, 41.

53. Quoted from Robert McG. Thomas Jr.'s obituary, R. M. Thomas, *New York Times,* January 8, 2000, p. 15.

54. Emmanuelle Rioux, "Les Zazous," pp. 15–29.

55. Veillon, *La Mode,* pp. 236–239; Jean-Pierre Rioux, "Survivre," *L'Histoire,* Vol. 80 (1985): 94.

56. Giolitto, *Histoire de la Jeunesse,* pp. 490, 492; Jean-Claude Loiseau, *Les Zazous* (Paris: Grasset, 1990), p. 156.

57. Emmanuelle Rioux, "Les Zazous," p. 96; Jean-Claude Loiseau just mentions "camps" in *Les Zazous,* p. 164.

58. Quoted in Azéma, *From Munich to the Liberation,* p. 117.

59. Robert Zaretsky, *Nîmes at War: Religion, Politics and Public Opinion in the Gard, 1938–1944* (State College: Penn State Press, 1995), pp. 215–216.

60. Jackson, *The Dark Years,* p. 228.

61. H. R. Kedward, *In Search of the Maquis: Rural Resistance in Southern France, 1942–1944* (Oxford: Clarendon, 1995).

62. Archives Départementales du Gard, 6 U 10 series.

63. Fabrice Virgili, *Shorn Women: Gender and Punishment in Liberation France,* trans. John Flower (New York: Berg, 2002).

64. Charles de Gaulle, "Bayeux Speech," June 16, 1946, www.charles-de-gaulle.org.

CHAPTER 10 RECONSTRUCTION AT HOME AND OVERSEAS: 1945–1958

1. Robert Paxton, *Vichy France: Old Guard and New Order 1940–1944* (New York: Norton, 1972), pp. 329–331, 381.

2. Herrick Chapman, "The Liberation of France as a Moment in State-Making," in Kenneth Mouré and Martin C. Alexander, eds., *Crisis and Renewal in France 1918–1962* (New York: Berghahn Books, 2002), pp. 179, 182–183.

3. Jean-Pierre Rioux, *The Fourth Republic 1944–1958,* trans. Godfrey Rogers (Cambridge, England: Cambridge University Press, 1987), p. 18; Dominque Veillon, *Vivre et survivre en France 1939–1947* (Paris: Payot, 1995), p. 289; Danielle Voldman, "La France en ruines," *L'Histoire,* Vol. 179 (July–August 1994): 98–105, and "Crise du logement et intervention de l'Etat: l'ordonnance du 11 octobre 1945," in "La bataille des squatters et l'invention du droit au logement. 1945–1955," no. 7, *Les Cahiers du GRMF* (1992), p. 24.

4. Veillon, *Vivre et survivre,* p. 289; Thomas R. Christofferson with Michael S. Christofferson, *France during World War II: From Defeat to Liberation* (New York: Fordham University Press, 2006), p. 178.

5. Voldman, "Crise du logement," p. 24; Jean-Jacques Becker, *Histoire politique de la France depuis 1945,* 8th ed. (Paris: Armand Colin, 2003), p. 18.

6. Becker, *Histoire politique,* p. 10.

7. Veillon, *Vivre et survivre,* p. 298, Becker, *Histoire politique,* p. 40.

8. Michèle Manceaux, "En 1950 au lavoir de Salers (Cantal) Jacqueline Bouvier fait sa lessive, en 1961 à la Maison Blanche," *Marie-Claire,* Vol. 77 (March 1961): 44–49, 46.

9. Andrew Shennan, *Rethinking France: Plans for Renewal 1940–1946* (Oxford: Oxford University Press, 1989), pp. 34–37, 40, 41.

10. David Coward, *A History of French Literature: From Chansons de Geste to Cinema* (Oxford: Blackwell, 2002), p. 320–325.

11. Sarah Fishman, *We Will Wait: Wives of French Prisoners of War, 1940–1945* (New Haven, CT: Yale University Press, 1992), pp. 113–115.

12. Maurice Larkin, *France since the Popular Front. Government and People, 1936–1996* 2d ed. (Oxford: Clarendon, 1997), p. 135.

13. Becker, *Histoire politique,* pp. 27–28.

14. Ibid., pp. 35, 39.

15. Robert Aldrich, *Greater France: A History of French Overseas Expansion* (New York: St. Martin's Press, 1996), p. 282.

16. Benjamin Stora, *Algeria 1830–2000: A Short History,* trans. Jane Marie Todd (Ithaca, NY: Cornell University Press: 2001), p. 21.

17. Larkin, *France since the Popular Front,* p. 156.

18. H. R. Kedward, *France and the French: A Modern History* (New York: Overlook Press, 2006), pp. 376–379; Jean-François Sirinelli et al., *Dictionnaire historique de la vie politique française au vingtième siècle,* 1st ed. (Paris: Presses Universitaires de France, 1995), pp. 261–262; Thierry Bouclier, *Les années Poujade. Une histoire du poujadisme 1953–1958* (Paris: Editions Rémi Perrin, 2006).

19. Tony Judt, *Past Imperfect: French Intellectuals 1944–1956* (Berkeley: University of California Press, 1992), p. 119.

20. Quoted in Ibid., p. 117.

21. Quoted in Annie Cohen-Solal, *Sartre: A Life,* trans. Anna Cagnoni (New York: Pantheon, 1987), p. 328.

22. Quoted in John Foley, *Albert Camus: From the Absurd to Revolt* (Durham, England : Acumen Publishing, 2008), p. 112.

23. Herbert R. Lottman, *Albert Camus: A Biography* (Berkeley, CA: Gingko Press), p. 532.

24. Adrian Jones, "Illusions of Sovereignty: Business and the Organization Committees of Vichy France," *Social History,* Vol. 11, no. 1 (January 1986): 1–31; Henry Rousso, "L'Activité industrielle en France de 1940 à 1944: Economie 'nouvelle' et occupation

allemande," *Bulletin de l'Institut d'histoire du temps présent,* Vol. 38 (December 1989): 25–68.

25. Larkin, *France since the Popular Front,* p. 186; Sima Lieberman, *The Growth of European Mixed Economies 1945–1970* (New York: Wiley, 1977), p. 11.

26. Veillon, *Vivre et survivre,* p. 304.

27. Lawrence Wylie, *Village in the Vaucluse,* 3d ed. (Cambridge, MA: Harvard University Press, 1974) pp. 32, 142–147.

28. Nicole Rudolf and Brian Newsome, "Rise of the Grandes Ensembles: Government, Business, and Housing in Postwar France," *The Historian,* Vol. 66, no. 4 (Winter 2004): 793–816; Jean-Louis Cohen, "Burning Issues in the Banlieues," trans. Julie Rose, *Log* (Winter–Spring 2006): 90–99.

29. Becker, *Histoire politique,* pp. 21–22.

30. Rioux, *Fourth Republic,* p. 356.

31. Rémi Lenoir, "Family Policy in France since 1938," in John S. Ambler, ed., *The French Welfare State: Surviving Social and Ideological Change* (New York: New York University Press,1991), pp. 158, 159; Lisa Greenwald, *The Women's Liberation Movement in France and the Origins of Contemporary French Feminism 1944–1981* (Ph.D. Dissertation, Emory University, 1996), p. 7.

32. Borne, *Histoire de la société française,* p. 81.

33. Archives Nationales, 1418 W 25.

34. Ministère de la Justice, Compte Général de l'administration de la justice civile et commerciale et de la justice criminelle (Années 1944 à 1947) (Melun: Imprimerie Administrative), p. xx.

35. Michael Sibalis, "Homophobia, Vichy France and the 'Crime of Homosexuality' : The Origins of the Ordinance of 6 August 1942," *GLQ : A Journal of Gay and Lesbian Studies* Vol. 8, no. 3(2002): 302.

36. Karen Adler, *Jews and Gender in Liberation France* (Cambridge, England: Cambridge University Press, 2003), p. 86.

37. Ibid., pp. 71, 69, 98, 84.

38. Robert Gildea, *France since 1945* (Oxford: Oxford University Press), p. 80.

39. Claire Duchen, *Women's Rights and Women's Lives in France, 1944–1968* (London: Routledge, 1994), pp. 53–57; Greenwald, *The Women's Liberation Movement,* pp. 55–57.

40. Patricia E. Prestwich, "Modernizing Politics in the Fourth Republic: Women in the Mouvement républicain populaire, 1944–1958," in Mouré and Alexander, eds., *Crisis and Renewal in France,* p. 204.

41. François Cribier, "Itinéraires professionnels et usure au travail: une génération de salariés parisiens," *Le Mouvement Social,* Vol. 124 (July–September 1983): 21.

42. Fishman, *We Will Wait,* pp. 157, 161.

43. Dominique Borne, *Histoire de la société française depuis 1945,* 3d ed. (Paris: A. Colin, 1992), pp. 81–82.

44. Roger Cousinet, "Preface," in Paulette Bernège and Marie-Louise Cordillot, *Guide d'enseignement ménager: pédagogie, installation des cours* (Paris: La Maison Rustique, 1947), pp. 5–6.

45. Duchen, *Women's Rights and Women's Lives,* pp. 70–71; Bernège and Cordillot, *Guide d'enseignement ménager,* pp. 7–9.

46. Madeleine Guilbert, "Aspects de l'emploi feminine," *Avenirs,* Vol. 93–95 (April–June 1958), p. 26.

47. Rebecca Pulju, "Consumers for the Nation: Women, Politics and Consumer Organizing in France 1944–1965," *Journal of Women's History,* Vol. 18, no. 3 (2006), pp. 68–90.

48. Jenny Leclercq, *Le contrôle des naissances et le malaise conjugal* (Paris: Editions Select, 1946).

49. Jacques Derogy, *Des enfants malgré nous* (Paris: Editions de Minuit, 1956), pp. 9–11.

50. Greenwald, *The Women's Liberation Movement,* pp. 66–68.

51. Simone de Beauvoir, *La force de l'âge* (Paris: Gallimard, 1960), pp. 585, 576.

52. Simone de Beauvoir, *The Second Sex,* trans. H. M. Parshley (New York: Vintage, 1989), p. xiv.

53. Ibid., p. 725.

54. Ibid., p. 267.

55. Greenwald, *The Women's Movement,* pp. 76–84.

56. Larkin, *France since 1936,* p. 236.

57. Thanks to Bob Buzzanco, Department of History, University of Houston, author of *Masters of War: Military Dissent and Politics in the Vietnam Era* (Cambridge, England: Cambridge University Press, 1996).

58. James F. McMillan, *Dreyfus to de Gaulle: Politics and Society in France 1898–1969* (London: Edward Arnold, 1985), pp. 153–154.

59. Todd Shepard, *The Invention of Decolonization: The Algerian War and the Remaking of France* (Ithaca, NY: Cornell University Press, 2006), pp. 6–7.

60. Raphaëlle Branche, *La torture et l'armée pendant la guerre d'Algérie* (Paris: Gallimard, 2001), pp. 13, 117.

61. Ibid., pp. 26, 118, 121, 127.

62. "French Seize a Book on Torture Charges," *New York Times,* March 28, 1958; Donald M. Reid, "The Question of Henri Alleg," *International Historical Review* (September 2007): 573-586.

63. Luis Lema, "Torture in Algeria: The Report That Was to Change Everything," *Le Temps* (Switzerland), August 19, 2005, printed on the ICRC website: http://www.icrc.org/Web/Eng/siteeng0.nsf/html/algeria-history-190805.

CHAPTER 11 DE GAULLE FOUNDS A NEW REPUBLIC: 1958–1969

1. Jean Lacouture, *De Gaulle,* 3 vols. (Paris: Seuil,1984–1986), vol. 3, pp. 270–282.

2. De Gaulle, quoted in Charles G. Cogan, *Charles de Gaulle. A Brief Biography with Documents* (Boston and New York: Bedford/St. Martin's, 1996), p. 91; Maurice Agulhon, *The French Republic, 1879–1992,* trans. Antonia Nevill (Oxford, England, and Cambridge, MA: Blackwell, 1993), pp. 392–393.

3. H. R. Kedward, *France and the French: A Modern History* (New York: The Overlook Press, 2005), pp. 388–389.

4. Robert Gildea, *France since 1945* (Oxford: Oxford University Press, 2002), p. 53.

5. Ibid., p. 54.

6. Agulhon, *The French Republic,* pp. 405–406; Gildea, *France since 1945,* p. 55.

7. Jean Garrigues, ed., *La France de la Ve République 1958–2008* (Paris: Armand Colin, 2008), p. 425.

8. Kedward, *France and the French,* pp. 390–391.

9. Sylvie Thénault, *Histoire de la guerre d'indépendance algérienne* (Paris: Flammarion, 2005), pp. 165–171.
10. Kedward, *France and the French,* p. 342.
11. Matthew Connelly, *A Diplomatic Revolution: Algeria's Fight for Independence and the Origins of the Post-Cold War Era* (New York: Oxford University Press, 2002), pp. 119–141.
12. Alistair Horne, *A Savage War of Peace, Algeria 1954–1962* (New York: Penguin Books, rev. ed. 1987), p. 363.
13. Ibid., p. 366.
14. Quoted in Ibid., pp. 368–369.
15. Quoted in Martin Thomas, Bob Moore, and L. J. Butler, *Crises of Empire: Decolonization and Europe's Imperial States, 1918–1975* (London: Hoddar Education, 2008), p. 237.
16. Thénault, *Histoire de la guerre,* pp. 32–35.
17. Albert Camus, *Carnets,* vol. 3 (Paris: Gallimard, 1969), p. 154.
18. Quoted in Thomas et al., *Crises of Empire,* p. 236.
19. Quoted in James D. Le Sueur, *Uncivil War: Intellectuals and Identity Politics during the Decolonization of Algeria* (Philadelphia: University of Pennsylvania Press, 2001), p. 111.
20. Thénault, *Histoire de la guerre,* pp. 91, 96.
21. Agulhon, *The French Republic,* p. 399.
22. Quoted in Cogan, *Charles de Gaulle,* p. 196.
23. Horne, *A Savage War,* p. 462.
24. Kedward, *France and the French,* p. 344.
25. Jim House and Neal McMaster, *Paris 1961: Algerians, State Terror and Memory* (Oxford: Oxford Univeristy Press, 2006), p. 214.
26. Todd Shepard, *The Invention of Decolonization: The Algerian War and the Remaking of France* (Ithaca, NY: Cornell University Press, 2006), pp. 121–122.
27. Thénault, *Histoire de la guerre,* p. 266.
28. Shepard, *Invention of Decolonization,* pp. 231–234.
29. Irwin Wall, *France, the United States and the Algerian War* (Berkeley: University of California Press, 2001), p. 2; Thénault, *Histoire de la guerre,* p. 267.
30. Aldrich, *Greater France,* pp. 301–302; Frederick Cooper, *Decolonization and African Society: The Labor Question in French and British Africa* (Cambridge, England: Cambridge University Press, 1996), pp. 424–431.
31. Quoted in Kedward, *France and the French,* p. 386.
32. Quoted in Gildea, *France since 1945,* p. 247.
33. Quoted in Ibid., p. 257.
34. "Chinese Checkers," *Time Magazine,* January 31, 1964.
35. Quoted in Cogan, *Charles de Gaulle,* p. 151.
36 Gildea, *France since 1945,* p. 100.
37. Martin Evans and Emmanuel Godin, *France, 1815–2003* (London: Arnold, 2004), p. 157.
38. Gildea, *France since 1945,* p. 101; Evans and Godin, *France,* p. 157.
39. Jean Chicoye, "Tant par mois pour nos robots domestiques," *Constellation,* Vol. 31 (March 1959): 32–36.
40. Gildea, *France since 1945,* pp. 103–105.
41. Quoted in Kedward, *France and the French,* p. 405.
42. Evans and Godin, *France,* p. 158.

43. Kedward, *France and the French,* pp. 409–410.

44. Neil McMaster, *Colonial Migrants and Racism: Algerians in France, 1900–62* (London: MacMillan, 1997), p. 194.

45. MacMaster, *Colonial Migrants,* p. 195.

46. Jeremy D. Popkin, *A History of Modern France,* 3d ed. (New York: Prentice Hall, 2005), p. 300.

47. Kristin Ross, *Fast Cars, Clean Bodies: Decolonization and the Reordering of French Culture* (Cambridge, MA: MIT Press, 1993), pp. 53–54.

48. Ellen Furlough, "Packaging Pleasures: Club Méditerranée and French Consumer Culture, 1950–1968," *French Historical Studies,* Vol. 18, no. 1 (Spring, 1993): 65–81.

49. Keith A. Reader with Khursheed Wadia, *The May Events in France* (New York: St. Martin's Press, 1993), pp. 10–11.

50. Marc Rohan, *Paris '68: Graffiti, Posters, Newspapers and Poems of the Events of May 1968* (London: Impact Books, 1988), pp. 66, 76, 86, 92, 104, 110; Jules Besançon, *Journal mural, mai 68: Sorbonne, Odéon, Nanterre, etc.* (Paris: Tchou, 1968), pp. 34, 87, 174.

51. Reader, *May Events,* p. 18.

52. Kedward, *France and the French,* p. 428.

53. Evans and Godin, *France,* p. 159.

54. Robert Aldrich and Gary Witherspoon, eds., *Who's Who in Contemporary Gay and Lesbian World History from World War II to Present Day* (London and New York: Routledge, 2001), p. 285.

55. Georges Sidéris, "Folles, Swells, Effeminates, and Homophiles in Saint-Germain-des-Prés of the 1950s: A New 'Precious' Society?" in Jeffrey Merrick and Michael Sibalis, eds., *Homosexuality in French History and Culture* (Philadelphia: The Haworth Press, 2001), pp. 219–231.

56. Ross, *Fast Cars,* pp. 161–178.

57. Frantz Fanon, *The Wretched of the Earth,* trans. Constance Farrington (New York: Grove Press, 1963), p. 312.

58. Richard Ivan Jobs, *Riding the New Wave: Youth and the Rejuvenation of France after the Second World War* (Stanford, CA: Stanford University Press, 2007).

59. Agulhon, *The French Republic,* p. 431.

CHAPTER 12 A NEW FRANCE IN A NEW EUROPE:
1969–1981

1. Roy Jenkins, *A Life at the Centre* (New York: MacMillan, 1991), p. 460.

2. Valéry Giscard d'Estaing, *Le pouvoir et la vie* (Paris: Compagnie Douze, 1988), p. 137.

3. Dorothy Pickles, *Problems of Contemporary French Politics* (London: Methuen, 1982), p. 88.

4. A. Sanguinetti quoted in D. L. Hanley, A. P. Kerr, and N. H. Waites, *Contemporary France: Politics and Society since 1945* (London: Routledge, 1989), p. 46.

5. Jean-François Sirinelli et al., *Dictionnaire historique de la vie politique française au XXe siècle* (Paris: Presses Universitaires de France, 1995), pp. 400–402.

6. Ibid., pp. 400–402.

7. Ibid., p. 406.

8. Ibid., p. 417.

9. Valéry Giscard d'Estaing, *French Democracy*, trans. Vincent Cronin (Garden City, New York: Doubleday, 1977), p. 4.
10. Ibid., pp. 20–24.
11. Ibid., pp. 61–66.
12. See the Front National's website at www.frontnational.com.
13. H. R. Kedward, *France and the French: A Modern History* (New York: The Overlook Press, 2005), pp. 423–424, 448.
14. Ibid., pp. 443–445.
15. Ibid., pp. 445–446. See also the 2007 documentary "Les Lip, l'imagination au pouvoir," and the film's website, www.liplefilm.com; Philippe Lançon, "Montre sacrée," *Libération*, May 3, 2007.
16. Tyler Stovall, *The Rise of the Paris Red Belt* (Berkeley: University of California Press, 1990), p. 167.
17. Gino Raymond, *The French Communist Party during the Fifth Republic: A Crisis of Leadership and Ideology* (New York: Palgrave Macmillan, 2005), p. 26.
18. Stovall, *The Red Belt*, pp. 145–167.
19. See François Furet, *The Passing of an Illusion: The Idea of Communism in the Twentieth Century*, trans. Deborah Furet (Chicago: University of Chicago Press, 1991).
20. Frank Costigliola, *France and the United States: The Cold Alliance since World War II* (New York: MacMillan, 1992), p. 187.
21. Kedward, *France and the French*, p. 450.
22. Charles Sowerwine, *France since 1870: Politics, Culture, Society*, 2d ed. (London: Palgrave, 2009), p. 347; Robert Gildea, *France since 1945* (Oxford: Oxford University Press, 2002), pp. 175–176.
23. Michel Dreyfus, *L'Europe des socialistes* (Brussels: Editions Complexe, 1991), p. 267.
24. Costigliola, *France and the United States*, pp. 160–179.
25. Claude Wauthier, *Quatre présidents et l'Afrique* (Paris: Seuil, 1998).
26. Brian Titley, *Dark Age: The Political Odyssey of Emperor Bokassa* (Montreal: McGill Queen's University Press, 2002), chap. 10; Wauthier, *Quatre présidents*, pp. 301–338.
27. Andrew Knapp and Vincent Wright, *The Government and Politics of France*, 5th ed. (New York: Routledge, 2006), pp. 113–114; Sowerwine, *France since 1870*, p. 379.
28. Sirinelli, *Dictionnaire*, p. 407.
29. Nicholas Atkin, *The Fifth French Republic* (London: Palgrave, 2005), p. 126.
30. Gabrielle Hecht, *The Radiance of France: Nuclear Power and National Identity after World War II* (Cambridge, MA: The MIT Press, 1998), p. 2.
31. Ibid., pp. 210–227.
32. Sowerwine, *France since 1870*, p. 359; Roger Price, *A Concise History of France* (Cambridge, England: Cambridge University Press, 1993), p. 286.
33. Hecht, *The Radiance of France*, pp. 227–234.
34. Michael Bess, *The Light-Green Society: Ecology and Technological Modernity in France 1960–2000* (Chicago: University of Chicago Press, 2003), pp. 100–102.
35. Hecht, *The Radiance of France*, p.329
36. Bess, *Light-Green Society*, p. 102.
37. Rebecca Pulju, "The Woman's Paradise: Gender and Consumer Culture in France, 1944-1965" (Ph. D Dissertation, University of Iowa, 2005), pp. 173–186; Sowerwine, *France since 1870*, p. 349; Françoise Cribier, "Changes in the Experiences of Life between Two Cohorts of Parisian Pensioners, Born in Circa 1907 and 1921," *Aging and Society*, Vol. 25 (2005): 6.

38. Christiane Rochefort, *Les petits enfants du siècle* (Paris: Editions Bernard Grasset, 1961), p. 86.

39. Rebecca Pulju, "Consumers for the Nation: Women, Politics, and Consumer Organization in France," *Journal of Women's History,* Vol. 18, no. 3 (2006): 68–90.

40. Jean Fourastié, *Les trentes glorieuses ou la révolution invisible de 1946 à 1975* (Paris: Fayard, 1979), pp. 10–22.

41. Maurice Larkin, *France since the Popular Front: Government and People, 1936–1996,* 2d ed. (Oxford: Oxford University Press, 1997), p. 298.

42. Arnaud Régnier-Loilier and France Prioux, "Does Religious Practice Influence Family Behaviors?" *Population & Societies,* Vol. 447 (July–August 2008): 1–2.

43. Suzanne Berger, "Religious Transformation and the Future of Politics," in Charles S. Maier, ed., *Changing Boundaries of the Political: Essays on the Evolving Balance between State and Society, Public and Private in Europe* (Cambridge, England: Cambridge University Press, 1987), p. 112.

44. Ibid., pp. 114–115.

45. Régnier-Loilier and Prioux, "Religious Practice," p. 2.

46. Jean Garrigues, ed., *La France de la Ve République, 1958–2008* (Paris: Armand Colin, 2008), p. 470.

47. www.diplomatie.fr, "Label France," no. 54 (2004), "What Schools for Tomorrow?"

48. M. J. Neuman and S. Peer, *Equal from the Start: Promoting Educational Opportunity for All Preschool Children—Learning from the French Experience* (New York: French-American Foundation, 2002).

49. Garrigues, *La France de la Ve République,* p. 425.

50. Atkin, *The Fifth French Republic,* p. 123.

51. Geoff Hare, "Radio," in Hugh Dauncey, ed., *French Popular Culture: An Introduction* (New York: Oxford University Press, 2003), p. 49.

52. Jean-Pierre Piriou, "Radio and Television," in Pierre L. Horn, ed., *Handbook of French Popular Culture* (New York: Greenwood Press, 1991), pp. 216–218.

53. Jody Rosen, "Charles Aznavour," www.salon.com/people/feature/1999/07/15/aznavour; André J. Prévos, "Popular Music," in Horn, ed., *Handbook of French Popular Culture,* pp. 215–228; Rupert Smith, "Les misérables," *The Guardian,* November 4, 2002; Chris Tinker, "Music," in Dauncey, ed., *French Popular Culture,* p. 93.

54. Quoted in Jean-Louis Dumas, *Histoire de la pensée. Philosophies et philosophes,* Vol. 3 (Paris: Tallandier, 1990), p. 433.

55. Tony Judt, *Postwar: A History of Europe since 1945* (New York: Penguin, 2005), p. 562.

56. Rémy Rieffel, *Les intellectuels sous la Ve République,* Vol. 3 (Paris: Calmann-Lévy, 1993), p. 210.

57. John F. Sweets, "Chaque livre un événement: Robert Paxton and the French, from briseur de glace to iconoclaste tranquille," in Sarah Fishman et al., eds., *France at War: Vichy and the Historians* (London: Berg Publishers, 2000), p. 22.

58. Miranda Pollard, "Whose Sorrow? Whose Pity? Whose Pleasure? Framing Women in Occupied France," in Melanie Hawthorne and Richard Joseph Golsan, eds., *Gender and Fascism in Modern France* (Hanover, NH: University Press of New England, 1997), p. 145.

59. Giscard, *French Democracy,* p. 32.

60. Elaine Audet, "Françoise Giroud, une femme influente au féminisme ambigu," http://sisyphe.org/article.php3?id_article=277, January 20, 2003.

61. Simone Veil, *Les hommes aussi s'en souviennent. Discours du 26 novembre 1974, suivi d'un entretien avec Annick Cojean* (Paris: Stock, 2004), pp. 1–2, 9–40.

62. Ibid., p. 72.

63. Ibid., p. 73.

64. Michael Sibalis, "Gay Liberation Comes to France: The Front Homosexuel d'Action Révolutionnaire (FHAR)," *French History and Civilization*, Vol. 1 (2005): 267–276.

65. Sowerwine, *France since 1870*, pp. 353, 355–356.

66. Sibalis, "Gay Liberation Comes to France," p. 279.

67. Ibid., p. 271.

68. Jean Le Bitoux, "The Construction of a Political and Media Presence: The Homosexual Liberation Groups in France between 1975 and 1978," in Jeffrey Merrick and Michael Sibalis, eds., *Homosexuality in French History and Culture* (Philadelphia: The Haworth Press, 2001), pp. 249–264.

69. Ibid., p. 262.

70. http://www.insee.fr/fr/themes/tableau.asp?reg_id=0&ref_id=NATCCI02124.

71. Martin Crowley, " 'Like the French of France': Immigration and Translation in the Later Novels of Marguerite Duras," in James S. Williams, ed., *Revisioning Duras: Film, Race, Sex* (Liverpool: Liverpool University Press, 2000), p. 127.

72. Kedward, *France and the French*, pp. 443–444.

73. MacMaster, *Colonial Migrants and Racism: Algerians in France, 1900–62* (London: MacMillan, 1997), p. 212; Paul Silverstein, *Algeria in France: Transpolitics, Race, and Nation* (Bloomington: Indiana University Press, 2004), pp. 130–131.

74. Brian Newsome, "The Rise of the Grandes Ensembles: Government, Business, and Housing in Postwar France," *The Historian*, Vol. 66, no. 4 (Winter 2004): 815.

75. C. Wihtol de Wenden, *Les immigrés et la politique* (Paris: Presses de la FNSP, 1988); Gérard Noiriel, *Le creuset français. Histoire de l'immigration, XIXe–XXe siècles* (Paris: Seuil, 1988); R. Kastoryano, *Etre Turc en France. Réflexions sur familles et communauté* (Paris: CIEMI/L'Harmattan, 1986); Gregory Mann, *Native Sons: West African Veterans and France in the Twentieth Century* (Durham, NC: Duke University Press, 2006).

76. Larkin, *France since the Popular Front*, p. 368; Bruno Jobert, "Democracy and Social Policies: The Example of France," in John S. Ambler, *The French Welfare State: Surviving Social and Ideological Change* (New York: New York University Press, 1991), p. 250.

77. Sowerwine, *France since 1870*, p. 350.

CHAPTER 13 THE REPUBLIC OF THE CENTER: 1981–1995

1. Michel Winock, *Le siècle des intellectuals* (Paris: Seuil, 1997), p. 606.

2. See Henrik Uterwedde, "Mitterand's Economic and Social Policy in Perspective," in Mairi Maclean, ed., *The Mitterand Years: Legacy and Evaluation* (London: Macmillan, 1998), p. 134; Ben Clift, "The French Socialists, Dirigisme and the Troubled Europeanisation of Employment Policy," in Emmanuel Godin and Tony Shafer, eds., *The French Exception* (London: Bergahn, 2004), p. 109.

3. See Emmanuel Le Roy Ladurie, *Histoire de France des régions* (Paris: Seuil, 2001), p. 106ff.

4. See Robert Gildea, *France since 1945* (Oxford, Oxford University Press, 2002), esp. chap. 6; also Olivier Donnat, Denis Cogneau, *Les pratiques culturelles des français, 1973–1989* (Paris: La Découverte, La Documentation française, 1990).

5. See Phillippe Poirier, *L'Etat et la culture en France au XX siècle* (Paris: Livres de poche, 2000), pp. 160–162.
6. See Guy Austin, "Socialist Film Policy and the Heritage Film," in Maclean, ed., *The Mitterand Years*, pp. 276–286.
7. Roger Celestin and Eliane DalMolin, *France from 1851 to the Present* (London: Palgrave, 2007), p. 359.
8. Alain Finkelkraut, *La défaite de la pensée* (Paris: Gallimard, 1987), pp. 154–155.
9. See Gildea, *France since 1945*, p. 163.
10. Chris Warne, "The Impact of World Music in France," in Alec Hargreaves and Mark McKinney, eds., *Post-Colonial Cultures in France* (London: Routledge, 1997), pp. 133–149.
11. Azouz Begag, *Béni, ou le paradis perdu*, quoted in Alec Hargreaves, "Writers of Maghrebi Immigrant Origin," in Hargreaves and McKinney, eds., *Post-Colonial Cultures*, pp. 230–231.
12. H. R. Kedward, *France and the French* (New York: Overlook Press, 2005), p. 506.
13. David Blatt, "Immigrant Politics in a Republican Nation," in Hargreaves and McKinney, eds., *Post-Colonial Cultures*, p. 48.
14. Rogers Brubaker, *Citizenship and Nationhood in France and Germany* (Cambridge, MA: Harvard University Press, 1992), p. 149.
15. Ibid., pp. 143–144.
16. See Pierre Bourdieu et al., *La misère du monde* (Paris: Seuil, 1993).
17. See Uterwedde, "Mitterand's Economic and Social Policy," pp. 133–150.
18. See Kenneth Mouré, "The French Economy since 1930," in Martin Alexander, ed., *French History since Napoleon* (London: Arnold, 1999), pp. 364–390.
19. Sudhir Hazareesingh, *Political Traditions in Modern France* (Oxford: Oxford University Press, 1994), p. 118.
20. Quoted in Brubaker, *Citizenship*, p. 154.
21. Furet coined the celebrated phrase; see Sue Collard's essay, "The Elusive French Exception," in Godin and Chafer, eds., *The French Exception*, pp. 30–46.
22. See Kedward, *France and the French*, pp. 553–557; John Bowen, *Why the French Don't Like Headscarves: Islam, the State and Public Space* (Princeton, NJ: Princeton University Press, 2006).
23. See Siân Reynolds, "Women and Political Representation during the Mitterand Presidency—Or the Family Romance of the Fifth Republic," in Maclean, ed., *The Mitterrand Years*, pp. 185–197.
24. See Joan Wallach Sott, *Parité: Sexual Equality and the Crisis of French Universalism* (Chicago: University of Chicago, 2005).
25. See Pierre Rosanvallon, *La nouvelle question sociale. Repenser l'Etat-providence* (Paris: Seuil, 1995), p. 83.
26. Reynolds, "Women and Political Representation," p. 196.
27. Kedward, *France and the French*, p. 538
28. See Richard Derderian, "Broadcasting from the Margins," in Hargreaves and McKinney, eds., *Post-Colonial Cultures in France*, p. 108.
29. Claude Wauthier, *Quatre présidents et l'Afrique. De Gaulle, Pompidou, Giscard d'Estaing, Mitterrand* (Paris: Seuil, 1995), pp. 616, 631–634, 640.
30. See Rousso and Conan, *Vichy, un passé qui ne passe pas* (Paris: Fayard, 1994).

31. Pierre Perrineau, quoted in Emmanuel Godin, "The Front National as a French Exception?," in Godin and Chafer, eds., *The French Exception*, p. 62.
32. Quoted in Collard, "The Elusive French Exception," p. 33.

CHAPTER 14 FRANCE SINCE 1995

1. Mairi Maclean, ed., *The Mitterrand Years: Legacy and Evaluation* (London: Macmillan, 1998), p. 248.
2. H. R. Kedward, *France and the French* (New York: Overlook Press, 2005), p. 589.
3. See Alain Duhamel, *Les peurs françaises* (Paris: Seuil, 1993).
4. See Philip Thody, *Le Franglais: Forbidden English, Forbidden American* (London: Athlone Press, 1995).
5. Dennis Ager, *Francophonie in the 1990s: Problems and Opportunities* (Bristol: Multilingual Matters, 2001).
6. Yves Tavernier, *Rapport d'information sur les moyens et les structures de diffusion de la francophonie*. 2592 (Paris: Librairies-Imprimeries réunies, 2000).
7. *Le Canard Enchaîné*, March 27, 1996.
8. Kedward, *France and the French*, pp. 606–607.
9. Quoted in Steven L. Kaplan, *Good Bread Is Back* (Chapel Hill, NC: Duke University Press, 2006), p. 81.
10. Quoted in Roger Celestin and Eliane DalMolin, *France from 1851 to the Present* (London: Palgrave, 2007), p. 383.
11. See *Le Monde*, ed., *Les grands entretiens du Monde*, Vol. 3 (December 1996), p. 9.
12. See Kedward, *France and the French*, p. 594ff.
13. See Ben Clift, "The French Socialists, Dirigisme and the Troubled Europeanisation of Employment Policy," in Emmanuel Godin and Tony Chafer, eds., *The French Exception* (London: Bergahn, 2004), pp. 106–120.
14. Kedward, *France and the French*, p. 603.
15. Quoted in Ibid., p. 643.
16. Sponsored by the group Ni Putes Ni Soumises.
17. Tony Judt, *The Burden of Responsibility* (Chicago: University of Chicago Press, 1998), p. 10.
18. Nicholas Hewitt, ed., *The Cambridge Companion to Modern French Culture* (Cambridge, England: Cambridge University Press, 2003), p. 11.
19. Quoted in Kedward, *France and the French*, p. 569.
20. Quoted in Emmanuel Godin, "The Front National as a French Exception?," in Godin and Shafer, eds., *The French Exception*, p. 72.
21. See Nicholas Sarkozy, *Testimony: France in the Twenty-First Century*, trans. Philip Gordon (New York: Pantheon, 2007).
22. See Jane Bryant, "French Foreign and Defence Policy: Exceptional in Methods and Rhetoric," in Godin and Chafer, eds., *The French Exception*, pp. 121–135.
23. Quoted in Celestin and DalMolin, *France from 1851 to the Present*, p. 378.
24. Assia Djebar, *Discours de réception*, http://www. Academie-francaise.fr/immortels/index.html, June 22, 2006.

Index

Page numbers followed by *f* indicate figures.